AF814417

QUE Bee

From Doubts to Distinction
Your ICSE 2026 Exams Partner

GIST OF THE TEXTBOOK
Crisp & Complete Theory - No need to go back to bulky textbooks!

ALL TYPES OF LATEST PATTERN QUESTIONS
MCQs | Case-based | Assertion-Reason | Fill-ups; All in one place!

KEY WORDS HIGHLIGHTED
Important points and formulae neatly highlighted never miss what matters

10 YEARS' PYQS ANSWERS
Previous Year Question Papers with solutions

COUNCIL-STYLE ANSWERS
Write responses like an examiner expects

SAMPLE PAPER
Practice in real-exam mode. Perfect your timing, strategy and confidence.

arihant
SUCCESS AND NOTHING LESS

ARIHANT PRAKASHAN
(School Division Series)

卐 ADMINISTRATIVE & PRODUCTION OFFICES

Regd. Office
'Ramchhaya' 4577/15, Agarwal Road, Darya Ganj, New Delhi -110002
Tele: 011- 47630600, 43518550; Fax: 011- 23280316

卐 Head Office
Kalindi, TP Nagar, Meerut (UP) - 250002, Tel: 0121-7156203, 7156204

卐 SALES & SUPPORT OFFICES
Agra, Ahmedabad, Bengaluru, Bareilly, Chennai, Delhi, Guwahati, Hyderabad, Jaipur, Jhansi, Kolkata, Lucknow, Nagpur & Pune.

PO No : TXT-XX-XXXXXXX-X-XX

Published By Arihant Publications (India) Ltd.

For further information about the books published by Arihant, log on to www.arihantbooks.com or e-mail at info@arihantbooks.com

Follow us on

卐 PRICE ₹275.00

PRODUCTION TEAM

Publishing Manager
Keshav Mohan

Project Head
Yojna Sharma

Project Coordinator
Amit Singh

Cover Designer
Bilal Hashmi

Inner Designer
Ankit Tyagi

Page Layouting
Subhash Chaprana

Proof Reader
Manshi, Ishan

QUE Bee

ICSE
PHYSICS
Class 10

Types of Questions & their Respective Number

Type of Questions	Total Number
Multiple Choice Questions (MCQs)	208
Assertion-Reason (A-R)	60
Fill-ups	62
Very Short Answer Questions (VSA)	123
Short Answer Type Questions (SA)	100
Long Answer Type Questions (LA)	56
Case Based Questions	34
Numericals	116
TOTAL NO. OF QUESTIONS	**759**

Created by
S. Gregory
25 Yrs. Experienced
HOD Physics
St. Thomas English Medium School, Meerut

Contributor
Priyasha Gupta

From Learner to Leader

Step-Into the Spotlight

QUE Bee is more than just a book - it's a platform for young achievers like you to guide future toppers. If you've cracked the code to smart study or have insights that can make learning easier for others, this is your moment to shine!

What Can You Share?

- Your study techniques, time management tips, or motivation hacks
- Feedback or suggestions to make QUE Bee even better
- Real experiences that can guide other students through the exam maze

What's in It for You?

- Your name will be featured in our exclusive Student Panel in the next edition
- Win exciting & surprise rewards for impactful suggestions
- **Get published** - your photo, Ideas-or even interviews can be featured in the book
- **Become a student icon** - recognized and followed by peers across schools

Let your learning become someone else's ladder.
Be remembered. Be featured. Be the guide.

SCAN TO SHARE YOUR IDEA

QUE Bee

Index

Latest
Course Structure

There will be ***one*** *paper of* ***two hours*** *duration carrying 80 marks and Internal Assessment of practical work carrying 20 marks.*

Note: *Unless otherwise specified, only S I. Units are to be used while teaching and learning, as well as for answering questions.*

Force, Work, Power and Energy

(i) Turning forces concept; moment of a force; forces in equilibrium; centre of gravity; [discussions using simple examples and simple numerical problems].

Elementary introduction of translational and rotational motions; moment (turning effect) of a force, also called torque and its cgs and SI units; common examples - door, steering wheel, bicycle pedal, etc.; clockwise and anti-clockwise moments; conditions for a body to be in equilibrium (translational and rotational); principle of moment and its verification using a metre rule suspended by two spring balances with slotted weights hanging from it; simple numerical problems; Centre of gravity (qualitative only) with examples of some regular bodies and irregular lamina.

(ii) Uniform circular motion

As an example of constant speed, though acceleration (force) is present. Differences between centrifugal and centripetal force.

(iii) Work, energy, power and their relation with force.

Definition of work. $W = FS \cos\theta$; special cases of $\theta = 0^0$, 90^0. $W = mgh$. Definition of energy, energy as work done. Various units of work and energy and their relation with SI units.[erg, calorie, kW h and eV]. Definition of Power, $P = W/t$; SI and cgs units; other units; kilowatt (kW), megawatt (MW) and gigawatt (GW); and horse power (1hp=746W) [Simple numerical problems on work, power and energy].

(iv) Different types of energy (e.g. chemical energy, Mechanical energy, heat energy, electrical energy, nuclear energy, sound energy, light energy).

Mechanical energy: potential energy $U = mgh$ (derivation included) gravitational PE, examples; kinetic energy $K = \frac{1}{2} mv^2$ (derivation included); forms of kinetic energy: translational, rotational and vibrational - only simple examples. [Numerical problems on K and U only in case of translational motion]; qualitative discussions of electrical, chemical, heat, nuclear, light and sound energy, conversion from one form to another; common examples.

(v) Machines as force multipliers; load, effort, mechanical advantage, velocity ratio and efficiency; simple treatment of levers, pulley systems showing the utility of each type of machine.

Functions and uses of simple machines: Terms- effort E, load L, mechanical advantage $MA = L/E$, velocity ratio $VR = VE/VL = dE / dL$, input (Wi), output (Wo), efficiency (η), relation between η and MA,VR (derivation included); for all practical machines $\eta < 1$; $MA < VR$.

Lever: principle. First, second and third class of levers; examples: MA and VR in each case. Examples of each of these classes of levers as also found in the human body.

Pulley system: single fixed, single movable, block and tackle; MA, VR and η in each case.

(vi) Principle of Conservation of energy.

Statement of the principle of conservation of energy; theoretical verification that $U + K =$ constant for a freely falling body. Application of this law to simple pendulum (qualitative only); [simple numerical problems].

Light

(i) Refraction of light through a glass block and a triangular prism - qualitative treatment of simple applications such as real and apparent depth of objects in water and apparent bending of sticks in water. Applications of refraction of light.

Partial reflection and refraction due to change in medium. Laws of refraction; the effect on speed (V), wavelength (λ) and frequency (f) due to refraction of light; conditions for a light ray to pass undeviated.

Values of speed of light (c) in vacuum, air, water and glass; refractive index $\mu = c/V$, $V = f\lambda$. Values of μ for common substances such as water, glass and diamond; experimental verification; refraction through glass block; lateral displacement; multiple images in thick glass plate/mirror; refraction through a glass prism simple applications: real and apparent depth of objects in water; apparent bending of a stick under water. (Simple numerical problems and approximate ray diagrams required).

(ii) Total internal reflection: Critical angle; examples in triangular glass prisms; comparison with reflection from a plane mirror (qualitative only). Applications of total internal reflection.

Transmission of light from a denser medium (glass/water) to a rarer medium (air) at different angles of incidence; critical angle (C) $\mu = 1/\sin C$. Essential conditions for total internal reflection. Total internal reflection in a triangular glass prism; ray diagram, different cases - angles of prism (60°60°60°, (60°30°90°, (45°45°90°; use of right angle prism to obtain $\delta = 90°$ and 180°(ray diagram); comparison of total internal reflection from a prism and reflection from a plane mirror.

(iii) Lenses (converging and diverging) including characteristics of the images formed (using ray diagrams only); magnifying glass; location of images using ray diagrams and thereby determining magnification.

Types of lenses (converging and diverging), convex and concave, action of a lens as a set of prisms; technical terms; centre of curvature, radii of curvature, principal axis, foci, focal plane and focal length,; detailed study of refraction of light in spherical lenses through ray diagrams; formation of images - principal rays or construction rays; location of images from ray diagram for various positions of a small linear object on the principal axis; characteristics of images. Sign convention and direct numerical problems using the lens formula are included.(derivation of formula not required).

Scale drawing or graphical representation of ray diagrams not required.

Power of a lens (concave and convex) – [simple direct numerical problems]: magnifying glass or simple microscope: location of image and magnification from ray diagram only [formula and numerical problems not included]. Applications of lenses.

(iv) Using a triangular prism to produce a visible spectrum from white light; Electromagnetic spectrum. Scattering of light.

Deviation produced by a triangular prism; dependence on colour (wavelength) of light; dispersion and spectrum; electromagnetic spectrum: broad classification (names only arranged in order of increasing wavelength); properties common to all electromagnetic radiations; properties and uses of infrared and ultraviolet radiation. Simple application of scattering of light e.g. blue colour of the sky.

Sound

(i) Reflection of Sound Waves; echoes: their use; simple numerical problems on echoes.

Production of echoes, condition for formation of echoes; simple numerical problems; use of echoes by bats, dolphins, fishermen, medical field. SONAR.

(ii) Natural vibrations, Damped vibrations, Forced vibrations and Resonance - a special case of forced vibrations.

Meaning and simple applications of natural, damped, forced vibrations and resonance.

(iii) Loudness, pitch and quality of sound:

Characteristics of sound: loudness and intensity; subjective and objective nature of these properties; sound level in dB (as unit only); noise pollution; interdependence of: pitch and frequency; quality and waveforms (with examples).

Electricity and Magnetism

(i) Ohm's Law; concepts of emf, potential difference, resistance; resistances in series and parallel, internal resistance.

Concepts of pd (V), current (I), resistance (R) and charge (Q). Ohm's law: statement, V=IR; SI units; experimental verification; graph of V vs I and resistance from slope; ohmic and non-ohmic resistors, factors affecting resistance (including specific resistance) and internal resistance; super conductors, electromotive force (emf); combination of resistances in series and parallel and derivation of expressions for equivalent resistance. Simple numerical problems using the above relations. [Simple network of resistors].

(ii) Electrical power and energy.

Electrical energy; examples of heater, motor, lamp, loudspeaker, etc. Electrical power; measurement of electrical energy, $W = QV = VIt$ from the definition of pd. Combining with Ohm's law $W = VIt = I^2 Rt = (V^2/R)t$ and electrical power $P = (W/t) = VI = I^2R = V^2/R$. Units: SI and commercial; Power rating of common appliances, household consumption of electric energy; calculation of total energy consumed by electrical appliances; $W = Pt$ (kilowatt × hour = kW h), [simple numerical problems].

(iii) Household circuits – main circuit; switches; fuses; earthing; safety precautions; three-pin plugs; colour coding of wires.

House wiring (ring system), power distribution; main circuit (3 wires-live, neutral, earth) with fuse / MCB, main switch and its advantages - circuit diagram; two-way switch, staircase wiring, need for earthing, fuse, 3-pin plug and socket; Conventional location of live, neutral and earth points in 3 pin plugs and sockets. Safety precautions, colour coding of wires.

(iv) Magnetic effect of a current (principles only, laws not required); electromagnetic induction (elementary); transformer.

Oersted's experiment on the magnetic effect of electric current; magnetic field (B) and field lines due to current in a straight wire (qualitative only), right hand thumb rule – magnetic field due to a current in a loop; Electromagnets: their uses; comparisons with a permanent magnet; Fleming's Left Hand Rule, the DC electric motor- simple sketch of main parts (coil, magnet, split ring commutators and brushes); brief description and type of energy transfer(working not required): Simple introduction to electromagnetic induction; frequency of AC in house hold supplies, Fleming's Right Hand Rule, AC Generator - Simple sketch of main parts, brief description and type of energy transfer(working not required). Advantage of AC over DC. Transformer- its types, characteristics of primary and secondary coils in each type (simple labelled diagram and its uses).

Heat

(i) Calorimetry: meaning, specific heat capacity; principle of method of mixtures; Numerical Problems on specific heat capacity using heat loss and gain and the method of mixtures.

Heat and its units (calorie, joule), temperature and its units (°C, K); thermal (heat) capacity $C' = Q/\Delta T$... (SI unit of C): Specific heat Capacity $C = Q/m\Delta T$ (SI unit of C) Mutual relation between Heat Capacity and Specific Heat capacity, values of C for some common substances (ice, water and copper). Principle of method of mixtures including mathematical statement. Natural phenomenon involving specific heat. Consequences of high sp. heat of water. [Simple numerical problem].

(ii) Latent heat; loss and gain of heat involving change of state for fusion only.

Change of phase (state); heating curve for water; latent heat; sp latent heat of fusion (SI unit). Simple numerical problems. Common physical phenomena involving latent heat of fusion.

Modern Physics

(i) Radioactivity and changes in the nucleus; background radiation and safety precautions.

Brief introduction (qualitative only) of the nucleus, nuclear structure, atomic number (Z), mass number (A).Radioactivity as spontaneous disintegration. α, β and γ - their nature and properties; changes within the nucleus. One example each of α and β decay with equations showing changes in Z and A. Uses of radioactivity - radio isotopes. Harmful effects. Safety precautions. Background radiation.

Radiation: X-rays; radioactive fallout from nuclear plants and other sources.

Nuclear Energy: working on safe disposal of waste. Safety measures to be strictly reinforced.

(ii) *Nuclear fission and fusion; basic introduction and equations.*

List of
Important Topics

On the basis of analysis of last 9 Years' Board Examination Papers we have identified Important Topics from each chapter.

Chapter 1: Force

- ***Types of Force*** *2025- 7 Marks, 2023- 1 Mark*
- ***Moment of Force*** *2024- 1 Mark, 2023- 4 Marks, 2020- 2 Marks, 2019- 5 Marks, 2018- 3 Marks, 2017- 2 Marks)*
- ***Centre of Gravity and uniform Circular Motion*** *2024- 6 Marks, 2023- 1 Mark)*

Chapter 2: Work, Power and Energy

- ***Work*** *2025- 1 Mark, 2024- 2 Marks, 2023- 1 Mark, 2018- 6 Marks*
- ***Power & Energy*** *2025 -5 Marks, 2024- 2 Marks, 2023- 4 Marks, 2019- 2 Marks, 2018- 6 Marks, 2017- 2 Marks*
- ***Energy Sources & Conservation of Energy*** *2024- 4 Marks, 2023- 1 Mark, 2020- 6 Marks, 2019- 3 Marks)*

Chapter 3: Machines

- ***Machines*** *2025-7 Marks, 2024- 8 Marks, 2023- 3 Marks, 2020- 5 Marks, 2019- 4 Marks, 2018- 4 Marks, 2017- 8 Marks*

Chapter 4: Refraction of Light

- ***Refraction of Light at Plane Surfaces*** *2025-8 Marks, 2024- 6 Marks, 2023- 5 Marks, 2020- 9 Marks, 2019- 5 Marks, 2018- 2 Marks, 2017- 4 Marks)*
- ***Prism and Total Internal Reflection*** *2025-6 Marks, 2024- 7 Marks, 2023- 2 Marks, 2020- 3 Marks, 2019- 4 Marks, 2018- 10 Marks, 2017- 9 Marks)*

Chapter 5: *Lenses*

- ***Lens and Technical Terms Related to Lens*** *2023- 4 Marks*
- ***Formation of Images and Lens Formula*** *2025-8 Marks, 2024- 7 Marks, 2023- 1 Mark, 2020- 4 Marks, 2019- 9 Marks, 2018- 11 Marks, 2017- 3 Marks)*

Chapter 6: Spectrum of Light

- ***Prism*** *2025-5 Marks, 2024- 1 Mark, 2023- 4 Marks, 2020- 2 Marks*
- ***Electromagnetic Spectrum*** *2025-7 Marks, 2024- 4 Marks, 2023- 2 Marks, 2019- 2 Marks*

Chapter 7: Sound

- ***Sound Waves & Vibrations*** *2025-7 Marks, 2024- 10 Marks, 2023- 3 Marks, 2020- 8 Marks, 2019- 3 Marks, 2018- 11 Marks, 2017- 12 Marks*
- ***Characteristics of Sound*** *2025-3 Marks, 2023- 4 Marks, 2020- 3 Marks, 2019- 9 Marks, 2017- 3 Marks*

Chapter 8: Electricity

- ***Electricity & Resistance*** *2025-5 Marks, 2024- 11 Marks, 2023- 5 Marks, 2020- 6 Marks, 2019- 8 Marks, 2018- 5 Marks, 2017- 3 Marks*
- ***Electrical Power & Energy*** *2025-4 Marks, 2023- 2 Marks, 2020- 5 Marks, 2017- 2 Marks*
- ***Domestic Circuits*** *2025-5 Marks, 2024- 3 Marks, 2023- 2 Marks, 2020- 2 Marks, 2019- 3 Marks, 2018- 8 Marks, 2017- 4 Marks*

Chapter 9: Electromagnetism

- ***Magnetic Effect of Current*** *2025-7 Marks, 2024- 5 Marks, 2023- 4 Marks, 2020- 4 Marks, 2018- 5 Marks*
- ***Electromagnetic Induction*** *2025-3 Marks, 2024- 4 Marks, 2019- 2 Marks*

Chapter 10: Heat

- ***Heat and Calorimetry*** *2025-5 Marks, 2024- 1 Mark, 2023- 5 Marks, 2020- 7 Marks, 2019- 7 Marks, 2018- 9 Marks, 2017- 10 Marks*
- ***Change of Phase and Latent Heat*** *2025-6 Marks, 2024- 9 Marks, 2023- 1 Mark, 2020- 7 Marks, 2019- 9 Marks, 2018- 5 Marks, 2017- 3 Marks)*

Chapter 11: Radioactivity and Nuclei

- ***Radioactive Substance*** *2023- 2 Marks, 2018- 6 Marks, 2017- 2 Marks*
- ***Changes with in Nucleus during α, β and γ-decay*** *2025-6 Marks, 2024- 4 Marks, 2023- 2 Marks, 2020- 6 Marks, 2019- 2 Marks)*
- ***Use of Radioactivity and Source of Harmful Radiation and Nuclear Energy*** *2025-2 Marks, 2024- 5 Marks, 2023- 3 Marks, 2020- 1 Mark, 2019- 3 Marks*

01

FORCE

Force may be defined as an external agency or cause (a push or a pull), which changes or tends to change the state of rest or of uniform motion or the direction of motion of a body or size of a body or shape of a body.
Its SI unit is **newton (N)** or kilogram-force (kgf), where 1 kgf = g N, if g is the acceleration due to gravity (9.8 ms^{-2}).

Motion of Rigid Body

- **Translational Motion or Linear Motion** When a force is applied on a stationary rigid body which is free to move and the body starts moving in a straight path in the direction of applied force, then its motion is called translational motion.

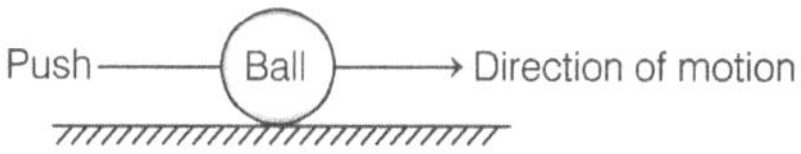

Translational motion of a ball

e.g. On pushing a ball lying on a floor as shown in figure, it starts moving.

- **Rotational Motion** When a force is applied on fixed point of a body which is pivoted at a point, then body starts rotating about that point. Such motion is called rotational motion and the force applied is called turning force.
  e.g. Rotational motion of a wheel.

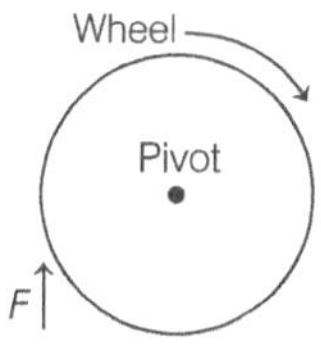

Rotational motion of a wheel

Torque or Moment of a Force

- The turning effect produced by a force on a rigid body fixed about a point (pivot or fulcrum) is called **moment of a force** or **torque**. It is the product of the magnitude of the force and the perpendicular distance of the line of action of force from the axis of rotation.

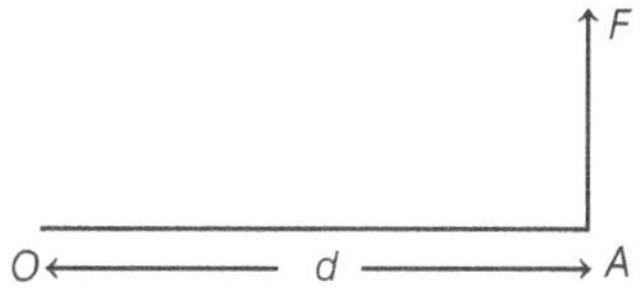

Torque (Moment of force) = Perpendicular distance of line of action of force from axis of rotation × Force

or $\tau = \mathbf{d} \times F$

where, d is the perpendicular distance.

- It is a **vector** quantity.
- Its SI unit is **newton-metre (N-m)** and CGS unit is **dyne-cm**.

$$1 \text{ N-m} = 10^7 \text{ dyne-cm}$$
$$\text{kgf} \times \text{m} = 9.8 \text{ N-m}$$
$$1 \text{ gf} \times \text{cm} = 980 \text{ dyne-cm}$$

REVISION NOTES

Clockwise and Anti-Clockwise Moments

If the turning effect on the body is anti-clockwise, then the moment of force is called **anti-clockwise moment** and is taken positive as shown in figure.

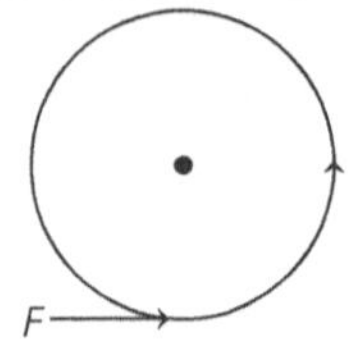

Anti-clockwise (positive)

On the other hand, if the turning effect on the body is clockwise, then the moment of force is called **clockwise moment** and is taken negative as shown in figure.

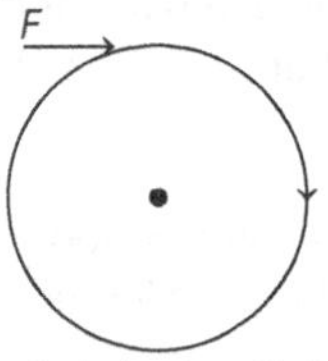

Clockwise (negative)

Common Examples of Moment of Force

Some common examples of moment of force are given as below

(i) It is easier to **open the door** by applying force near the outer edge, away from the hinges or axis of rotation.

(ii) For **turning a steering wheel**, a force is applied tangentially on the rim of the wheel.

(iii) In a bicycle, the toothed wheel is rotated by applying less **force on the foot pedal** which is at a large distance from the axle of rear wheel.

Equilibrium of Bodies

When a number of forces acting on a body produce no change in its state of rest or linear or rotational motion, the body is said to be in a state of equilibrium.

(i) **Static Equilibrium** When a body remains in a state of rest under the influence of several force, the body is in static equilibrium.

e.g. If a book is lying on a table, the weight of the book exerted on the table vertically downwards is balanced by an equal and opposite force of reaction exerted by the table on the book vertically upwards. Thus, the book is in static equilibrium.

(ii) **Dynamic Equilibrium** When a body remains in the same state of motion under the influence of several forces, the body is said to be dynamic equilibrium.

e.g. An aeroplane moving at a constant height with a constant speed.

(iii) **Neutral Equilibrium** A body is said to be in neutral equilibrium if on being slightly displaced, it remains in its new position.

e.g. When a cone lying on a horizontal surface along slant height, then it is said that the cone is disturbed from its equilibrium position and it will acquire the equilibrium whenever it is released.

Conditions for Equilibrium

- A resultant of all the forces acting on the body should be equal to zero.
- The resultant moment of all the forces acting on the body about the point of rotation should be zero, i.e. the sum of the anticlockwise moments about the axis of rotation must be equal to the sum of the clockwise moments about the same axis.

Couple

- A pair of equal and opposite forces acting along parallel lines (not on the same line of action) forms a couple.
- A couple always produces a rotational motion in a rigid body.
- Some examples of couple are

  (i) Opening a tap. (ii) Steering of a four wheeler. (iii) Tightening a screw with a screwdriver.

Moment of Couple

The moment of couple is defined as the product of force and the perpendicular distance between the lines of action of forces (or couple arm).

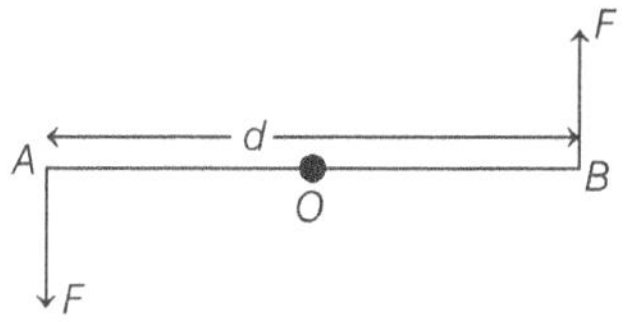

i.e. Moment of couple = Magnitude of either force × Perpendicular distance between the line of action of forces (or couple arm)

$$\text{Moment of couple} = F \times d$$

Its SI unit is **newton-metre** (N-m).

Principle of Moment

According to the principle of moment, if different forces act on a body which is capable to rotate about an axis, but no rotation takes place, then the algebraic sum of moments of all the forces is zero or the body is in equilibrium.

Sum of the anti-clockwise moments = Sum of the clockwise moments

Centre of Gravity

Centre of gravity of a rigid body is the point at which its whole weight can be supposed to act.

(i) Its position depends upon the distribution of mass of the body.

(ii) It may be inside or outside the body. e.g. The centre of gravity of a uniform straight wire is at its mid-point. But, if this wire is bent into the form of a circle, then its centre of gravity will be at the centre of circle.

(iii) If the body is of symmetrical shape whose weight is distributed uniformly, then the centre of gravity of the body lies at its geometrical centre. e.g. In case of a ring, the centre of gravity lies at its centre, where there is no material.

Centre of gravity of some regular objects

Object	Figure	Centre of Gravity
Uniform rod		Mid-point of rod
Circular disc	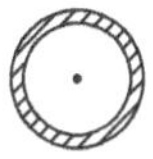	Geometric centre
Sphere (solid or hollow)	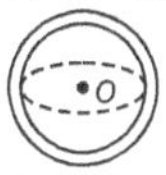	Geometric centre of the sphere
Cylinder	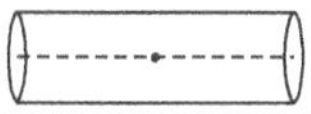	Mid-point on the axis of the cylinder
Circular ring		Centre of the ring
Rectangle or parallelogram	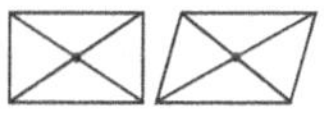	The point of intersection of the diagonals

Object	Figure	Centre of Gravity
Triangular lamina	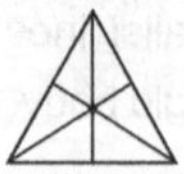	The point of intersection of medians (centroid)
Hollow cone		At a height $\left(\frac{h}{3}\right)$ from the base on its axis
Solid cone		At a height $\left(\frac{h}{4}\right)$ from the base on its axis
Cube/Cuboid	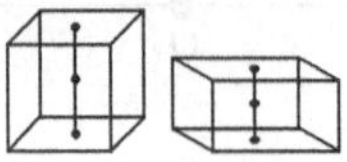	At the point of intersection of diagonals

Uniform Circular Motion

- When a body moves with a constant speed in a circular path, then its motion is known as uniform circular motion.
- However, the direction of motion of the body which is tangential to the circle changes at every point of the circular path (as shown below).
- Due to continuous change in direction of motion, the velocity is no longer uniform (only magnitude remains same) hence, due to change of its velocity, the motion is said to be an accelerated motion.

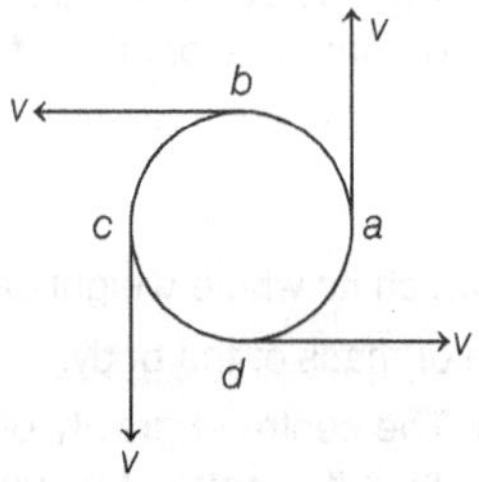

Direction of velocity in a circular path

Centripetal Force

The force which keeps a body moving with a uniform speed along a circular path and directed along the radius towards the centre is called centripetal force.

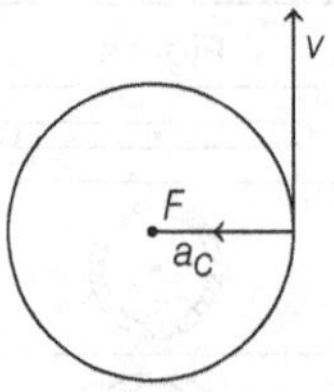

Uniform circular motion

Centripetal force acts on a body of mass m,

$$F = \frac{mv^2}{r}$$

where, v = speed of body and r = radius of circular path.

Centrifugal Force

It is the apparent force that draws a rotating body away from the centre of rotation. It is caused by the inertia of the body as the body's path is continually redirected.

The centrifugal force is in the opposite direction to the direction of centripetal force, but it is not the force of reaction of centripetal force. The centrifugal force is not a real force but it is a fictitious force (or virtual force).

EXAM ORIENTED QUESTIONS

TYPE - 1   01 Mark

Multiple Choice Questions

Q.1 A body is acted upon by two equal and opposite forces, that are not along the same straight line. The body will **[ICSE 2025]**

(a) remain stationary
(b) have only rotational motion
(c) have only rectilinear motion
(d) have both rectilinear and rotational motion

Ans. (b) When two equal and opposite forces not acting along the same line acts on a body, it forms a couple.
A couple is always needed to produce rotation in a body.

Q.2 The diagrams below show a force $F = 40$ N acting on a rod AB pivoted at A in different directions. Choose the correct option.

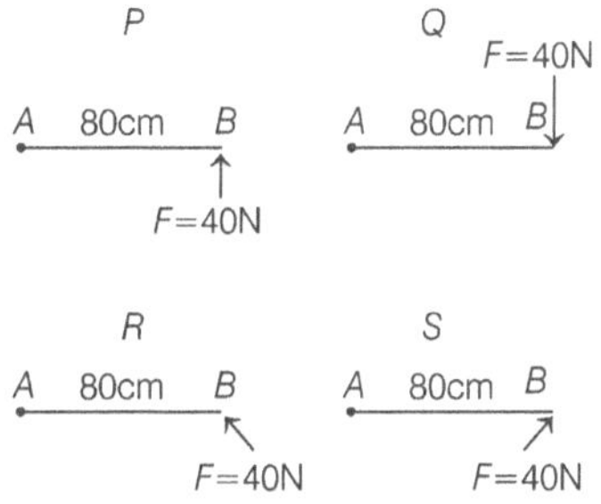

(a) P and S have opposite moments
(b) The magnitude of the moment of force is maximum in R.
(c) The magnitude of the moment of force is maximum in P and Q.
(d) The moment of force in R is negative.

Ans. (c) In P and Q, force is completely perpendicular to the rod, making torque maximum, even though they act in opposite directions with respect to each other.

Q.3 The relation between CGS and SI unit of moment of force is **[ICSE 2022 Sem-I]**

(a) 1 N-m = 10^5 dyne-cm   (b) 1 N-m = 10^5 dyne
(c) 1 N-m = 10^7 dyne-cm   (d) 1 dyne-cm = 10^7 N-m

Ans. (c) We know that,

$$1 \text{ newton} = 10^5 \text{ dyne}$$
$$1 \text{ N-m} = 10^5 \times 10^2 \text{ dyne-cm}$$
$$1 \text{ N-m} = 10^7 \text{ dyne-cm}$$

Q.4 SI unit of moment is **[ICSE Specimen 2023]**

(a) kgf-m   (b) N-m
(c) gf-m   (d) N-cm

Ans. (b) The unit for a moment in SI is the newton-metre (N-m).

Q.5 Clockwise moment produced by a force about a fulcrum is considered to be **[ICSE Specimen 2023 Sem-I]**

(a) positive
(b) negative
(c) zero
(d) None of these

Ans. (b) The clockwise moment sign convention is always interpreted negatively.

Q.6 Which weight creates a clockwise moment and which weight creates an anti-clockwise moment in the given figure?

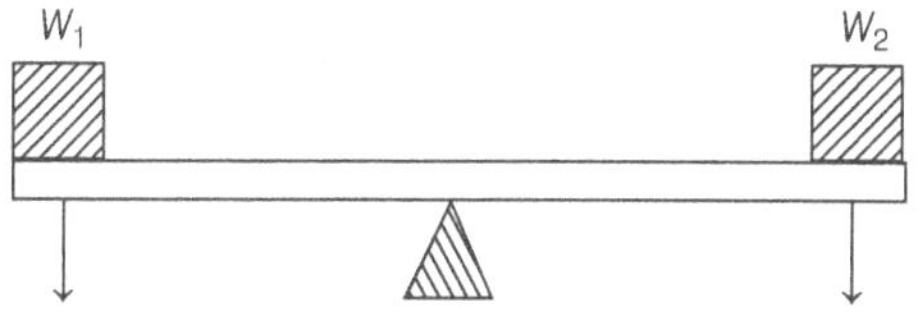

(a) W_1 creates a clockwise moment, W_2 creates an anti-clockwise moment
(b) W_2 creates a clockwise moment, W_1 creates an anti-clockwise moment
(c) Both W_1 and W_2 create clockwise moments
(d) Both W_1 and W_2 create an anti-clockwise moments

Ans. (b) In the given figure, W_2 produces a clockwise moment by acting on the right side of the pivot, while W_1 produces an anti-clockwise moment on the left side of the pivot.

Q.7 A pupil balances a non-uniform object on a knife edge. To do this, a weight is suspended from the left-hand end of the object. Where is the centre of the gravity of the object?

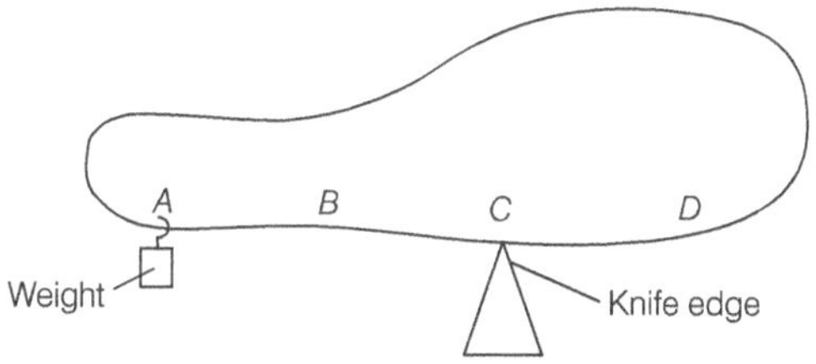

(a) A (b) B
(c) C (d) D

Ans. (d) For the system to balance, the sum of moment of anti-clockwise direction has to be equal to the sum of moment of clockwise direction. The weight in this case is generating moment of anti-clockwise direction.
The centre of gravity should be at the right hand side of pivot, i.e. at point D.

Q.8 A moment of couple has a tendency to rotate the body in an anti-clockwise direction. Then, the moment of couple is taken as **[ICSE Specimen 2025,23]**

(a) positive (b) negative
(c) maximum (d) zero

Ans. (a) A moment of couple has a tendency to rotate the body in an anti-clockwise direction. Then, the moment of couple is taken as positive.

Q.9 The line joining the centre of gravity of a cuboid and the centre of the earth will fall within the base of the body even after being disturbed by an external force, then the body is said to be in

(a) neutral equilibrium (b) stable equilibrium
(c) unstable equilibrium (d) dynamic equilibrium

Ans. (b) Since, the line joining the centre of gravity and centre of earth passes through the base of the body and the body will regain its position after being disturbed. So, the body is in stable equilibrium.

Q.10 A tractor is being used on rough ground. What is the safest position for its centre of gravity?

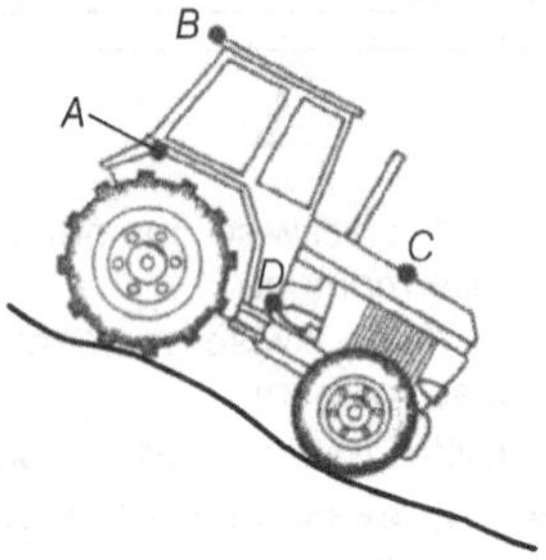

(a) *A* (b) *B* (c) *C* (d) *D*

Ans. (d) The centre of gravity should be as low as possible so that the tractor can be more stable.

Q.11 In which of the following body postures can the centre of gravity lie outside the body?

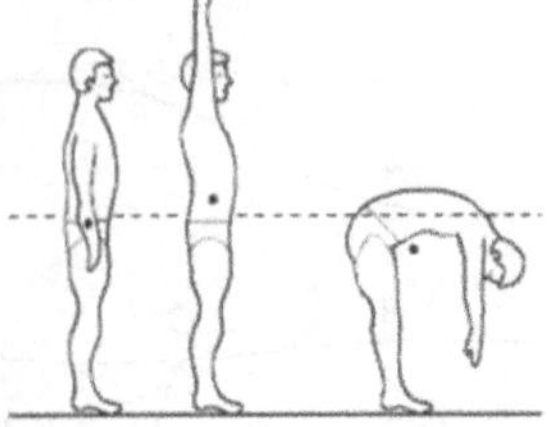

(a) Standing upright
(b) Performing a headstand
(c) Bending forward in a yoga pose.
(d) In all posture, centre of gravity will be inside the human body.

Ans. (c) When bending forward into an inverted *V* or *U* shape during yoga poses, the centre of gravity may shift outside the body due to the redistribution of weight.

Q.12 In the diagram below, four cones are depicted, each with a height of 12 cm. The position of the centre of gravity is indicated by dots located at 9 cm, 8 cm, 4 cm and 3 cm from the apex of each cone. Which of these cones is completely solid?

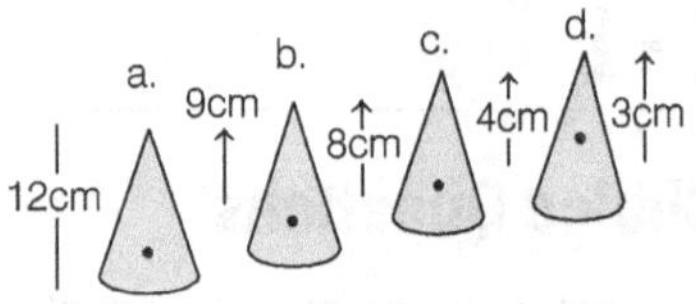

(a) 9 cm (b) 8 cm
(c) 4 cm (d) 3 cm

Ans.(a) For a completely solid cone, the centre of gravity lies at a height of $\frac{h}{4}$ from the base, where h is the height of the cone. Given that the height of each cone is 12 cm, the centre of gravity of a solid cone should be at $\frac{12}{4}$ = 3 cm from the base or 9 cm from the apex.

Q.13 A body is describing a uniform circular motion. Which of the following quantities is constant?

(a) Speed (b) Acceleration
(c) Velocity (d) Momentum

Ans. (a) Speed

Q.14 A particle is acted upon by a force of constant magnitude which is always perpendicular to the velocity of the particle. The motion of the particle takes place in a plane. It means that

(a) its velocity is constant
(b) its kinetic energy is constant
(c) its acceleration is constant
(d) it moves in a straight line

Ans. (b) According to given situation, the particle is performing uniform circular motion. The force acting on the particle perpendicular to its velocity is centripetal force. As the speed is constant in uniform circular motion, its kinetic energy is constant.

Q.15 Butter separates from milk, when milk is churned at a high speed. This is because of

(a) centripetal force (b) centrifugal force
(c) frictional force (d) adhesive force

Ans. (b) When the milk is churned at a high speed, then due to centrifugal force, the denser particles are pulled outwards. The lighter particles, i.e. butter settles at centre.

Q.16 A rectangular window pane, 2 m wide is hinged at one side. A force of 50 N is applied. Perpendicularly at the mid-point of its free edge to open it. What is the moment of the force about the hinge?

(a) 25 N-m (b) 50 N-m(c) 100 N-m (d) 75 N-m

Ans. (b) Moment of the force required = $50 \times \frac{2}{2}$ = 50 N-m

Q.17 A door requires a minimum moment of 32.5 Nm in order to open it.

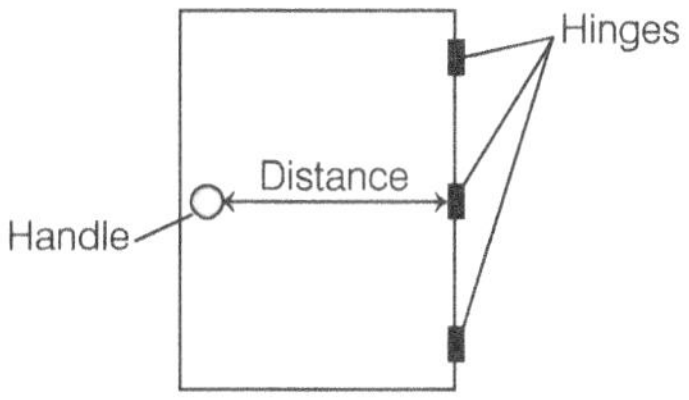

What is the minimum distance of the handle from the hinges, if the door is to be pulled open with a force at the handle not greater than 50 N?

(a) 0.33 m (b) 0.65 m
(c) 0.77 m (d) 1.54 m

Ans. (b) Moment = Force × Perpendicular distance

$$\text{Perpendicular distance} = \frac{\text{Moment}}{\text{Force}} = \frac{32.5}{50} = 0.65 \text{ m}$$

Q.18 A door lock is opened by turning the level (handle) of length 0.2 m . If the moment of force produced is 1 N-m, then the minimum force required is **[ICSE 2024]**

(a) 5 N (b) 10 N (c) 20 N (d) 0.2 N

Ans. (a) Given, $\tau = 1$ N-m and $d = 0.2$ m

The moment of force is given by

$$\tau = F \times d \Rightarrow 1 = F \times 0.2$$

$$\text{Minimum force, } F = \frac{1}{0.2} = \frac{10}{2} = 5 \text{ N}$$

Q.19 A uniform metre scale is suspended at 50 cm mark from a rigid support with a weight of 150 gf attached at 5 cm mark as shown in figure. To balance the scale, a weight of 450 gf should be attached at mark

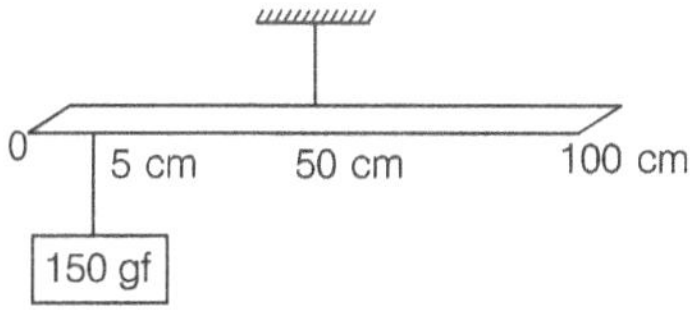

(a) 65 cm (b) 90 cm
(c) 95 cm (d) 100 cm

Ans. (a) Let the weight of 450 gf be attached at distance d as shown below

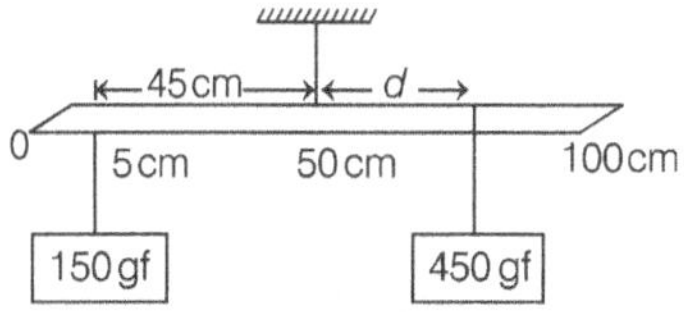

Applying principle of moment, in equilibrium,

Sum of anti-clockwise moment = Sum of clockwise moment

$$\Rightarrow \quad 45 \times 150 = d \times 450$$

$$\Rightarrow \quad d = \frac{45 \times 150}{450} = 15 \text{ cm}$$

The distance of weight from zero mark = 50 + 15 = 65 cm

Q.20 An iron bar is 1.2 m long and weighs 40 N. It is pivoted at one end. Given that the centre of gravity of the iron bar is 72 cm from the pivot.

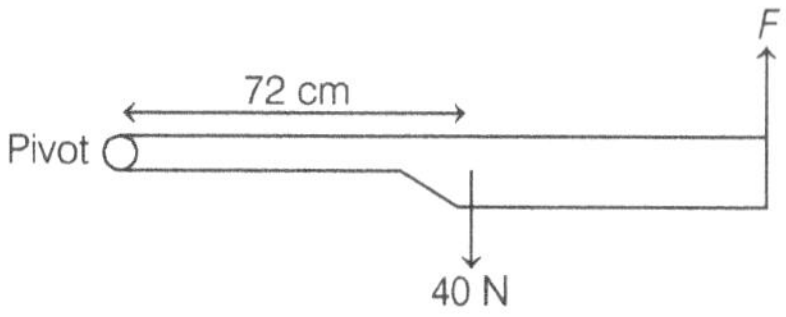

What is the magnitude of the force, F needed at the other end to keep it in equilibrium?

(a) 24 N (b) 30 N (c) 40 N (d) 48 N

Ans. (a) When the iron bar is pivoted at 72 cm mark, it is in equilibrium.

When the pivot is moved to A,

Clockwise moment = 40 × 0.72 = 28.8 N m

To be in equilibrium.

Anti-clockwise moment = 28.8

$$F \times 1.2 = 28.8$$

$$F = 24 \text{ N}$$

Q.21 A ball of mass 1 kg is tied to a string of length 2 m and rotated in a circular path with a uniform speed of 10 ms^{-1}. The centripetal force and centrifugal force acting on the body are, respectively

(a) 50 N each, both acting tangentially to the circle
(b) 50 N each, both acting toward the centre of circle
(c) 50 N each, both acting away from the centre of circle
(d) 50 N each, centripetal force is acting towards centre of circle while centrifugal force acting opposite to it

Ans. (d) Given, mass, $m = 1$ kg

Radius of circle, $r = l = 2$ m

Speed, $v = 10 \text{ ms}^{-1}$

$$\text{Centripetal force, } F = \frac{mv^2}{r} = \frac{1 \times 10^2}{2} = 50 \text{ N}$$

The magnitude of centripetal and centrifugal forces are equal but their directions are opposite. i.e. Centripetal force acts towards centre of circle while centrifugal force acts away from the centre of circle.

TYPE - 2 01 Mark

Assertion-Reason Type Questions

Direction (Q. Nos. 1-5) In the following questions two statements are given as Assertion and Reason.

(a) Both A and R are true and R is the correct explanation of A.
(b) Both A and R are true but R is not the correct explanation of A.

(c) A is true but R is false.
(d) A is false but R is true.

Q.1 Assertion (A) The moment of force depends on the perpendicular distance between the line of action of the force and the axis of rotation.
Reason (R) Torque is the product of force and the perpendicular distance from the axis of rotation.

Ans. (a) Moment of force (torque)
= Force × Perpendicular distance.
If the distance increases, torque increases.

Q.2 Assertion (A) Torque depends on both the force applied and the perpendicular distance from the axis of rotation.
Reason (R) Torque is the product of force and the perpendicular distance from the pivot point.

Ans. (a) Torque (moment of force) is given by $\tau = \mathbf{F} \times \mathbf{d}$, where F is the applied force and d is the perpendicular distance from the axis.

Q.3 Assertion (A) The centre of gravity of an irregularly shaped object always lies at its geometric centre.
Reaon (R) The centre of gravity depends on the distribution of mass within the object.

Ans. (d) The centre of gravity of an irregularly shaped object does not always coincide with its geometric centre. It depends on the distribution of mass within the object.

Q.4 Assertion (A) The centre of gravity of a body is the point where its entire weight appears to act.
Reason (R) The centre of gravity always lies within the body.

Ans. (c) The centre of gravity is where the entire weight acts, but it can lie outside the body (e.g., in a ring or hollow sphere).

Q.5 Assertion (A) A body in uniform circular motion is said to be accelerating.
Reason (R) The direction of velocity changes continuously in uniform circular motion.

Ans. (a) In circular motion, speed remains constant, but the direction changes. This change in direction will cause change in velocity which will produce acceleration.

TYPE - 3 — 01/02 Marks

Fill in the Blanks

Q.1 For a body to be in equilibrium under the action of forces, the net force and net .... (torque, momentum, work) must be zero. **[1]**

Ans. torque

Q.2 In uniform circular motion the centrifugal force acts .... (towards the centre/away from the centre/along the tangential direction). **[1][ICSE 2025]**

Ans. away from the centre

Q.3 The principle of moments states that for equilibrium, the sum of clockwise moments is equal to the sum of .... (anti-clockwise, vertical, horizontal) moments. **[1]**

Ans. anti-clockwise

Q.4 For a circular disc the position of centre of gravity is along the .... (tangent of the circle, geometric centre) **[1]**

Ans. geometric centre

Q.5 When a body remains in a state of rest under the influence of several forces, the body is in .... (static/dynamic) equilibrium. **[1]**

Ans. static

Q.6 In translational motion, a rigid body moves in a .... (circular, straight, curved) path when a force acts in the .... (opposite direction, same direction). **[2]**

Ans. straight, same direction

Q.7 In rotational motion, a body rotates about a .... (pivot, axis, point) when a force is applied tangentially to its .... (rim, centre, surface) **[2]**

Ans. pivot, rim

TYPE - 5 — 02 Marks

Very Short Answer Type Questions

Q.1 (i) Define moment of force. **[1]**
(ii) Write the relationship between the SI and CGS unit of moment of force. **[1][ICSE 2020]**

Ans. (i) The turning effect produced by a force on a rigid body about a point, pivot or fulcrum is called moment of force or torque.

(ii) ∵ Force = Mass × Acceleration

$$\therefore \frac{\text{SI unit of force}}{\text{CGS unit of force}} = \frac{\text{kg} \times \text{ms}^{-2}}{\text{g} \times \text{cms}^{-2}} = \left(\frac{\text{kg}}{\text{g}}\right)\left(\frac{\text{m}}{\text{cm}}\right) = 10^3 \times 10^2 = 10^5$$

∴ SI unit of force (Newton) = 10^5 CGS unit of force (dyne)

or 1 Newton = 10^5 dyne

Q.2 The picture below shows a boy climbing a rope ladder hanging from the branch of a tree. The boy in the picture finds it difficult to climb the ladder as it turns about the axis where he is holding. The instructor tells the boy to stretch the body with the hands stretched up and make the body parallel to the ladder and climb.

(i) Which force caused the ladder to turn? **[1]**

(ii) How does keeping the body parallel to the ladder make climbing easier? **[1]**

Ans. (i) His own weight causes the torque on his body and turns about his hands holding the ladder.

(ii) By stretching and keeping the body parallel to the rope decreases the torque arm, reducing the torque and makes it easier to climb.

Q.3 The diagram shows wheel *O* pivoted at point *A*. Three equal forces F_1, F_2 and F_3 acts at point *B* on the wheel.

(i) Which force will produce maximum moment about *A*? **[1]**

(ii) Give a reason for your answer in (i). **[1][ICSE 2023]**

Ans.

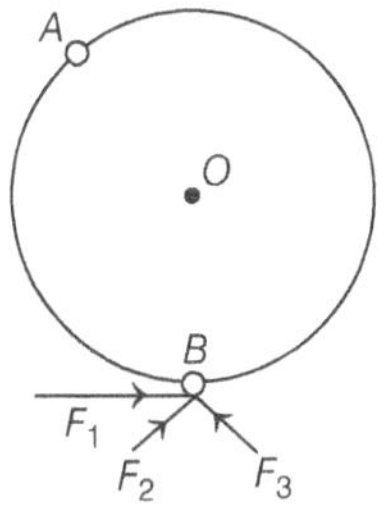

(i) About point *A*, force F_1 would result in the maximum moment $\tau = F \times d$. As, $F_1 = F_2 = F_3$ τ depends only on distance

(ii) F_1 has the greatest distance between the point of application of force and *A*. As a result, the maximum moment of force would be produced.

Q.4 Figure shows a system for raising a heavy piece of metal into a vertical position.

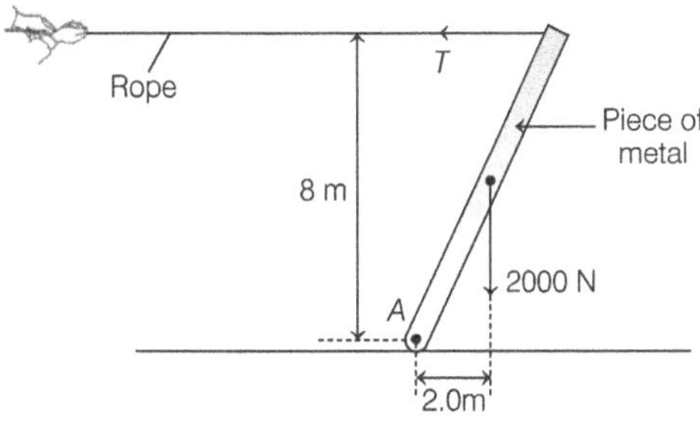

A man pulls the rope with a horizontal force *T*. The piece of metal has a weight of 2000 N and is freely pivoted at *A*. The system is in equilibrium

(i) By taking moments about *A*, calculate *T*. **[1]**

(ii) The force *T* and the force that the rope exerts on the man are related by Newton's third law. State the relationship between these forces. **[1]**

Ans. (i) Anti-clockwise moment = Clockwise moment

$$T \times 8 = 2000 \times 2 \Rightarrow T = 500 \text{ N}$$

(ii) The two forces are equal in magnitude but opposite in direction.

Q.5 (i) Define couple. **[1]**

(ii) State the SI unit of moment of couple. **[1][ICSE 2019]**

Ans. (i) A couple is a pair of forces equal in magnitude, oppositely directed and displaced by perpendicular distance or moment. The simplest kind of couple consists of two equal and opposite forces whose lines of action do not coincide and these forces produce turning effect.

(ii) The SI unit of moment of couple is N-m.

Q.6 Anu and Amy purchased ice creams in plastic balls and cones, respectively, during their outing at the science fair. After consuming their ice creams, Anu stated that regardless of whether they were filled with ice cream or empty, the centre of gravity of the objects would remain unchanged. Do you agree with Anu ? Why?

Ans. No, we do not agree with Anu.

The reason is that in the case of the plastic ball, since it has an equal distribution of mass around the centre of gravity irrespective of the fact that it is fully filled or fully empty, the centre of gravity remains in the same position.

But in case of a hollow cone and a solid cone, the mass distribution is not the same for the two. So, the centre of gravity for the cone shifts when it turns from solid to a hollow cone.

Q.7 A non-uniform kite is hanging freely from the branch of a tree as shown. Study the figure and answer the following **[2] [ICSE 2025]**

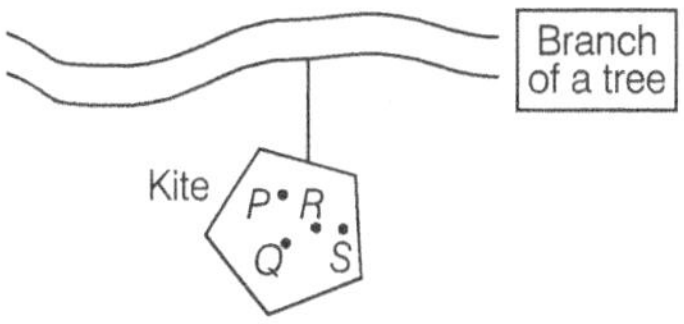

(a) Fill in the blank.

.... (*P*, *Q*, *R* or *S*) is the most probable position of its centre of gravity.

(b) Support your answer to (a) with a reason.

Ans. (a) *Q*.

(b) For a stable equilibrium of a body, the centre of gravity should be as low as possible and also near the geometric centre of the body and in the above case *Q* is the most appropriate point for the centre of gravity of the kite.

Q.8 What is the position of centre of gravity of a triangular lamina? When this triangular lamina is suspended freely from any one vertex, what is the moment of force produced by its own weight in its rest position? **[ICSE 2023]**

Ans. The centre of gravity of a triangular lamina is located at the point of intersection of its medians.

The moment of force produced by the weight of the triangular lamina in its rest position when suspended freely from any one vertex is equal to the torque produced by the weight of the lamina.

Q.9 Will the centre of gravity of a hollow sphere filled half with mercury and half with oil be identical to that of an empty hollow sphere? Give reasons for your answer.

Ans. No, the centre of gravity will not be the same.An empty hollow sphere has its centre of gravity at the geometric centre. However, when it is half filled with mercury and half with oil, the centre of gravity shifts downward. This happens because mercury is much denser than oil, so the lower half becomes heavier.

As a result, the centre of gravity moves closer to the mercury filled part of the sphere.

Q.10 In a gold atom (atomic number 79), an electron revolves around the nucleus in a circular orbit. There is a strong electrostatic force between the positively charged nucleus and the negatively charged electron. Though the total positive charge possessed by the nucleus is much higher than the negative charge of the electron, there is no displacement of the electron in the direction of the force.

(i) Name the force responsible for the movement of the electron around the nucleus in its own orbit. **[1]**

(ii) In the absence of such force, what would happen to the movement of the electron? **[1]**

Ans. (i) Centripetal force which is electrostatic force.

(ii) The electron would have moved in straight line along the tangent to the circular path.

Q.11 With reference to their direction of action, how does a centripetal force differ from a centrifugal force?

Ans. With reference to their direction of action, centripetal force is directed towards the centre of circle, whereas centrifugal force is opposite to the centripetal force (i.e. radially outward).

TYPE - 6 — 03 Marks

Short Answer Type Questions

Q.1 A metal rod *AB* of length 80 cm is balanced at 45 cm from the end *A* with 100 gf weights suspended from the two ends. **[Latest Specimen 2025]**

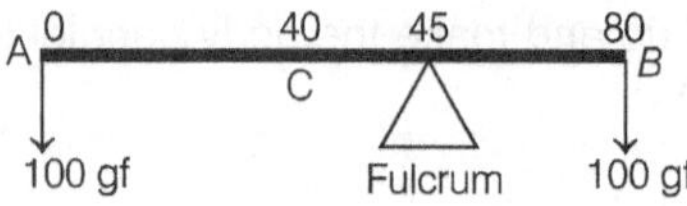

(i) If this rod is cut at the centre *C*, then compare the weight of *AC* to the weight of *BC*. **[1]**

(ii) Give a reason for your answer in (i) **[2]**

Ans. (a) Weight of *AC* < Weight of *BC*

(b) Even though the weights present are the same at both ends, the torque arm of *B* is less than the torque arm of *A*.

This means the moment of the weight of the rod acts from side *B* and the centre of gravity lies beyond 45. Thus, more weight is concentrated between *C* to *B*.

Q.2 Akash takes a uniform meter scale and suspends a weight of 2 N at one end '*X*' and a weight of 5 N on the other end '*Y*'. He then balances the ruler horizontally on a knife edge placed at 70 cm from *X*. Draw a diagram of the arrangement and calculate the weight of the ruler. **[3][ICSE 2025]**

Ans.

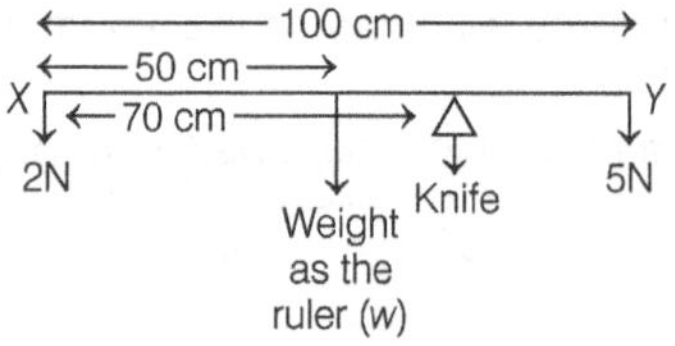

From the principle of moment, we know that sum of anti-clockwise moment = sum of clockwise moment.

$\therefore \quad (2 \times 70) + w \times 20 = 5 \times 30$

$\Rightarrow \quad 140 + 20w = 150$

$\Rightarrow \quad w = \dfrac{150 - 140}{20} = 0.5 \text{ N}$

$\therefore$ The weight of the ruler is 0.5 N.

Q.3 (i) Describe an experiment to verify the principle of moments. You may include a diagram in your answer. **[2]**

(ii) Figure shows a spanner tightening a nut.

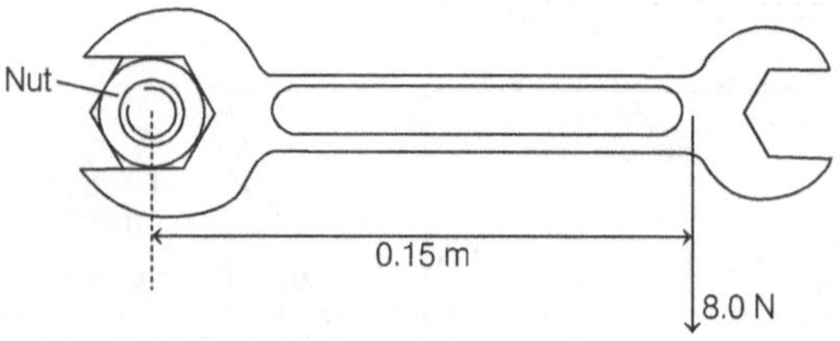

A force of 8.0 N is applied to the spanner at a perpendicular distance of 0.15 m from the centre of the nut.

Calculate the moment of the force acting on the nut. **[1]**

Ans. (i)

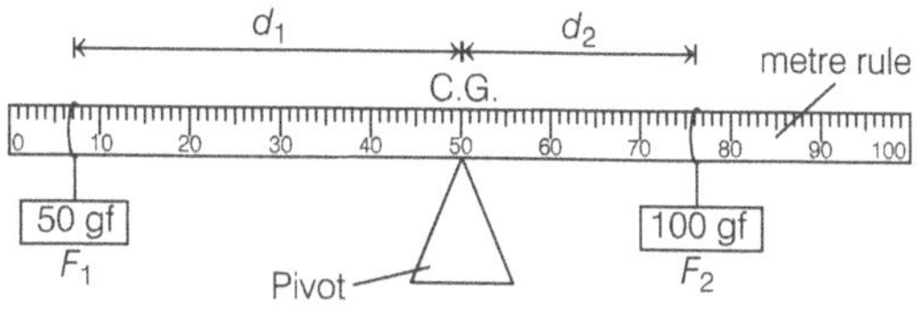

Set up the apparatus as shown with a pivot at 50 cm mark. Balance the metre rule by adjusting the distances d_1 and d_2. Calculate the anti-clockwise moment ($F_1 \times d_1$) and the clockwise moment ($F_2 \times d_2$). If it is found that,

Anti-clockwise moment = Clockwise moment

i.e. $F_1 \times d_1 = F_2 \times d_2$

then, it verfies the principle of moments

At the end, use the weights of different values and repeat the experiment.

(ii) Moment = force × moment arm

$= 8.0 \times 0.15 = 1.2$ Nm

Q.4 (i) Define centre of gravity. **[1]**

(ii) A hollow icecream cone has height 6 cm.

(a) Where is the position of its centre of gravity from the broad base? **[1]**

(b) Will its position change when it is filled completely with honey. Write yes or no. **[1]**

[ICSE 2024]

Ans. (i) The centre of gravity of a body is the point above which the algebraic sum of the moments of weights of all the particles constituting the body is zero.

(ii) (a) At the height $\left(\frac{h}{3}\right) = \frac{6}{3} = 2$ cm from the broad base.

(b) Yes

Q.5

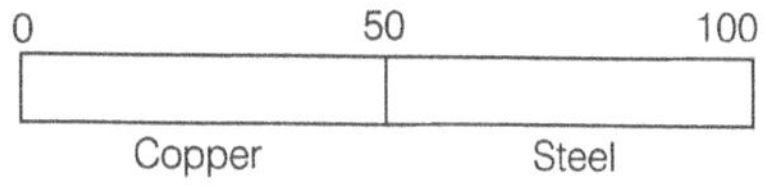

A metre rod made of copper and steel as shown in the diagram. Weights of copper and steel are 10 N and 8 N respectively.

(i) On which part does the centre of gravity lie (0 to 50 or 50 to 100). **[1]**

(ii) Justify your answer. **[2] [ICSE Specimen 2024]**

Ans. (i) Centre of gravity of the given rod lie between 0 to 50.

(ii) Centre of gravity lies towards high mass or weight.

Here,

$$W_{Copper} > W_{Steel}$$
$$10 \text{ N} > 8 \text{ N}$$

Q.6 Pavel took an earthen pot which was filled with water up to its brim. The earthen pot was conical in shape and kept with its apex in downward direction.

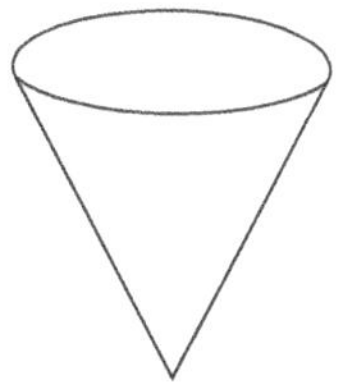

(i) If the vertical height of the earthen pot is 12 cm, where does its centre of gravity lie? **[1]**

(ii) Pavel poured out all the water from the pot. How will its centre of gravity shift towards the open end or towards its apex? **[1]**

(iii) Pavel wanted to grow a plant in the given pot. So, he filled it completely again with some soil. What will be the new position of its centre of gravity? **[1]**

Ans. (i) The centre of gravity of a uniform solid cone lies at a height of $\frac{h}{4}$ from its base along its central axis. Given that the vertical height of the earthen pot is 12 cm, the centre of gravity will be at $\frac{12}{4} = 3$ cm from the base (or 9 cm from the apex).

(ii) When Pavel pours out all the water from the pot, the pot becomes hollow and the centre of gravity of hollow cone is $\frac{h}{3}$. Hence, its centre of gravity shift towards the apex of the cone.

(iii) When Pavel fills the pot with soil, the cone again becomes a solid cone. The centre of gravity of solid cone as $\frac{h}{4}$ that's why the centre of gravity shift towards the same position as before.

Q.7 A uniform half metre ruler balances horizontally on a knife edge at 29 cm mark when a weight of 20 gf is suspended from one end.

(i) Draw a diagram of the arrangement. **[1]**

(ii) What is the weight of the half metre ruler? **[2]**

[ICSE 2017]

Ans. (i)

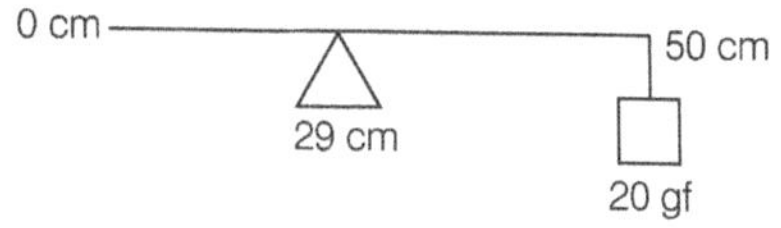

(ii) The centre of gravity of a uniform half metre rule is 25 cm.

The rule balances horizontally on a knife-edge at 29 cm mark when a weight of 20 gf is suspended from 50 cm end.

The difference in the centre of gravity and the point of balance = 29 – 25 = 4 cm (y)

The weight is suspended at one of the extremes.

Let us assume at the 50 cm end

Therefore, the distance from the point of knife edge to the weight.

$$50 - 29 = 21\,\text{cm}\ (x)$$

$$\therefore \text{ Weight of metre rule} = \frac{x}{y} \times \text{suspended weight}$$

$$= \frac{21}{4} \times 20$$

$$= 105\ \text{gf}$$

The weight of the half metre rule is 105 gf.

Q.8 **A stone of mass *m* is rotated in a horizontal circular path with a uniform speed by tying a strong string with the help of your hand. Answer the following questions**

(i) **Is the stone moving with a uniform or variable speed?** **[1]**

(ii) **Is the stone moving with a uniform acceleration? In which direction does the acceleration act?** **[1]**

(iii) **What kind of force acts on the hand and state its direction?** **[1][ICSE 2016]**

Ans. (i) The stone is moving with a uniform speed and variable velocity.

(ii) No, the stone is not moving with a uniform acceleration, because the direction of acceleration changes. Acceleration always acts towards the centre of the circular path.

(iii) Reaction force of centripetal force, radially in outwards direction from the centre of the circle.

TYPE - 7 — 04 Marks

Long Answer Type Questions

Q.1 Explain the moment of a force with diagram for

(i) the steering wheel of a car. **[2]**

(ii) the pedal and the rear wheel of a bicycle. **[2]**

Ans. (i) For turning a steering wheel, a force is applied tangentially on rim of the wheel.

The sense of rotation of wheel is changed by changing the point of application of force without changing the direction of force.

In Fig. (a), when force F is applied at the point A of the wheel, the wheel rotates anti-clockwise, while in Fig. (b), the wheel rotates clockwise when the force F in same direction is applied at the point B of the wheel.

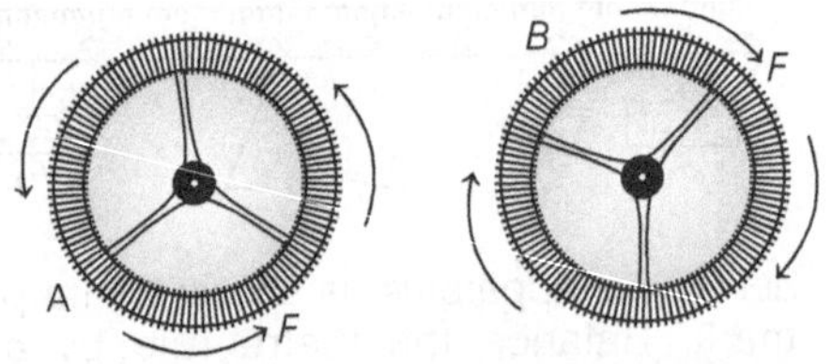

Fig. (a) Anti-clockwise rotation Fig. (b) Clockwise rotation

(ii) In the case of a bicycle wheel, a small force is applied at the pedal which is at large distance from the axle. Since, in one revolution, the pedal moves through a large distance than the links of the chain. Thus, the applied force gets multiplied and is passed on the rear wheel.

The two pedals provide two such forces and form a torque, i.e. moment of force which rotates the wheel.

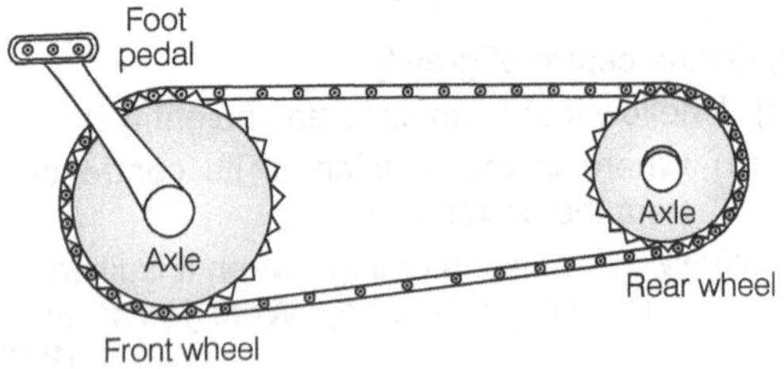

Q.2 (i) **Explain how the concept of a couple is used in steering a car.** **[1]**

(ii) **If the distance between two forces is increased, how will it affect the moment of the couple?** **[1]**

(iii) **Why is a couple said to produce only rotational motion and not translational motion?** **[2]**

Ans. (i) In steering a car, a couple is applied when forces are exerted in opposite directions on the steering wheel to turn it.

(ii) Increase in the distance (d) between the forces increases the moment of the couple, making it more effective.

(iii) A couple produces only rotational motion because the equal and opposite forces cancel out any translational effects.

Q.3 (i) **Name the different types of equilibrium?** **[1]**

(ii) **Mention two essential conditions required for a body to be in equilibrium.** **[2]**

(iii) **Define the principle of moments and describe its significance in maintaining equilibrium.** **[1]**

Ans. (i) There are three types of equilibrium static equilibrium, dynamic equilibrium and neutral equilibrium.

(ii) The body will be in equilibrium if resultant of all forces acting on the body is zero.

Resultant moment of all forces acting on the body about the point of rotation should be zero.

(iii) The principle of moment states that for a body to be in equilibrium. The sum of clockwise moments about a point must be equal to the sum of anti-clockwise moments about the same point.

The principle of moments helps in keeping objects balanced and stable. It ensure that when the turning effects of force on both sides of a pivot are equal, the object remains in equilibrium and does not rotate. This is important in daily life, engineering and construction.

Q.4 (i) **State what is meant by the moment of a force about a point and state how it is calculated? [1]**

(ii) **The figure below shows a crane lifiting some bricks during the building of a house.**

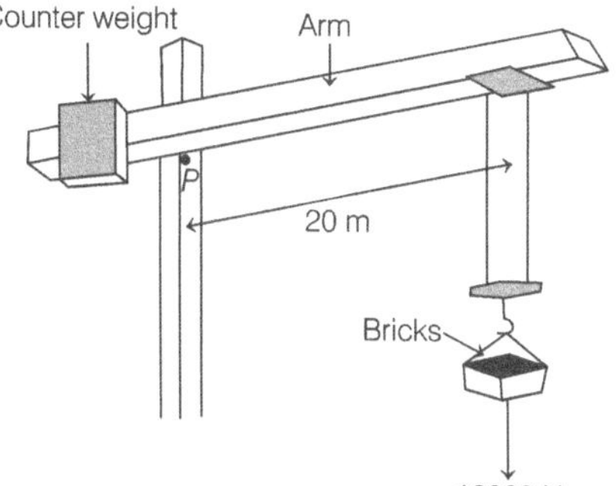

The weight of the bricks produces a turning effect or moment, on the arm of the crane about the point *P*. The weight of the bricks is 12000 N.

(a) **Calculate the moment of this force, using the distance, marked on the figure above. [1]**

(b) **Explain, why the counter weight is necessary? [1]**

(c) **Suggest one advantage of being able to move the counterweight along the arm. [1]**

Ans. (i) The moment of a force about a point (known as pivot) is the turning effect about the point.

Moment of a force about a point is the product of the force and the perpendicular distance of the force from that point.

(ii) (a) Moment = force × perpendicular distance

$$= 12000 \text{ N} \times 20 \text{ m} = 240000 \text{ N-m}$$

(b) The load will produce a clockwise moment about the pivot. Therefore a counter weight is needed to produce an opposing moment in order to prevent the arm from topping over.

(c) By adjusting the distance of the counter weight from the pivot, the anti-clockwise moment produced by the counter weight can be varied. This allows the crane to carry different loads.

Q.5 (i) **Which of the following remains constant in a uniform circular motion, speed or velocity or both? [1]**

(ii) **Name the force required for a uniform circular motion. State its direction. [1]**

(iii) **Explain, the motion of a planet around the sun in a circular path. [2]**

Ans. (i) Speed remains constant in a uniform circular motion.

(ii) Centripetal force is required for a uniform circular motion. Centripetal force is always directed towards the centre.

(iii) For a planet moving around the sun in a circular path, the gravitational force of attraction between the planet and the sun provides the necessary centripetal force.

TYPE - 8 — 03/04 Marks

Case Based Questions

Q.1

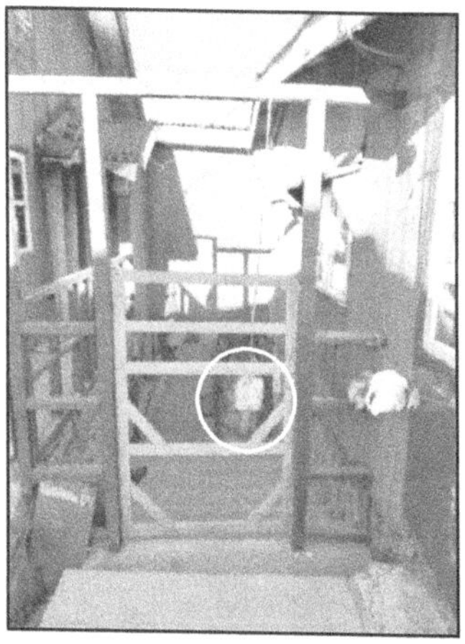

Bandish and Parag, on a trek to Sandakpu, halted at a tea house in Tumbling. The picture above shows the entrance door of the tea house. They saw the tumbrel filled with water hanging from top rigid support passing through the door. On enquiring about the tumbrel, the owner of the tea house, he said that it acts as a pullback (door closure) after opening and releasing the door. [Competency Based Qus.]

(i) **Explain how the tumbrel helps to close the door on its own. [1]**

(ii) **Name the principle involved. [1]**

(iii) **Why does the owner of the tea house use water instead of a solid weight? [1]**

(iv) **Where is the tumbrel attached in the set up? [1]**

Ans. (i) Initially, the centre of gravity of the tumbrel is vertically below the fixed support, so the torque on the door is zero as the torque arm is zero.

But when you push the door to open it, the tumbrel moves away and now there is some torque arm which acts on the door to bring it back to its original position.

(ii) Principle of moments.

(iii) Water is easily available, adjustable and adds the required weight to pull the door without causing damage.

(iv) The tumbrel is hanging from a top rigid support and connected to the door.

Q.2 **A technician is designing a metal plate of irregular shape. To determine its centre of gravity, he hangs the plate from different points and traces the vertical line passing through the hanging point. The intersection of these lines is the centre of gravity.**

(i) Why does the technician hang the plate from different point ? **[1]**

(ii) How would the centre of gravity change if the metal plate had an extra mass attached at one end ? **[1]**

(iii) What is the significane of the intersection point of the lines drawn? **[1]**

Ans. (i) The technician does this to accurately located the centre of gravity, as it lies at the intersection of all such vertical lines.

(ii) The centre of gravity would shift toward the heavier end because the additional mass increases the weight distribution on that side.

(iii) The intersection point is the exact location of the centre of gravity of the irregular shape.

TYPE - 9

Numerical Questions

Q.1 **Calculate the resultant torque from the following diagram.** **[2][ICSE Specimen 2017]**

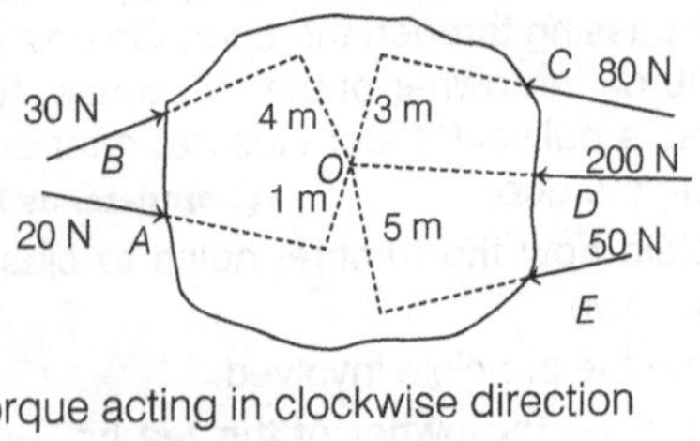

Sol. Total torque acting in clockwise direction

$$= -(30 \times 4 + 50 \times 5)$$

$$= -(120 + 250) = -370 \text{ N-m}$$

Total torque acting in anti-clockwise direction

$$= +(20 \times 1 + 80 \times 3)$$

$$= +(20 + 240)$$

$$= +260 \text{ N-m}$$

$$\text{Resultant torque} = (-370 + 260) \text{ N-m}$$

$$= -110 \text{ N-m (clockwise direction)}$$

200 N will not produce torque as there is no perpendicular distance.

Q.2 **(i) Name the force which produces maximum moment about.** **[1]**

(ii) Calculate this moment in SI unit. **[1][ICSE Specimen 2023]**

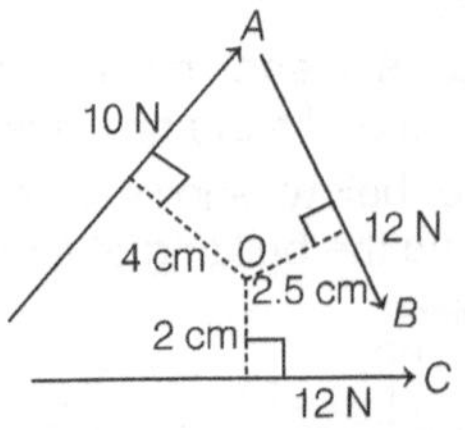

Sol. (i) The force $F = 10$ N which produces maximum moment about O.

(ii) Moment of force A,

$$F = 10 \text{ N}, \; d = 4 \text{ cm} = 0.04 \text{ m}$$

$$\tau = 10 \times 0.04 = 0.4 \text{ N-m}$$

Moment of force B,

$$F = 12 \text{ N}, d = 2.5 \text{ cm} = 0.025 \text{ m}$$

$$\tau = 12 \times 0.025 = 0.3 \text{ N-m}$$

Moment of force C,

$$F = 12 \text{ N}, d = 2 \text{ cm} = 0.02 \text{ m}$$

$$\tau = 12 \times 0.02 = 0.24 \text{ N-m}$$

Q.3 **If the moment of force F about the centre of a wheel O is 6 N-m, then calculate the moment of F about A.** **[2][ICSE Specimen 2023]**

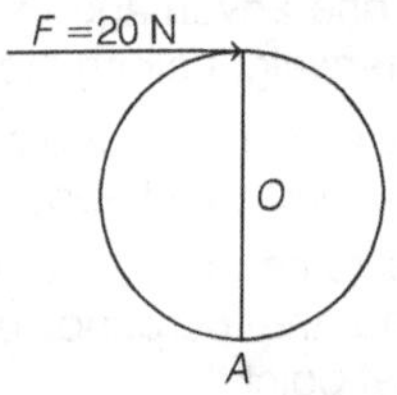

Sol. Moment of force, $\tau = 6$ N-m point at O.

Force, $F = 20$ N

As we know, $\tau = r \times F$

$$r = \frac{\tau}{F} = \frac{6}{20} \text{ m} = 0.3 \text{ m}$$

When the rotation occur at point A, then $r' = 2r$

$$= 2 \times 0.3 \text{ m}$$

$$r' = 0.6 \text{ m}$$

Hence, the moment of force about A,

$$\tau = r' \times F = 20 \times 0.6 = 12 \text{ N-m}$$

Q.4 A metre rod is half made of copper and half made of iron. If the mass of the copper part is 900 g and the mass of iron is 800 g, then calculate the position at which the rod can remain in equilibrium. **[2]**

[Competency Based Que.]

Sol.

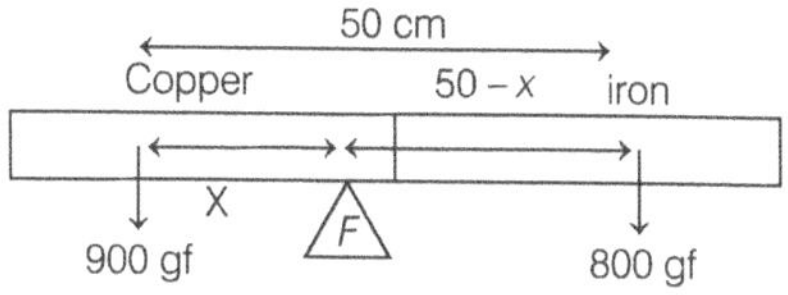

The distance between their CG is 50 cm

$$900 \times x = 800(50 - x)$$

$\therefore \quad 900x = 40000 - 800x$

$\therefore \quad 1700x = 40000$

$\therefore \quad x = \frac{40000}{1700} = \frac{400}{17} = 23.53$ cm

It will be balanced at a distance (25+23.53) cm = 48.53 cm from the end of copper.

Q.5 A uniform metre scale is in equilibrium position. Calculate the mass of the ruler. **[2][ICSE Specimen 2017]**

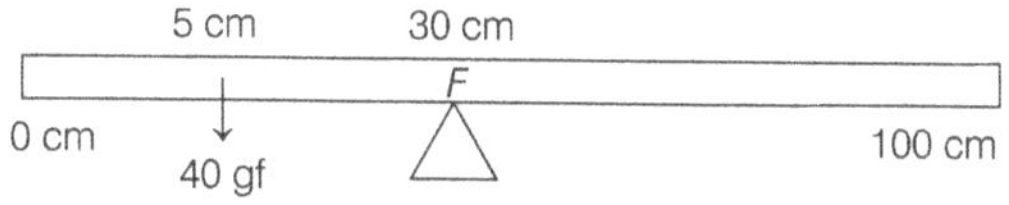

Sol. Let m be the mass of scale in gram.

$\therefore$ Weight of scale = m gf

By principle of moment, we get

$$40 \times (30 - 5) = m \times (50 - 30)$$

[$\because$ centre of gravity of scale is 50 cm]

$\Rightarrow \quad 40 \times 25 = m \times 20 \Rightarrow m = 50$ g

Q.6 A non-uniform beam of weight 120 N pivoted at one end is shown in the diagram below. Calculate the value of F to keep the beam in equilibrium. **[ICSE 2024] [2]**

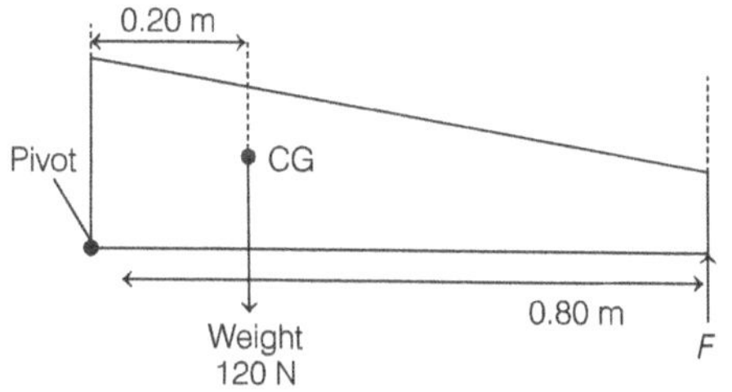

Sol. By principle of moments above O,

$$F_1 d_1 = F_2 d_2$$

$$120 \times (0.20) = F_2 \times (0.80)$$

$$F_2 = \frac{120 \times 0.20}{0.80} = 30 \text{ N}$$

Q.7 A rectangular iron door of a building has a width of 3 m and can rotate about its hinges along one side. A force of 100 N is applied perpendicularly at the mid-point of the door to open it.

(i) Calculate the torque required to open the door. **[1]**

(ii) Determine the minimum force needed to open the door and identify the point of application of this force. **[2]**

Sol. (i) Given, $F = 100$ N, distance of point of application of force, $r = \frac{1}{2} \times$ breadth of door

$$= \frac{1}{2} \times 3 = 1.5 \text{ m} \qquad \text{...(i)}$$

Moment of force (torque) needed to open the door

$= F \times r = 100 \text{ N} \times 1.5$ m

$= 150$ Nm

(ii) The force required will be least if it is applied at the farthest point from the hinges. Therefore the force should be applied normally at the free end of the door i.e., at a distance of 3 m from the hinges.

Let the force required be F' newton, then

Moment of force $= F' \times 3$ N $\qquad$ ...(ii)

From Eqs. (i) and (ii)

$$F' \times 3 = 150$$

$$F' = \frac{150}{3} = 50 \text{ N}$$

Q.8 A half metre rod is pivoted at the centre with two weights of 20 gf and 12 gf suspended at a perpendicular distance of 6 cm and 10 cm from the pivot respectively as shown below. **[ICSE 2018]**

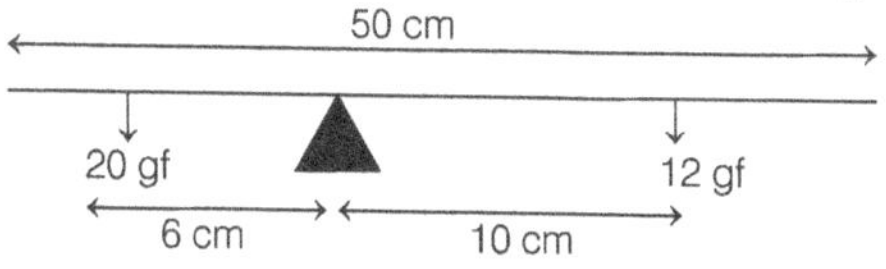

(i) Which of the two forces acting on the rigid rod causes clockwise moment? **[1]**

(ii) Is the rod in equilibrium? **[1]**

(iii) The direction of 20 gf force is reversed. What is the magnitude of the resultant moment of the forces on the rod? **[1]**

Sol. (i) The force 12 gf rotates the rod clockwise.

(ii) The clockwise moment = 20gf × 6 cm

= 120 gf cm

The anti-clockwise moment

= 12 gf × 10 cm

= 120 gf cm

Hence, the rod is in equilibrium.

(iii) On reversing the direction of force, 20 gf will also produce clockwise moment, total clockwise moment will then be (20 gf × 6 cm + 12 gf × 10 cm)

$= 240$ gf cm

Q.9 The force F is necessary to hold steady, in the position shown, a mass of W kg. The mass of lifiting bar is negligible otherwise stated. ($g = 10\ ms^{-2}$)

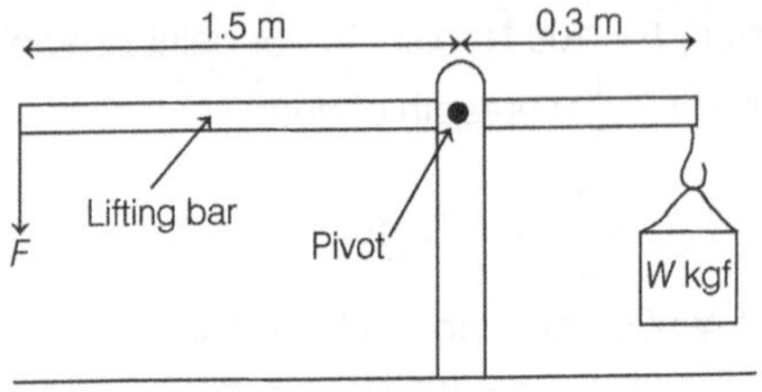

(i) If $W = 60$ kgf, what is F? **[1]**

(ii) If $W = 100$ kgf, and $F = 150$ N, which side and where should another mass of 10 kg be suspended from the pivot to keep the bar in the same position? **[2]**

Sol. (i) Taking moment about the pivot,

anticlockwise moment = clockwise moment

$$F \times 1.5 = 60 \times 10 \times 0.3$$

$$F = 120 \text{ N}$$

(ii) Let d be the distance of the 10 kg mass from the pivot.

Clockwise moment $= 100 \times 10 \times 0.3 = 300$ N m

Anti-clockwise moment produced by F

$= 150 \times 1.5 = 225$ Nm

To be in equilibrium,

$$(10 \times 10 \times d) + 225 = 300$$

$$d = 0.75 \text{ m}$$

The mass of 10 kg should be suspended to the left side 0.75 m from the pivot.

Q.10 The adjacent diagram shows a wheel of diameter 40 cm fixed on a wall capable of rotating around its centre O. If the wheel rotates in an anti-clockwise direction, then

(i) calculate the clockwise moment. **[1]**

(ii) state whether $X = 100$ gf or $X < 100$ gf or $X > 100$ gf. **[1]**

(iii) Given a reason for your answer. **[1]**

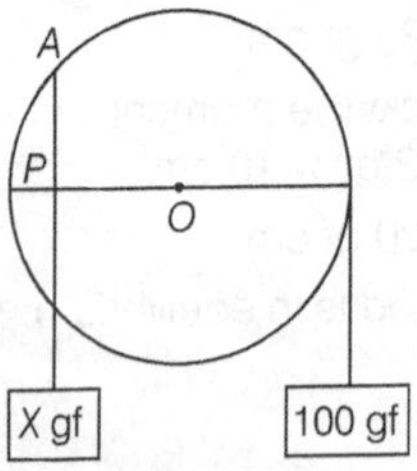

[ICSE Specimen 2023]

Sol. (i) Clockwise moment $= 100 \times 20 = 2000$ gf cm

(ii) $X > 100$ gf

(iii) Anti-clockwise moment should be greater than clockwise rotation.

Q.11 A uniform metre scale is in equilibrium as shown in the figure given below.

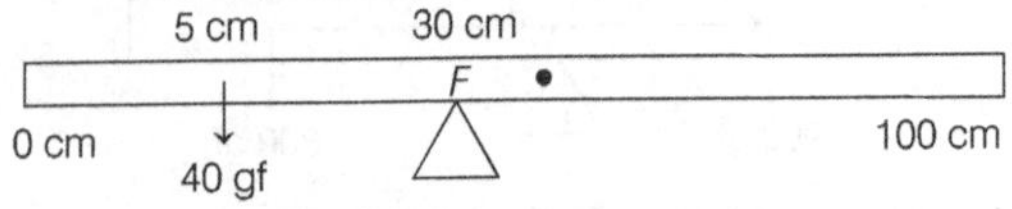

(i) Calculate the weight of the metre scale. **[2]**

(ii) Which of the following option is correct to keep the ruler in equilibrium, when 40 gf-wt is shifted to 0 cm mark? F is shifted towards 0 cm or F is shifted 100 cm. **[1][ICSE 2019]**

Sol.

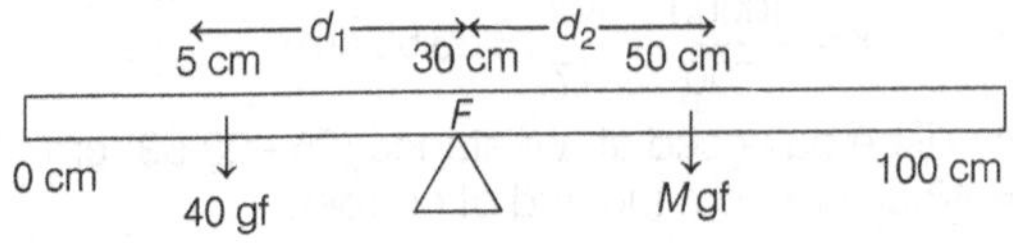

(i) At 50 cm,

Mass of the metre scale = M gf

Now, $F_1d_1 = F_2d_2$

$$(40 \text{ gf})(30 - 5) = F_2(50 - 30)$$

$$F_2 = 50 \text{ gf}$$

$$F_2 = 0.49 \text{ N}$$

$\therefore$ $F_2 = Mg$

$$0.49 = M \times 9.8$$

$$M = \frac{0.49}{9.8} = 0.05 \text{ kg}$$

(ii) F is shifted towards 0 cm.

Q.12 An uniform metre rule rests horizontally on a knife edge at the 60 cm mark when a weight of 10gf is suspended from one end. Draw a diagram of the arrangement.

(i) At which end of the scale, this mass must be suspended to maintain equilibrium? **[2]**

(ii) What is the mass of the metre scale? **[1]**

Sol. (i) Let M gram be the mass of the rule. Since the density of the rule is uniform, its weight Mgf will act at its middle point i.e., at the 50 cm mark (fig).

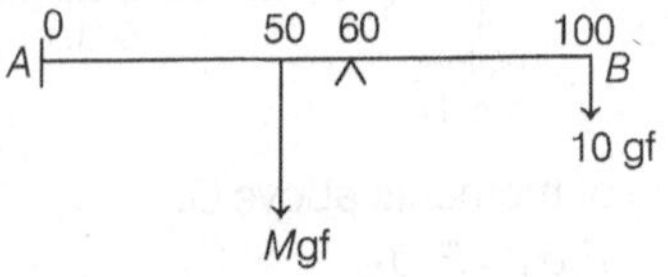

The weight of the rule produces an anti-clockwise moment about the knife edge O. In order to balance it, 10 gf weight is to be suspended at the end B to produce a clockwise moment.

(ii) From the principle of moments,

Anti-clockwise moment = Clockwise moment

$M \times (60 - 50) = 10 \times (100 - 60)$

$M \times 10 = 10 \times 40$

$\therefore$ Mass of rule, $M = 40$ g

Q.13 A couple consists of two forces of magnitude $F = 20$ N each, separated by a perpendicular distance $d = 0.4$ m.

Answer the following

(i) Calculate the moment of the couple using the formula. **[1]**

(ii) If the distance between the forces is doubled, then find the new moment of the couple. **[1]**

(iii) If the magnitude of the forces is halved, while keeping the distance the same as in part (i), calculate the new moment of the couple. **[1]**

Sol. (i) Given,

$F = 20$ N, $d = 0.4$ m

$M = F \times d$

$M = 20 \times 0.4 = 8$ Nm

(ii) New distance,

$d' = 2 \times 0.4 = 0.8$ m

$M' = F \times d'$

$M' = 20 \times 0.8$

$= 16$ Nm

(iii) New force, $F' = \dfrac{20}{2} = 10$ N

Distance = 0.4 m

$M'' = F' \times d$

$M'' = 10 \times 0.4 = 4$ Nm

Q.14 (i) Calculate the centripetal force acting on the car if its mass is 1000 kg. Velocity is 10 m/s and radius of circle is 50 cm. **[1]**

(ii) If the car's speed is doubled, how will the centripetal force change? **[1]**

(iii) Why do passengers in the car feel pushed outward while turning? **[1]**

Sol. (i) Given, $M = 1000$ kg, $v = 10$ m/s, $r = 50$ m

$$F = \frac{mv^2}{r}, \quad F = \frac{1000 \times 10^2}{50} = \frac{1000 \times 100}{50} = 2000 \text{ N}$$

(ii) If the car's speed is doubled ($v = 20$ m/s) the centripetal force will be

$$F' = \frac{mv^2}{r} = \frac{1000 \times 20^2}{50}$$

$$= \frac{1000 \times 400}{50} = 8000 \text{ N}$$

(iii) Passengers feel pushed outward due to their inertia, as they tend to move in a straight line while the car is turning. This sensation is perceived as centrifugal force.

02

WORK, POWER AND ENERGY

Work

- It is said to be done when a force produces displacement in the direction in which it acts. e.g. A man pulling a car, a horse pulling a cart, a cyclist while pedaling a bicycle, etc, are examples of work.

  Work done by a force is $\boxed{W = Fs\cos\theta}$

  where, F = Force applied on the body, s = Displacement produced and θ = Angle between direction of force and direction of displacement.
- The SI unit of work is **joule** (J) and CGS unit is **erg**. It is a **scalar quantity**.
- **1 joule** of work is said to be done when a force of 1 newton, displaces an object by 1 metre along with the direction of force.
- 1 erg of work is said to be done when a force of 1 dyne displaces an object by 1 centimetre along with the direction of force.

Positive, Negative and Zero Work

- When the force F and displacement s are in the **same direction** (angle between direction of force and displacement is 0°), work done will be **positive**, i.e. work is done by the force.
  e.g. a boy pulls an object towards himself.

  $$\boxed{W = +F \times s}$$

- When the force F and displacement s are in opposite direction (angle between direction of force and displacement is 180°), work done will be **negative**, i.e. work is done against the force.

  e.g. frictional force acts in the direction opposite to the direction of displacement, so work done by friction will be negative.

  $$\boxed{W = -F \times s}$$

- When the force and displacement are in perpendicular direction (angle between direction of force and displacement is 90°), work done is zero.

  e.g. a coolie carrying load on his head. In this case, gravitational force is acting vertically downward (weight of load) and displacement is along horizontal direction, i.e. force and displacement are perpendicular to each other.

  Thus, work done by gravitational force is zero.

  $$\boxed{W = 0}$$

Units of Work

- 1 kJ (kilo-joule) = 10^3 J,
- 1 MJ (mega-joule) = 10^6 J
- 1 GJ (giga-joule) = 10^9 J
- **Relation between Joule and Erg**

  $$1 \text{ joule} = 1 \text{ newton} \times 1 \text{ metre} \Rightarrow 1 \text{ joule} = 10^5 \text{ dyne} \times 10^2 \text{ centimetre}$$

  $$\therefore \quad 1 \text{ joule} = 10^7 \text{ erg}$$

Energy

- The energy of a body is its ability to do work. A body capable of doing work is said to possess energy. Work and energy are directly related to each other. The SI unit of energy is **joule** (J) and in CGS unit is **erg**. It is a **scalar quantity**.

REVISION NOTES

- The larger units of energy are watt hour (Wh) and kilowatt hour (kWh)

$$1\text{ Wh} = 3600\text{ J} \Rightarrow 1\text{ kWh} = 3.6 \times 10^6\text{ J}$$

- Other unit of energy are calories and eV.

$$1\text{cal} = 4.18\text{J} \quad \Rightarrow \quad 1\text{eV} = 1.6 \times 10^{-19}\text{ J}$$

- The energy possessed by a body due to its position and state of motion is called **mechanical energy**.
- Mechanical energy is of two types, kinetic energy and potential energy.
- The total mechanical energy of a body is equal to the **sum of its kinetic energy** and **potential energy**.

Kinetic Energy

- The energy possessed by a body by virtue of its state of motion is called kinetic energy.
- It is generally denoted by KE. It is expressed as

$$\boxed{\text{KE} = \frac{1}{2}mv^2}$$

where, m = mass of the body, v = speed of the body.

- Kinetic energy K and momentum $p (= mv)$ are related as $K = \dfrac{p^2}{2m}$
- **Work-Energy Theorem** Work done by a body or on a body is equal to change in its kinetic energy. If initial speed (velocity) of a body is u and final speed (velocity) of a body is v, then according to work-energy theorem,
  Work done by all the forces acting on the body (ΔW) = Change in kinetic energy of the body (ΔK)

$$\boxed{\Delta W = \frac{1}{2}mv^2 - \frac{1}{2}mu^2}$$

Forms of Kinetic Energy There are three forms of kinetic energy as mentioned below

(i) **Translational Kinetic Energy** The kinetic energy which acts on a body when it is moving in a straight line is called its translational kinetic energy.
e.g. A car moving in a straight path, freely falling body, molecule of a monoatomic gas, etc.

(ii) **Rotational Kinetic Energy** If a body rotates about an axis, the motion is called rotational motion and the kinetic energy possessed due to rotational motion is called rotational kinetic energy. e.g. A rotating wheel, a spinning top, etc.

(iii) **Vibrational Kinetic Energy** The kinetic energy which comes into play when an object vibrates to and fro about its mean position is called vibrational kinetic energy, e.g. A wire clamped at both ends when plucked at the middle vibrates.

Potential Energy

The energy possessed by a body by virtue of its position (configuration) is called the potential energy. e.g. A body placed at a height above the ground, a wound up watch spring. It is usually denoted by the symbol U.

Forms of Potential Energy Mainly there are two types of potential energy such as

(i) **Gravitational Potential Energy** It is the amount of work done in raising a body from the ground to a point at height h, against gravity.

It is expressed by $\boxed{U = mgh}$

where, m is the mass of the object, g is acceleration due to gravity and h is the height through which the object is raised.

(ii) **Elastic Potential Energy** The energy possessed by a body in its deformed state due to the change in its shape and size is called elastic potential energy. e.g. Energy possessed by a compressed spring.

Different Forms of Energy

We get energy in various forms. Some of these forms are

(i) **Chemical Energy** It is the energy possessed by fossil fuels such as coal, petroleum and natural gases. A battery also has chemical energy in it.

(ii) **Mechanical Energy** It is the energy possessed by a body due to its **position** and state of **motion**. A moving ball, a body at rest, etc., have mechanical energy.

(iii) **Heat Energy** The energy released on burning fuels such as coal, oil, gas, etc., is called heat energy.

(iv) **Electrical Energy** The energy possessed by a charged body due to the movement of free electrons is called electrical energy.

(v) **Nuclear Energy** When a heavy nucleus of an element splits into two smaller nuclei or when two lighter nuclei fuses to form a single heavy nucleus, a tremendous amount of energy is released, which is known as nuclear energy.

(vi) **Light Energy** It is a form of energy which we receive from the sun and also from other luminous sources which helps us in seeing the objects around us when it reflected from the surface of the objects.

(vii) **Sound Energy** The mechanical energy possessed by a vibrating body which is capable of producing a sensation of hearing in human ears when it travels through a material medium is known as sound energy.

Law of Conservation of Energy

- The law of conservation of energy states that **energy can neither be created nor be destroyed, it can only be transformed from one form to another**.
- The total energy before and after transformation always remains constant.

Transformation of Energy

One form of energy can be converted into other form of energy and this phenomenon is called transformation of energy. When an object is dropped from some height, its potential energy gradually converts into kinetic energy. When an object is thrown upwards, its kinetic energy gradually converts into potential energy.

Some examples of **energy transformation** are as follows.

(i) Green plants prepare their own food (stored in the form of chemical energy) by using solar energy through the process of **photosynthesis**.

(ii) When we throw a ball, the muscular energy which is stored in our body, gets converted into kinetic energy of the ball.

(iii) The wound spring in the toy car possesses potential energy. As the spring is released, its potential energy changes into kinetic energy due to which the toy car moves.

(iv) In a stretched bow, potential energy is stored. As it is released, the potential energy of the stretched bow gets converted into the kinetic energy of arrow which moves in the forward direction with large velocity.

Rate of Doing Work : Power

- The rate of doing work by a machine is called the power of the machine.

Thus, $$\text{Power} = \frac{\text{Work}}{\text{Time}}$$

- If a machine does a total amount of work W by exerting a force on a body for a total time-interval t, then the average power delivered by the machine is given by

$$P = W/t$$

- The unit of power is **watt** (W) in honour of **James Watt**.
- We express larger rate of energy transfer in **kilowatt (kW)**.

$$1\text{ W} = 1\text{ Js}^{-1}$$

or $$1\text{kW} = 1000\text{ W} = 1000\text{ Js}^{-1} \Rightarrow 1\text{ MW} = 10^6\text{ W},$$

$$1\text{ HP (horse power)} = 746\text{ W} = 0.746\text{ kW}$$

- **Average Power** It is defined as the ratio of total work done by the total time taken.
A machine may perform work at different rates at different intervals of time. In such situation, average power is considered by dividing the total energy consumed by the total time taken.

$\therefore$ $$\text{Average power} = \frac{\text{Total energy consumed}}{\text{Total time taken}}$$

REVISION NOTES

EXAM ORIENTED QUESTIONS

TYPE - 1   01 Mark

Multiple Choice Questions

Q.1 A coolie raises a load upwards against the force of gravity, then the work done by the load is **[ICSE 2022 Sem-I]**

(a) zero (b) positive work

(c) negative work (d) None of these

Ans. (c) The coolie raises load in the upward direction and the force of gravity is in downward direction.

So, work done $= |F||s|\cos 180^\circ = -|F||s|$

$\therefore$ Negative work

Q.2 A force F moves a load from A to C as shown in the figure below. For the calculation of the work done, which of these lengths would you use as the displacement ? **[ICSE 2024]**

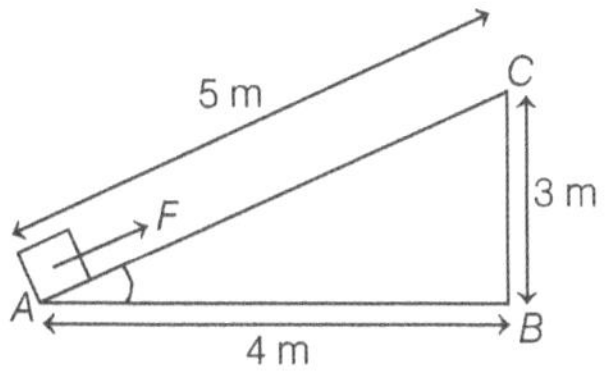

(a) 3 m (b) 4 m (c) 5 m (d) 7 m

Ans. (c) Work done = Force × Displacement in the direction of force.

Since, the force acting on the object is along the slope of the inclined plane so, the displacement considered is 5m.

Q.3 What is the correct energy transformation during burning of a candle? **[ICSE 2025]**

(a) Heat → Kinetic + Potential

(b) Heat → Chemical + Light

(c) Chemical → Heat + Light

(d) Mechanical → Chemical + Heat

Ans. (c) When a candle burns, a chemical reaction occurs where wax reacts with oxygen which converts the chemical potential energy into heat and light.

Q.4 The kinetic energy of a given body depends on the **[ICSE Specimen 2025]**

(a) position

(b) centre of gravity of the body

(c) momentum

(d) displacement

Ans. (c) The kinetic energy of a body is $KE = \frac{p^2}{2m}$

$KE \propto (\text{momentum})^2$

Q.5 When a bell fixed on a cycle rings, then the energy conversion that takes place is **[ICSE 2024]**

(a) gravitational potential energy to sound energy

(b) kinetic energy to sound energy

(c) sound energy to electrical energy

(d) sound energy to mechanical energy

Ans. (b) When a bell fixed on a cycle rings, then the energy conversion that takes place is kinetic energy to sound energy.

Q.6 The usable form of mechanical energy is **[ICSE Specimen 2022 Sem-I]**

(a) elastic potential energy

(b) kinetic energy

(c) gravitational potential energy

(d) None of these

Ans. (b) Usable form of mechanical energy is kinetic energy.

Q.7 The energy conversion in washing machine is from **[ICSE 2023]**

(a) magnetic to electrical

(b) electrical to mechanical

(c) electrical to magnetic

(d) magnetic to electrical

Ans. (b) In washing machine, there is a motor which converts electrical energy into mechanical energy.

Q.8 In an electric cell while in use, the change in energy is from **[ICSE Specimen 2022 Sem-I]**

(a) chemical to mechanical

(b) chemical to electrical

(c) electrical to mechanical

(d) electrical to chemical

Ans. (b)

Q.9 For burning of coal in a thermoelectric station, the energy conversions taking place are **[ICSE Specimen 2025]**

(a) chemical to heat to mechanical

(b) chemical to heat to mechanical to electrical

(c) chemical to heat to light

(d) heat to chemical to mechanical

Ans. (b) In thermoelectric station, the energy conversion taking place is chemical to heat to mechanical to electrical.

Q.10 The energy conversion, when an oscillating pendulum moves from mean to extreme position is **[ICSE Specimen 2023]**

(a) kinetic to potential
(b) potential to kinetic
(c) potential to kinetic to potential
(d) kinetic to potential to kinetic

Ans. (a) When pendulum goes from mean position to extreme position, its velocity becomes zero and kinetic energy changes to potential energy.

Q.11 A 300 N force is applied to a box in the direction *XY* in order to move it up a ramp of the dimensions shown.

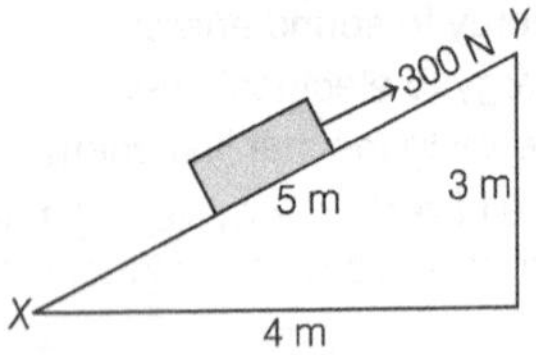

How much work is done when moving the box from *X* to *Y* ?

(a) 900 J (b) 1200 J
(c) 1500 J (d) 3000 J

Ans. (c) Work = Force × Distance moved in the direction of the force = (300)(5) = 1500 J

Q.12 A stationary box is pushed by a 120 N force along a horizontal surface as shown below.

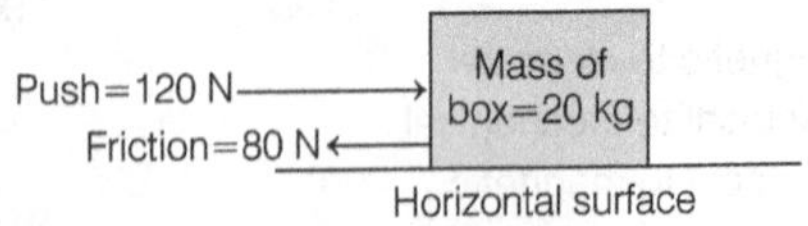

If the friction between the box and the surface is 80 N and the mass of the box is 20 kg, calculate the work done by the force in the first four seconds.

(a) 640 J (b) 1280 J
(c) 1920 J (d) 3200J

Ans. (c) To find distance moved, find area under $v-t$ graph.

Since friction is 80 N, only 40 N is used in moving the box. Apply Newton's second law.

Resultant force = ma

$$120 - 80 = 20a$$

$$a = 2\ \text{m s}^{-2}$$

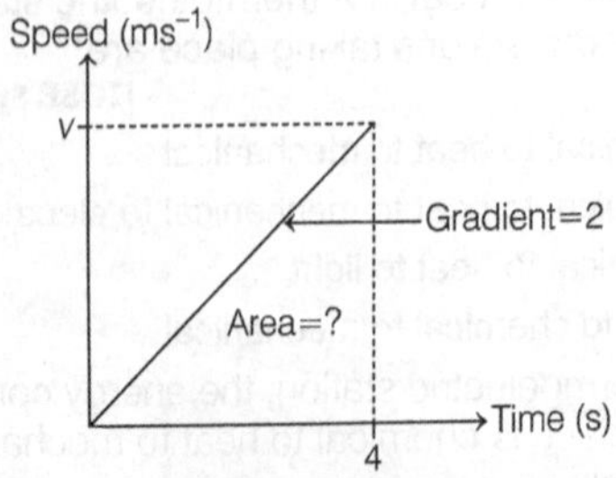

$$v = a \times t \Rightarrow v = 4 \times 2 = 8\ \text{ms}^{-1}$$

$$\text{Area} = \frac{1}{2} bh \Rightarrow s = \frac{1}{2} t \times v$$

$$\text{Distance travelled} = \frac{1}{2} \times 8 \times 4 = 16\ \text{m}$$

$$\text{Work done} = 120\,\text{N} \times 16\,\text{m} = 1920\ \text{J}$$

Q.13 The given figure depicts the graph of work done *versus*, displacement under a constant force of 10N. Which of the following option is true? **[Competency Based Que.]**

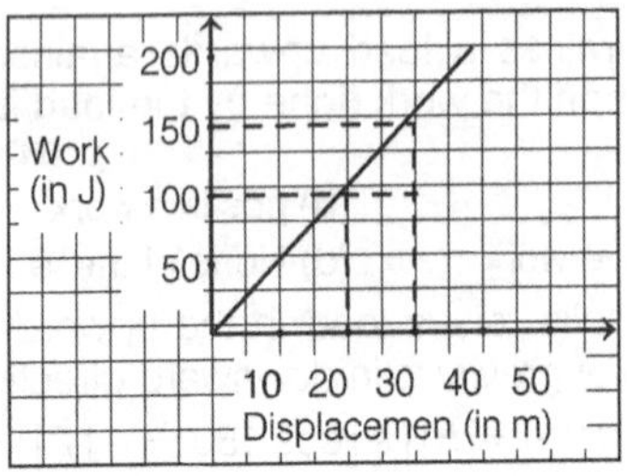

(a) Force is acting at an angle of 0° with the displacement.
(b) Force is acting at an angle of 45° with the displacement.
(c) Force is acting at an angle of 60° with the displacement.
(d) Force is acting at an angle of 90° with the displacement.

Ans. (c) Given $F = 10$ N

$$W = Fd\cos\theta$$

From the graph, corresponding to 150 J of work, the displacement is 30 m.

$$150 = 10 \times 30\cos\theta$$

$$\therefore \quad \cos\theta = \frac{1}{2} \Rightarrow \theta = 60°$$

Q.14 When the speed of a moving object is doubled, then its kinetic energy **[ICSE 2023]**

(a) remains the same (b) decreases
(c) is doubled (d) becomes four times

Ans. (d) If v becomes 2 v, then KE $= \frac{1}{2} m\,(2v)^2 = \frac{4}{2} mv^2 = 4$ times the initial kinetic energy.

Q.15 Which of the following is the correct expression for gain in kinetic energy, if initial velocity is not zero? **[ICSE Specimen 2023]**

(a) $K = \frac{1}{2} mv^2$ (b) $K = \frac{mv^2}{4}$

(c) $K = \frac{mv^2}{2t}$ (d) $K = \frac{1}{2} m(v^2 - u^2)$

Ans. (d) Gain in kinetic energy

$$= \frac{1}{2} mv^2 - \frac{1}{2} mu^2 = \frac{1}{2} m(v^2 - u^2)$$

Q.16 The diagram shows a flight of stairs.

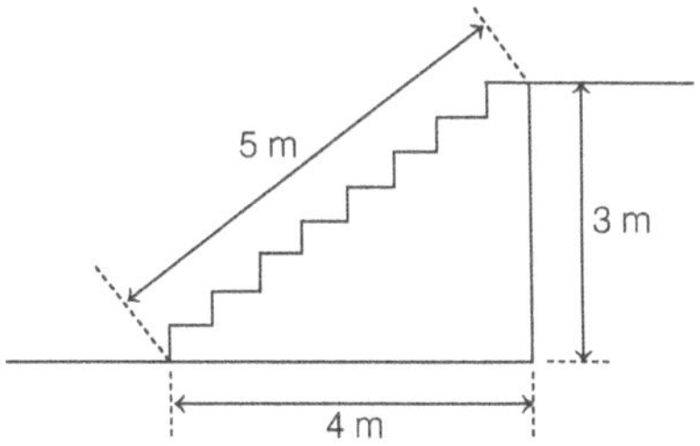

How much useful work is done by a person weighing 600 N when climbing the stairs?

(a) 120 J (b) 1800 J
(c) 2400 J (d) 3000 J

Ans. (b) By conservation of energy,

Useful work done = Gain in gravitational potential energy

$= mgh = (600\text{N})(3\text{m}) = 1800 \text{ J}$

Q.17 A ball bearing is placed on a smooth track at a point *P*. When the ball bearing is released from rest, it moves down and passes a point *Q*.

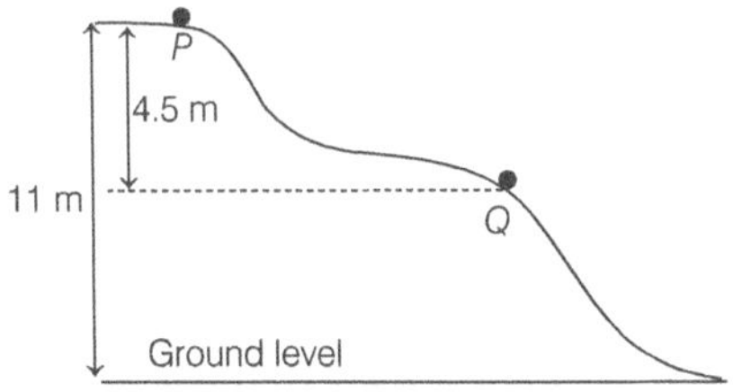

Choose the correct answer for *Q*.

	GPE	KE	Total energy
(a)	45*m* J	65*m*J	110*m* J
(b)	0 J	65*m* J	65*m* J
(c)	45*m* J	0 J	45*m* J
(d)	65*m* J	45*m* J	110*m* J

Ans. (d) Total energy = (11)(10)*m* = 110*m* J

At *Q*,

GPE lost = K.E. gained = (4.5)(10)*m* = 45*m* J

GPE = 65*m* J

Q.18 Which among the following is a vector quantity? **[ICSE 2025]**

(a) Work (b) Power
(c) Energy (d) Moment of couple

Ans. (d)

Q.19 A student takes 25 s to run up 50 steps each of 0.2 m high. If the mass of the student is 50 kg, calculate the rate of work done by the student.

(a) 200 W (b) 1000 W
(c) 800 W (d) 5000 W

Ans. (a) Since KE gained is converted to GPE, work done by the student is equal to the GPE gained.

$$P = \frac{E}{t} = \frac{mgh}{t}$$

$$= \frac{50 \times 10 \times (0.2 \times 50)}{25} = 200 \text{ W}$$

Q.20 An athlete keeps fit by doing press-ups.

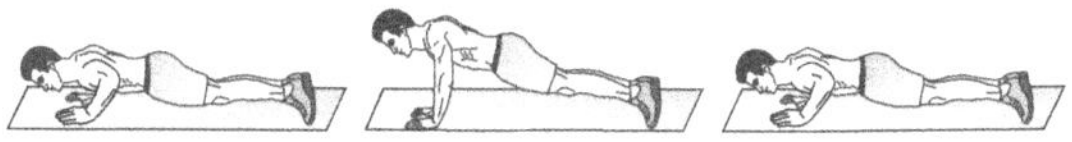

He applies a force of 300 N as he pushes up to a distance of 0.5 m. He does 10 press-ups in 30 s. What is the average power output in 30 s?

(a) 5 W (b) 50 W
(c) 150 W (d) 1500 W

Ans. (c) Average power output $= \dfrac{\text{Work Done}}{\text{Time}}$

Total work done = Force × Distance × Quantity

= (300)(0.5)(10)

Average power output

$$= \frac{1500}{30} = 50 \text{ W}$$

Q.21 When a 300 N force is applied to a box weighing 600 N, then box moves 3.0 m horizontally in 20 s.

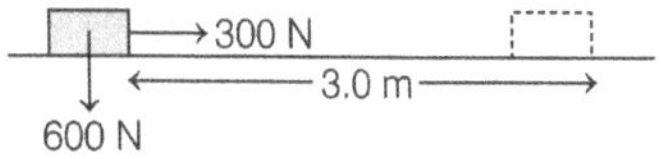

What is the average power?

(a) 45 W (b) 90 W
(c) 900 W (d) 1800 W

Ans. (a) Average power $= \dfrac{\text{Work done}}{\text{Time}}$

$$= \frac{F \times d}{t} = \frac{300 \times 3.0}{20}$$

= 45 W

Q.22 The power of a vehicle moving at a speed of 20 ms^{-1} is 24 kW. What is the total force acting on the vehicle at this speed?

(a) 1200 N
(b) 2400 N
(c) 2000 N
(d) 4800 N

Ans. (a) Power $= \dfrac{\text{work done by the engine}}{\text{time}}$

$$= \frac{\text{force} \times \text{distance moved}}{\text{time}}$$

∴ Power = force × speed

24 × 1000 = force × 20

force = 1200 N

TYPE - 2 01 Mark

Assertion-Reason Type Questions

Directions (Q. Nos. 1-5) In the following questions, a statement of assertion (A) is followed by a statement of reason (R). Mark the correct choice as

(a) Both A and R are true and R is the correct explanation of A.
(b) Both A and R are true but R is not the correct explanation of A.
(c) A is true but R is false.
(d) A is false but R is true.

Q.1 **Assertion** (A) When the displacement is zero, then the workdone is zero. So, if the work done is zero, then it necessarily means the displacement is zero.

Reason (R) Work done is calculated by the relation $W = FS\cos\theta$ **[Compelency Based Que.]**

Ans. (d) The assertion (A) states that when displacement is zero, work done is zero, which is correct. However it also says that if work done is zero, then displacement must be zero, which is incorrect. Work done is given by $W = FS\cos\theta$. If work done is zero, it can happen in two cases:

I. When displacement S is zero.
II. When the force and displacement are perpendicular ($\theta = 90^\circ$).

So, work done can be zero even when displacement is not zero.

Q.2 **Assertion (A)** While climbing stairs, a person performs negative work against the force of gravity.

Reason (R) Negative work occurs when the direction of force opposes the direction of the displacement.

Ans. (a) In this case, negative work is done as force of gravity acts in the direction opposite to displacement.

Q.3 **Assertion** (A) A stone rolling down a hill converts its kinetic energy into potential energy.

Reason (R) The potential energy of an object decreases as it is converted to kinetic energy.

Ans. (d) As stone is falling down, its potential energy decreases and kinetic energy increases as per law of conservation of energy.

Q.4 **Assertion** (A) A person driving the motorcycle increases the speed on approaching a hilly road.

Reason (R) To provide more potential energy to the motorcycle. So that it may go up against gravity of earth.

Ans. (c) The person increases the speed, to provide more kinetic energy to the motorcycle, which gets converted to potential energy as it drives up on hilly road.

Q.5 **Assertion** (A) Kinetic energy of a body does not depend upon the direction of motion.

Reason (R) Kinetic energy is of three forms translational kinetic energy, rotational kinetic energy and vibrational kinetic energy.

Ans. (b) Kinetic energy is the energy possessed by a body due to its motion. It is a scalar quantity and does not depend on the direction of motion of the body.

TYPE - 3 01/02 Marks

Fill in the Blanks

Q.1 Work is said to be done when a force is applied on an object and the object .... [moves, stops, vibrates] in the direction of the applied force.

Ans. moves

Q.2 The potential energy of an object is given by the formula ...., [mgh, $1/2mv^2$, $1/2mgh$], where m is mass, g is acceleration due to gravity, and h is height.

Ans. mgh

Q.3 Unit of power used in mechanical engineering is .... [watt/horse power/erg per second] **[ICSE Specimen 2025]**

Ans. horse power.

Q.4 Work is said to be positive when the displacement is .... [opposite to, along, perpendicular to] the direction of force, and it is negative when the displacement is ....[opposite to, along, perpendicular to] the direction of force. **[2]**

Ans. along, opposite to

Q.5 If a machine does 500 joules of work in 10 seconds, its power is .... (50 W, 500 W) and the SI unit of power is .... [joule, watt]. **[2]**

Ans. 50 W, watt

TYPE - 4 02 Marks

Very Short Answer Type Questions

Q.1 Figure shows a boat stationary in still water in a narrow tunnel.

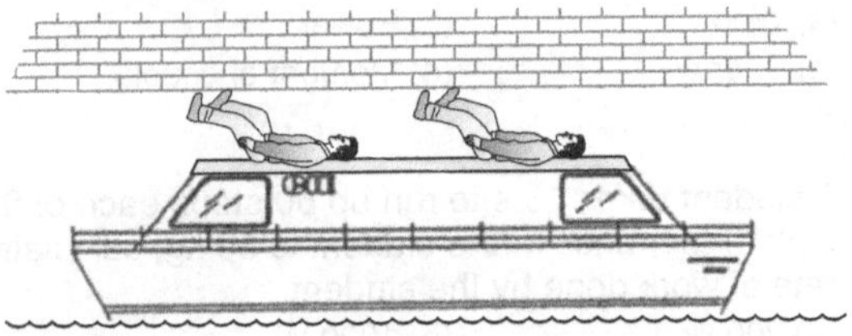

To move the boat, two men lie on the top of it and push against the tunnel roof with their legs.

They exert a total forwards force of 1680 N on the boat.

(i) The men push the boat 50.0 m to the end of the tunnel. Calculate the work done on the boat by the men. **[1]**

(ii) Explain why the kinetic energy of the boat at the end of the tunnel is less than the work done on the boat by the men. **[1]**

Ans. (i) Work done = Force × Distance moved

$$= 1680 \times 50.0 = 84000 \text{ J}$$

(ii) The work done by the men on the boat appears in the form of the kinetic energy of the boat but some of this energy is lost due to the resistance of water.

Q.2 Draw a graph of potential energy *versus* height for a body thrown vertically upwards. [Assume no friction is present] **[ICSE Specimen 2025]**

Ans. The potential energy of a body at height h,

$$U = mgh$$

$$U \propto h$$

∴ The graph of U *versus* h is given below

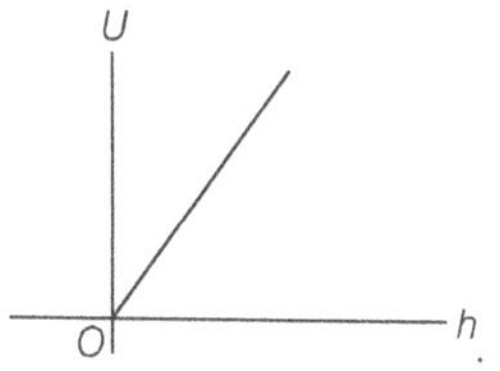

Q.3 State the energy changes in the following devices while in use

(i) a loudspeaker **[1]**

(ii) a glowing electric bulb. **[1]**

Ans. (i) In a loudspeaker, electrical energy is converted into sound energy.

(ii) In a glowing electric bulb, electrical energy is converted into light and heat energy.

Q.4 (i) What should be the angle between the direction of force and the direction of displacement, for work to be negative? **[1]**

(ii) Name the physical quantity obtained using the formula $\frac{U}{h}$, where U is the potential energy and h is the height. **[1][ICSE 2023]**

Ans. (i) 180°

(ii) As gravitational potential energy $U = mgh$

Hence, $\frac{U}{h} = mg$

∴ The physical quantity obtained is weight of the object.

Q.5 State the relation between the kinetic energy and momentum of a body.

Ans. Kinetic energy, $\text{KE} = \frac{1}{2}mv^2$

where m = mass of the body

v = velocity of a body

Linear momentum, $p = mv$

$$\text{KE} = \frac{1}{2}\frac{mv^2 \times m}{m} = \frac{m^2v^2}{2m}$$

$$\Rightarrow \quad \text{KE} = \frac{1}{2}\frac{p^2}{m}$$

Q.6 Two bodies A and B have same kinetic energy. Compare their velocities if mass of A is four times the mass of B. **[ICSE Specimen Paper 2024]**

Ans. **Considering body *A***

Let mass of body $A = m_a = 4m$

Let kinetic energy of body $A = K$

Let velocity of body $A = v_a$

Considering body *B*

Mass of body $B = m_b = m$

[∵ mass of A is four times the mass of B]

Kinetic energy of body $B = K$ [∵ A and B have same kinetic energy]

Let velocity of body $B = v_b$

Given, A and B have same kinetic energy,

$$\therefore \quad \frac{1}{2}4mv_a^2 = \frac{1}{2}mv_b^2$$

$$4mv_a^2 = mv_b^2$$

$$\frac{v_a^2}{v_b^2} = \frac{1}{4} \Rightarrow \frac{v_a}{v_b} = \sqrt{\frac{1}{4}}$$

$$\frac{v_a}{v_b} = \frac{1}{2}$$

Hence, $v_a : v_b = 1:2$ or velocity of body B is two times the velocity of body A.

Q.7 (i) State the energy conversion taking place in a solar cell. **[1]**

(ii) Give one disadvantage of using a solar cell. **[1]**

Ans. (i) In solar cell, solar energy is converted into electrical energy.

(ii) The main disadvantage of solar cell is that it is not a constant source of energy.

Q.8 Regenerative braking involves harnessing the energy that is typically lost when a car decelerates and brakes and instead using it to recharge the car's batteries. Unlike traditional braking systems that simply dissipate energy, regenerative braking allows some of that energy to be recycled.

(i) What is the energy conversion process that results in the wastage of energy in a normal car during braking? **[1]**

(ii) How does regenerative braking differ from normal braking in terms of energy conversion? **[1] [Competency Based Que.]**

Ans. (i) During braking in a normal car, the car's kinetic energy is converted into heat energy due to friction between the brake pads and the wheels. This heat energy is then lost to the surroundings, which result in energy wastage.

(ii) Regenerative braking is different because instead of converting kinetic energy into heat and wasting it, it converts kinetic energy into electrical energy. This electrical energy is stored in the car's battery and can be used later. This makes regenerative braking more efficient than normal braking, as it helps to save energy rather than losing it as heat.

TYPE - 5 — 03 Marks

Short Answer Type Questions

Q.1 For each of the following scenarios, state whether the work done by gravity is positive, negative or zero.

(i) a person walks on a levelled road. **[1]**

(ii) a person climbs a ladder. **[1]**

(iii) a car in neutral gear is coming down the slope. **[1]**

Ans. (i) No work is done.

(ii) Negative work is done.

(iii) Positive work is done.

Q.2 (i) Derive a relationship between the SI and CGS unit of work. **[2] [ICSE 2018]**

(ii) A force acts on a body and displaces it by a distance s in a direction at an angle θ with the direction of force. What should be the value of θ to get the maximum positive work? **[1]**

Ans. (i) SI unit of work is joule and CGS unit of work is erg.

Since, work = force × displacement

$$1 \text{ joule} = 1 \text{ newton} \times 1 \text{ metre}$$
$$= 10^5 \text{ dyne} \times 100 \text{ cm}$$
$$= 10^7 \text{ dyne} \times \text{cm} = 10^7 \text{ erg}$$
$$1 \text{ joule} = 10^7 \text{ erg}$$

(ii) Work $= F \cdot s \cdot \cos\theta$

For maximum work, $\cos\theta = 1$ or $\theta = 0°$

Q.3

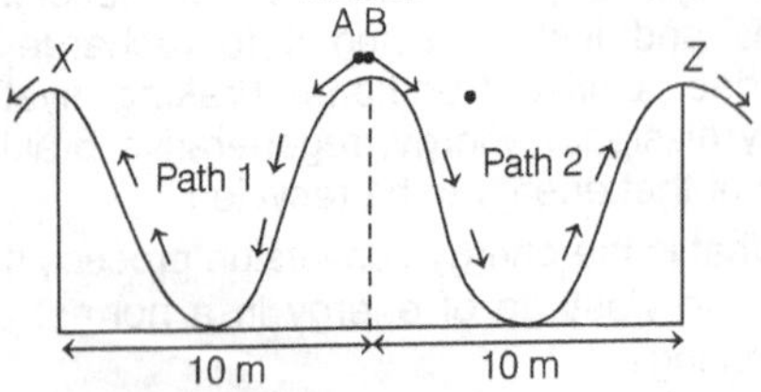

Two identical marbles A and B are rolled down along path 1 and path 2, respectively. Path 1 is frictionless and path 2 is rough. **[ICSE 2024]**

(i) Which marble will surely reach the next peak ? **[1]**

(ii) Along which path(s), the mechanical energy will be conserved? **[1]**

(iii) Along which path(s) is the law of conservation of energy obeyed? **[1]**

Ans. (i) Marble *A*

(ii) Along path 1, the mechanical energy will be conserved.

(iii) Law of conservation of energy is obeyed in both the paths.

Q.4 The figure below shows the path of a ball thrown into the air from point *A* to point *D*.

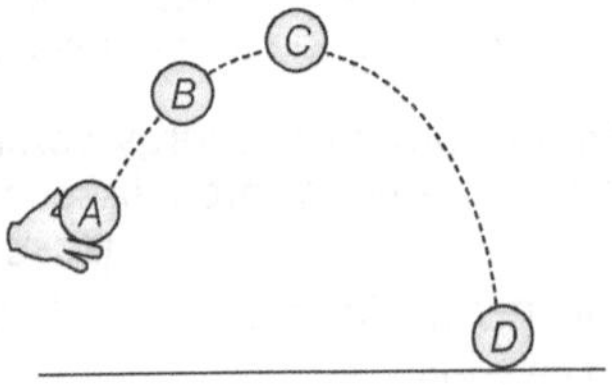

(i) State at which points *A, B, C* or *D* the ball travels the slowest. **[1]**

(ii) The ball gains gravitational potential energy when it moves from *A* to *C*.

(a) Explain why the gain in gravitational potential energy is not equal to the total input energy from the hand. **[1]**

(b) When kinetic energy is converted to gravitational potential energy, why is some useful kinetic energy wasted? **[1]**

Ans. (i) Point *C*.

(ii)(a) The ball gains kinetic energy from the hand. Besides upward direction, it also has a forward direction. Therefore only part of the kinetic energy is converted to gravitational potential energy.

(b) There is frictional force which opposes the direction of motion.

Q.5 Figure illustrates the journey of a cyclist from point *A* to point *B*. Points *A* and *B* are at the same height.

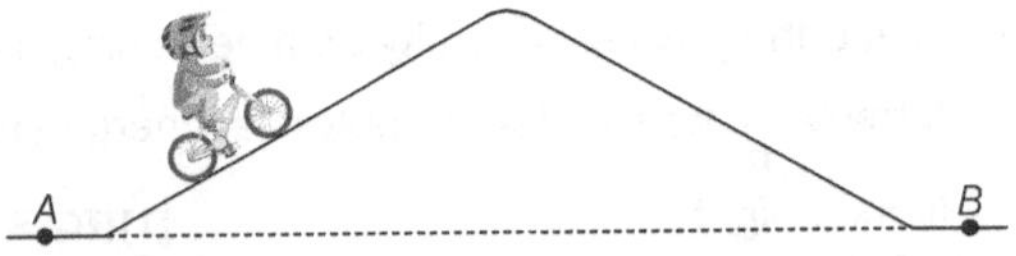

The cyclist starts from rest at *A* and pedals up and over a hill. Near the bottom of the hill, she starts to brake apply and comes to rest at *B*.

(i) Describe the energy changes that take place as she pedals up the hill at constant speed. **[1]**

(ii) Explain how the law of conservation of energy applies to the complete journey from *A* to *B*. **[1]**

(iii) At one point in the journey, the gravitational potential energy of the cyclist has increased by

5400 J. The mass of the cyclist is 60 kg. The acceleration due to gravity is $10 m/s^2$.

Calculate the height above *A* of the cyclist at this point. **[1]**

Ans. (i) During the cyclist's upward movement his chemical energy changes into gravitational potential energy and heat energy.

(ii) During the cyclist's movement from $A \rightarrow B$ his energy only changes from one form to another and some energy is lost in the form of heat but the total energy remains constant at all points of his journey.

(iii) Gravitational potential energy $= mgh$

$$5400 = 60 \times 10 \times h$$

$$h = 9.0$$

$\therefore$ Height above $A = 9.0$ m.

TYPE - 6 04 Marks

Long Answer Type Questions

Q.1 (i) A satellite is revolving around the earth in a circular orbit. Explain why the work done by the force of gravity on the satellite is zero. **[1]**

(ii) If both force and displacement are vector quantities, why is work considered as a scalar quantity? **[1]**

(iii) Two individuals, *A* and *B* each with a mass *m*, move to the top of a building of height *h*. Person *A* takes the stairs, while *B* uses an elevator. Compare and calculate the work done by each. **[1]**

(iv) Identify which of the following-work, energy or power-is a vector quantity. **[1]**

Ans. (i) The gravitational force on the satellite due to the earth acts along the radius of the circular orbit towards the centre of the earth, while the direction of velocity and hence the direction of displacement of the satellite is along the tangent of the circular path followed by the satellite. Hence, force and the displacement are mutually perpendicular to each other. Therefore, the work done at any instant is zero.

(ii) While calculating the work done, we only consider the products of magnitudes of the force applied and the magnitude of displacement along the direction of the force applied. Hence, work done is a scalar quality.

(iii) Work done by both *A* and *B* is same and is equal to *mgh*.

(iv) None of the quantities is a vector. All are scalar quantities.

Q.2 A bowling ball is released at point *A* and is allowed to move freely along a frictionless track.

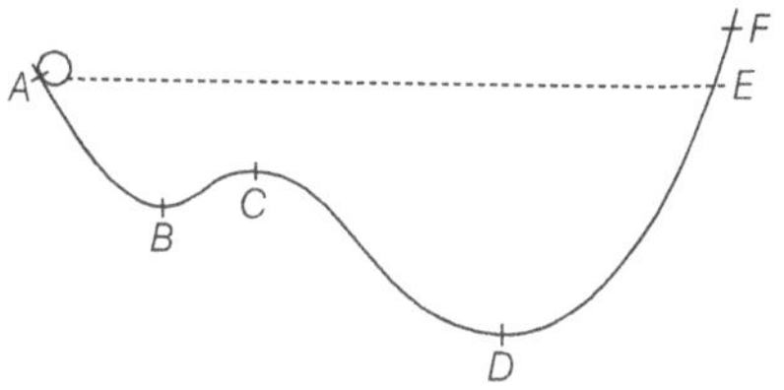

(i) At which point will the bowling ball possess the greatest speed? **[1]**

(ii) At which of the two points, *B* or *C*, will the bowling ball gain more gravitational potential energy and more kinetic energy? **[1]**

(iii) Point *E* is at the same level as point *A*. What can you say about the speed of the bowling ball at point *E*? Explain your answer. **[1]**

(iv) Will the bowling ball reach point *F*? If not, explain what will happen. **[1]**

Ans. (i) Point *D*.

(ii) The bowling ball has more kinetic energy at *B* than *C*. However, it has more gravitational potential energy at *C* than *B*.

(iii) By principle of conservation of energy, the bowling ball at point *E* will have the same amount of gravitational potential energy as at point *A*. Since all kinetic energy has to be converted to potential energy to reach point *E*, the speed of the bowling ball at point *E* is temporarily zero.

(iv) The highest point the bowling ball can reach is *E*. Because by the law of conservation of energy the maximum potential energy the body can posses when it reaches point *E* should be same as that of point *A*. At point *E* all the kinetic energy is converted into potential energy and hence velocity becomes momentarily zero at *E* and from the point the ball again falls back and gains kinetic energy and the process goes on.

Q.3 An object of mass *m* is allowed to fall freely from point *A* as shown in the figure. Calculate the total mechanical energy of the object at

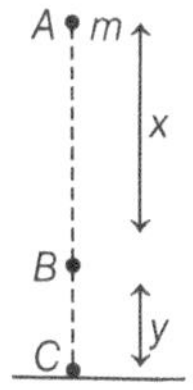

(i) Point *A* **[1]**

(ii) Point *B* **[1]**

(iii) Point *C* **[1]**

(iv) State the law which is verified by your calculations in parts (i), (ii) and (iii). **[1]**

Ans. (i) Mechanical energy at point A,

$$(ME)_A = (KE)_A + (PE)_A$$
$$= 0 + mg(x + y)$$
$$= mg(x + y)$$

(ii) Mechanical energy at point B,

$$PE = mgy$$
$$KE = \frac{1}{2}mv_B^2 = mgx$$
$$\therefore \quad ME = mg(x + g)$$

(iii) Mechanical energy at point C,

$$PE = 0$$
$$KE = \frac{1}{2}mv_C^2 = mg(x + y)$$
$$\therefore \quad ME = mg(x + y)$$

(iv) **For conservation of energy** According to the law of conservation of energy, energy can neither be created nor be destroyed but it can be changed from one form to another.

TYPE - 7 — 03/04 Marks

Case Based Questions

Q.1 The mass of the block P is 5 kg. It is to be moved along an inclined plane AC of length 8 m, which makes an angle of 30° with the horizontal. A force of 50 N is applied on the block to move it through the inclined plane AC, as shown in the diagram.

[Competency Based Que.] [ICSE CFPQ]

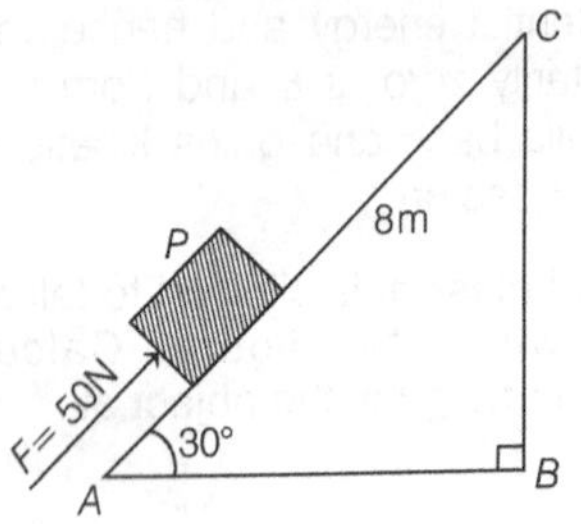

(i) What is the work done by the force along the inclined plane? **[1]**

(ii) Find the gain in potential energy of block P if it is directly lifted to C from the ground. (Take, $g = 10\text{ ms}^{-2}$) **[1]**

(iii) We know that potential energy is gained due to the work done on the body against gravity. Then, in this case, why are the work done on the block and the increase in the potential energy of the block different? **[1]**

Ans. (i) $W = F \times s = 50 \times 8 = 400$ J

(ii) Potential energy is given by $PE = mgh$

Here, the height gained h is the vertical component of the inclined plane.

$$h = s\sin\theta$$

Substituting values

$$h = 8 \times \sin 30° = 8 \times 0.5 = 4\text{ m}$$

Now, calculating the potential energy

$$PE = 5 \times 10 \times 4 = 200\text{ J}$$

(iii) This is because while pushing the block along the inclined plane, some energy is wasted to overcome the friction between the block and the inclined plane.

Q.2 The figure below shows a simple pendulum of mass 200 g. It is displaced from the mean position A to the extreme position B. The potential energy at the position A is zero. At the position B, the pendulum bob is raised by 5 m. **[ICSE Specimen, 2025, 20]**

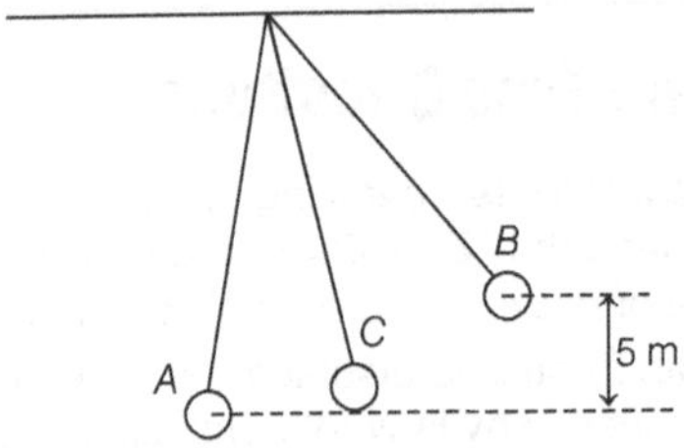

(i) What is the potential energy of the pendulum at the position B? **[1]**

(ii) What is the total mechanical energy at point C? **[1]**

(iii) What is the speed of the bob at the position A when released from B? **[1]**

(Take, $g = 10\text{ ms}^{-2}$ and there is no loss of energy)

Ans. Mass of simple pendulum, $m = 200\text{ g} = 02$ kg.

(i) Since, B is in extreme position, so total energy at B is maximum, hence total energy at B is present in the form of its potential energy.

Potential energy, $U = mgh$

$$= 02 \times 10 \times 5 = 10\text{ J}$$

(ii) Since, total mechanical energy (E) remains conserved, hence total mechanical energy at C is

$$E = U = 10\text{ J}$$

(iii) At point A, whole of the potential energy of the bob is converted into its kinetic energy.

So, $\frac{1}{2}mv^2 = U$

$$\Rightarrow \frac{1}{2} \times 02 \times v^2 = 10$$
$$\Rightarrow \quad v^2 = \frac{10}{0.1} = 100$$
$$\Rightarrow \quad v = \sqrt{100}$$
$$\Rightarrow \quad v = 10\text{ m/s}$$

TYPE - 8

Numerical Questions

Q.1 If kinetic energy of a moving body is 40 J, then what will be its kinetic energy when its velocity is doubled? **[2][ICSE Specimen 2023]**

Sol. $KE = \frac{1}{2}mv^2$

If the velocity is doubled ($2v$), the new (KE) will be

$$KE' = \frac{1}{2}m(2v)^2 = \frac{1}{2}m\,4v^2$$

$$= 4 \times \left(\frac{1}{2}mv^2\right) = 4\,KE$$

Since, the KE is 40 J, the new K.E will be

$$K.E' = 4 \times 40 = 160\text{ J}$$

So, when the velocity is doubled, the KE becomes 160 J.

Q.2 David pushes a washing machine from rest with constant force 100 N for a distance of 5 m. The mass of the washing machine is 60 kg and the friction is negligible.

(i) How much work has David done? **[1]**

(ii) Find the acceleration of the washing machine. **[1]**

(iii) What is the final kinetic energy of the washing machine? **[1]**

(iv) Find the speed of the washing machine after travelling 0.5 m. **[1]**

Sol. (i) Work done = 100 N × 5 m = 500 J

(ii) $F = ma$

$100 = 60a$

Acceleration, $a = 1.67\text{ ms}^{-2}$

(iii) Final kinetic energy = Work done = 500 J

(iv) Work done = 100 N × 0.5 m = 50 J

$\therefore$ KE gained = 50 J

$$\Rightarrow \frac{1}{2}(60)v^2 = 50$$

Speed, $v = 1.3\text{ ms}^{-1}$

Q.3

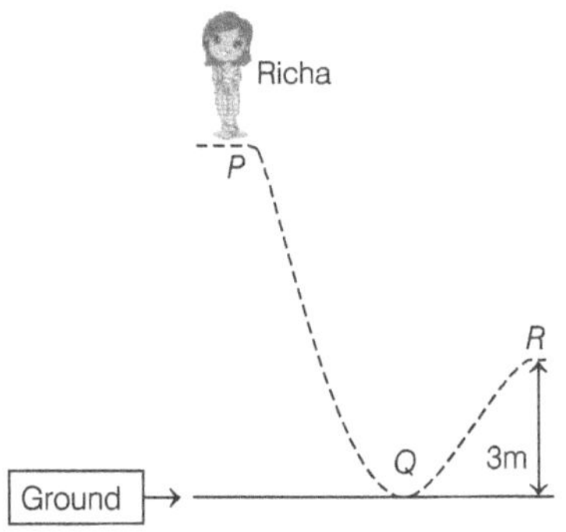

Richa weighing 40 kgf leaves point *P* on her skateboard and reaches point *Q* on the ground with velocity 10 ms^{-1}. Calculate **[4][ICSE 2025]**

(i) the kinetic energy of Richa at point *Q*.

(ii) the vertical height of point *P* above the ground. (Use *g* as 10 m/s^2 and neglect friction

(iii) the kinetic energy of Richa at point *R*. (While moving from *Q* to *R*, she loses 500 J of energy against friction)

Sol. (i) Weight of Richa = 40 kgf

$= 40 \times 10$ N

$= 400$ N

$\therefore$ Mass of Richa $= \frac{400}{10} = 40$ kg

$\therefore$ Kinetic energy of Richa when she reaches point *Q*

$= \left(\frac{1}{2} \times 40 \times 10^2\right)$ J.

$= 2000$ J.

(ii) From conservation of energy,

we know PE = KE

$$\Rightarrow \quad mgh = \frac{1}{2}mv^2 = 2000\text{ J}$$

where, h = length of *PQ*.

$$\therefore \quad h = \frac{2000}{400} = 5\text{ m}$$

(iii) PE of Richa at point $R = (400 \times 3)$ J = 1200 J

Loss of energy = 500 J

$\therefore$KE + 500 = 1200, by law of conservation of energy

$\therefore$ KE = 700 J, at point *R*.

Q.4 A body of mass 10 kg is kept at a height of 5 m. It is allowed to fall and reach the ground. **(ICSE 2019)**

(i) What is the total mechanical energy possessed by the body at the height of 2 m assuming it is a frictionless medium? **[2]**

(ii) What is the kinetic energy possessed by the body just before hitting the ground? (Take, $g = 10\text{ m/s}^2$). **[2]**

Sol. (i) Given, mass of body, $m = 10$ kg

Height, $h = 5$ m

So, potential energy at height of 5 m

$= mgh = 10 \times 10 \times 5 = 500$ J

If it falls to a height of 2 m, the increase in kinetic energy will be equal to the decrease in potential energy, so the total mechanical energy will be equal to potential energy.

Hence, total mechanical energy (ME) is 500 J.

(ii) From principle of conservation of energy when body is about to reach the ground, the entire potential energy will be converted to kinetic energy. So, kinetic energy (KE) = 500 J.

Q.5 A block of mass 30 kg is pulled up a slope (shown diagram) with a constant speed by applying a force of 200 N parallel to the slope. A and B are the initial and final positions of the block. Calculate the force of friction offered by the surface AB.

[Competency Based Que.]

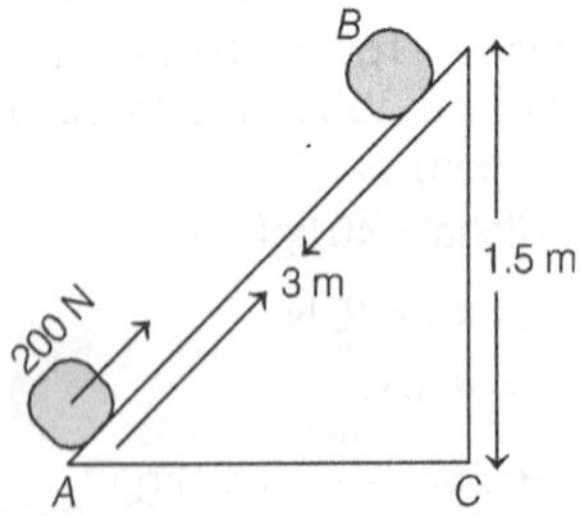

Sol. Given,

$m = 30$ kg, $g = 10$ m/s^2

height, $h = 1.5$ m, force applied, $F = 200$ N

Distance moved along the slope, $s = 3$ m

We know that,

Gravitational PE gained by the block as it rises by a height 1.5 m from the ground is

$$W = mgh$$
$$= 30 \times 10 \times 1.5$$
$$= 450 \text{ J}$$

Total work done by the applied force,

$W = F \times S = (200 \times 3)\text{ J} = 600$ J

$\therefore$ The work done against friction,

$W_{\text{friction}} = (600 - 450)\text{ J} = 150$ J

$\therefore$ The force of friction, f is

$$W_{\text{friction}} = F \times S$$
$$150 = f \times 3$$
$$\therefore \quad f = \left(\frac{150}{3}\right)\text{N}$$
$$\therefore \quad f = 50 \text{ N}$$

Q.6 A ball of mass m is dropped freely from point A. It is given that $AB = BC = CD = h$. If the acceleration due to gravity at the given place is g, then what will be its

(i) potential energy at point A?

(ii) kinetic energy at point C?

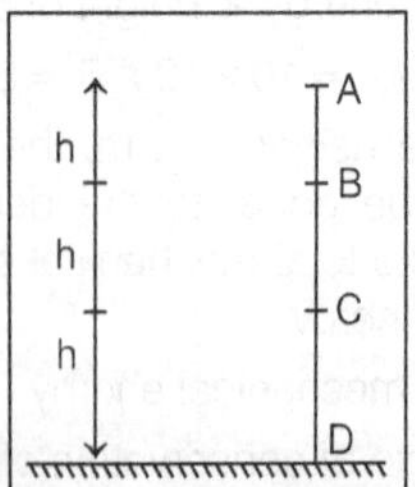

Sol. Given,

A ball of mass m is dropped freely from point A.

The distance $AB = BC = CD = h$

Acceleration due to gravity $= g$.

(i) **Potential energy at point** A

Gravitational potential energy at some height h from the ground is given by

$$\text{PE} = mgh'$$

At point A, the height of the ball from the ground is $3h$.

$\therefore$ $\text{PE}_A = mg(3h) = 3mgh$

(ii) Kinetic energy at point C.

By the law of conservation of energy, total mechanical energy remain constant. When the ball reaches at point C, it has fallen from height $3h$ to h, meaning it has descended by $2h$.

$\therefore$ The loss in PE

$$\text{PE}_{\text{lost}} = mg(2h) = 2mgh$$

The lost energy is converted into KE at point C.

$$\therefore \quad \text{KE}_C = 2mgh$$

Q.7 A metal ball of mass 60 g falls on a concrete floor from a vertical height of 2.8 m and rebounds to a height of 1.3 m. Find the change in KE in SI units.

[2] [ICSE Specimen Paper, 2018]

Sol. Potential energy of a ball at height $h_1 = 2.8$ m

$$\text{PE}_1 = mgh_1$$
$$= \frac{60}{1000} \times 10 \times 2.8 = 1.68 \text{ J}$$

$\therefore$ Kinetic energy just before striking the ground

$$= \text{KE} = 1.68 \text{ J}$$

Potential energy at height = 1.3 m

$$\text{PE}_2 = mgh_2 = \frac{60}{1000} \times 10 \times 1.3 \text{ m}$$
$$= 0.78 \text{ J}$$

$\therefore$ Kinetic energy just after rebounding = 0.78 J

$\therefore$ Change in kinetic energy $= \text{KE}_1 - \text{KE}_2$

$$= (1.68 - 0.78) = 0.9 \text{ J}$$

Q.8 A stationary car at ground level drives up a long bridge with a uniform acceleration of 5 ms^{-2} for the first 5 s. It then moves with an acceleration of 2 ms^{-2} for the next 5 s. The mass of the car is 1800 kg.

(i) Draw a speed-time graph to illustrate the motion of the car during the 10 s and hence deduce the total distance travelled in this time. **[1]**

(ii) Calculate the resultant force required to produce the acceleration of 5 ms^{-2}. How much work is done by this force in the first 5 s? **[1]**

(iii) What is the car's final kinetic energy? **[1]**

(iv) If the highest point of the bridge has a height of 8 m above ground level, what is the gravitational potential energy gained by the car at this point? **[1]**

Sol. (i)

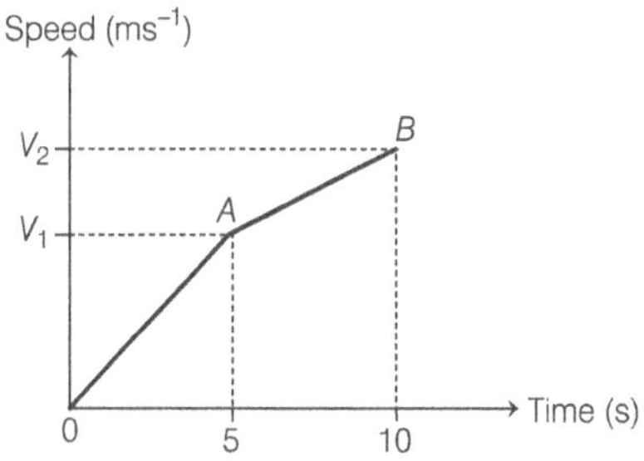

From the slope of the speed-time graph, we get

$$\frac{v_1 - 0}{5 - 0} = 5$$

$$\therefore \quad v_1 = 25 \text{ m s}^{-1}$$

Similarly, $\frac{v_2 - v_1}{10 - 5} = 2$

$$v_2 - 25 = 10$$

$$v_2 = 35 \text{ m s}^{-1}$$

Total distance travelled is the area under the curve *OABC*

$$\therefore \quad d = \frac{1}{2}(5)(25) + \frac{1}{2}(5)(25 + 35) = 212.5 \text{ m}$$

(ii) Resultant force = ma

$$= 1800 \times 5 = 9000 \text{ N}$$

Distance travelled in the first 5 s = Area of triangle

$$= \frac{1}{2} \times 5 \times 25 = 62.5 \text{ m}$$

Work done = $9000 \times 62.5 = 562500$ J

(iii) Final KE = $\frac{1}{2} mv^2$

$$= \frac{1}{2}(1800)(35)^2 = 1102500 \text{ J}$$

(iv) GPE = mgh

$$= 1800 \times 10 \times 8 = 144000 \text{ J}$$

Q.9 (i) **A stone of mass 64.0 g is thrown vertically upward from the ground with an initial speed of 20.0 m/s. The gravitational potential energy at the ground level is considered to be zero. Apply the principle of conservation of energy and calculate the potential energy at the maximum height attained by the stone. (Take, $g = 10 \text{ ms}^{-2}$)** **[2]**

(ii) **Using the same principle, state what will be the total energy of the body at its half-way point?** **[1]**

Sol. (i) Given, mass, $m = 64.0 \text{ g} = 0.064$ kg

Velocity, $v = 20.0$ m/s, $g = 10 \text{ m/s}^2$

According to principle of conservation of energy, PE at the maximum height will be the same as the KE imparted by the thrower.

$$\therefore \text{PE} = \text{KE} = \frac{1}{2} mv^2$$

$$= \frac{1}{2} \times 0.064 \times (20)^2 = 12.8 \text{ J}$$

(ii) According to principle of conservation of energy, the total energy of the body at any point remains same.

So, TE = 12.8 J , at it half-waypoint

Q.10 **Two students are conducting experiments with identical 100 g mass simple pendulums, each raising the bob 5m above the mean position. The graph depicting the relationship between distance from the mean position and velocities is presented in the diagram.**

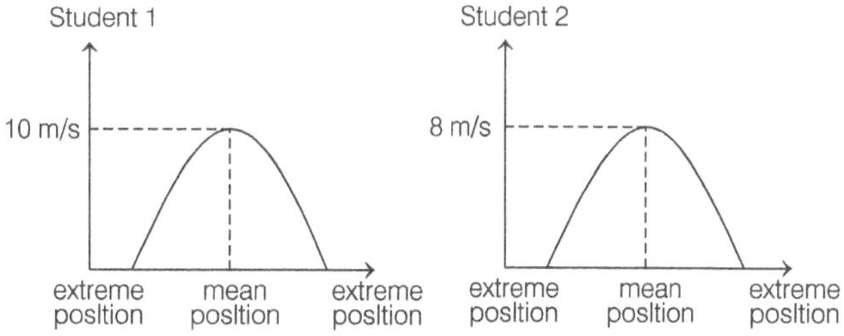

(i) **Demonstrate, using mathematical calculations, that the path followed by student 1 is devoid of friction.**

(ii) **Does the situation involving student 2 exhibit a breach of the law of conservation of energy?**

Sol. (i) At the extreme positions.

$$\text{PE} = mgh = \frac{100}{1000} \times 10 \times 5 = 5 \text{ J}$$

KE = 0, since $v = 0$

At the mean position

$$\text{KE} = \frac{1}{2} mv^2$$

$$= \frac{1}{2} \times \frac{100}{1000} \times 10 \times 10 = 5 \text{ J}$$

PE = 0, since $h = 0$

So, from the above calculations we can conclude that the path followed by student 1 is devoid of friction. Since there is no loss in energy during the conversion of the PE into KE.

(b) At the extreme positions,

$$\text{PE} = mgh = \frac{100}{1000} \times 10 \times 5 = 5 \text{ J}$$

KE = 0

At the mean position,

$$\text{KE} = \frac{1}{2} \times \frac{100}{1000} \times 8 \times 8 = 32 \text{ J}$$

PE = 0

No, the situation involving student 2 does not exhibit a breach of the law of conservation of energy because in this case, some work has to be done by the PE against the force of friction between bob and the air molecules and the rest is converted into KE. So, the total energy remains conserved according to the law of conservation of energy.

Q.11 **A pump is used to lift 600 kg of water from a depth of 75 m in 10 s. Calculate**

(i) the work done by the pump. **[1]**

(ii) the power at which the pump works. **[1]**

(iii) the power rating of the pump, if its efficiency is 40% . **[1]**

(Take, $g = 10\ \text{ms}^{-2}$)

Sol. Mass of water = 600 kg

Height to which the water has to be raised = 75 m

Time = 10 s

(i) Work done by the pump = mgh

$$W = mgh$$
$$W = 600 \times 10 \times 75$$
$$W = 450000$$
$$W = 4.5 \times 10^5\ \text{J}$$

(ii) Power at which pump works

$$= \frac{\text{Work done}}{\text{Time taken}} = \frac{mgh}{t}$$
$$= \frac{600 \times 10 \times 75}{10} = 45000\ \text{W}$$
$$= 45\ \text{kW} \qquad [\because 1\ \text{kW} = 1000\ \text{W}]$$

(iii) $\text{Efficiency} = \dfrac{\text{Useful power}}{\text{Power input}}$

Efficiency = 40% = 0.4

$$\Rightarrow \quad 0.4 = \frac{45\ \text{kW}}{\text{Power input}}$$
$$\text{Power input} = \frac{45\ \text{kW}}{0.4}$$
$$\text{Power input} = 112.5\ \text{kW}$$

Q.12 **A car of mass 120 kg is moving at a speed 18 km/h and it accelerates to attain a speed of 54 km/h in 5 s. Calculate** **[ICSE 2023]**

(i) the work done by the engine. **[2]**

(ii) the power of the engine. **[1]**

Sol. (i) Given, $m = 120$ kg, $v_1 = 18$ km/h

$$= \frac{18 \times 1000}{60 \times 60}\ \text{m/s}$$
$$v_1 = 5\ \text{m/s}$$
$$v_2 = 54\ \text{km/h} = 15\ \text{m/s}$$

and $t = 5$ s

$$\text{Work done} = \text{Change in KE} = \frac{1}{2} m (v_2^2 - v_1^2)$$
$$= \frac{1}{2} \times 120 \times (15^2 - 5^2) = 12000\ \text{J}$$

(ii) $\text{Power} = \dfrac{\text{Work done}}{\text{Time}}$

$$= \frac{12000}{5} = 2400\ \text{W}$$

Q.13 **Calculate the power spent by a crane, while lifting a load of mass 2000 kg, at velocity of 1.5 ms^{-1}. (Take, $g = 10\ \text{ms}^{-2}$)** **[2]**

Sol. $\text{Power} = F \cdot v = mgv = 2000 \times 10 \times 1.5$

$$= 30000\ \text{W}$$

Q.14 **Sumit does 600 J of work in 10 min and Amit does 300 J of work in 20 min. Calculate the ratio of the powers delivered by them.** **[2][ICSE 2024]**

Sol. **For Sumit**

Work, $W = 600$ J

Time, $t = 10\ \text{min} = 10 \times 60 = 600$ s

$$\text{Power} = \frac{W}{t} = \frac{600}{600}$$
$$P_s = 1\ \text{W}$$

For Amit

Work, $W = 300$ J

Time, $t = 20\ \text{min} = 20 \times 60 = 1200$ s

$$\text{Power} = \frac{W}{t} = \frac{300}{1200}$$
$$P_A = \left(\frac{1}{4}\right) \text{W}$$

Ratio of the powers, $\dfrac{P_S}{P_A} = \dfrac{1}{\frac{1}{4}} = 4$

Q.15 **(i) A fire engine pumps 10 kg of water per second to a height of 10 m and then projects the water with a speed of 12 m s^{-1}. Calculate the average power of the fire engine.** **[1]**

(ii) An escalator 16 m long is inclined at 30° to the horizontal.

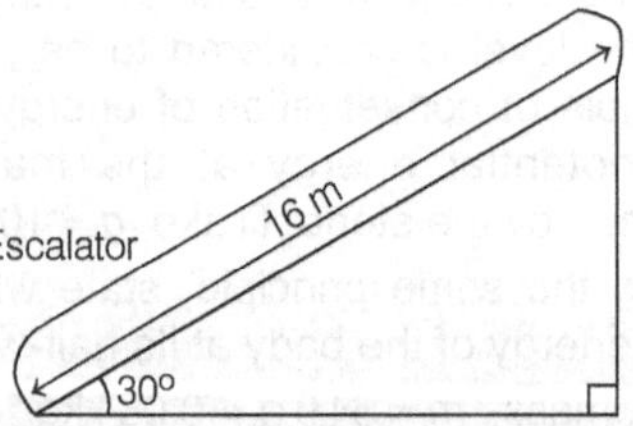

If 1500 people of average mass 70 kg each are carried up in 50 minutes,

(a) find the increase in potential energy of the people carried by the escalator in one hour, **[1]**

(b) what is the useful output power of the escalator? **[1]**

Sol. (i) Total energy converted = GPE + KE

Average power of the fire engine

$$= \frac{\text{Total energy converted}}{\text{Time taken}}$$

$$= \frac{(10 \times 10 \times 10) + \left(\frac{1}{2} \times 10 \times 12^2\right)}{1} = 1720 \text{ W}$$

(ii) (a) Height raised after travelling 16 m

$= 16 \times \sin 30° = 8$ m

Increase in potential energy in 1 h

= Increase in potential energy per minute × 60 mins

$$= \frac{(1500 \times 70) \times 10 \times 8}{50} \times 60 = 10080000 \text{ J}$$

(b) Useful output power $= \frac{10080000}{60 \times 60} = 2800$ W

Q.16 A hydro-electric power station stores its power output by using a pumped storage system. The high level reservoir is 100 m above the low level reservoir as shown below.

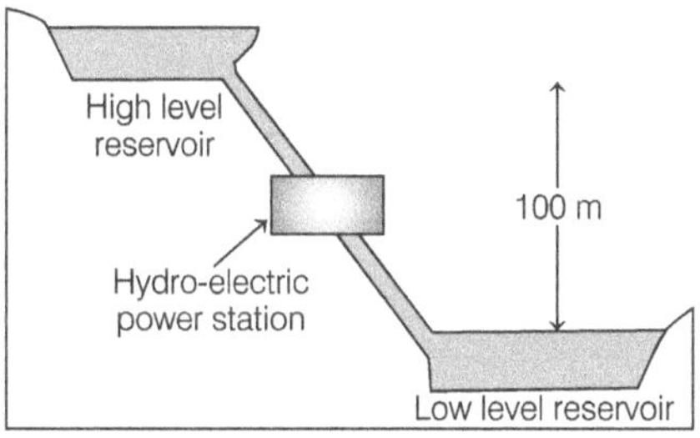

Assuming that there is no energy loss in this process. find the amount of water pumped from the low level reservoir to the high level reservoir from 12 : 00 mid-night to 5:00 am. If the power output and the average electrical energy supplied by this power station is

(i) 5×10^6 W, **[2]**

(ii) 1.5×10^{10} J/h. **[2]**

Sol. (i) Total energy E supplied by the power station for 5 h is

$$E = P \times t$$

where, $P = 5 \times 10^6$

and $t = 5 \text{ h} = (5 \times 3600)$ s

$\therefore \quad E = (5 \times 10^6) \times (5 \times 3600)$

$E = 9 \times 10^{10}$ J

Le the total amount of water pumped be m kg in 5 h.

The energy supplied by the power station is equal to the gain in gravitational potential energy by the water when it is raised by a height of 100 m.

$\therefore \quad E = mgh$

$\Rightarrow \quad 9 \times 10^{10} = m \times 10 \times 100$

$\Rightarrow \quad m = 9 \times 10^7$ kg

(ii) Total energy E, suplied for 5 h is

$E = 1.5 \times 10^{10} \times 5$

$\therefore \quad E = 7.5 \times 10^{10}$ J

To find amount of water pumped, m we know that energy supplied by the system = gained gravitational potential energy by the water

$\therefore \quad E = mgh$

$7.5 \times 10^{10} = m \times 10 \times 100$

or, $\quad m = 7.5 \times 10^7$ kg

03

MACHINES

Machine

- It is a device which helps us to do the work at one point and deliver it at another point with a view of accomplishing the work conveniently.
- Machines act as **force multiplier**, i.e. the net effort produced by the machines is much more than the effort applied.
- A jack is used to lift a bus or car, pulleys are used to lift heavy loads. In all such examples, the effort is much less than the load. So, we can say that machines act as a force multiplier.
- Simple machines can be classified (or categorised) into two major classes, one is lever and other is inclined plane.

Classification of Machine

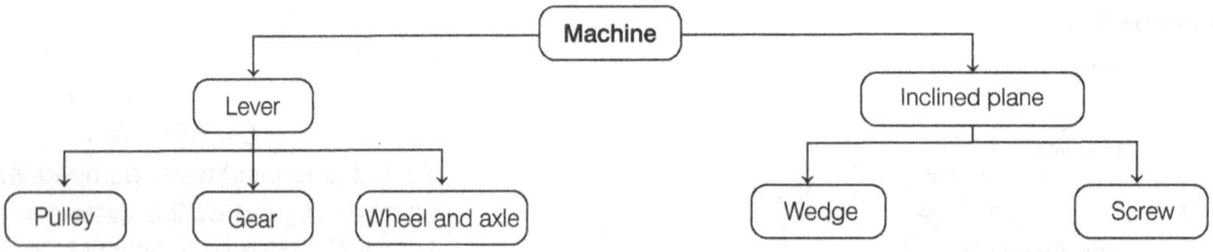

Terms Related to Machine

- **Load** It is the resistive or opposing force against which the machine does the work. It is denoted by L.
- **Effort** It is the force applied on the machine to overcome the load. It is denoted by E.
- **Mechanical Advantage (MA)** It is the ratio of the load to the effort. It is denoted by MA. It is expressed as

$$\boxed{\text{MA} = \frac{L}{E}}$$

(i) If MA > 1 (i.e. $L > E$), then machine works as force multiplier.

(ii) If MA < 1 (i.e. $L < E$), then machine gains speed, i.e. machine can help us to achieve greater movement of load by smaller movement of effort.

(iii) If MA = 1 (i.e. $L = E$), then machine changes the direction of effort, i.e. machine can change the direction of effort to a more convenient direction.

- Being a ratio of two like quantities (both load and effort are same type of forces) MA has **no unit**.
- **Velocity Ratio (VR)** It is defined as the ratio of velocity of the effort to the velocity of the load. It is denoted by VR. It is expressed as

$$\boxed{\text{VR} = \frac{\text{Velocity of effort } (v_E)}{\text{Velocity of load } (v_L)}}$$

- In terms of distance moved by a particular force, velocity ratio is the ratio of the distance moved by the effort to the corresponding distance moved by the load, keeping the time same.

$$\therefore \quad \boxed{\text{VR} = \frac{v_E}{v_L} = \frac{d_E/t}{d_L/t} = \frac{d_E}{d_L}}$$

Here, d_E and d_L are the distances moved in same time t by the effort and the load, respectively.

- Being a ratio of two like quantities, velocity ratio also has no unit.

- **Input Work** The work done on the machine by the effort is called the work input (W_{input} or W_i).

Input Work = Work done by the effort on the machine

- **Output Work** The work done by the machine on the load is called output work.

Output Work = Work done on the load by the machine

- **Efficiency** (η) It is the ratio of the work done on the load by the machine to the work done on the machine by the effort. It is denoted by η.

It is expressed as

$$\eta = \frac{\text{Work done on the load}}{\text{Work done by the effort}} = \frac{W_{output}}{W_{input}}$$

and in percentage as

$$\eta = \frac{W_{output}}{W_{input}} \times 100\ \%$$

- **Relation between** η**, MA and VR**

$$\eta = \frac{\text{Load} \times \text{Displacement of load}}{\text{Effort} \times \text{Displacement of effort}} = \frac{\frac{L}{E}}{\frac{d_E}{d_L}} = \frac{\text{MA}}{\text{VR}}$$

$\therefore$ When expressed in percentage,

$$\eta = \frac{\text{MA}}{\text{VR}} \times 100\%$$

Ideal Machine

- An ideal machine is that in which there is no loss of energy in any manner.
- A machine whose parts are weightless and frictionless, such that whatever the energy given to it, is same as the energy produced by it, is called as an ideal machine. The efficiency of an ideal machine is 100%. An ideal machine cannot be made practically.

Actual Machine

- In an actual machine, the output energy is always less than the input energy, i.e. there is always some loss of energy during its operation.
- The loss of energy in a machine is due to following three reasons
  (i) The moving parts of the machine are neither weightless nor smooth or frictionless.
  (ii) Different parts of the machine are not perfectly rigid.
  (iii) The elastic materials are not perfectly elastic.

Therefore, for an actual machine, $\eta < 1$ or MA < VR.

Lever

A lever is a straight or bent rigid rod which can be turned or rotated about a fixed point called fulcrum. It is one of the most common and simple machine.

Principle of a Lever

- A lever works on the principle of moment. In the equilibrium position of the lever, by the principle of moment, moment of load about the fulcrum = moment of effort about the fulcrum
- The two moments are always in opposite directions.
- Consider a lever (i.e. a straight rod) *AB* with balanced point at *F* (fulcrum for the lever). A load *L* acts at point *A* of the lever and effort *E* acts at point *B* as shown in the diagram.

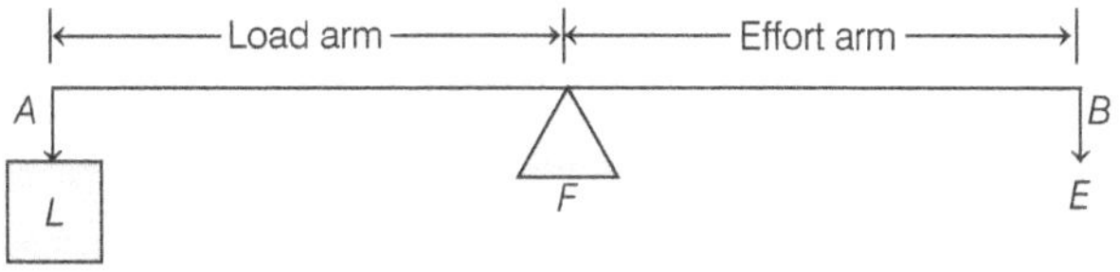

Lever

In figure, the moment of load is anti-clockwise while the moment of effort is clockwise.

Thus, we can write $\boxed{\text{Load} \times \text{Load arm} = \text{Effort} \times \text{Effort arm}}$

This is also called **principle of lever.**

or $$L \times AF = E \times BF$$

or $$\frac{L}{E} = \frac{BF}{AF}$$

$$\therefore \quad \boxed{\text{Mechanical Advantage (MA)} = \frac{L}{E} = \frac{\text{Effort arm}}{\text{Load arm}} = \frac{BF}{AF}}$$

This relation is known as the **law of levers.**

From the above equation, it is clear that, if

(i) Effort arm = Load arm, MA = 1

(ii) Effort arm < Load arm, MA < 1

(iii) Effort arm > Load arm, MA > 1

Note Mechanical advantage of a lever can be increased either by increasing its effort arm or by decreasing its load arm.

Class I Levers

- In this type of lever, the effort (E) and the load (L) are situated on either side of the fulcrum (F).
  Ex. A see-saw, a pair of scissors, crowbar.

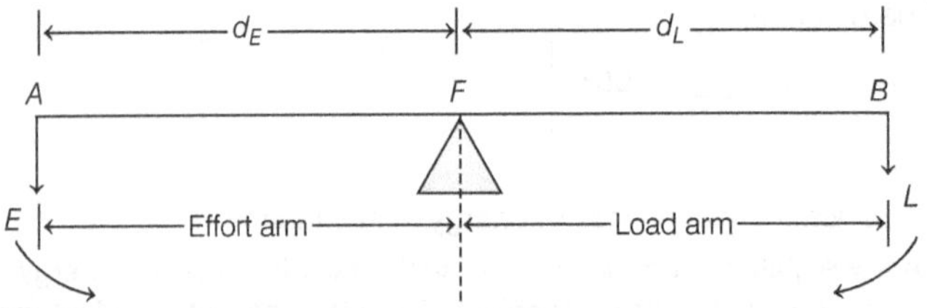

Class I Lever

- MA of class I lever $= \dfrac{\text{Effort arm}}{\text{Load arm}}$
- VR of class I lever $= \dfrac{d_E}{d_L}$

Characteristics of a Class I Lever

Some characteristics of class I lever are as follows

(i) Fulcrum lies in between the load and the effort.

(ii) By moving the fulcrum towards the load, i.e. by decreasing load arm, mechanical advantage can be increased.

(iii) For class I lever, the mechanical advantage and velocity ratio can have any value either greater than 1 or equal to 1 or less than 1.

Class II Levers

- In this type of lever, the load is situated between fulcrum and effort. e.g. A nut cracker, A bottle opener.

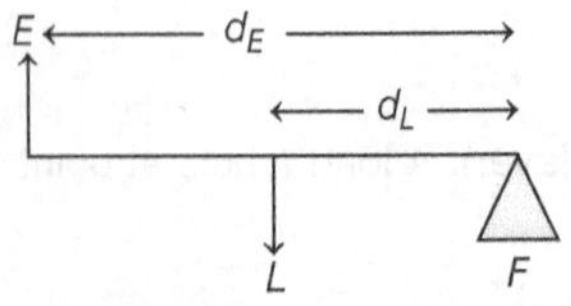

(i) Representation of various force in class II lever

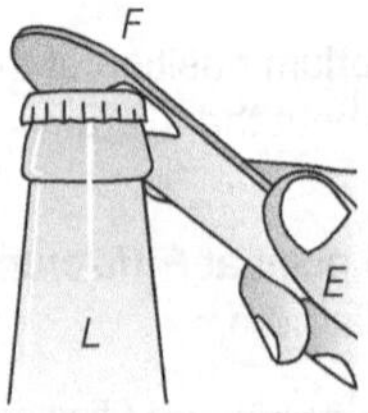

(ii) Bottle opener

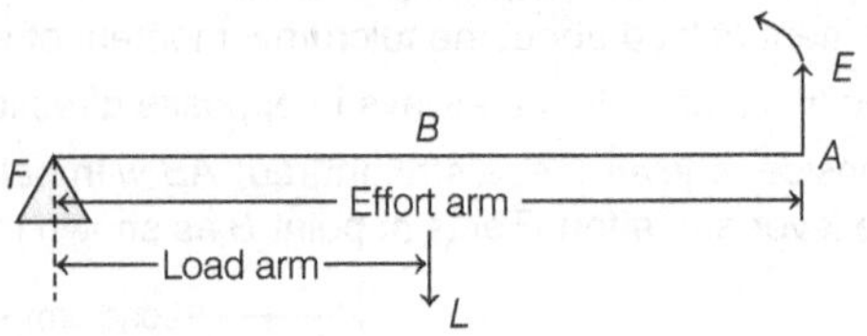

(iii) Class II Lever

Characteristics of a Class II Lever

Some characteristics of class II lever are as follows

(i) Mechanical advantage and velocity ratio are always more than one because the effort arm is always longer than the load arm.

(ii) If load is moved towards the fulcrum, then load arm decreases and consequently the mechanical advantage increases.

(iii) Class II levers always act as a force multiplier.

Class III Levers

- In this type of lever, effort is situated between the load and the fulcrum. e.g. Sugar tongs, foot treadle, etc.

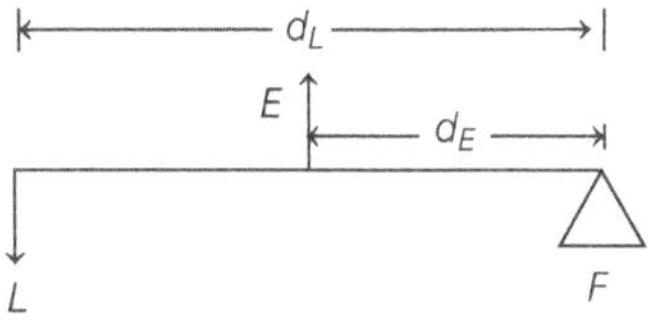

(i) Representation of various force in class III lever

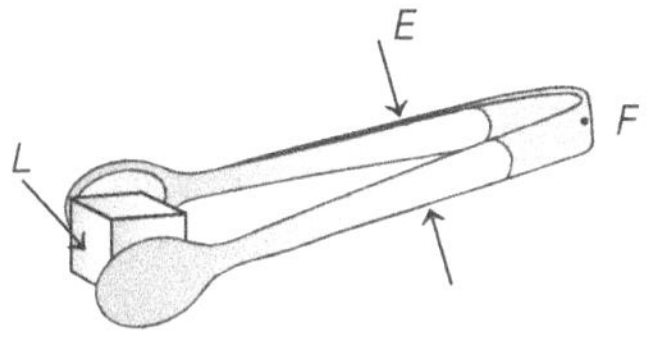

(ii) Sugar tongs

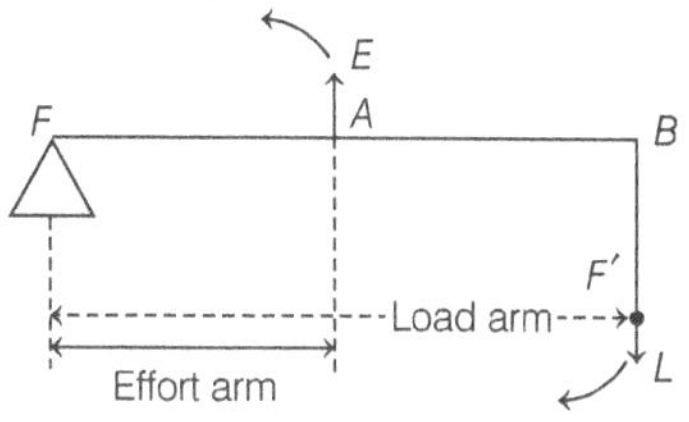

(iii) Class III lever

Characteristics of Class III Lever

Some characteristics of class III lever are as follows

(i) Mechanical advantage and velocity ratio are always less than one, because the effort arm is always smaller than the load arm.

(ii) These levers are also called **speed multiplier** as the load moves through a larger distance as compared to the effort.

Lever	MA	VR
Class I	Either greater than, equal to or less than one	Either greater than, equal to or less than one.
Class II	Always more than one.	Always more than one.
Class III	Always less than one.	Always less than one.

Examples of each Class of Lever as Found in Human Body

1. **Example of Class-I Lever** Class I lever is found in the action of nodding of the head. In this action, the spine acts as the fulcrum *F*, load *L* at its front part and effort *E* is at its rear part as shown in the figure (a).
2. **Example of class-II Lever** Class II lever in human body is found in raising the weight of the body on toes. In this action, load *L* is in the middle, fulcrum *F* is at one end and effort *E* by muscles is at the other end as shown in the figure (b).

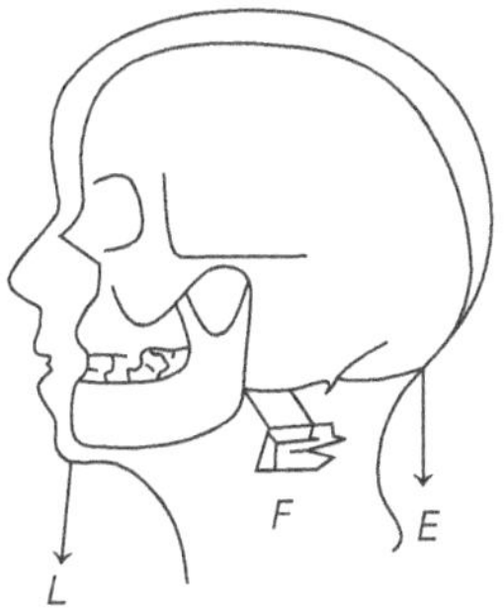

Fig (a)

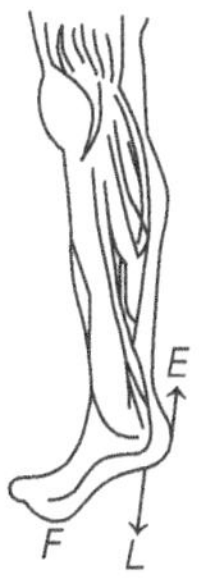

Fig (b)

3. **Example of class-III Lever** Class-III lever in human body is found in raising a load by forearm. The elbow joint acts as fulcrum *F* at one end, biceps exerts the effort *E* in the middle and a load *L* on the palm is at the other end as shown in the figure.

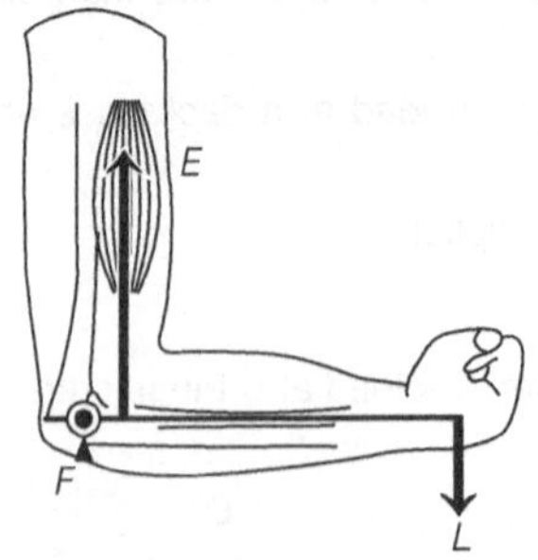

Pulley

Pulley is a wheel on an axle that is designed to support movement and change the direction of a cable or belt along its circumference.

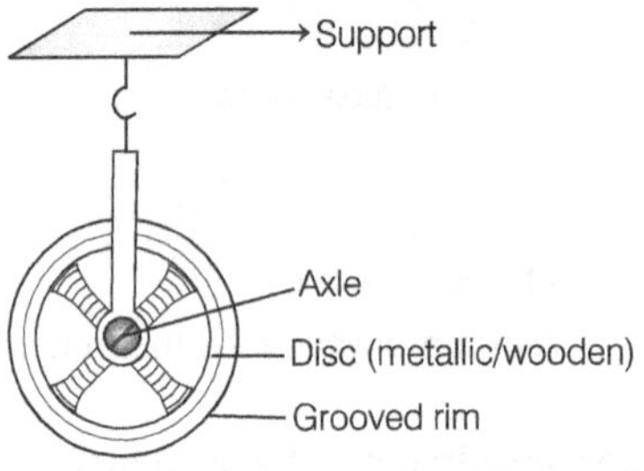

Pulley

A single pulley can be used in two ways as (i) a fixed pulley and (ii) a movable pulley

Single Fixed Pulley

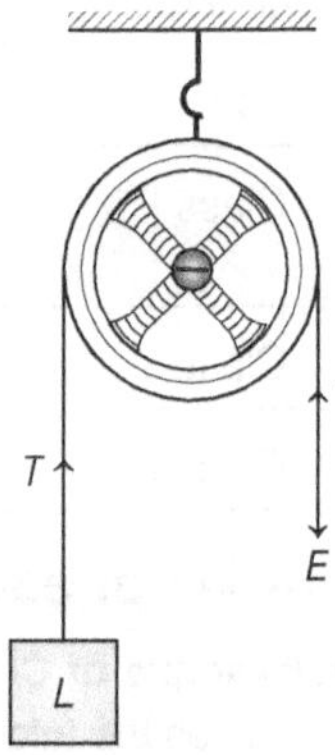

Single fixed pulley

- A pulley which has its axis of rotation fixed in position is called single fixed pulley.
- A fixed pulley is used only to change the direction of effort to be applied, i.e. with its use, the effort can be applied in a more convenient direction.
- Mechanical Advantage $MA = \frac{\text{Load}}{\text{Effort}} = \frac{T}{T} = 1$

  ($\because$ load, $L = T$, effort, $E = T$, if pulley is not rotating)
- Velocity Ratio (VR) $= \frac{d_E}{d_L} = \frac{d}{d} = 1$ ($d_E = d$ and $d_L = d$)
- Efficiency $(\eta) = \frac{MA}{VR} = 1$ or 100%

Single Movable Pulley

- A pulley whose axis of rotation is not fixed in position is called a movable pulley.

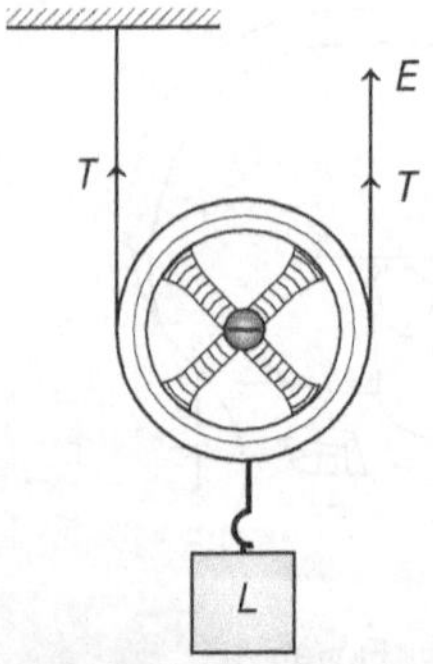

Single movable pulley

- Load is balanced by $T + T = 2T$
- Mechanical Advantage $(\text{MA}) = \dfrac{\text{Load}}{\text{Effort}} = \dfrac{2T}{T} = 2$ $\quad (\because L = 2T \text{ and } E = T)$
- Velocity Ratio $(\text{VR}) = \dfrac{d_E}{d_L} = \dfrac{2d}{d} = 2$ $\quad (\because d_E = 2d \text{ and } d_L = d)$
- Efficiency $(\eta) = \dfrac{\text{MA}}{\text{VR}} = \dfrac{2}{2} = 1$ or 100%

Combination of Pulleys

The combination can be made in two ways

(i) Using one fixed pulley and several movable pulleys.

(ii) Using several fixed pulleys in two blocks known as block and tackle system.

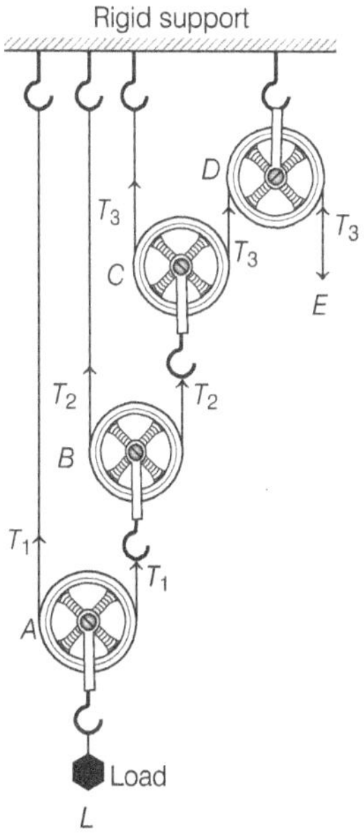

Using One Fixed Pulley and Several Movable Pulleys

According to the diagram, we see that one end of each string passing over a movable pulley is fixed, so the other end of string moves up twice the distance moved by the axle of the movable pulley.

- If there are n movable pulleys with one fixed pulley, then the mechanical advantage of this system is

$$\boxed{\text{MA} = 2^n}$$

So, mechanical advantage of system which has one fixed pulley and three movable pulleys $= 2^3 = 8$

So, velocity ratio of system which has one fixed pulley and three movable pulleys $= 2^3 = 8$

Efficiency of this combination, $\boxed{\eta = \dfrac{\text{MA}}{\text{VR}} = \dfrac{2^n}{2^n} = 1 \text{ or } 100\%}$

Using Several Fixed Pulleys in Two Blocks (Block and Tackle System)

- In this system, two blocks of pulleys are used while usually upper block is fixed and the lower block is movable.
- If the total number of pulleys used in both the blocks is n and the effort is being applied in the downward direction, then

$$\text{Load} = nT \text{ and Effort} = T$$

- Mechanical Advantage $\boxed{\text{MA} = \dfrac{\text{Load}}{\text{Effort}} = n}$
- In a block and tackle system, if the load moves up through a distance d, the effort end moves through a distance nd because each section of the string supporting the load is loosened by a length d, i.e. if $d_L = d$, then $d_E = nd$

$\therefore$ Velocity Ratio $\boxed{\text{VR} = \dfrac{nd}{d} = n}$

Efficiency of this combination, $\boxed{\eta = \dfrac{\text{MA}}{\text{VR}} = \dfrac{n}{n} = 1 \text{ or } 100\%}$

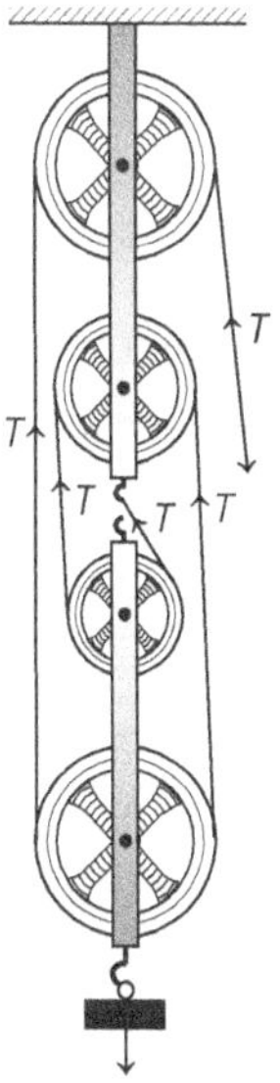

Block and tackle for four pulleys

EXAM ORIENTED QUESTIONS

TYPE - 1

01 Mark

Multiple Choice Questions

Q.1 In which simple machine is the direction of application of effort conveniently changed?

(a) Lever (b) Pulley

(c) Inclined plane (d) Screw

Ans. (b) A pulley changes the direction of effort force, making it convenient to pull loads.

Q.2 Mechanical Advantage (MA), load (L) and effort (E) are related as **[ICSE Specimen 2022 Sem-I]**

(a) $MA = L \times E$ (b) $MA = E/L$

(c) $MA \times E = L$ (d) $MA \times L = E$

Ans. (c) $MA = \frac{L}{E}$

$\therefore \quad MA \times E = L$

Q.3 Class II lever are designed to have

(a) MA = VR (b) MA > VR

(c) MA > 1 (d) MA < 1

Ans. (c) In class II lever, the effort arm is always longer than the load arm, so its Mechanical Advantage (MA) is always more than 1, i.e. MA > 1.

Q.4 A lever for which mechanical advantage is always less than 1 has

(a) fulcrum at the mid-point between load and effort

(b) load between effort and fulcrum

(c) effort between fulcrum and load

(d) load and effort acting at the same point

Ans. (c) The mechanical advantage of a lever is less than 1, when its effort arm is less than load arm. i.e. The effort is between fulcrum and load.

Q.5 The correct relationship between Mechanical Advantage (MA), Velocity Ratio (VR) and efficiency (η) is

(a) $MA = \eta \times VR$ (b) $VR = \eta \times MA$

(c) $\eta = MA \times VR$ (d) None of these

Ans. (a) Efficiency of a machine,

$$\eta = \frac{\text{Output work}}{\text{Input work}} = \frac{L \times d_L}{E \times d_E} = \frac{L}{E} \times \frac{1}{d_E / d_L}$$

Since, $\frac{L}{E} = MA$ and $\frac{d_E}{d_L} = VR$

$$\Rightarrow \quad \eta = \frac{MA}{VR} \text{ or } VR \times \eta = MA$$

Q.6 Which of the following is a class III lever? **[ICSE 2024]**

(a) Pair of scissors (b) Wheelbarrow

(c) Crowbar (d) Human forearm

Ans. (d) In third class lever, effort is situated between the load and the fulcrum. Human forearm is a class III lever.

Q.7 A movable pulley is used as

(a) a force multiplier

(b) a speed multiplier

(c) a device to change the direction of effort

(d) an energy multiplier

Ans. (a) By using a single movable pulley, a load can be lifted with an effort equal to half the load. So, it acts as a force multiplier.

Q.8 A single fixed pulley is used because **[ICSE 2022 Sem-I]**

(a) it changes the direction of applied effort conveniently

(b) it multiplies speed

(c) it multiplies effort

(d) its efficiency is 100%

Ans. (a) A single fixed pulley is used to lift load by changing the direction of the lifting force into a convenient direction.

Q.9 For a lever, a graph is plotted with load on Y-axis and effort on X-axis. Which of the following represents the slope of the graph? **[ICSE 2025]**

(a) Mechanical advantage

(b) Velocity ratio

(c) 1/ Velocity ratio

(d) 1 Mechanical advantage

Ans. (a) Mechanical advantage $= \frac{\text{Load}}{\text{Effort}}$

and slope of a graph $= \frac{\Delta Y}{\Delta X}$

Q.10 A woman draws water from a well using a fixed pulley. The mass of the bucket and the water together is 10 kg. The force applied by the woman is 200 N. The mechanical advantage is (Take, $g = 10 \text{ m/s}^2$) **[ICSE 2022 Sem-I]**

(a) 2 (b) 20

(c) 0.05 (d) 0.5

Ans. (d) Given load = weight of water

$$L = 10 \times 10 = 100 \text{ N}$$

Effort = force applied

$$E = 200 \text{ N}$$

Now, $MA = \frac{\text{Load}}{\text{Effort}} = \frac{100}{200} = 0.5$

Q.11 During his experiments with a single movable pulley, Jas determined the effort, mechanical advantage and efficiency as X, Y and Z, respectively. Subsequently, after lubricating the pulley thoroughly, he recalculated the effort, MA and efficiency. X', Y' and Z' respectively. Which of the following relationships accurately represents the scenario? **[Competency Based Que.]**

(a) $X' > X$ (b) $Y' < Y$ (c) $Z' > Z$ (d) $Z' = Z$

Ans. (c) In the above scenario, the effort reduces since lubrication reduces friction. The mechanical advantage increases since the effort decreases and hence the overall efficiency of the system increases.

Q.12 A pulley system has MA = 4. If a load of 10 kgf is pulled by a distance of 2 m in 10 s, calculate the power developed by the effort.

(a) 15 W (b) 20 W (c) 25 W (d) 5 W

Ans. (d) MA = 4

Load (L) = 10 kgf

$$MA = \frac{L}{E} \Rightarrow E = \frac{10}{4}\text{ kgf} = \left(\frac{10}{4} \times 10\right)\text{N}$$

∴ Work done is moving effort by a distance of 2 m

$$= \left(\frac{100}{4} \times 2\right)\text{J} = 50\text{ J}$$

$$\therefore \text{ Power developed} = \frac{W}{t} = \frac{50}{10} = 5\text{ W}$$

Q.13 A person draws 10 kg water from a well at depth of 5 m using a single fixed pulley by applying an effort of 120 N. Then, the efficiency of the machine is (Take, $g = 10\text{ ms}^{-2}$)

(a) 83% (b) 87% (c) 75% (d) 92%

Ans. (a) Weight of water = 10 × 10 = 100 N

$$\therefore \quad \eta = \frac{\text{Work output}}{\text{Work input}} = \frac{L \times d_L}{E \times d_E} = \frac{100 \times 5}{120 \times 5}$$

$$\eta = \frac{100}{120} \times 100 \simeq 83\%$$

Q.14 In the diagram shown below, the velocity ratio of the arrangement is **[ICSE 2022 Sem-I]**

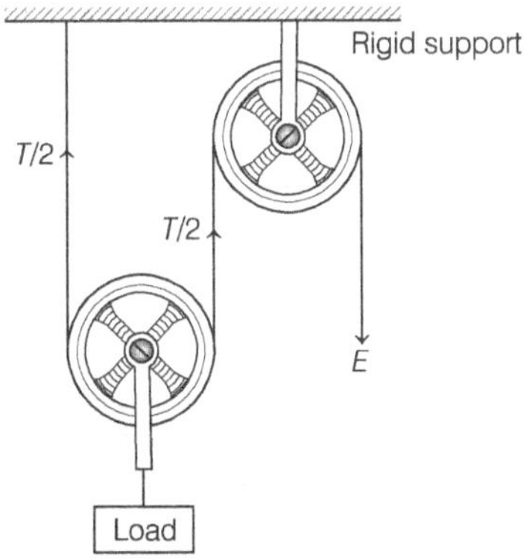

(a) 1 (b) 2 (c) 3 (d) 0

Ans. (b) Velocity Ratio (VR) $= \frac{d_E}{d_L} = \frac{2d}{d} = 2$

Q.15 The diagrams below show four pulley systems. State which of the options following the diagrams is true.

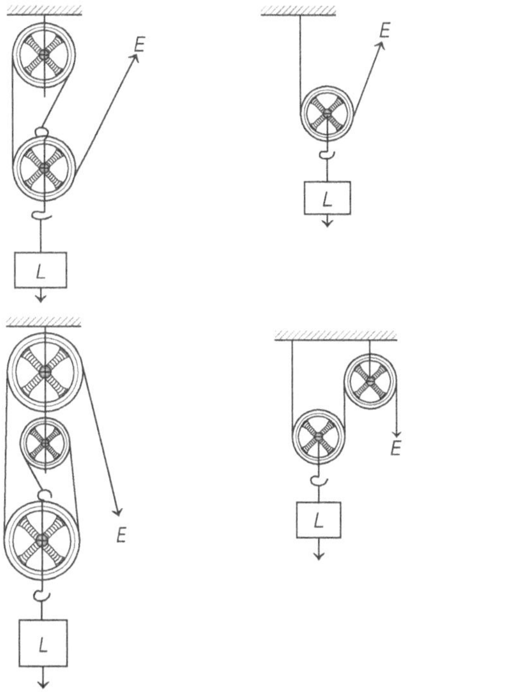

(a) There are three pulley systems with VR = 2 and one pulley system with VR = 1.

(b) There are two pulley systems with VR = 2, one pulley system with VR = 3 one pulley system with VR = 1.

(c) There are two pulley systems with VR = 2, one pulley system with VR = 3 and one pulley system with VR = 4.

(d) There are two pulley systems with VR = 2 and two pulley system with VR = 3.

Ans. (d) For the systems having effort in the downward direction, the VR is equal to the number of pulleys and for the system having effort in the upward direction the VR is equal to the number of strands of strings supporting the load.

Q.16 A pulley system has a single fixed pulley and a single movable pulley. Its mechanical advantage is

(a) 1 (b) 2 (c) 3 (d) 4

Ans. (b) A single fixed pulley has mechanical advantage as

$$MA_f = \frac{T}{T} = 1$$

The single movable pulley has mechanical advantage

$$MA_m = \frac{2T}{T} = 2$$

So, the given pulley system has mechanical advantage as, $MA = MA_f \times MA_m = 1 \times 2 = 2$

Q.17 If a block and tackle system with convenient direction has 3 movable pulleys, then its velocity ratio **[ICSE Specimen 2022 Sem-I]**

(a) is either 6 or 7 (b) should be 6

(c) should be 7 (d) is 3

Ans. (a) Given, Number of movable pulleys = 3

∴ So, total pulleys can be double the movable or plus one.

Q.18 The adjacent diagram shows the movable block of a block and tackle system with effort in a convenient direction. From the diagram we can conclude that the number of pulleys used in the fixed block are **[ICSE Specimen 2025]**

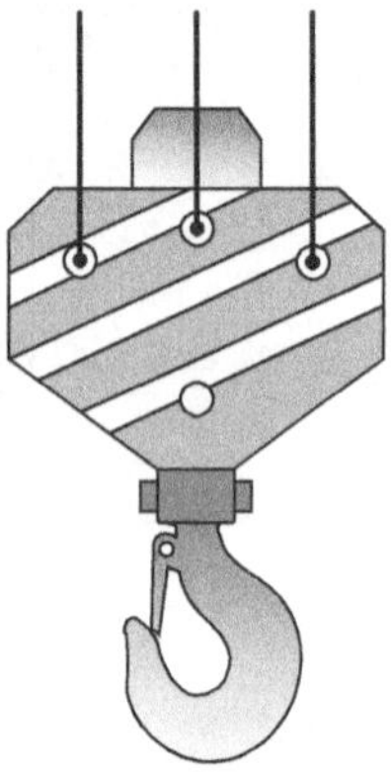

(a) 1 (b) 3 (c) 2 (d) 4

Ans. (c) The minimum number of fixed pulleys required to hold two strands of ropes in movable pulley in given case is 2.

TYPE - 2 01 Mark

Assertion-Reason Type Questions

Directions (Q. Nos. 1-4) In the following questions two statements are given as Assertion and Reason.

(a) Both A and R are true and R is the correct explanation of A.

(b) Both A and R are true but R is not the correct explanation of A.

(c) A is true but R is false.

(d) A is false but R is true.

Q.1 Assertion (A) The efficiency of an ideal machine is 100%.

Reason (R) In an ideal machine, the work output is always equal to the work input.

Ans. (a) In an ideal machine, there is no energy loss, so the work output equals to the work input, resulting in 100% efficiency.

Q.2 Assertion (A) The efficiency of a machine decreases when there are energy losses due to friction and other factors.

Reason (R) Efficiency is the ratio of useful work output to total work input, including losses.

Ans. (a) Because it mathematically explains the energy loss due to friction and other factors.

Q.3 Assertion (A) Mechanical advantage is the ratio of the load to the effort in a machine.

Reason (R) It quantifies how much a machine amplifies force, allowing users to accomplish tasks with less effort than if they were directly applied.

Ans. (b) Because the Reason is also another definition of the mechanical advantage.

Q.4 Assertion (A) Moving parts of machines are perfectly frictionless.

Reason (R) Actual machines operate with some energy loss because of friction and other factors.

Ans. (d) Moving parts are not perfectly frictionless, which leads to energy loss in actual machines.

TYPE - 3 01/02 Marks

Fill in the Blanks

Q.1 A machine in which the mechanical advantage is less than 1 used to .... [increase speed, reduce effort]

Ans. increase speed

Q.2 In a lever, the .... [effort, fulcrum] is the fixed point around which the lever rotates.

Ans. fulcrum

Q.3 The .... [efficiency, MA, VR] of a machine is the ratio of the load to the effort applied, while the .... (MA, VR, efficiency) is the ratio of the distance moved by the effort to the distance moved by the load in the same time.

Ans. MA, VR

Q.4 In an ideal machine, the .... [efficiency, MA, VR] equals the .... [efficiency, VR, MA] because there is no energy losses.

Ans. MA, VR

Q.5 In class .... [I/II/III] lever the MA and the VR are always more than one whereas in class........... [I/II/III] lever the MA and VR are always less than one.

Ans. II, III

Q.6 In a block and tackle system, increase in the weight of the movable block .... [decreases, does not affect, increases] the efficiency of the pulley system. **[ICSE Specimen 2025]**

Ans. decreases

TYPE - 4 02 Marks

Very Short Answer Type Questions

Q.1 Why is a jack screw provided with a long arm? **[2]**
[ICSE 2017]

Ans. $\tau = F_x \perp d = E_x d_E$

Jack screw is provided with a long arm so that by applying less effort to this long arm, a heavy load can be lifted.

Q.2 Copy the diagram of the forearm given below, indicate the positions of load, effort and fulcrum. **(2)**
[ICSE 2008]

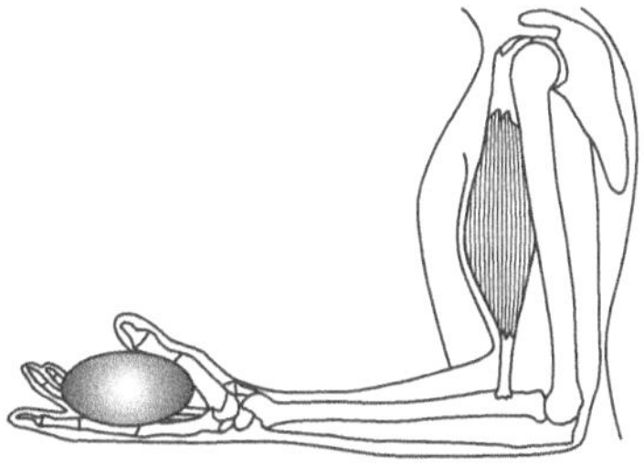

Ans. The below diagram shows the position of load *L*, effort *E* and fulcrum *F*.

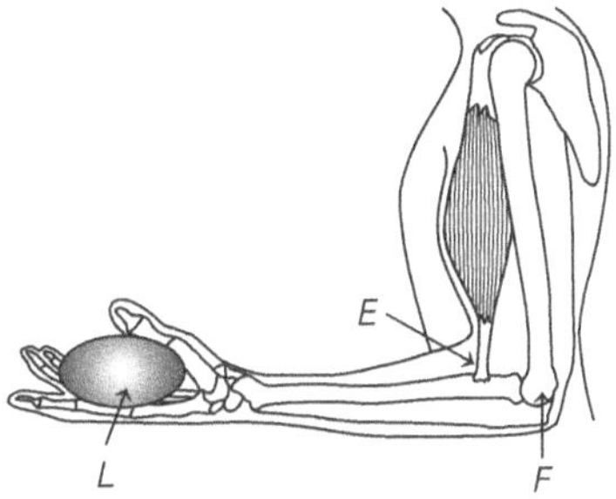

Q.3 What is the relationship between the mechanical advantage and the velocity ratio for

(i) ideal machine? **[1]**

(ii) practical machine? **[1]**

Ans. (i) For an ideal machine, the work done by the machine is equal to the work done on the machine. Therefore, mechanical advantage is equal to velocity ratio. i.e. MA = VR.

(ii) For practical machine, mechanical advantage is less than velocity ratio as efficiency is less than 1.

Q.4 The diagram below shows a claw hammer used to remove a nail.

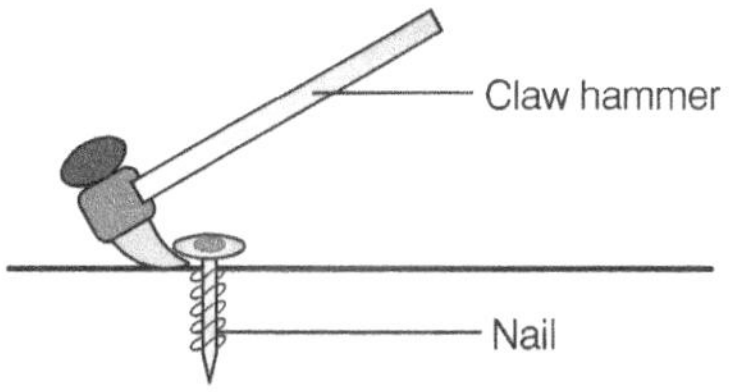

(i) To which class of lever does it belong? **[1]**

(ii) Give one more example of the same class of lever mentioned by you in part (i) for which the mechanical advantage is greater than one. **[1]**

Ans. (i) A claw hammer used to remove a nail is a class I lever.

(ii) A longer crow bar is an example of class I lever, that have mechanical advantage greater than one.

Q.5 The diagram below shows a lever in use **[ICSE 2018]**

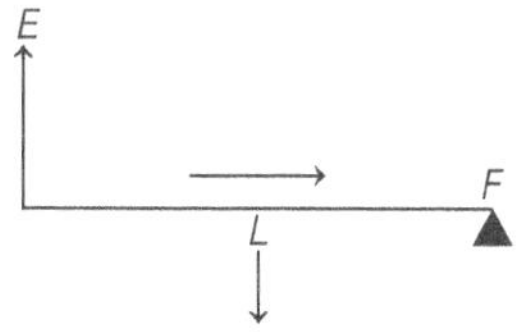

(i) To which class of levers does it belong? **[1]**

(ii) Without changing the dimensions of the lever, if the load is shifted towards the fulcrum, what happens to the mechanical advantage of the lever? **[1]**

Ans. (i) It belongs to class II lever because load is situated between fulcrum and effort.

(ii) If load is shifted towards the fulcrum, then mechanical advantage will increase as load arm decreases.

Q.6

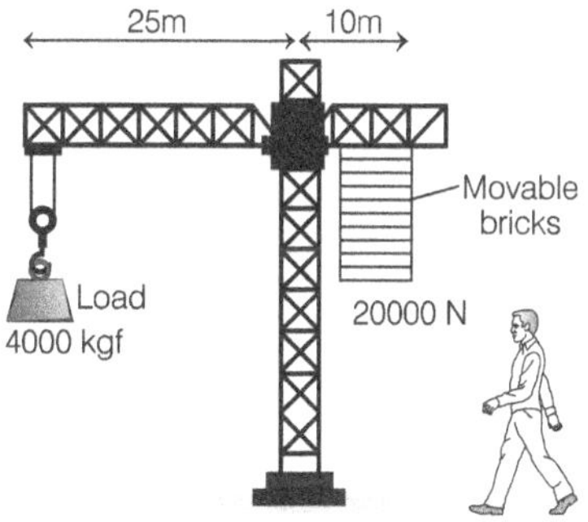

Study the diagram and answer the questions that follow.

(i) In the diagram, is the worker attempting to raise or lower the load? **[1]**

(ii) Justify your answer (i) with the necessary calculation. **[1][Competency Based Que.]**

Ans. (i) The worker is attempting to lower the load.

(ii) Moment of load about the fulcrum

$$= (4000 \times 10) \times 25$$
$$= 10^6 \text{ Nm}$$

Moment of effort about the fulcrum

$$= 20000 \times 10$$
$$= 2 \times 10^5 \text{ Nm.}$$

Since, the moment of load about the fulcrum is more, so it can be concluded that the load is being lowered.

Q.7 The graph shows load against effort for a lever with load and effort on the same side of the fulcrum.

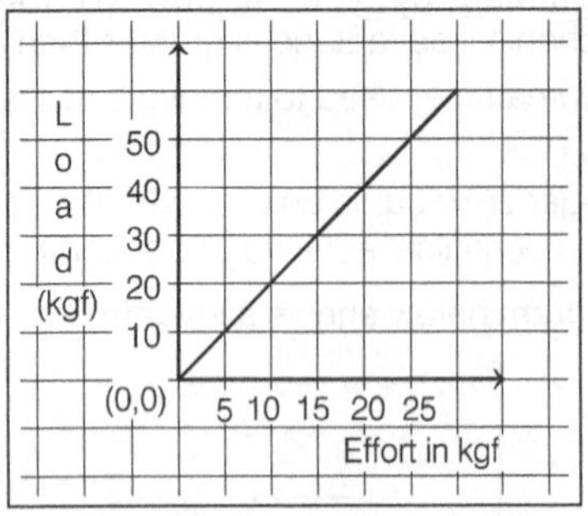

(i) Which feature of the load and effort graph must be calculated to determine mechanical advantage? **[1]**

(ii) Which class does this lever belong to? **[1]**

[Competency Based Ques.]

Ans. (i) The slope of the graph must be calculated to determine the mechanical advantage.

(ii) $MA = \frac{\text{Load}}{\text{Effort}} = \frac{\Delta L}{\Delta E} = \frac{50-20}{25-10} = \frac{30}{15} = 2.$

Since the mechanical advantage is always greater than 1 as can be seen from the graph so the lever belongs to the II class.

Q.8 (i) Why is the mechanical advantage of a lever of the second order always greater than one? **[1]**

(ii) Name the type of single pulley that has a mechanical advantage greater than one. **[1]**

Ans. (i) $MA = \frac{E_{arm}}{L_{arm}}$

The effort arm is always greater than the load arm, so the mechanical advantage of class II lever is always greater than one.

(ii) Single movable pulley is the type of pulley whose mechanical advantage is greater than unity.

Q.9 A type of single pulley is very often used as a machine, even though it does not give any gain in mechanical advantage.

(i) Name the type of pulley used. **[1]**

(ii) For what purpose is such a pulley used? **[1]**

Ans. (i) The pulley which is used in the arrangement is single fixed pulley.

(ii) Single fixed pulley is used only to change the direction of the force applied.

Q.10 Meera chooses to use a block and tackle system of 9 pulleys instead of a single movable pulley to lift a heavy load. **[ICSE 2024]**

(i) What is the advantage of using a block and tackle system over a single movable pulley? **[1]**

(ii) Why should she connect more number of pulleys in the upper fixed block? **[1]**

Ans. (i) Block and tackle systems can reduce the effort.

(ii) She connects more number of pulleys in the upper fixed block, so that effort can be applied in the downward direction.

TYPE - 5 03 Marks

Short Answer Type Questions

Q.1 A pair of scissors and a pair of pliers belong to the same class of levers.

(i) Which one has mechanical advantage less than one? **[2]**

(ii) State the usefullness of such a machine whose mechanical advantage is less than 1. **[1]**

Ans. (i) Both the scissors and the pair of pliers belong to class I lever, since in both the case the fulcrum lies between the load and the effort.

For the pair of scissors the mechanical advantage and the velocity ratio both are less than one because the effort arm is shorter than the load arm.

(ii) For a pair of scissors since the velocity ratio is less than one so it acts as a speed multiplier so that the blades of the scissors move longer on the cloth when the handless of it are moved a little.

Q.2 Draw a block and tackle system of pulleys with velocity ratio equal to 3. **[ICSE 2025]**

Ans.

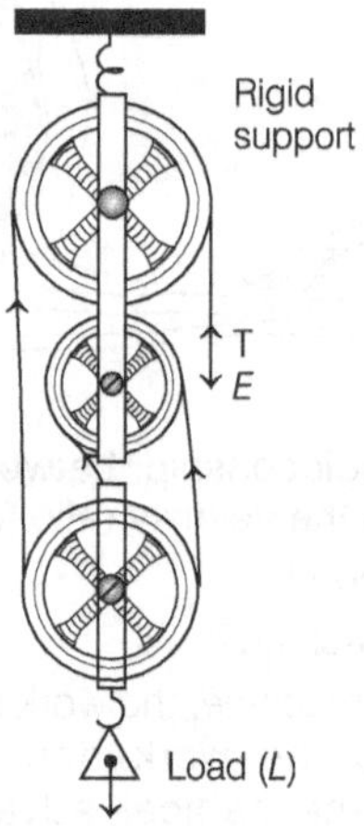

Q.3 Three levers X, Y, Z of equal lengths are shown in the diagram. **[ICSE 2025]**

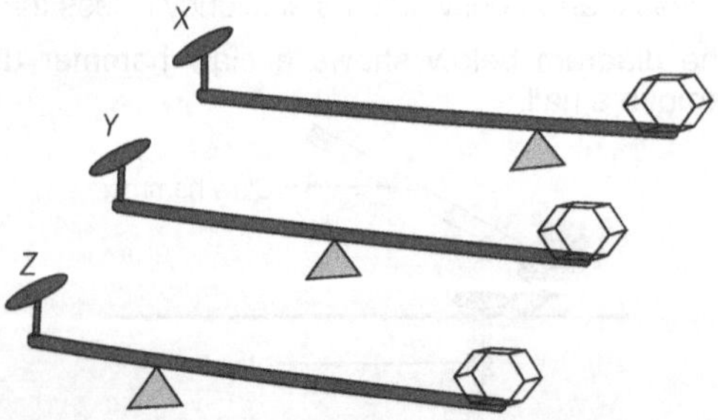

(a) Which class of lever do these belong to?

(b) Among these (*X*, *Y* or *Z*) which one will give the maximum mechanical advantage? Justify your answer.

Ans. (a) Class I lever.

(b) Mechanical advantage = $\frac{\text{Effort arm}}{\text{Load arm}}$

Since the effort arm is greatest and the load arm is the least for *Z*, so *Z* will have the maximum mechanical advantage.

Q.4 From the diagram given below, answer the questions that follow:

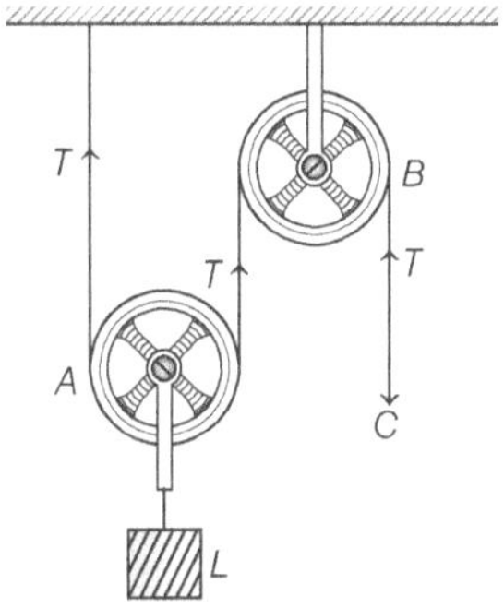

(i) What kind of pulleys are *A* and *B*? **[1]**

(ii) State the purpose of pulley *B*. **[1]**

(iii) What effort has to be applied at *C* to just raise the load *L* = 20 kgf?

(Neglect the weight of pulley *A* and friction) **[1]**

[ICSE 2016]

Ans. (i) According to the question, *A* is a movable pulley while *B* is a fixed pulley.

(ii) The purpose of pulley *B* is to change the point of application of effort in the convenient direction.

(iii) Given, load = 20kgf, MA = 2

and we know that,

$$\text{MA} = \frac{\text{Load}}{\text{Effort}}$$

$$\Rightarrow \quad \text{Effort} = \frac{\text{Load}}{\text{MA}}$$

$$= \frac{20}{2} = 10 \text{ kgf}$$

Q.5 A block and tackle system of pulleys has velocity ratio 4.

(i) Draw a labelled diagram of the system indicating clearly, the direction of load and effort. **[2]**

(ii) What is the value of the mechanical advantage of the given pulley system if it is an ideal pulley system? **[1] [ICSE 2023]**

Ans. (i)

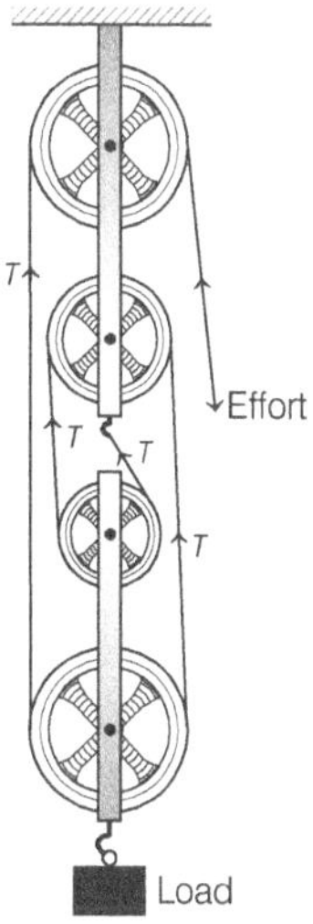

(ii) $\text{MA} = \frac{\text{Load}}{\text{Effort}} = \frac{4T_L}{T_E} = 4$

Q.6 A block and tackle system of pulleys has velocity ratio 4.

(i) Draw a labelled diagram of the system indicating clearly, the direction of the load and effort. **[2]**

(i) Calculate the potential energy of the load 100 kgf lifted by this pulley to a height 5 m. (g = 10 ms²) **[2]**

[ICSE Specimen 2025]

Ans. (i) Refer to the diagram of the previous question.

(ii) Potential energy of the load is given as = *mgh*

where, $mg = 100 \text{ kgf} = (100 \times 10) \text{ N} = 1000 \text{ N}$.

$h = 5 \text{ m}$.

$\therefore \quad \text{PE} = (1000 \times 5) \text{ J} = 5000 \text{ J}$.

TYPE - 6 — 04 Marks

Long Answer Type Questions

Q.1 The figure below shows a pulley arrangement.

[ICSE 2019]

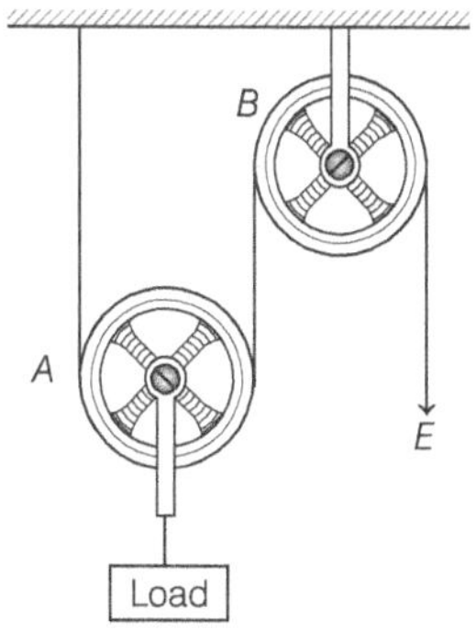

(i) Copy the figure and mark the direction of tension on each strand of the string. **[1]**

(ii) What is the velocity ratio of the arrangement? **[1]**

(iii) It the tension acting on the string is T, then what is the relationship between T and effort E? **[1]**

(iv) If the free end of the string moves through a distance x, then find the distance by which the load is raised. **[1]**

Ans. (i)

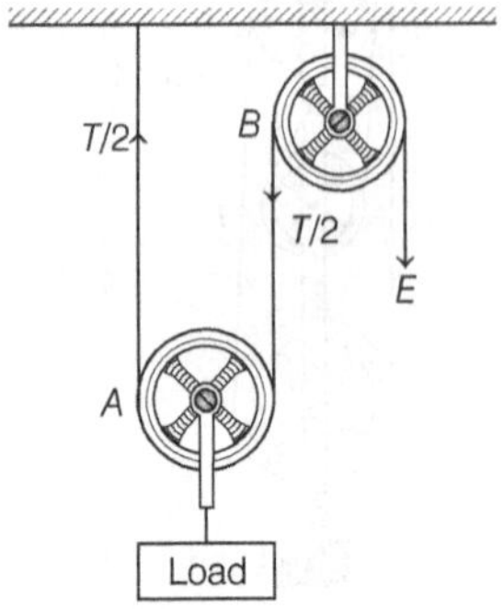

(ii) The system has one fixed pulley and one movable pulley. Thus, the velocity ratio is given by

$$VR = 2^1 = 2$$

(iii) The relation between T and effort E is given by

$$\frac{T}{2} = E \Rightarrow T = 2E$$

(iv) If the free end of the string moves through a distance x, then the load is raised by $\frac{x}{2}$ distance.

Q.2 A block and tackle system has VR = 5

(i) Draw a neat labelled diagram of a system indicating the direction of its load and effort. **[2]**

(ii) Rohan exerts a pull of 150 kgf. What is the maximum load he can raise with this pulley system, if its efficiency is 75%? **[2] [ICSE 2015]**

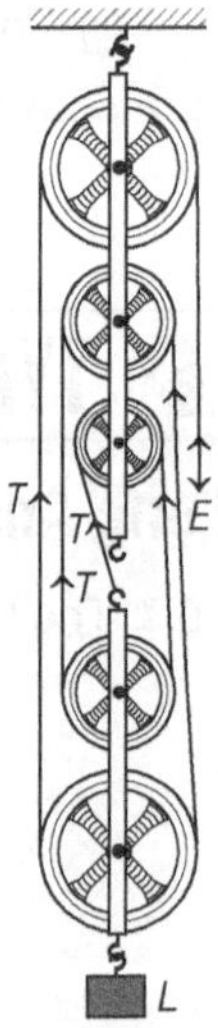

Ans. (i) Velocity ratio is always equal to the number of strands of tackle supporting the load. For velocity ratio 5, there will be 5 strands supporting the load.

(ii) Here, $E = 150$ kgf, $\eta = 75\% = 0.75$,

$$VR = 5$$

$$MA = L/E = VR \times \eta = 5 \times 0.75 = 3.75$$

$$L/150 = 3.75$$

$$L = 3.75 \times 150 = 562.5 \text{ kgf}$$

Q.3 (i) An effort is applied on the bigger wheel of a gear having 32 teeths. It is used to turn a wheel of 8 teeths. Where is it used? **[2]**

(ii) A pulley system has three pulleys. A load of 120 N is overcome by applying an effort of 50 N. Calculate the mechanical advantage and efficiency of this system. **[2] [ICSE 2016]**

Ans. (i) If an effort is applied on the bigger wheel of gear having 32 teeths to turn a wheel of 8 teeths, it acts as speed multiplier. It is used in bicycles and car to gain speed.

(ii) According to question,

Load = 120 N, Effort = 50 N

So, mechanical advantage $= \frac{\text{Load}}{\text{Effort}} = \frac{120}{50} = 2.4$

% efficiency $= \frac{MA}{VR} \times 100 \Rightarrow \frac{2.4}{3} \times 100 = 80\%$

Q.4 Given are two pulleys. **[ICSE 2024]**

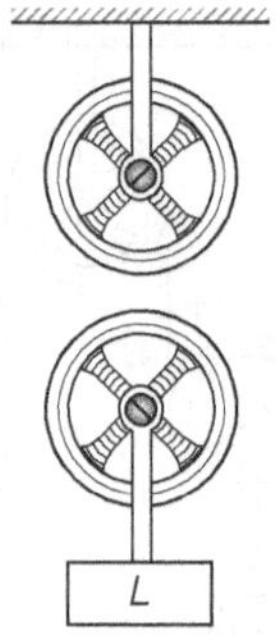

(i) Copy and complete the labelled diagram connecting the two pulleys with a tackle to obtain velocity ratio = 2. **[2]**

(ii) Its load is 48 kgf and efficiency is 80%, then calculate

(a) mechanical advantage. **[1]**

(b) effort needed to lift the load. **[1]**

Ans. (i)

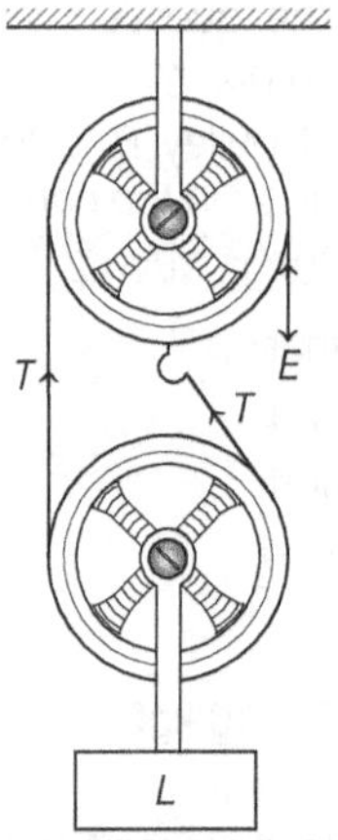

(ii) (a) Mechanical advantage,

$$MA = VR \times \eta$$

$$= 2 \times \frac{80}{100} = \frac{160}{100} = 1.6$$

(b) Effort $= \frac{\text{Load}}{MA} = \frac{48}{1.6} = 30$ kgf

Q.5 (i) Draw a diagram to show a block and tackle pulley system having a velocity ratio of 3 marking the direction of load L, effort E and tension T. **[2]**

(ii) The pulley system drawn lifts a load of 150 N. When an effort of 60 N is applied, find its mechanical advantage. **[1]**

(iii) Is the above pulley system an ideal machine or not? **[1] [ICSE 2018]**

Ans. (i) The labelled diagram of the system is shown below

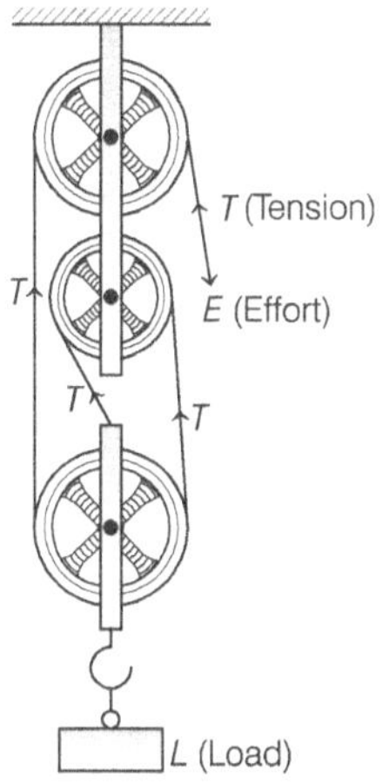

(ii) Given, load $L = 150$ N

Effort $E = 60$ N

We know that, Mechanical Advantage,

$$MA = \frac{\text{Load}}{\text{Effort}} = \frac{150}{60} = 2.5$$

(iii) No, the above pulley system is not an ideal machine, because velocity ratio (VR = 3) is not equal to mechanical advantage.

Q.6

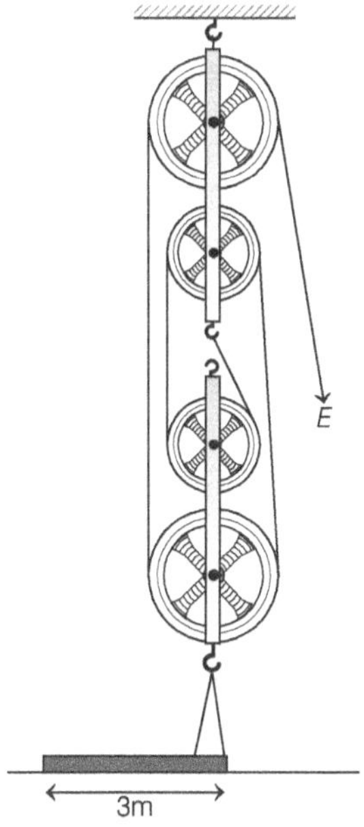

The diagram above shows a pulley used to lift an iron beam of length 3m and weight 100 kgf, lying on the ground.

(i) Calculate the minimum effort needed to just lift the beam off the ground. [Assume no loss of energy **[2]**

(ii) When the beam is being lifted from the ground, with the other end touching the ground, state with a reason whether the effort needed keeps on increasing, decreasing or remains constant. **[2]**

[Competency Based]

Ans. (i) When the beam is just lifted from its one end, it acts as a lower as long as its other end is touching the ground.

Weight of the beam is 100 kgf which acts at the centre.

$\therefore \quad 100 \times 1.5 = x \times 3$

where, x is the weight acting in the load end of the pulley system.

$$\therefore \quad x = \frac{100 \times 1.5}{3} = 50 \text{ kgf}$$

So, 50 kgf is the effective load for the pulley.

Now, MA of the pulley system = 4.

$$\therefore \quad 4 = \frac{\text{Load}}{\text{Effort}} = \frac{50}{E}$$

$$\therefore \quad E = 12.5 \text{ kgf}$$

(ii) The effort needed remains the same, since the ratio between the effort arm and the load arm remains the same while the beam is being lifted.

Q.7 Two boys are playing with a see-saw as shown in the figure.

The lighter boy sits farther away from the mid-point as compared to the heavier boy, such that the moments of both of them are same.

Complete the table, using the lables from the figure. The first label is done for you. **[Competency Based Que.]**

S.No.	Description	Label
(i)	Load	a
(ii)	Effort	
(iii)	Effort arm	
(iv)	Load arm	
(v)	Fulcrum	

Ans.

S.No.	Description	Label
(i)	Load	*a*
(ii)	Effort	*b*
(iii)	Effort arm	*e*
(iv)	Load arm	*d*
(v)	Fulcrum	c

TYPE - 7 — 03/04 Marks

Case Based Questions

Q.1 At construction sites, workers utilize a variety of tools and equipments based on the principles of levers to complete tasks efficiently. For instance, levers help simplify jobs like lifting heavy loads, removing nails, and cutting materials. Imagine a construction team using tools such as hammers, wheel barrows, and pry bars while building a new structure. These tools represent different classes of levers, each designed to maximize efficiency and reduce physical effort.

(i) Identify the class of lever represented by a hammer used to pull out nails from wooden planks. **[1]**

(ii) Explain how a wheel barrow, commonly used in construction sites, functions as a second class lever. **[1]**

(iii) Describe the role of pry bar as a lever lifting heavy objects during construction tasks. **[1]**

Ans. (i) First class lever.

(ii) In a wheel barrow, the load (materials being transported) is placed between the fulcrum and the effort. This arrangement always has a mechanical advantage greater than one, making it easier to lift heavy loads with less effort since it acts as a force multiplier.

(iii) The pry bar which is also commonly known as crow bar is a first class lever in which the effort arm is greater than the load arm and hence it acts as a force multiplier in which a large load can be lifted with a less effort.

Q.2 At a construction site, workers use several wheel barrows of exactly the same dimensions having a mass of 15 kg to effectively carry a large amount of load from one location of the site to another. The maximum load the wheelbarrows can carry at once, apart from its own weight, is 30 kgf. The workers are instructed to carry the maximum amount of load while using the wheel barrows.

(i) Which class of lever does the above mentioned tool belong to? Give another example of the same class of lever. **[1]**

(ii) If the distance between the fulcrum and load of the wheelbarrows is 20 cm and that of the effort and the load is 40 cm then find the minimum effort required to keep the leg of the wheelbarrow just off the ground. **[1]**

(iii) Give an example each of the other two classes of levers not mentioned in part (i) which have application at construction sites. **[1]**

Ans. (i) Class II lever.

Nut cracker is another example of class II lever.

(ii) Given, load arm = 20 cm

The distance between the load and the effort is 40 cm but for a class II lever, load lies between the effort and the fulcrum, so

Effort arm = (20 + 40) cm = 60 cm

The mass of the wheelbarrow is 15 kg

$\therefore$ The weight of the wheelbarrow = 15 kf.

$\therefore$ Total load = (15 + 30) kgf = 45 kgf

So, according to the principle moment

Load $\times$ Load arm = Effort $\times$ Effort arm

$$\Rightarrow \quad 45 \times 20 = E \times 60$$

$$\Rightarrow \quad E = 15 \text{ kgf}$$

So, the minimum effort needed to keep the leg just off the ground is 15 kgf.

(iii) Class I lever - A crowbar or pry bar.

Class III lever - A spade used to lift coal or soil.

TYPE - 8

Numerical Questions

Q.1 Crane A lifts a heavy load in 5 s, whereas another crane B does the same work in 2 s. Compare the power of crane A to that of crane B. **[ICSE 2020] [2]**

Sol. Time taken to lift load by crane A, $t_1 = 5\text{s}$

Time taken by crane B to do the same work, $t_2 = 2\text{s}$

$$\therefore \quad \frac{\text{Power of crane } A}{\text{Power of crane } B} = \frac{W_1/t_1}{W_2/t_2}$$

$$\frac{P_A}{P_B} = \frac{t_2}{t_1} \quad [\because W_1 = W_2]$$

$$\Rightarrow \quad \frac{P_A}{P_B} = \frac{2}{5}$$

$$\Rightarrow \quad P_A = \frac{2}{5}P_B$$

Thus, power of crane A is two-fifth of crane B.

Q.2 A lever is shown below.

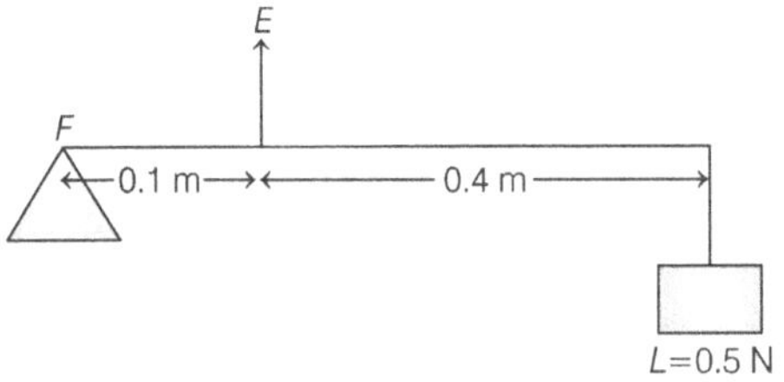

(i) Identify the type of lever. **[1]**

(ii) Calculate its mechanical advantage. **[1]**

[ICSE Specimen 2024]

Sol. (i) The given lever is class III lever.

(ii) $$\text{MA} = \frac{\text{Effort arm}}{\text{Load arm}}$$

$$\text{MA} = \frac{0.1 \text{ m}}{(0.1 + 0.4)\text{m}} = \frac{0.1}{0.5} = 0.2$$

Q.3 The diagram below shows a lever in use.

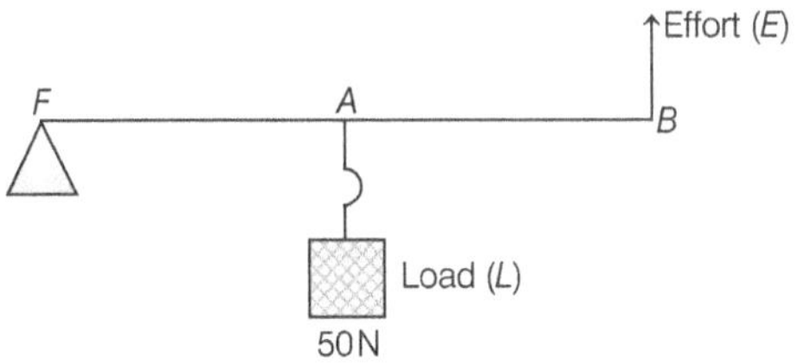

(i) To which class of lever does it belong? **[1]**

(ii) If $FA = 40$ cm, $AB = 60$ cm, then find the mechanical advantage of the lever. **[1]**

(iii) Find the value of effort **[1]**

Sol. (i) It belongs to class II lever.

(ii) Effort arm $FB = FA + AB$

$= 40 + 60 = 100$ cm

Load arm $= FA = 40$ cm

$$\therefore \quad \text{MA} = \frac{\text{Effort arm}}{\text{Load arm}}$$

$$= \frac{FB}{FA} = \frac{100}{40} = 2.5$$

(iii) $E \times E_{\text{arm}} = L \times L_{\text{arm}}$

$E \times 100 = 50 \times 40$

$E = -20\,N$

Q.4 A fire tong is used to lift a coal of weight 2 kgf by applying an effort at a distance of 10 cm from the fulcrum. The arms of the fire tong is 20 cm long.

(i) Calculate the mechanical advantage of the fire tongs. **[1]**

(ii) The effort needed to lift the coal. **[1]**

Sol. (i) $$\text{MA} = \frac{\text{Effort arm}}{\text{Load arm}} = \frac{10}{20} = 0.5$$

(ii) From the principle of moment, we know

Effort × Effort arm = Load × Load arm

$$\Rightarrow \quad \text{Effort} = \frac{2\text{kgf} \times 20\text{cm}}{10 \text{ cm}} = 4\text{kgf}$$

So, 4 kgf effort is needed to lift the coal.

Q.5 A pulley system with VR = 4 is used to lift a load of 175 kgf through a vertical height of 15 m. The effort required is 50 kgf in the downward direction. (Take, $g = 10 \text{ m/s}^2$). Calculate

(i) distance moved by the effort. **[1]**

(ii) work done by the effort. **[1]**

(iii) MA of the pulley system. **[1]**

(iv) efficiency of the pulley system. **[1] [ICSE 2017]**

Sol. Given, VR = 4,

load = 175 kgf,

Load arm = 15 m,

Effort = 50 kgf

Applying the formula,

$$L \times d_L = E \times d_E$$

where, L = Load, d_L = Load arm,

E = Effort and d_E = Effort arm.

$$\text{Also, VR} = \frac{\text{Distance moved by effort}}{\text{Distance moved by load}} = \frac{d_E}{d_L}$$

$$\Rightarrow \quad 4 = \frac{d_E}{15}$$

(i) Distance moved by the effort,

$$d_E = 15 \times 4 = 60 \text{ m}$$

(ii) Work done,

$$W = F \times s = E \times d_E$$

$$= 50 \times 60 = 3000 \text{ J}$$

(iii) $MA = \frac{Load}{Effort} = \frac{175}{50} = 3.5$

(iv) Efficiency, $\eta = \frac{MA}{VR} \times 100$

$= \frac{3.5}{4} \times 100\,\% = 87.5\%$

Q.6 The maximum pull a man can exert on a block and tackle system of velocity ratio 3 is 200 kgf.

(a) Find the maximum load the man can raise, if the efficiency of the pulley is 60%. **[2]**

(b) If the effort is moved by a distance of 60 cm, then how much does the load move? **[1]**

Sol. (a) Given, VR = 3, $\eta = 60\% = \frac{60}{100} = 0.6$

$\eta = \frac{MA}{VR}$; So, $MA = 0.6 \times 3 = 1.8$

Now, $MA = \frac{Load}{Effort}$,

Effort given by the man = 200 kgf

So, the maximum load the man can raise is $L = 1.8 \times 200 = 360$ kgf

(b) $VR = \frac{\text{distance moved by effort } (d_E)}{\text{distance moved by load } (d_L)}$

$\therefore \quad d_L = \frac{60}{3} = 20$ cm

So, the distance moved by load is 20 cm.

Q.7 A pulley system has a velocity ratio 5. Draw a neat labelled diagram of the pulley system to lift a load by applying the effort in a convenient direction. Mark the tension in your diagram.

(i) If the efficiency of the system is 80%, find its mechanical advantage. **[2]**

(ii) If a load of 10 kgf is pulled up by a distance of 2 m in 10 s, calculate the power developed of effort (given, $g = 10\ ms^{-2}$). **[2]**

[ICSE Specimen 2017]

Ans.

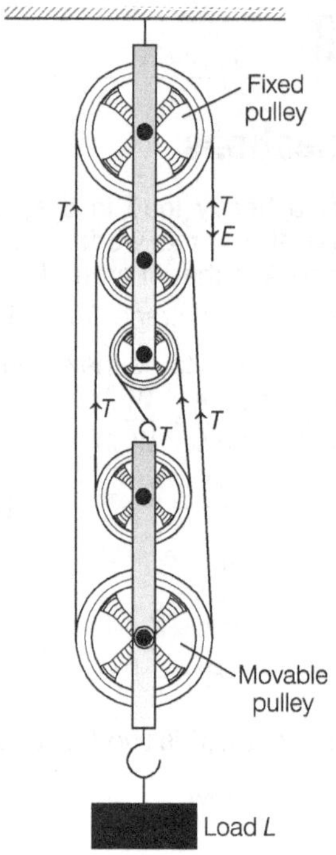

(i) VR = 5, $\eta = 80\% = 0.80$

$MA = VR \times \eta = 5 \times 0.8 = 4$

(ii) Load (L) = 10 kgf

$MA = \frac{Load}{Effort} \Rightarrow 4 = \frac{10\ kgf}{Effort}$

$\Rightarrow \quad Effort = \frac{10}{4} = 2.5$ kgf

Distance travelled by effort,

$d_E = d_L \times VR = (2 \times 5)\ m = 10\ m$

$\therefore$ Work done by effort

$W = (2.5 \times 10) \times 10\ J = 250\ J$

$\therefore \quad$ Power developed at effort $= \frac{250\ J}{10\ s} = 25\ W$

04

REFRACTION OF LIGHT

Refraction of Light at Plane Surfaces

- The change in path of a light ray as it passes obliquely from one transparent medium to another transparent medium is called **refraction of light**.
- The angle formed between the incident ray and the normal is called **angle of incidence** and the angle formed between the refracted ray and the normal is called **angle of refraction**.

(i) When a ray of light travels from a **rarer medium** to a **denser medium**, it bends **towards** the **normal**.

i.e. $\angle r < \angle i$

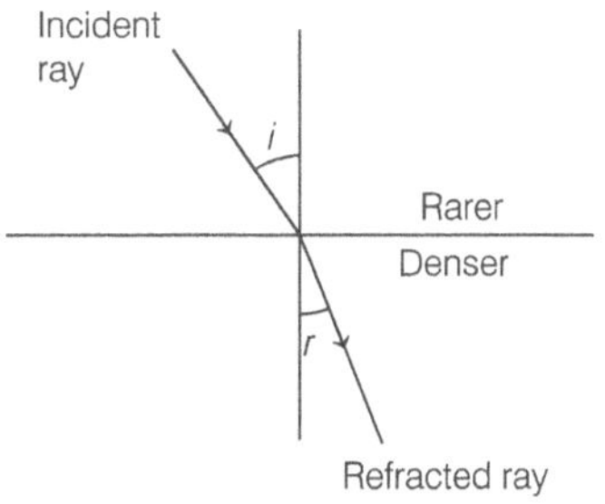

(ii) When a ray of light travels from a **denser medium** to **rarer medium,** it **bends away** from the normal.

i.e. $\angle r > \angle i$

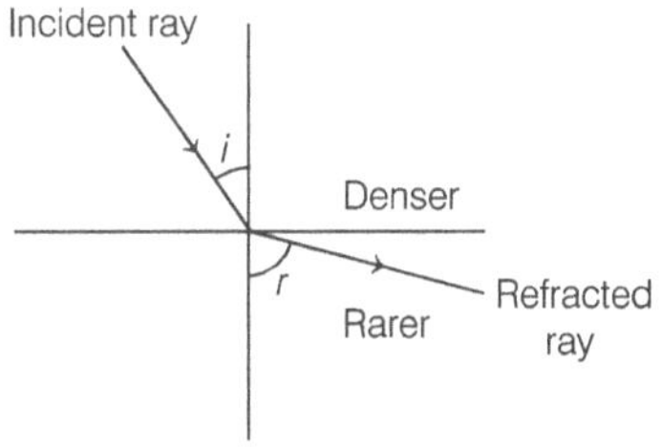

(iii) The ray of light which is incident normally on the surface separating the two media, passes undeviated.

i.e. $\angle i = \angle r = 0°$

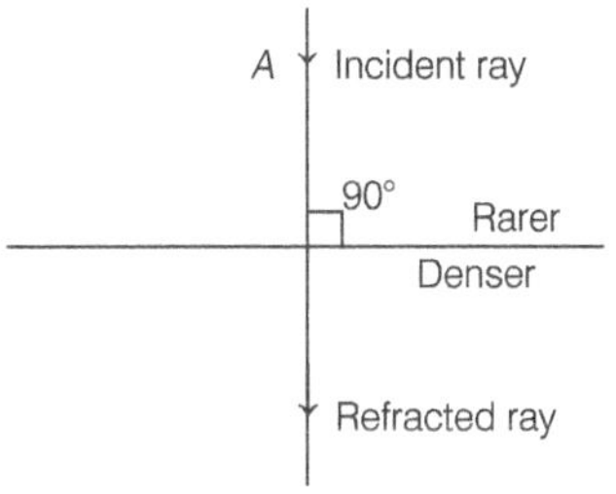

Causes of Refraction

- The speed of light is lesser in optically denser medium and greater in optically rarer medium.
- When light enters a denser medium, its speed reduces and it bends towards the normal.
- When it enters a rarer medium, its speed increases and it bends away from the normal.

Partial Reflection and Refraction due to Change in Medium

Partial reflection and refraction occurs when a light wave is travelling between two media. Some of the wave is reflected back and the rest is refracted through the other medium.

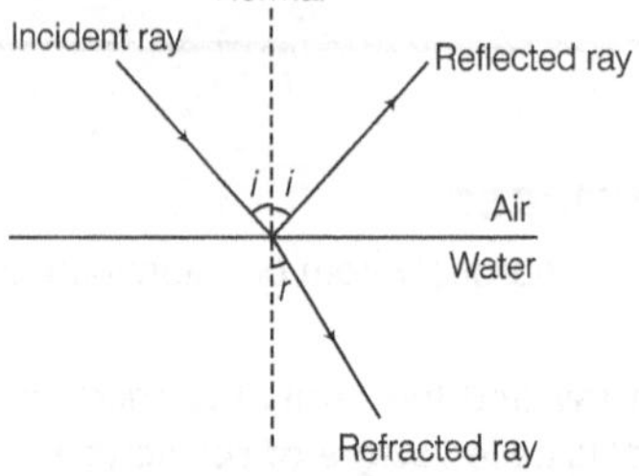

Laws of Refraction

(i) **First law** The incident ray, the refracted ray and the normal at the point of incidence, all lie in the same plane.

(ii) **Second law** The ratio of sine of angle of incidence to the sine of angle of refraction is constant for a given pair of media. This constant is known as refractive index of the second medium with respect to first medium.

It is expressed as $${}_1\mu_2 = \frac{\sin i}{\sin r} = \text{constant.}$$

This is also known as **Snell's law.**

Refractive Index

- The refractive index of the medium is the ratio of the velocity of light in vacuum (or air) to the velocity of light in that medium.

$$\mu = \frac{\text{Velocity of light in vacuum } (c)}{\text{Velocity of light in medium } (v)}$$

- ${}_1\mu_2$ represents refractive index of medium 2 with respect to medium 1, when light is going from medium 1 to medium 2.

$${}_1\mu_2 = \frac{\mu_2}{\mu_1} = \frac{\sin i}{\sin r}$$

- The refractive index of a medium with respect to vacuum, is called absolute refractive index of the medium. The absolute refractive index of a medium is simply called its refractive index.

For glass/water pair, $${}_w\mu_g = \frac{{}_a\mu_g}{{}_a\mu_w}$$

The refractive index has no unit as it is the ratio of two similar quantities.

Relation between Refractive Index and Wavelength

$$\mu = \frac{\text{Speed of light in air } (c)}{\text{Speed of light in medium } (v)} = \frac{f\lambda_0}{f\lambda}$$

$$\Rightarrow \quad \mu = \frac{\lambda_0}{\lambda} \Rightarrow \lambda = \frac{\lambda_0}{\mu} \quad \text{or} \quad \lambda \propto \frac{1}{\mu} \text{ or } \mu \propto \frac{1}{\lambda}$$

where, λ = wavelength of the light in medium and μ = refractive index of medium.

Refractive indices of a few media

Material	Refractive Index
Air	1.0003
Water	1.33
Glass	1.5
Diamond	2.42

Relation between Speed, Frequency and Wavelength of Light

The equation that relates wavelength and frequency

$$c = f\lambda$$

where, c = speed of light in vacuum, f = frequency of light and λ = wavelength of light

Effect on Speed, Wavelength and Frequency due to Refraction of Light

(i) Speed of light increases when light passes from denser to rarer medium and it decreases when light passes from rarer to denser medium.

(ii) Frequency is a characteristic of light, therefore it remains same as light travels from one medium to another.

(iii) Wavelength of light increases when light passes from denser to rarer medium (as its speed also increases) and it decreases when light passes from rarer to denser medium (as its speed also decreases).

Principle of Reversibility of Light

- If light travels from medium 1 to medium 2 along a certain path and if the path is reversed while travelling from medium 2 to medium 1 then it will retrace its original path.

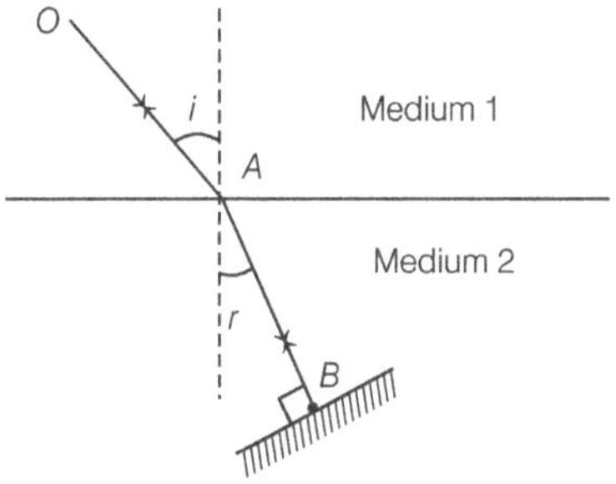

Reversibility of light

Refraction of Light Through Glass Slab

When a light ray enters in a glass slab, then the emergent ray is parallel to the incident ray but it is shifted sideward slightly. In this case, refraction takes place twice, first when the ray of light enters the glass slab from air and second when ray of light emerges from glass slab to air.

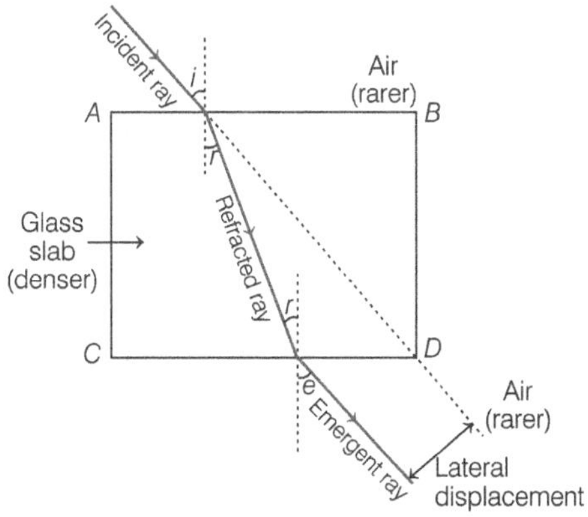

REVISION NOTES

Here, the ray emerges parallel to incident ray but is shifted laterally slightly.

where, i = Angle of incidence, r = Angle of refraction and e = Angle of emergence.

- Here, Angle of incidence = Angle of emergence
- If incidence rays fall normally on the surface of glass slab, then there is no bending of the ray of light.

Lateral Displacement

The perpendicular separation between the incident ray and the emergent ray is called lateral displacement. The lateral displacement depends on

(i) the thickness of the glass block. (ii) the angle of incidence.

(iii) the refractive index of glass.

Multiple Images in Thick Glass Plate/Mirror

- When an object is placed in front of thick glass mirror, then its multiple images are formed. It happens due to multiple reflection and refraction from two layers top and bottom surfaces.
- A small fraction of incident light (nearly 4%) is reflected in the direction *BP*. While a large fraction (nearly 96%) is refracted along *BB′*.
- The ray *BB′* is strongly reflected back by the silvered surface *NP*. A large fraction of this ray is refracted in air and forms a virtual image A_2.
- Image A_2 is the brightest because it is formed due to first strong reflection by the silvered surface.
- The brightness of rest of the virtual images formed by both surfaces gradually decreases due to multiple reflection.

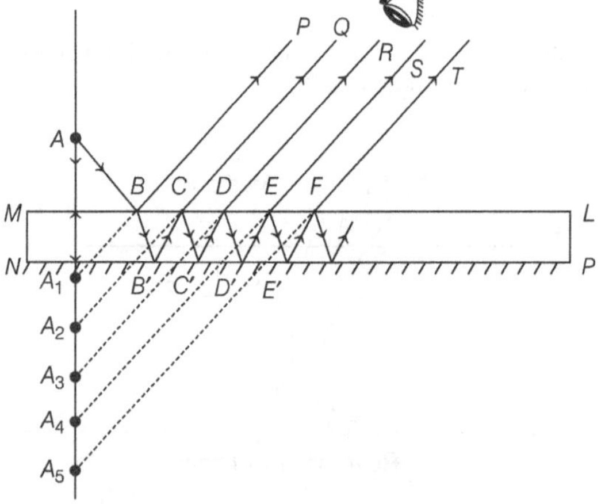

Simple Applications of Refraction of Light

Simple applications of refraction of light are given below

Real and Apparent depths

- Due to law of refraction of light, the apparent depth of the image as seen from the rarer medium which is placed in a denser medium is less than its real depth.
- According to the situation shown in the figure.

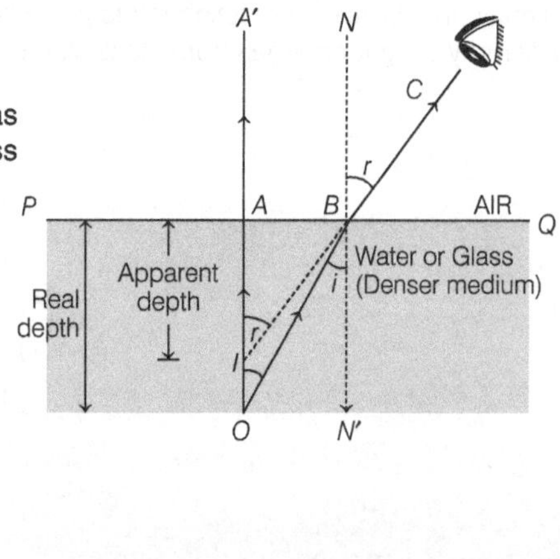

$$\text{Refractive index, } \mu = \frac{OA}{IA} = \frac{\text{Real depth}}{\text{Apparent depth}}$$

$$\Rightarrow \quad \boxed{\text{Apparent depth} = \frac{\text{Real depth}}{\mu}}$$

Further, Shift, OI = Real depth − Apparent depth

Or $\quad \text{Shift} = \text{real depth} \times \left(1 - \frac{1}{\mu}\right)$

The apparent depth of an object depends upon

(i) refractive index of the medium,

(ii) thickness of the denser medium and

(iii) the colour of the incident light.

Apparent Bending of Stick Under Water

Consider a straight stick *ABO*, which is placed obliquely in water. The portion of the stick *OB* under water appears to be bent and raised up to *LB*. This is due to the refraction of light while passing from water to air.

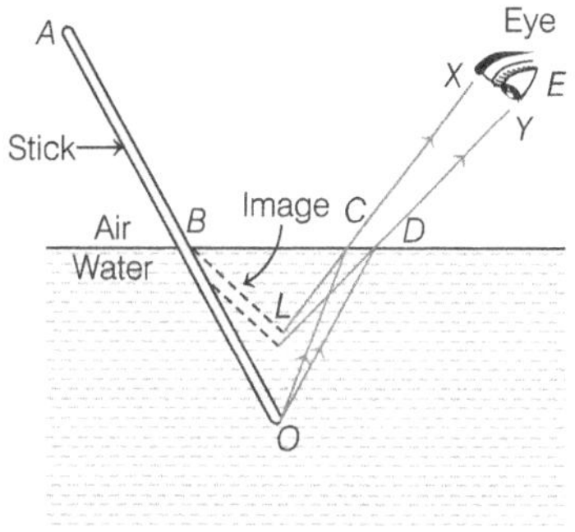

Prism

- A transparent refracting medium bounded by at least two lateral surface, inclined to each other at certain angle is called a prism.
- It has two triangular bases and three rectangular lateral surfaces.
- The angle between two lateral surfaces is called **angle of prism (*A*)**.

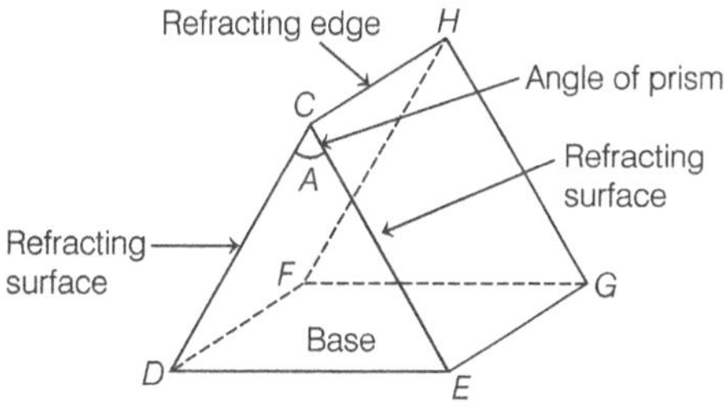

Prism

- The two rectangular plane inclined surfaces through which the light passes are known as **refracting surfaces**.
- The line along which the two surfaces (refracting) meet is called the **refracting edge**.

Refraction of Light through a Glass Prism

In the diagram given below, a ray of light *PQ* is entering from air to glass at the first surface *AB*. The light ray on refraction gets bend towards the normal. At the second surface *AC*, the light ray enters from glass to air, so it bends away from the normal.

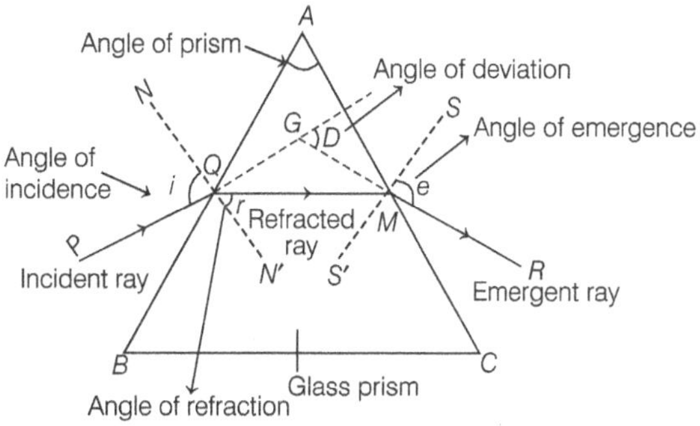

Refraction of light through a triangular glass prism

The diagram shows refraction through a prism,

where, PQ = incident ray, QR = refracted ray,

RS = emergent ray, $\angle A$ = angle of prism,

$\angle i$ = angle of incidence, $\angle r, \angle r'$ = angle of refractions,

$\angle e$ = angle of emergence and $\angle D$ = angle of deviation.

Angle of Deviation

- It is the angle, which the emergent ray (produced backward) makes with the incident ray (produced forward).
- It is given by $\angle D = \angle i + \angle e - \angle A$.

For minimum deviation $\angle D_{min}$,

$$\angle i = \angle e$$

$$\therefore \quad \angle D_{min} = \angle i + \angle i - \angle A$$

$$\angle D_{min} = 2\angle i - \angle A$$

There are four factors on which the value of angle of deviation produced by the prism depends. These are as follow

(i) **Dependence of Angle of Deviation on the Angle of Incidence** (i) Experimentally, it has been observed that with the increase in the incident angle, the angle of deviation first decreases, then reach a minimum value and then it also increases. This is depicted in i-D graph shown below.

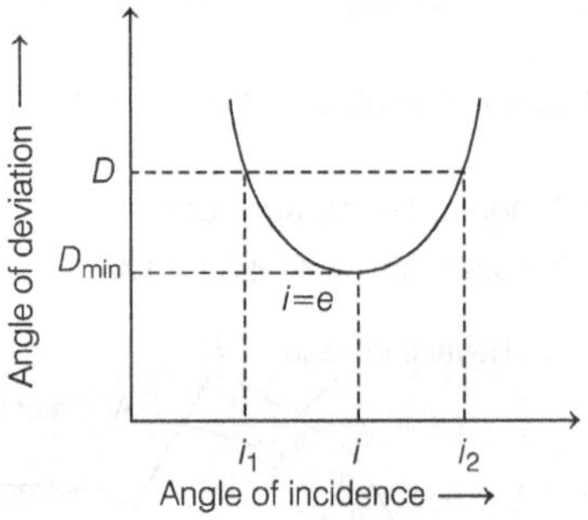

(ii) **Dependence of Angle of Deviation on the Refractive Index** (μ) Experimentally, it is found that as the refractive index of the material decreases, the angle of deviation decreases.

(iii) **Dependence of Angle of Deviation on the Colour or Wavelength of Light** (λ) For a given prism, the violet light deviates the most whereas the red light deviates the least.

(iv) **Dependence of Angle of Deviation on the Angle of Prism** (A) The angle of deviation (D) increases with increase in the angle of prism.

Critical angle

Critical angle for a pair of given media in contact can be defined as, **"the angle of incidence in denser medium for which angle of refraction in rarer medium is 90°"**. The value of critical angle depends on the nature of two media in contact.

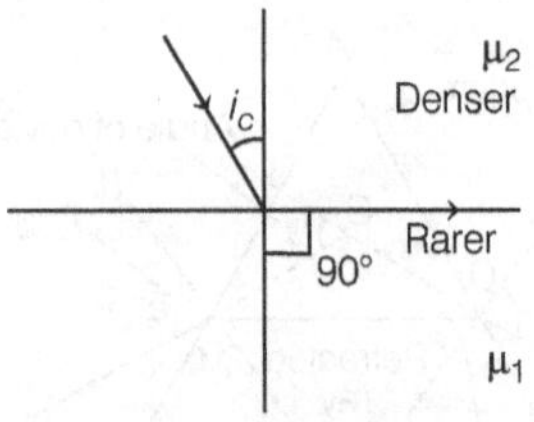

$$^1\mu_2 = \frac{1}{\sin i_c}$$

REVISION NOTES

The critical angle for a given pair of media depends on their refractive index, which in turn depends on the following two factors.

(i) **Effect of Colour of Light** As violet light has the highest value of refractive index, while red light has the least value of refractive index. So, the critical angle for a pair of media is least for violet light and most for red light. Therefore, the critical angle increases with increase in the wavelength of light.

(ii) **Effect of Temperature** When the temperature of medium is increased, its refractive index decreases, due to which, the critical angle for that pair of media increases. Therefore, the critical angle increases with an increase in temperature.

Total Internal Reflection (TIR)

- When a ray of light travelling from a denser medium to rarer medium, is incident at the interface of the two media at an angle greater than the critical angle, then the ray is totally reflected back to denser medium.
  This phenomenon is called **Total Internal Reflection (TIR).**

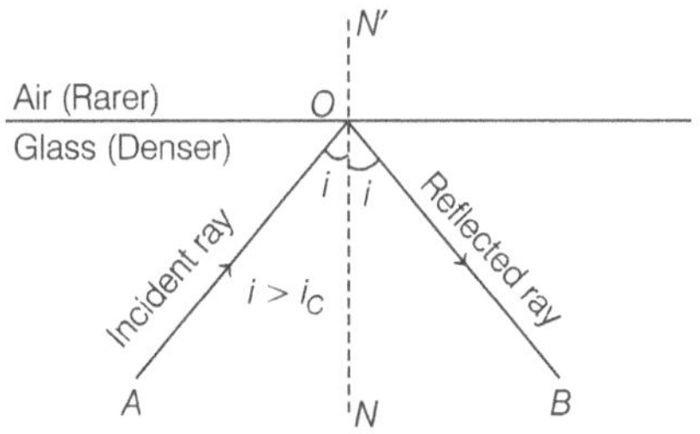

The necessary conditions for the total internal reflection are

(i) The light must travel from a denser medium to a rarer medium.

(ii) The angle of incidence must be greater than the critical angle for the pair of media.

Total internal reflection through a 45°, 90°, 45° prism

- A prism with an angle of 90° between its two refracting surfaces and the other two angles each equal to 45° is called a total reflecting prism because the light incident normally on any of its faces suffers total internal reflection inside the prism.
- This prism is used for the following three purposes

(i) **To deviate a ray of light through 90°.**

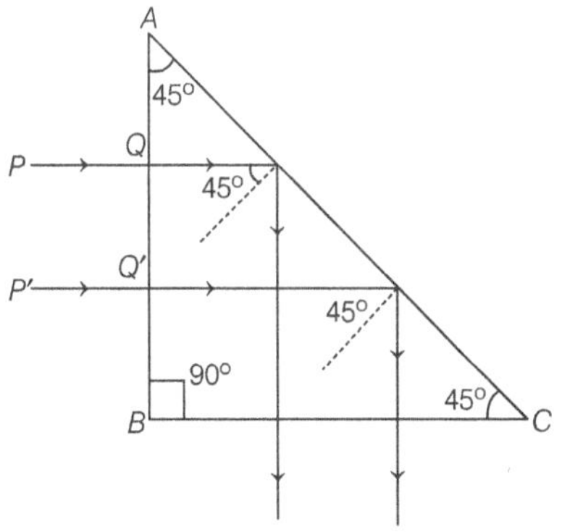

(ii) **To deviate a ray of light through 180°.**

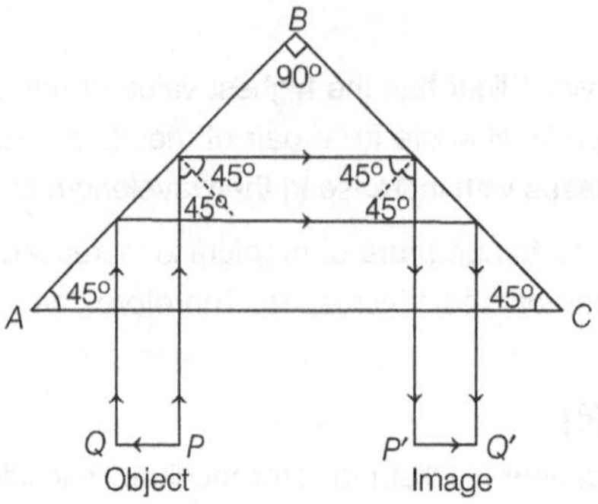

(iii) **To erect an inverted image without deviation.**

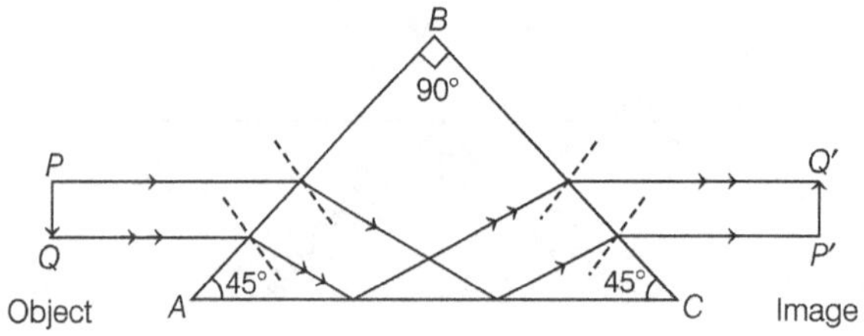

Total Internal Reflection through a Prism with Each Angle as 60°, i.e. an Equilateral Prism

- A prism with each angle of 60° can be used to deviate a light ray through 60° by total internal reflection.

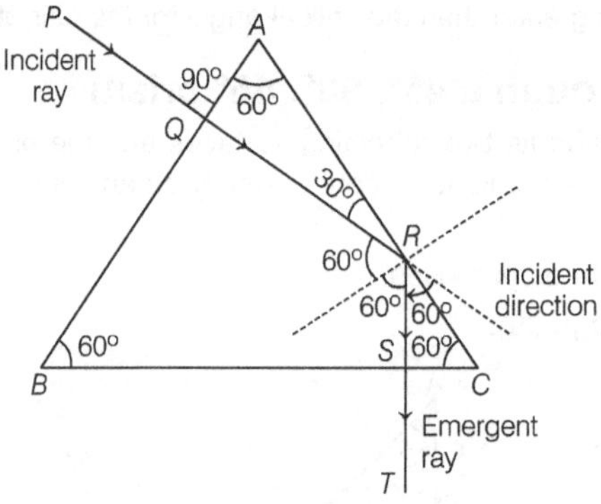

Total Internal Reflection and Refraction through a 30°, 60°, 90° Prism

(i) Incident normally on face *BC* (side opposite to 30°)

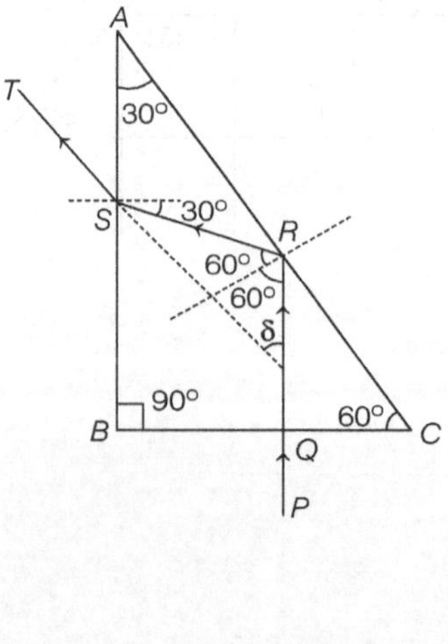

(ii) Incident normally on face *AB* (side opposite to 60°)

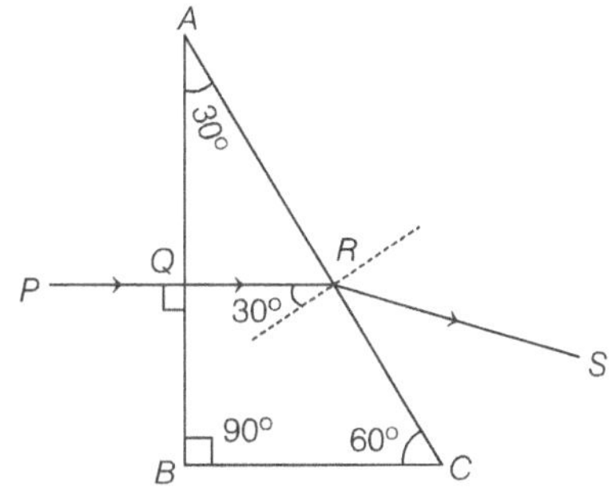

(iii) Incident normally on face *AC* (side opposite to 90°).

(a) Incident normally in the portion *AD*.

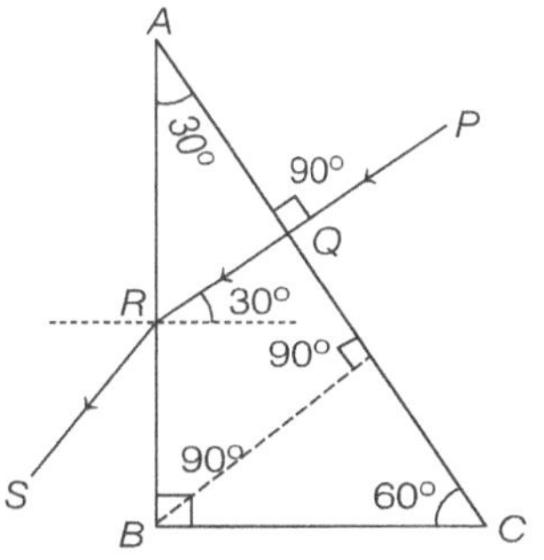

(b) Incident normally in the portion *DC*.

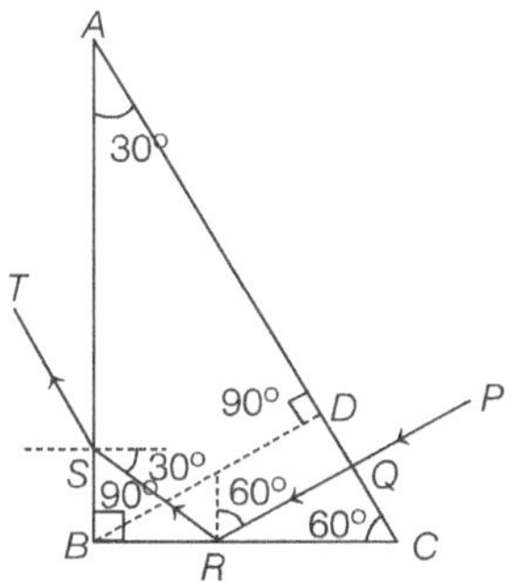

Comparison between Total Internal Reflection and Reflection from a Plane Mirror

Total internal reflection	Reflection from a plane mirror
It occurs only when light passes from a denser medium to a rarer medium at an angle of incidence greater than critical angle for that pair of media.	It occurs only when light is incident on a plane mirror from any medium at any angle of incidence.
The incident ray is totally reflected back.	The incident ray is partially reflected and partially refracted.
There is no loss of energy.	The energy of the reflected beam is always less than the energy of the incident beam.

EXAM ORIENTED QUESTIONS

TYPE - 1   01 Mark

Multiple Choice Questions

Q.1 When a ray of light passes from one optical medium to another, which of the following physical quantities does not change? **[ICSE 2025]**

(a) Amplitude of the wave (b) Frequency of the wave
(c) Wavelength of the wave (d) Speed of the wave

Ans. (b)

Q.2 When a ray of light travels normal to the given surface, then the angle of refraction is **[ICSE Specimen 2023]**

(a) 180° (b) 90° (c) 0° (d) 45°

Ans. (c) When a light ray travels normal to the surface, it will continues undeviated and the angle of refraction with the normal will be zero.

Q.3 In the diagram shown below, **[ICSE Specimen 2021]**

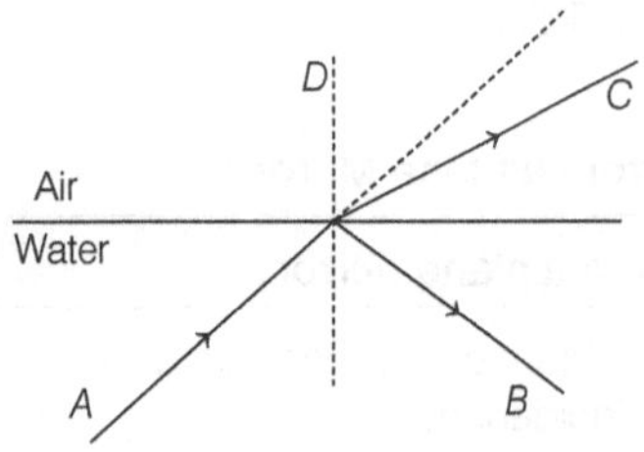

(a) *B* is incident ray and *C* is refracted ray.
(b) *A* is incident ray and *B* is refracted ray.
(c) *C* is incident ray and *B* is refracted ray.
(d) *A* is incident ray and *C* is refracted ray.

Ans. (d)

Q.4 A ray of light is incident normally on a face of an equilateral prism. The ray gets totally reflected at the second refracting surface. The total deviation produced in the path of the ray is **[ICSE 2025]**

(a) 30° (b) 60° (c) 90° (d) 120°

Ans. (d)

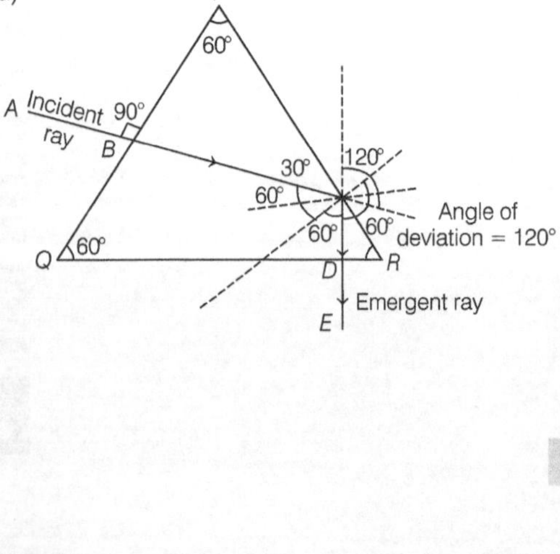

Q.5 A ray of light in glass is incident on the surface at an angle *c*. The angle *c* is the critical angle.
Which diagram shows what happens to the light?

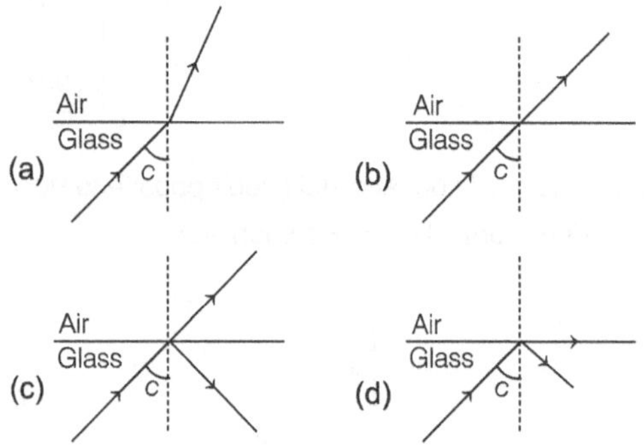

Ans. (d) A ray of light incident at the critical angle in a denser medium is partially reflected ($i = r$) and partially refracted at right angle with the less denser medium.

Q.6 A ray of light is incident on the surface of a glass block, as shown in the diagram adjacent.

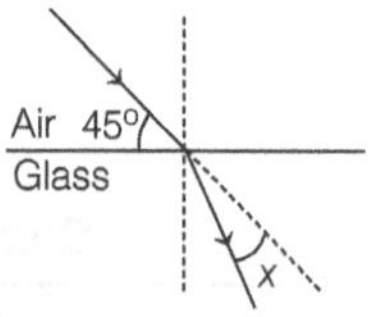

The refractive index of the glass is 1.5. The light ray changes direction when entering the glass. What is the angle *x* through which the ray moves?
[Take, $\sin 28° = \frac{\sqrt{2}}{3}$]

(a) 30° (b) 28° (c) 17° (d) 15°

Ans. (c) $n = \frac{\sin i}{\sin r} \Rightarrow 1.5 = \frac{\sin 45°}{\sin r}$

$\Rightarrow r = 28°$

So, angle $x = 45° - 28° = 17°$

Q.7 The refractive index of a diamond is 2.4. It means that **[ICSE 2022 Sem-I]**

(a) the speed of light in vacuum is equal to $\frac{1}{2.4}$ times the speed of light in diamond
(b) the speed of light in diamond is 2.4 times the speed of light in vacuum
(c) the speed of light in vacuum is 2.4 times the speed of light in diamond
(d) the wavelength of light in diamond is 2.4 times the wavelength of light in vacuum

Ans. (c) We know that,

$$\text{Refractive index} = \frac{\text{speed of light in air}}{\text{speed of light in medium}}$$

So, speed of light in vacuum is equal to 2.4 times speed of light in diamond.

Q.8 A ray of light passes obliquely from an optical medium of refractive index 1.33 to another medium of refractive index 1.5. While passing from the first medium to the second, the light ray will **[Competency Based Ques.]**

(a) bend towards the normal.
(b) bend away from the normal.
(c) move along the normal.
(d) suffer total internal reflection.

Ans. (a) When a ray of light travels from a rarer medium to a denser medium, the ray of light will bend towards the normal due to decrease in the speed of the ray of light.

Q.9 Light passes from air into a block of glass, as shown.

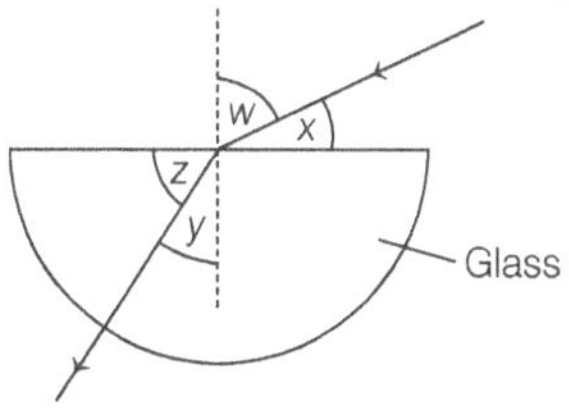

Which expression is equal to the refractive index of glass?

(a) $\frac{\sin w}{\sin y}$ (b) $\frac{\sin w}{\sin z}$ (c) $\frac{\sin y}{\sin w}$ (d) $\frac{\sin z}{\sin x}$

Ans. (a) The refractive index is defined as. $n = \frac{\sin i}{\sin r}$

when applied on the given diagram this expression becomes, $n = \frac{\sin w}{\sin y}$

Q.10 A ray of light enters a glass block at an angle of incidence i, producing an angle of refraction r in the glass.

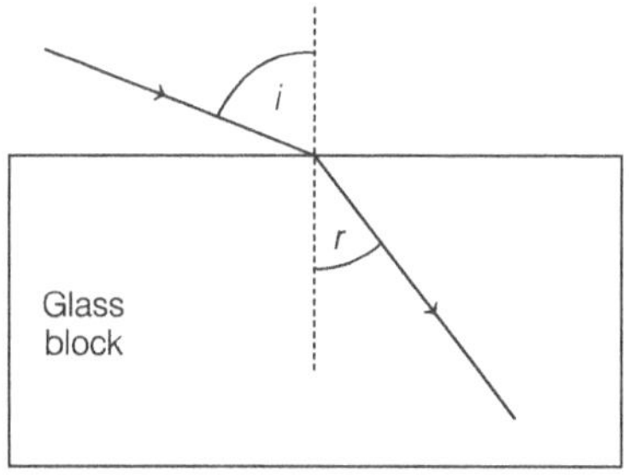

Several different values of i and r are measured and a graph is drawn of $\sin i$ against $\sin r$.
Which graph is correct?

(a)
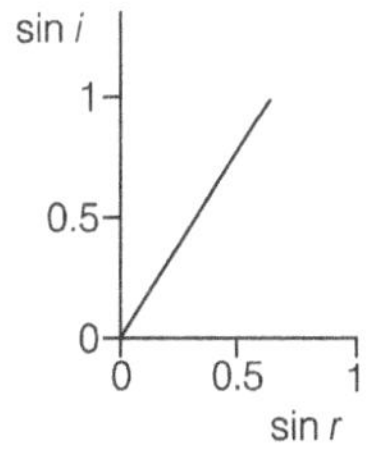

(b)
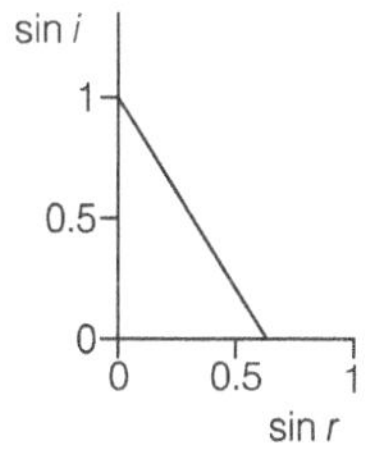

(c)
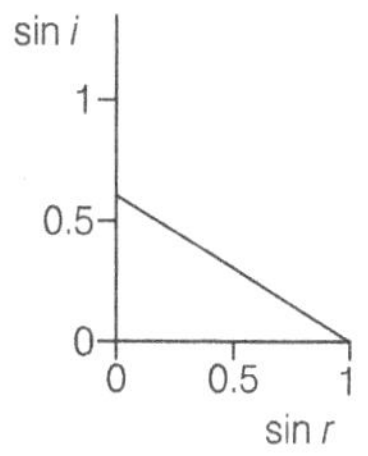

(d)
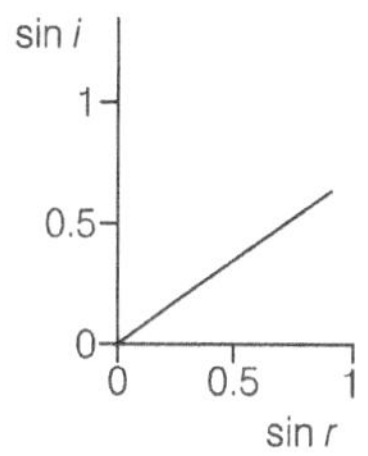

Ans. (a) The slope of the graph between $\sin i$ and $\sin r$ passing through the origin gives the refractive index of glass.

The refractive index of glass is greater than 1. Since only graph (a) gives a slope value greater than 1. Therefore, graph (a) is correct.

Q.11 When light enters from air to glass, it bends toward the normal. If red, blue, and yellow colours are allowed to enter the same glass block at the same angle of incidence, then for which colour, the value of $\angle i - \angle r$, be greater? **[Competency Based Ques.]**

(a) Green (b) Red
(c) Blue (d) Yellow

Ans. (c)Since, blue colour has shorter wavelength. So, it will bend the most towards normal. As a result, the value of $\angle i - \angle r$ will be greater for blue light.

Q.12 A ray of light IM is incident on a glass slab $ABCD$ as shown in the figure. The emergent ray for this incident ray is **(ICSE 2021 Sem-I)**

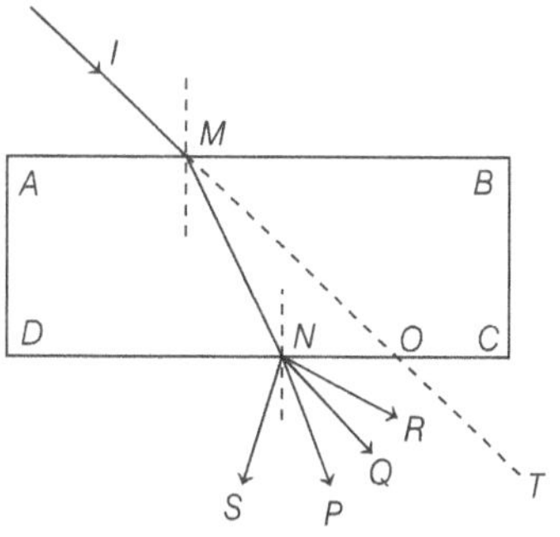

(a) NQ (b) NR
(c) NP (d) NS

Ans. (a) Here, the emergent ray will be away from the normal but parallel to the incident ray.

Q.13 The phenomenon of light that causes the diamond to glitter is **[ICSE Specimen 2023]**

(a) refraction (b) total internal reflection
(c) reflection (d) absorption

Ans. (b) The critical angle is very small for diamond due to its high refractive index so most of the light with an incident angle greater than the critical angle will under go multiple reflection due to which diamond shines. This phenomenon is called total internal reflection.

Q.14 Small air bubbles rising up a fish tank appear silvery when viewed from some particular angle is due to the **[ICSE 2023]**

(a) reflection (b) refraction
(c) dispersion (d) total internal reflection

Ans. (d) If the angle of incidence is larger than the critical angle, a light beam that is travelling from an optically denser (water) to a rarer (air) medium reflects back into the denser medium.

Q.15 An endoscope uses optic fiber to transmit high resolution images of internal organs without loss of information. The principle of light that is used by the optic fiber is based on **[ICSE Specimen 2025]**

(a) refraction (b) reflection
(c) scattering (d) total internal reflection

Ans. (d) The phenomenon of light governing the working of optical fibre is based on total internal reflection.

TYPE - 2 01 Mark

Assertion-Reason Type Questions

Directions (Q. Nos. 1-7) In the following questions, a statement of assertion (A) is followed by a statement of reason (R). Mark the correct choice as

(a) Both A and R are true and R is the correct explanation of A.
(b) Both A and R are true but R is not the correct explanation of A.
(c) A is true but R is false.
(d) A is false but R is true.

Q.1 Assertion (A) The refractive index of a medium is a dimensionless quantity.
Reason (R) The refractive index is the ratio of the speed of light in a vacuum to the speed of light in the medium.

Ans. (a) The refractive index is a ratio of two similar quantities (speeds) making it dimensionless.

Q.2 Assertion (A) The refractive index of glass is greater than that of water.
Reason (R) The refractive index of a medium depends on the speed of light in that medium.

Ans. (a) The refractive index (n) is given by the formula.

$$n = \frac{\text{Speed of light in vacuum}}{\text{Speed of light in medium}}$$

Since light travels slower in glass than in water, so refractive index of glass is higher than the water.

Q.3 Assertion (A) A ray of light bends towards the normal when it enters a denser medium from a rarer medium.
Reason (R) The speed of light is greater in a denser medium compared to a rarer medium.

Ans. (c) Light bends towards the normal when it slows down in a denser medium. However, the speed of light is lesser in a denser medium not greater.

Q.4 Assertion (A) For a glass block, the *i versus r* graph is a straight line.
Reason (R) When a ray of light undergoes refraction, it follows Snell's law. **[Competency Based Ques.]**

Ans. (d) The Assertion is false because the *i versus r* graph is a straight line only for small angles.
When a ray of light undergoes refraction, it obeys Snell's law.

i.e. $$\frac{\sin i}{\sin r} = \mu = \text{constant.}$$

Hence, Reason is true.

Q.5 Assertion (A) A glass slab does not change the direction of a light ray emerging from it.
Reason (R) The emergent ray is parallel to the incident ray due to lateral displacement.

Ans. (a) Due to refraction of light at two parallel surfaces of a glass block, the emergent ray and the incident ray are parallel (i.e. they are in the same direction). But the emergent ray is laterally shifted from the path of the incident ray. This shift is called lateral displacement.

Q.6 Assertion (A) When light passes through a triangular prism, it is observed that for two angles of incidence, the angle of deviation is the same.
Reason (R) According to the principle of reversibility, the light retraces the path in reversing the direction. **[Competency Based Que.]**

Ans. (a)

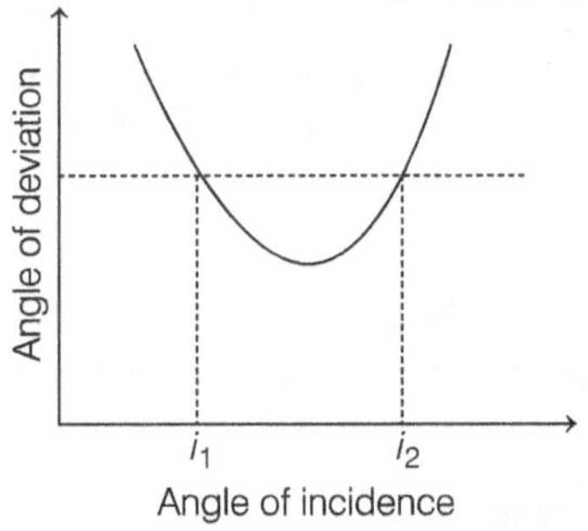

From the above diagram, it is cleared that for the two angles of incidence, the angle of deviation is the same. Hence, assertion is true.

When the incident angle becomes equal to the emergent angle of the ray, the emergent angle becomes equal to the incident angle due to principle of reversibility of light.

Q.7 Assertion (A) The critical angle for total internal reflection is smaller in water than in glass.
Reason (R) The refractive index of water is smaller than that of glass.

Ans. (d) The critical angle is given by

$$\sin C = \frac{1}{n}$$

Since, the refractive index of glass (≈ 1.5) is higher than that of water (≈ 1.33), So, critical angle for glass is smaller than for water.

TYPE - 3 — 01/02 Marks

Fill in the Blanks

Q.1 The refractive index of a medium is defined as the ratio of the speed of light in .... (water, vacuum) to the speed of light in the medium.

Ans. vacuum

Q.2 Refractive index of a medium is independent of .... (temperature/angle of incidence/ wave length of light). **[ICSE 2025]**

Ans. angle of incidence

Q.3 The angle of incidence in the denser medium for which the angle of refraction in the rarer medium is .... (0°, 90°, 45°) is called the .... (critical, refractive, incident) angle.

Ans. 90°, critical

Q.4 The phenomenon of .... (total internal, partial) reflection occurs when the angle of incidence is greater than the .... (critical, refractive)

Ans. total internal, critical

TYPE - 4 — 02 Marks

Very Short Answer Type Questions

Q.1 (i) What is meant by refraction of light? **[1]**

(ii) What is the cause of refraction of light? **[1]**

Ans. (i) The change in the direction of light, when it passes from one medium to another medium is called refraction of light.

(ii) The main cause of refraction of light is due to different speeds of light in different media.

Q.2 A ray of light is moving from a rarer medium to a denser medium and strikes a plane mirror placed at 90° to the direction of the ray as shown in the diagram.

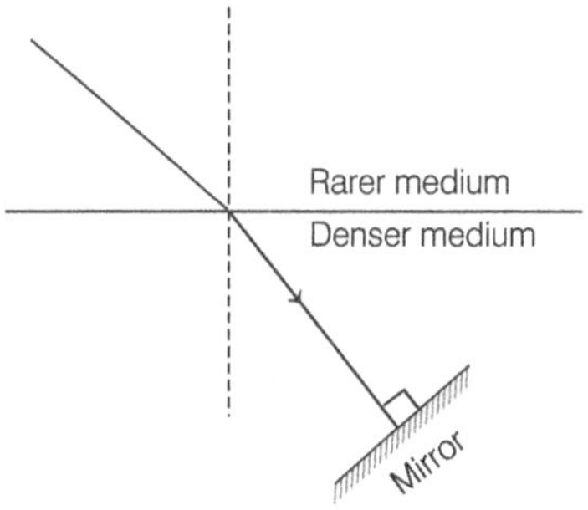

(i) Copy the diagram and mark arrows to show the path of the ray of light after it is reflected from the mirror. **[1]**

(ii) Name the principle you have used to mark the arrow to show the direction of the ray. **[1]**

Ans. (i) The diagram is redrawn and the path of ray of light is shown below

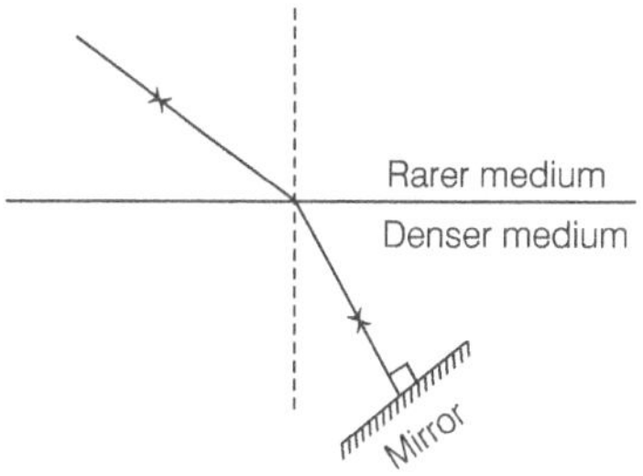

(ii) The principle of reversibility of light have used to mark the arrow to show the direction of the ray.

Q.3 A ray of light falls normally on a rectangular glass slab. Draw a ray diagram showing the path of the ray till it emerges out of the slab.

Ans. When a ray of light falls normally on a rectangular glass slab, then angle of incidence, $i = 0$

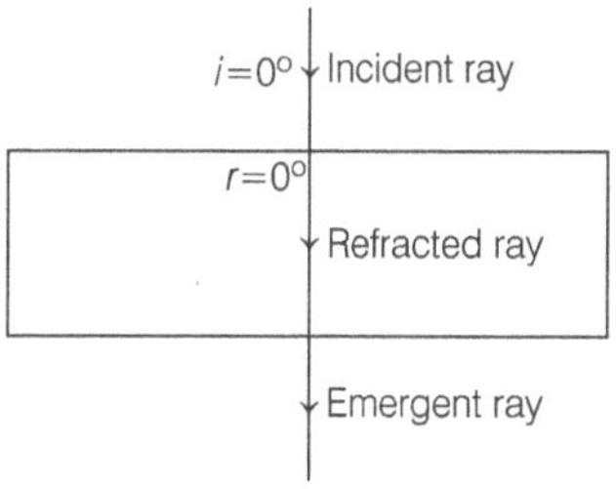

∴ By Snell's law, $_a\mu_g = \dfrac{\sin i}{\sin r}$

$$\Rightarrow \quad _a\mu_g = \frac{\sin 0^\circ}{\sin r} = \frac{0}{\sin r}$$

$$\Rightarrow \quad _a\mu_g \times \sin r = 0$$

$$\because \quad _a\mu_g \neq 0,$$

$$\therefore \quad \sin r = 0 \Rightarrow r = 0^\circ$$

Hence, when a ray of light falls normally on a rectangular glass slab, then it emerges out of the slab undeviated which is shown in the figure.

Q.4 In the given diagram, PQ is a ray of light incident on a rectangular glass block.

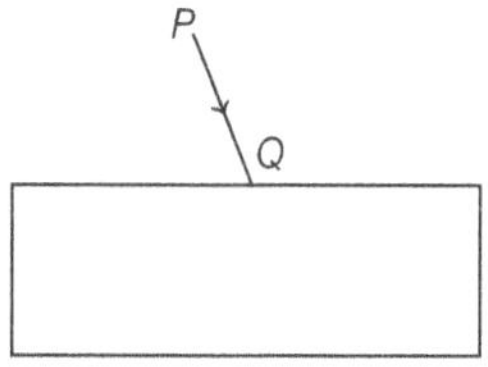

(i) Copy the diagram and complete the path of the ray of light through the glass block. In your diagram, mark the angle of incidence by letter *i* and the angle of emergence by the letter *e*. **[1]**

(ii) How are the angles *i* and *e* related to each other? **[1]**

Ans. (i)

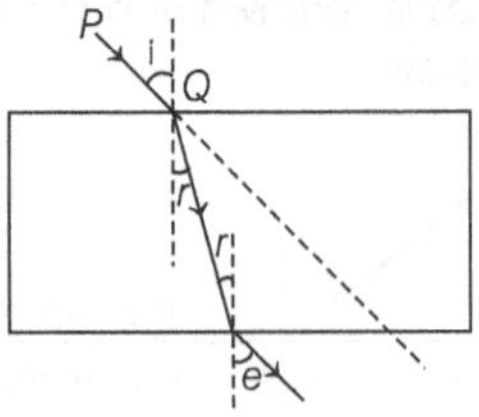

(ii) The angle of incidence $\angle i$ is equal to angle of emergent $\angle e$, i.e. $\angle i = \angle e$.

Q.5 How is the refractive index of a material related to

(i) real and apparent depth? **[1]**

(ii) velocity of light in vacuum or air and the velocity of light in a given medium? **[1] [ICSE 2017, 11]**

Ans. (i) If an object is placed under water (any denser medium), when observed it from the air (or a rarer medium), it appears to be raised up.

The ratio of real depth and apparent depth is equal to the refractive index of the medium.

$$\text{Refractive index, } \mu = \frac{\text{Real depth}}{\text{Apparent depth}}$$

(ii) The refractive index of the medium is the ratio of the velocity of light in vacuum (or air) to the velocity of light in that medium.

$$\mu = \frac{\text{Velocity of light in vacuum } (c)}{\text{Velocity of light in medium } (v)}$$

Q.6 (i) What is the relation between the refractive index of water with respect to air $({}_a\mu_w)$ and the refractive index of air with respect to water $({}_w\mu_a)$? **[1]**

(ii) If the refractive index of water with respect to air $({}_a\mu_w)$ is $\frac{5}{3}$. Calculate the refractive index of air with respect to water $({}_w\mu_a)$. **[1][ICSE 2019]**

Ans. (i) Refractive index of water with respect to air,

$${}_a\mu_w = \frac{\mu_w}{\mu_a} \quad \ldots(i)$$

and refractive index of air with respect to water,

$${}_w\mu_a = \frac{\mu_a}{\mu_w} \quad \ldots(ii)$$

From Eqs. (i) and (ii), we get

$${}_a\mu_w = \frac{1}{{}_w\mu_a}$$

(ii) Refractive index of water with respect to air,

$${}_a\mu_w = \frac{1}{\text{Refractive index of air with respect to water } ({}_w\mu_a)}$$

$$\text{Given, } {}_a\mu_w = \frac{5}{3}$$

$$\therefore \quad {}_a\mu_w = \frac{1}{{}_w\mu_a}$$

$$\therefore \quad {}_w\mu_a = \frac{3}{5}$$

Q.7 A pond appears to be 2.7 m deep. If the refractive index of water is $\frac{4}{3}$, find the actual depth of the pond. **[ICSE 2020]**

Ans. Apparent depth of pond, $d = 2.7$m

$$\text{Refractive index of water, } \mu = \frac{4}{3}$$

$$\text{We know that, } \mu = \frac{\text{Actual depth}}{\text{Apparent depth}}$$

$$\Rightarrow \quad \frac{4}{3} = \frac{\text{Actual depth}}{2.7}$$

$$\therefore \text{ Actual depth } = \frac{4}{3} \times 2.7 = 3.6 \text{ m}$$

Q.8 Complete the path of the monochromatic light ray *AB* incident on the surface *PQ* of the equilateral glass prism *PQR* till it emerges out of the prism due to refraction. **[ICSE 2020]**

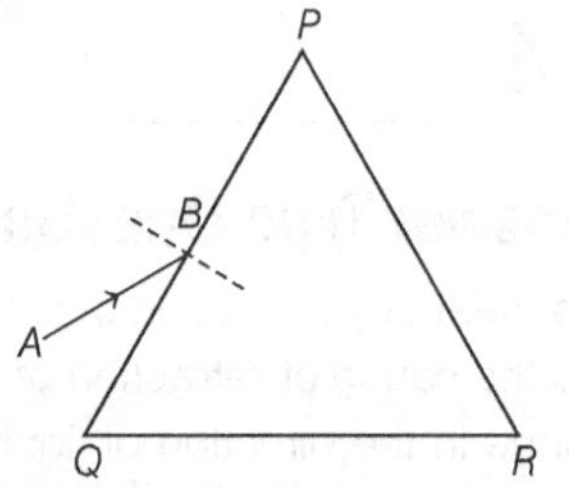

Ans. The complete path of a monochromatic light *AB* incident on the surface *PQ* of the equilateral glass prism *PQR* till it emerges out of the prism due to refraction is given below.

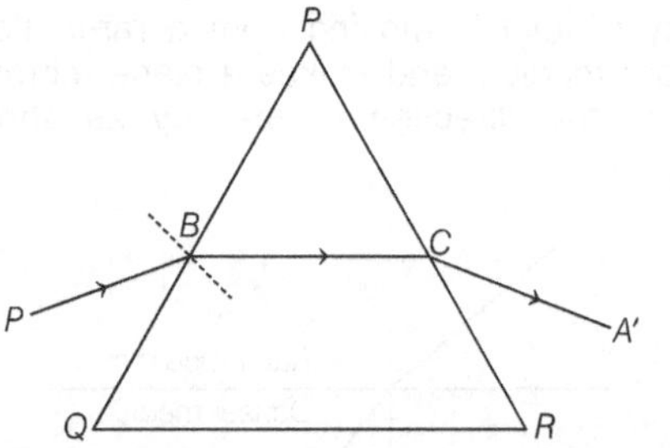

Q.9 Draw a ray diagram to show the refraction of a monochromatic ray through a prism when it suffers minimum deviation. **[ICSE 2017]**

Ans. When a ray of light passes through a prism, it bends towards the thicker part of the prism.

Let the incident ray PQ falls on the face AB of prism and emerges out from the face AC as RS.

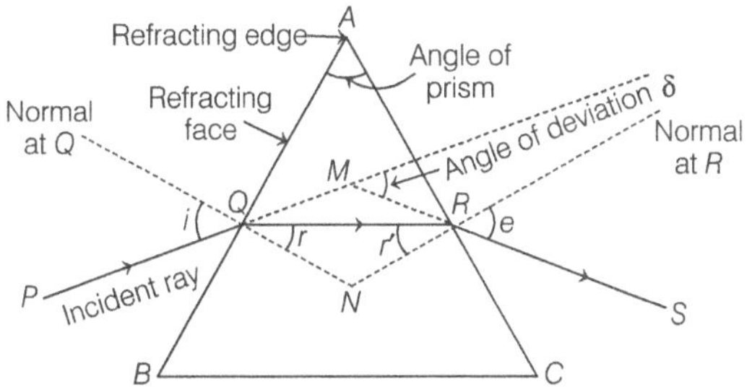

Here,

PQ = Incident ray,

QR = Refracted ray,

RS = Emergent ray,

$\angle A$ = Angle of prism,

$\angle i$ = Angle of incidence,

$\angle r, \angle r'$ = Angles of refraction,

$\angle e$ = Angle of emergence

and $\angle \delta$ = Angle of deviation.

Angle of Deviation (δ) It is the angle which the emergent ray (produced backward) makes with the incident ray (produced forward). It depends upon the angle of prism. When the refracted ray (QR) travel parallel to the base (BC). The prism is said to be in minimum deviation position.

At that position QR || BC

Q.10 **A ray of light enters a rectangular glass slab submerged in water at an angle of incidence 55°. Does this ray undergo total internal reflection when it moves from water to glass? Justify your answer. (The critical angle for glass-water interface is 54°.)** **[2] [ICSE 2025]**

Ans. Yes, the ray will undergo total internal reflection as the critical angle of the glass-water interface is less than the angle of incidence of the ray of light.

Q.11 **(i) State the relation between the critical angle and the absolute refractive index of a medium.** **[1]**

(ii) Which colour of light has a higher critical angle? Red light or green light. **[1]**

Ans. (i) The relation between the critical angle C and the absolute refractive index (μ) of medium is given by

$$\mu = \frac{1}{\sin C}$$

or $$\sin C = \frac{1}{\mu}$$

(ii) As $\mu_{green} > \mu_{red}$. Therefore, critical angle C for red colour is higher than that of green colour light.

Q.12 **A ray of light enters a glass slab $PQRS$, as shown in the diagram. The critical angle of the glass is 42°. Copy this diagram and complete the path of the ray till it emerges from the glass slab**

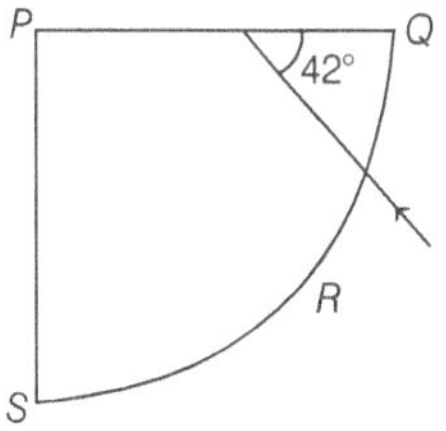

Mark the angles in the diagram wherever necessary.

Ans. The diagram is redrawn as

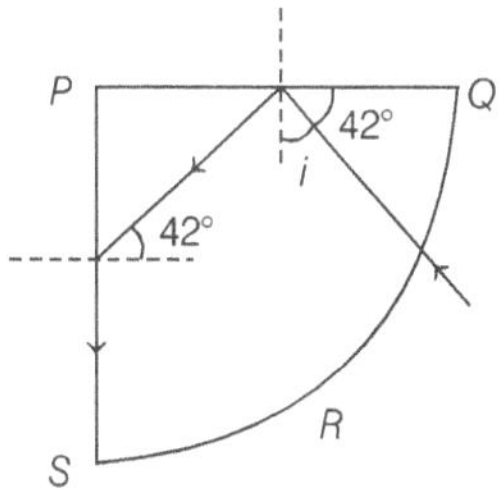

$$i = 90° - 42° = 48°$$

$\because$ $i > i_c$

$\therefore$ Total internal reflection takes place.

Q.13

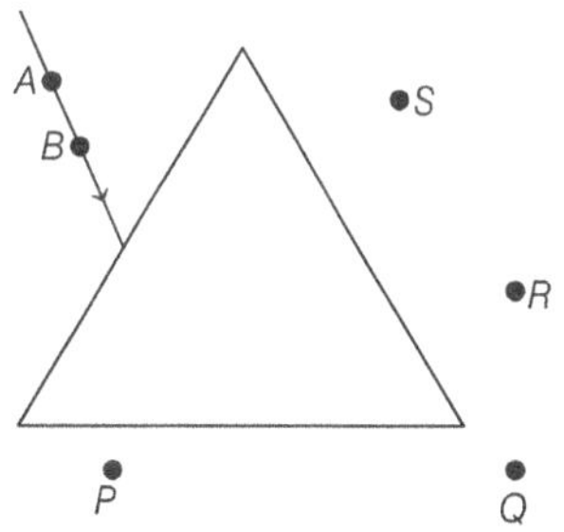

Observe the diagram and answer the following

(a) State the correct eye position from the points P, Q, R and S to see the images of the points A and B in the same line through the prism.

(b) If the ray, after entering the prism, suffers total internal reflection, then which would be the appropriate position out of P, Q, R, and S to see the image due to TIR? **[1][Competency Based Que.]**

Ans. (a)

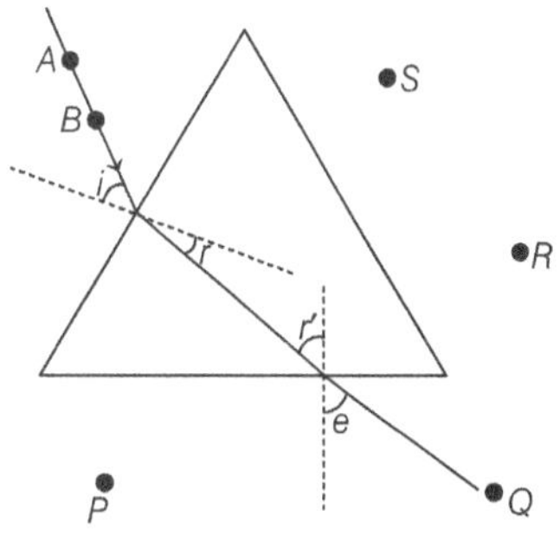

The correct eye position should be at point Q to see the images of points A and B after refraction through the prism.

(b)

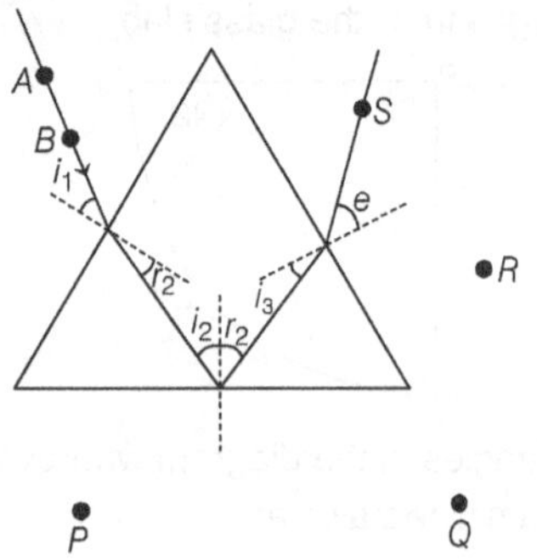

The correct eye position should be at point S to see images of point A and B after TIR through the prism.

Q.14 The following diagram shows a 60°, 30°, 90° glass prism of critical angle 42°. Copy the diagram and complete the path of incident ray AB emerging out of the prism marking the angle of incidence on each surface. **[ICSE 2018]**

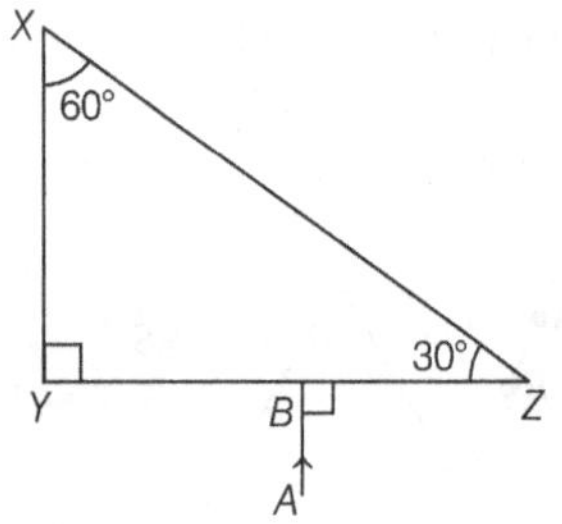

Ans. Given, $i_C = 42°$

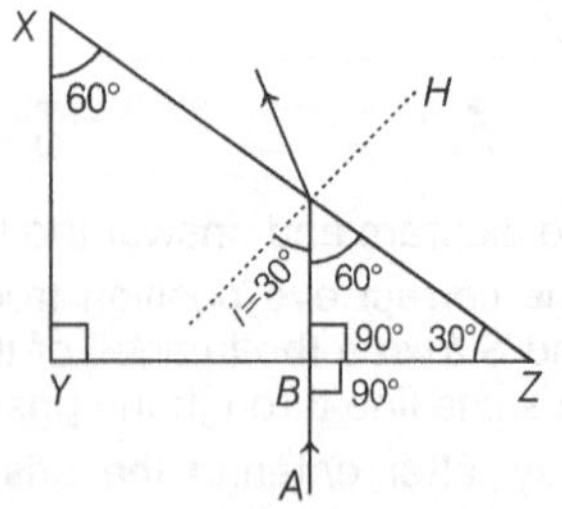

As angle of incidence on face XZ is less than i_C, so ray is refracted.

TYPE - 5

03 Marks

Short Answer Type Questions

Q.1 (i) Write a relationship between angle of incidence and angle of refraction for a given pair of media. **[1]**

(ii) When a ray of light enters from one medium to another having different optical densities, it bends. Why does this phenomenon occur? **[1]**

(iii) Write one condition, where ray of light does not bend when entering in a medium of different optical density. **[1] [ICSE 2016]**

Ans. (i) For a given pair of media, the relationship between the angle of incidence and angle of refraction is given by $_1\mu_2 = \frac{\sin i}{\sin r}$

where, i = angle of incidence,

r = angle of refraction,

$_1\mu_2$ = refractive index of the second medium with respect to the first medium.

(ii) The phenomenon of refraction occurs, because light travels at different speeds in different medium. If a ray of light travels through air and enter a more dense medium, such as water, it slows down and bends towards the normal.

(iii) When a ray of light is incident normally to the surface, then it passes undeviated from one medium to another medium without any bending.

Q.2 A diver in water looks obliquely at an object AB in air.

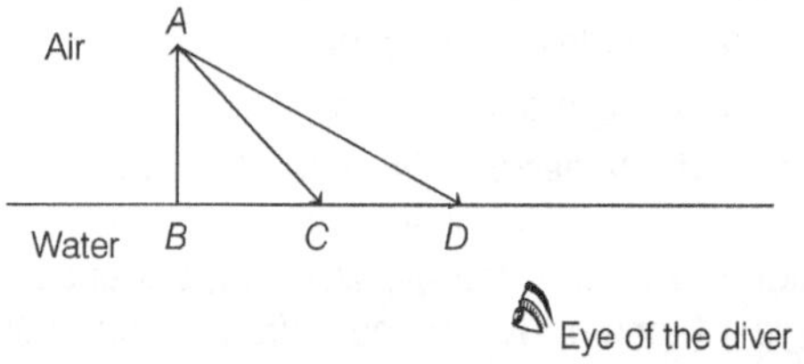

(i) Does the object appear taller, shorter or of the same size to the diver? **[1]**

(ii) Show the path of two rays AC and AD starting from the tip of the object as it travels towards the diver in water and hence obtain the image of the object. **[2] [ICSE 2020]**

Ans. (i) When a diver in water looks obliquely at an object AB in air, then object AB appears taller than its actual size, because when the ray is coming from the rarer medium to the denser medium, then they deviate towards the normal, hence they produced larger image.

(ii)

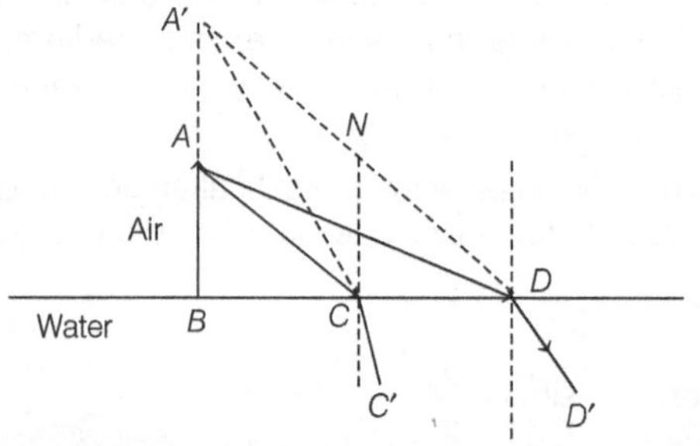

When the rays of light coming from the rarer medium to the denser medium, then it bends towards the normal. Hence, path of rays *AC* and *AD* are shown in above figure.

The image of object *AB* is shown in the figure as *A′B*.

Q.3 A ray of monochromatic green light enters a liquid from air as shown in the figure given below.

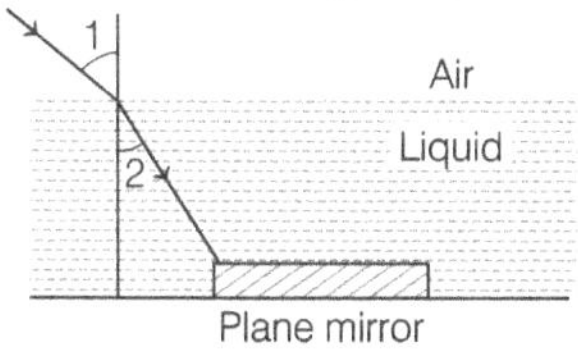

The angle 1 is 45° and angle 2 is 30°.

(i) Determine the refractive index of the liquid. **[1]**

(ii) Represent in the diagram showing the path of the ray after it strikes the mirror and re-enters air. Mark in the diagram wherever necessary. **[1]**

(iii) Draw the diagram again if plane mirror becomes normal to the refracted ray inside the liquid. Name the principle used. **[1]**

Ans. According to Snell's law,

(i) Refractive index of liquid, $\dfrac{\sin i}{\sin r} = \dfrac{\sin \angle 1}{\sin \angle 2}$

$$= \frac{\sin 45^\circ}{\sin 30^\circ} = \frac{\frac{1}{\sqrt{2}}}{\frac{1}{2}} = 1.4$$

(ii) The path of the reflected and refracted rays is shown below.

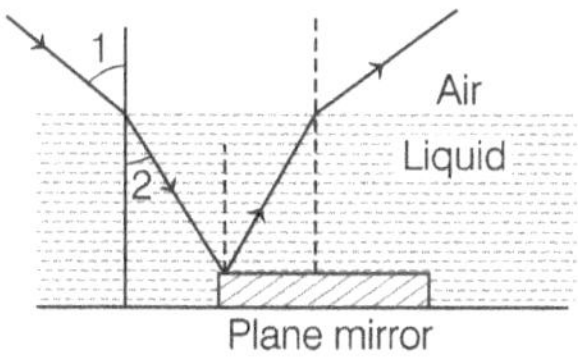

(iii) The principle used is the principle of reversibility of light.

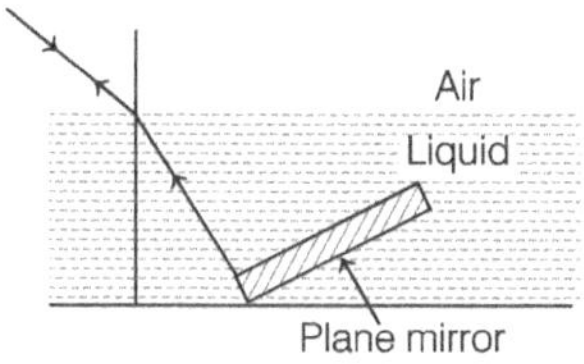

Q.4 (i) Refractive index of glass with respect to water is $\frac{9}{8}$. Find the refractive index of water with respect to glass. **[1]**

(ii) Name the principle used to find the value in part (a). **[1]**

(iii) If we change the temperature of water, then will the ratio $\frac{9}{8}$ remain the same ? Write Yes or No. **[1]**

Ans. (i) Given, ${}^{w}\mu_g = \dfrac{9}{8} \Rightarrow {}^{g}\mu_w = \dfrac{1}{{}^{w}\mu_g} = \dfrac{1}{\frac{9}{8}} = \dfrac{8}{9}$

(ii) Principle of reversibility of light.

(iii) No, if the temperature rises, the refractive index of medium will decrease and *vice-versa*.

Q.5 Light travels a distance of $10x$ units in time t_1 in vacuum and it travels a distance of x units in time t_2 in a denser medium. Using this information, answer the question that follows.

(i) Light covers a distance of $20x$ units in time t_1 in diamond. State true or false. **[1]**

(ii) Calculate the refractive index of the medium in terms of t_1 and t_2. **[2][ICSE 2024]**

Ans. (i) False.

Since, the velocity of light decreases in a denser medium like diamond, so it will cover less distance in the same amount of time compared to vacuum.

(ii) Velocity of light in vacuum, $v_1 = \dfrac{10x}{t_1}$

Velocity of light in denser medium, $v_2 = \dfrac{x}{t_2}$

$\therefore$ Refractive index of medium, $\mu = \dfrac{v_1}{v_2} = \dfrac{\frac{10x}{t_1}}{\frac{x}{t_2}}$

$$\mu = \frac{10x}{t_1} \times \frac{t_2}{x} = \frac{10t_2}{t_1}$$

Q.6 The diagram below shows two parallel rays-*A* (Orange) and *B* (Blue) incident from air, on air-glass boundary.

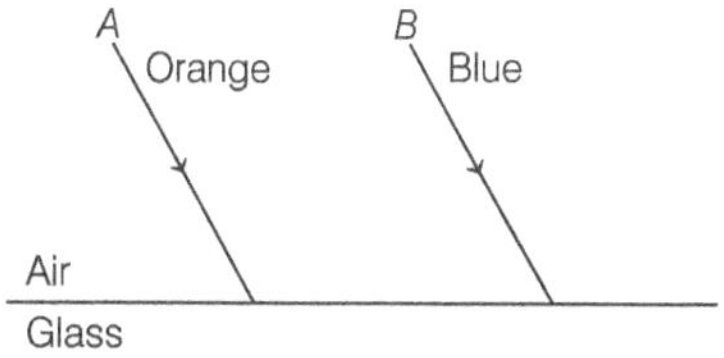

(i) Copy and complete the path of the rays *A* and *B*. **[1]**

(ii) How do the speeds of these rays differ in glass? **[1]**

(iii) Are the two refracted rays in glass parallel? Give a reason. **[1][2023]**

Ans. (i)

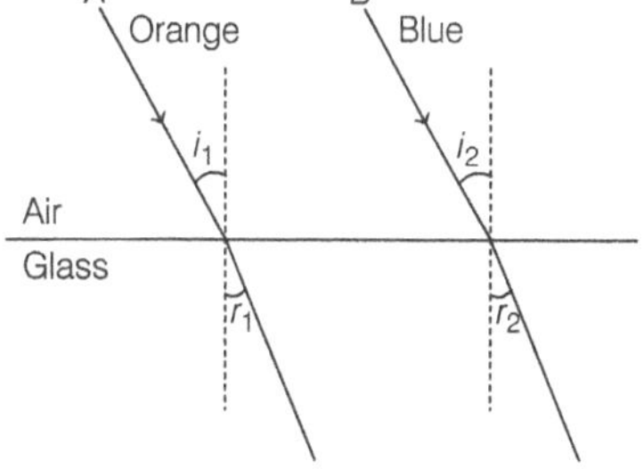

(ii) Speed of orange light is more than speed of blue light in glass medium.

(iii) No, the two refracted rays are not parallel this is due to the fact that $v_{Orange} > v_{Blue}$ blue i.e, the speed of orange light is more, so the orange light bends less and blue light bends more in glass medium.

Q.7

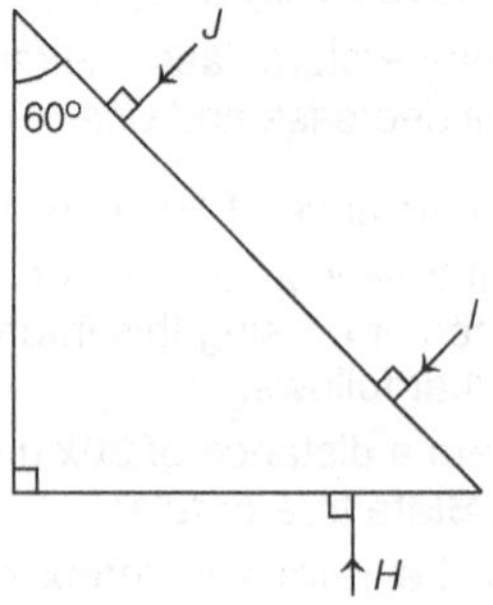

(i) Out of the three rays (*I*, *J*, *H*) shown in the diagram, which ray will suffer total internal reflection, while inside the prism? (Critical angle of the prism is 42°.)

(ii) Copy the diagram to complete the path of the ray which you have named in (a) till it comes out of the prism **[ICSE 2025]**

Ans. (i) Ray *J*

(ii)

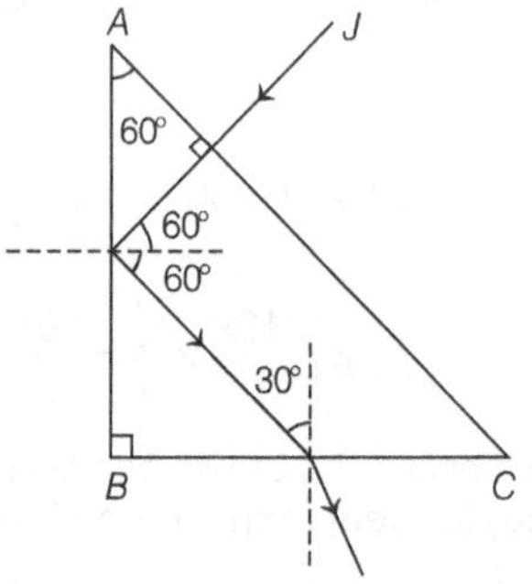

Q.8 (i) State the laws of refraction of light. **[2]**

(ii) Write a relation between the angle of incidence (i), angle of emergence (e), angle of prism (A) and angle of deviation (δ) for a ray of light passing through an equilateral prism. **[1]**

Ans. (i) The laws of refraction of light are

(a) The incident ray, the refracted ray and the normal at the point of incidence all lie in the same plane.

(b) The ratio of sine of angle of incidence to the sine of angle of refraction is a constant for a pair media.This constant is known as refractive index, i.e. $\mu = \frac{\sin i}{\sin r}$.

(ii) A ray of light passing through an equilateral prism have the following relation $\angle i + \angle e = \angle A + \angle \delta$ where, the symbols have their usual meaning.

Q.9 When sunlinght passes through water droplets in the atmosphere, it gets dispersed into its constituent colours forming a rainbow. A similar phenomenon is observed when white light passes through a prism.

(i) Which colour will show the maximum angle of deviation and which colour will show the minimum angle of deviation? **[2]**

(ii) If Instead of sunlight, a green coloured ray is passed through a glass prism. What will be the colour of the emergent ray? **[1][ICSE Specimen]**

Ans. (i) Violet shows maximum angle of deviation. Red shows minimum angle of deviation.

(ii) Green colour

Q.10 (i) A coin kept inside water ($\mu = 4/3$) when viewed from air in a vertical direction appears to be raised by 3.0 mm. Find the depth of the coin in water. **[2]**

(ii) How is the critical angle related to the refractive index of a medium? **[1][ICSE 2023]**

Ans. (i) Given, $\mu = 4/3$

and the shift = 3 mm

Let the real depth be x mm, then

$$\text{Apparent depth} = \frac{x}{\mu} = \frac{x}{4/3} = \frac{3x}{4}$$

Shift = Real depth – Apparent depth

$$\Rightarrow \quad x - \frac{3x}{4} = 3\text{ mm}$$

$$\Rightarrow \quad 4x - 3x = 12\text{ mm}$$

$$\Rightarrow \quad x = 12\text{ mm}$$

So, the depth of the coin in water is 12 mm.

(ii) The relation between the critical angle i_c and the absolute refractive index (μ) of medium is given by $\mu = \frac{1}{\sin i_c}$ or $\sin i_c = \frac{1}{\mu}$.

Q.11 The refractive index of water is 1.33 at a certain temperature. When the temperature of water is increased by 40 °C, the refractive index changes to x.

(i) State whether $x < 1.33$ or $x > 1.33$ **[1]**

(ii) State two differences between normal reflection and total internal reflection. **[2] [ICSE Specimen 2025**

Ans. (i) As, refractive index $\propto \frac{1}{\text{temperature}}$

$$\therefore \quad x < 1.33$$

(ii) Two differences between normal reflection and total internal reflection

Normal reflection	Total internal reflection
It occurs only when light is incident on a plane mirror from any medium at any angle of incidence.	It occurs only when light passes from a denser medium to a rarer medium at an angle of incidence greater than critical angle for that pair of media.
The incident ray is partially reflected and partially refracted.	The incident ray is totally reflected back.

Q.12 A rectangular glass block of refractive index 1.5 has an air bubble trapped inside it as shown in the diagram. When seen from the surface *AB*, it appears to be 4 cm deep. **[ICSE 2025]**

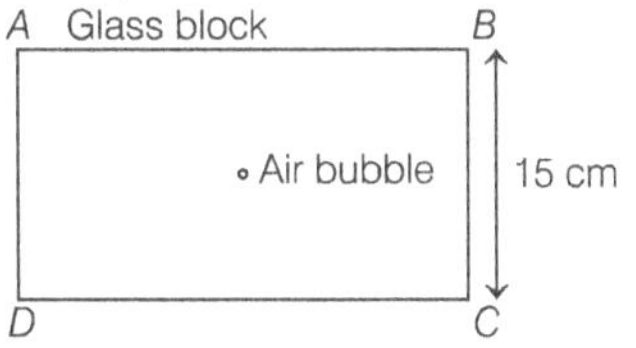

(i) Calculate the actual depth of the air bubble from the surface *AB*.

(ii) For which colour of light, blue or yellow, the apparent depth will be greater?

(iii) Turning the glass block upside down, does not change the apparent depth of the air bubble. State true or false.

Ans. (i) Refractive index of a medium with respect to air,

$$\mu = \frac{\text{Real depth or actual depth}}{\text{Apparent depth}}$$

$$\therefore \quad 1.5 = \frac{\text{Actual depth}}{4}$$

$\Rightarrow$ Actual depth $= (1.5 \times 4) = 6$ cm

(ii) Apparent depth $\propto \frac{1}{\text{RI}}$

$\therefore$ The apparent depth will be greater for yellow light, since its refractive index for yellow light is lower.

(iii) When the glass block is turned upside down, the real depth of the air bubble becomes 9 cm.

$\therefore$ Apparent depth $= \frac{9}{1.5} = 6$ cm.

$\therefore$ The statement is false.

Q.13 The diagram below shows the path of a blue ray through the prism.

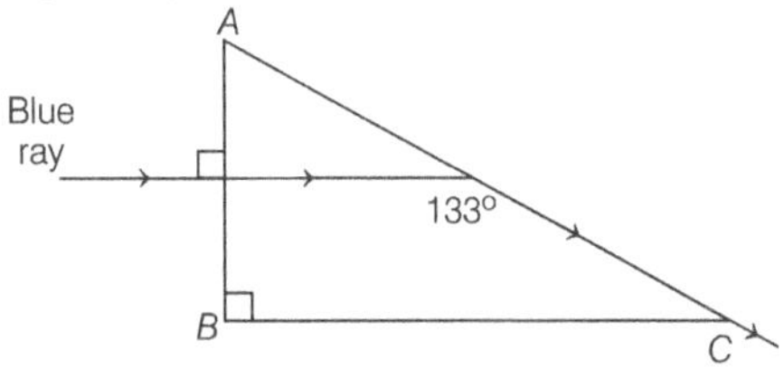

(i) Calculate the critical angle of the material of the prism for blue colour. **[1]**

(ii) What is the measure of the angle of this prism (*A*)? **[1]**

(iii) Which colour should replace the blue ray, for the ray to undergo total internal reflection ? **[1]**

[ICSE 2024]

Ans.

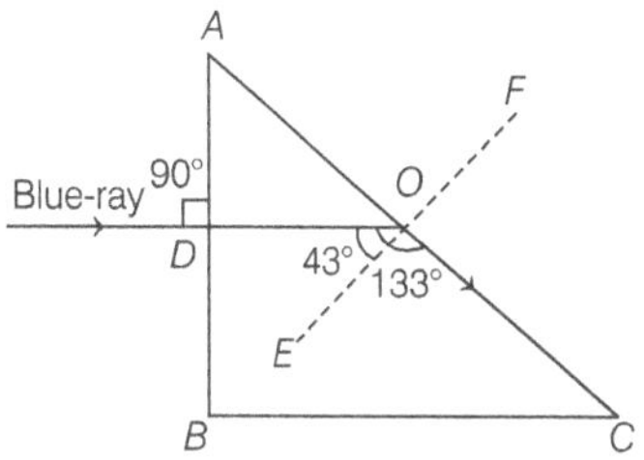

(i) From the figure,

$$\angle EOD = \angle DOC - \angle EOC$$
$$= 133° - 90°$$
$$\angle EOD = 43°$$

So, the critical angle of the material of the prism for blue colour will be 43°.

(ii) From the figure,

$$\angle DOA = \angle EOA - \angle EOD$$
$$= 90° - 43° = 47°$$

So, $\angle DAO = 90° - 47°$

$$= 43°$$

The prism angle = 43°

(iii) Violet or indigo

Q.14 *ABC* is a glass block whose two sides, *AB* and *BC*, are at right angles to each other. A ray of light is incident on the surface *AB*, as shown in the diagram, and suffers total internal reflection before falling on the surface *BC*. Finally, the light ray emerges out along the surface *BC*.

(i) What is the angle of incidence at the surface *AB*? **[1]**

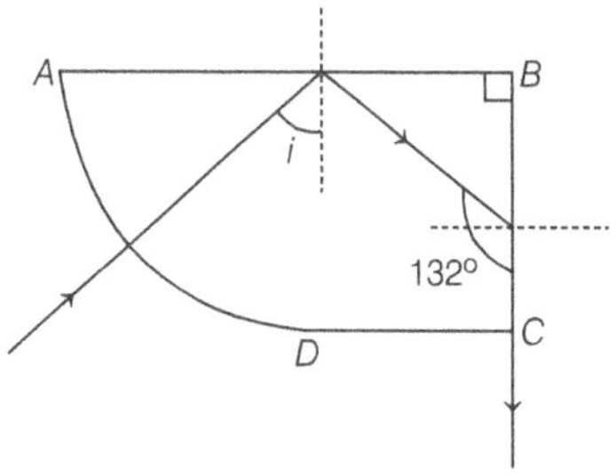

(ii) What is the critical angle for the glass block *BC*? **[1]**

(iii) What would happen to the critical angle if the temperature of the glass block is increased? **[1] [Competency Based Que.]**

Ans. (i)

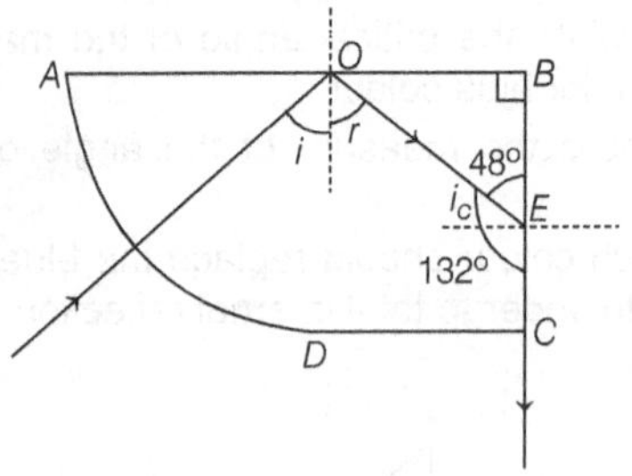

The incident ray undergo total internal refraction on surface *AB*.

∴ Apply law of reflection at surface *AB*,

$$\angle i = \angle r \qquad \ldots(i)$$

The angle between reflected ray and the surface *BC*, i.e. < *BEO*

$$180^\circ - 132^\circ = 48^\circ$$

By alternate angle property, since normal to surface *AB* and the surface *BC* are parallel to each other.

i.e., $\angle r = \angle BEO$

∴ $\angle r = 48^\circ$

From Eqs. (i)

$$\angle i = 48^\circ$$

(ii) The critical angle for glass block *BC*,

$$\angle i_C = 90^\circ - 48^\circ = 42^\circ$$

(iii) We know that,

$$i_C = \sin^{-1}\left(\frac{1}{n}\right)$$

Since, the refractive index decreases with increase in temperature. Therefore, from the above equation critical angle will increase, if the temperature of the glass block in increased.

TYPE - 6 — 04 Marks

Long Answer Type Questions

Q.1 Two rays *PQ* and *RS* are incident on a rectangular glass block as shown in the diagram. Observe the diagram and answer the questions that follow. **[ICSE 2025]**

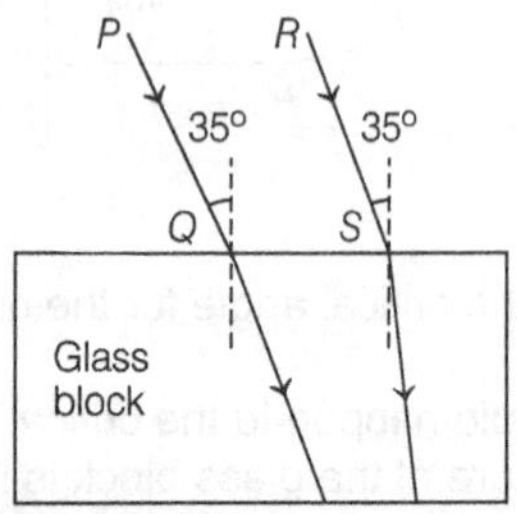

Which of these two rays will

(i) have greater lateral displacement on emerging out of the block?

(ii) travel with greater speed in the block?

(iii) scatter more in the atmosphere?

Ans. (i) Ray *RS*

Since, it bends more inside the glass block.

(ii) Ray *PQ*.

Since, it bends less inside the glass block and hence has a lower refractive index as compared to ray *RS*.

(iii) The light ray having greater refractive index will suffer less deviation as compared to the light having lower refractive index.

Therefore, *PQ* having lower refractive index will scatter more.

Q.2 **Jatin puts a pencil into a glass container having water and is surprised to see the pencil in a different state.**

(i) What change is observed in the appearance of the pencil? [2]

(ii) Name the phenomenon responsible for the change. [1]

(iii) Draw a ray diagram showing how the eye sees the pencil. [1] (ICSE 2015)

Ans. (i) When a pencil is dipped into a glass container having water, it appears to be bent upward.

(ii) This appearance in the shape of pencil when dipped in water is due to refraction of light.

(iii) Ray diagram to show appearance of bending of pencil due to refraction of light.

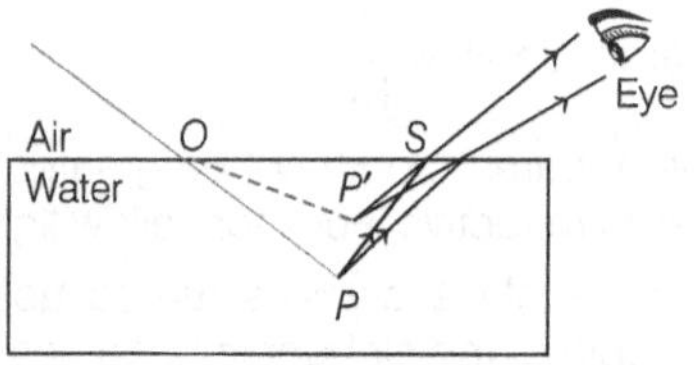

Q.3

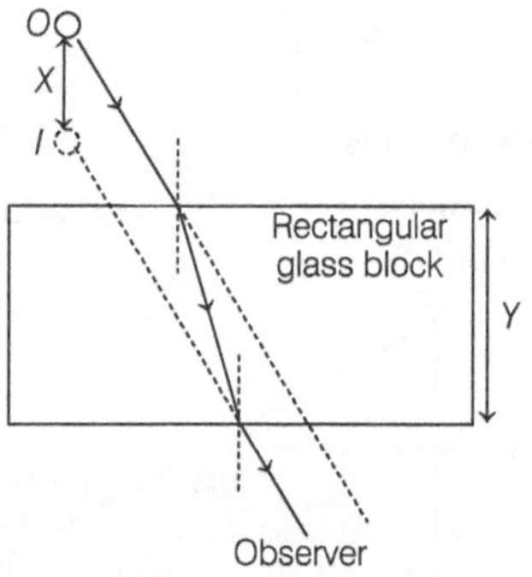

The above diagram shows that an observer sees the image of an object *O* at *I*.

(i) Name and define the phenomenon responsible for seeing the image at a different position. **[2]**

(ii) State the effect on *X* when **[2]**

(a) *Y* increases

(b) *Y* decreases **[ICSE Specimen 2023]**

Ans. (i) The perpendicular separation between the incident ray and the emergent ray is called lateral displacement.

(ii) Lateral displacement is directly proportional. The thickness of the slab. Therefore, in the diagram,

(a) When *Y* increases, *X* also increases.

(b) When *Y* decreases, *X* also decreases.

Q.4 You are doing an experiment on the refraction of light in your Physics laboratory. *ABCD* is a rectangular block. A ray of light is incident obliquely on the surface *AB*.

(i) Draw the path of the ray of light through the glass block and also show how it emerges from the block. [The diagram should show the lateral displacement suffered by the ray.] **[2]**

(ii) Which two pairs of angles remain the same during the experiment? **[1]**

(iii) If the same experiment is performed first with red and then with blue light, which colour will suffer greater lateral displacement?

[1][Comptency Based Qus.]

Ans. (i)

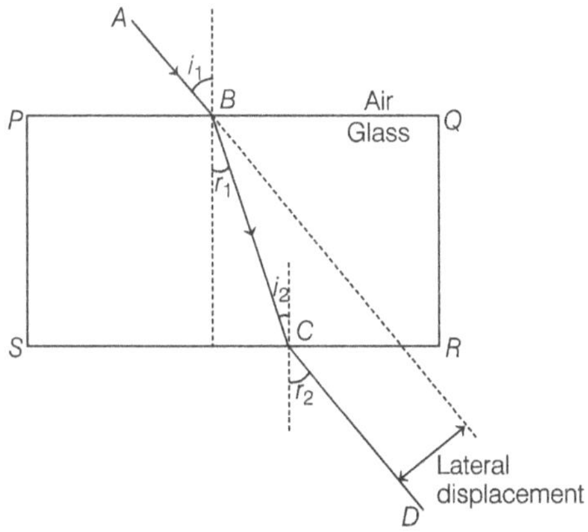

(ii) Since, the two surfaces *PQ* and *SR* is parallel.

$\therefore \quad \angle i_1 = \angle r_2$

and $\quad \angle r_1 = \angle i_2$

(iii) Lateral displacement is maximum for blue light because it has a higher refractive index than red light.

Q.5 A student traces the path of a ray of blue light as it enters and as it leaves a glass prism. Given figure shows the trace obtained by the student.

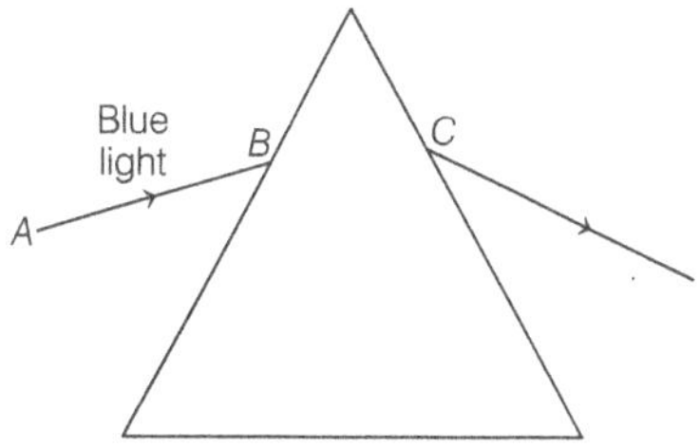

(i) On figure draw and label, at the point *B*, the normal, the angle of incidence *i* and the angle of refraction *r*.

(ii) State, in terms of the properties of light waves, why the light refracts at *B* ?

(iii) The angle of incidence for the ray of blue light at *B* is 45°. The refractive index of the glass is 1.5. Calculate the angle of refraction at *B*.

(iv) The student performs another experiment with a ray of red light along the line *AB*.

On figure, show the path taken by this ray of light as it passes through and leaves the prism.

Ans. (i) Blue light bends more towards the normal than red light when it enters a denser medium due to its shorter wavelength compared to red light.

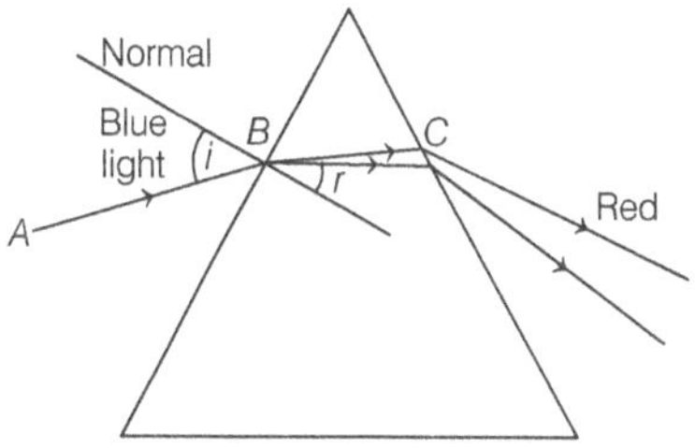

(ii) The light refracts at *B* because of the decrease in its speed as it passes from a less dense (air) to a more dense medium (glass).

(iii) $$n = \frac{\sin i}{\sin r}$$

$$\sin r = \frac{\sin i}{n} = \frac{\sin 45^\circ}{1.5}$$

$$r = 28.13^\circ$$

$\therefore$ Angle of refraction $\approx 28^\circ$

(iv) Refer to figure in (i).

Q.6 *PQ* and *PR* are two light rays emerging from the object *P* as shown in the figure.

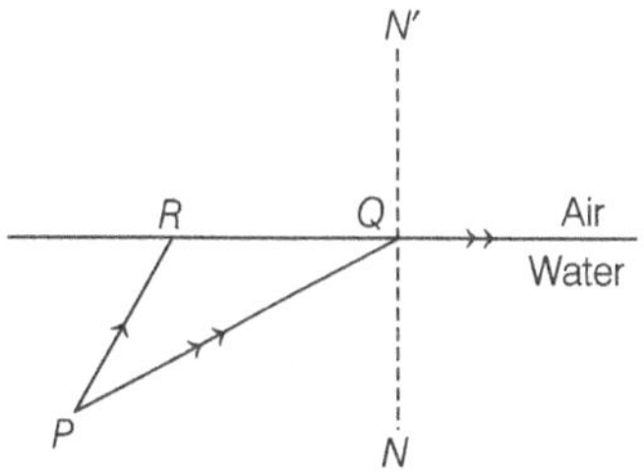

(i) What is the special name given to the angle of incidence ($\angle PQN$) of ray PQ? **[1]**

(ii) Copy the ray diagram and complete it to show the position of the image of the object P, when seen obliquely from above. **[2]**

(iii) Name the phenomenon that occurs, if the angle of incidence $\angle PQN$ is increased still further. **[1]**

Ans. (i) The special name given to the angle of incidence $\angle PQN$ of ray PQ is critical angle.

(ii) The complete diagram is shown below

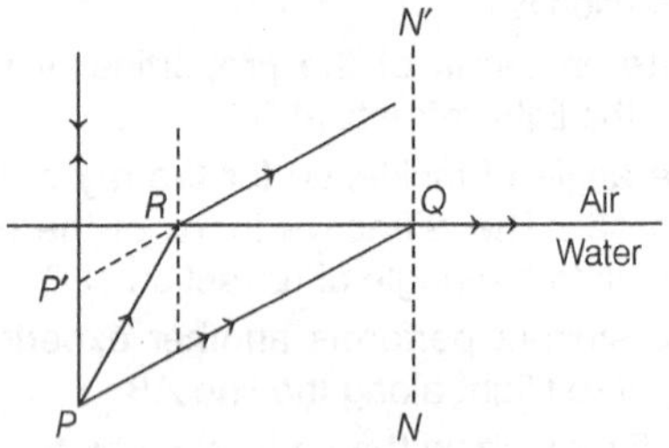

The image of the object P will be formed at P' when seen obliquely from above.

(iii) Total internal reflection occurs, if the angle of incidence $\angle PQN$ is increased still further.

Q.7 (i) In the given diagram, a ray of light PQ is incident normally on one face AB of an equilateral glass prism. What are the angles of incidence at the faces AB and AC? **[2]**

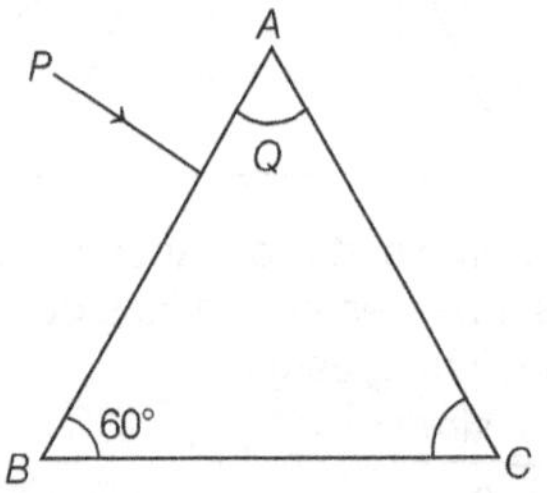

(ii) Complete the ray diagram showing its emergence into air after passing through the prism. **[2]**

Ans. (i) The angle of incidence at the face AB is 0°. The angle of incidence at the face AC is 60°.

(ii)

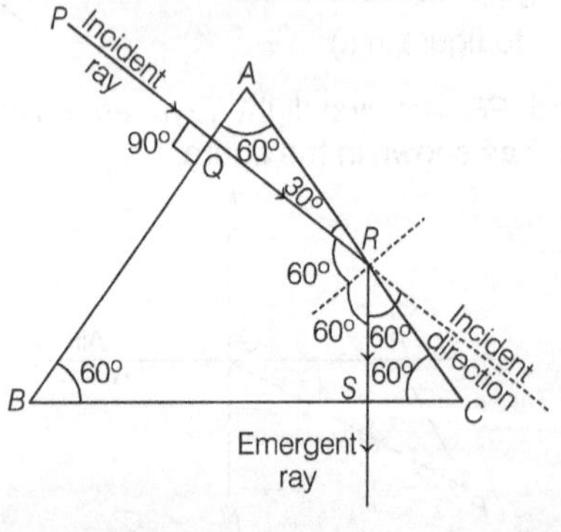

Q.8 Figure shows a ray of light entering a semi-circular glass block and striking the glass surface at M, the mid-point of the straight face.

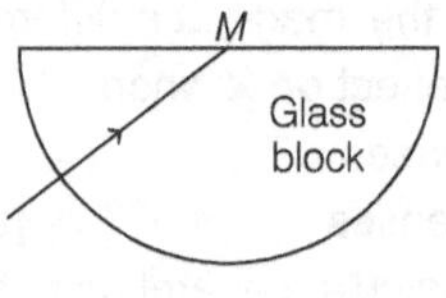

(i) The ray of light strikes the glass surface at M with an angle of incidence C equal to the critical angle of light in glass.

(a) State what is meant by critical angle? **[1]**

(b) On given fig. mark and label the angle C. **[1]**

(ii) Figure below shows a second ray of light striking M.

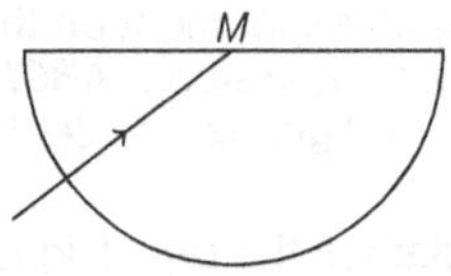

This ray has an angle of incidence at M smaller than the critical angle.

On figure continue this ray of light after it strikes the glass surface at M. **[1]**

(iii) The refractive index of this glass is 1.5. A third ray of light enters the block from air with an angle of incidence of 30°. Calculate the angle of refraction. **[1]**

Ans. (i) (a) The critical angle is the angle of incidence in the optically denser medium for which the angle of refraction in the less dense medium is 90°.

(b)

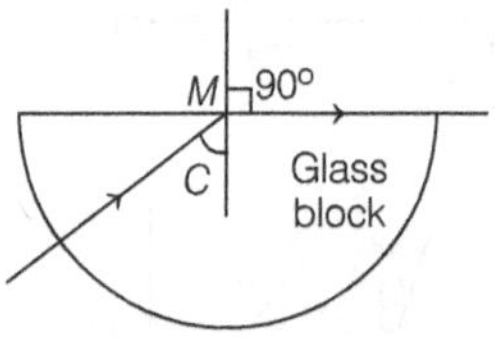

(ii)

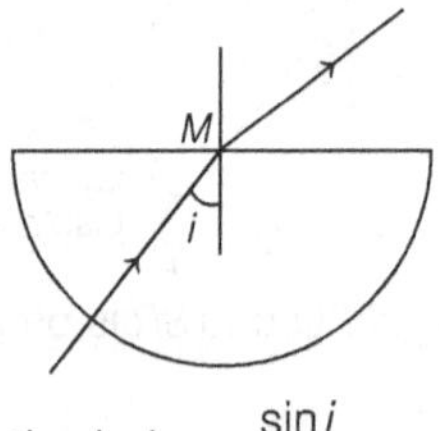

(iii) Refractive index $= \dfrac{\sin i}{\sin r}$

$$1.5 = \frac{\sin 30^\circ}{\sin r}$$

$$r = 19^\circ$$

Q.9

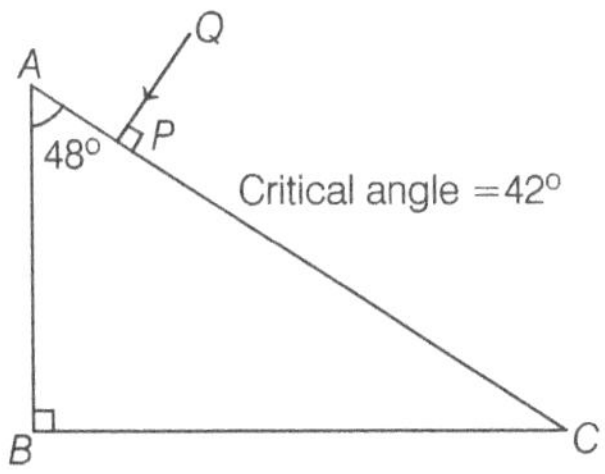

The above diagram shows a glass prism of a critical angle 42°.

(a) Redraw the diagram and complete the path of the light ray *PQ* till it emerges out of the prism. **[2]**

(b) Also, calculate the net angle of deviation of the ray *PQ* when it emerges from the prism. **[2]**

[Competency Based]

Ans. Given, critical angle is 42°.

(a)

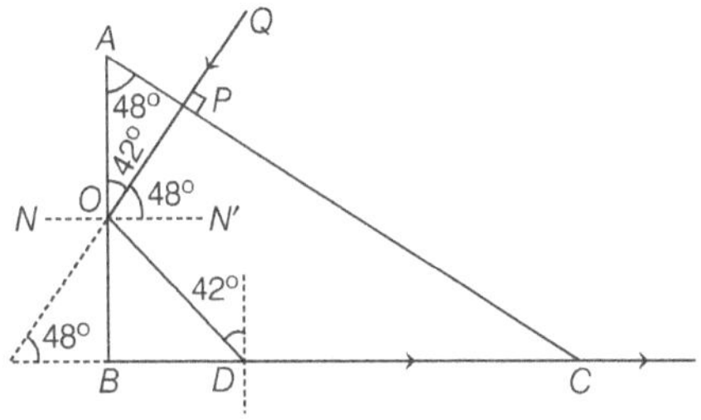

The incidence ray makes an angle 48° with the normal NN′ which is greater than critical angle 42°. So, it will undergo TIR at surface *AB*.

Now, inside the prism incidence ray *OD* is equal to the critical angle (i.e., 42°). Therefore, the angle of refraction becomes 90° and will pass along surface *BC*.

The angle of deviation is the angle between incidence ray and emergent ray. From the above diagram, it is cleared that $\angle D = 48°$.

TYPE - 7

03/04 Marks

Case Based Questions

Q.1 A student is conducting an experiment to study the refraction of light through a rectangular glass slab. She places a laser light at an angle of incidence of 40° on one side of the slab. The light beam refracts into the slab and exits from the opposite side. She observes that the incident and emergent rays are parallel to each other but displaced.

(i) What is the phenomenon observed by the student when the light beam bends as it enters the glass slab? Explain why this bending occurs? **[1]**

(ii) If the angle of refraction inside the glass slab is 25°, calculate the refractive index of the glass with respect to air. Use the formula **[1]**

$$n = \frac{\sin i}{\sin r}$$

(Take, sin 40° = 0.6428 and sin 25° = 0.4226)

(iii) Why are the incident and emergent rays parallel to each other but displaced? Explain this observation? **[1]**

Ans. (i) The phenomenon observed by the student is refraction of light. This bending occurs because light travels at different speeds in different media. When light enters a denser medium like glass from air, it slows down and bends towards the normal.

(ii) Given,

Angle of incidence, $i = 40°$

Angle of refraction, $r = 25°$

Using Snell's law,

$$n = \frac{\sin i}{\sin r}$$

Substituting values,

$$n = \frac{\sin 40°}{\sin 25°}$$

$$n = \frac{0.6428}{0.4226} \approx 1.52$$

Thus, the refractive index of the glass is 1.52.

(iii) The incident and emergent rays are parallel because the light undergoes refraction twice, first when entering the glass slab and second when exiting it.

These refractions cancel out the angular deviation but result in a lateral shift of the light beam, causing the rays to be displaced but parallel.

Q.2 Let *ABC* represent the principal section of prism and ray *PQ* is incident on surface *AB*. As it enters in the prism it bends towards the normal line. The refracted ray *QR* again suffer refraction on the surface *AC* and emerges along *RS* as shown in figure.

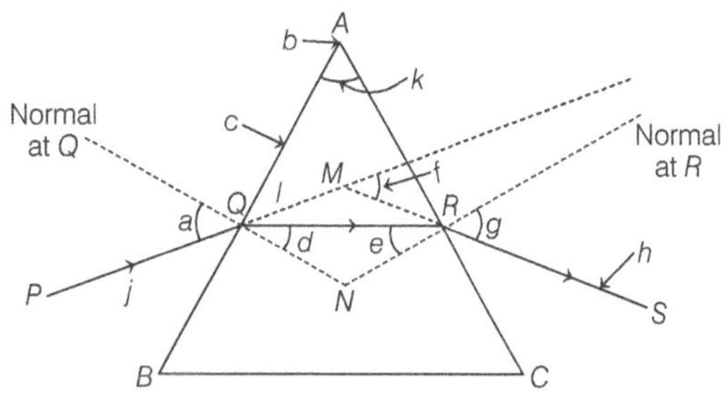

S.No	Description	Label
(i)	The emergent ray	*h*
(ii)	The refracted ray inside the prism	
(iii)	Angle between emergent and original incident ray	
(iv)	Refracting edge.	

Ans.

S.No	Description	Label
(i)	The emergent ray	*h*
(ii)	The refracted ray inside the prism	*i*
(iii)	Angle between emergent and original incident ray	*f*
(iv)	Refracting edge	*b*

Q.3 A student performs an experiment to study the refraction of a light ray by a transparent material *M* which is semi-circular in shape. He directs a light ray into the semi-circular block as shown below.

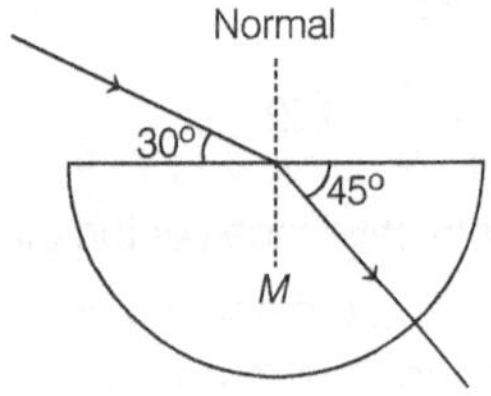

(Take, $\sin 55° = \sqrt{\frac{2}{3}}$)

(i) Find the angle of incidence *i* and angle of refraction *r* of the light ray. **[1]**

(ii) What is the refractive index of the material *M*? **[1]**

(iii) What is the critical angle, *C*, of material *M*? **[1]**

(iv) Complete the diagram below to show the critical angle *C* and the angle of refraction. **[1]**

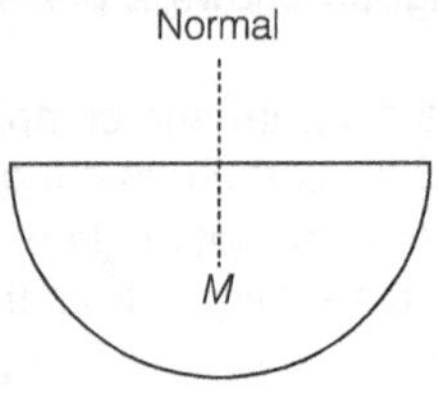

Ans. (i) Angle of incidence (i) = 90° − 30° = 60°

Angle of refraction (r) = 90° − 45° = 45°

(ii) Refractive index $= \frac{\sin i}{\sin r} = \frac{\sin 60°}{\sin 45°} = \sqrt{\frac{3}{2}}$

(iii) $\sin C = \sqrt{\frac{2}{3}}$

$\sin C = \sin 55°$

$C = 55°$

(iv)

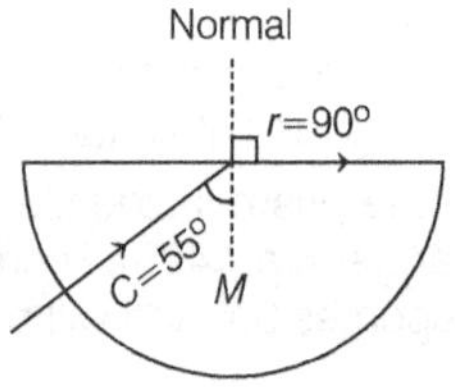

05

LENSES

Lens

- Lens is a transparent refracting medium bounded by two surfaces of which one or both surfaces are spherical.
- Lenses are of two types **convex** lens and **concave** lens

1. Convex or Converging Lens

- A lens which is thicker at the centre and thinner at its ends is called convex lens.
- A convex lens is also known as **converging lens** because it converges a parallel beam of light rays passing through it.
- Convex lenses are of three types as shown below

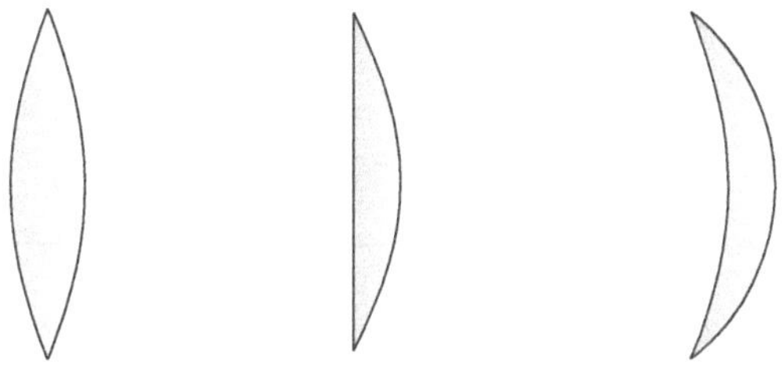

(a) Bi-convex lens (b) Plano-convex lens (c) Concavo-convex lens

(a) A **double-convex or bi-convex or equi-convex** lens has two outward curving sides and is simply called convex lens.

(b) The **plano-convex** lens is flat on one side and curved outward on the other side.

(c) The **concavo-convex** lens has one surface convex and the other surface concave.

2. Concave or Diverging Lens

- A lens which is thinner at the centre and thicker at its ends is called a concave lens.
- A concave lens is also known as **diverging lens** because it diverges a parallel beam of light rays passing through it.
- Concave lenses are of three types as shown below

(a) Bi-concave lens (b) Plano-concave lens (c) Convexo-concave lens

(a) **A double-concave or bi-concave or equi-concave** lens has two inward curving sides and is simply called concave lens.

(b) **The plano-concave** lens has a flat surface on one side and an inwardly curved surface on the other side.

(c) **The convexo-concave** lens has one surface concave and the other surface convex.

Action of a Lens as a Set of Prism Converging and Diverging Action of Lenses

- The converging and diverging action of lenses can be explained by considering a lens made up of large number of different small angle prisms.
- A converging lens can be supposed to be made up of a number of prisms with the base of each prism **towards** the centre of the lens.
- A diverging lens can be supposed to be made up of a number of prisms with the base of each prism **away from** the centre of the lens.

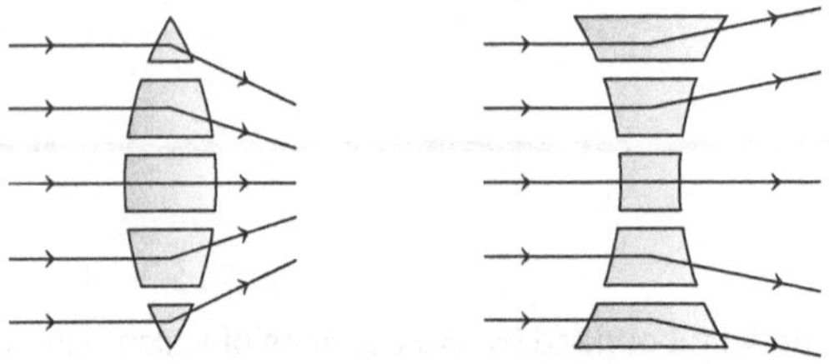

Converging action of convex lens

Diverging action of concave lens

Some Definitions Related to Lenses

Optical Centre

- The centre point of a lens is known as its optical centre.
- It is represented by *O*.
- It is a point of the lens, directed to which incident rays refract without any deviation in the path.

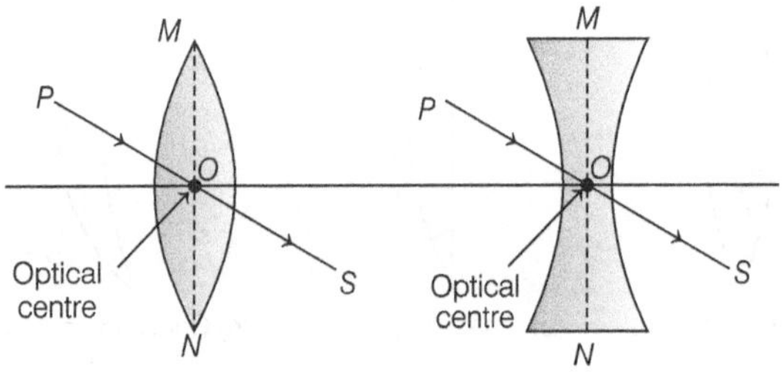

Convex lens

Concave lens

Centres of Curvature

- The centres of the two imaginary spheres of which the lens is a part are called centres of curvature of the lens.
- It is represented by *C* or 2*F*.
- A lens has two centres of curvature with respect to its two curved surfaces.

Radii of Curvature

- The radii of the two imaginary spheres of which the lens is a part are called radii of curvature of the lens.
- A lens has two radii of curvature. These may or may not be equal.

Aperture

- The effective diameter of the circular outline of a spherical lens is called its aperture.
- The length *MN* represents the aperture of lens.

Principal Axis

- The imaginary line joining the two centres of curvature is called principal axis of a lens.
- Principal axis also passes through the optical centre.

- Line XX' represents the principal axis in the figure.

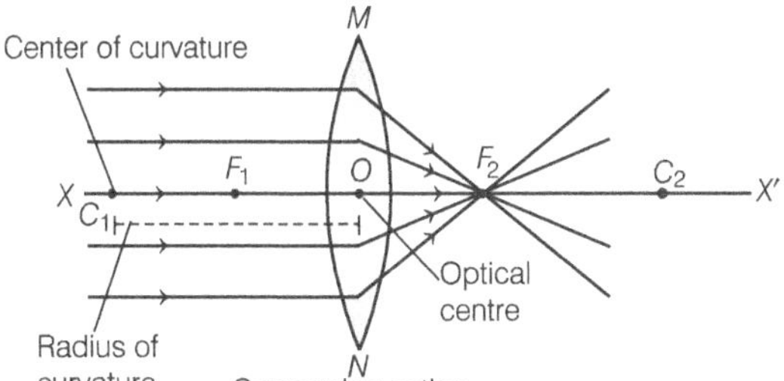

Converging action of a convex lens

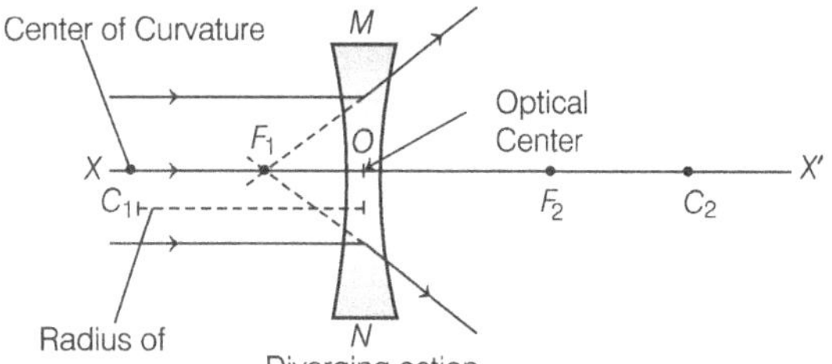

Diverging action of a concave lens

Principal Focus

- Lens has two principal foci

(i) **First Principal Focus** It is a point on the principal axis of lens at which the rays starting from or directed towards, become parallel to the principal axis after refraction from the lens.

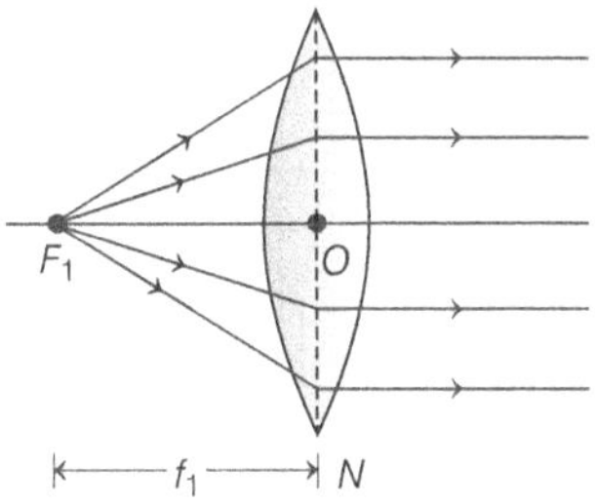

Convex lens

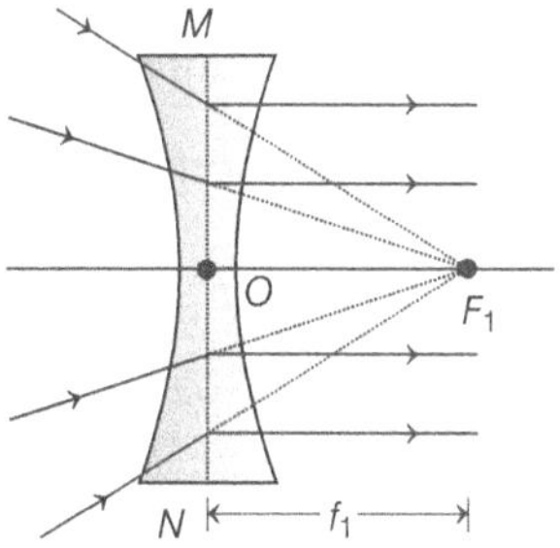

Concave lens

(ii) **Second Principal Focus** It is the point on the principal axis at which the rays coming parallel to the principal axis, converge on the other side of lens (convex) or appear to meet on the same side of lens (concave), after refraction from the lens.

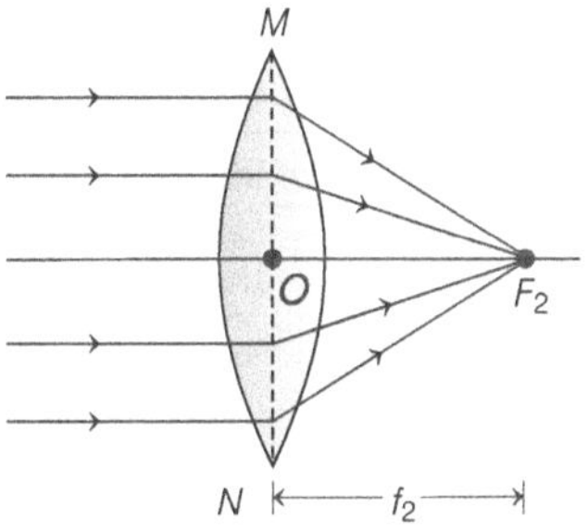

Convex lens

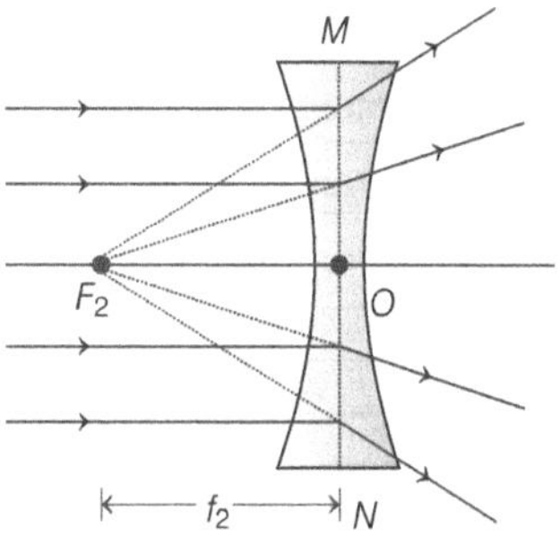

Concave lens

- Both the foci of convex lens are real while that of concave lens are virtual.

Focal Length of Lens

- The distance between focus and optical centre of lens is called focal length of lens.

Focal Plane

- The plane passing through the focus perpendicular to the principal axis is called focal plane.

Ray Diagrams for Principal or Construction Rays

- For drawing ray diagrams in lenses like spherical mirrors, we consider any two of the following rays
  (i) Rays which are parallel to the principal axis after refraction, will pass through principal focus in case of convex lens and will appear to be coming from principal focus in case of concave lens.

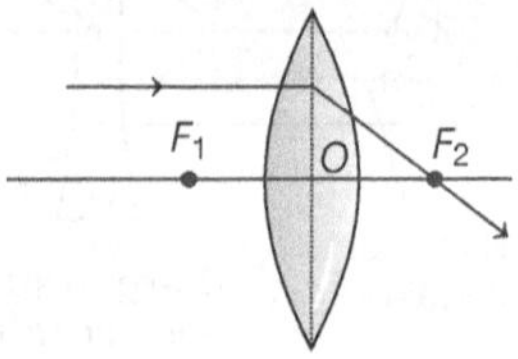

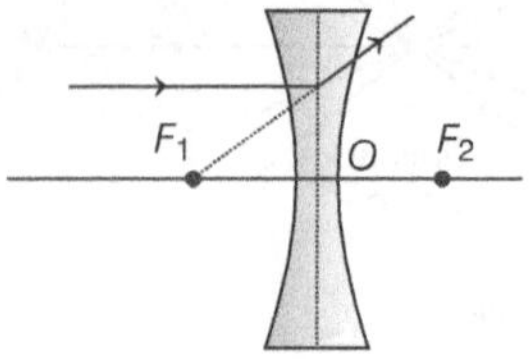

  (ii) Ray passing through or directed towards the focus will emerge parallel to the principal axis.

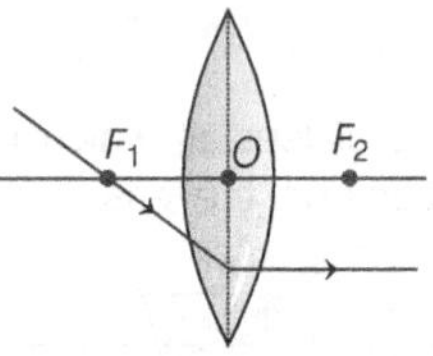

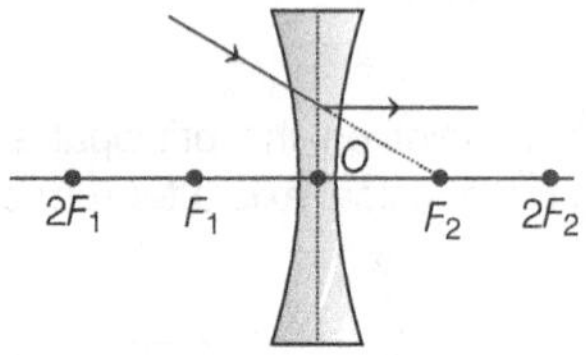

  (iii) Ray directed towards optical centre will emerge out undeviated.

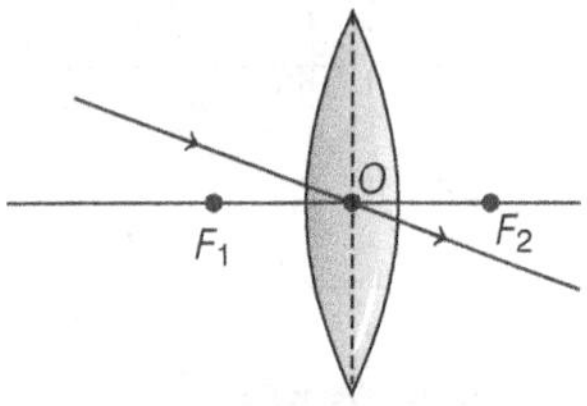

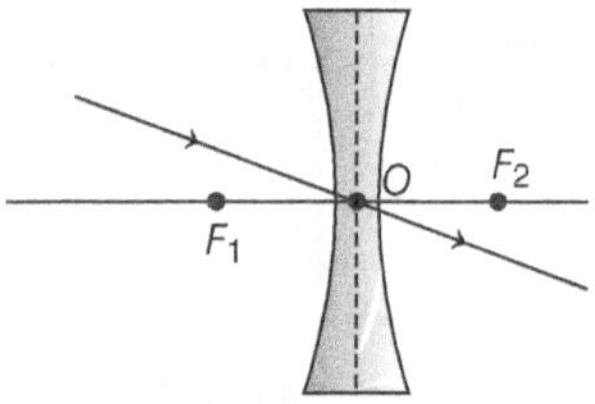

Characteristics and Location of Images of a Convex Lens

The table given below illustrates the ray diagrams along with the position and nature of image, formed by convex lens for various positions of the object.

Formation of Image by Convex Lens for Different Positions of Object

Position of Object	Ray Diagram	Position of Image	Nature and Size of Image
At infinity	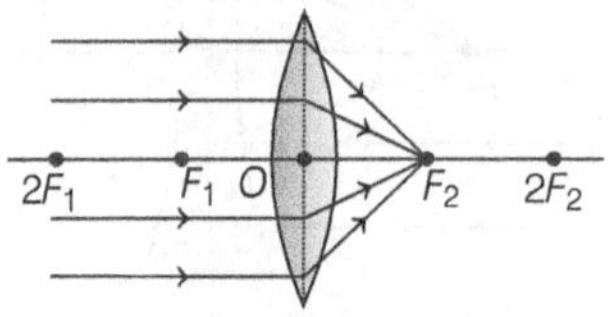	At F_2	Real, inverted and extremely diminished
Beyond $2F_1$ (at finite distance)	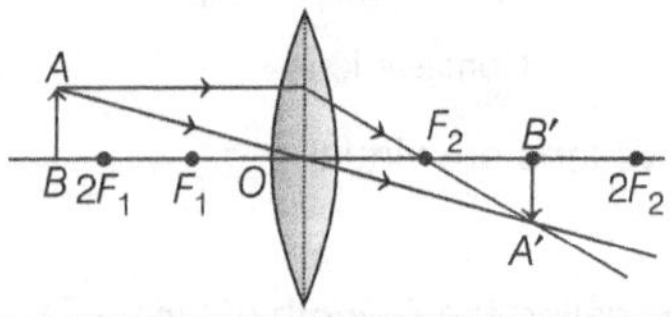	Between F_2 and $2F_2$	Real, inverted and diminished
At $2F_1$	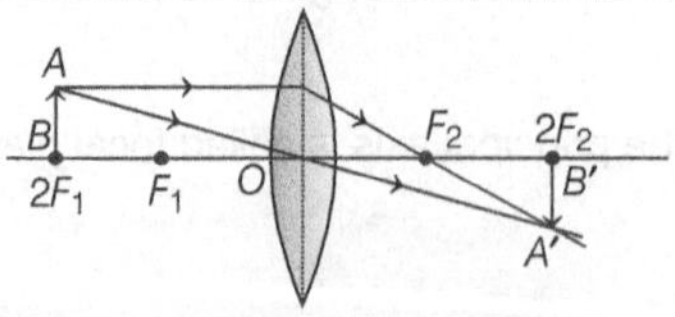	At $2F_2$	Real, inverted and of same size as that of object

Position of Object	Ray Diagram	Position of Image	Nature and Size of Image
Between F_1 and $2F_1$	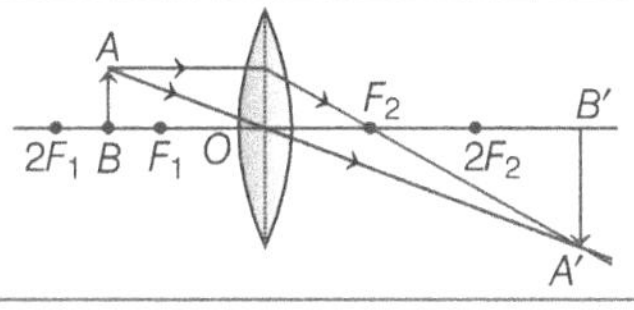	Beyond $2F_2$	Real, inverted and magnified
At F_1	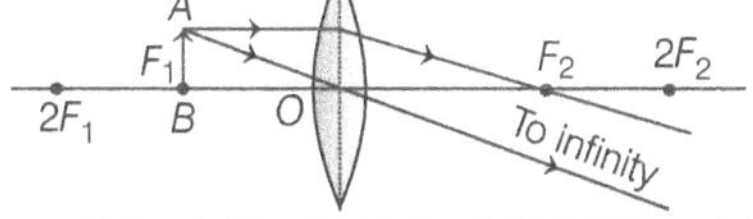	At infinity	Real, inverted and highly magnified
Between optical centre O and F_1	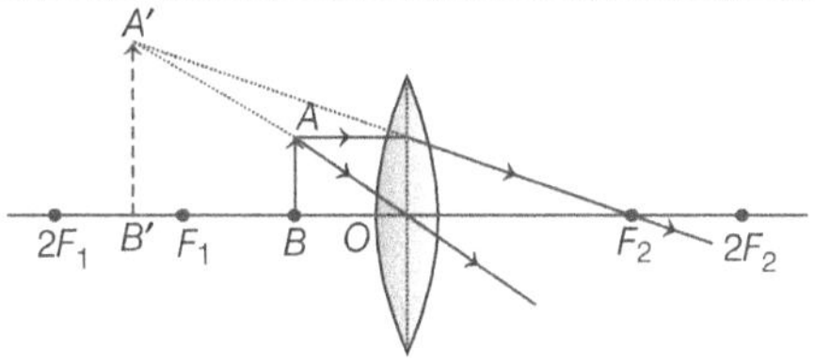	On same side of the lens as the object	Virtual, erect and magnified

Characteristics and Location of Images for a Concave Lens

For studying the image formation by concave lens,there are only two positions of object that are considered. The table given below illustrates the ray diagrams along with the position and nature of image formed by concave lens for the above two positions of the object.

Formation of Image by Concave Lens for Different Positions of Object

Position of Object	Ray Diagram	Position of Image	Nature and Size of Image
At infinity	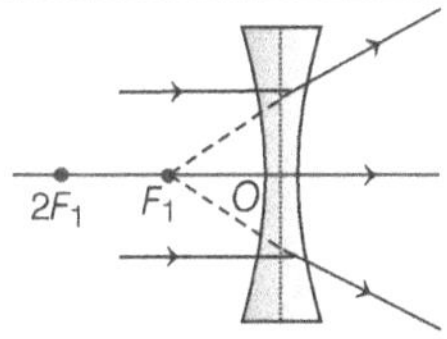	At focus on the same side of the lens as the object	Virtual, erect and highly diminished
At finite distance	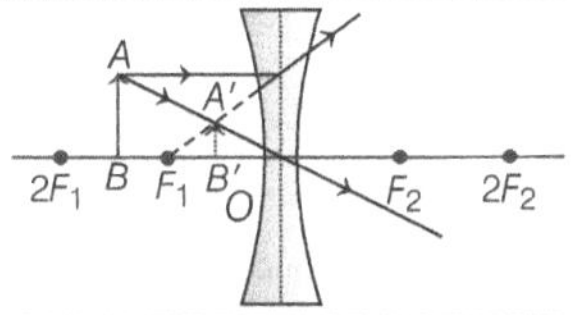	Between the focus and optical centre, on the same side of the lens as the object	Virtual, erect and diminished

Sign Convention for Spherical Lenses

(i) All the distances are measured from the optical centre O of the lens.

(ii) The principal axis of the lens is taken as X-axis and the optical centre as origin.

(iii) Distances measured in the direction of the incident light are taken as **positive** and opposite to the direction of incident light as **negative**.

(iv) The heights measured upwards with respect to X-axis and normal to the principal axis of the lens are taken as **positive** and the heights measured downwards are taken as **negative**.

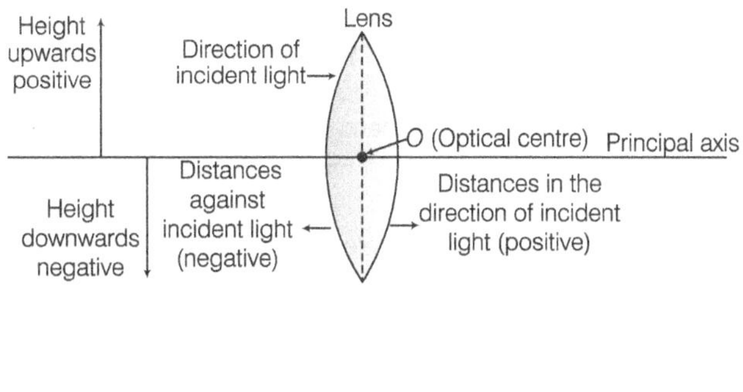

Lens Formula

- This formula gives the relationship between object distance (u), image distance (v) and the focal length (f).
- The lens formula is expressed as $$\frac{1}{v}-\frac{1}{u}=\frac{1}{f}$$
- The lens formula is general and is valid in all situations for any thin spherical lens.

Magnification by Lenses

- The ratio of height of image (h_i) and the height of object (h_o) is called magnification (m).
- Magnification, $$m=\frac{h_i}{h_o} \quad \text{or} \quad m=\frac{v}{u}$$
- Magnification is **positive**, when image formed is **virtual** and magnification is **negative**, when image formed is **real.**

Power of a Lens

- The ability of a lens to converge or diverge light rays is called power (P) of lens. It is defined as the reciprocal of the focal length,

  i.e. $$P=1/f \text{ (in metre)}$$
- Its **SI unit** is **dioptre** (D).
- The power of convex lens is positive and that of concave lens is negative.

Magnifying Glass or Simple Microscope

Microscope is an optical instrument which forms large image of close and minute objects.

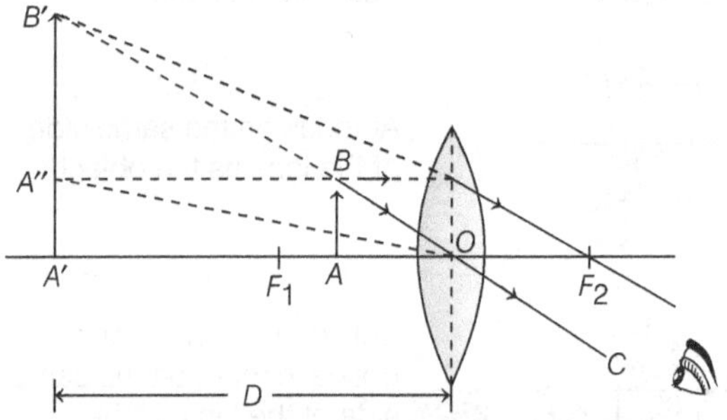

Ray diagram for location of image and magnification

- When an object AB is placed in front of a convex lens. The position of lens is so adjusted that the object AB lies in between its optical centre O and focus F_1 and the image formed is at the distance of distinct vision (D).
- The characteristics of image formed is virtual, magnified and erect.

$$\text{Magnifying power } M=1+\frac{D}{f}$$

Application of Lenses

Some applications of lenses are discussed as follows

(i) We usually use spectacles when our eyesight weakens. They either consist of convex lens or concave lens or both. A person suffering from long sightedness, i.e. hypermetropia, use convex lens while a person suffering from short sightedness, i.e. myopia, uses concave lens.

(ii) They are used in a spectroscope which uses convex lens for obtaining pure spectrum.

(iii) In telescope, camera, slide projector, etc., convex lens is used which forms a real and inverted image of an object.

(iv) In galilean telescope, a concave lens is used as an eyelens to obtain an erect final image of the object.

(v) Convex lens of short focal length fitted in a steel frame with a handle, is used as a magnifying glass.

EXAM ORIENTED QUESTIONS

TYPE - 1   01 Mark

Multiple Choice Questions

Q.1 Which of the following diagrams shows the correct path of light through the lens?

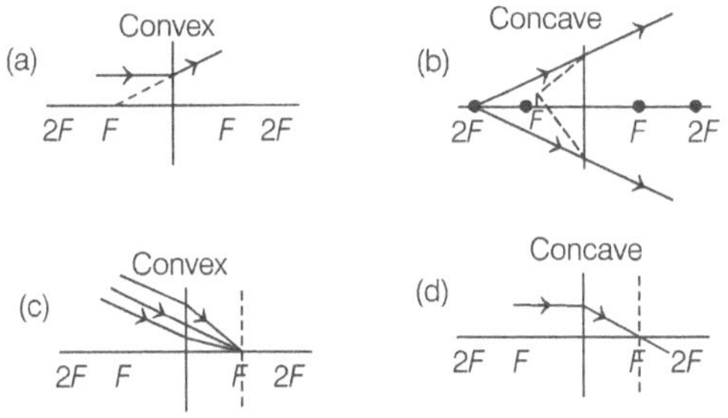

Ans. (b)

Q.2 Which of the following lenses is a converging lens?

(a) Concave lens
(b) Plano-concave lens
(c) Cylindrical lens
(d) Convex lens

Ans. (d) A convex lens is converging lens because it is thicker at the centre and thinner at the edge.

Q.3 For a real image formed by a convex lens, the ratio of $I : O = 2:5$, then the object is I is the height of the image and O is the height of the object) **[ICSE 2025]**

(a) between O and F
(b) beyond $2F$
(c) at F
(d) between F and $2F$

Ans. (b) Here the image formed is real and diminished which depicts that the object is kept beyond $2F$.

Q.4 For the object placed between the optical centre and focus of a convex lens, the image is

(a) real and enlarged
(b) real and diminished
(c) virtual and enlarged
(d) virtual and diminished

Ans. (c) When an object is placed between the optical centre and focus of a convex lens, then the image formed is virtual and enlarged. It is formed in the same side as object.

Q.5 A block of glass is pushed into the path of the light as shown below. Then, the converging point X will **[ICSE 2024]**

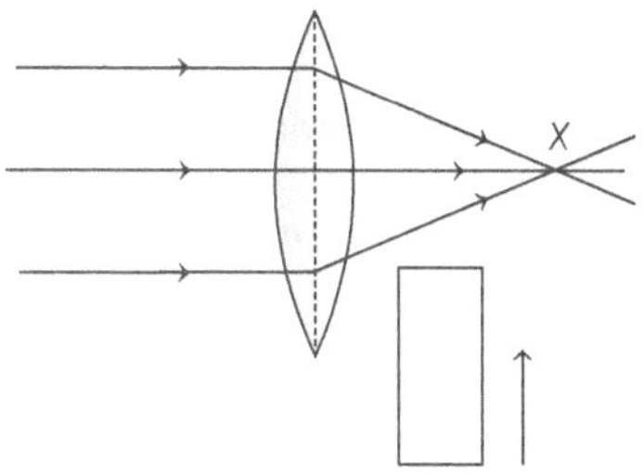

(a) move away from the slab
(b) move towards the slab
(c) not shift
(d) move towards the left side of the lens

Ans. (a) When the oblique rays of light from the lens enters the glass slab, it bends towards the normal which shift the converging point X farther to the right of the lens.

Q.6 From the diagram shown below, identify the characteristics of the image that will be formed. **[ICSE Specimen 2022 Sem-I]**

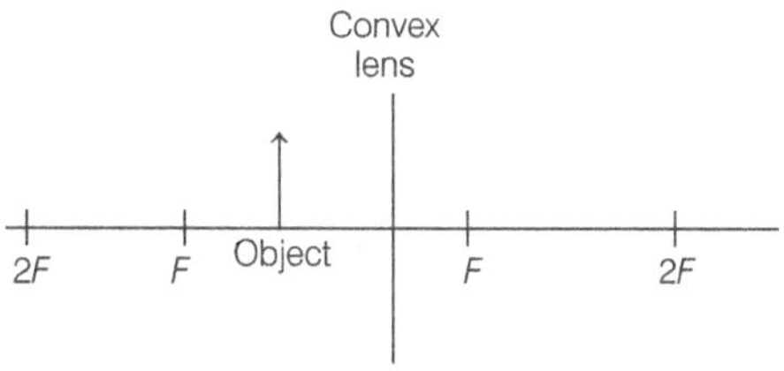

(a) Real
(b) Diminished
(c) Formed within the focal length
(d) Virtual

Ans. (d) As it is a convex lens and the object is placed between focal point and centre of curvature, the image formed will be enlarged, virtual and erect.

Q.7 The image when obtained from a concave lens of focal length f is magnified up to n times the size of the object. What is the distance of the object from the lens ?

(a) $\left(\frac{1-n}{n}\right)f$ (b) $\left(\frac{1+n}{n}\right)f$

(c) $\left(1-\frac{1}{n}\right)f$ (d) $\left(1+\frac{1}{n}\right)f$

Ans. (a) Using the lens formula,

$$\frac{1}{v}-\frac{1}{u}=\frac{1}{f} \Rightarrow \frac{u}{v}-1=\frac{u}{f} \quad \ldots(i)$$

As, $m=\frac{v}{u}=n$ (given)

$\Rightarrow \frac{u}{v}=\frac{1}{n}$

Substituting the above values in Eq. (i), we get

$$\Rightarrow \left(\frac{1}{n}-1\right)=\frac{u}{f} \Rightarrow u=\left(\frac{1-n}{n}\right)f$$

Q.8 Linear magnification m produced by a concave lens is **[ICSE 2024]**

(a) $m<1$ (b) $m>1$
(c) $m=1$ (d) $m \leq 2$

Ans. (a) Linear magnification, $m=\frac{v}{u}=\frac{h_i}{h_o}$

The image formed by a concave lens is always virtual and diminished.

i.e. $h_i < h_o$

So, $m<1$

Q.9 On reducing the focal length of a lens, its power
(a) decreases
(b) increases
(c) remains same
(d) first increase, then decrease

Ans. (b) Since, power $(P)=\frac{1}{\text{focal length }(f)}$

So, as f is reduced, the power of lens P will increase.

Q.10 Assuming all lenses shown below are of the same material, state which lens has the maximum power. **[ICSE Specimen 2022 Sem-I]**

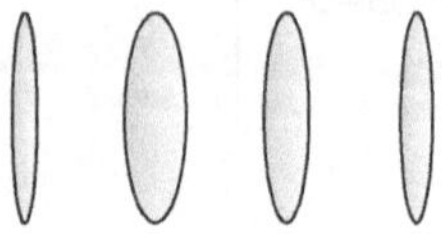

P Q R S

(a) R (b) P (c) Q (d) S

Ans. (c) Lens Q, because thicker lens has a shorter focal length and power of a lens is the reciprocal of the focal length.

Q.11 Find power of both the lenses A and B, if both have the focal length of 50 cm?

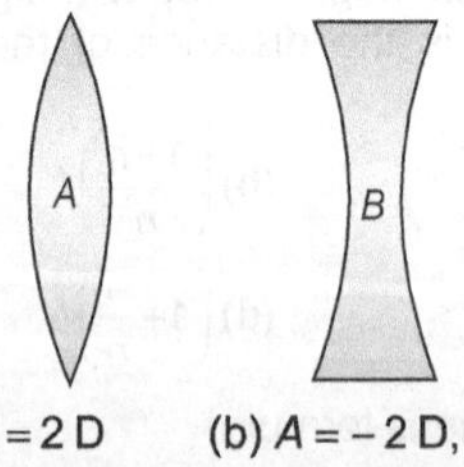

(a) $A=2$ D, $B=2$ D (b) $A=-2$ D, $B=+2$ D
(c) $A=+2$ D, $B=-2$ D (d) $A=-2$ D, $B=-2$ D

Ans. (c) Power, $P=\frac{100}{f(\text{cm})}$ D

$A=+2$ D, $B=-2$ D

A is convex lens, have the power +2 D, because it has positive focal length.

B is concave lens, with power –2 D as it has negative focal length.

Q.12 Which among the two lenses with power –3D and 4D respectively can form a real image?
(a) Only the lens with power –3D
(b) Only the lens with power 4D
(c) Both the lenses
(d) None of the above

Ans. (b) Only the lens with power 4D.

A negative power indicates a concave lens, which cannot form real images. Therefore, the lens with power 4D (positive) is a convex lens and can form a real image. So, the lens with power 4D can form a real image.

Q.13 For an object placed at a distance 20 cm infront of a convex lens, the image is at a distance 20 cm behind the lens. The focal length of the convex lens is

(a) 20 cm (b) 10 cm
(c) 15 cm (d) 40 cm

Ans. (b) Given, object distance, $u=-20$ cm

Image distance, $v=20$ cm

Using lens formula, $\frac{1}{v}-\frac{1}{u}=\frac{1}{f}$

$$\Rightarrow \frac{1}{(20)}-\frac{1}{(-20)}=\frac{1}{f}$$

$$\Rightarrow f=\frac{20}{2}=10 \text{ cm}$$

Q.14 An object of height 10 cm is placed in front of a concave lens of focal length 20 cm, at a distance of 25 cm from the lens. Is it possible to capture this image on a screen? Select a correct option from the following. **[ICSE 2021 Sem-I]**

(a) Yes, as the image formed will be real.
(b) Yes, as the image formed will be erect.
(c) No, as the image formed will be virtual.
(d) No, as the image formed will be inverted.

Ans. (c) Given, object size, $h_1=10$ cm

Object distance, $u=-25$ cm

Focal length, $f=-20$ cm

By lens formula, $\frac{1}{v}-\frac{1}{u}=\frac{1}{f}$

$$\frac{1}{v}+\frac{1}{25}=\frac{-1}{20} \Rightarrow \frac{1}{v}=\frac{-1}{25}-\frac{1}{20}$$

$$\Rightarrow \frac{1}{v}=\frac{-4-5}{100} \Rightarrow \frac{1}{v}=\frac{-9}{100}$$

$$\Rightarrow v=\frac{-100}{9} \text{cm}=-11.11 \text{cm}$$

Image will form at 11 cm in front of lens.

Magnification, $m = \frac{h_{image}}{h_{object}} = \frac{-v}{u}$

$\Rightarrow \quad h_{image} = \frac{-(-11.11)}{25} \times 10 = 4.444$ cm

Image formed will be virtual and not possible to capture on a screen.

Q.15 A convex lens has focal length 12 cm with an object at a distance of 20 cm in front of the lens. A student obtains a blurred image on the screen placed at a distance of 23 cm in front of the lens. In order to obtain the clear image, he has to move the screen

(a) towards the lens.
(b) away from the lens.
(c) to a position very far away from the lens.
(d) either towards or away from the lens.

[ICSE Specimen 2025)

Ans. (b) By lens formula,

For convex lens,

$f = +12$ cm

$u = -20$ cm

$\frac{1}{f} = \frac{1}{v} - \frac{1}{u}$

$\Rightarrow \quad \frac{1}{12} = \frac{1}{v} - \frac{1}{(-20)}$

$\Rightarrow \quad \frac{1}{12} = \frac{1}{v} + \frac{1}{20}$

$\Rightarrow \quad \frac{1}{v} = \frac{1}{12} - \frac{1}{20}$

$\Rightarrow \quad \frac{1}{v} = \frac{5-3}{60} = \frac{2}{60}$

$\Rightarrow \quad \frac{1}{v} = \frac{1}{30}$

$\Rightarrow \quad v = 30$ cm

Image will be formed at a distance 30 cm. So, in order to obtain a clear image, he has to move the screen 7 cm away from the lens.

Q.16 Two thin lenses of power 3D and – 2D are placed in contact, then power and focal length of the lens combination is

(a) + 2D, + 100 cm (b) +1D, + 100 cm
(c) + 5D, + 20 cm (d) + 1D, – 100 cm

Ans. (b) Given, power of lenses are $P_1 = 3$D and $P_2 = -2$D.

Power of combination of the lens,

$$P = P_1 + P_2 = 3\text{D} - 2\text{D} = +1\text{D}$$

Combined focal length $= \left(\frac{1}{P} \times 100\right)$ cm

$= \frac{1}{1} \times 100$

$= 100$ cm

Q.17 The maximum magnifying power of a convex lens of focal length 5 cm can be

(a) 25 (b) 10
(c) 1 (d) 6

Ans. (d) Given, focal length, $f = 5$ cm

Since, magnifying power, $m = 1 + \frac{D}{f}$

Here, $D = 25$ cm (least distance of distinct vision)

$\Rightarrow \quad m = 1 + \frac{25}{5} = 6$ cm

Hence, the maximum magnifying power of a convex lens of focal lenght 5 cm is 6.

TYPE - 2   01 Mark

Assertion-Reason Type Questions

Directions (Q. Nos. 1-5) In the following questions two statements are given as Assertion and Reason.

(a) Both A and R are true and R is the correct explanation of A.
(b) Both A and R are true but R is not the correct explanation of A.
(c) A is true but R is false.
(d) A is false but R is true.

Q.1 Assertion (A) A convex lens always produces a real and inverted image.

Reason (R) The convex lens converges light rays to a point called the principal focus.

Ans. (d) A convex lens can also produce a virtual and erect image when the object is placed between the focus and the optical centre (*O*) of the lens.

Q.2 Assertion (A) A convex lens of short focal length bends the light rays through large angles by focusing them closer to the optical centre.

Reason (R) A concave lens of very short focal length causes higher divergence than the one with a longer focal length.

Ans. (b) Convex lens with a short focal length has a greater curvature and thus, a stronger bending power causing light rays to converge more sharply and focus closer to the lens.

Concave lens with a very short focal length also has a greater curvature, causing light rays to diverge more strongly compared to a concave lens with a longer focal length.

Q.3 Assertion (A) The power of a lens is positive for a concave lens.

Reason (R) Power is the reciprocal of the focal length in metres.

Ans. (d) The power of a concave lens is negative as it has a negative focal length.

Q.4 Assertion (A) The SI unit of power of lens is diopter.

Reason (R) The power of a concave lens is positive and that of a convex lens is negative.

Ans. (c) The SI unit of the power of a lens is indeed the diopter and the power of a concave lens is considered negative while that of convex lens is positive.

Q.5 Assertion (A) Power of convex lens is positive and that of a concave lens is negative.

Reason (R) Focal length of convex lens is positive and that of a concave lens is negative.

Ans. (a) $P = \frac{1}{f}$, if f is negative, then power will be also negative. Focal length of convex lens is positive and that of a concave lens is negative.

TYPE - 3 — 01/02 Marks

Fill in the Blanks

Q.1 The focal length of a lens is the distance from the .... [object, centre of lens] to the focal point. **[1]**

Ans. centre of lens

Q.2 A concave lens forms a .... [real, virtual] image when the object is at infinity. **[1]**

Ans. virtual

Q.3 The focal length of a thin convex lens is .... [more/less] than that of a thick convex lens. **[1]**

Ans. more

Q.4 The radius of the sphere whose part is the lens surface is called the .... [centre of curvature/ radius of curvature] of that surface. **[1]**

Ans. radius of curvature

Q.5 According to sign convention, distances measured in the direction of incident light are .... [negative/positive]. **[1]**

Ans. positive

Q.6 A virtual image formed by a concave lens is always .... (diminished, enlarged, inverted) and appears on the .... [same, opposite, refracted] side of the lens as the object. **[2]**

Ans. diminished, same

Q.7 The power of a lens is measured in ...... (diopter, joule, metre) and it is given as the reciprocal of its .... [focal length, curvature, thickness] in metre.

Ans. diopter, focal length **[2]**

Q.8 The image formed by simple microscope is always .... [magnified/diminished] and .... [real/virtual]. **[2]**

Ans. magnified, virtual

TYPE - 4 — 02 Marks

Very Short Answer Type Questions

Q.1 Define convex lens and give its nature of refraction.

Ans. A lens which is thicker at the centre and thinner at its end is called convex lens.

It is also called converging lens as it converges the light rays passing through it.

Q.2 (i) Refer to the diagram given below. A lens with two different refractive indices is shown. If the rays are coming from a distant object, then how many images will be seen? **[ICSE Specimen 2025] [1]**

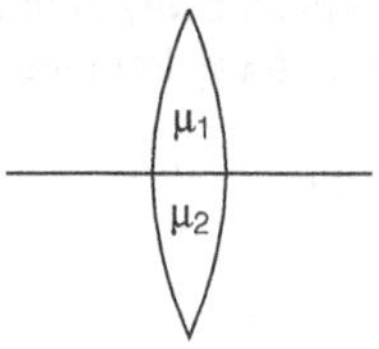

(ii) A glass lens always forms a virtual, erect and diminished image of an object kept in front of it. Identify the lens. **[1]**

Ans. (i) As the lens is made of the materials two different refractive indices so number of images formed will be two because the upper and the lower part of the lens bends the refracted rays by different angles.

(ii) In a concave lens, the image formed is always virtual, erect and diminished. So, it is a concave lens.

Q.3 A double convex lens with refractive index μ_1 inside two liquids of refractive indices μ_2 and μ_3 are shown in the diagrams below. The refractive indices are such that $\mu_2 > \mu_1$ and $\mu_1 > \mu_3$. **[ICSE Specimen 2025]**

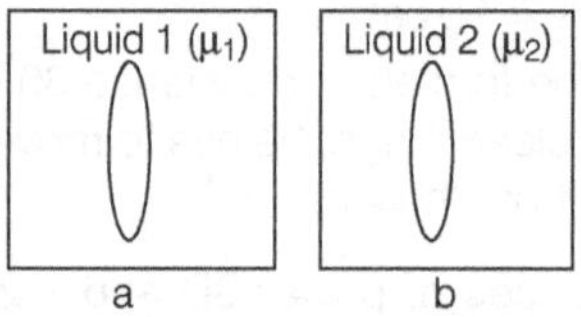

How would a parallel incident beam of light refract when it comes out of the lens in each of the cases shown above?

(i) in Fig. a. (ii) in Fig. b.

Ans. (i) In this case, $\mu_1 > \mu_3$, that is the refractive index of material of lens is greater than that of the medium in which it is kept. So, it will act as a converging lens. So the rays will converge after refraction.

(ii) In this case $\mu_2 > \mu_1$, that is the refractive index of the material of the lens is less than that of the medium in which it is kept. So, it will act as a diverging lens. So, the rays will diverge after refraction.

Q.4 (i) An object is placed infront of a converging lens at a distance greater than twice the focal length of the lens. Draw a ray diagram to the formation of the image. **[1]**

(ii) An object is placed infront of a convex lens such that the image formed has the same size as that of the object. Draw a ray diagram to illustrate this. **[1]**

Ans. (i) The ray diagram to show the formation of the image is shown below.

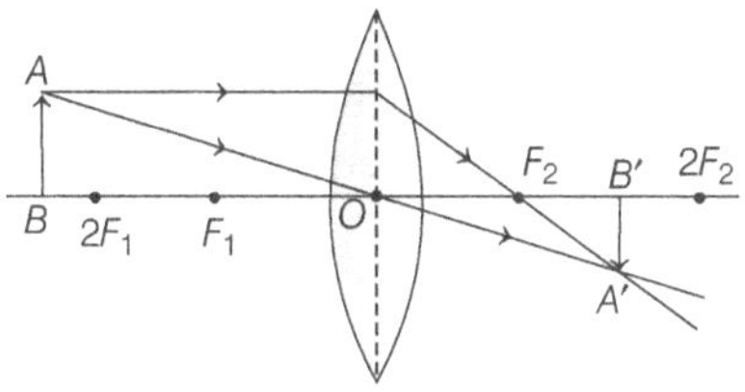

(ii) The ray diagram to show the formation of the image is shown below.

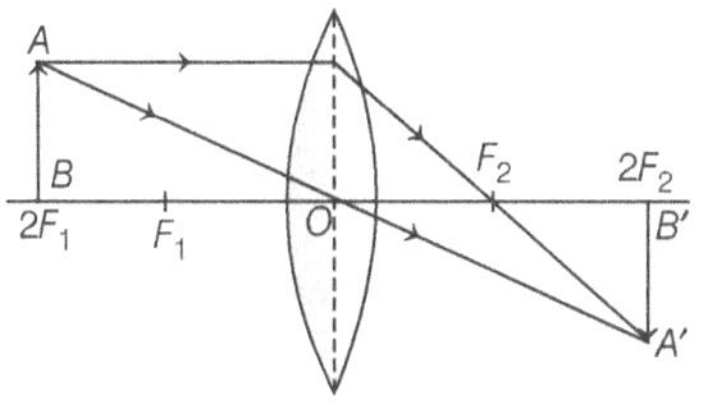

Q.5 An object *AB* is placed between $2F_1$ and F_1 on the principal axis of a convex lens as shown in the diagram.

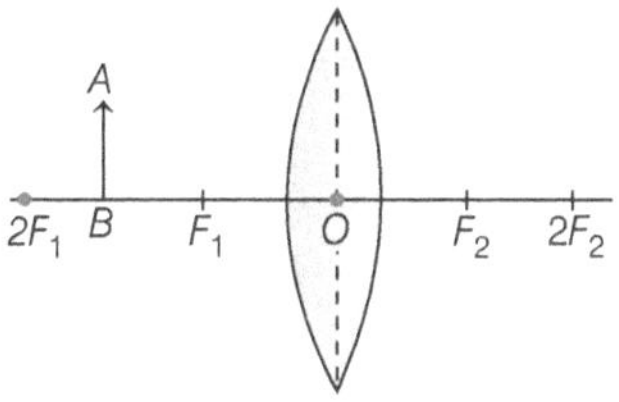

Copy the diagram and using two rays starting from point *A*, obtain the image of the object formed by the lens.

Ans. The formation of image is shown below.

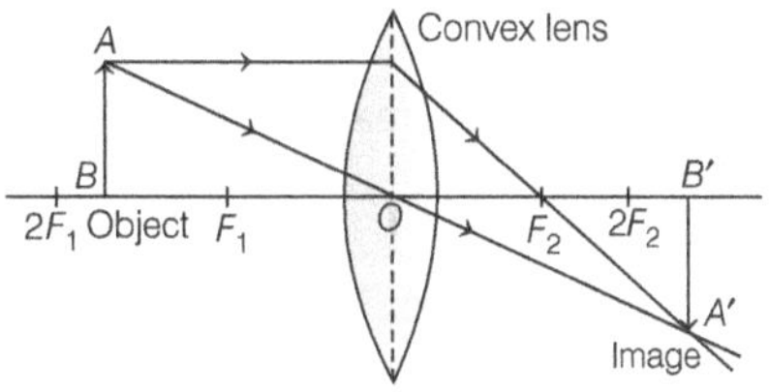

Q.6 *AB* is an object and *PQ* is its real, inverted image. The lengths of *AB* and *PQ* are equal. This is possible when a lens is present between the object and its image.

(i) What kind of lens is used here? Also, state the position of the lens and where it is to be placed. **[1]**

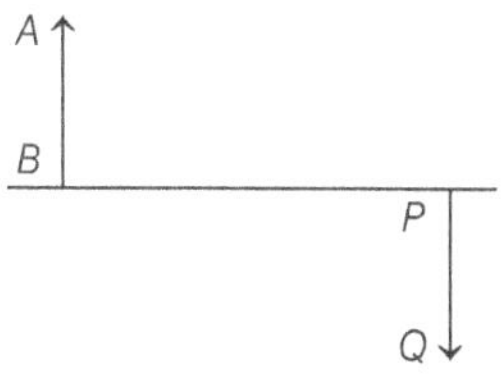

(ii) Name a device where this lens action is used. **[1]**

Ans. (i) Convex lens (converging lens).

The converging lens should be placed halfway between the object *AB* and the image *PQ* such that it has a focal length which is equal to one fourth of the distance between *P* and *B*, since only when an object is placed at a distance $2F$ infront of a lens, an image of the same size as the object is formed at a distance of $2F$ behind the lens.

(ii) Camera

Q.7 Name the part of a lens through which a ray of light passes without suffering any deviation.

Ans. When a ray of light passes through optical centre of the lens (both concave and convex), it will emerge out undeviated (as shown in figure).

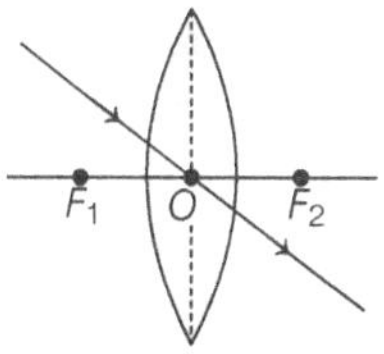

Convex lens

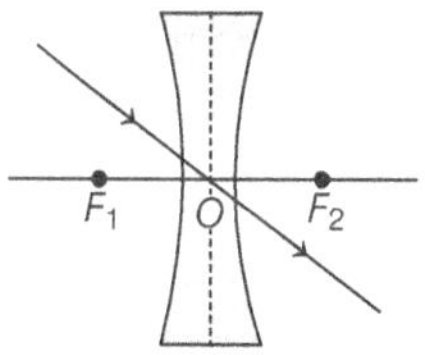

Concave lens

Q.8 (i) If the lens is placed in water instead of air, how does its focal length change? **[1]**

(ii) Which lens, thick or thin has greater focal length? **[1]**

Ans. (i) The refractive index of water is more than air.

When lens is placed in water, its focal length increases.

(ii) A thin lens has greater focal length.

Q.9 State two characteristics of the image of an extended source, formed by a concave lens. **[2]**

Ans. The two characteristics of the image of an extended source formed by a concave lens are

(i) virtual, erect and

(ii) highly diminished, if the object is at infinity and diminished, if the object is between optical centre and infinity.

Q.10 State the position of the object in front of a converging lens, if

(i) it produces a real and same size image of the object. **[1]**

(ii) it is used as a magnifying lens. **[1] [ICSE 2018]**

Ans. (i) To get real and same size image, object is placed at $2F$.

(ii) To use a converging lens as magnifying lens, object must be placed between lens and first focus.

Q.11 (i) Is it possible for a concave lens to form an image of size two times that of the object? Write Yes or No. **[1]**

(ii) What will happen to the focal length of the lens, if a part of the lens is covered with an opaque paper? **[1] [ICSE 2023]**

Ans. (i) No, because concave lens always produces a diminished image.

(ii) The focal length of the lens will not change. The focal length of a lens is a characteristic property of the lens itself and is determined by its shape and refractive index. Thus, covering a portion of the lens with opaque paper will not alter the lens's inherent optical properties.

Q.12 (i) In a reading glass, what is the position of the object with respect to the convex lens used? **[1]**

(ii) Why can we not use concave lens for the same purpose? **[1] [ICSE 2024]**

Ans. (i) In a reading glass, the object is placed between lens and its focus i.e., near the convex lens because convex lens acts as a magnifying lens for this position of object.

(ii) We cannot use concave lens for reading because image formed by the concave lens is virtual erect and highly diminished.

TYPE - 5

03 Marks

Short Answer Type Questions

Q.1 (i) An object is placed at $2F$ position of a convex lens. Draw a ray diagram showing the formation of the image. **[ICSE 2025]**

(ii) How will the size of the image change if we, only replace the lens in the above arrangement with another lens of a greater focal length? **[4]**

Ans. (i)

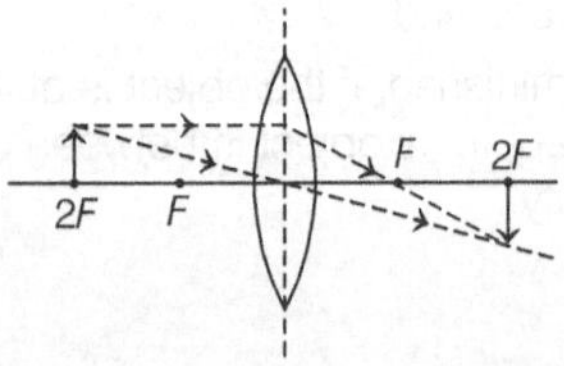

(ii) Since the size of the image in the above case is same as that of the object so it will remain same even if the lens is replaced with a lens of a different focal length.

Q.2 A lens produces a virtual image between the object and the lens.

(i) Name the lens. **[1]**

(ii) Draw a ray diagram to show the formation of this image. **[2] [ICSE 2016]**

Ans. (i) Concave lens is the lens which produces a virtual image between the object and the lens.

(ii) The ray diagram is given below.

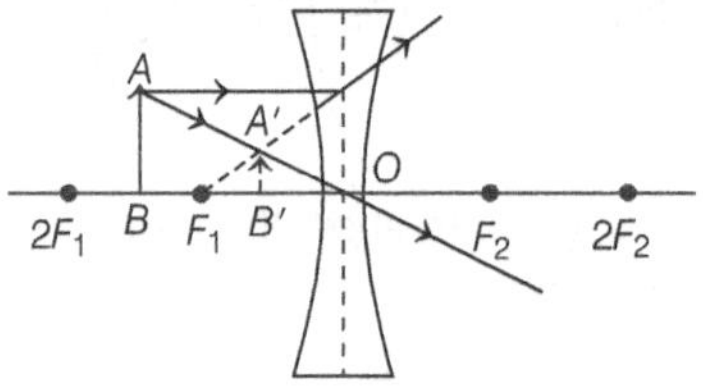

Q.3 A virtual diminished image is formed when an object is placed between the optical centre and the principal focus of a lens.

(i) Name the type of lens which forms the above image. **[1]**

(ii) Draw a ray diagram to show the formation of the image with the above stated characteristics. **[2]** **[ICSE 2019]**

Ans. (i) When an object is placed between the optical centre and the principal focus of a concave lens, then virtual and diminished image of object is formed.

(ii) Ray diagram

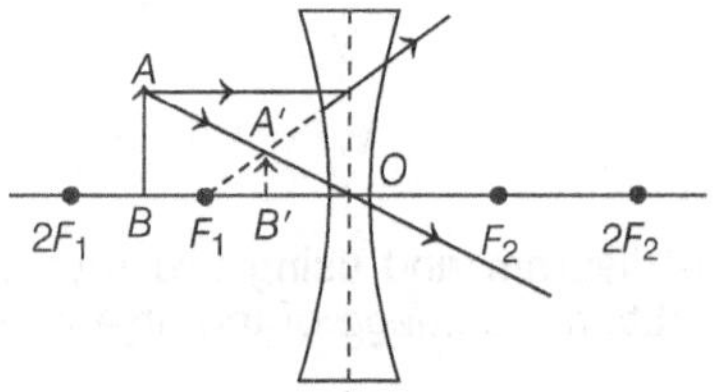

where, f = principal focus

and O = optical centre of lens.

Q.4 A lens forms an erect, magnified and virtual image of an object.

(i) Name the lens. **[1]**

(ii) Draw a labelled ray diagram to show the image formation. **[2]**

Ans. (i) A convex lens forms an erect, magnified and virtual image of an object when the object is placed between the focus and optical centre.

(ii) The ray diagram showing the formation of image is shown below.

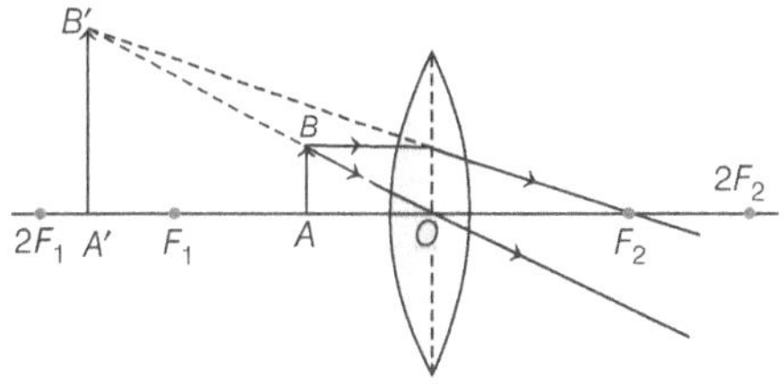

Q.5 Figure below shows a lens treated as a combination of two prisms and a glass block.

(i) Name the lens formed by the combination. **[1]**

(ii) Draw the refraction of two incident rays parallel to its principal axis. **[1]**

(iii) What is the linear magnification produced by the given lens? **[1]**

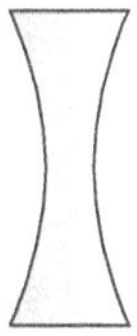

Ans. (i) The lens formed by the combination is a concave lens.

(ii) The ray diagram is shown below.

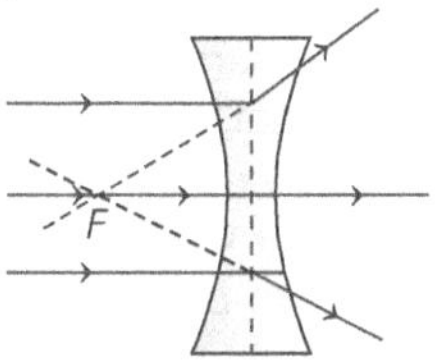

(iii) Since, concave lens always forms a diminished image, hence its linear magnification is always less than one.

Q.6 A convex lens of power +5 D has an object placed at a distance of 50 cm in front of the lens.

(i) State the nature of the image formed. **[2]**

(ii) What is the definite distance, towards or away from the lens, the object should move so that the image is not seen? **[1] [Competency Based Que.]**

Ans. (i) $f = \frac{1}{P} = \frac{1}{5} = 0.2$ m

$\therefore \quad f = 20$ cm

Since, the object is placed beyond $2f$, so the image will be formed infront of the lens and it will be real, inverted and diminished.

(ii) 30 cm towards the lens.

The object should be moved 30 cm towards the lens so that it is placed at the focus of the lens. At f, the magnification is so large that practically the image is not seen.

Q.7 (i) Describe the characteristics of the image formed by a magnifying glass when the object is placed between its optical centre and the focal point. **[2]**

(ii) Why is the image formed by a simple microscope virtual and erect? **[1]**

Ans. (i) When the object is placed between the optical centre and the focal point of the convex lens, the image formed is virtual, erect and magnified. The image appears on the same side of the lens as the object.

(ii) The image is virtual and erect because the light rays diverge after passing through the lens. These diverging rays appear to come from a point on the same side as the object, which forms a virtual image that cannot be projected on a screen.

Q.8 State two applications each of

(i) convex lens

(ii) concave lens

Ans. (i) A convex lens is used

(a) as a magnifying glass.

(b) in spectacles to correct hypermetropia.

(ii) Concave lens is used

(a) in spectacles to correct myopia.

(b) as an eye lens in terrestrial telescope.

TYPE - 6   04 Marks

Long Answer Type Questions

Q.1 The diagram below shows an object *AB* kept in front of the lens. The path of one ray coming from the object is shown. **[ICSE Specimen 2023]**

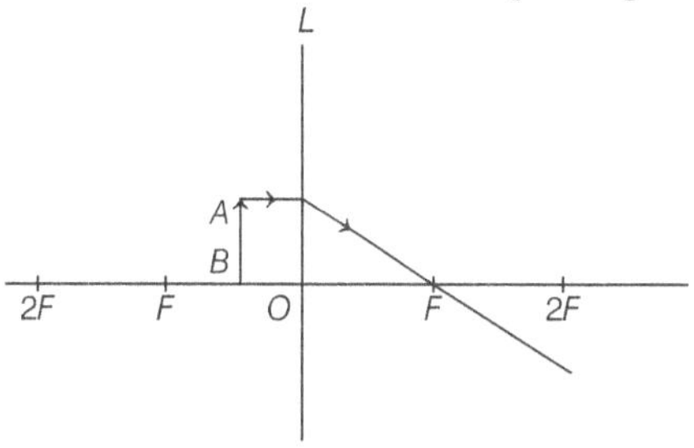

(i) Name the lens *L*. **[1]**

(ii) Redraw and complete the ray diagram showing the formation of the image. **[2]**

(iii) In which optical instrument is this kind of image formed? **[1]**

Ans. (i) It is convex lens.

(ii)

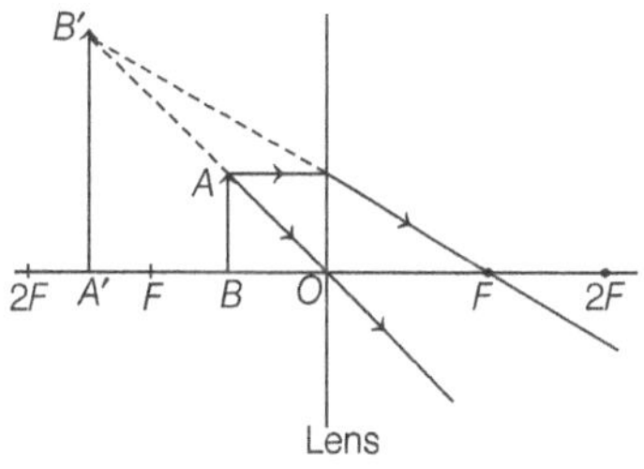

(iii) Simple microscope (Magnifying glass)

Q.2 **A thin converging lens forms a real magnified image and a virtual magnified image of an object in front of it.**

(i) Write the positions of the objects in each case. [1]

(ii) Draw ray diagrams to show the image formation in each part. [2]

(iii) How will the following be affected on cutting this lens into two halves along the principal axis? [1]

(a) Focal length

(b) Intensity of the image formed by half lens

Ans. (i) (a) Object is placed between F and $2F$.

(b) Object is placed between optical centre and F.

(ii) The ray diagrams are shown below.

(a)

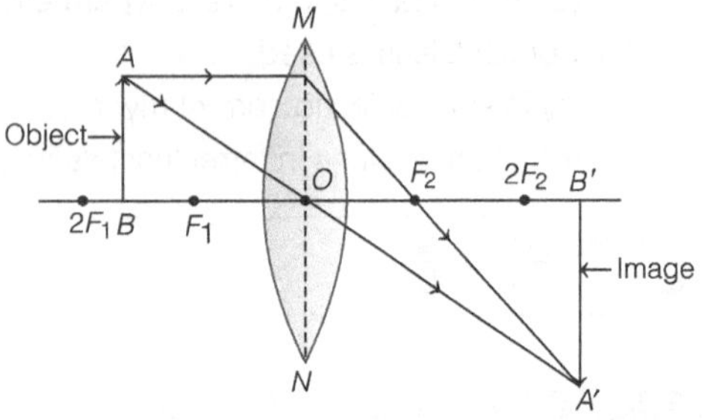

(b)

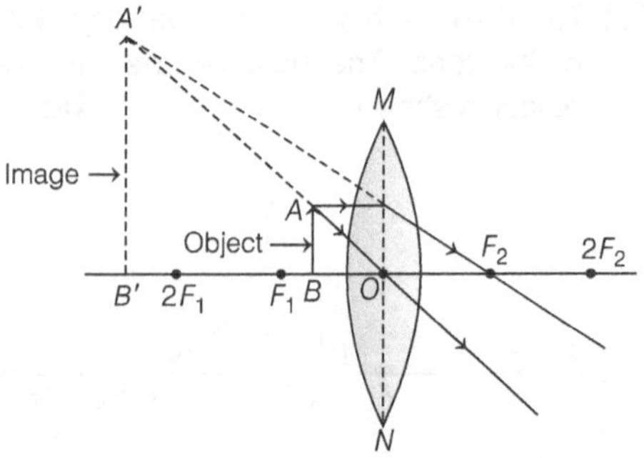

(iii) (a) There will be no change in focal length.

(b) Intensity will reduce.

Q.3 **A student wants to project the image of a candle flame on the walls of school laboratory by using a lens.**

(i) Which type of lens should he use and why? [1]

(ii) At what distance in terms of focal length F of the lens should he place the candle flame, so as to get

(a) a magnified and

(b) a diminished image respectively, on the wall? [1]

(iii) Draw ray diagrams to show the formation of the image in each case. [2]

Ans. (i) He should use a convex lens as real images are formed by it.

(ii) (a) For magnified image, he should place the candle flame between focus (F) and centre of curvature ($2F$) of lens.

(b) To get diminished image, he should place the candle flame beyond centre of curvature ($2F$) of lens.

(iii) (a) For magnified image

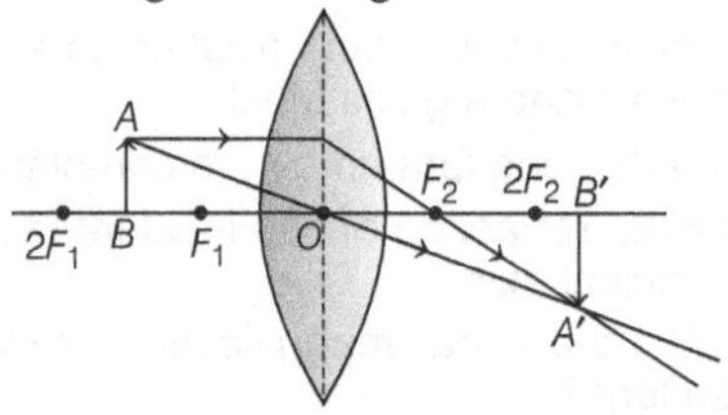

(b) For diminished image

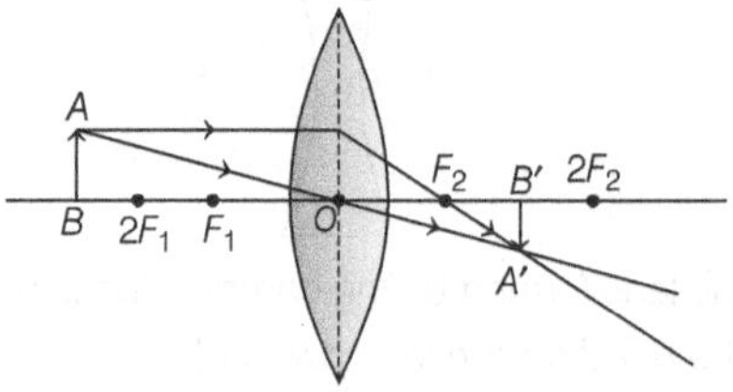

Q.4 **A student wants to burn a piece of paper using a convex lens in day light, rather than using match stick or any direct flame. Will he be able to, if yes justify your answer with a ray diagram?**

Ans. Yes, he will be able to burn a piece of paper using a convex lens in day light without using match sticks or any flame. A convex lens is a converging lens, which means it gathers parallel rays of sunlight and focus them at a single point, known as the focus (F) of the lens. When the paper is placed at this focal point, the radiation from the concentrated sunlight heats it up significantly. If the temperature at the focus exceeds the ignition temperature of the paper, it will catch fire.

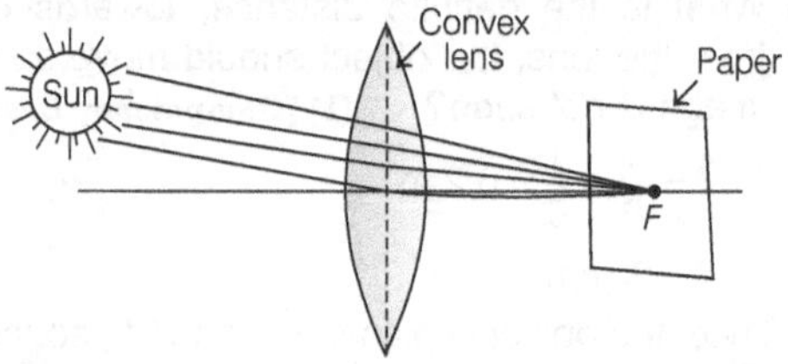

TYPE - 7

03/04 Marks

Case Based Questions

Q.1 **A ray is directed towards a lens as shown in the figure below. The lens is being depicted as a combination of a glass slab and two prisms.**

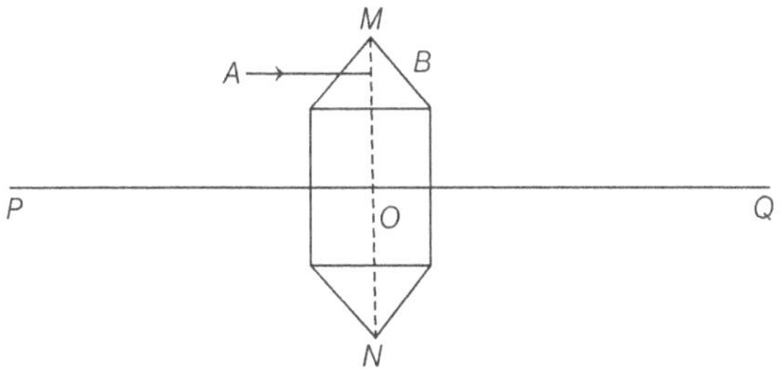

Answer the following questions.

(i) Name the lens which is formed by this combination. **[1]**

(ii) What is the line PQ called? **[1]**

(iii) Complete the path of the ray. **[1]**

(iv) The incident ray after refraction actually meets or appears to meet line PQ at a point. What is this point called? **[1]**

Ans. (i) The lens is convex lens.

(ii) The line PQ is called principal axis.

(iii)

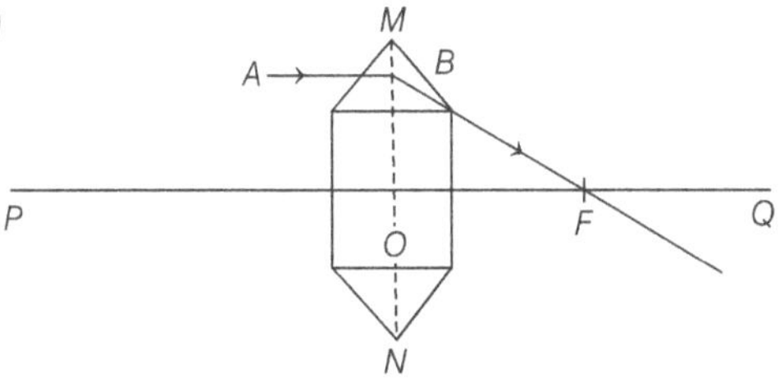

(iv) When an incident ray parallel to the principal axis falls on a convex lens, then after refraction, the emergent ray actually meets at a point on line PQ. This point is known as the focus of the lens.

Q.2 A convex lens is widely used in magnifying glasses, cameras and optical instruments. It converges light rays passing through it and forms different types of images based on the object's position. A student conducted an experiment using a convex lens of focal length 15 cm and placed an object at different positions to observe image formation.

(i) If the object is placed at infinity, what will be the nature and position of the image? **[1]**

(ii) How can a convex lens be used as a magnifying glass? **[1]**

(iii) What will happen to the image if the convex lens is replaced with a concave lens? **[1]**

Ans. (i) When the object is at infinity, the image is formed at the focal point (F). It is real, inverted and highly diminished (point-sized).

(ii) A convex lens acts as a magnifying glass when object is placed between F (focus) and the optical centre.

The image formed is virtual, erect and magnified.

(iii) If the convex lens is replaced with a concave lens, the image will always be virtual, erect and diminished regardless of the object's position.

Q.3 A lens is a piece of any transparent material bounded by two curved surfaces. There are two types of lenses, convex lens and concave lens

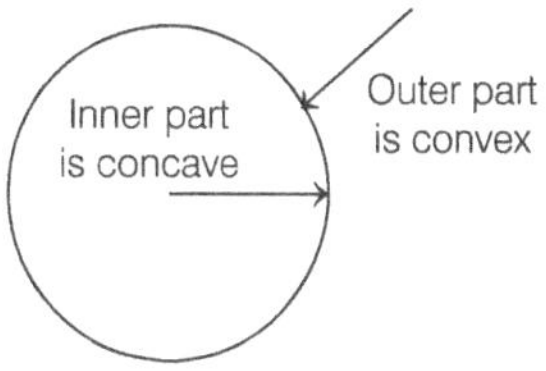

Convex lens is made up of a transparent medium bounded by two spherical surfaces such that it is thicker at the middle and thinner at the edges. Concave lens is also made up of a transparent medium such that it is thicker at edge and thinner at the middle. The mid-point of the lens is called the optical centre.

A convex lens converges a parallel beam of light on the other side after refraction, whereas a concave lens spreads it out.

(i) Which type of lenses are shown in given figures (a) and (b).

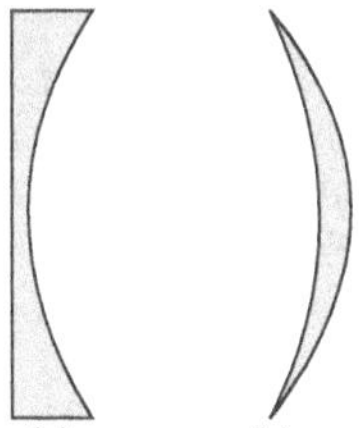

(a) (b)

(ii) Why is a convex lens called a converging lens and a concave lens is called a diverging lens. **[1]**

(iii) Give one practical application each of a convex lens and a concave lens. **[1]**

Ans. (i) (a) Plano-concave lens.

(b) Concave - convex lens.

(ii) A convex lens converges a parallel beam of light on the other side after refraction, whereas a concave lens diverges the parallel rays after refraction. Hence, the convex lens is called converging and concave lens is called diverging.

(iii) **Practical applications**

I Convex lens used in magnifying glasses and cameras.

II Concave lens used in eyeglasses for correcting myopia (near sightedness).

TYPE - 8

Numerical Questions

Q.1 A convergent beam of light passes through the diverging lens of focal length 0.2 m and comes to a point 0.3 m behind the lens. Find the position of the point at which the beam would converge in the absence of the lens. **[2]**

Sol. Given, focal length, $f = -\ 02\text{m}$

$$v = +\ 0.3\text{m}$$

From lens formula,

$$\frac{1}{v} - \frac{1}{u} = \frac{1}{f}$$

$$\frac{1}{u} = \frac{1}{v} - \frac{1}{f} = \frac{1}{0.3} - \frac{1}{(-02)} = \frac{25}{3}$$

$$u = \frac{3}{25} = 0.12 \text{ m}$$

∴ The beam converges at a distance of 0.12 m to the right of the diverging lens which mean that this point acts as an object for the image which is formed at 0.3 m to the right of the lens, in the presence of the diverging lens. This means that in the absence of the lens, the beam will converge at a distance of 0.12 m to the right of the lens.

Q.2 An object is placed in front of a concave lens at a distance of 45 cm from it. If its image is formed at a distance of 30 cm from the lens, calculate the focal length of the lens?

Sol. From lens formula, we know that

$$\frac{1}{v} - \frac{1}{u} = \frac{1}{f}$$

where v is the image distance, u is the object distance and f is the focal length of the lens.

Here, $v = -\ 30$ cm, $u = -\ 45$ cm.

$$\therefore \quad \frac{1}{f} = \frac{1}{(-30)} - \frac{1}{(-45)} = \frac{-1}{30} + \frac{1}{45} = \frac{-1}{90}$$

$$\therefore \quad f = -\ 90 \text{ cm}$$

∴ The focal length of the concave lens is 90 cm.

Q.3 A 6 cm tall object is placed perpendicular to the principal axis of a convex lens of focal length 25 cm. The distance of the object from the lens is 40 cm. By calculation, determine

(i) the position and **[2]**

(ii) the size of the image formed. **[1]**

Sol. Given, height of object, $h_o = 6$ cm

Focal length of lens, $f = 25$ cm

Distance of object, $u = -\ 40$ cm

(i) Using lens formula, $\frac{1}{f} = \frac{1}{v} - \frac{1}{u}$

$$\Rightarrow \quad \frac{1}{v} = \frac{1}{f} + \frac{1}{u} = \frac{1}{25} + \frac{1}{(-40)}$$

$$= \frac{8-5}{200} = \frac{3}{200}$$

$$v = \frac{200}{3} = 66.67 \text{ cm}$$

(ii) ∴ Magnification, $m = \frac{h_i}{h_o} = \frac{v}{u}$

$$\Rightarrow \quad h_i = \frac{v}{u} \times h_o = \frac{66.67}{-40} \times 6 = -\ 10 \text{ cm}$$

Therefore, the size of the image fomed is 10 cm and is real, inveted and magnified.

Q.4 An object is placed at a distance 24 cm in front of a convex lens of focal length 8 cm.

(i) What is the nature of the image so formed?. **[1]**

(ii) Calculate the distance of the image from the lens. **[1] [ICSE Specimen 2025]**

Sol. For convex lens, $f = 8$ cm, $u = -\ 24$ cm

(i) As $u > 2f$, so the image formed is real, inverted and smaller size than the object.

(ii) By lens formula, $\frac{1}{f} = \frac{1}{v} - \frac{1}{u}$

$$\Rightarrow \quad \frac{1}{8} = \frac{1}{v} - \frac{1}{(-24)}$$

$$\Rightarrow \quad \frac{1}{v} = \frac{1}{8} - \frac{1}{24} = \frac{1}{12} \Rightarrow v = 12 \text{ cm}$$

So, the image is formed at 12 cm, infront of the lens.

Q.5 An object of height 20 cm is placed in front of a lens at a distance of 50 cm. Its virtual, diminished image is formed at a distance of 15 cm. **[ICSE 2023]**

(i) Identify the type of the lens. **[1]**

(ii) Calculate the focal length of the lens. **[2]**

Sol. (i) It is concave lens because only concave lens can form virtual and diminished image.

(ii) Lens formula, $\frac{1}{f} = \frac{1}{v} - \frac{1}{u}$

In case of concave lens, u and v both are negative.

$$\text{Therefore,} \quad \frac{1}{f} = \frac{1}{-15} - \frac{1}{-50}$$

$$= \frac{-10+3}{150} = \frac{-7}{150}$$

$$\Rightarrow \quad f = \frac{150}{-7}$$

$$\therefore \quad f = -\ 21.42 \text{ cm}$$

Q.6 At what distance should an object be placed from a convex lens of focal length 18 cm to obtain an image at 36 cm from it? What will be the magnification produced in this case? **[4]**

Sol. For a convex lens, image can be formed at either side of the lens and so v can be both, positive as well as negative.

Given, Focal length of lens, $F = 18$ cm

Distance of image, $v = \pm 36$ cm

Distance of object, $u = ?$

Magnificaiton produced, m = ?

From lens formula, $\frac{1}{v} - \frac{1}{u} = \frac{1}{f}$

Case I

$v = 36$ cm

$\frac{1}{u} = \frac{1}{v} - \frac{1}{f}$

$\frac{1}{u} = \frac{1}{36} - \frac{1}{18} = \frac{1-2}{36} = \frac{-1}{36}$

$\therefore \quad u = -36$ cm

Then, magnification, $m = \frac{v}{u} = \frac{36}{-36} = -1$

Therefore, the image is real, inverted and of the same size as the object.

Case II

$v = -36$ cm

$\frac{1}{u} = \frac{1}{v} - \frac{1}{f}$

$\frac{1}{u} = \frac{1}{-36} - \frac{1}{18} = \frac{-1-2}{36} = \frac{-3}{36} = -\frac{1}{12}$

$\therefore \quad u = -12$ cm

Then, magnification, $m = \frac{v}{u} = \frac{-36}{-12} = 3$

Therefore, the image is virtual, erect and enlarged.

Q.7 A lens of focal length 20 cm forms an inverted image at a distance of 60 cm from the lens. **[ICSE 2020]**

(i) Identify the lens. **[1]**

(ii) How far is the lens present infront of the object? **[2]**

(iii) Calculate the magnification of the image. **[1]**

Sol. (i) A convex lens forms both erect and inverted images while a concave lens always forms erect image, hence the lens must be of a convex lens.

(ii) Real and inverted image, for a convex lens is always formed in front of the lens. Hence, v is taken to be positive.

Given, $v = 60$ cm, $f = 20$ cm

By lens formula, $\frac{1}{v} - \frac{1}{u} = \frac{1}{f}$

$\Rightarrow \quad \frac{1}{60} - \frac{1}{u} = \frac{1}{20}$

$\Rightarrow \quad \frac{1}{u} = \frac{1}{60} - \frac{1}{20}$

$= -\frac{2}{60} = -\frac{1}{30}$

$\Rightarrow \quad u = -30$ cm

Hence, the lens is at a distance of 30 cm in front of the object.

(iii) Magnification of the image,

$$m = \frac{v}{u} = \frac{60}{(-30)} = -2$$

Q.8 (i) One half of a convex lens of focal length 10 cm is covered with a black paper. Can such a lens produce an image of a complete object placed at a distance of 30 cm from the lens? Draw a ray diagram to justify your answer. **[2]**

(ii) A 4 cm tall object is placed perpendicular to principal axis of a convex lens of focal length 20 cm. The distance of the object from the lens is 15 cm. Find the nature, position and the size of the image. **[2]**

Sol. (i) Yes, a lens can form a complete image but of less intensity and brightness because only the upper part of the lens can refract the rays coming from the object.

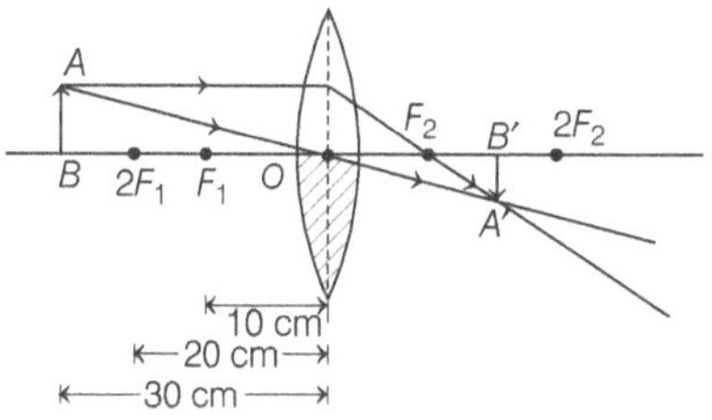

(ii) Given, height of object, $h_o = 4$ cm, focal length, $f = 20$ cm and distance of object, $u = -15$ cm

Using lens formula,

$\frac{1}{f} = \frac{1}{v} - \frac{1}{u}$

$\Rightarrow \quad \frac{1}{v} = \frac{1}{f} + \frac{1}{u} = \frac{1}{20} + \frac{1}{(-15)} = \frac{3-4}{60} = \frac{-1}{60}$

$\therefore \quad v = -60$ cm

As we know that, magnification,

$$m = \frac{h_i}{h_o} = \frac{v}{u}$$

$\Rightarrow \quad h_i = h_o \times \frac{v}{u} = 4 \times \frac{-60}{-15} = 16$ cm

Image formed is virtual, erect and magnified.

Q.9 A convex lens forms a real and inverted image of a needle at a distance of 20 cm from the lens. If the image is of the same size as that of the needle, then where should the needle be placed in front of the lens. Also find the power of the lens. **[3]**

Sol. Given, image distance, $v = 20$ cm

As, height of image (h_i) = Height of object (h_o)

So, magnification, $m = -1$

(image is of the same size, real and inverted)

As we know, $m = \frac{v}{u}$

$\Rightarrow \quad -1 = \frac{20}{u}$, so $u = -20$ cm.

Using $\frac{1}{u} + \frac{1}{v} = \frac{1}{f}$, we get value of f

$$\frac{1}{f} = \frac{1}{20} + \frac{1}{20} = \frac{2}{20}$$

$= 10$ cm

Now, power of lens, $P = \frac{100}{f(\text{in cm})}$

$$= \frac{100}{10} = +10\text{ D}$$

Q.10 **The power of a lens is – 5 D.**

(i) Find its focal length. **[1]**

(ii) Name the type of lens. **[1] [ICSE 2018]**

Sol. Given, power of a lens = – 5 D

(i) We know that,

Power of lens, $P = \frac{1}{f(\text{focal length})}$

or $\quad f = \frac{1}{P} \Rightarrow f = \frac{1}{-5}$

$= -0.2$ m $= -20$ cm

(ii) The power of lens is negative, therefore lens is concave.

Q.11 **(i) A child is using a spectacle with power of – 2.5 D. What is meant by the negative sign?** **[1]**

(ii) Find the focal length of the lens used. **[1]** **[ICSE 2018]**

Sol. (i) Negative sign shows that child is using a concave lens in spectacle, that is the child has short sightedness.

(ii) Power, $P = \frac{1}{\text{Focal length}}$

$$P = \frac{1}{f} \Rightarrow -2.5\text{ D} = \frac{1}{f}$$

$\Rightarrow \quad f = \frac{1}{-2.5} = -0.4\text{ m} = -40$ cm

Q.12 **Two lenses have power of (i) + 2D (ii) –4 D. What is the nature and focal length of each lens?** **[2]**

Sol. (i) Given, $P = +2$ D

Since, power is positive, so the lens is convex lens.

Focal length, $f = \frac{1}{P} = \frac{1}{2} = 0.5\text{ m} = 50$ cm

(ii) Given, $P = -4$ D

Since, power is negative, so the lens is concave lens.

Focal length, $f = \frac{1}{P} = \frac{1}{-4} = -0.25\text{ m} = -25$ cm

Q.13 **Rohit while playing with an old lens, discovers that if he holds the lens 20 cm away from a wall opposite to a window, he can see sharp but inverted images of the outside world on the wall. What is the power of the old lens hold by him?** **[2]**

Sol. Since, the rays from far away objects in outside world get focussed at principal focus, the distance between lens and wall is equal to focal length, i.e. 20 cm.

$\therefore$ Power of lens, $P = \frac{100}{f\text{ (in cm)}} = \frac{100}{20} = 5$ D

Q.14 **(i) If the focal length of a convex lens used as a magnifying glass is 10 cm and the least distance of distinct vision *D* for a person is 25 cm, calculate the magnifying power *M* of the lens.** **[1]**

(ii) If the focal length is halved, how does the magnifying power change? Calculate new magnifying power. **[1]**

Sol. (i) Given, $f = 10$ cm, $D = 25$ cm

We know that, $M = 1 + \frac{D}{f}$

On substituting the given values,

$$M = 1 + \frac{25}{10}$$

$$M = 1 + 2.5 = 3.5$$

So, the magnifying power is 3.5.

(ii) If the focal length is halved,

$$f = \frac{10}{2} = 5\text{ cm}$$

$$M = 1 + \frac{25}{5} = 1 + 5 = 6$$

The new magnifying power is 6.

SPECTRUM OF LIGHT

Prism

- Prism is a **transparent** refracting medium bounded by at least **three lateral surfaces**, inclined to each other at a certain angle. It has **two triangular** and **three rectangular** surfaces.
- The angle between two lateral surfaces through which the refraction occurs is called the **angle of prism** (*A*).

Deviation Produced by a Triangular Prism

- When a ray of light is incident on the prism at its surface, it gets bent towards its base after refraction.
- The deviation produced by a triangular prism is shown below

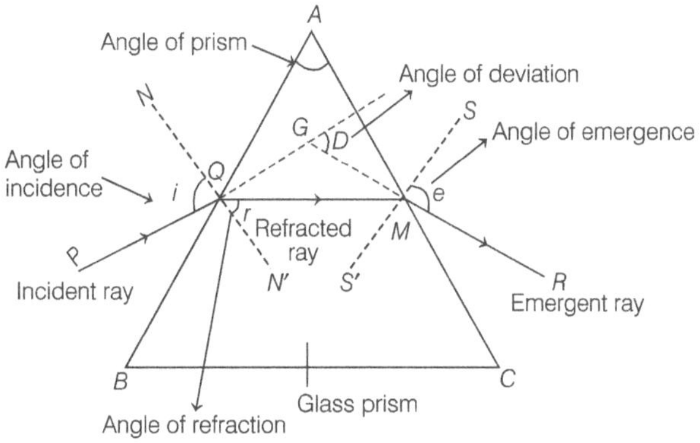

Deviation of light ray through a triangular glass prism

- In the diagram given above, a **ray of light *PQ* enters** from **air to glass** at the **first surface *AB***. As a result, the light ray undergoes refraction and is bent towards the normal.
- At the **second surface** *AC*, the light ray goes from glass to air, causing it to bend away from the normal.
- **Angle of deviation (*D*)** The angle between the direction of incident ray and the emergent ray is called angle of deviation.
- **Angle of deviation depends on three factors**
  (i) Angle of incidence (i) at the first surface
  (ii) Angle of the prism (A)
  (iii) Refractive index of the material of the prism (μ)

Because the refractive index depends on the colour (or wavelength λ) of light used, the angle of deviation depends on the colour of incident light.

Dependence of Deviation on Colour or Wavelength of Light

- Light of different colours has different speeds in a medium. The speed of light in a transparent medium decreases with the decrease in the wavelength of light. [$v = f\lambda$; f is constant; $v \propto \lambda$]
- Therefore, the refractive index of glass increases with decrease in the wavelength of light, so the deviation increases with decrease in the wavelength.
- Thus, in the visible spectrum, red colour (λ = 8000Å) is deviated the least and violet (λ = 4000 Å) is deviated the most.

Dispersion of White Light by a Glass Prism

- The phenomenon of splitting of white light into its constituent colours, when it passes through a prism is called **dispersion of light.**
- This band of seven colours so obtained, the **VIBGYOR** (V = violet, I = indigo, B = blue, G = green, Y = yellow, O = orange and R = red) is called **spectrum**. In other words, the band of seven colours formed on a white screen when a beam of white light is passed through a glass prism is called spectrum.

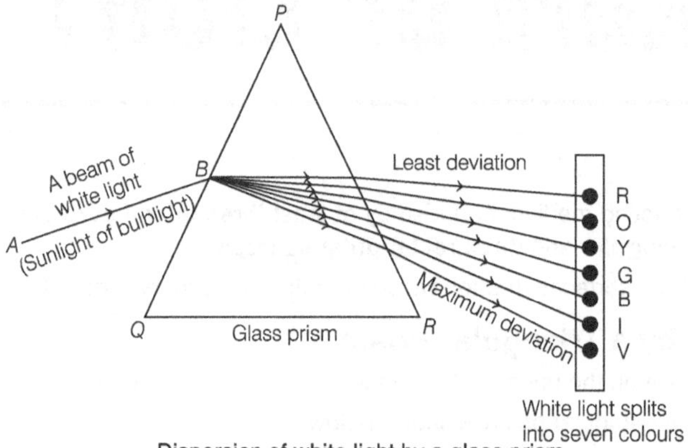

Dispersion of white light by a glass prism

Note **Isaac Newton** was the first one to use a glass prism to obtain the **spectrum of** light.

Cause of Dispersion

- The main causes of dispersion is that the light rays of different wavelength travel with different speeds in any media apart from vacuum or air.
- **Red light** has the **maximum wavelength** and **violet light** has the **minimum wavelength.** So in any medium, red light travels fastest and deviates the least, while violet light travels slowest and deviates the most.

i.e. $$\text{Wavelength} \propto \text{Velocity} \propto \frac{1}{\text{Deviation}}$$

Electromagnetic Spectrum

- The complete arrangement of electromagnetic waves in the increasing order of their wavelengths or decreasing order of their frequencies is known as the electromagnetic spectrum.
- Range of wavelength of electromagnetic spectrum varies from 10^{-12} m to 10^{4} m, i.e. from γ-rays to radio waves.
- The spectrum which has defined boundaries, i.e. various bands of colours do not overlap with each other is called **pure spectrum** whereas, the spectrum which do not have defined boundaries is called **impure spectrum.**
- The portion of the spectrum which lies between the red and the violet regions is called **visible spectrum** and the portion of the spectrum which lies beyond the red and violet regions is called **invisible spectrum.**

Broad Classification of Spectrum in the Increasing Order of Wavelength

The figure shown below shows the various parts of the electromagnetic spectrum with approximate wavelength range.

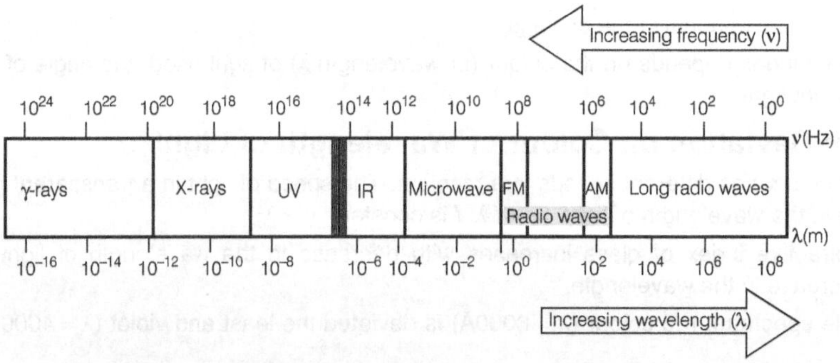

- The table given below shows the various parts of the electromagnetic spectrum with approximate wavelength range, frequency range, their sources of production and detection.

Type	**Wavelength Range** (m)	**Frequency Range** (Hz)	**Production** (Source)	**Detection**
Gamma rays	0.6×10^{-14} to 1×10^{-10}	3×10^{18} to 5×10^{22}	Nuclear origin	Photographic film, ionisation chamber
X-rays	1×10^{-13} to 3×10^{-8}	1×10^{16} to 3×10^{21}	X-rays tubes or excitation of inner shell electron	Photographic film, geiger tubes
Ultraviolet	6×10^{-9} to 4×10^{-7}	8×10^{14} to 5×10^{16}	Excitation of atoms spark and arc lamp	Photocells, photographic film
Visible light	4×10^{-7} to 8×10^{-7}	4×10^{14} to 8×10^{14}	Excitation of valency electrons in atoms	Human eye, photocells, photographic plate
Infrared	8×10^{-7} to 1×10^{-3}	3×10^{11} to 4×10^{14}	Vibrations of atoms and molecules	Thermopile, bolometer, infrared photographic films
Microwave	10^{-3} to 0.3	3×10^{9} to 3×10^{11}	Klystron valve or magnetron valve	Point contact diodes
Radio wave	0.3 to 6×10^{2}	5×10^{5} to 10^{9}	Oscillating circuit or rapid acceleration and retardation of electrons in aerials	Receiver's aerial

Properties Common to all Electromagnetic Spectrum

(i) The electromagnetic waves of entire wavelength range **do not require any material medium** for their propagation.

(ii) They all travel with the same speed in vacuum which is same as the speed of light in vacuum, i.e. $\mathbf{3 \times 10^{8}}$ **m/s.**

(iii) They exhibit the properties of reflection and refraction.

(iv) These waves are not deflected by the electric and magnetic fields.

(v) These waves are transverse waves.

Properties and Uses of Infrared Waves

These waves were discovered by **Herschel.** These waves are also called **heat waves**. These waves are produced from the heat radiating bodies and molecules.

They have high penetration power. Their frequency range is from $\mathbf{3 \times 10^{11}}$ **Hz to** $\mathbf{4 \times 10^{14}}$ **Hz.**

Uses of infrared waves are given below

(i) These are used in physical therapy.

(ii) These are used in satellite for army purpose.

(iii) These are used in weather forecasting.

(iv) These are used for producing dehydrated fruits.

(v) These are used in solar water heater, solar cells and cooker.

(vi) These are used in infrared camera.

Properties and Uses of Ultraviolet Rays

These rays were discovered by **Ritter** in 1801. These are produced by special lamps and very hot bodies. The sun is an important source of UV-rays but fortunately absorbed by ozone layer. Their frequency range is from $\mathbf{10^{14}}$**Hz to** $\mathbf{10^{16}}$**Hz.**

Uses of ultraviolet rays are given below

(i) These are used in burglar alarm.

(ii) These are used in checking mineral sample.

(iii) These are used to study molecular structure.

(iv) To kill germs in water.

(v) To sterilise surgical instruments.

Note The relation among frequency (ν), speed (c) and wavelength (λ) of electromagnetic waves is

$$\text{Frequency }(\nu) = \frac{\text{Speed of EM wave }(c)}{\text{Wavelength }(\lambda)}$$

Scattering of Light

- The deviation of light from its path randomly in all directions, when it falls on suspended particles present in atmosphere is called scattering of light. It is the absorption and re-emission of light by medium particle
- The colour of scattered light depends on the size of scattering particles and wavelength of light.
- When sunlight enters our atmosphere, dust particles and air present in the atmosphere deflects the light in all directions causing the scattering of light.
- **Very fine particles** scatter mainly **blue light** while particles of **larger size scatter** light of longer wavelength (red light). If the size of the scattering particles is large enough, then the scattered light may even appear white, as all the wavelength colours scatter equally.

Some Phenomena Based on Scattering of Light

Red colour of Sun at sunrise and sunset

At the time of sunrise and sunset, light from the Sun has to travel the longest distance of atmosphere to reach the observer. Since, the blue light of short wavelength is scattered more, much of it is lost, while the red light of long wavelength is scattered a little, so it is not much lost and **Sun appears red**.

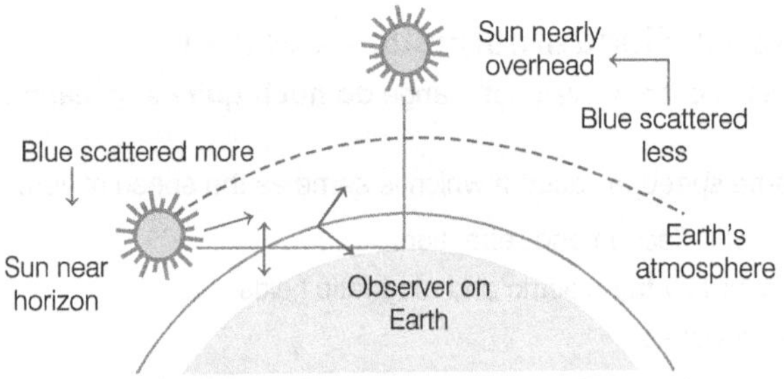

Reddening of the sun at sunrise and sunset

White colour of sky at noon

At noon, the Sun is directly above our head, so we get light rays directly from the Sun after travelling the shortest distance, without much scattering of any particular colour. So, all the colours reach our eye. Hence, the sky is seen white.

Blue colour of sky

The size of particles present in the atmosphere is smaller so they scatter light of shorter wavelength. They are more effective in scattering blue colour. So, when sunlight passes through the atmosphere, blue colour is scattered most, making the colour of sky blue.

If earth had no atmosphere, then there would be no scattering and the sky would have looked dark and black.

Danger signals are red

Colour of dark signals is kept red because red colour is scattered least by atmospheric particles. So it travels longer distances without being scattered. Hence, it is visible from long distances.

Tyndall effect

The earth's atmosphere is a **heterogeneous mixture** of minute particles of smoke, tiny water droplets, suspended particles of dust and molecules of air. When a beam of light strikes such fine particles, the path of the beam become visible. This effect is called Tyndall effect.

Tyndall effect can also be observed when **sunlight passes through a canopy of a dense forest.**

EXAM ORIENTED QUESTIONS

TYPE - 1   01 Mark

Multiple Choice Questions

Q.1 Which one of the following combinations is the correct ascending order of electromagnetic waves in terms of wavelength? **[ICSE 2025]**

(a) Gamma-rays, visible light, microwaves
(b) Microwaves, visible light, gamma-rays
(c) Gamma-rays, microwaves, visible light
(d) Microwaves, gamma-rays, visible light

Ans. (a)

Q.2 The deviation produced by an equilateral prism does not depend on the **[ICSE 2022 Sem-I]**

(a) angle of incidence (b) size of the prism
(c) material of the prism (d) colour of light used

Ans. (b)

Q.3 Light rays are deviated by a prism.

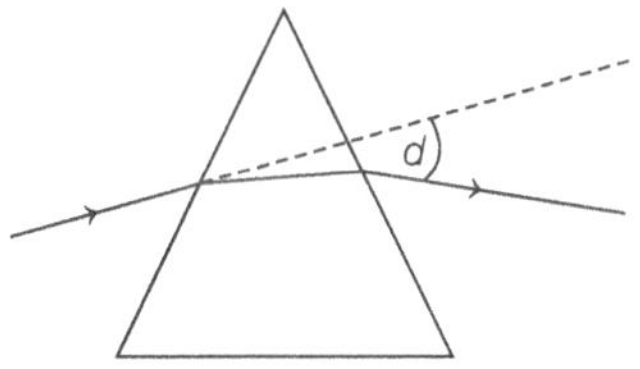

The deviation angle d is measured for light rays of different frequency ν, including blue light and red light. Which graph is correct?

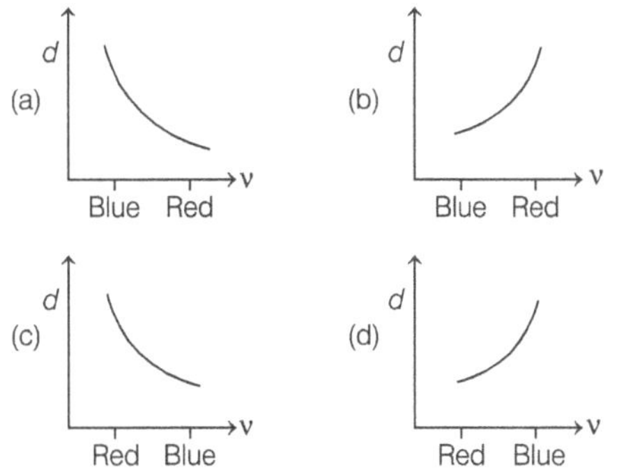

Ans. (d) A glass prism causes dispersion of the component colours of white light as it passes through it. The blue colour refracts more than the red colour. So, the angle of deviation of the blue colour is greater than that of the red colour.

Also, the frequency of the blue colour is greater than that of the red colour.

Q.4 White light is dispersed by a prism. Inside the prism, compared to the blue light, the red light

(a) slows down less and refracts more **[ICSE Spec. 2025]**
(b) slows down more and refracts less
(c) slows down more and refracts more
(d) slows down less and refracts less

Ans. (d) Red light has the longest wavelength among visible light and travels faster inside the prism than blue light, which has a shorter wavelength. Since, red light slows down less, it bends (refracts) less compared to blue light. On the other hand, blue light slows down more and bends more.

Q.5 In the spectrum of white light by a prism, the colour at the extreme end opposite to the base of prism is

(a) violet (b) yellow (c) red (d) blue

Ans. (c) On passing white light through a prism, the band of colours obtained on screen is called spectrum. Starting from the base, the order of colours is violet, indigo, blue, green, yellow, orange and red. So, red is at the extreme end opposite to the base of prism.

Q.6 If a red monochromatic light and a white light is allowed to pass through the following different optical objects. Choose the correct option.

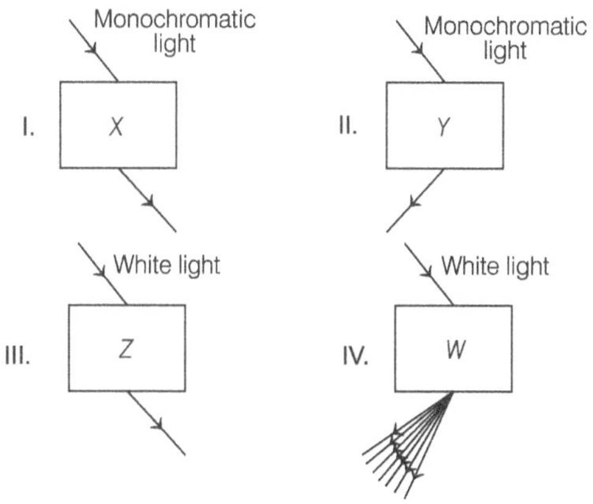

(a) X and Y are glass prisms
(b) Z and W are glass slabs
(c) X, Y and Z are glass slabs and W is glass prism
(d) X and Z are glass slabs and Y and W are glass prisms

Ans. (d) Monochromatic light through glass slab emerged out parallely and monochromatic light through glass prism emerged out at an angle.

White light through glass slab emerged out parallely but through glass prism dispersed in the form of spectrum.

Q.7 Which diagram correctly shows the dispersion of white light by a glass prism?

(a)

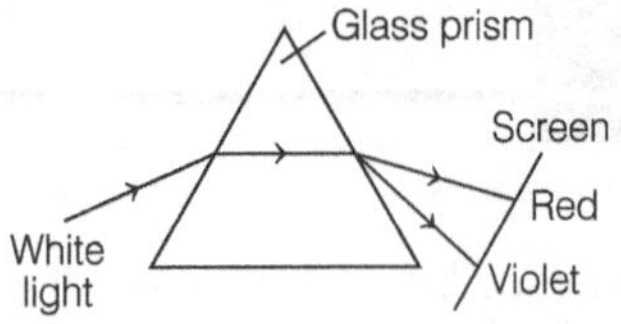

(b)

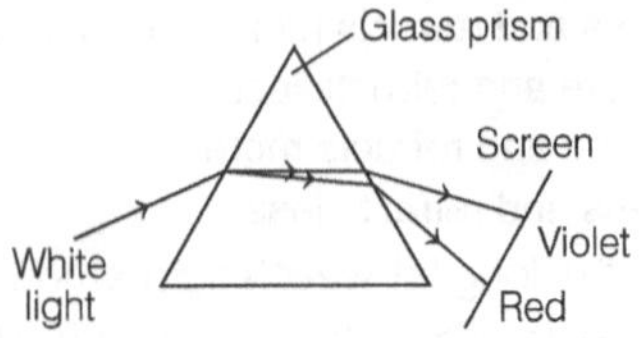

(c)

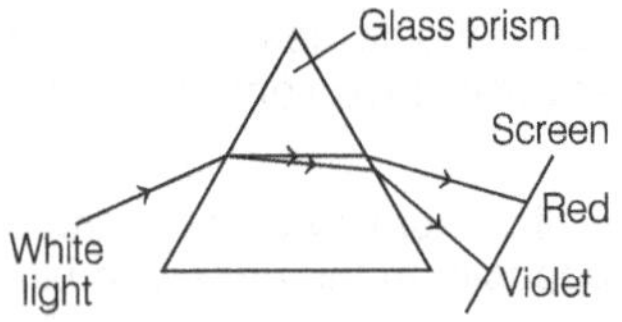

(d)

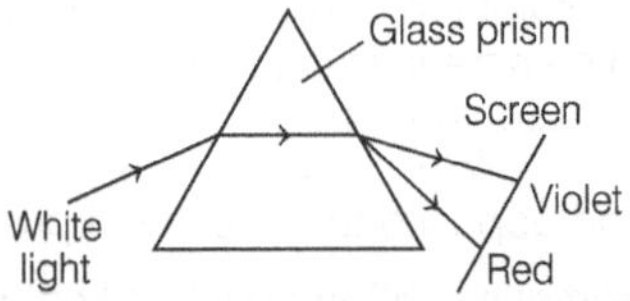

Ans. (c) The dispersed light rays always bend (refract) towards the thicker part (base) of the prism. Red is deviated least from its original path whereas violet is deviated the most.

Q.8 The main cause of dispersion of light is that
(a) they travel with same speed in different media.
(b) they travel with different speed in different media.
(c) they all have same wavelength in different media.
(d) they all have same frequency in different media.

Ans. (b) They travel with different speed in different media.

Q.9 The wavelength range of white light is **[ICSE 2022 Sem-I]**
(a) 4000 nm to 7000 nm (b) 400 nm to 700 nm
(c) 40 nm to 70 nm (d) 4 nm to 7 nm

Ans. (b) The white light or the visible band of spectrum lies in the wavelength range of 400 nm to 700 nm.

Q.10 Speed of blue light in water is **[ICSE 2023]**
(a) more than green light (b) more than orange light
(c) more than violet light (d) more than red light

Ans. (c)

Q.11 Which is correct w.r.t. the increasing order of their wavelength?
(a) Gamma rays < Visible light < Radio waves
(b) UV-rays < X-rays < Microwaves
(c) Radio waves < Gamma rays < Visible light
(d) Microwaves < UV-rays < Infrared ray

Ans. (a)

Q.12 Which of the following EM waves is used in amplitude modulation?
(a) Infrared waves (b) Ultraviolet rays
(c) Radio waves (d) Gamma rays

Ans. (c)

Q.13 Which one of the following EM waves is useful in sterilising surgical instruments?
(a) Microwave (b) UV-rays
(c) X-rays (d) Infrared waves

Ans. (b) UV-rays

Q.14 To an astronaut in a spaceship, the Earth appears
(a) white (b) red
(c) blue (d) black

Ans. (c) Due to scattering of sunlight by the Earth's atmosphere, the Earth appears blue to an astronaut in a spaceship.

Q.15 The scattering of light when it passes through a colloidal solution is called
(a) Tyndall effect (b) Colloidal effect
(c) Atmospheric refraction (d) Scattering

Ans. (a) Tyndall effect

Q.16 The size of the particles in the atmosphere is comparable to the wavelength of blue light. In this context, which of the colours will be scattered the most?
(a) Blue (b) Violet (c) Yellow (d) Red

Ans. (a) Blue light gets scattered the most.

Q.17 What would happen, if the earth had no atmosphere?
(a) Scattering of the light through fine particles
(b) Scattering of the light through large particles
(c) Sky appears dark
(d) Sky appears blue

Ans. (c) The colour of the scattered light depends on the size of scattering particles. If earth had no atmosphere, there would not have been any scattering of light. Then, the sky would have looked black.

Q.18 The wavelength of red light is 800 nm. If speed of light is 3×10^8 ms^{-1}, then its frequency is
(a) 3×10^{14} Hz (b) 3.75×10^{14} Hz
(c) 4.25×10^{14} Hz (d) 4.8×10^{14} Hz

Ans. (b) Given, $\lambda = 800\text{ nm} = 800\times 10^{-9}$ m

$c = 3\times 10^{8}\text{ ms}^{-1}$

Since, frequency,

$$\nu = \frac{c}{\lambda} = \frac{3\times 10^{8}}{800\times 10^{-9}} = 3.75\times 10^{14}\text{ Hz}$$

TYPE - 2 01 Mark

Assertion-Reason Type Questions

Directions (Q. Nos. 1-5) In the following questions two statements are given as Assertion and Reason.

(a) Both A and R are true and R is the correct explanation of A.
(b) Both A and R are true but R is not the correct explanation of A.
(c) A is true but R is false.
(d) A is false but R is true.

Q.1 Assertion (A) A prism splits white light into its constituent colours.

Reason (R) Different colours of light have different speeds in a prism.

Ans. (a) A prism causes dispersion of light because the refractive index of the prism material varies with the wavelength of light. This results in different colours bending by different amounts.

Q.2 Assertion (A) Infrared radiations travel long distances through a dense fog and mist.

Reason (R) Infrared radiations undergo minimal scattering in the Earth's atmosphere.

[ICSE Speciemen 2025]

Ans. (a) The infrared radiations have long wavelengths. So, they undergo minimal scattering in earth's atmosphere and travel long distances in dense fog and mist.

Q.3 Assertion (A) Very fine particles scatter mainly red light, while particles of large size scatter light of shorter wavelengths (Blue).

Reason (R) The colour of the scattered light depends on the size of the scattering particles.

Ans. (d) Very fine particles scatter mainly blue light while particles smaller in size, scatter shorter wavelength.

Q.4 Assertion (A) Sometimes the sky appears reddish in the evening.

Reason (R) Red, being longer in wavelength, scatter more than the other colours.

(a) A and R are true, and R is the reason for A.
(b) A and R are true, and R is not the reason for A.
(c) A is true, but R is false.
(d) A is false, but R is true.

Ans. (c) Red light scatters the least, while shorter wavelengths like blue scatters more. During sunset, the sun's light travels a longer distance through the atmosphere, and shorter wavelengths (blue and violet) scatter away.

This leaves mostly red and orange light, making the sky appear reddish.

Q.5 Assertion (A) When a fine beam of sunlight enters a smoke-filled room through a small hole, makes the particles visible.

Reason (R) The phenomenon of scattering of light by the colloidal particles gives rise to Tyndall effect, which makes the particles visible.

Ans. (a)

TYPE - 3 01/02 Marks

Fill in the Blanks

Q.1 The colors of light that deviates the least while passing through a prism is .... (red/blue/violet)

Ans. red

Q.2 In a prism, the colour that bends the most is .... (red/yellow/violet)

Ans. violet

Q.3 .... (Infrared, UV-rays, Microwaves) are used in weather forecasting whereas .... (Infrared/X-rays /UV-rays) are useful in checking mineral samples.

Ans. Infrared, UV-rays

Q.4 Very fine particles in the atmosphere mainly scatter .... (red/blue/green) light while particles of larger size scatter .... (yellow/red/blue)

Ans. blue, red

TYPE - 4 02 Marks

Very Short Answer Type Questions

Q.1 (i) What do you mean by dispersion and spectrum? **[1]**

(ii) Draw the diagram to show dispersion of white light by the glass prism. **[1]**

Ans. (i) The splitting of light into its component colours is called dispersion.

The band of the coloured components of a light beam is called spectrum.

(ii)

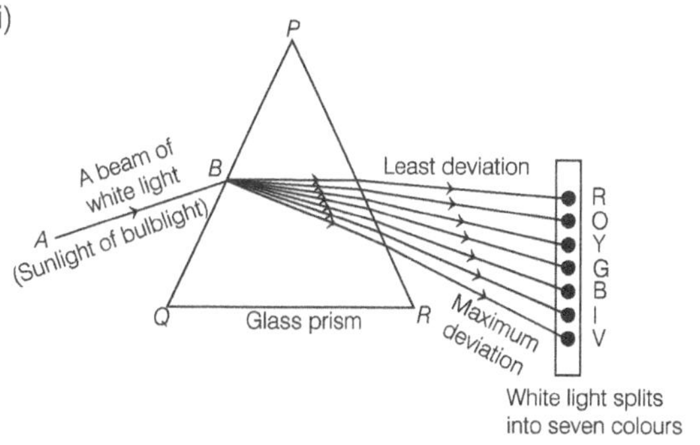

Q.2 (i) Why is the ratio of the velocities of light of wavelengths 4000 Å and 8000 Å in vacuum 1 : 1? **[1]**

(ii) Which of the above wavelengths has a higher frequency? **[1] [ICSE 2018]**

Ans. (i) In vacuum light or any electromagnetic wave velocity is always constant 3×10^8 m/s and it does not depend on wavelength or frequency.

(ii) The light of wavelength 4000 Å will have higher frequency.

Q.3 The wavelengths for the light of red and blue colours are nearly 7.8×10^{-7}m and 4.8×10^{-7}m, respectively.

(i) Which colour has the greater speed in a vacuum? **[1]**

(ii) Which colour has a greater speed in glass? **[1]** **[ICSE 2020]**

Ans. Given, wavelength of light for red colour,

$$\lambda_R = 7.8 \times 10^{-7}\text{m}$$

Wavelength of light for blue colour,

$$\lambda_B = 4.8 \times 10^{-7}\text{m}$$

$$\therefore \quad \lambda_R > \lambda_B$$

(i) Speed of light in vacuum is independent to the wavelength of light. Hence, red colour of light has equal speed in vacuum as the blue colour of light.

(ii) For same medium, speed of light is directly proportional to its wavelength. Therefore, speed of red colour of light is greater than speed of blue colour of light as $\lambda_R > \lambda_B$.

Q.4 (i) Name a prism required for obtaining a spectrum of ultraviolet light. **[1]**

(ii) Name the radiations which can be detected by a thermopile. **[1]**

Ans. (i) Quartz prism is required for obtaining a spectrum of ultraviolet light.

(ii) Infrared radiations can be detected by a thermopile.

Q.5 (i) Name the high energetic invisible electromagnetic waves, which help in the study of the structure of crystals. **[1]**

(ii) State an additional use of the waves mentioned in part (i). **[1] [ICSE 2015]**

Ans. (i) X-rays are used to study the structure of a crystal.

(ii) Uses of X-rays are

I. In surgery for the detection of fractures, foreign bodies like bullets, stones in human body, etc.

II. For detecting faults, cracks, flaws and holes in the final products of metals.

III. To cure untrackable skin diseases and malignant growths.

Q.6 An electromagnetic radiation is used for photography in fog. **[ICSE 2019]**

(i) Identify the radiation. **[1]**

(ii) Why is this radiation mentioned by you, ideal for this purpose? **[1]**

Ans. (i) Infrared radiations are used in photography in fog and mist and also at night.

(ii) Because infrared radiation have long wavelength. As they are having low frequency the energy associated with them is also low. So, they do not scatter much and can penetrate appreciably through fog.

Q.7 (a) Why does the sky appear blue during the day? **[1]**

(b) What happens to the blue colour of the sky at higher altitudes? **[1]**

Ans. (a) The sky appears blue because the particles in the atmosphere scatter shorter wavelengths of light, such as blue, more effectively than longer wavelengths.

(b) At higher altitudes, the sky appears black because there are fewer air particles to scatter the light.

TYPE - 5   03 Marks

Short Answer Type Questions

Q.1 The diagram below shows the extreme colours of a visible spectrum (*X* and *Y*). **[ICSE Specimen 2023]**

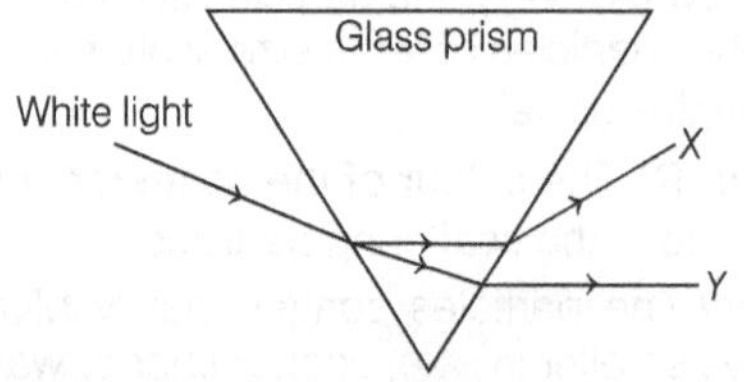

(i) Identify the colours *X* and *Y*. **[1]**

(ii) Which colour has greater speed in vacuum? **[2]**

Ans. (i) *X* is violet colour and *Y* is red colour.

(ii) In prism all the colours have same speed, while when they passes through the another medium like water the red light have the greatest speed.

Q.2 When sunlight passes through water droplets in the atmosphere it gets dispersed into its constituent colours forming a rainbow. A similar phenomenon is observed when white light passes through a prism.

(i) Which colour will show the maximum angle of deviation and which colour will show the minimum angle of deviation? **[2]**

(ii) If instead of sunlight, a green-coloured ray is passed through a glass prism. What will be the colour of the emergent ray? **[1]**

[ICSE Specimen 2025, 24]

Ans. (i) When sunlight passes through water droplets in the atmosphere or through a prism, violet light shows the maximum angle of deviation, while red light shows the minimum angle of deviation.

(ii) The colour of emergent ray will be green. A prism does not change the colour of light. It just disperses white light into its constituent colours.

Q.3 A type of electromagnetic wave has wavelength 50 Å.

(i) Name the wave. **[1]**

(ii) What is the speed of the wave in vacuum? **[1]**

(iii) State one use of this type of wave. **[1]**

Ans. (i) The wave is X-ray as its range is 0.1 Å to 100 Å.

(ii) The speed of wave in vacuum is 3×10^8 m/s.

(iii) X-rays are used for detection of fractures in bone, teeth etc.

Q.4 Below is an incomplete table showing the arrangement of electromagnetic spectrum in the increasing order of their wavelength. Complete the table

Gamma ray
X-ray
UV-rays
Visible rays
Infrared
A
Radio waves

(i) Identify the radiation *A*. **[1]**

(ii) Name the radiation used to detect fracture in bones. **[1]**

(iii) Name one property common to both *A* and radio waves. **[1]**

Ans. (i) Radiation *A* is microwaves

(ii) X-rays

(iii) Radio waves and microwaves travel at the same speed through a vacuum.

Q.5 Give one use of each of the electromagnetic radiations given below

(i) Microwave, (ii) Ultraviolet radiation, **[2]**

(iii) Infrared radiation. **[1] [ICSE Specimen 2018]**

Ans. (i) Microwaves are used for analysis of atomic and molecular structure.

(ii) Ultraviolet radiations are used for sterilizing purposes.

(iii) Infrared radiations are used for therapeutic purposes by doctors.

Q.6 (i) Name the radiations **[4] [ICSE 2025]**

(a) for which a quartz prism is used to study the spectrum.

(b) which are used in remote sensing devices.

(c) which are used in traffic signals in India.

(b) Name one property common to all electromagnetic radiations.

Ans. (i) (a) Ultraviolet radiation

(b) Infrared radiation

(c) Visible light

(ii) All electromagnetic waves travel with the same speed in vacuum that is 3×10^8 m/s.

TYPE - 6 04 Marks

Long Answer Type Questions

Q.1 The refraction of a monochromatic ray through a prism is shown in the figure.

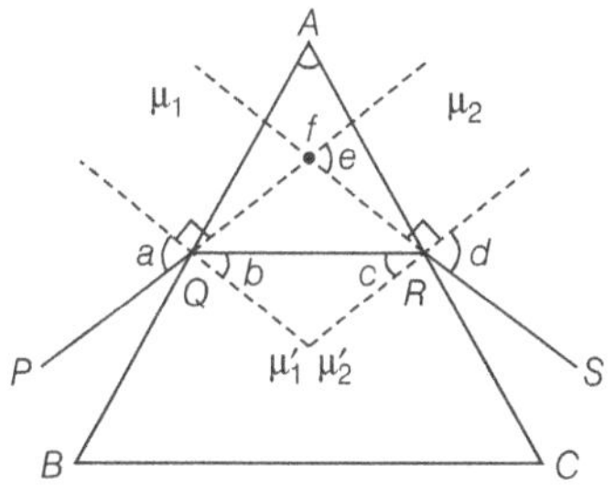

Complete the table, using the labels from the figure. The first label is done for you.

Description	Label
Angle of incidence	*a*
Angle of refraction	
Angle of emergence	
Angle of deviation	
Angle of prism	

Ans.

Description	Label
Angle of incidence	*a*
Angle of refraction	*b*
Angle of emergence	*d*
Angle of deviation	*e*
Angle of prism	*f*

Q.2 The diagram below shows two parallel rays *A* (orange) and *B* (blue) incident from air, on air-glass boundary. **[ICSE 2023]**

(i) Copy and complete the path of the rays *A* and *B*. **[1]**

(ii) How do the speeds of these rays differ in glass? **[1]**

(iii) Are the two refracted rays in glass parallel? Give a reason. **[2]**

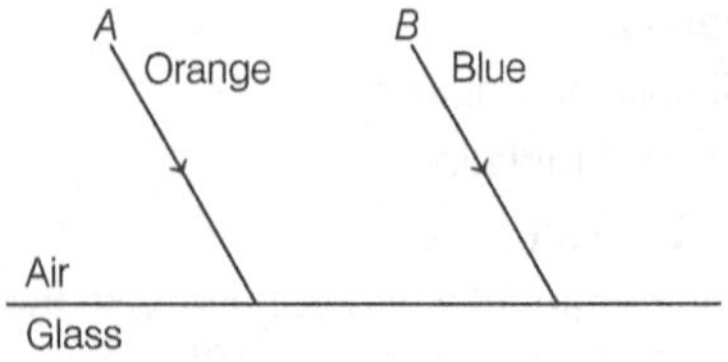

Ans. (i)

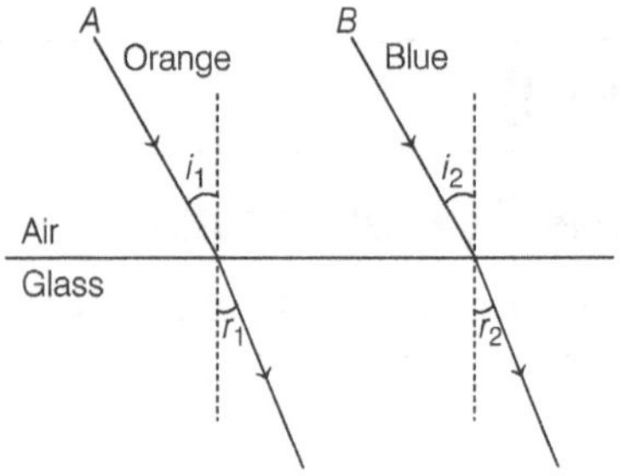

(ii) Since, the refractive index of glass is less for orange light and it is more for blue light ($\mu_O < \mu_B$) in glass, the orange light travels faster than blue light.

(iii) The two refracted rays inside glass are not parallel. The reason is that the speed of orange light in glass is more, while it is less for the blue light, so the orange ray bends less, and the blue ray bends more (i.e. angle of refraction r_1 for orange is more than angle of refraction r_2 for blue ray).

($\mu_O < \mu_B$) in glass, the orange light travels faster than blue light.

Q.3 (i) Infrared radiations are used in warfare. Explain with reason. Why? **(2)**

(ii) A ray of white light is incident at 45° on an equilateral prism in the diagram below.

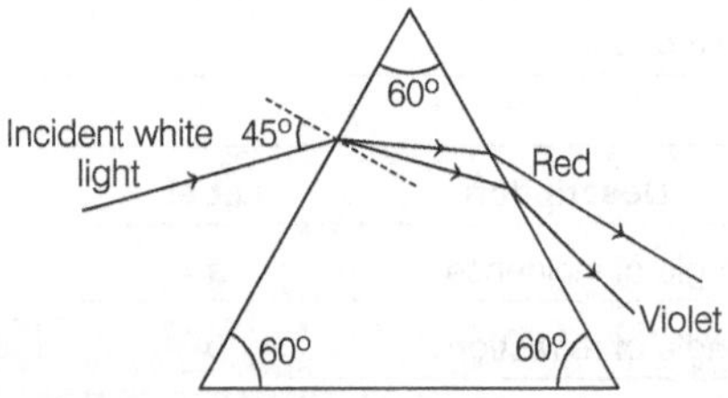

(a) Name the phenomenon exhibited by the ray of light when it enters and emerges out of the prism. **[1]**

(b) State the cause of the above phenomenon mentioned by you. **[1] [ICSE 2023]**

Ans. (i) Infrared radiations are used as signals during warfare as they are not visible and they are not absorbed much in the medium. They have more λ and less scattering. Therefore, they can be used as signals on distant objects obscured by atmospheric haze.

(ii) (a) When white light ray passes through a prism, it disperses into seven different colours and this phenomenon is called dispersion.

(b) When white light ray passes through a glass prism, its constituent colours (red, orange, yellow, green, blue, indigo, violet) travel with different speeds in the prism because the refractive index is colour dependent. Their angle of deviation are different. This causes the dispersion of light.

Q.4 X-rays, microwaves, ultraviolet and infrared are different types of radiation in the electromagnetic spectrum.

(i) Write the name of one of these types of radiation in each of the boxes, placing them in order of increasing wavelength. **[1]**

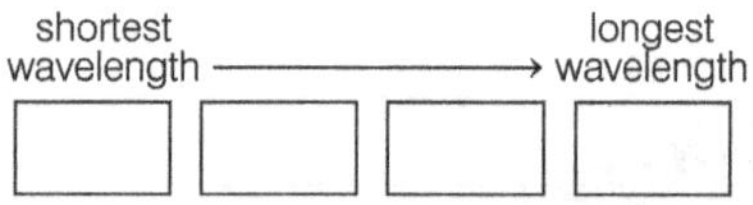

(ii) State two uses of ultraviolet radiation. **[1]**

(iii) State two properties that all types of radiation in the electromagnetic spectrum have in common. **[2]**

Ans. (i) X-rays , ultraviolet , infrared, microwaves

(ii) (a) Checking for counterfeit notes.

(b) Sterilising medical equipment.

(iii) (a) All electromagnetic waves are unaffected by electric or magnetic fields.

(b) All electromagnetic waves travel with the same speed in a vacuum.

Q.5 Fig. shows some of the colours in the visible part of the electromagnetic spectrum.

Red	Orange	Yellow	Green	Blue

(i) State which colour in Fig. has

(a) the largest wavelength, **[1]**

(b) the highest frequency. **[1]**

(ii) Visible light, infrared, ultraviolet and radio waves are four components of the electromagnetic spectrum. **[2]**

State two other components of the electromagnetic spectrum and describe a different use that is made of each component.

Ans. (i) (i) Red (ii) Blue

(ii) 1. Component : Microwaves

Description of use Satellite televisions use microwaves to receive television programmes *via* satellites in space because microwaves are highly directional and can penetrate haze, rain, snow, clouds and smoke.

2. Component : Gamma rays

Description of use These high energy rays are used to treat cancer by killing the cancer cells in cancerous tumours.

TYPE - 7 03/04 Marks

Case Based Questions

Q.1 **A glass prism is placed on a table, and a narrow beam of white light is passed through it. The emergent light shows a band of seven colours on a screen.**

(i) Why does the white light split into seven colours when passed through the prism? [1]

(ii) Name the phenomenon responsible for the splitting of light? [1]

(iii) Arrange the seven colours of light in increasing order of their wavelengths? [1]

(iv) Which colour deviates the least, and which deviates most? [1]

Ans. (i) The white light splits into seven colours due to phenomenon of dispersion different colours of light have different wavelengths, and they refract by different amounts when passing through the prism.

(ii) The phenomenon is called dispersion of light.

(iii) The seven colours in increasing order of wavelength are; violet, indigo, blue, green, yellow, orange, red.

(iv) Red colour deviates the least and violet colour deviates most.

Q.2 **The figure given below shows a thin beam of white light from a source *S* striking on one face of prism.**

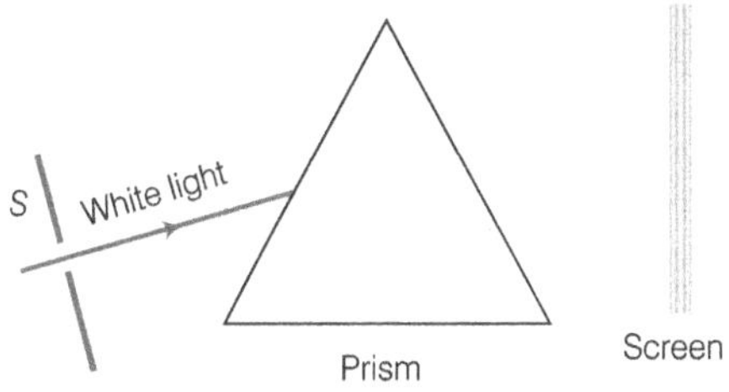

(i) In order to show the effect of the prism on the beam, complete the diagram, so that it can represent what is seen on the screen. [1]

(ii) Assume if a slit is placed between the prism and the screen to pass only the light of green colour, then what observation will you get on the screen? [1]

(iii) State the conclusion that you draw from the observation in part (ii) above. [1]

Ans. (i) As we can see in the figure, a pattern of seven colours is formed on the screen with red on the top and violet at the bottom.

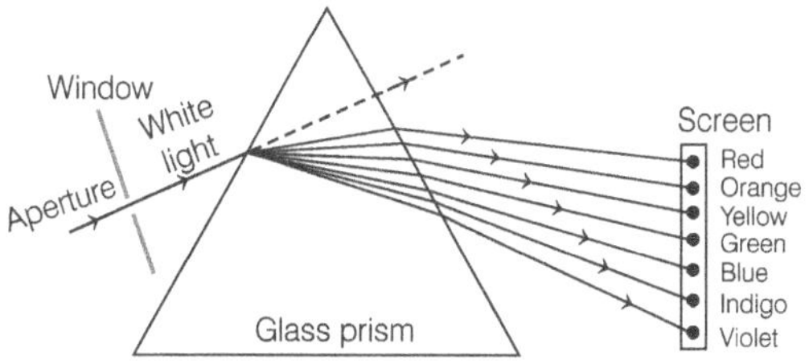

(ii) Since, a green filter transmits only green light. Therefore, it is placed between the prism and the screen, the spectrum on the screen will appear dark except for the region near the green part in the original spectrum.

(iii) It proves that the prism by itself produces no colour.

TYPE - 8

Numerical Questions

Q.1 **An electromagnetic wave of frequency 40 MHz travel in free space in the *x*-direction. Determine the wavelength of the wave. [2]**

Ans. Given, frequency, $\nu = 40 \text{ MHz} = 40 \times 10^6$ Hz

Speed of wave, $v = 3 \times 10^8$ m / s

$\because$ Wavelength of wave,

$$\lambda = \frac{\text{Speed of wave } (v)}{\text{Frequency } (\nu)}$$

Substituting the given values, we get

$$\lambda = \frac{3 \times 10^8}{40 \times 10^6} = 7.5 \text{ m}$$

Q.2 **What is the wavelength of an electromagnetic wave whose frequency is 10^{15} Hz? Name this electromagnetic wave. [3]**

Ans. Given, frequency, $\nu = 10^{15}$ Hz,

Speed of wave, $v = 3 \times 10^8 \text{ms}^{-1}$

Using the relation,

$\because$ Wavelength of wave,

$$\lambda = \frac{\text{Speed of wave } (v)}{\text{Frequency } (\nu)}$$

Substituting the given values, we get

$$\lambda = \frac{3 \times 10^8}{10^{15}}$$

$$= 3 \times 10^{-7} \text{ m} = 300 \text{ nm}$$

Such a wave is infrared wave, whose wavelength varies from 10 nm to 400 nm.

Q.3 The wavelength of electromagnetic radiation is 900 nm. Find its frequency.
(Take, speed of radiation = $3 \times 10^8 ms^{-1}$) **[2]**

Ans. Given, wavelength, $\lambda = 900 nm$

$$= 900 \times 10^{-9} m$$

$$= 9 \times 10^{-7} m$$

Speed of radiation, $v = 3 \times 10^8 ms^{-1}$

As we know,

$$\text{Frequency, } \nu = \frac{\text{Speed of electromagnetic radiation}}{\text{Wavelength}}$$

Substituting the given values, we get

$$\nu = \frac{3 \times 10^8}{9 \times 10^{-7}} = 0.33 \times 10^{15}$$

$$= 3.3 \times 10^{14} Hz$$

Q.4 A radio can tune into any station in 7.5 MHz to 12 MHz band, what is the corresponding wavelength band? **[3]**

Ans. Given, frequency range = 7.5 MHz to 12 MHz

$$= 7.5 \times 10^6 \text{ Hz to } 12 \times 10^6 \text{ Hz}$$

Speed of radio waves, $v = 3 \times 10^8 ms^{-1}$

From the relation,

Speed of wave (v) = Wavelength (λ) $\times$ Frequency (ν)

$$\Rightarrow \quad \lambda = \frac{v}{\nu}$$

$$\therefore \quad \lambda_1 = \frac{3 \times 10^8}{7.5 \times 10^6} = 40 \text{ m}$$

and

$$\lambda_2 = \frac{3 \times 10^8}{12 \times 10^6} = 25 \text{ m}$$

$\therefore$ The corresponding wavelength band is 40 m-25 m.

07

SOUND

Sound is a form of energy which causes a **sensation of hearing**. It is produced by vibrating objects. Sound requires a medium for its propagation.

Reflection of Sound Wave

The **bouncing back of the sound** wave on striking a surface such as a wall, metal sheet, plywood, etc., is called the reflection of sound wave.

Echo

- The sound heard after reflection from a distant obstacle (such as a cliff, a hillside, wall of a building, edge of a forest, etc.) after the original sound has ceased, is called an echo.
- The sensation of sound persists in our ears for about 0.1 s after the exciting stimulus ceases to act. Hence, to hear an echo distinctly, the reflected sound must reach the ears at least 0.1 s after the original sound.

To **hear the echo distinctly**, following three conditions must be satisfied

(i) The **minimum distance** between the source of sound (or observer) and the reflector in air must be **17 m.** It is different in different medium depending upon the speed of sound in that medium.

(ii) The **size of the reflector** must be large enough as compared to the wavelength of the sound wave.

(iii) The **intensity of sound** should be such that the reflected sound reaching the ear is sufficiently loud to be audible.

Determination of Speed of Sound By Echo

- The phenomenon of echo can be used to determine the speed of sound in air.
- Let d be the distance between the observer and the obstacle and v be the speed of sound. Then, the total distance travelled by the sound to reach the obstacle and then to come back is $2d$ and the time taken is given by

$$\text{Time taken} = \frac{\text{Total distance travelled by the sound}}{\text{Speed of sound}} = 2d/v \quad \text{or } d = vt/2$$

$$\therefore \text{ Speed of the sound, } \boxed{v = 2d/t \text{ ms}^{-1}}$$

As we know, the minimum distance between the source and sound to hear echo is 17 m.

$$\therefore \quad v = \frac{2 \times 17}{0.1} = 340 \text{ ms}^{-1}$$

Use of Echoes by Bats, Dolphins and Fisherman

- The **sounds produced by flying bats** get reflected from an obstacle in front of it. By hearing the echoes, bats are able to detect obstacles in the dark. Hence, they can fly safely without colliding with the obstacles. This process of detecting obstacles is called **sound ranging**.
- **Dolphins** detect their enemies and obstacles by **emitting ultrasonic waves** and hearing their echo. They use ultrasonic waves for hunting their prey.
- A **fisherman** sends a **pulse of ultrasonic waves** from a source into the sea and receives the waves reflected from the shoal of fish via a detector.

Use of Echoes in Medical Field

- Echoes of the ultrasonic waves are used to investigate the internal organs of human body such as liver, gall bladder, pancreas, kidneys, uterus, heart, etc. This is called **ultrasonography**.
- Ultrasonic waves are made to reflect from various part of the heart and form the image of the heart. This technique is called **echocardiography**.

SONAR

- The SONAR stands for **Sound Navigation And Ranging.** Sonar is an apparatus used to find the depth of a sea or to locate the underwater things like shoals of fish, shipwrecks and enemy submarines.
- It uses **ultrasonic waves** to measure the distance, direction and speed of underwater objects.
- It consists of three parts; a **transmitter**, a **detector** and a **receiver**.

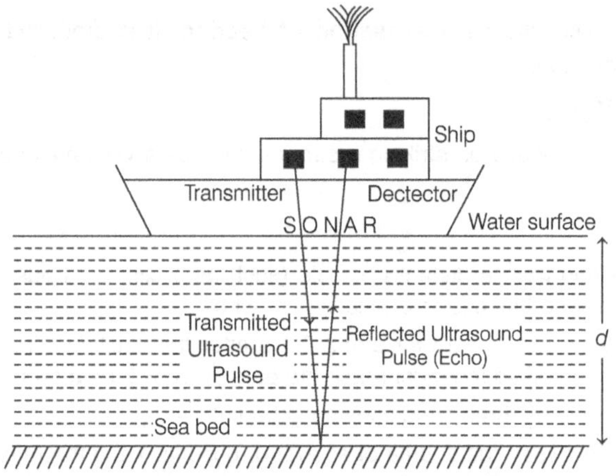

To measure the depth of a sea by using SONAR

(i) The **transmitter** produces and transmits ultrasonic waves. These waves travel through the water towards the bottom of the sea.

When these waves strike the bottom of the sea or any other object, they are reflected back in the form of echo and are sensed by the detector.

(ii) The **detector** converts the ultrasonic waves into electrical signals which are appropriately interpreted.

(iii) The distance of the object that reflected the sound wave can be calculated by knowing the **speed of sound wave** in water and **the time interval** between transmission and reception of the ultrasound.

This will give us the depth of the sea. This method is called **echo-ranging.**

Characteristics of Sound

Loudness

- Loudness is the characteristic by virtue of which a loud sound can be distinguished from a faint one, both having the **same pitch and quality**.
- Loudness of sound depends on the square of the **amplitude of the wave**.
- Loudness is directly proportional to the **surface area of vibrating body**.
- Loudness **decreases** with **increase in distance** of the source of sound.
- The unit of loudness is **phon** and its level is expressed in **decibel (dB).**

Intensity

- Intensity of a sound wave at a point of the medium is **the amount of sound energy passing per second normally through unit area at that point.**
- Its unit is **watt/m^2**.
- **Greater the energy carried by a sound wave, greater is the intensity of sound.**

- The intensity of sound wave in air is proportional to
  (i) The **square of the amplitude** of vibration $(a)^2$.
  (ii) The **square of the frequency** of vibration $(\nu)^2$.
  (iii) The **density of air**.

Note For a sound wave, **loudness has a subjective nature** since it depends on the sensitivity of hearing of a listener while **intensity** is a measurable quantity and hence has **an objective nature**.

Pitch (or shrillness) and Frequency

- **Pitch** is that characteristic of sound by which **an acute (or shrill)** note can be distinguished from a **grave (or flat)** note of some loudness and quality.

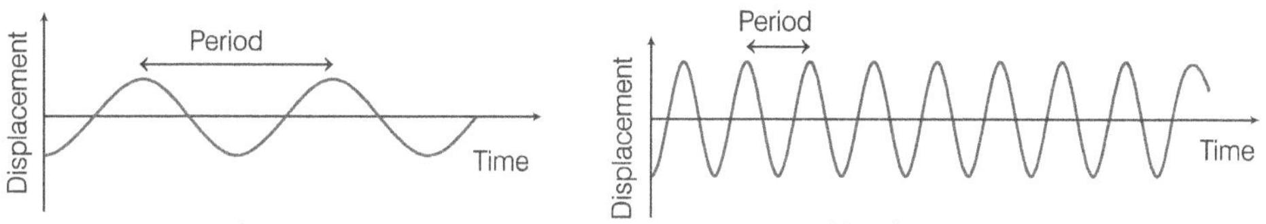

Low frequency wave High frequency wave

- Pitch is considered only in **reference to musical sounds**. Each musical note has a **definite pitch**.
- If the **pitch is high**, the sound is **shrill** and if the **pitch** is low, the sound is flat.

Quality and Waveforms

- **Quality (or timbre)** of a sound is that characteristic which **distinguishes the two sounds of the same loudness and same pitch**, but emitted by two different sources.
- The quality of a musical sound **depends on the waveform**.
- The resultant vibration obtained by the superposition of the principal (or fundamental) vibration and the subsidiary (or secondary) vibrations, gives the waveform of the sound which we hear.
- Quality of a musical sound **depends on the number of the subsidiary notes and their relative amplitudes** present along with the principal note.

(a) Shape of sound waves produced by a note played on flute
(b) Shape of sound waves when the same note is played on violin

Music and Noise

- **Music** is a pleasant, continuous and uniform sound produced by **regular and periodic vibrations**. e.g., Sound produced by a musical instrument. Their sound level is usually **between 10 dB to 30 dB**.
- **Noise** is a sound produced by an **irregular succession of disturbances** and is usually discontinuous. Usually sounds of level **above 120 dB** are termed as noise. It is discordant and unpleasant to the ears.

Noise Pollution

- The disturbance caused in the environment due to **undesirable loud and harsh sound of level above 120 dB** from various sources such as loudspeakers, sirens, moving vehicles, etc., is known as **noise pollution**.
- It causes headache and permanent damage to the ears of listener.

Natural Vibrations

The **periodic vibrations** of a body in the **absence of any external force** on it, are called natural or free vibrations.

Some examples of natural vibrations are as follows

(i) If a **tuning fork** is struck against a hard rubber pad, then it vibrates with its **natural frequency**.

(ii) A **free suspended pendulum** vibrating about its mean position.

Forced Vibrations

The vibrations of a body which take place under the **influence of an external periodic force** acting on it, are called **forced vibrations**.

Some examples of forced vibrations are as follows

(i) When stem of vibrating **tuning fork is pressed on top of table**.

(ii) When, an **artist plays guitar** string with his fingers, **forced vibration** is caused in the air column present inside the hollow box.

Damped Vibrations

The **periodic vibrations** of a body of **decreasing amplitude** in the presence of a **resistive force** are called damped vibrations. The amplitude decreases due to the frictional force. e.g., A simple pendulum vibrating in air.

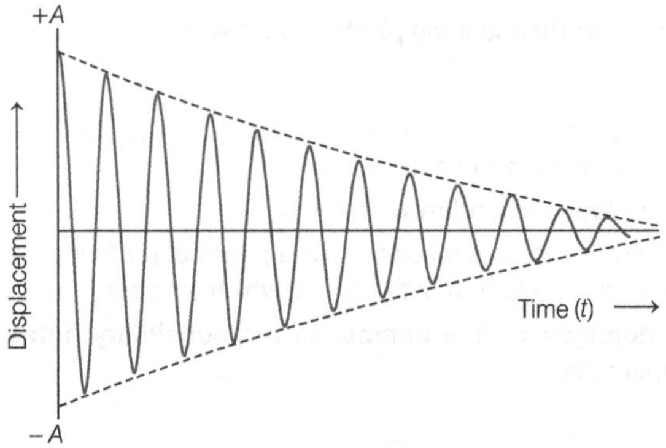

Damped vibrations

Resonance

- **Resonance is a special case of forced vibrations.**
- When the **frequency** of the externally applied periodic force on a body is equal to its **natural frequency**, the body readily begins to vibrate with an **increased amplitude**. This phenomenon is known as accoustic resonance.
- The vibrations of large amplitude are called **resonant vibrations.**

Some examples of resonance are

(i) Resonance in air column and tuning fork

(ii) Resonance in a bridge

(iii) Resonance in radio and TV receiver

EXAM ORIENTED QUESTIONS

TYPE - 1 — 01 Mark

Multiple Choice Questions

Q.1 Which one of the following diagnostic methods uses reflection of sound? **[ICSE 2021]**

(a) CT Scan
(b) Electrocardiogram
(c) Echocardiogram
(d) MRI

Ans. (c) An echocardiogram uses the reflection of ultrasound waves to create images of the heart and its structures. The reflected sound waves are analysed to provide information about heart function, size and motion.

Q.2 Select a correct option with respect to echo depth sounding. **[ICSE 2021]**

(a) Infrasonic waves are used.
(b) The frequency of the waves used is between 20 Hz and 20,000 Hz.
(c) Ultrasonic waves are used.
(d) Supersonic waves are used.

Ans. (c) Echo depth sounding uses ultrasonic waves (above 20,000 Hz) because they provide accurate and precise measurements.

Q.3 A man who is standing at a point X between two parallel walls (as shown in the diagram) fires a starting pistol.

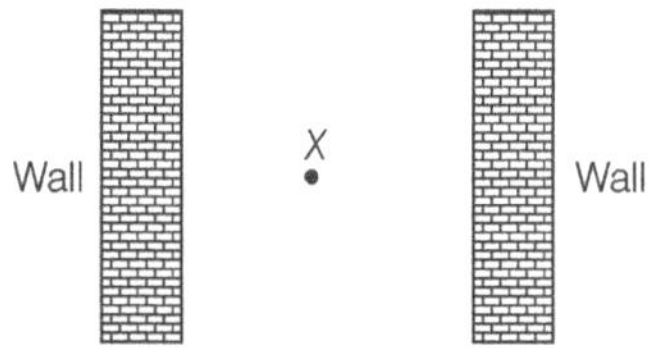

He hears the first echo after 0.6 s and another one after 0.8 s. How long after firing the pistol will he hear the next echo?

(a) 1.2 s
(b) 1.4 s
(c) 1.6 s
(d) 2.4 s

Ans. (b) The third echo is heard $(0.8 + 0.6) = 1.4$ s after firing the pistol. Note that both 0.6 s and 0.8 s (for first two echoes) are measured from the firing of the pistol.

The third echo will arrive at X at the same time from the reflections of the 2 walls.

Q.4 A bat sends sound waves and it gets reflected by a small insect within 0.3 s.

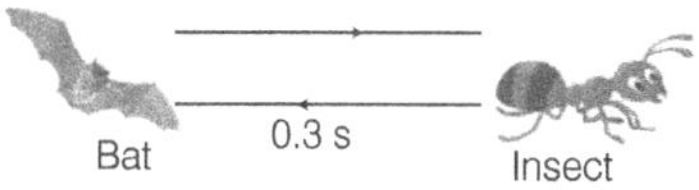

How far is the insect from the bat?
(Take, speed of sound in air = 340 m/s)

(a) 17 m (b) 35 m
(c) 51 m (d) 68 m

Ans. (c) Given, speed of sound, $v = 340\,\text{ms}^{-1}$

Total time taken, $t = 0.3$ s

The sound waves travel from bat to insect and again after reflection, they travel from insect to bat in 0.3 s.

$$\therefore \quad 2d = 340 \times 0.3$$

$$\Rightarrow \quad d = \frac{102}{2} = 51\,\text{m}$$

Hence, the insect is 51 m away from the bat.

Q.5 A submarine produces an ultrasonic wave of speed $1500\,\text{ms}^{-1}$. A man sends a signal from transmitter and it detects an object 1600 m below the submarine.

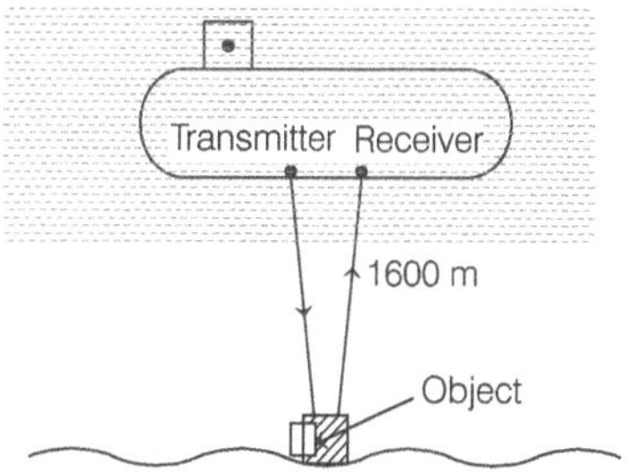

What will be the time taken for receiver to receive signal sent from transmitter?

(a) 2.5 s (b) 2.4 s
(c) 2.1 s (d) 2.0 s

Sol. (c) Given, $v = 1500\,\text{ms}^{-1}$, $s = 1600$ m

As sound waves will have to travel twice the distance between object and submarine, so

$$d = 2d' = 2 \times 1600\,\text{m}$$
$$= 3200\,\text{m}$$

$$\text{Time taken } (t) = \frac{\text{Total distance } (d)}{\text{Speed of ultrasonic wave } (v)}$$

$$= \frac{3200}{1500} = 2.13$$

$$\simeq 2.1\,\text{s}$$

Q.6 Two sound waves *X* and *Y* have the same amplitude and the same wave pattern but their frequencies are 60 Hz and 120 Hz respectively, then

[ICSE Specimen 2025]

(a) *X* will be shriller and *Y* will be grave
(b) *X* will be grave and *Y* will be shriller
(c) *X* will differ in quality than *Y*
(d) *X* is louder than *Y*

Ans. (b) Lower frequency (*X*, 60 Hz) produces a grave sound, while higher frequency (*Y*, 120 Hz) produces a shriller sound.

Q.7 Two notes are produced from two different musical instruments, such that they have same loudness and same pitch. The produced notes differ in their

[ICSE 2023]

(a) waveform (b) frequency
(c) wavelength (d) speed

Ans. (a) Two notes of the same pitch and loudness, played from different instruments do not sound the same because the waveforms are different and therefore differ in quality or tone.

Q.8 Sumit, a teenager enjoys playing his music player loudly. However, his grandmother consistently lowers the volume of the music player. Analyse the wave to identify which characteristic of the wave has been altered when the grandmother reduces the volume.

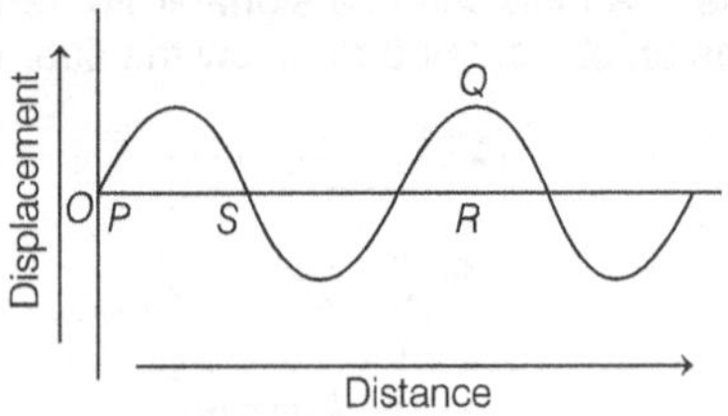

(a) The length *PS* becomes more **[Competancy Based Que]**
(b) The length *SR* becomes less
(c) The length *QR* becomes less
(d) The length *PR* becomes less

Ans. (c) When the loudness of the sound is reduced, the amplitude of the wave reduced and *QR* represents the amplitude of the the given diagram.

Q.9

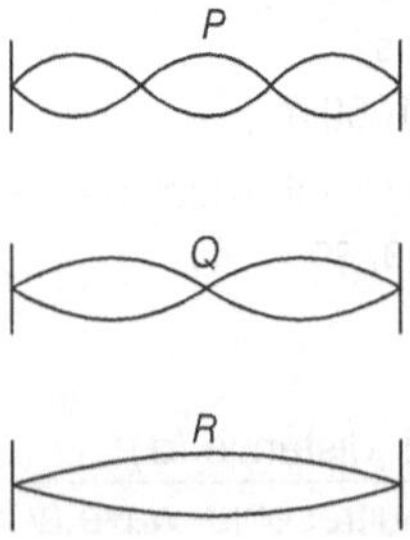

[Competancy Based Que.]

What is the ratio of wavelength between *P*, *Q* and *R*?
(a) 3 : 2 : 1 (b) 1 : 2 : 3
(c) 6 : 3 : 2 (d) 2 : 3 : 6

Ans. (d) Frequency of *P*, *Q* and *R* are respectively 3*f*, 2*f* and *f*.

Now, $\lambda \propto \frac{1}{f}$

$$\Rightarrow \lambda_P : \lambda_Q : \lambda_R = \frac{1}{3f} : \frac{1}{2f} : \frac{1}{f} = 2 : 3 : 6$$

Q.10 When a body vibrates under a periodic force, the vibrations of the body are always
(a) natural vibrations (b) damped vibrations
(c) forced vibrations (d) resonant vibrations

Ans. (c) When the external periodic force is applied to the vibrating body, the body vibrates without damping and gradually acquires the frequency of the applied periodic force.

Q.11 A child plays a note on a trumpet. She then plays a louder note of higher pitch. How do the amplitude and frequency of the second sound compare with the first?

	Amplitude of second sound	Frequency of second sound
(a)	larger	larger
(b)	larger	smaller
(c)	smaller	larger
(d)	smaller	smaller

Ans. (a) The loudness and pitch of sound depend on amplitude and frequency of sound wave respectively.

Q.12 Pendulums *A*, *B*, *C* and *D* are tied to a flexible string *PQ* and are at rest. Pendulum *C* is disturbed. Which of the following statements is true?

[ICSE Specimen 2022 Sem-I]

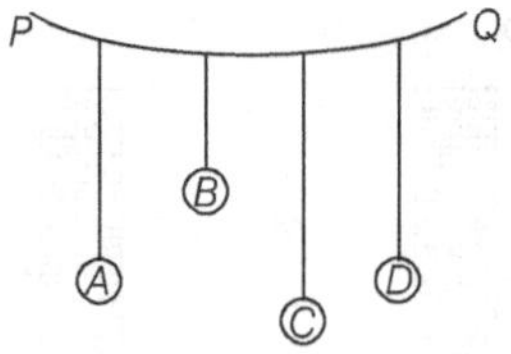

(a) Only pendulum *C* will start vibrating.
(b) Pendulums *A*, *B* and *D* will also start vibrating but *A* and *D* will vibrate with the maximum amplitude.
(c) Pendulums *A*, *B* and *D* will also start vibrating.
(d) Vibrations of pendulum *C* are forced vibrations.

Ans. (b) Pendulums *A*, *B* and *D* will also start vibrating but *A* and *D* will vibrate with the maximum amplitude, Since, *A* and *D* have the same length. So resonance occurs between *A* and *D* which makes them vibrates with the greater amplitude.

Q.13 When the stem of vibrating tuning fork is pressed on a table, the tabletop starts vibrating. These vibrations are definitely an example of **[ICSE 2024]**
(a) resonance (b) natural vibrations
(c) forced vibrations (d) damped vibrations

Ans. (c) When the stem of vibrating tuning fork is pressed on a table, the tabletop starts vibrating. These vibrations are definitely an example of forced vibrations.

Q.14

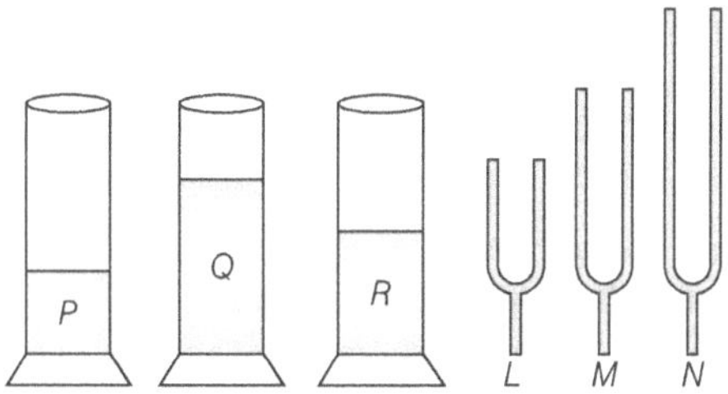

The above picture shows three cylinders filled with water to a different extent. The tuning forks *L*, *M* and *N* in vibration produce louder sound when held above the mouth of the cylinders. Which combination is correct for hearing a louder sound of the tuning fork? **[Comptency Based Que.]**

(a) L – R, M – Q, N – P (b) L – P, M – Q, N – R
(c) L – R, M – P, N – Q (d) T – Q, M – R, N – P

Ans. (d) For a tuning fork, shorter the prongs, higher is the frequency and for the cylinders. Shorter the air column, higher will be the frequency. So, to hear louder sound, that is for resonance to occur *L* should be held near *Q*, *M* should be held near *R* and *N* should be held near *P*.

TYPE - 2 — 01 Mark

Assertion-Reason Type Questions

Directions (Q. Nos. 1-6) In the following questions two two statements are given as Assertion and Reason.

(a) Both A and R are true and R is the correct explanation of A.
(b) Both A and R are true but R is not the correct explanation of A.
(c) A is true but R is false.
(d) A is false but R is true.

Q.1 Assertion (A) As the level of water in a tall measuring cylinder kept under running tap rises, the pitch of sound gradually increases. **[ICSE 2025]**

Reason (R) Frequency of sound is inversely proportional to the length of the water column.

Ans. (a) Both A and R are true and R is the correct explanation of A because as the water level rises, the air column decreases which increases the frequency of vibration of the air column thereby increasing the pitch of the sound.

Q.2 Assertion (A) SONAR is used to detect objects underwater by emitting ultrasonic waves.

Reason (R) Ultrasonic waves have frequencies about 20,000 Hz and can travel distances in water without significant loss of energy.

Ans. (a) SONAR emits ultrasonic waves, which help to detect underwater objects because of their high frequency and ability to travel without much attenuation.

Q.3 Assertion (A) As the amplitude of sound increases, the loudness of sound decreases.

Reason (R) The loudness of sound depends on the amplitude of wave.

Ans. (d) As the amplitude of sound increases, the loudness of sound increases. Loudness is directly proportional to the amplitude of the sound wave.

Q.4 Assertion (A) The ratio of amplitudes of two waves is 3 : 4. So, the ratio of loudness of the two waves will be 9 : 16.

Reason (R) The loudness of a wave is directly proportional to the square of amplitude of the wave.

Ans. (a) Both Assertion and Reason are true and Reason is the correct explanation of Assertion because $I \propto a^2$.

$$\therefore \quad \frac{I_1}{I_2} = \frac{3^2}{4^2} = \frac{9}{16}$$

$$\Rightarrow \quad I_1 : I_2 = 9 : 16.$$

Q.5 Assertion (A) A sound level 70 dB is twice as loud as a sound level of 35 dB.

Reason (R) Sound level in dB follows a linear scale, where each 10 dB increase represents a doubling of loudness.

Ans. (c) Sound level in decibels (dB) is based on a logarithmic scale, not a linear scale. Each increase of 10 dB represents a ten times increase in sound intensity or perceived loudness, not a doubling. Therefore, a sound level of 70 dB is ten times louder than a sound level of 35 dB, not twice as loud.

Q.6 Assertion (A) The pitch of the sound produced by vibrating string can be changed.

Reason (R) The pitch of the sound can be changed by changing the length, tension and thickness of vibrating string.

Ans. (a) The pitch of the sound produced by a vibrating string can be changed by changing the length, tension and thickness of the vibrating string.

TYPE - 3 — 01/02 Marks

Fill in the Blanks

Q.1 The pitch of a sound depends on its .... (amplitude, frequency, wavelength). **[1]**

Ans. frequency

Q.2 The unit of loudness or sound intensity is .... (watt, decibel, hertz). **[1]**

Ans. decibel

Q.3 The amplitude of a sound wave determines its .... (loudness, intensity) and .... (frequency, waveform) determines its pitch. **[2]**

Ans. loudness, frequency.

Q.4 When a body vibrates at its ...... (natural, forced) frequency and another body in contact or proximity starts vibrating at the same frequency, the phenomenon is called .... (resonance/damping) **[2]**

Ans. natural, resonance

Q.5 In resonance, the .... (vibrational, rotational) energy of a vibrating system is transferred to another system of the same nature frequency. **[1]**

Ans. vibrational

TYPE - 4 02 Marks

Very Short Answer Type Questions

Q.1 A bucket kept under a running tap is getting filled with water. A person sitting at a distance is able to get an idea that when the bucket is going to be filled.

(i) What change takes place in the sound to give this idea? **[1]**

(ii) What causes the change in the sound? **[1]**

[ICSE 2013]

Ans. (i) The frequency of the sound appears to be increased as the air column of bucket is filled with water.

(ii) The change in the sound is caused because air column gradually decreases while water gets filled in the bucket.

Q.2 A student went to a hill station early in the morning, he could hear the echo of his clap after 0.1 s. When he went to the same place in the afternoon, he could not hear the echo at all. Then, explain the reason for his changed observation.

Ans. There is a rise in temperature in the afternoon and the speed of sound increases with increase in temperature. As speed increases, time taken by reflected sound will be less, may be less than 0.1 s in the afternoon. So, the student could not hear the echo at all in the afternoon.

Q.3 Rohan conducted experiments on echo in different media. He observed that a minimum distance of x metres is required for the echo to be heard in oxygen and y metres in benzene. Compare x and y and justify your answer.

Speed of sound in oxygen = 340 ms^{-1}

Speed of sound in benzene = 200 ms^{-1} **[ICSE 2024]**

Ans. The minimum distance for an echo to be heard for oxygen is $\left(\frac{340 \times 0.1}{2}\right)$ m = 17m and for benzene it is $\left(\frac{200 \times 0.1}{2}\right)$ m = 10 m. Therefore, $x > y$.

Q.4 (i) Name the waves used for echo depth sounding. **[1]**

(ii) Give one reason for their use in the above purpose. **[ICSE Specimen 2025] [1]**

Ans. (i) Ultrasonic waves

(ii) They travel long distance without deviation or not easily absorbed by the medium or can be confined to a narrow beam.

Q.5 Which characteristic of sound is affected due to the larger surface area of a school bell?

Ans. The larger surface area of a school bell can affect the amplitude or loudness of the sound produced by the bell. When the surface area of a bell is increased, it allows for a larger amount of air to be displaced when the bell is struck, resulting in a larger sound wave and a louder sound.

Q.6 John is trying to create musical notes using water-filled bottles, as shown in the picture.

Which of the bottles is likely to produce a musical note with the highest pitch? Give reasons.

[Competency Based Que.]

Ans. Less air means higher pitch, and more air means lower pitch. Bottle *A* has the most water and therefore the least air inside it.

Since, sound is produced by the vibration of air, less air vibrates faster, resulting in a higher frequency and hence a higher pitch.

Q.7 When Shyam, the band leader, struck both the bass drum and the kettle drum with equal force, the bass drum emitted a sound measuring 120 dB, whereas the kettle drum produced a sound of 90dB. Explain this discrepancy in the loudness. **[Competency Based Que.]**

Ans. The loudness of sound depends upon the surface area of the vibrating body. A larger vibrating area sends forth a greater amount of energy. So, when the bass drum which has a larger surface area is stuck with same force that of kettle drum, the bass drum produces a louder sound.

Q.8 (i) Three musical instruments give out notes at the frequencies listed below.

Flute: 400 Hz, Guitar: 200 Hz, Trumpet: 500 Hz. Which one of these has the highest pitch? **[1]**

(ii) With which of the following frequencies does a tuning fork of 256 Hz resonate? 288 Hz, 341 Hz, 333 Hz, 512 Hz **[1] [ICSE 2011]**

Ans. (i) Trumpet having highest frequency of 500 Hz have highest pitch, because pitch is directly proportional to the frequency.

(ii) The frequency 512 Hz will resonate a tuning fork of 256 Hz as 512 Hz is an integral multiple of the natural frequency of the tuning fork.

Q.9 Seismic waves have different frequencies. During earthquakes, why are short-length buildings more prone to damage caused by high-frequency seismic waves? **[Competency Based Que.]**

Ans. Shorter the length of a building, greater will be the frequency with which it vibrates. So, when high-frequency seismic waves hit short length buildings, they are more prone damage.

Q.10 A metal foot ruler is held at the edge of a table. It is pressed at its free end and then released. It vibrates.

(i) Name the vibrations produced. **[1]**

(ii) State one way to increase the frequency of these vibrations. **[1] [ICSE 2023]**

Ans. (i) The vibrations produced are known as damped vibration.

(ii) Reducing the length of the free end from the table's edge will increase the vibration frequency.

Q.11 Ashish, Sameer, Aditya and Mohit were sitting on the terrace of Ashish's house listening to the songs playing on Aditya's mobile phone. Mohit, sitting in one corner, a little distance away from the others, requests to increase the volume of the songs. But Aditya says the volume is full. Sameer, being a smart guy, gets up, goes into the kitchen, brings an empty steel glass, places the mobile phone inside it and solves the problem. What is the reason for Sameer to keep the mobile phone in the glass? **[Competency Based Que.]**

Ans. The steel glass acts as a resonator which increases the loudness of vibration of sound which solves the problem.

TYPE - 5   03 Marks

Short Answer Type Questions

Q.1 (i) Give one example of forced vibration. **[1]**

(ii) State two necessary conditions for hearing a distinct echo. **[2] [ICSE Specimen 2017]**

Ans. (i) When guitar is played, the artist forces the strings of the guitar to execute forced vibrations.

(ii) The two conditions for an echo to be heard are

(a) The minimum distance between source and reflecting surface should be 17 m.

(b) To hear a distinct echo, the interval between original and reflected sound must be 0.1 s.

Q.2 Rohit playing a flute and Anita playing a piano emit sounds of same pitch and loudness. **[ICSE 2022 Sem-II]**

(i) Name one characteristic that is different for waves from the two different instruments. **[1]**

(ii) If now the loudness of the sound from flute becomes four times that of the sound from piano, then write the value of the ratio $A_F : A_P$ (where, A_F = amplitude of sound wave from flute, A_P = amplitude of sound wave from piano) **[2]**

Ans. (i) The quality of sound is that characteristic of sound which enables us to distinguish one sound from another having the same pitch and loudness.

(ii) Given, $(\text{Loudness})_{\text{flute}} = 4 \times (\text{Loudness})_{\text{piano}}$

We know that,

$$\text{Loudness} \propto (\text{Amplitude})^2$$

$$\Rightarrow \frac{(\text{Loudness})_{\text{flute}}}{(\text{Loudness})_{\text{piano}}} = \frac{(\text{Amplitude})^2_{\text{flute}}}{(\text{Amplitude})^2_{\text{piano}}}$$

$$\Rightarrow \frac{(\text{Amplitude})_{\text{flute}}}{(\text{Amplitude})_{\text{piano}}} = \frac{A_F}{A_P} = \sqrt{4}$$

$$\Rightarrow \frac{A_{\text{flute}}}{A_{\text{piano}}} = 2$$

or $\quad A_{\text{flute}} : A_{\text{piano}} = 2:1$

Q.3 (i) What are the factors on which the following characteristics of a musical note depend?

(a) Intensity

(b) Timbre **[1]**

(ii) How does a trawlerman catch fish in deep water? **[2]**

Ans. (i) Factors on which the given characteristics of musical note depends are

(a) Intensity depends upon

I. frequency   II. amplitude.

(b) Timbre depends upon

I. waveform of sound   II. frequency

III. resonance and sound pressure.

(ii) A trawlerman sends ultrasonic waves in deep water, which on striking the shoal of fish, return back to him. He notes the time t taken by the waves in going and coming back, then he calculates the depth of water d by using the relation, $d = \frac{vt}{2}$

where, v is the velocity of ultrasonic waves in water. This helps them in catching the fishes easily.

Q.4 (i) Define pitch. **[1]**

(ii) Two wires *AB* and *CD* of same length are stretched by same amount. Which wire will produce sound of greater pitch on plucking? **[1]**

(iii) Given a reason for your answer. **[1]**

[ICSE Specimen 2022 Sem-II]

Ans. (i) It is that characteristic of sound by which we can distinguish between different sounds of the same loudness.

(ii) When both wires are stretched by same amount, wire *AB* will produce sound of greater pitch on plucking.

(iii) Pitch depends upon the frequency of the wave. More the frequency of the wave, higher is its pitch. In the given case, both the wires are of same length but wire *AB* is thinner than wire *CD*. So, wire *AB* will vibrate faster and have higher frequency than wire *CD*. Thus, pitch of wire *AB* is more compared to wire *CD*.

Q.5 It is observed that during march past we hear a base drums distinctly from a distance compared to the side drums.

(i) Name the characteristic of sound associated with the above observation. **[1]**

(ii) Give a reason for the above observation. **[2]**

[ICSE 2019]

Ans. (i) Loudness and intensity

(ii) Side drums have smaller surface area as compared to bass drums and as loudness of sound is directly proportional to the surface area of vibrating body. So, bass drum can be heard from a larger distance.

Q.6 A change in amplitude of a sound wave is noticed.

[ICSE Specimen 2022 Sem-II]

(i) Which characteristic of sound is affected due to the above change? **[1]**

(ii) How is amplitude related to your answer to part (i) above? **[1]**

(iii) What happens to the quality of the sound? **[1]**

Ans. (i) Loudness

(ii) Loudness is proportional to the square of its amplitude, i.e. $L \propto (a)^2$.

(iii) The quality of the sound does not change because quality is dependent on the waveform.

Q.7 The displacement-time graph of a sound wave produced by a vibrating wire is shown below. **[2]**

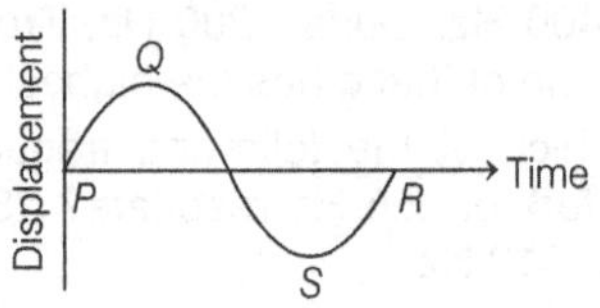

(i) How will you adjust the tension in the wire, to reduce the length of *PR*?

(ii) Which characteristic of sound is affected by the reduction in the length of *PR*? **[ICSE 2025]**

Ans. (i) The frequency of note produced by a stretched string is related to the tension in the string as $f \propto \sqrt{T}$.

When the length *PR* is reduced, the wavelength of the wave is reduced thereby increasing the frequency of the wave.

So, the tension must be increased in case if *PR* has to be reduced.

(ii) The pitch of the vibration of sound increases when the length *PR* is reduced.

Q.8 Study the diagram and answer the following.

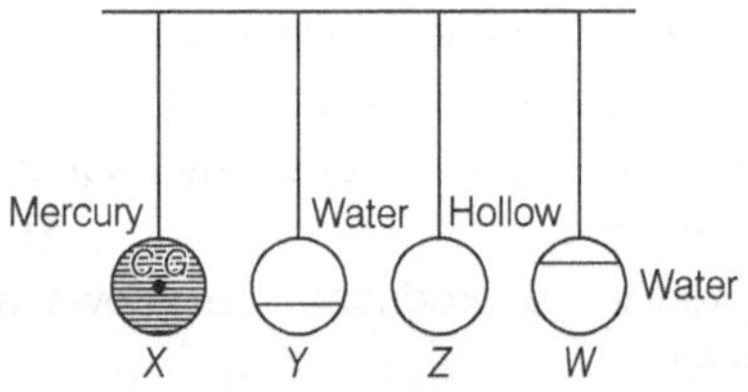

(i) Arrange the following pendulums according to their natural frequencies (use < > =). **[1]**

(ii) If pendulum *Z* is initiated into oscillation, which pendulum among the others will exhibit the highest amplitude of vibration? **[1]**

(iii) Give reasons for your answer.

[Comptency Based Que.]

Ans. (i) $X = Y = Z = W$

(ii) All the pendulum will exhibit same amplitude of vibration.

(iii) The reason being that all the pendulums have same length and hence will have equal natural frequency as frequency of a simple pendulum is independent of the mass of the bulb and is only dependent on the length of the bob and the acceleration due to gravity. **[1]**

Q.9 A submarine in the sea, sends ultrasonic ping and a stopwatch is started simultaneously. The stopwatch stops on receiving the reflected wave from an obstacle and reads 1 minute 40 seconds. Calculate the distance of the obstacle from the submarine. (Speed of sound in water 1500 ms^{-1}) **[ICSE 2025]**

Ans. Let the total distance travelled by the ultrasonic wave from sending to receiving the signal be $2d$ m

Total time taken = 1 m 40 s = 100 s.

Speed of the ultrasonic wave in water = 1500 ms^{-1}.

$\therefore \quad 2d = (1500 \times 100)$ m

$\Rightarrow \quad d = 75000$ m = 75 km.

$\therefore$ The distance of the obstacle from the submarine = 75 km.

TYPE - 6 — 04 Marks

Long Answer Type Questions

Q.1 We are able to see the TV channels clearly when we set TV on auto-tuning. **[ICSE 2023]**

(i) Which phenomenon led to the clear visibility of the channels due to auto-tuning? **[1]**

(ii) Define the above phenomenon mentioned by you. **[1]**

(iii) Give any one more example of this phenomenon. **[2]**

Ans. (i) The phenomenon led to the clear visibility of the channels due to auto-tuning is called resonance.

(ii) Resonance is a phenomenon that occurs when an object is subjected to an external force at its natural frequency, causing it to vibrate with a large amplitude.

(iii) Example of resonance is in musical instruments, where the natural frequency of the instruments components, such as strings or air columns, can resonate with the applied force of the musician playing the instrument, creating the characteristic sound of the instrument.

Q.2 (i) When a tuning fork (vibrating) is held close to ear, one hears a faint hum. The same (vibrating tuning fork) is held such that its stem is in contact with the table surface, then one hears a loud sound. Explain. **[2]**

(ii) What do you understand by intensity of sound? How is it different from loudness? **[2]**

Ans. (i) When a tuning fork is held close to ear, then one hears a faint hum because it produces damped vibration. When the stem of vibrating tuning fork is in contact with the table surface, then table surface starts vibrating with same frequency but of larger amplitude because the table has a greater surface area and loudness of sound is directly proportional to the surface area of a body.

(ii) **Intensity of Sound** It is the amount of sound energy passing per second normally through a unit area.

Loudness is a measure of the response of the ear to the sound. Even when two sounds are of equal intensity, we may hear one as louder than the other, as our ear detects it better. Therefore, loudness depends both on the intensity of sound and the response of the ear to that sound.

Q.3 The diagrams given below show two sound boxes A and B with wires of same length (l) and tension (10 kgf) but different cross-sectional areas. Simultaneously, vibrating tuning forks of frequency 300 Hz are placed on the boxes A and B. The paper rider falls off in case of B but not in case of A. **[4][ICSE 2025]**

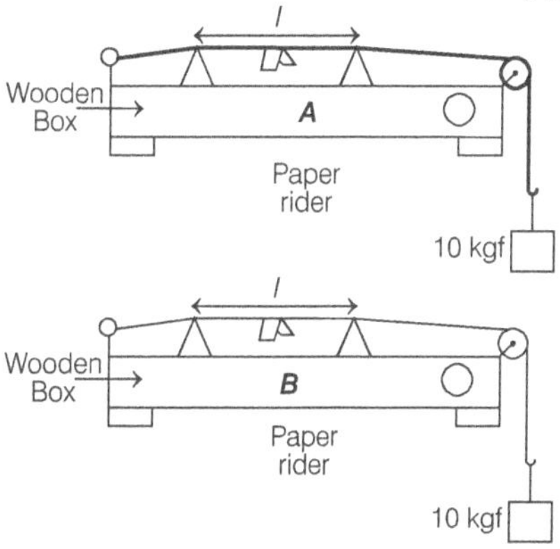

(i) Name and explain the phenomenon responsible for the falling off of the paper rider in B.

(ii) The wire A resonates with a tuning fork of frequency f. Is f greater than, less than or equal to 300 Hz? Justify your answer.

Ans. (i) The wire B undergoes resonance which is responsible for the falling off of the paper rider in B.

Refer to theory on page 96 (Resonance).

(ii) f will be less than 300 Hz. because frequency of a stretched string is inversely proportional to the radius of the string. Since, the string in A has a greater radius, so it will have smaller resonant frequency as compared to the resonant frequency of B.

TYPE - 7 — 03/04 Marks

Case Based Questions

Q.1 A boy standing in front of a wall produces two whistles per second. He notices that the sound of his whistling coincides with the echo. The echo is heard only once when whistling is stopped. (The speed of sound in air = 320 m/s) **[ICSE 2022 Sem-I]**

(i) The time in which the boy hears the echo is **[1]**

(a) 1 s (b) 0.5 s (c) 1.5 s (d) 2 s

(ii) The distance at which the boy is standing from the wall is **[1]**

(a) 160 m (b) 240 m (c) 320 m (d) 80 m

(iii) If the speed of sound is increased by 16 ms^{-1} and the boy moves 4 m away from the wall, then in how much time will he hear the echo of the first whistle? **[1]**

(a) 0.525 s (b) 0.5 s

(c) 0.48 s (d) 0.3 s

(iv) In which of the following timings of reflection of the whistle, the echo cannot be heard? **[1]**

(a) 0.05 s (b) 0.12 s (c) 0.2 s (d) 0.11 s

Ans. (i) (b) Echo heard by the boy is only once when whistle stops.

$$\therefore \quad t = \frac{1}{2}\text{ s} = 0.5\text{ s}$$

(ii) (d) $\text{Time} = \frac{2d}{v}$

$$\Rightarrow \quad d = \frac{\text{Time} \times v}{2} \Rightarrow d = \frac{0.5 \times 320}{2} = 80\text{ m}$$

(iii) (b) If the speed of sound = (320 + 16) ms^{-1} = 336 m/s

Distance between boy and wall = $d + 4$ = 84 m

$$\text{Time of echo, } t = \frac{2(d+4)}{v}$$

$$= \frac{2 \times 84}{336} = 0.5\text{ s}$$

(iv) (a) An echo can be heard only if the time gap is at least 0.1 seconds.

So, only value less than 0.1s means the echo cannot be heard. Hence 0.05 is less than 0.1s so 0.05 is correct answer.

Q.2 A boat equipped with a SONAR starts its operation at P and moves slowly towards Q. Along the straight path, the SONAR's transmitter/receiver continuously sends ultrasonic waves down to the seabed and detects all corresponding reflected sound waves from the seabed. A timer records the time of sending and receiving.

The following graph shows the readings of the time interval t recorded by the transmitter/receiver when the boat is at the various positions.

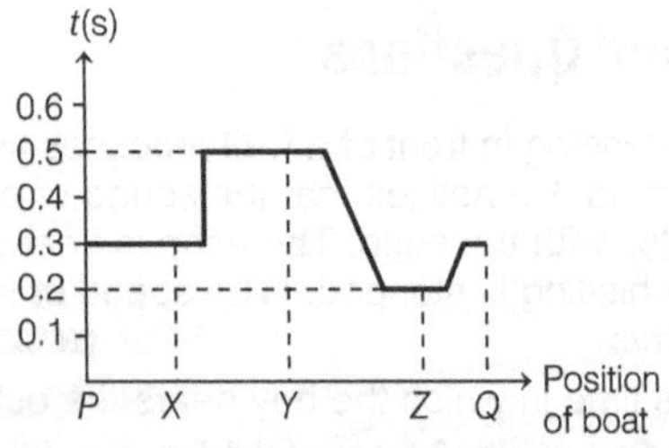

(i) What does time interval t tell you? **[1]**

(ii) Given that the speed of sound in sea water is 1540 ms^{-1}, find the depth of the sea at the various positions X, Y and Z shown in the graph. **[1]**

(iii) Use the findings from (ii) and sketch the shape of the seabed along PQ. **[1]**

Ans. (i) The time interval t is the time taken for the ultrasonic waves to travel down to the seabed and return back to the receiver.

(ii) $\text{Depth at } X = 1540 \times \frac{0.3}{2} = 231\text{ m}$

$\text{Depth at } Y = 1540 \times \frac{0.5}{2} = 385\text{ m}$

$\text{Depth at } Z = 1540 \times \frac{02}{2} = 154\text{ m}$

(iii)

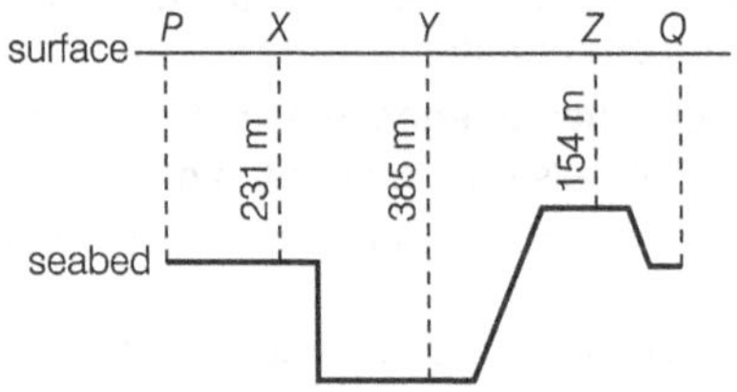

3. Examine the graph depicting the transmitted (T) and reflected (R) waves from submarines A and B, which are equipped with a device emitting ultrasonic sounds. Study the graph and answer the following. (Speed of sound in water is 1500 m/s)

(i) Name the device used here. **[1]**

(ii) Why is ultrasonic sound used in this device? **[1]**

(iii) Which submarine is closer to the ship? Calculate the distance of the closest submarine. **[1]**

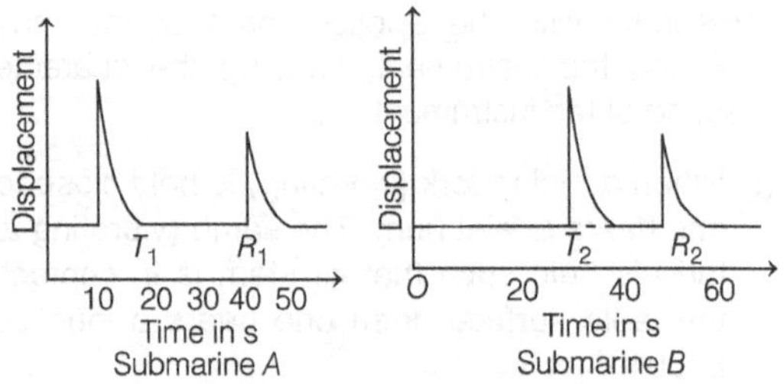

Ans. (i) Sound Navigation and Ranging (SONAR).

(ii) Ultrasonic waves have high energy and hence can travel a long distance without much loss.

(iii) Submarine A transmits signal at 10 s and receives it at 40 s and submarine B transmits signal at 30 s and receives it at 50 s.

So, submarine B is closer to the ship.

Speed of sound in water = 1500 m/s

Time taken for the signal to travel = 20 s

$$\therefore \text{ Distance of submarine } B = \frac{vt}{2}$$

$$= \frac{1500 \times 20}{2} = 15000\text{ m}$$

4.

The above picture shows a mother pushing her daughter sitting on a swing. The swing is going through the positions *A*, *B*, *C* where, *A* and *C* are extreme positions and *B* is the mean position.

(i) Which is the right position i.e. at *A*, *B* or *C*, for the mother to give a constant periodic push to the swing every time in the forward direction to increase the amplitude of the swing? **[1]**

(ii) Name the phenomenon involved in this. **[1]**

(iii) Explain with this example how this phenomenon helps to increase the amplitude of the swing. **[1]**

[ICSE Speciemen 2025]

Ans. (a) Position *A*

(b) Resonance

(c) The natural frequency of the swing matches with the frequency of the force applied by the mother which increases the amplitude of vibration of the swing.

Q.5 In the given diagram, a vibrating tuning fork is kept near the mouth of burette filled with water. The length of the column is adjusted by opening the tap of the burette. At a length of 5 cm of the air column, a sound is heard. **[ICSE 2024]**

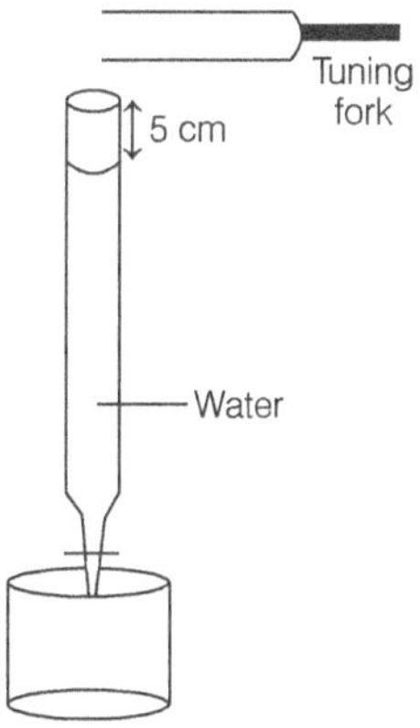

(i) Name the phenomenon illustrated by the above experiment. **[1]**

(ii) Why is a loud sound heard at this particular length? **[1]**

(iii) If the present tuning fork is replaced with a tuning fork of higher frequency, should the length of the air column be increased or decreased to produce a loud sound? Give a reason. **[1]**

Ans. (i) Resonance

(ii) A loud sound is heard at this particular length because the frequency of the air column becomes equal to the frequency of the tuning fork.

(iii) The frequency of air column is inversely proportional to the length of air column, i.e. $f \propto \frac{1}{l}$.

When the present tuning fork is replaced with a tuning fork of higher frequency, the length of air column should be decreased to produce loud sound (or higher frequency).

Q.6 This question is about the sound produced by a mobile phone and the energy changes while it is operating.

(i) The sound produced by a ringing phone consists of two notes, one after the other.

Figure shows the trace on an oscilloscope screen produced by the first of the notes.

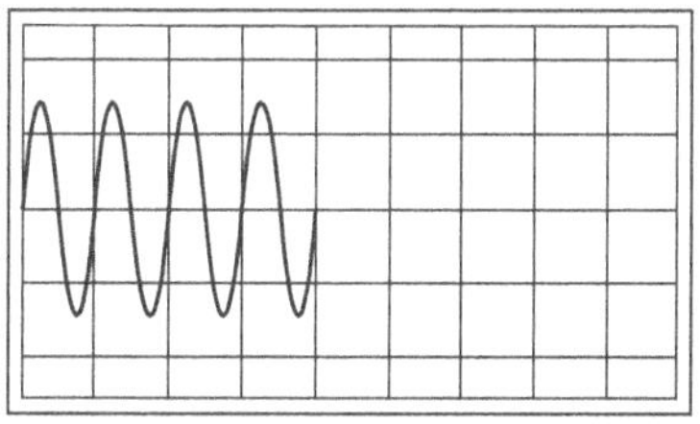

The second note is louder and has a higher pitch.

(a) On figure continue the trace to show what happens when the second note is sounding. **[1]**

(b) Explain the differences between the two traces. **[2]**

(ii) The mobile phone contains a rechargeable battery. Energy is stored inside the battery as it is charged.

(a) Describe the useful energy change that takes place inside the battery as it is charged from the mains. **[1]**

(b) Describe the useful energy changes occurring inside the mobile phone as sound is being produced. **[2]**

Ans. (i) (a)

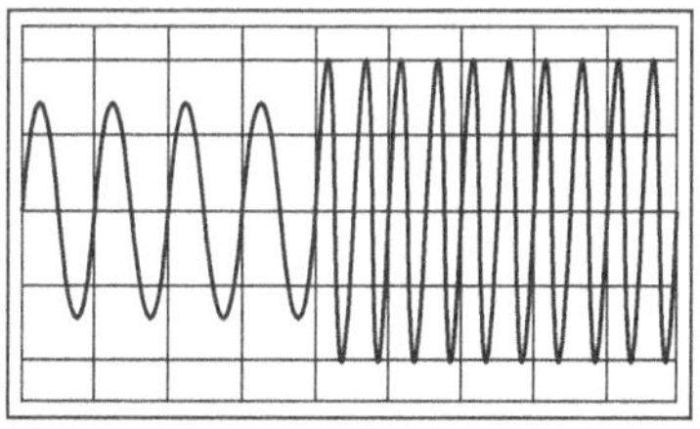

(b) The second trace has a larger amplitude and a smaller period. This is because a louder sound has got a greater amplitude and a sound with a higher pitch has got a higher frequency.

(ii) (a) Electrical energy from the mains is converted to chemical energy in the battery.

(b) Electrical energy from the mains is converted to sound energy in the speaker.

Q.7

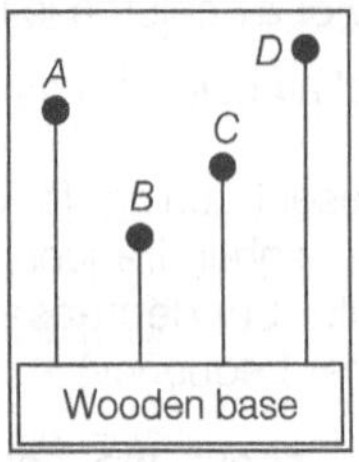

The adjacent diagram shows four solid plastic balls with wires fitted on a wooden base. A person shakes the wooden base to and fro (forward and backward) periodically. It is observed that even the balls start vibrating. It is also observed that all balls vibrate, but only one ball vibrates vigorously.

(a) Explain, why only one ball vibrates vigorously? [2]

(b) If f_A, f_B, f_C and f_D are the natural frequencies of vibration of the wires, then arrange them in the increasing order of their frequencies and give reasons for the same. [2]

Ans. (a) The natural frequency of the ball is equal to the frequency of the wooden base.

(b) $f \propto \frac{1}{l}$ or frequency is inversely proportional to the length of the wire.

$\therefore \quad f_B > f_C > f_A > f_D$

TYPE - 8

Numerical Questions

Q.1 An observer stands at a distance of 850 m from a cliff and fires a gun. After what time gap will he hear the echo, if sound travels at a speed of 350 ms^{-1} in air? [2]

Ans. Given, distance between sound source and cliff, $d = 850$ m

Total distance travelled by the sound = $2d$

Speed, (v) = 350 m/s and Time, (t) = ?

$$\because \quad v = \frac{2d}{t}$$

$$\Rightarrow \quad t = \frac{2d}{v} = \frac{2 \times 850}{350} = 4.86 \text{ s}$$

Q.2 John fires a gun towards a hill and hears its echo after 5 s. He then moves 320 m towards the hill and fires his gun again. This time he hears the echo after 3 s. Calculate the velocity of sound.

[ICSE Specimen 2017] [3]

Ans. At position-I

$(\text{Distance})_1 = d$ m and $t_1 = 5$ s

$$\therefore \quad v_1 = \frac{2d}{5}$$

At position-II

$(\text{Distance})_2 = (d - 320)$m and $t_2 = 3$ s

$$\therefore \quad v_2 = \frac{2(d-320)}{3}$$

As velocity of sound in air is the same.

$$\therefore \quad v_1 = v_2$$

$$\frac{2d}{5} = \frac{2(d-320)}{3}$$

$$3d = 5(d - 320)$$

$$3d = 5d - 1600$$

$$2d = 1600 \Rightarrow d = 800 \text{ m}$$

$$\therefore \text{Velocity of sound} = \frac{2 \times 800}{5} = 320 \text{ ms}^{-1} \text{ in air.}$$

Q.3 Uttam and Nitesh are standing at a distance of 12 m and 20 m respectively, from a cliff. They start shouting their names. They want to hear clear echo of their sound?

(i) Will Nitesh and Uttam be able to hear a clear echo of their own sound? [2]

(ii) Can you explain the condition for a sound to form an echo? [2]

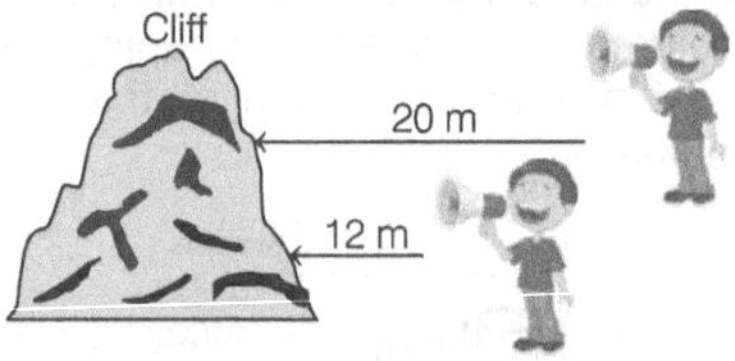

Ans. (i) We know that, we can hear two sounds separately, if the time gap between there two sounds is more than 0.1 second.

Now, check whether Uttam will hear his sound or not.

Calculate the time taken to hear the echo for Uttam.

$$\because \quad t = \frac{2d}{v}$$

Here, $d = 12$ m, $v = 340$ m/s

$$\because \quad t = \frac{2 \times 12}{340} = 0.07 \text{ s}$$

Here, clearly observe that 0.07 s < 0.1 s.

Therefore, Uttam will not be able to hear his clear echo.

Now, check whether Nitesh will hear his sound or not.

$\therefore \quad t = \frac{2d}{v} = \frac{2 \times 20}{340} = 0.117$ s

Here, 0.117 s > 0.1 s

Hence, Nitesh will be able to hear his clear echo.

(ii) Conditions for an echo to be heard

(a) The time gap between source and reflector must be greater than 0.1 second.

(b) The size of reflector must be large enough as compared to wavelength of sound.

Q.4 **A sound made on the surface of a lake takes 3s to reach a boatman. How much time will it take to reach a diver inside the water at the same depth?**
(Take, velocity of sound in air = 300 ms^{-1}, velocity of sound in water = 1440 ms^{-1}) **[ICSE 2013] [2]**

Ans. Given, time of sound to reach at boatman, $t = 3$ s

Velocity of sound in air, $v_a = 300$ m/s

Velocity of sound in water, $v_w = 1440$ m/s

Time taken by diver, $t_d = ?$

$\therefore$ Depth of lake, $d_l = v_a \times t$ [as given in question]

$= 300 \times 3 = 900$ m

Time taken by sound in water to reach diver,

$$t_w = \frac{d_l}{v_w} = \frac{900}{1440} = 0.62 \text{ s}$$

Q.5 **An ultrasonic wave is sent from a ship towards the bottom of the sea. It is found that the time interval between the sending and the receiving of the wave is 1.5 s. Calculate the depth of the sea, if the velocity of sound in sea water is 1400 ms^{-1}.** **[2]**

Ans. Given, time interval, $t = 1.5$ s,

Velocity, $v = 1400$ m/s

Let d = distance travelled by ultrasonic waves during 1.5 s.

So, $d = v \times t = 1400 \times 1.5 = 2100$ m

Therefore, the depth of the sea will be given by

$$= \frac{d}{2} = \frac{2100}{2} = 1050 \text{ m}$$

Q.6 **Calculate the distance covered by the ultrasonic wave having a velocity of 1.5 kms^{-1} in 14 s, when it is received after reflection by the receiver of the SONAR.** **[ICSE 2023] [2]**

Ans. Distance covered by the ultrasonic wave can be calculated using formula Distance = Velocity × Time

Here, velocity of the ultrasonic wave is given as 1.5 km/s.

Time taken for it to travel to the target and back is 14 s.

Since, the actual distance covered will be half of the total distance travelled by the wave, so we can calculate the distance covered by the ultrasonic wave as

$$\text{Distance} = \frac{\text{Velocity} \times \text{Time}}{2} = \frac{1.5 \times 14}{2} = 10.5 \text{ km}$$

$\therefore$ The distance covered by ultrasonic wave is 10.5 km when it is received after reflection by the receiver of the SONAR.

Q.7 **A person standing in front of a cliff fires a gun and hears its echo after 3s. The speed of sound in air is 336 ms^{-1}.**

(i) Calculate the distance of the person from the cliff. **[1]**

(ii) After moving a certain distance from the cliff, he fires the gun again and this time the echo is heard 1.5 s later than the first. Calculate the distance that the person moved. **[ICSE Specimen 2025] [2]**

Ans. (i) Given, $t = 3$ s and speed of sound, $v = 336$ m/s

Let d = distance of person from cliff.

$\therefore \quad 2d = v \times t \Rightarrow 2d = 336 \times 3$

$\Rightarrow \quad d = 504$ m

(ii) Let the extra distance moved by person from the cliff = x

$t = 3 + 1.5 = 4.5$ s

$\therefore \quad 2(d + x) = v \times t$

$\Rightarrow \quad 2(504 + x) = 336 \times 4.5$

$\therefore \quad x = 252$ m

Q.8 **(i) A man standing between two cliffs produces a sound and hears two successive echoes at intervals of 3 s and 4 s, respectively. Calculate the distance between the two cliffs. The speed of sound in the air is 330 ms^{-1}.** **[2]**

(ii) Why will an echo not be heard when the distance between the source of sound and the reflecting surface is 10 m? **[1]**

Ans. (i) Given, time taken from nearer cliff, $t_1 = 3$ s

Time taken from another cliff, $t_2 = 4$ s

Velocity of sound in air, $v_a = 330$ m/s

Total distance, $d = ?$

Distance of man from nearer cliff,

$$d_1 = \frac{v_a \times t_1}{2} = \frac{330 \times 3}{2} = 495 \text{ m}$$

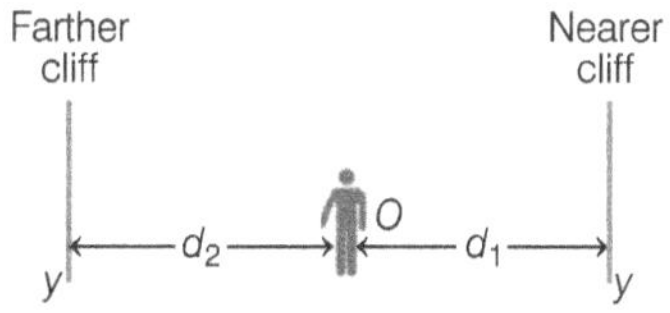

Distance of man from another cliff,

$$d_2 = \frac{v_a \times t_2}{2} = \frac{330 \times 4}{2} = 660 \text{ m}$$

Total distance between two cliffs,

$d = d_1 + d_2 = 495 + 660 = 1155$ m

(ii) An echo will not be heard when the distance between the source of sound and the reflecting surface is 10 m because to hear the echo distinctly, the minimum distance of the obstacle from the observer should be 17 m.

Q.9 A pendulum has a frequency of 4 vibrations per second. An observer starts the pendulum and fires a gun simultaneously. He hears the echo from the cliff after 6 vibrations of the pendulum. If the velocity of sound in air is 340 m/s, find the distance between the cliff and the observer. **[ICSE 2019] [3]**

Ans. Given, frequency of pendulum, $\nu = 4\,\text{Hz}$

Velocity of sound in air, $v_s = 340$ m/s

As we know that

Time period, $T = \frac{1}{\text{Frequency}} = \frac{1}{4}\,\text{s}$

Time in which echo is heard, $t = 6 \times \frac{1}{4} = 1.5$ s

According to the question, $2d = v_s \times t$

$\Rightarrow \quad d = \frac{v_s \times t}{2} = \frac{340 \times 1.5}{2} = 255$ m

Q.10 A person is standing at the sea shore. An observer on the ship which is anchored in between a vertical cliff and the person on the shore fires a gun. The person on the shore hears two sounds, 2 s and 3 s after seeing the smoke of the fired gun. If the speed of sound in the air is 320 ms^{-1}, then calculate

(i) the distance between the observer on the ship and the person on the shore. **[2]**

(ii) the distance between the cliff and the observer on the ship. **[2]**

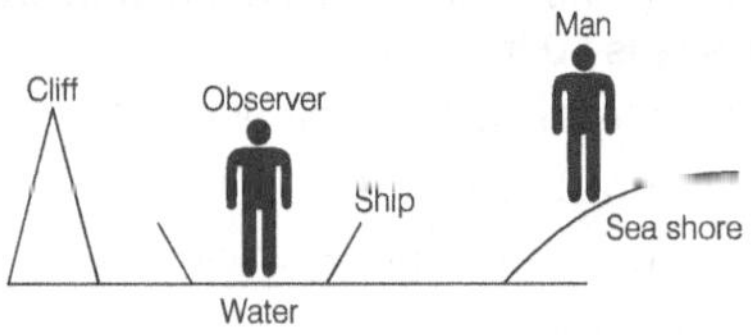

[ICSE 2018]

Ans.

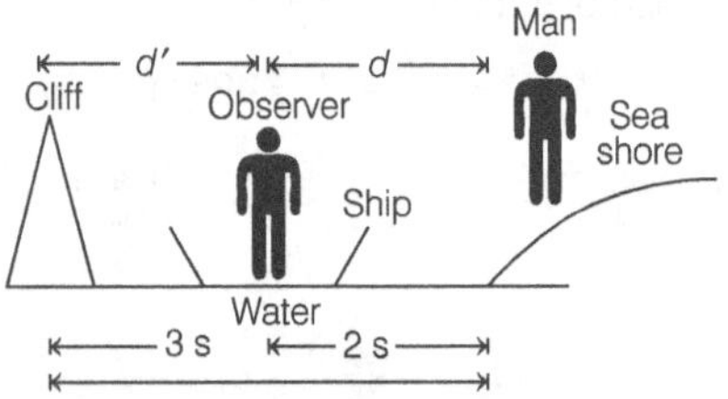

(i) Observer hears direct sound in 2 s.

As, velocity $= \frac{\text{distance}}{\text{time}}$

$\Rightarrow \quad 320 = \frac{d}{2}$

$\Rightarrow \quad d = 320 \times 2$

$= 640$ m

$\therefore$ Distance between person and observer

$= 640$ m

(ii) Observer hears reflected sound in 3 s. This means that when the observer fires the gun, sound from the observer hils and cliff and reaches the man an the shore in total 3 seconds.

$\therefore \quad 2d' + d = 3 \times 320$

$\Rightarrow \quad 2d' + 640 = 960$

$\Rightarrow \quad d' = \frac{960 - 640}{2}$

$\Rightarrow \quad d' = 160$ m

$\therefore$ The distance between the cliff and the observer in the ship is 160 m.

Q.11 Figure below shows a student clapping in front of a vertical wall. The wall reflects the sound.

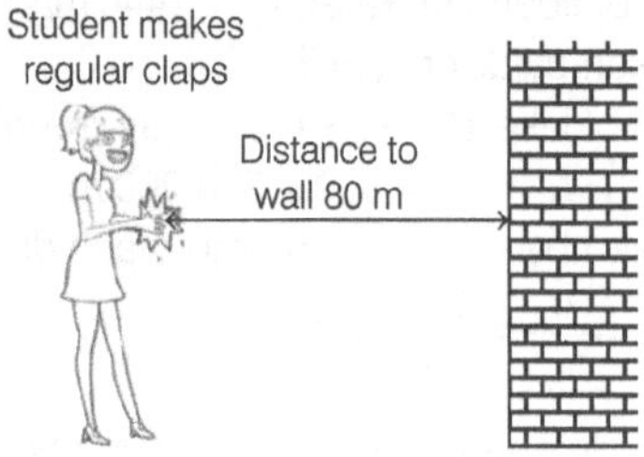

The student changes the number of claps made in 1 minute until the reflection of each clap returns to her at exactly the same time as she makes the next clap.

The speed of sound in air is 330 m/s.

(i) Explain what is meant by speed. **[1]**

(ii) Calculate the time between claps. **[1]**

(iii) Calculate the number of claps in 1 minute. **[1]**

Ans. (i) The distance travelled per unit time is known as the speed.

(ii) Speed $= \frac{2 \times \text{Distance}}{\text{Time}}$

$\Rightarrow$ Time $= \frac{2 \times \text{Distance}}{\text{Speed}}$

$= \frac{2 \times 80}{330} = 0.48$

$\therefore$ Time $= 0.48$ s

(iii) No. of claps in 1 minute

$= \frac{60}{0.48} = 125$

$\therefore$ Number of claps $= 125$

08

ELECTRICITY

Electric Charge

- Charge is an intrinsic property of matter which can be detected when there is an excess or deficiency of electrons in a body. A body is said to be **negatively charged** if it gains electrons while it is said to be **positively charged** if it loses electrons.
- Electric Charge is denoted by Q or q. The SI unit of electric charge is **coulomb (C).**
- The total charge acquired by a body is an integral multiple of magnitude of charge on a single electron. This principle is called **quantisation of charge**. The possible value of charge on a body can be $\boxed{q = \pm ne.}$

  where, q = total charge, n = number of electrons lost or gained by the body

  and e = charge on one electron $(-1.6 \times 10^{-19}\text{ C})$.

Electric Current

- It is defined as the rate of flow of electric charge through any cross-section of a conductor in unit time.

  Electric current, $\boxed{I = \dfrac{\text{Charge }(q)}{\text{Time }(t)} = \dfrac{ne}{t}}$

  where, n = number of electrons flowing through the conductor.
- The SI unit of electric current is **ampere** (A) and it is a **scalar quantity**.
- When 1 coulomb of charge flows through any cross-section of a conductor in 1 second, then the electric current flowing through it is said to be 1 ampere.

$$\boxed{1\text{ ampere} = \frac{1\text{ coulomb}}{1\text{ second}} \Rightarrow 1\text{ A} = 1\text{C s}^{-1}}$$

- Smaller units of current are **miliampere** $(1\text{ mA} = 10^{-3}\text{ A})$ and **microampere** $(1\mu\text{A} = 10^{-6}\text{ A})$.
- The conventional **direction of electric current** is taken as the opposite to the direction of the flow of electrons.

Electric Potential

- Potential is the electric state of a conductor that determines the direction of flow of charge when two conductors are placed in contact and joined by a conducting wire.
- Conductor with higher concentration of electrons is said to be at lower potential and conductor with lower concentration of electrons is said to be at higher potential.
- Electrons flow from a body at lower potential to a body at higher potential.
- Electric current always flows from a body at higher potential to a body at lower potential.
- Electric potential at a point is defined as the amount of work done to bring a unit positive charge from infinity to that point.
- If work done in moving a positive charge q from infinity to the point is W, then electric potential V of that point is

$$\boxed{V = \frac{W}{q}}$$

- It is a **scalar quantity**. The SI unit of electric potential is **volt (V)**.

Electric Potential Difference (ΔV)

- The electric potential difference between two points is defined as the work done in moving a unit positive charge from one point to another point.
- Let W be the work done in moving a charge q from point B to point A, then the potential difference $(V_B - V_A)$ between these two points is given by $\boxed{\Delta V = V_B - V_A = \frac{W}{q}}$
- The electric potential difference between two points in a current carrying conductor is said to be **1 volt**, if 1 joule of work is done in moving 1 coulomb of electric charge from one point to another point.

$$1 \text{ volt} = \frac{1 \text{ joule}}{1 \text{ coulomb}} \Rightarrow 1 \text{ V} = 1 \text{ JC}^{-1}$$

- Smaller units of electric potential, $1 \text{ mV} = 10^{-3}\text{V}$, $1\mu\text{V} = 10^{-6}$ V and larger units of electric potential, $1 \text{ kV} = 10^3$ V, $1\text{MV} = 10^6$ V

Ohm's Law

- According to this law, the electric current flowing through a conductor is directly proportional to the potential difference applied across its ends, providing the physical conditions (such as temperature, dimensions, etc.) remain unchanged.
- If V is the potential difference applied across the ends of a conductor through which current I flows, then according to Ohm's law, $V \propto I$ [at constant temperature]

or $\boxed{V = IR}$ or $\boxed{I = \frac{V}{R}}$

where, R is the constant of proportionality is called **resistance of the conductor** at a given temperature.

V-I Graph

The graph between the potential difference V and the corresponding current I is found to be a straight line passing through the origin for metallic conductors.

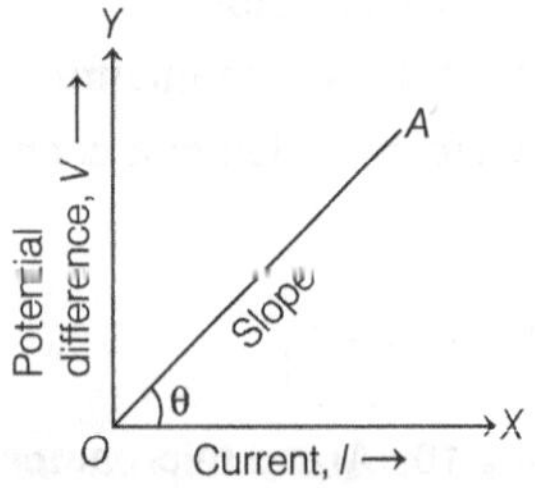

V-I graph for metal conductor

Resistance (R)

- It is that property of a conductor by virtue of which it opposes/resists the flow of charges/flow of current through it. Its SI unit is **ohm,** it is represented by the Greek letter Ω.

  Resistance of a conductor is given by $R = \frac{V}{I}$.
- From the above formula, it is clear that **current is inversely proportional to resistance.** If resistance is doubled, then current gets halved and if resistance is halved, then current gets doubled.
- It is said to be **1 ohm**, if a potential difference of 1 volt across the ends of the conductor makes a current of 1 ampere to flow through it.

  i.e. $$1 \text{ ohm} = \frac{1 \text{ volt}}{1 \text{ ampere}} \Rightarrow 1\Omega = \frac{1 \text{ V}}{1 \text{ A}} = 1 \text{ VA}^{-1}$$
- The reciprocal of resistance is known as **conductance (G)** and its SI unit is **siemen (S).**

$$\Rightarrow \boxed{G = \frac{1}{R}}$$

Factors Affecting the Resistance of a Conductor

The resistance of a conductor depends on the following factors

(i) **Length of the Conductor** The resistance (R) of a conductor is directly proportional to its length (l),

i.e. $$R \propto l \qquad \text{...(i)}$$

Resistance increases with increase in length of conductor.

(ii) **Area of Cross-section of the Conductor** The resistance of a conductor (R) is inversely proportional to its area of cross-section (A),

i.e. $$R \propto \frac{1}{A} \qquad \text{...(ii)}$$

Resistance of thicker wire is smaller as compared to thin wire.

(iii) **Nature of the Material of the Conductor** The resistance also depends upon the nature of the material of the conductor of which it is made. Some materials offer low resistance whereas others offer high resistance.

Hence, from Eqs. (i) and (ii), we get $R \propto \frac{l}{A}$ or $R = \rho \frac{l}{A}$

where, ρ is the constant of proportionality called resistivity.

(iv) **Effects of Temperature** Resistance of a conductor increases linearly with increase in temperature while resistance of a semiconductor and insulators decrease with increase in temperature.

Specific Resistance (Resistivity) and Conductivity

- The resistance offered by a conductor of unit length and unit cross-sectional area is called **resistivity**. Its SI unit is **ohm-metre**.
- The resistivity of a material does not depend on its length or thickness but depends on the nature of the substance and temperature.
- **Conductivity** is defined as the reciprocal of resistivity of a conductor. Its SI unit is **ohm per metre (Ω m^{-1})** or **siemen per metre** (S m^{-1}).
- It is expressed as $\boxed{\sigma = \frac{1}{\rho}}$

Ohmic and Non-ohmic Resistors

- The conductors which obey Ohm's law are called **ohmic resistors (**or **linear resistance)**. e.g. Silver, nichrome, copper, iron, etc. The *V-I* graph for these resistor is a straight line passing through the origin.

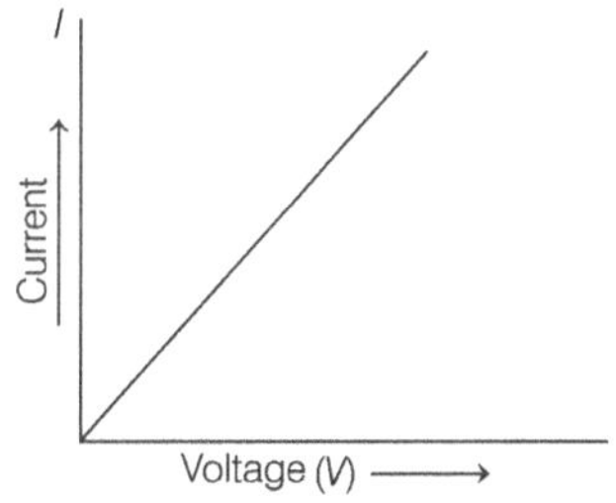

V-I graph of ohmic resistors

- Whereas those conductors which do not obey Ohm's law are known as **non-ohmic resistors** (or **non-linear resistance**). e.g. Triode valve, junction diode, transistor, etc. The *V-I* graph for these resistors is a curve line.

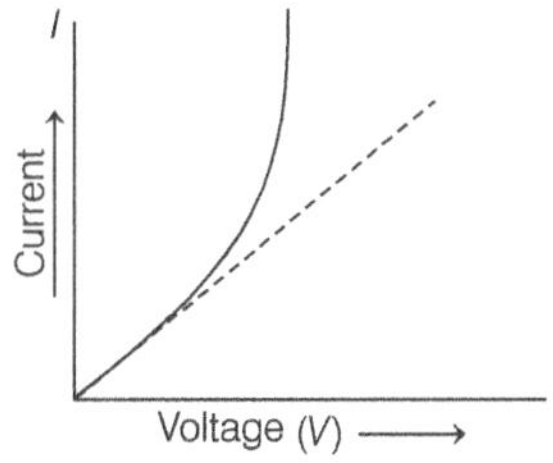

V-I Graph of non-ohmic resistor

Superconductors

A substance which has zero resistance below a certain temperature is known as a superconductor. e.g., Mercury below 4.2 K, lead below 7.25 K.

Electromotive Force (EMF) of a Cell (ε)

- The work done by the cell in moving a unit positive charge through the whole circuit (including the cell) is called the electromotive force (emf) of the cell. If during the flow of q coulomb of charge in an electric circuit, the work done by the cell is W, then

$$\text{emf of the cell, } \varepsilon = \frac{W}{q}$$

- Its unit is **joule/coulomb** or **volt**.

Internal Resistance (r)

- It is defined as the resistance offered by the electrolyte of the cell to the flow of current through it. It is denoted by r. Its unit is also ohm.
- **Internal resistance of a cell depends on the following factors**
  (i) It is directly proportional to the separation between the two plates of the cell.
  (ii) It is inversely proportional to the plate area dipped into the electrolyte.
  (iii) It depends on the nature, concentration and temperature of the electrolyte and increases with increase in concentration and decreases with increase in temperature of electrolyte.

Terminal Potential Difference (V)

Terminal potential difference of a cell is defined as the potential difference between the two terminals of the cell in a closed circuit (i.e. when current I is drawn from the cell). It is represented by V and its unit is **volt**. It is always less than the emf of the cell, while discharging

i.e. $$V = \varepsilon - Ir$$

Relationship among EMF, Terminal Voltage and Internal Resistance

In the given circuit,

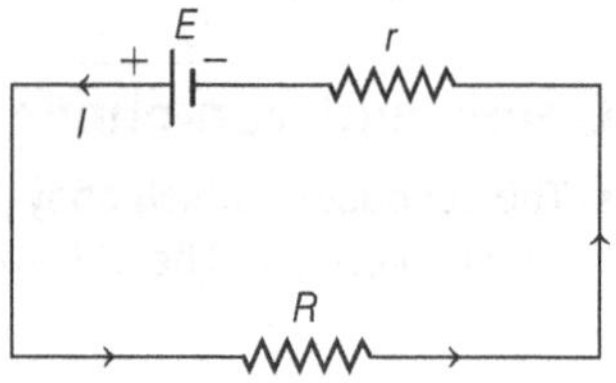

- Total resistance of circuit $= R + r$
- Current drawn from the cell, $I = \dfrac{E}{R + r}$
- EMF of the cell $E = I(R + r)$.
  where, r is the internal resistance, R is external resistance and I is current through the circuit.
- Terminal voltage of the cell, $V = IR = E - Ir$
- Voltage drop due to internal resistance $= Ir$
- Internal resistance , $$r = \frac{E - V}{I} = \frac{E - V}{V/R} = \left(\frac{E}{V} - 1\right) R$$

Combination of Resistors

(i) **Series Combination of Resistors** When two or more resistors are connected end to end, they are said to be connected in series. This is also known as **maximum** effective **resistance.**

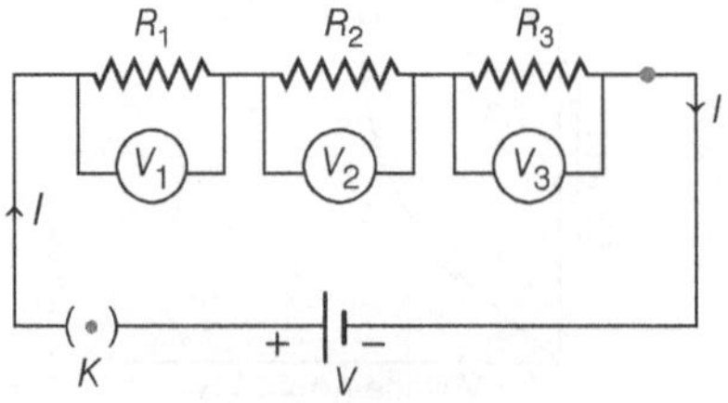

$$V = V_1 + V_2 + V_3$$

The equivalent resistance in series combination is given as

$$R_{eq} = R_1 + R_2 + R_3$$

(ii) **Parallel Combination of Resistors** When one end of the given resistors is connected at one point and other end is connected to other point, then it is called parallel combination of resistors.

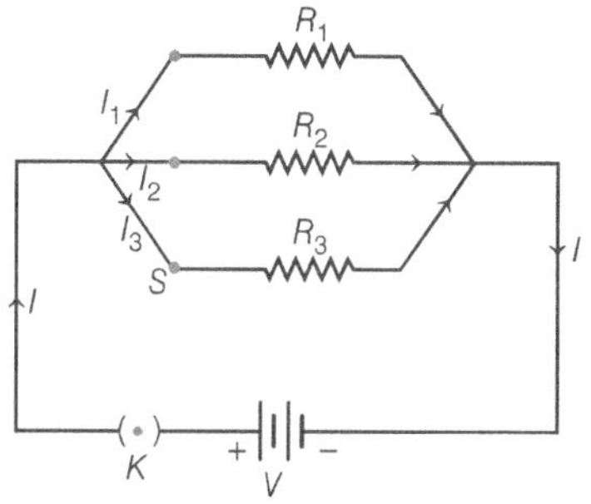

This is also known as **minimum effective resistance.**

The equivalent resistance of parallel combination of resistors is given as

$$\Rightarrow \quad \frac{1}{R_{eq}} = \frac{1}{R_1} + \frac{1}{R_2} + \frac{1}{R_3}$$

Electrical Energy

- The energy consumed during the flow of electric current in a circuit is called electrical energy.

$\therefore$ It can be given as

$$W = q \times V \qquad \text{...(i)}$$

From definition of current, we know that

$$I = \frac{q}{t} \text{ or } q = I \times t \qquad \text{...(ii)}$$

From Ohm's law, $\frac{V}{I} = R$ or $V = IR$ ... (iii)

Substituting the values of q and V in Eq. (i), we get

$$W = (I \times t) \times IR = I^2RT = VIt = \frac{V^2t}{R}$$

$\therefore$ Electric energy, $$E = W = I^2Rt = VIt = \frac{V^2t}{R}$$

- SI unit of electrical energy is **joule (J)**, where, 1 joule = 1 volt × 1 ampere × 1 second.

Applications of Electric Energy

(i) When an electric current is passed through a metallic wire, it gets heated up due to its resistance and the electrical energy is converted into heat energy.

(ii) When an electric current is passed through an electric motor, its coil begin to rotate. The electrical energy is converted into mechanical energy.

(iii) When an electric current is passed through an electric lamp, the filament of the bulb gets heated and it glows. Thus, electrical energy is converted into heat and light energy.

(iv) When the output of a microphone (sound to electrical energy) which is in the form of electric pulses is passed to a loud speaker, the electrical energy is converted into sound energy.

Heating Effect of Electric Current

- When an electric current is passed through a conductor, heat is produced in it. This is known as heating effect of electric current. This is obtained by the **transformation of electrical energy into heat energy**, e.g. electric heater, electric iron, etc.

  It can be given as, $\boxed{H = I^2Rt}$
- The SI unit of heat is **Joule.**

Electric Power

- It is defined as the amount of electric energy consumed in a circuit per unit time.
- If W be the amount of electric energy consumed in a circuit in t seconds, then the electric power is given by

$$\boxed{P = \frac{W}{t} = VI = \frac{V^2}{R} = I^2R} \qquad \left[\because W = VIt \text{ and } I = \frac{V}{R}\right]$$

- The SI unit of electric power is **watt** (W).
- It is said to be **1 watt**, if 1 ampere current flows through a circuit having 1 volt potential difference.

  i.e. 1 watt = 1 volt × 1 ampere = 1 VA
- Electrical energy is the product of power and time, i.e. $E = P \times t$. So, its unit will be **watt hour (W-h).**

  One watt-hour is the energy consumed in which 1 watt of power is used for one hour.
- **Bigger units of power** are as given below

  1 kilowatt (kW) $= 10^3$ W, 1 megawatt (MW) $= 10^6$ W and 1 gigawatt (GW) $= 10^9$ W
- **Practical unit of power** is horse power.

$$1 \text{ HP} = 746 \text{ W}$$

- **Commercial unit of electrical energy**

  One kilowatt hour is the electrical energy consumed by an appliances of 1000 watts when used for one hour.

$$1 \text{ kWh} = 1000 \text{ W-h} = 1000 \times 3600 \text{ W-s} = 3.6 \times 10^6 \text{ W-s} = 3.6 \times 10^6 \text{ J}$$

- Number of units consumed by electric appliances $= \dfrac{\text{watt} \times \text{hours}}{1000}$
- Cost of electricity = Energy consumed (in kWh) × Rate in rupees per unit.

Power Rating of Common Appliances

The electrical appliances such as electric bulb, geyser bulb, heater, etc., are rated with power and voltage. We calculate the following two quantities such as

(i) Resistance of the filament of the bulb (coil),

$$R = \frac{V^2}{P} = \frac{(\text{Voltage rating of appliance})^2}{\text{Power rating of appliance}}$$

(ii) Safe limit of current through the filament of the bulb (coil),

$$I = \frac{P}{V} = \frac{\text{Power rating of appliance}}{\text{Voltage rating of appliance}}$$

Household Consumption of Electrical Energy

The electrical energy consumed by a household appliance in a certain time (t) is given as

$$\text{Energy (in kWh)} = \text{Power (in kW)} \times \text{Time (in h)} = \frac{\text{Power (in W)} \times \text{Time (in h)}}{1000} = \frac{V\,(\text{volt}) \times I\,(\text{ampere}) \times t\,(\text{hour})}{1000}$$

Now, cost of the electricity will be given as,

Cost of electricity = Energy consumed (in kWh) × Rate in rupee per unit.

House Wiring (Ring) System

- In a house, the wiring is commonly done by the **ring system**. A ring system of wiring connects a lamp, a socket with switch and a fan is shown below.

- In this system, the wires starting from the main fuse box run around all the rooms of the house and then come back to the fuse box again forming the ring.

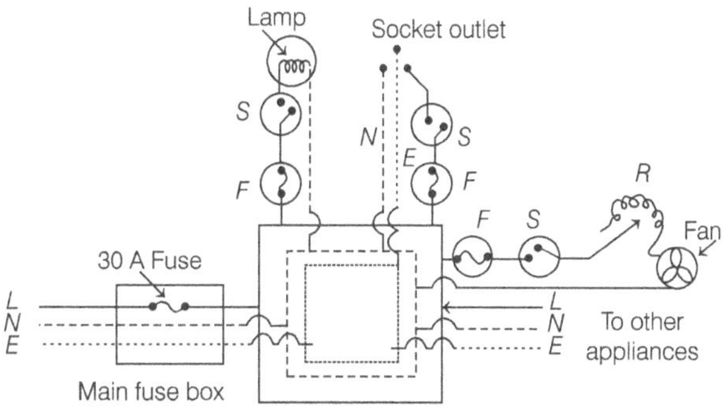

- In this system, the terminal of the appliance is connected to the live wire through a separate fuse and at a separate switch while the other terminal is directly connected to neutral wire.

Advantages of the Ring System

The advantages of the ring system are given as

(i) Each appliance can operate independently, without affecting the other appliances connected in the system.

(ii) To install a new appliance in a room, a new line up to the distribution box is not required but it can be directly connected to the ring circuit of the room.

(iii) In this system, all the plugs and sockets used can be of same size but each socket should have its own fuse of rating suitable for the appliance connected with it.

Power Distribution

The electric power is generated at the power generating stations. The power from these stations is transmitted over long distances at a high voltage to minimise the loss of energy in the form of heat in the line wires used for transmission.

This is because at high voltages the value of current is very less. Therefore, from the relation of the heating effect produced, i.e. $H = I^2RT$, will also be less at low current. Hence, the energy loss will be least.

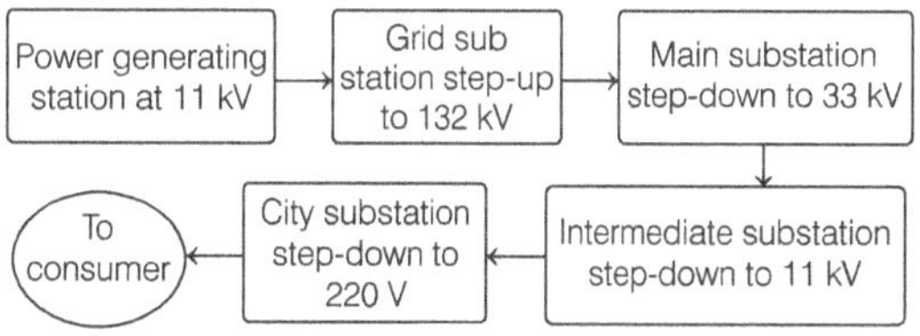

Block diagram representing the power distribution

Components of House Hold Circuit

Main Circuit

- The main circuit has three wires such as **live (or phase) wire (*L*)**, **neutral wire (*N*)** and the **earth wire (*E*)**. The neutral and the earth wires are connected together at the local substation, so that the neutral and the earth wires are at the same potential (0V).
- The live wire carries current from the source to the distribution board, while the neutral wire is for the return path of current. The connections are made to the distribution board through a **main fuse** and a **main switch.**

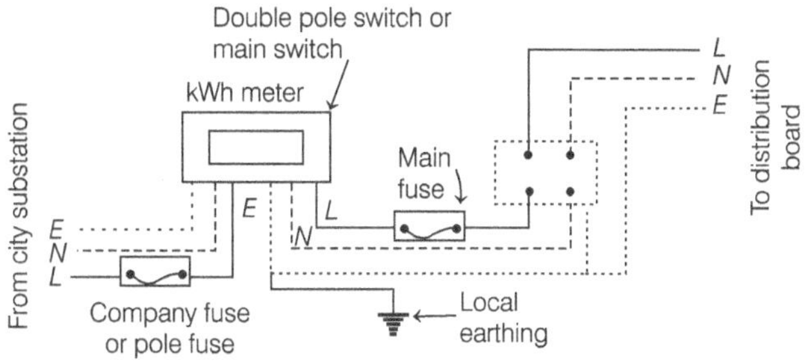

A schematic diagram of main circuit

Switch

In an electrical circuit, switch is used to start or stop the flow of current.

Two-Way Switch

- It uses two or more switches present in different locations to control one lamp. They all are wired, so that operation of either switch will control the lights. This given figure illustrates that how light is controlled from two different locations.

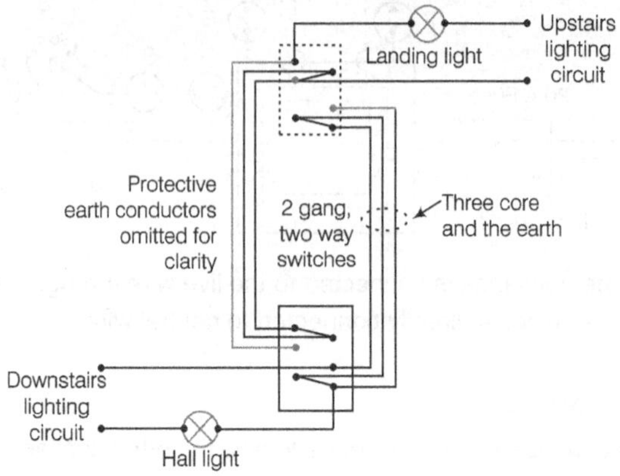

Staircase Wiring

- It is a dual control switch system in which the double-pole type switches are used at the top and bottom of a staircase.
- Staircase wiring or dual control switch has two pathways for making the switch ON/OFF. The following diagrams illustrate a dual switch with two switches S_1 and S_2. The circuit can be switched ON either using switch S_1 or S_2.

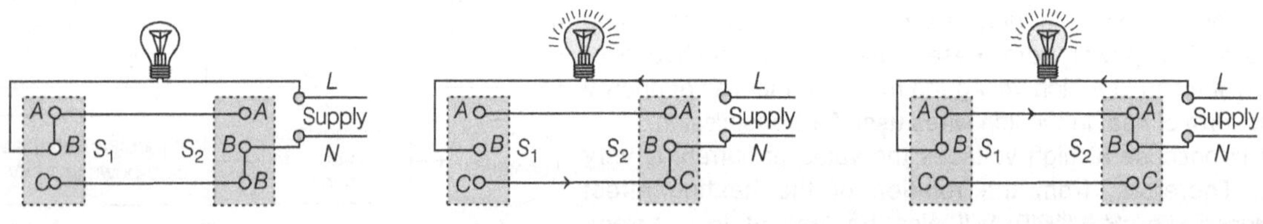

(a) Bulb OFF (b) Bulb ON through switch S_1 (c) Bulb ON through switch S_2

Earthing

- Earthing means to connect the metal case of the appliance to the earth (i.e. zero potential) by means of a metal wire called the **earth wire** (in green/yellow insulation cover). One end of the metal wire is buried in the earth. The appliances are connected to the earth by using the top pin of a 3-pin plug.
- Earthing saves us from electrical shocks.

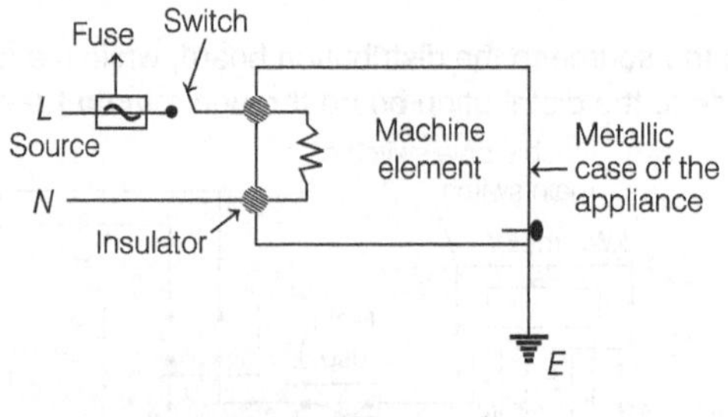

The symbol ⏚ is used for earthing or grounding the appliances.

Fuse

- Fuse is used as a safety device in household circuits and is based on heating effect of current. It is connected in series with the mains supply.
- A fuse consists of an alloy of **lead** and **tin** which has appropriate melting point and high resistance.

REVISION NOTES

When the current flowing through the circuit exceeds the safe limit, the temperature of the fuse wire increases, it gets melted and breaks the circuit. This helps in protecting the other circuit elements from hazards caused by heavy current.

MCB : Miniature Circuit Breaker

- In these days, instead of a fuse, an MCB is used for each individual circuit. If due to short circuit (or some fault), a heavy current flows in the circuit, the MCB falls down to switch OFF the circuit in a very short time ($\approx$ 25 ms). After repairing the fault in the circuit, the MCB is raised up.
- Thus, the use of MCB is more convenient and safe in comparison to a fuse.
  (i) It avoids the inconvenience of connecting a new fuse and wire.
  (ii) It is much safer due to its quick response.

Three-Pin Plug and Socket with Conventional Location of Wires

- In a three-pin plug, the **top pin is for earthing**, the **left pin is for live** and the **right pin is for neutral**.
- A **socket** is fixed in an electric circuit in which the plug is inserted. It has **three holes** whose inner walls are made up of hollow metallic tubes.
- The **upper bigger hole** in the socket is for the **earth connection**, while the **hole on the right side** is for connection to **live wire** and the **hole on left side** is for connection to the neutral wire of electric supply.

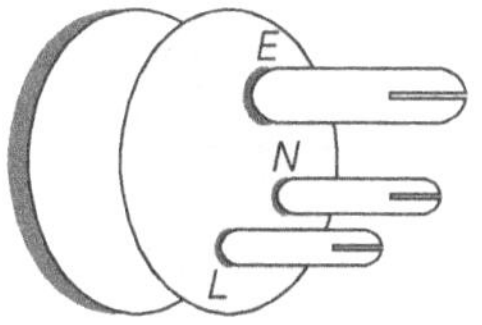

Three-pin plug

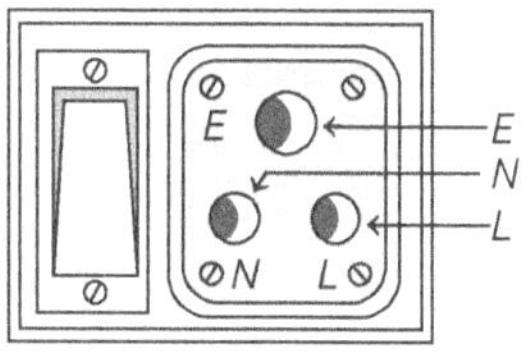

Socket

Safety precautions while using the switch

(i) A switch should not be touched with wet hands.
(ii) The switch should always be connected in the live wire.
(iii) Electrical appliances should be properly earthed.
(iv) Always use appropriate fuse rating in the live wire of the circuit.

Colour Coding of Wires

The colour coding of wires in a cable are as

Wires	Colour	
	Old Convention	**New Convention**
Live	Red	Brown
Neutral	Black	Light blue
Earth	Green	Green or Yellow

EXAM ORIENTED QUESTIONS

TYPE - 1 01 Mark

Multiple Choice Questions

Q.1 The graph plotted for potential difference (*V*) against current (*I*) for ohmic resistors is **[ICSE 2022 Sem-II]**

(a) a curve passing through the origin
(b) a straight line not passing through origin
(c) a straight line passing through origin
(d) a circle centred at the origin.

Ans. (c)

Q.2 The graph shows *I* against *V* relation for three conductors *A, B* and *C*. Choose the correct relation for the resistors of *A, B* and *C*. **[ICSE Specimen 2023]**

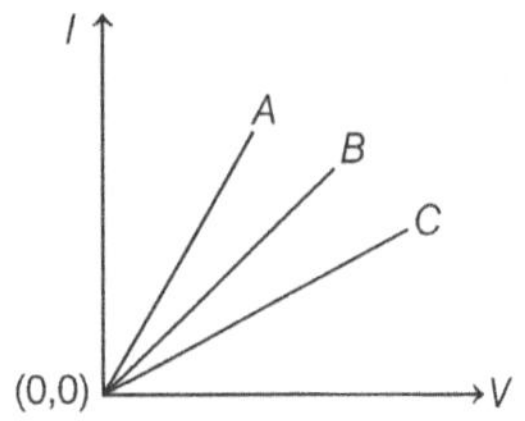

(a) $R_A > R_B > R_C$ (b) $R_B > R_C < R_A$
(c) $R_C > R_B < R_A$ (d) $R_C > R_B > R_A$

Ans. (d) $R_C > R_B > R_A$

Slope $= \frac{1}{V} = \frac{1}{R}$ is least for R_C

A is the best conductor, as it has the least resistance among *A, B* and *C*.

Q.3 The graph of voltage vs current for four different materials is shown below.

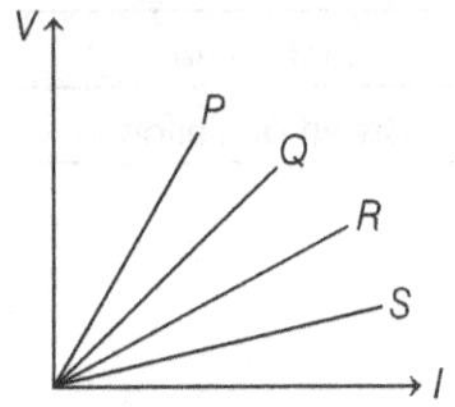

Which of these four materials would be used for making filament of a bulb? **[ICSE Specimen 2025]**

(a) Q (b) S
(c) P (d) R

Ans. (c) Resistance, R = Slope of *V*-*I* graph = $\tan\theta$

As, $\theta_P > \theta_Q > \theta_R > \theta_S$

$\Rightarrow R_P > R_Q > R_R > R_S$

The filament of a bulb is made up of high resistance material. So, material *P* is used to make its filament.

Q.4 The resistance of a cylindrical wire *P* is 80 Ω. A second wire *Q* is made from the same material. The cross-sectional area of *Q* is four times that of *P*. The length of *Q* is twice the length of *P*.

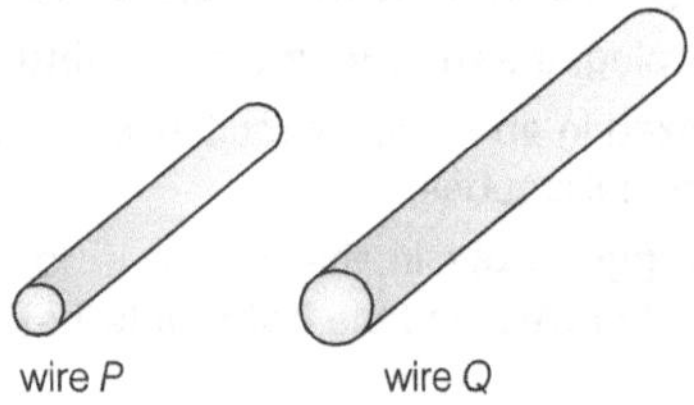

What is the resistance of wire *Q*?

(a) 10 Ω (b) 40 Ω
(c) 160 Ω (d) 640 Ω

Ans. (b) As $R \propto \frac{l}{A}$, if the length of the wire is doubled, the resistance is doubled. If the cross-sectional area is made four times, the resistance becomes one fourth. The combination of the two will reduce the resistance to half.

Q.5 The specific resistance of a conductor depends on its **[ICSE 2024]**

(a) length (b) material
(c) area of cross-section (d) radius

Ans. (b) Specific resistance is a characteristic property of the material of a conductor. Hence, specific resistance of conductor depends on its material.

Q.6 The potential difference between terminals of a cell in a closed electric circuit is **[ICSE 2024]**

(a) terminal voltage
(b) electromotive force
(c) voltage drop
(d) None of the above

Ans. (a) The potential difference between terminals of a cell in a closed electric circuit is terminal voltage. Its unit is volt.

Q.7 Which of the following is not a characteristic of parallel combination of resistors? **[ICSE 2022 Sem-II]**

(a) If one resistor is fused, the circuit does not become open.
(b) The total resistance R is given by the formula
$$\frac{1}{R} = \frac{1}{R_1} + \frac{1}{R_2} + \frac{1}{R_3} ....$$
(c) The total resistance becomes less than the least resistor, present in the combination.

(d) The current through each resistor always remains the same.

Ans. (d) In a parallel circuit, the current is divided among the different branches based on their individual resistance. Therefore, the current through each resistor will not be the same unless all resistors have the same resistance.

Q.8 When a current I flows through a wire of resistance R for time t, then the electrical energy produced is given by **[ICSE 2023]**

(a) I^2Rt (b) IR^2t (c) IRt (d) IRt^2

Ans. (a)

Q.9 One horse power is equal to **[ICSE Specimen 2022 Sem-II]**

(a) 100 W (b) 735 W (c) 764 W (d) 746 W

Ans. (d)

Q.10 A main switch in the main distribution board is present in **[ICSE 2022 Sem-II]**

(a) a live wire

(b) a neutral wire

(c) a live as well as neutral wire

(d) an earth wire

Ans. (c)

Q.11 Which of the following is the correct colour code of the three wires live, neutral and earth? **[ICSE Specimen 2023]**

(a)	Live : Green	Neutral : Red	Earth : Yellow
(b)	Live : Brown	Neutral : Red	Earth : blue
(c)	Live : Brown	Neutral : Blue	Earth : Yellow
(d)	Live : Blue	Neutral : Brown	Earth : Green

Ans. (c)

Q.12 According to the old convention, the colour of the earth wire is **[ICSE Specimen 2025]**

(a) black (b) green

(c) yellow (d) red

Ans. (b) According to old convention, the colour of live, neutral and earth wires are red, black and green respectively.

Q.13 Identify the option that displays the correct wiring with correct colour code. **[ICSE 2024]**

(a)

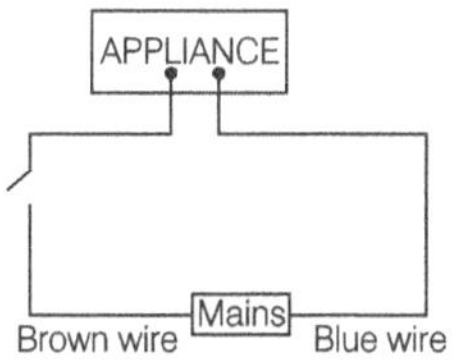

(b)

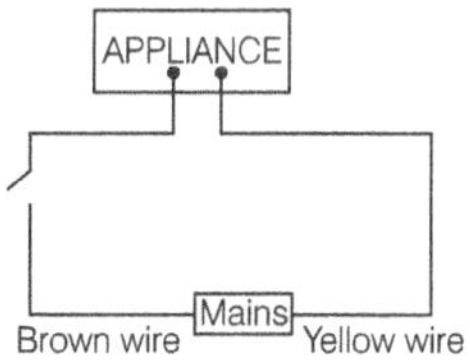

(c)

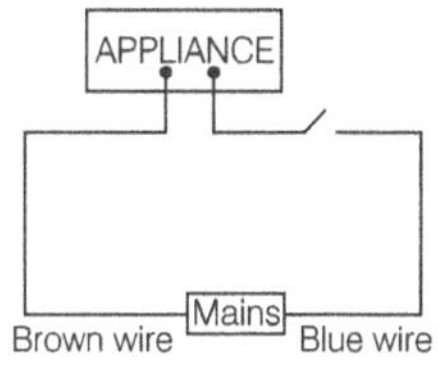

(d)

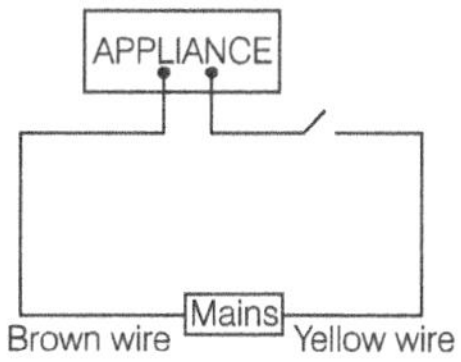

Ans. (a) The live wire is represented with brown colour, the neutral wire is represented as blue colour. Fuse or key is connected in live wire. So, option (a) is correct.

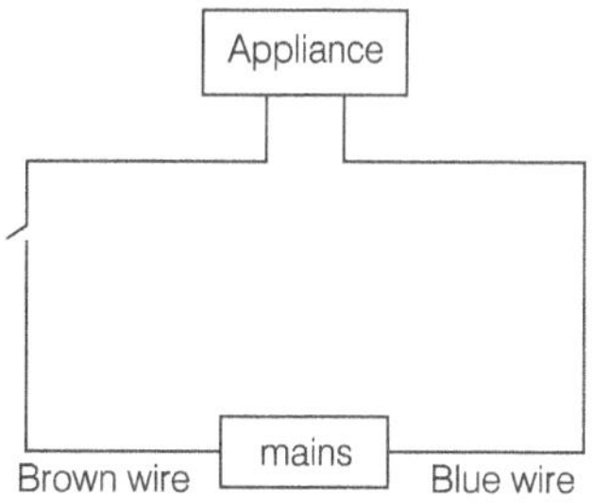

Q.14 The cable of an electric fan becomes so warm that the live wire makes electrical contact with the metal case. The case is earthed. The plug to the fan contains a 5 A fuse. There is a current of 4 A when the fan works normally.
What will happen?

(a) The current will run to earth and the fuse will not be affected.

(b) The fuse will melt and switch OFF the circuit.

(c) The metal case will become live and dangerous.

(d) The metal case will become very hot.

Ans. (b) The current now flows directly from the live wire to the earth *via* the metal case. Since, the main circuit in the fan is by passed, the resistance of this connection is going to much lower than before. Hence, a large current will flow and the fuse will overheat and blows.

Q.15 In the given circuits Y and Z, the resistors R_1 and R_2, are connected in **[ICSE 2025]**

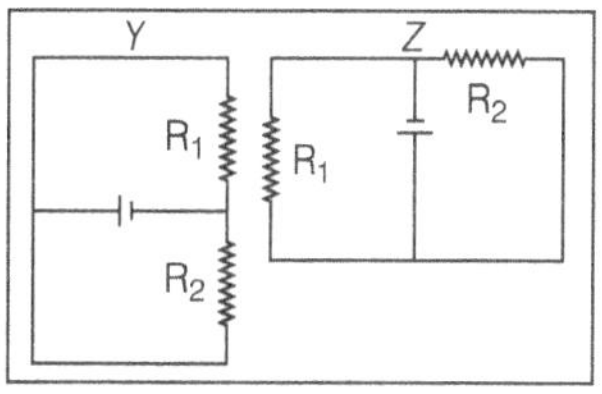

(a) series in both the circuits

(b) parallel in both the circuits

(c) parallel in Y and series in Z

(d) series in Y and parallel in Z

Ans. (b)

Q.16 A current of 2A flows through a conductor for 5 s. The total charge that flow is

(a) 2 C

(b) 5 C

(c) 10 C

(d) 0.4 C

Ans. (c) Total charge is given by $Q = I \times t$

where, $I = 2\text{A}$ and $t = 5\ \text{s}$

Thus, $Q = 2 \times 5 = 10\ \text{C}$

Q.17 In a closed circuit containing a bulb and a cell, the electromotive force (ε) and the terminal voltage (V) is related as **[ICSE 2025]**

(Given, I is current and r is internal resistance)

(a) V = ε + Ir (b) V = ε − Ir

(c) V = ε ÷ Ir (d) V = ε × Ir

Ans. (b)

Q.18 A wire has a resistance of 50 Ω. If its length is doubled and its cross-sectional area is halved, its new resistance will be

(a) 5 Ω (b) 10 Ω

(c) 200 Ω (d) 40 Ω

Ans. (c) Resistance (R) is proportional to the length (L) and inversely proportional to cross-sectional area (A) $R \propto \frac{L}{A}$. If L is doubled and A is halved, R becomes 4 × the original resistance.

Thus, $R = 50 \times 4 = 200\ \Omega$

Q.19 A cell has an emf of 6V and an internal resistance of 1Ω. When a resistor of 5Ω is connected across it, the current through the circuit is

(a) 1 A (b) 1.2 A

(c) 6 A (d) 0.5 A

Ans. (a) Total internal resistance = $R_{internal} + R_{external}$

$= 1 + 5 = 6\Omega$ Current is given by $I = \frac{E}{R_{total}} = \frac{6}{6} = 1\text{A}$

TYPE - 2

01 Mark

Assertion-Reason Type Questions

Directions (Q. Nos. 1-6) In the following questions two statements are given as Assertion and Reason.

(a) Both A and R are true and R is the correct explanation of A.

(b) Both A and R are true and R is not the correct explanation of A.

(c) A is true but R is false.

(d) A is false but R is true.

Q.1 Assertion (A) The resistance of a conductor increases with an increase in its length.

Reason (R) Resistance is directly proportional to the length of the conductor and inversely proportional to its cross-sectional area.

Ans. (a) The resistance (R) of a conductor is given by

$$R = \rho \frac{l}{A}$$

Where, ρ is the resistivity, L is the length, and A is the cross-sectional area. Since, $R \propto L$, if the length increases, resistance increases proportionally.

Q.2 Assertion (A) In a parallel circuit, the total resistance is less than the resistance of any of the individual branches.

Reason (R) The reciprocal of the total resistance in a parallel circuit is equal to the sum of the reciprocals of individual resistances.

Ans. (a) In parallel circuit, the total resistance (R_{total}) is calculated using

$$\frac{1}{R_{total}} = \frac{1}{R_1} + \frac{1}{R_2} + \ldots$$

This results in R_{total} being less than the smallest resistance in the branches because adding reciprocals increases the total value.

Q.3 Assertion (A) Electric toaster and fuse are the devices, which work on the principle of Joule's law of heating.

Reason (R) According to Ohm's law, $V \propto I$.

Ans. (b) Electric toasters and fuses work on Joule's law of heating, which states that the heat produced is proportional to the square of the current, resistance and the time.

∴ $H = I^2Rt$

Ohm's law states, $V = IR$

Q.4 Assertion (A) Alloys used in electrical heating devices like electric iron.

Reason (R) Alloys oxidise readily at high temperature.

Ans. (c) The resistivity of alloy is much more higher than those of the pure metals. So, the heating elements of electrical heating appliance such as electric iron and toaster etc., are made up of an alloy. Alloys do not oxidise readily at high temperature.

Q.5 Assertion (A) 80W bulb will glow brighter than 60W bulb when arranged in parallel.

Reason (R) The power dissipated across 80W bulb is more than 60 W bulb.

Ans. (a) ∵ $R_{60W} > R_{80W}$

So, 80 W bulb will glow brighter.

Q.6 Assertion (A) A switch will serve the purpose of making and breaking a circuit when it is connected to the neutral wire.

Reason (R) Neutral wire is at zero potential. **[Competency Based Que.]**

Ans. (d) A switch is always connected to the live wire, not the neutral wire. Connecting it to the neutral wire would not completely disconnect the device from the power supply, which can be dangerous.

TYPE - 3
01/02 Marks

Fill in the Blanks

Q.1 Emf of a cell is .... (greater than / less than / equal to) the terminal voltage when the cell is in open circuit. **[ICSE 2025]**

Ans. equal to

Q.2 In parallel circuit, the voltage across each resistor is .... (equal, different, double). **[1]**

Ans. equal

Q.3 The unit of electrical energy commonly used in household is .... (joule, watt, kilowatt-hour). **[1]**

Ans. kilowatt-hour

Q.4 Electrical power is transmitted from power stations to substations using .... [high/low/neutral] voltage to reduce energy loss.

Ans. high

Q.5 Two copper wires can have the different .... [resistivity/resistance] but will have same .... [resistance/resistivity]. **[2][Latest Specimen 2025]**

Ans. resistance, resistivity

Q.6 In metallic conductor, the drift velocity of electrons decreases if the .... [area/temperature] increases because of the resistivity .... [increases/ decreases] **[2]**

Ans. temperature, increases

Q.7 Two resistors connected in parallel have the same .... [current/voltage] across them but may carry different .... [current/voltages] **[2]**

Ans. voltage, current

TYPE - 4
02 Marks

Very Short Answer Type Questions

Q.1 A current flows through a metallic conductor for a long period of time. State the change you would expect in its **[2][ICSE 2025]**

(i) Resistance (ii) Resistivity

Ans. (i) Since the current flows for a long period of time so the resistance will increase due to the heating effect of current.

(ii) Since, resistivity is also dependent on temperature and it increases with the increase in temperature so the resistivity is also affected in the above case.

Q.2 Define specific resistance and state its SI unit. **[ICSE 2017]**

Ans. . Specific resistance or resistivity (ρ) of a conductor is defined as the resistance of a conductor of unit length and unit area of cross-section.

From the factors affecting the resistance of a conductor, the resistance is given by

$$R = \rho \frac{l}{A}$$

$$\Rightarrow \quad \rho = \frac{RA}{l} = \frac{\Omega\text{-m}^2}{\text{m}} = \Omega\text{-m}$$

Its SI unit is ohm-metre (Ω - m).

Specific resistance or resistivity is the characteristic property of a conducting material and it depends only on the nature of that material and temperature.

Q.3 A geyser is rated 240 W-220 V. Explain the meaning of this statement. **[ICSE 2023]**

Ans. A geyser is rated 240 W-220 V means that the geyser operates at 240 W when connected to a 220 V source.

Q.4 (i) At what frequency is AC supplied to residential houses? **[1]**

(ii) Name the wire in a household electrical circuit to which the switch is connected. **[1] [ICSE 2015]**

Ans. (i) The frequency of AC supplied to residential houses is 50 Hz.

(ii) An electrical switch is always connected to live wire.

Q.5 If live wire makes an accidental contact with the metal case, which circuit (*A* or *B*) in the diagram, illustrating an electric iron, is considered safe for the user (Assuming the fuse is present in the live wire in both circuits)? Justify your answer.

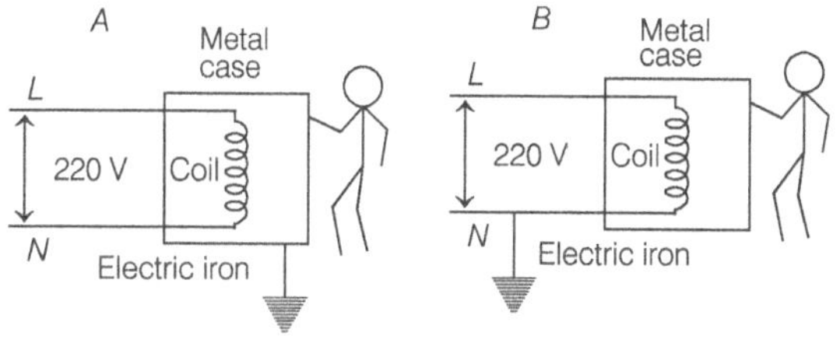

[ICSE Specimen 2025]

Ans. In circuit *A*, metal case is earthed. So, the person would not get electric shock but in circuit *B*, metal case is not earthed. So, the circuit will be completed through the body of the person giving him a shock. Therefore, circuit *A* is safe for the user.

Q.6 Redraw the diagram by linking points *A*, *B* and *C* to the points *X*, *Y*, and *Z* on the socket.
[Competency Based Que.]

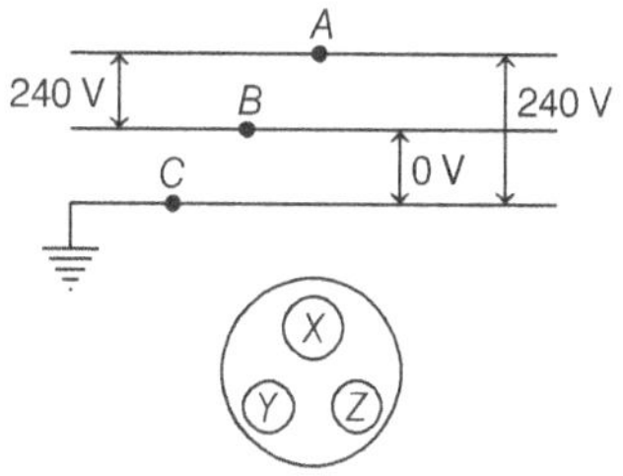

Ans.

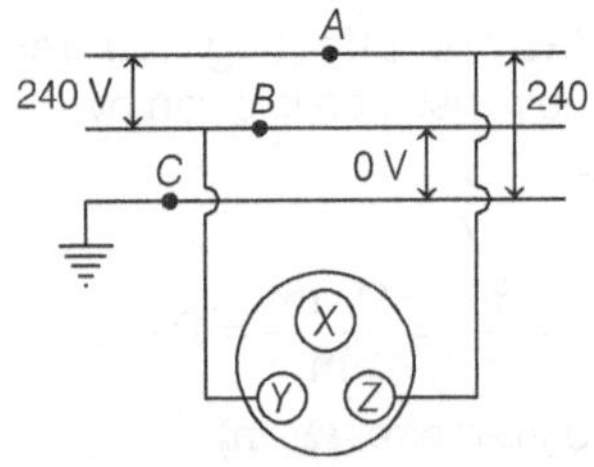

Q.7 (i) Which electrical component protects the electric circuit in case of excess current and which can also be used as a switch? **[1]**

(ii) Name the wire to which this electrical component is connected in an electric circuit. **[1] [ICSE 2023]**

Ans. (i) The miniature circuit breaker is an electrical part that functions as a switch and secures the electric circuit from excess current.

(ii) The wire connected to MCB is called the line wire or phase wire.

Q.8 According to the new colour convention which colour of wire is connected to **[2][ICSE 2025]**

(a) the metal body of the appliance

(b) the switch of the appliance?

Ans. (a) Green or Yellow (Earth) (b) Brown (Live).

Q.9 5 bulbs are connected in series in a room. One bulb is fused. It is removed and remaining 4 bulbs are again connected in series to the same circuit. What will be the effect on the following physical quantities? (Increases, decreases, remain same) **[ICSE 2024]**

(i) Resistance (ii) Intensity of light **[1+ 1]**

Ans. (i) Resistance decreases.

(ii) Intensity of light increases.

TYPE - 5 — 03 Marks

Short Answer Type Questions

Q.1 (i) Draw a graph of potential difference (V) versus current (I) for an ohmic resistor. **[1]**

(ii) How can you find the resistance of the resistor from this graph? **[1]**

(iii) What is a non-ohmic resistor? **[1][ICSE 2011]**

Ans. (i) The graph of potential difference (V) versus current (I) for an ohmic resistor is shown below

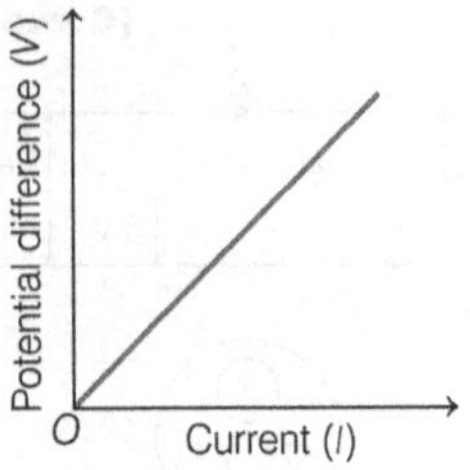

(ii) The resistance of the resistor is given by the slope of the straight line in the V-I graph.

(iii) The conductor which does not obey Ohm's law is known as non-ohmic resistor.

Q.2 The diagram shows wiring in a meter room of a building. **[3][ICSE 2025]**

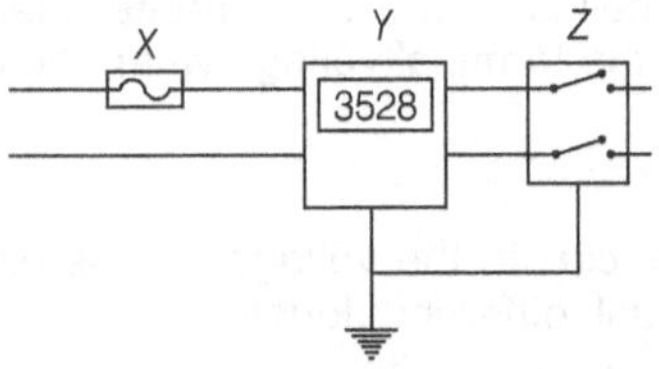

(i) What is the current rating of device X?

(ii) What is the difference between the switch Z shown in the diagram and the switches you use to operate different appliances at home?

(iii) What is the unit of the physical quantity displaced in Y?

Ans. (i) 5 ampere.

(ii) Switch Z is the main switch which is a double pole switch which helps in breaking the connection with both neutral and live wires simultaneously from the main supply which is not present in switches used for operating household appliances.

(iii) Kilowatt hour (kWh).

Q.3 Jack's friend Jones performs an experiment with a 6 V, 12 W lamp connected in series with a resistor R and a source of voltage 12 V.

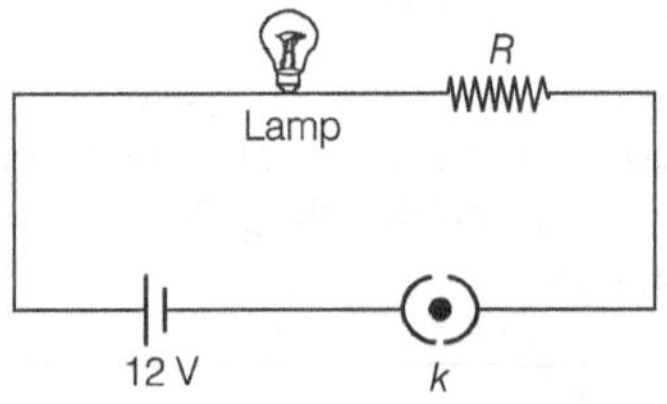

(i) What is the purpose of the resistor R? **[1]**

(ii) Calculate the value of the resistor R, for the proper working of the lamp. **[1]**

(iii) What is the current flowing through the circuit? **[1]**

Ans. (i) The given lamp is meant to be used on supply of voltage 6 V. Since, the source available is of voltage 12 V, so a resistor R is used in series with the lamp to reduce the current to its safe value for the lamp.

(ii) Maximum current which the lamp of rating 6 V, 12 W can withstand, is $I = \frac{P}{V} = \frac{12}{6} = 2$ A

Resistance of the filament of lamp, while in use,

$$R' = \frac{V^2}{P} = \frac{6^2}{12} = 3\Omega$$

On connecting a resistor R in series with the lamp, total resistance of circuit,

$$R_t = R + R' = (R + 3)\Omega$$

With supply of voltage 12 V, the current in the circuit should be $I = 2$ A

By Ohm's law, $V = IR_t$

$\therefore \quad 12 = 2(R + 3)$

or $\quad 12 = 2R + 6$ or $R = 3\Omega$

(iii) Current flowing through the circuit is 2A.

Q.4 (i) Write an expression for the electrical energy spent in the flow of current through an electrical appliance in terms of *I*, *R* and *t*. **[1]**

(ii) At what voltage is the alternating current supplied to our houses? **[1]**

(iii) How should the electric lamps in a building be connected? **[1][ICSE 2012]**

Ans. (i) The expression for the electrical energy, $E = I^2Rt$.

(ii) Alternating current supplied to our houses is at voltage 220 V.

(iii) The electric lamps in a building should be connected in parallel.

Q.5 (i) Name the electrical appliance shown in the diagram below. **[1]**

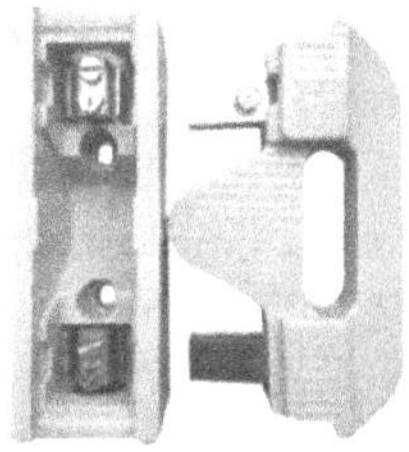

(ii) Name the material of the wire used in this device. **[1]**

(iii) Name two important characteristics of this wire. **[1]**
[ICSE Specimen Sem-II 2022]

Ans. (i) The electrical appliance shown in the diagram is called fuse.

(ii) The material used in fuse wire is made up of an alloy of lead (Pb) and tin (Sn) having a low melting point of 250°C.

(iii) Characteristics of fuse wire

(a) It has high resistivity. (b) It has low melting point.

Q.6 Purvi's friend Tim wants to connect a fuse to his oven. He wants to control the oven from two different locations. Shown below is his circuit diagram

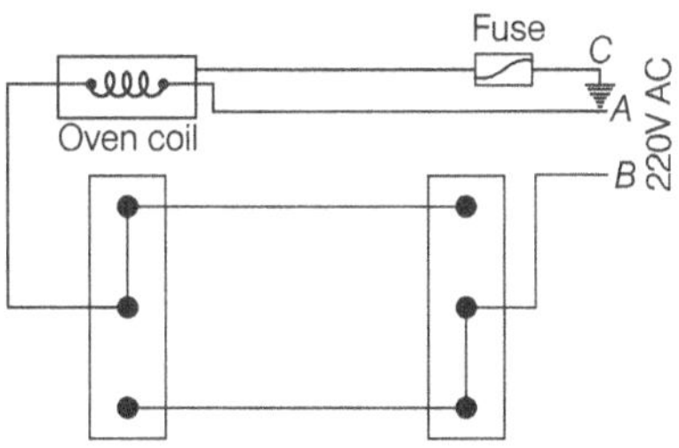

(i) Which one of the two, *A* or *B* should be a live wire? **[1]**

(ii) In the event of an overload, will the fuse serve its purpose? **[1]**

(iii) What is the meaning of the statement that the bulb is rated 600 W, 220V? **[1]**
[ICSE Specimen 2024]

Ans. (i) The switch is always connected to the live wire. In above diagram, wire *B* is connected to switch so wire *B* must be the live wire.

(ii) No, the fuse will not serve its purpose. In the diagram, the fuse is connected to the earth wire and not the live wire. In case of overload, the excess current will pass through the oven and damages it.

(iii) It means that if the bulb is operated on a 220 V supply, the electric power consumed by it is 600 W i.e., 600 J of electric energy is consumed by the bulb in 1s.

Q.7 (i) If one of the switches in a staircase wiring circuit is defective, describe what happens to the circuit. **[1]**

(ii) Write two advantages of using staircase wiring in buildings. **[2]**

Ans. (i) If one switch is defective, the circuit will not be completed and the bulb will not light regardless of the position of the other switch.

(ii) **Advantages**

(a) Convenient control of lights from multiple locations.

(b) Saves energy by allowing users to switch OFF lights from either end of the staircase, reducing unnecessary power consumption.

Q.8 The diagram below shows a bulb connected by dual control switches. Observe the diagrams and answer the questions that follow.

(i) Which of the above circuits will be able to switch ON or switch OFF the bulb using both switches?

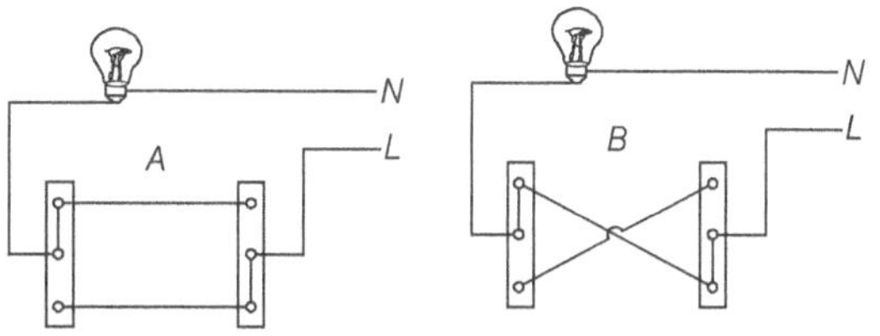

(ii) At present, in which circuit is the bulb glowing?

(iii) If we interchange the *L* and *N* wires in circuit *B*, will the circuit work? **[Competency Based Que.]**

Ans. (i) Both circuits will be able to switch ON and switch OFF the bulb using both switches.

(ii) The bulb is glowing in circuit *B* because the path is complete, allowing current to flow.

(iii) Yes, the circuit will function.

Q.9 Figure shows a main extension lead. The six sockets allow several electrical appliances to be connected to the main supply through one cable.

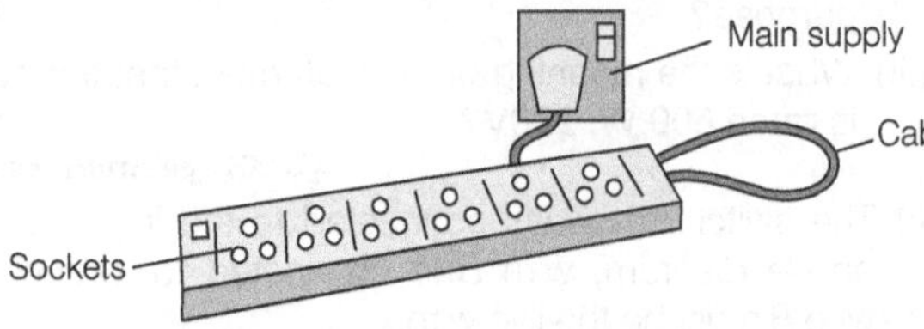

(i) The cable connects the sockets to the mains supply.
The cable contains three wires: live, neutral and earth. State what is meant by
(a) live,
(b) neutral and
(c) earth? **[1]**

(ii) Six powerful lamps are plugged into the sockets and switched ON, one by one. Describe why it can be dangerous when a fuse of the wrong value is used in the plug. **[1]**

(iii) Explain why your hands should be dry when you put a plug into a socket. **[1]**

Ans. (i) (a) The live wire means the wire at a high voltage.
(b) The neutral wire means the wire at zero voltage.
(c) The earth wire is at zero voltage and is connected to the ground.

(ii) A fuse of a wrong value can allow more current to pass through the cable. This would cause overheating and melting of the cable.

(iii) The hands of person should be dry when putting a plug into a socket to avoid an electric shock as water makes good contact of your body with electric current.

Q.10 Three wires with proper colour coding are connected to the three terminals of a three pin socket. Match the colour of the wire with the proper terminals *A*, *B* and *C* of the socket. **[ICSE 2022 Sem-II]**

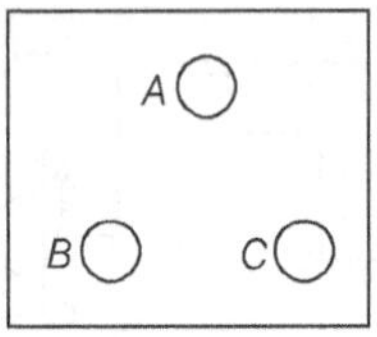

(i) Brown **[1]**
(ii) Green **[1]**
(iii) Light blue **[1]**

Ans. (i) Colour of the wire Brown-Terminal *C* (Live)
(ii) Colour of the wire Green- Terminal *A* (Earth)
(iii) Colour of the wire Light blue- Terminal *B* (Neutral)

TYPE - 6 — 04 Marks

Long Answer Type Questions

Q.1 The current in the transmission line used to supply electrical power to a village is 65 A. The power is transmitted at a voltage of 23000 V.

(i) Calculate the power supplied to the village. **[1]**

(ii) The transmission line has a resistance of 3.0 Ω Calculate
(a) the potential difference across a 3.0 Ω resistor that carries a current of 65 A. **[1]**
(b) the thermal energy (heat) produced in 1.0 s in a 3.0 Ω resistor that carries a current of 65 A. **[1]**

(iii) (a) State one advantage of transmitting electrical power at a high voltage.
(b) Suggest one reason why the main power supply to the houses in the village is at a voltage much lower than 23000 V. **[1]**

Ans. (i) Power = Voltage × Current
$= 23000 \times 65 = 1.5 \times 10^6$ W

(ii) (a) Potential difference, $V = IR = 65 \times 3.0 = 195$ V
(b) Heat energy = VIt
$= 195 \times 65 \times 1 = 12675$ J

(iii) (a) There is less energy loss at higher voltage. For constant power when v increases, I decreases, I^2RT decreases. So, less energy is dissipated.
(b) The main power supply to houses is at a voltage much lower than 23000 V to minimise the chance of electric shock.

Q.2 A schematic diagram of main circuit is given below

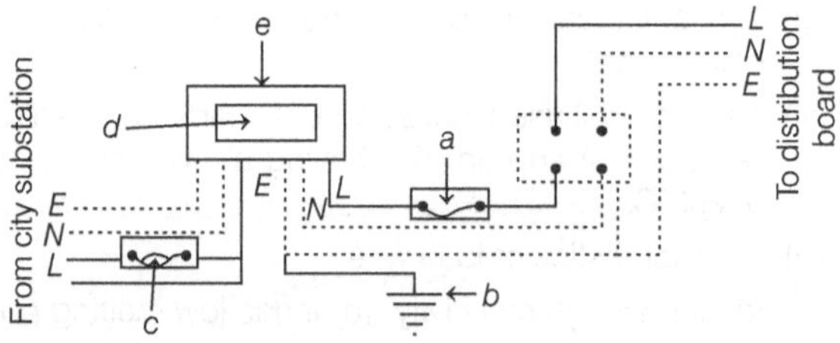

Complete the table using the labels from the figure. The first label is done for you. **[4]**

S.No.	Description	Label
(a)	Main fuse	*a*
(b)	kWh meter	
(c)	Local earthing	
(d)	Pole fuse	
(e)	Main switch	

Ans.

S.No.	Description	Label
(a)	Main fuse	*a*
(b)	kWh meter	*e*
(c)	Local earthing	*b*
(d)	Pole fuse	*c*
(e)	Main switch	*d*

Q.3 A fuse is one form of protection in an electrical circuit.

(i) State two other forms of protection that are included in household electrical circuits which can protect the consumer, the circuit or an electrical appliance. **[1]**

(ii) Figure shows a fusebox connected to part of a lighting circuit in a house.

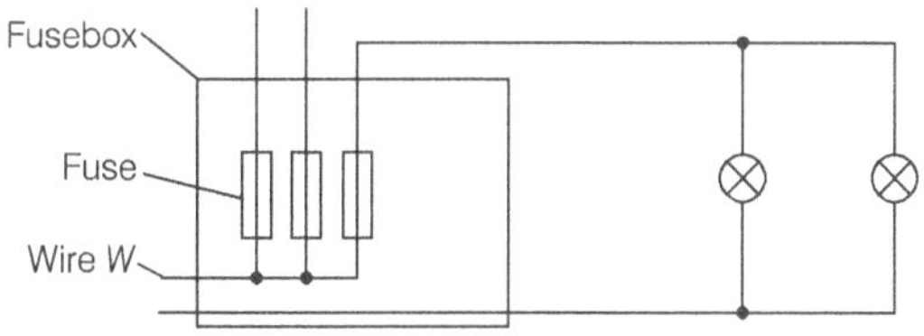

(a) State how figure shows that wire W is the live wire? **[1]**

(b) On figure, mark with a letter S, the correct position for a switch that controls both lamps. **[1]**

(c) The rating of the fuse in the lighting circuit is 5 A. **[1]**

Explain, what this means ?

Ans. (i) I. Circuit breaker

II. Earthing

(ii) (a) Fuse is connected at the live wire in series between the source and component / load / appliance.

(b)

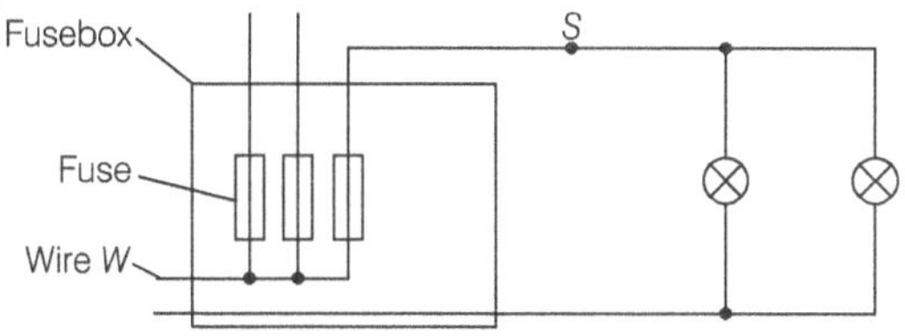

(c) Fuse blows up to break the circuit if current greater than 5A flows through it.

TYPE - 7

03/04 Marks

Case Based Questions

Q.1 Electrical resistivities of some substances at 20°C are given as below

Silver = 1.60×10^{-8} Ω-m, Copper = 1.62×10^{-8} Ω-m

Tungsten = 5.2×10^{-8} Ω-m, Iron = 10.0×10^{-8} Ω-m

Mercury = 94.0×10^{-8} Ω-m

Nichrome = 100×10^{-8} Ω-m

Answer the following questions using above data

(i) Among silver and copper, which one is a better conductor and why? **[1]**

(ii) Which material would you advise to be used in electrical heating devices and why? **[1]**

(iii) Among tungsten and nichrome which one has a higher resistivity and why it is preferred for heating elements? **[1]**

Ans. (i) Silver is a better conductor due to its lower resistivity.

(ii) Nichrome should be used in electrical heating devices due to very high resistivity, so it gets heated easily.

(iii) Nichrome has a higher resistivity (100×10^{-8} Ω-m) compared to tungsten (52×10^{-8} Ω-m). It is preferred for heating elements because its high resistivity ensures greater heat production and it has good resistance at high temperatures.

Q.2 The circuit depicted in the figure is employed for studying Ohm's Law. Instead of using a standard resistor, a student opts for a glass tube filled with mercury (tube 1), connected to the circuit through two electrodes E_1 and E_2. He records the readings of the ammeter and voltmeter, thereby calculates the resistance. The student repeats the experiment by substituting tube 1 with tube 2 which has more length and less area of cross-section. where the same amount of mercury fills the tube 2. **[Latest Specimen 2025]**

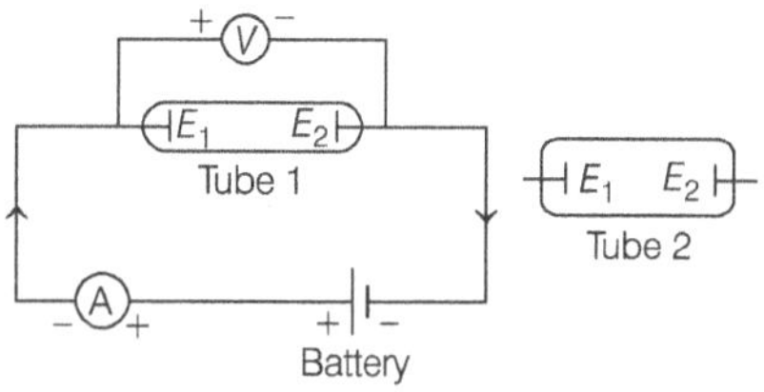

Neglecting internal resistance of the cell use (> or < or =) to compare

(i) the resistance in both the cases. **[1]**

(ii) the voltmeter readings in both the cases. **[1]**

(iii) the specific resistance in both the cases. **[1]**

Ans. (i) The resistance R is given by $R = \rho \dfrac{l}{A}$

For tube 1 and tube 2, the volume V of mercury is the same.

$$V = A \cdot l \Rightarrow A_1 \cdot l_1 = A_2 \cdot l_2$$

Since, $l_2 > l_1$ (longer tube), $A_2 < A_1$

(Smaller cross sectional area)

Thus, $R_2 > R_1$ (resistance increases with longer tube)

(ii) The voltage, $V = IR$

For the same current I, $V_2 > V_1$ because $R_2 > R_1$. Hence, the voltmeter reading is higher for tube 2.

(iii) Specific resistance (ρ) is material property and is independent of the dimensions of the tube.

So, specific resistance is the same for both cases.

Q.3 An electric bulb is a simple source of light. A bulb is a simple apparatus that converts electrical energy into light energy. A wire filament is used that glows on providing electricity.
An electric bulb is made up of positive and negative terminals embedded inside the glass. A thin wire which gives the light is connected to both terminals. When electricity is supplied to the terminals, the flow of electrons heats up the thin filament.

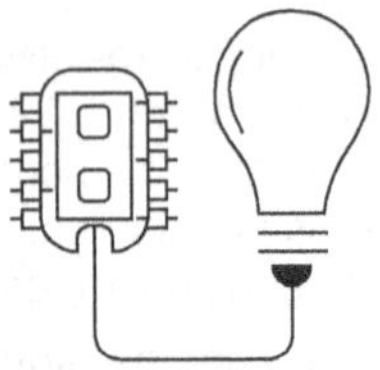

Electric switch has connected to electric bulb

↓

Electric bulb glows using electric switch after current passes through it.

(i) Name the phenomena on which the electric bulb is based. [1]

(ii) Name any other device which is based on this phenomena. [1]

(iii) Write the expression for calculating electrical power of bulb in terms of resistance and potential difference. [1]

Ans. (i) Heating effect of current

(ii) Electric fuse

(iii) $P = \dfrac{V^2}{R}$

TYPE - 8

Numerical Questions

Q.1 A music system draws a current of 400 mA, when connected to a 12 V battery.

(i) What is the resistance of the music system? **[1]**

(ii) The music system is left playing for several hours and finally the battery voltage drops and the music system stops playing when the current drops to 320 mA. At what battery voltage does the music system stop playing? **[1][ICSE 2016]**

Sol. Given, current, $I = 400$ mA $= 400 \times 10^{-3}$ A $= 0.4$ A

Voltage, $V = 12$ V

(i) Resistance of the music system is

$$R = \frac{V}{I} = \frac{12}{0.4} = \frac{120}{4} = 30\,\Omega$$

(ii) Resistance of music system, $R = 30\,\Omega$,

Current, $I = 320\text{mA} = 0.32$ A

By Ohm's law, $R = \dfrac{V}{I} \Rightarrow V = IR$

$\Rightarrow \quad V = 0.32 \times 30$

$\Rightarrow \quad V = 9.60\text{V}$

Q.2 Calculate the total resistance across AB. **[2][ICSE 2020]**

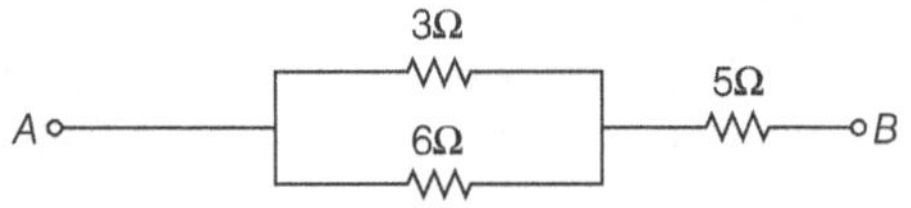

Sol. Total resistance between A and B.

$$R_{AB} = (3\,||\,6) + 5 = \frac{3 \times 6}{3+6} + 5 = 2 + 5 = 7\ \Omega$$

Q.3 You are given three resistors of magnitude 3 Ω each. You can join them either in a series or in parallel combination. How will you arrange them so that the equivalent resistance would become

(i) maximum (ii) minimum

[Competency Based Que.]

Ans. (i) maximum, when they are combined in series

$$R_{max} = 3 + 3 + 3 = 9\ \Omega$$

(ii) minimum, when they are combined in parallel

$$\frac{I}{R} = \frac{1}{3} + \frac{1}{3} + \frac{1}{3}$$

$$R_{min} = 1\Omega$$

Q.4 You have three resistors of values 2Ω, 3Ω and 5Ω. How will you join them, so that the total resistance is more than 7Ω?

(i) Draw a diagram for the arrangement. **[1]**

(ii) Calculate the equivalent resistance. **[1][ICSE 2018]**

Sol. To get total resistance more than 7 Ω, we can connect 2 Ω, 3 Ω and 5 Ω in series.

(i)

(ii) $R_{eq} = R_1 + R_2 + R_3$ [For series combination]

$R_{eq} = 2 + 3 + 5 = 10\,\Omega$

Q.5 A metal wire has a resistance of 60 Ω. It is cut into three equal lengths. Find the equivalent resistance when two parts are connected in parallel and the third part is in series with them. **[2][ICSE Specimen 2018]**

Sol. Resistance of wire = 60 Ω

When cut into three equal parts.

Resistance of each part $= \frac{60}{3} = r = 20\,\Omega$

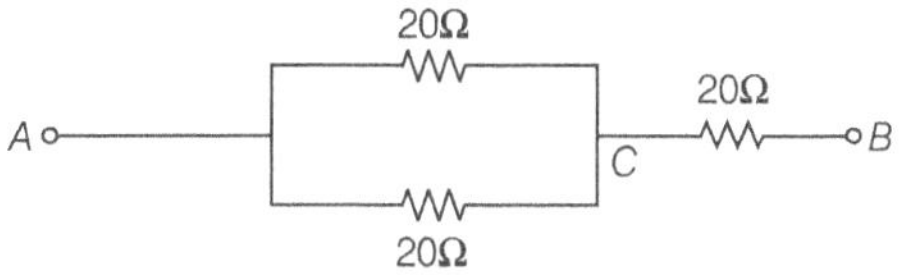

Resistance between A and C is given by

$$\frac{1}{R'} = \frac{1}{20} + \frac{1}{20} = \frac{2}{20} = \frac{1}{10} \Rightarrow R' = 10\,\Omega$$

Now resistance between A and B is

$$R'' = 10 + 20 = 30\,\Omega$$

Q.6 Find the equivalent resistance between points A and B. **[3][ICSE 2015]**

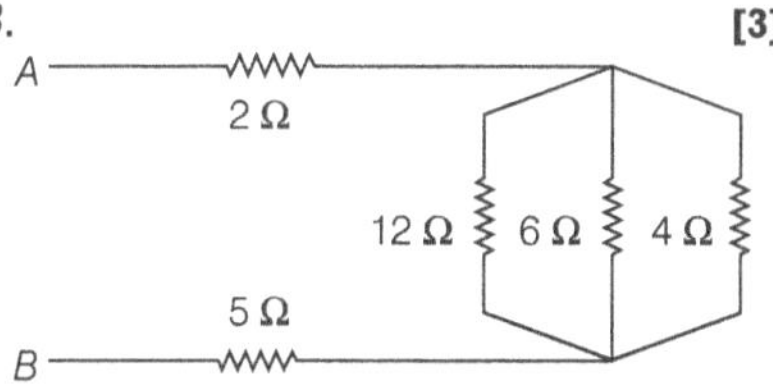

Sol.

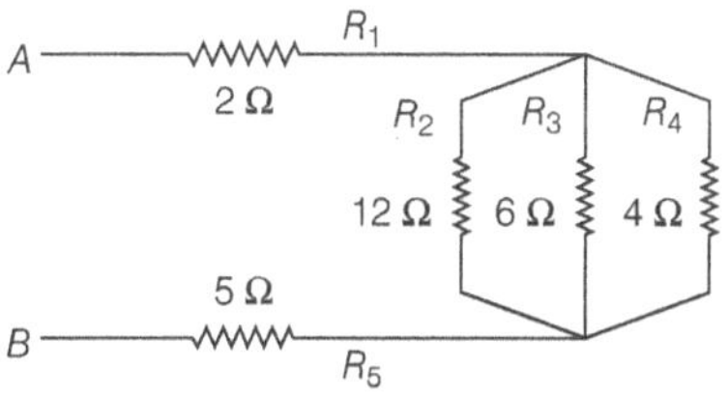

R_2, R_3 and R_4 are in parallel.

So, equivalent resistance corresponding to them

$$R_p = \frac{R_2R_3R_4}{R_3R_2 + R_3R_4 + R_4R_2}$$

$$= \frac{12 \times 6 \times 4}{6 \times 12 + 6 \times 4 + 4 \times 12}$$

$$R_p = \frac{288}{144} = 2\,\Omega$$

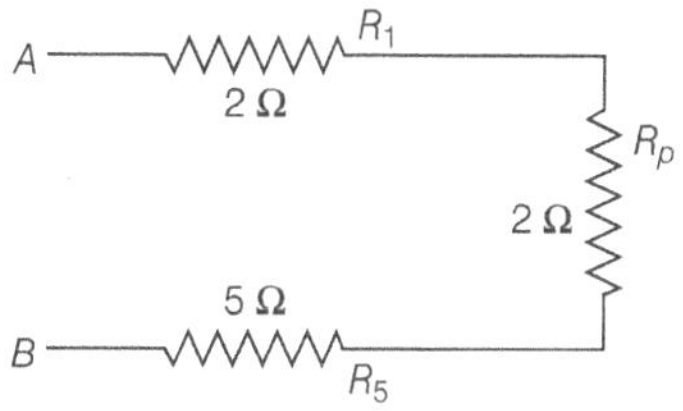

R_1, R_p and R_5 are in series.

Now, equivalent resistance will be given by,

$$R = R_1 + R_p + R_5$$
$$= 2 + 2 + 5$$
$$R = 9\,\Omega$$

Q.7

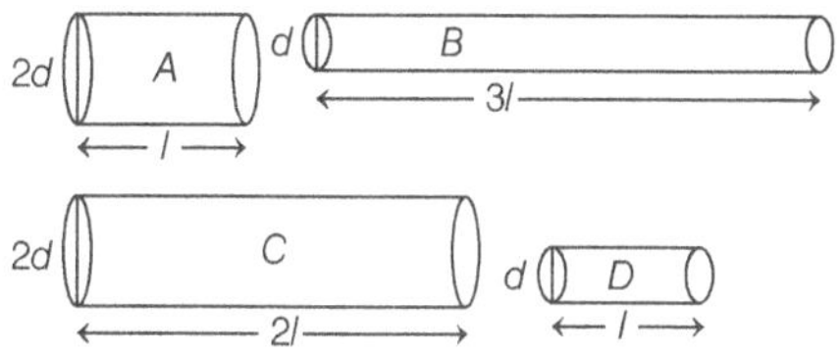

In the above diagram, calculate the ratio of the resistances A, B, C and D.

[4][Competency Based Que.]

Ans. The resistance R of a wire is given by

$$R = \rho \frac{l}{A}$$

where, ρ = resistivity,

l = length of the wire and

A = cross-sectional area

The cross - sectional area A of a cylindrical wire,

$$A = \pi r^2$$

where, r is the radius, given that diameter d and $2d$ are mentioned, we use

$$A = \pi\left(\frac{d}{2}\right)^2 = \frac{\pi d^2}{4} \Bigg\} \text{ For wires } B \text{ and } D$$

$$A = \pi\left(\frac{2d}{2}\right)^2 = \pi d^2 \Bigg\} \text{ For wires } A \text{ and } C$$

For wire A

Length = l, diameter = $2d$ and area = πd^2

$$\therefore \quad R_A = \rho \frac{l}{\pi d^2}$$

For wire B

Length = $3l$

diameter = d,

area $= \frac{\pi d^2}{4}$

$$R_B = \rho \frac{3l}{\frac{\pi d^2}{4}} = \rho \frac{12l}{\pi d^2}$$

For wire C

Length = $2l$

diameter = $2d$, area = πd^2

$$R_C = \rho \frac{2l}{\pi d^2}$$

For wire D

Length = l

diameter = d, area = $\frac{\pi d^2}{4}$

$$R_D = \rho \frac{l}{\frac{\pi d^2}{4}} = \rho \frac{4l}{\pi d^2}$$

∴ The ratio of resistances A, B, C and D are

$$A : B : C : D = \rho \frac{l}{\pi d^2} : \rho \frac{12l}{\pi d^2} : \rho \frac{2l}{\pi d^2} : \rho \frac{4l}{\pi d^2}$$

$$= 1 : 12 : 2 : 4$$

Q.8 There are two copper wires of length ratio 1 : 2 that have their cross-sectional areas in the ratio 1 : 4. What will be the ratio of their

(i) resistances? [2]

(i) specific resistances? [2]

[Competency Based Que.]

Ans. Given,

length ratio = $l_1 : l_2$

= 1:2

Cross-sectional area ratio = $A_1 : A_2 = 1 : 4$

(i) Using the resistance formula,

$$R_1 = \rho \frac{l_1}{A_1} \text{ and } R_2 = \rho \frac{l_2}{A_2}$$

$$\therefore \quad \frac{R_1}{R_2} = \frac{\rho \frac{l_1}{A_1}}{\rho \frac{l_2}{A_2}}$$

$$\therefore \quad \frac{R_1}{R_2} = \frac{l_1}{A_1} \times \frac{A_2}{l_2}$$

∵ Substituting given values

$$\therefore \quad \frac{R_1}{R_2} = \frac{1}{1} \times \frac{4}{2} = 2 : 1$$

(ii) Specific resistance (resistivity), ρ is a material property and depends only on the material.

Since both wires are made of copper, their specific resistances are equal.

$$\therefore \quad \frac{\rho_1}{\rho_2} = 1 : 1$$

Q.9 An electric bulb of resistance 500 Ω, draws a current of 0.4A. Calculate the power of the bulb and the potential difference at its end. [2][ICSE 2017]

Sol. Given, resistance of bulb, $R = 500\ \Omega$

Current, $I = 0.4$ A

Power, $P = ?$

Potential difference, $V = ?$

As we know power, $P = I^2R = (0.4)^2 \times 500$

Power, $P = 80$ W

∴ Potential difference, $V = IR$

$= 0.4 \times 500 = 200$ V

Q.10 A fuse is rated 5 A. Can it be used with a geyser rated 1540 W, 220 V. Write yes or no. Give supporting calculations to justify your answer. [2][ICSE 2024]

Sol. No, a 5A fuse cannot be used with a geyser rated at 1540 W, 220 V. The current drawn by the geyser is 7A, which exceeds the rating of the 5A fuse. Hence, there will be a risk of fire when the geyser is used with a 5A fuse.

Alternate solution

No, a 5A fuse cannot be used with a geyser rated at 1540 W, 220 V.

Current drawn by geyser,

$$I = \frac{P}{V} = \frac{1540}{220} = 7\text{A}$$

The current drawn by the geyser is 7A, which exceed the rating of 5A fuse. So, there will be a risk of fire when the geyser is used with a 5A fuse.

Q.11 (i) Calculate the Emf of a cell if 10 J of work is done to move a charge of 5C through the entire circuit. [1]

(ii) If the internal resistance of the cell is 1.5 Ω and the current flowing through the circuit is 2A, calculate the terminal voltage of the cell. [2]

Sol. (i) Given,

Work done, $W = 10$ J

Charge, $q = 5$ C

Using the formula, $\varepsilon = \frac{W}{q} = \frac{10}{5} = 2$ V

Emf of the cell = 2 V

(ii) Given,

Internal resistance, $r = 1.5\ \Omega$

Current, $I = 2$ A

Terminal voltage V is related to Emf by the formula

$$V = \varepsilon - Ir$$

Substituting the values

$$V = 2 - (2 \times 1.5) = 2 - 3 = -1\text{V}$$

Since, negative voltage indicates polarity reversal, terminal voltage = – 1V

Q.12 Observe the given circuit diagram and answer the questions that follows. **[ICSE Specimen 2025]**

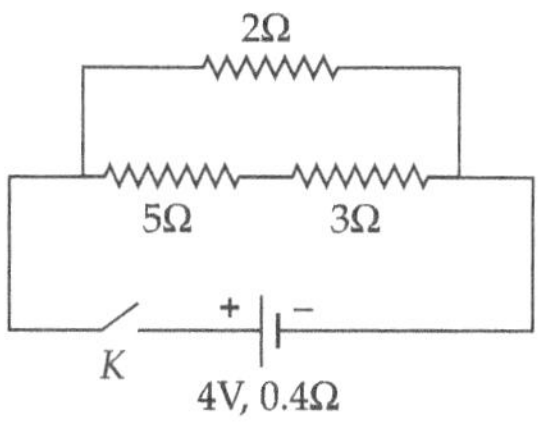

(i) Calculate the resistance of the circuit when the key K completes the circuit. **[1]**

(ii) Calculate the current through 3 Ω resistance when the circuit is complete. **[2]**

Sol. (i) When key K is closed, then the circuit diagram is as shown below.

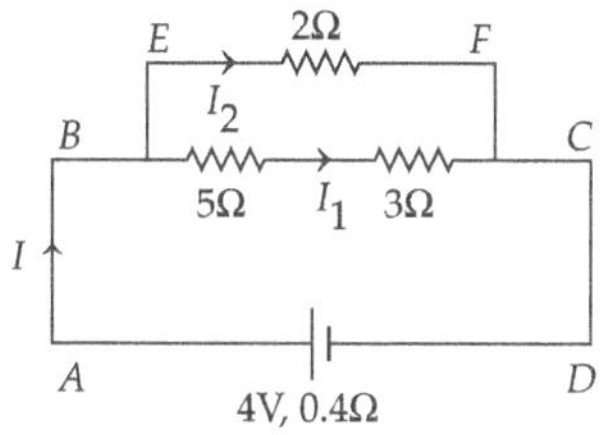

The resistance of the circuit is given as

$$R_{eq} = \frac{2 \times (5+3)}{2+(5+3)} + 0.4 = 2\Omega$$

(ii) Total current through the circuit is

$$I = \frac{V}{R} = \frac{4}{2} = 2\text{ A}$$

Now, the voltage across BC is given as

$$V_{BC} = V - I_r$$

where, r = internal resistance = 0.4 Ω

$\therefore$ $V_{BC} = (4 - 2 \times 0.4)\text{ V} = 3.2\text{ V}$

Now, $I = I_1 + I_2$

where $I_2 = \frac{V_{BC}}{2\Omega} = \frac{3.2}{2} = 1.6\text{ A}$

$\therefore$ $I_1 = I - I_2 = (2 - 1.6)\text{ A} = 0.4\text{A}$

$\therefore$ The current through 3Ω resistor is 0.4 A.

Q.13

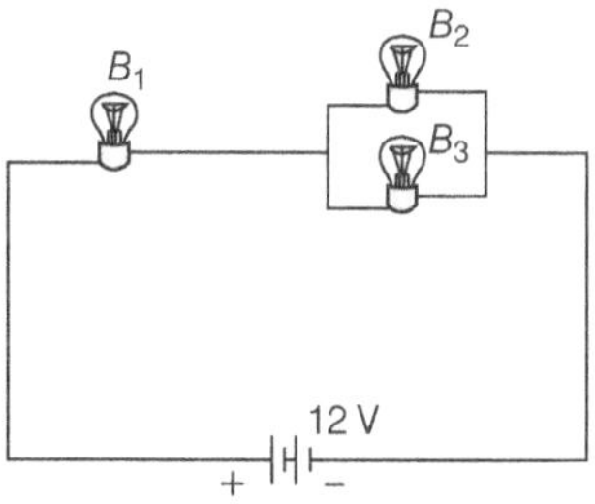

Three identical bulbs B_1, B_2, and B_3 each of power rating 18 W, 12 V are connected to a battery of 12 V. **[4][ICSE 2025]**

(i) Calculate

(a) the resistance of each bulb

(b) the current drawn from the cell

(ii) If the bulb B_3 is removed from the circuit, then will the brightness of the bulb B_1 increase, decrease or remain the same?

Sol. (i) (a) Power rating of each bulb = 18 W.

Since, all the bulbs have the same resistance so let each have a resistance of R Ω.

The maximum voltage that the bulbs can draw are 12 V.

$$\therefore \quad R = \frac{V^2}{P} = \frac{12 \times 12}{18} = 8\ \Omega$$

(b) The effective resistance in the circuit,

$$R_{EF} = R + \frac{R \times R}{R + R}$$

$$= R + \frac{R}{2} = \frac{3R}{2}$$

$$\therefore R_{EF} = 3 \times \frac{8}{2} = 12\ \Omega$$

$$\therefore \text{Current drawn} = \frac{\text{Supplied voltage}}{R_{EF}}$$

$$= \frac{12}{12} = 1\text{A}$$

(ii) If the bulb B_3 is removed from the circuit, then R_{EF} becomes $2R = 2 \times 12\ \Omega$

$= 24\ \Omega$

$$\therefore \text{Current drawn} = \frac{12}{24} = 0.5\text{ A}$$

So, the brightness of bulb B_1 will decrease.

Q.14 (i) Find the equivalent resistance between points A and B. **[2]**

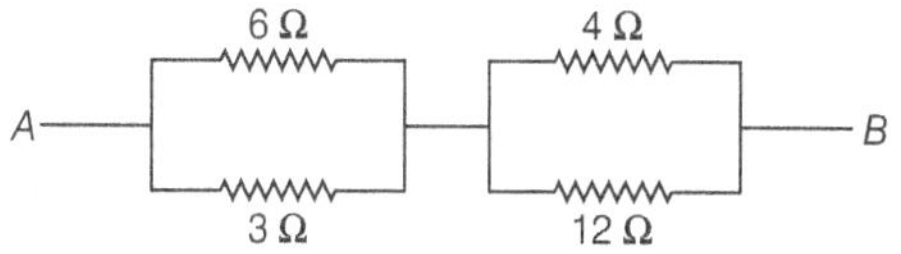

(ii) State whether the resistivity of a wire changes with the change in the thickness of the wire. **[1]**

[ICSE 2018]

Sol. (i)

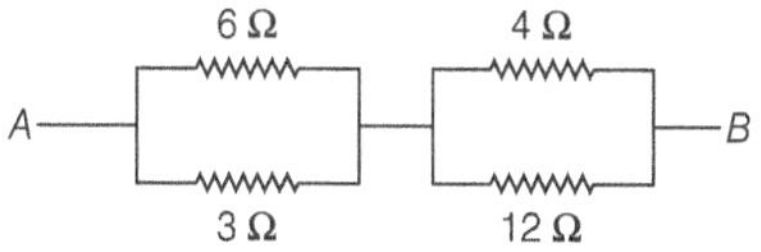

In the given circuit, 6 Ω and 3 Ω resistances are in parallel combination.

$$\therefore \quad \frac{1}{R_{p_1}} = \frac{1}{R_1} + \frac{1}{R_2}$$

$$R_{p_1} = \frac{R_1 \times R_2}{R_1 + R_2} = \frac{6 \times 3}{6+3} = \frac{18}{9} = 2\ \Omega$$

Similarly, 4Ω and 12Ω resistances are in parallel combination.

$$\therefore \quad R_{p_2} = \frac{R_3 \times R_4}{R_3 + R_4} = \frac{4 \times 12}{4 + 12} = \frac{48}{16} = 3\,\Omega$$

Now, we get new circuit as

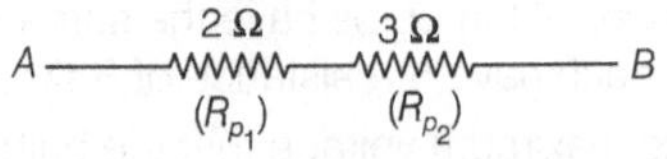

Here, 2 Ω and 3 Ω resistances are in series combination.

So, total resistance of circuit,

$$R_T = R_{p_1} + R_{p_2} = 2 + 3 = 5\,\Omega$$

(ii) Resistivity is a materials property, it does not change with change in thickness of wire.

Q.15

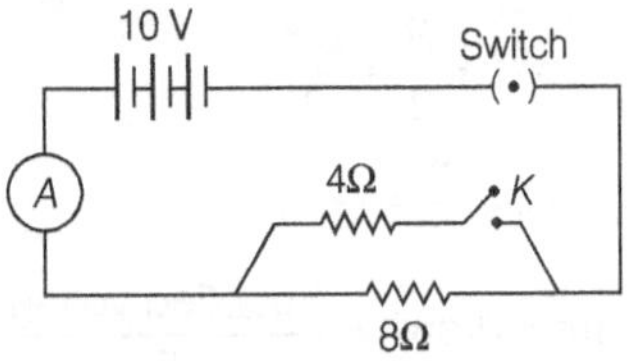

[ICSE 2017]

Calculate the reading of *A* when

(i) *K* is closed. **[1]**

(ii) *K* is open. **[1]**

Sol. (i) When *K* is closed, 4 Ω and 8 Ω are in parallel.

$$\text{Net resistance} = \frac{8 \times 4}{8 + 4} = \frac{32}{12} = \frac{8}{3}\,\Omega$$

$$I = \frac{V}{R} = \frac{10}{8/3} = \frac{15}{4}\,\text{A} = 3.75\,\text{A}$$

(ii) When *K* is open

Net resistance = 8 Ω

$$I = \frac{V}{R} = \frac{10}{8} = 1.25\,\text{A}$$

Q.16 **In Mrs. Pinto's flat there are 6 bulbs of 100 W each, a heater of 2 kW and 5 fans of 50 W each. If these are used everyday as shown below, calculate the cost of energy consumption for a month of 30 days at the rate of Rs. 3.50 per kWh.**

6 bulbs of 100 W each used 8 h per day

1 heater of 2 kW used half hour daily

5 fans of 50 W each are used 6 h everyday.

[3][ICSE Specimen 2017]

Sol. Electrical energy consumed by bulbs in one month

= (6 × 100W) × (8h × 30) / 1000 kWh = 144 kWh

Electrical energy consumed by heater in one month

= 2kW× (0.5× 30) = 30 kWh

Electrical energy consumed by fans in one month.

= (5 × 50) × (6 × 30) / 1000 = 45 kWh

Total energy consumed = (144 + 30 + 45) kWh

= 219 kWh

Cost of electricity = ₹ (219 × 3.50) = ₹ 766.5

Q.17

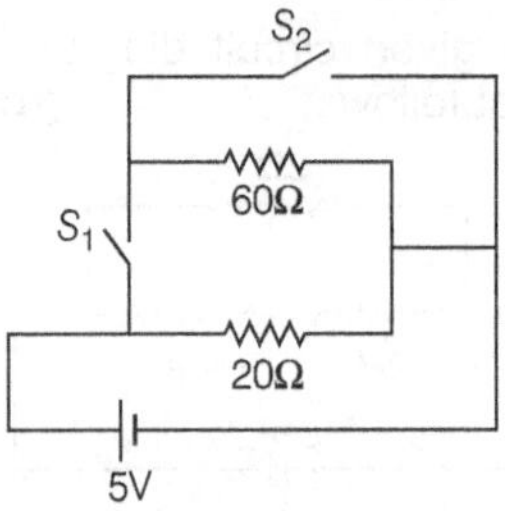

In the above circuit diagram, calculate the power consumed in the circuit when

(i) the switch S_1 is closed and the switch S_2 is open. [1]

(ii) the switch S_2 is closed and the switch S_1 is open.

[Competancy Based Que.]

Ans. (i) $R = \frac{20 \times 60}{20 + 60} = 15\,\Omega$

$$P = \frac{V^2}{R} = \frac{5 \times 5}{15} = \frac{5}{3} = 1.67\,\text{W}$$

(ii) $P = \frac{V^2}{R} = \frac{5 \times 5}{20} \Rightarrow P = \frac{5}{4} = 1.25\,\text{W}$

Q.18 **A student places a small electrical heater inside a cup of water, as shown in figure.**

The student determines the electrical power of the heater.

(i) In the space above the cup on figure draw the electrical circuit that the student uses. Include an ammeter, a voltmeter and a power supply. [1]

(ii) The voltage of the power supply is 12V and the current is 4.2 A.

(a) Calculate the electrical power input to the heater. [1]

(b) Calculate the energy input to the heater in 8.0 min. Give your answer in kW h. [1]

Sol. (i)

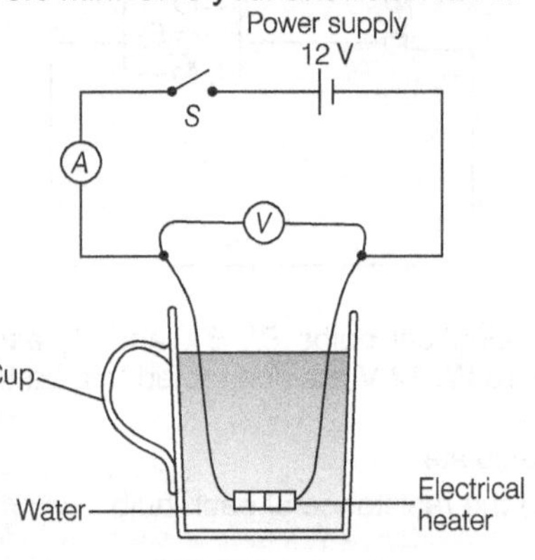

(ii) (a) Electrical power, $P = VI$

$= 12 \times 42 = 50.4$ W

(b) Energy, $E = P \times t$

$$= \frac{50.4}{1000} \times \frac{8}{60} = 0.0067 \text{ kWh}$$

Q.19 An appliance rated 440 W, 220 V is connected across 220 V supply. **[ICSE 2022 Sem-II]**

(i) Calculate the maximum current that the appliance can draw. **[1]**

(ii) Calculate the resistance of the appliance. **[1]**

Sol. (i) Given, power = 440 W

Voltage applied, $V = 220$ V

$$\text{Current} = \frac{\text{Power}}{\text{Voltage}}$$

$$I = \frac{440}{220} \text{ A} \Rightarrow I = 2 \text{ A}$$

(ii) Resistance of the appliance, power $(P) = \frac{V^2}{R}$

$$R = \frac{V^2}{P} = \frac{220 \times 220}{440}$$

$$R = 110\ \Omega$$

Q.20 In the circuit diagram given below, a cell of 9V and internal resistance 0.5 Ω is connected across a resistor of 2 Ω in series and two resistors 2 Ω and 6 Ω which are in parallel.

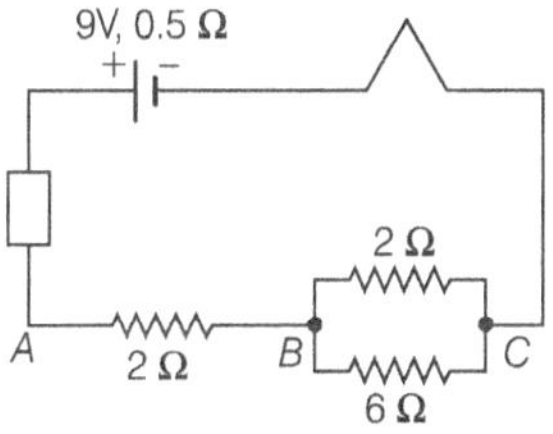

Find,

(i) the total resistance, **[1]**

(ii) the total current, **[1]**

(iii) the current in the 6 Ω resistor and **[1]**

(iv) the potential difference across the terminals of the cell. **[1][ICSE Specimen 2018]**

Sol. (i) Here, 6 Ω and 2 Ω resistors are in parallel so,

$$R_{eq} = \frac{R_1 R_2}{R_1 + R_2} = \frac{6 \times 2}{6 + 2} = \frac{12}{8} = 1.5\ \Omega$$

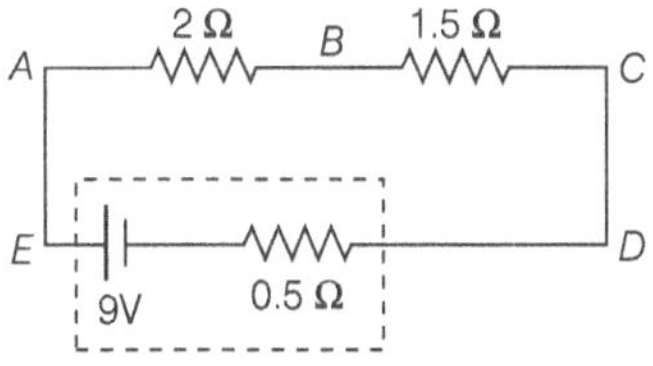

$$R + r = R_{eq} = 2 + 1.5 + 0.5 = 4\ \Omega$$

(ii) $I = \frac{V}{R} = \frac{9}{4} = 2.25$ A

(iii) $V_{BC} = 1.5 \times \frac{9}{4} = \frac{27}{8}$ V

$$I_{6\,\Omega} = \frac{27}{8 \times 6} = \frac{9}{16} \text{ A} = 0.5625\text{A}$$

(iv) $V_{\text{Battery}} = V - IR$

$$= 9 - \left(\frac{9}{4}\right)(0.5) = 7.875 \text{ V}$$

Q.21

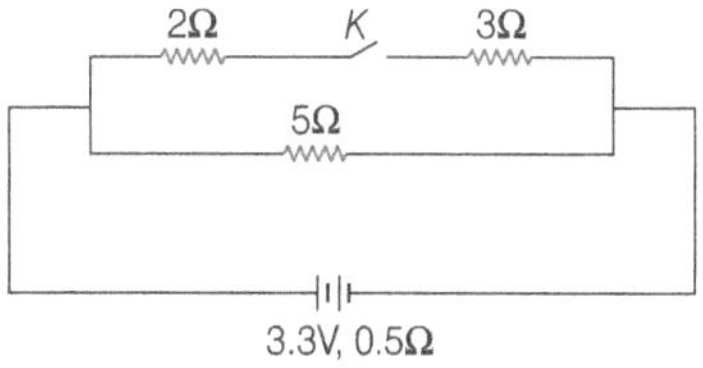

The above figure shows a circuit with the key K open. Calculate

(i) the resistance of the circuit when the key K is open. **[1]**

(ii) the current drawn from the cell when the key K is open. **[1]**

(iii) the resistance of the circuit when the key K is closed. **[1]**

(iv) the current drawn from the cell when the key K is closed. **[1][ICSE 2019]**

Sol.

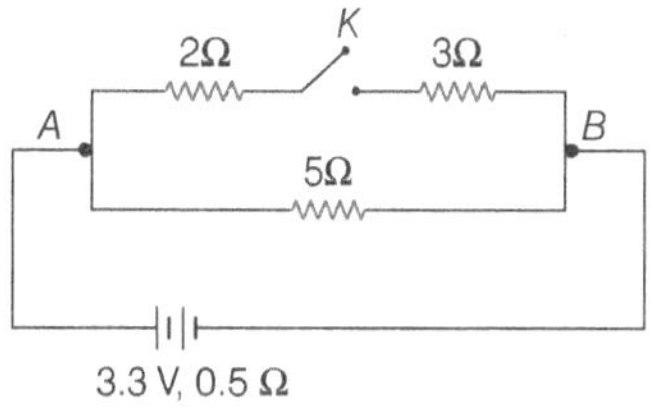

(i) When the key K is open, then 2 Ω and 3 Ω resistances are not in the circuit, i.e. this branch is not accounted in the circuit.

Now, equivalent resistance, $R_{eq} = 5 + 0.5 = 5.5\ \Omega$

(ii) According to the Ohm's law, $E = I(R + r)$

$$I = \frac{E}{R + r} = \frac{3.3}{5 + 0.5}$$

So, current $I = \frac{3.3}{5.5} = 0.6$ A

(iii)

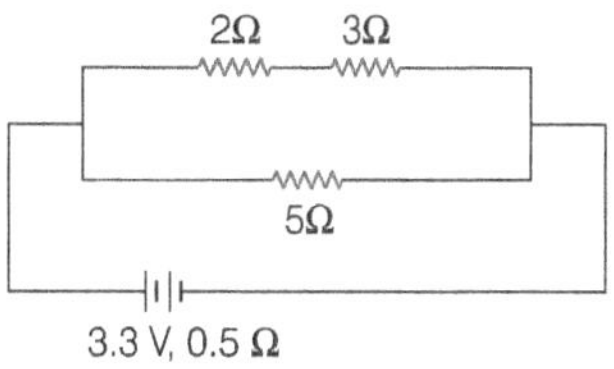

When the key K is closed, then resistance of the circuit is

$$R + r = R_{eq} = \frac{5 \times (2+3)}{5 + (2+3)} + 0.5 = \frac{25}{10} + 0.5$$
$$= 2.5 + 0.5 = 3\,\Omega$$

(iv) The current drawn from the cell when the key K is closed, $E = I(R + r)$

$$3.3 = I\,(3)$$
$$\therefore \quad I = \frac{3.3}{3} = 1.1\text{A}$$

Q.22 Figure shows part of a circuit containing three resistors X, Y and Z.

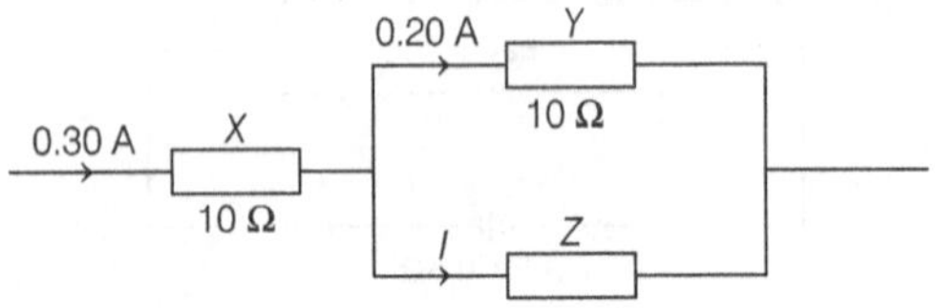

The resistance X and the resistance Y are each of 10Ω. The current through X in 0.30 A. The current through Y is 0.20 A.

(i) Calculate the potential difference across Y. **[1]**

(ii) Calculate the current I in resistor Z. **[1]**

(iii) Explain in words, rather than by calculation, how figure shows that the resistance of Z is larger than the resistance of Y. Use ideas about potential difference and current in your answer. **[1]**

(iv) Calculate the total resistance of the resistors X, Y and Z in this circuit. **[1]**

Sol. (i) $V = IR = 0.20 \times 10 = 2.0$

$\therefore$ Potential difference $= 2.0$ V

(ii) $I_X = I_Y + I_Z$

$$0.30 = 0.20 + I_Z$$
$$I_Z = 0.10$$

$\therefore$ Current in resistor $Z = 0.10$ A

(iii) The potential difference is the same across both the resistors Y and Z in parallel. So, smaller current through Z than Y shows that the resistance of Z is greater than the resistance of Y.

(iv) Potential difference across $X = 0.30 \times 10 = 3.0$ V

Total voltage $= 3.0 + 2.0 = 5.0$ V

$$\text{Total resistance} = \frac{\text{Total } V}{\text{Total } I} = \frac{5.0}{0.3} = 16.7\,\Omega$$

Q.23 An electric bulb is rated 240 V, 100 W.

(i) What information can you get from the above statement? **[1]**

(ii) What will happen, if this bulb is connected across 220 V? **[1]**

(iii) Calculate the resistance of the bulb. **[1]**

(iv) Also, find the energy consumed by the bulb in 10 minutes. **[1][ICSE 2022 Sem-II]**

Sol. (i) The above statement gives the information that when the electric bulb is put at 240 V of a potential difference, it consumes 100 W of power.

(ii) The bulb will consume less power.

(iii) $R = \frac{V^2}{P} = \frac{240 \times 240}{100} = 576\,\Omega$

(iv) Electrical energy (kWh) = kW × h

$$= \frac{100}{1000} \times \frac{10}{60} = \frac{1}{60}\text{kWh}$$

Q.24 The figure shows a circuit, when the circuit is switched ON, the ammeter reads 0.5 A.

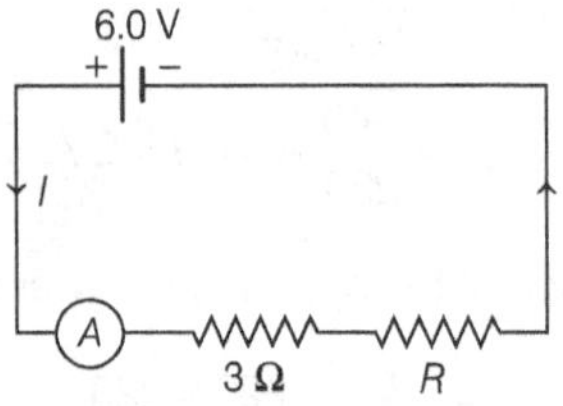

(i) Calculate the value of the unknown resistor R. **[1]**

(ii) Calculate the charge passing through the 3 Ω resistor in 120 s. **[1]**

(iii) Calculate the power dissipated in the 3 Ω resistor. **[1] [ICSE 2013]**

Sol. (i) $\because I = \frac{V}{R}$

$$\Rightarrow \quad 0.5 = \frac{6.0}{3 + R}$$
$$\Rightarrow \quad 3 + R = \frac{6}{0.5}$$
$$\Rightarrow \quad R = \frac{60}{5} - 3 = 9\,\Omega$$

(ii) $Q = I \times t = 0.5 \times 120 = 60$ C

(iii) $P = VI = I^2R = (0.5)^2 \times 3$

$$= 0.25 \times 3$$
$$= 0.75\text{ W}$$

Q.25 A bulb is marked 100 W, 220 V and an electric heater is marked 2000 W, 220 V.

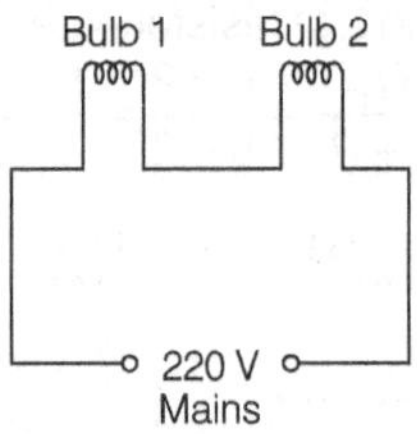

(i) What is the ratio between the resistances of these two devices? **[1]**

(ii) How does the power-voltage rating of a device help us to decide about the type of loads (connecting wires) to be used for it? **[1]**

(iii) In which of the two devices, a thicker connecting wire or load is required? **[1]**

Sol. Given, $P_1 = 100\text{ W}$, $V_1 = 220\text{ V}$

$P_2 = 2000\text{ W}, V_2 = 220\text{ V}$

(i) $P = \frac{V^2}{R} \Rightarrow R = \frac{V^2}{P}$

$$R_1 = \frac{(220)^2}{100}$$

and $$R_2 = \frac{(220)^2}{2000}$$

$$\therefore \frac{R_1}{R_2} = \frac{\frac{(220)^2}{100}}{\frac{(220)^2}{2000}} = \frac{2000}{100} = \frac{20}{1}$$

(ii) $I_1 = \frac{P_1}{V_1} = \frac{100}{220} = 0.45\text{ A}$

and $I_2 = \frac{P_2}{V_2} = \frac{2000}{220} = 9.1\text{ A}$

A wire having current 9.1 A is required for a heater.

(iii) The current flowing through the bulb is only 0.45 A, while through heater is 9.1 A. Hence, a heavy load is needed for the heater while for a bulb an ordinary thin connecting wire is required.

Q.26 (i) The diagram (a) and (b) given below are of a plug and a socket with arrow marked as 1, 2, 3 and 4, 5, 6 respectively on them. Identify and write live (L), neutral (N) and the earth (E) against the correct number. **[1]**

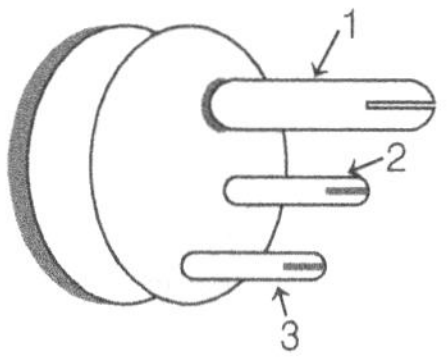

(a) Plug

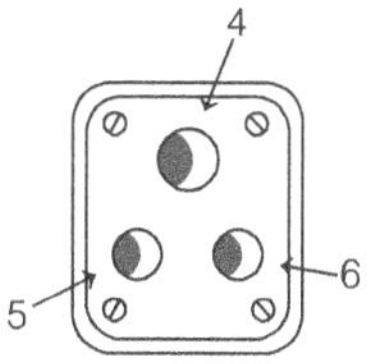

(b) Socket

(ii) Calculate the electrical energy consumed when a bulb of 40 W is used for 12.5 h everyday for 30 days. **[2] [ICSE 2009]**

Sol. (i) 1–Earth (E), 2–Neutral (N)

3–Live (L), 4–Earth (E)

5–Neutral (N)

6–Live (L)

(ii) Given, $P = 40\text{ W}, t = 12.5\text{ h}$

Number of days = 30

Electrical energy, $E = ?$

$\therefore \quad E = P \times t \times$ number of days

$= \frac{40}{1000} \times 12.5 \times 30$

$= 15\text{ kWh}$

09

ELECTROMAGNETISM

- The branch of physics which deals with study of electricity and magnetism and the interaction between them is known as electromagnetism.

Oersted's Experiment on the Magnetic Effect of Electric Current

- In 1820, Hans Oersted observed experimentally that, when an electric current is passed through a conducting wire, a magnetic field is produced around it. **The phenomenon of production of magnetic field around a current carrying conductor is called magnetic effect of current.**
- The presence of magnetic field at a point around a current carrying wire can be detected with the help of a compass needle, which shows deflection in presence of a magnetic field.

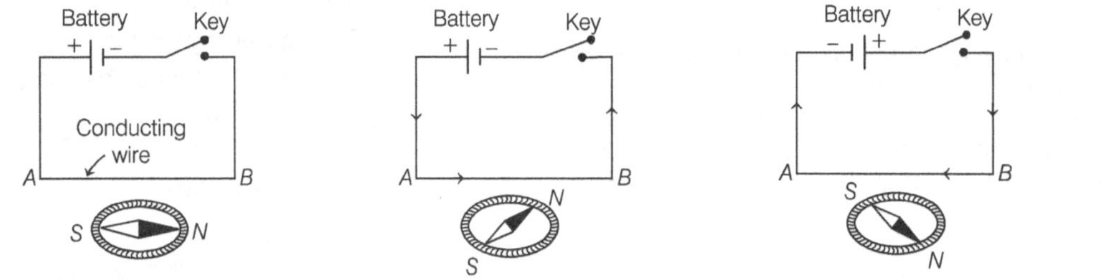

Fig.(a) No flow of current in wire

Fig.(b) Flow of current in wire

Fig.(c) Flow of current in wire in reverse direction as in Fig.(b)

Phenomenon of magnetic effect of electric current in a conducting wire

- On increasing the current in the wire and bringing the needle closer to the wire, the deflection of the needle increases.
- This experiment shows that, the magnetic field is produced due to electric current or flow of charges.

Magnetic Field

- The space around a magnet or a current carrying conductor in which its magnetic effect can be experienced i.e., its force can be detected, is called magnetic field.
- Magnetic field is a **vector** quantity. Its SI unit is **tesla** (T) named after an American engineer **Nikola Tesla**. Its CGS unit is **gauss** (G).

$$B = \frac{F}{I l}$$

$$1 \text{ tesla} = \frac{1 \text{ newton}}{1 \text{ ampere-metre}}$$

$$1 \text{T} = 1 \text{ N/A-m} = \text{kg /A-s}^2$$

$$1 \text{ tesla} = 10^4 \text{ gauss}$$

Magnetic Field due to a Current through a Straight Conductor

- The magnetic field lines around a current carrying straight conductor are **concentric circles** whose centres lie on the wire and lying in the plane perpendicular to straight wire.

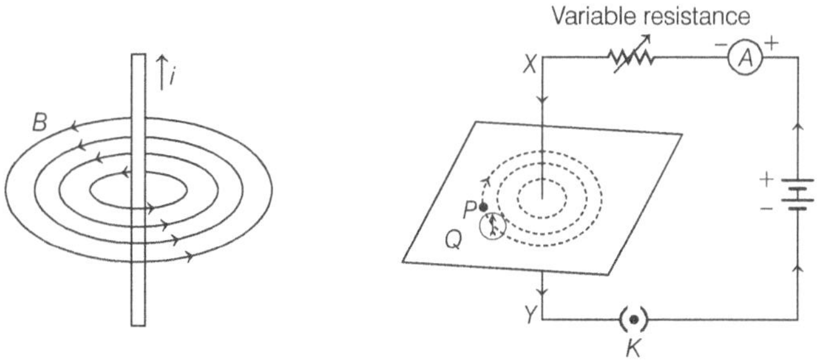

A pattern of concentric circles indicating the field lines of magnetic field around a straight conducting wire.

- The **strength of magnetic field *B*** produced by a straight current carrying wire at a given point is

$$\boxed{B \propto \frac{I}{r}}$$

Here, I is current flowing through the conductor and r is the distance of the point from conductor.

- Magnetic field at a point due to current in straight wire is **directly proportional to the amount of current flows in the wire** and **inversely proportional to its distance** from the wire.
- If the direction of current in a straight wire is known, then the direction of magnetic field produced by it is obtained by **Maxwell's right hand thumb rule**.

Maxwell's Right Hand Thumb Rule

- It states that, if you hold the current carrying straight wire in the grip of your right hand in such a way that the stretched thumb points in the direction of current, then the direction of the curl of the fingers will give the direction of the magnetic field. This rule is also called **Maxwell's corkscrew rule**.

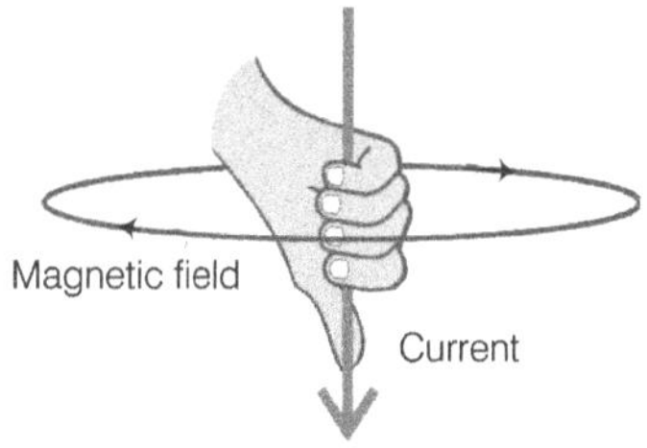

Maxwell's right hand thumb rule

Magnetic Field Due to a Current through a Circular Loop

- The magnetic field lines due to a circular coil is shown in given figure. At every point of a current carrying circular loop, the **concentric circles represent the magnetic field around** it. At the **centre of loop**, the field appears to be a **straight line**.

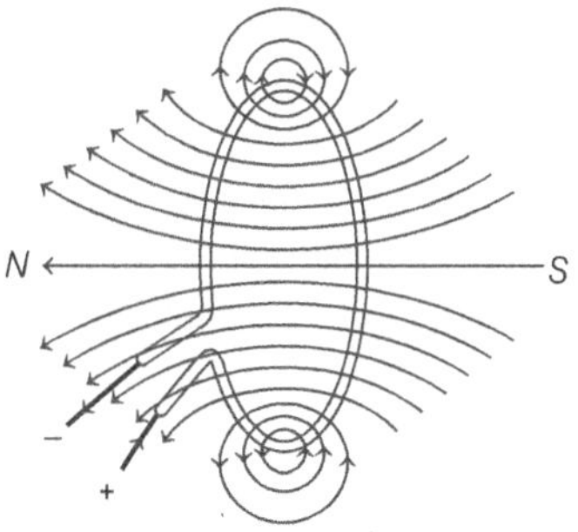

Magnetic field lines due to a current through a circular loop

- By looking at the direction of current in the face of loop, we can identify its polarity i.e, whether it will behave like North pole or South pole. If current around the face in loop is in **anti-clockwise direction,** then it will behave like North pole while in case of **clockwise direction** it will behave like South pole.

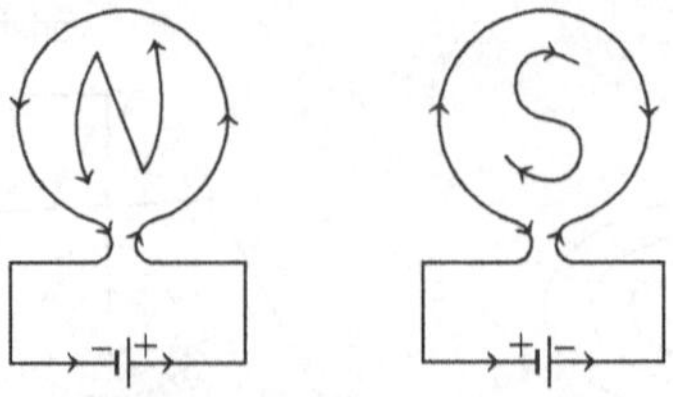

Anti-clockwise current (a) Clockwise current (b)

Polarities at the faces of a loop carrying current

(i) The strength of magnetic field (B) due to a current carrying circular wire is directly proportional to the amount of current (I) flowing through it

i.e. $B \propto I$

(ii) The strength of the magnetic field due to a current carrying circular wire is directly proportional to the number of turns (N) of the wire

i.e. $B \propto N$

Electromagnet

- An electromagnet is a solenoid that works like a magnet when current flows through it. It consists of a long insulated copper wire wound around a soft iron core. The magnetic effect remains, till the current is flowing through the solenoid.

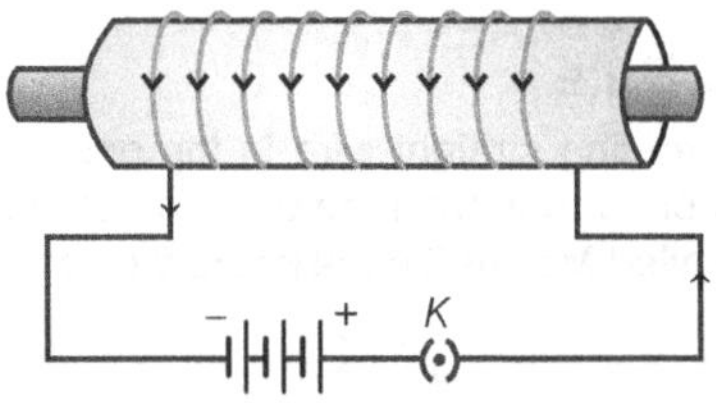

The **strength of an electromagnet** increases with

(i) increase in number of turns in the coil

(ii) increase in the amount of current flowing through the coil.

(iii) decrease in the air gap between poles.

Uses of Electromagnet

Following are the uses of electromagnet

(i) It is used for lifting and transporting large masses of iron scrap, girder, plates, etc.

(ii) It is used for loading the furnace with iron.

(iii) It is used for separating the magnetic substances such as iron from debris and raw materials.

(iv) It is used for removing pieces of iron from wounds.

Force on a Current-Carrying Conductor in a Magnetic Field

- When a current carrying conductor is placed in a magnetic field in a direction other than the magnetic field, it experiences a force.
- The force acting on a current carrying conductor in a magnetic field is due to interaction between magnetic field due to current carrying conductor and external magnetic field in which the conductor is placed.
- The direction of force which acts on a current carrying conductor placed in a magnetic field is given by Fleming's left hand rule.

- The **magnitude of force** acting on a current-carrying wire placed in a magnetic field in the direction perpendicular to its length is given by

$$\boxed{F = Bil}$$

where, B is the magnetic field strength, i is the current and l is the length of the conductor.
- Fleming Left Hand Rule states that, if the forefinger, thumb and middle finger of left hand are stretched mutually perpendicular to each other and the forefinger points along the direction of external magnetic field, middle finger indicates the direction of current, then thumb points in the direction of force acting on the conductor.

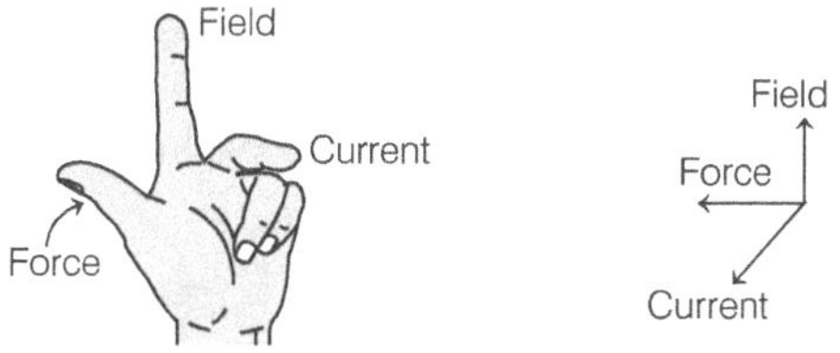

Fleming's left hand rule

Electric Motor

- It is a rotating device which is used for **converting electrical energy into mechanical energy**.
- It is based on the principle that when a current carrying rectangular coil is placed in a magnetic field, a force (torque) acts on the coil, which rotates it continuously.The direction of the force is obtained from the Fleming's left hand rule.

Construction of Electric Motor

The main parts of electric motor are described below

(i) **Armature** It is a rectangular coil wound around a soft iron core which is kept in-between the poles of a permanent magnet. When current flows through armature coil, then magnetic force acts on it and it rotates along its axis.

(ii) **Split Rings** These are the parts of a ring, fixed to the coil. These are used to reverse the direction of current flowing through armature coil every time, it passes through the vertical position.

(iii) **Brushes** These are made up of carbon/copper, these are pressed tightly against split rings. Their main function is to connect the coil with the current supply.

(iv) **Magnet** It is a strong horse-shoe magnet either permanent or electromagnet. Its function is to produce magnetic field, so that magnetic force can act on armature coil.

(v) **DC Source** It is a battery connected to the brush, to flow the electric current in armature coil, so that magnetic force can act on it.

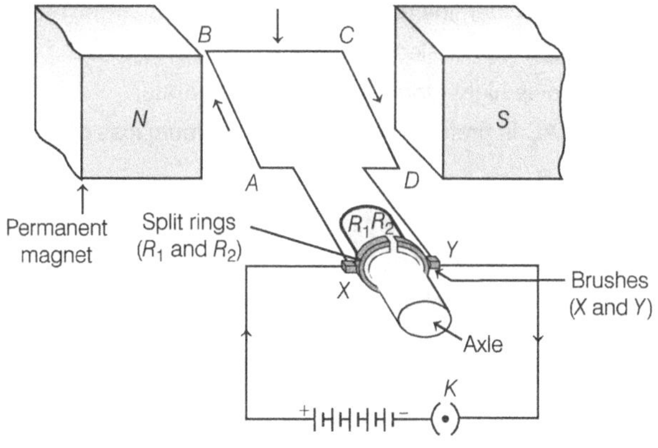

A schematic diagram of an electric motor

REVISION NOTES

Electromagnetic Induction

- Electromagnetic induction is the phenomenon in which an emf is induced in a conductor, if there is a change in magnetic field around the conductor.
- The emf produced here is called **induced emf**. If the circuit is closed, then electric current flows in the circuit due to this emf, known as **induced current**.
- This effect is the reverse effect of magnetic effect of electric current and it was discovered by Michael Faraday.
- The direction of induced current in a straight conductor is given by Fleming's right hand rule.
- **Fleming's Right Hand Rule** states that, if the forefinger, middle finger and thumb of the right hand are stretched at right angles to each other, with the forefinger in the direction of the magnetic field and the thumb in the direction of the motion of the wire, then the current in the wire is in the direction of the middle finger.

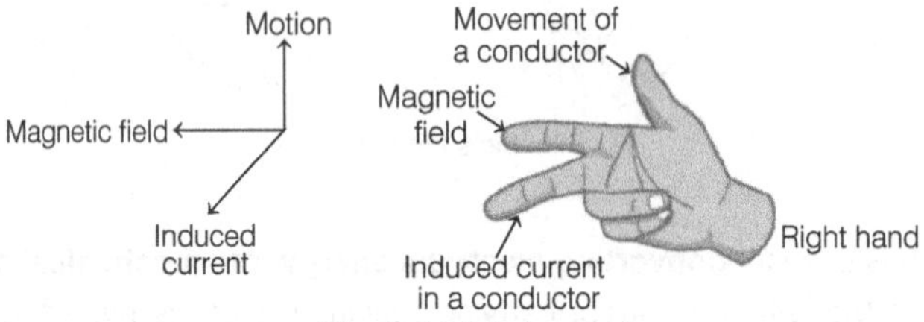

Fleming's right hand rule

Direct Current and Alternating Current

- **Direct Current (DC)** An electric current whose magnitude is either constant or variable but the direction of flow in a conductor remains the same is called direct current. It is denoted by DC. Sources of DC are voltaic cell, a dry cell, battery, DC generator, etc.
- **Alternating Current (AC)** An electric current whose magnitude changes with time and direction reverses periodically is called alternating current. It is denoted by AC. Alternating current is used in house hold circuit.
- The number of cycles completed by the AC in one second is called the frequency of AC. The frequency of AC in India is 50 Hz which means that AC changes its polarity after $\frac{1}{100}$ second as it completes one cycle.

Note *The major difference between AC and DC is that DC always flows in one direction, while AC reverses its direction periodically.*

Advantages of AC over DC

(i) With the help of a transformer, the magnitude of an AC can be increased or decreased.

(ii) AC can be easily converted into DC by using a device called **rectifier**.

(iii) The cost of generation of AC is less than the cost of generation of DC.

(iv) AC can be controlled without much loss of electric power as compared to DC.

(v) The efficiency of an AC generator is higher than that of a DC generator.

(vi) For long distance transmission, AC is preferred as it causes minimum loss of energy during transmission.

AC Generator

- It generates Alternating current (AC) which changes its direction after equal intervals of time.
- The different parts of AC generator are explained as below

(i) **Armature** It is a coil having large number of turns of insulated copper wire wound over a soft iron core.

(ii) **Field Magnet** It is a powerful magnet that provides a uniform magnetic field perpendicular to the axis of rotation of coil between the North and South poles.

(iii) **Slip Rings** In an AC generator, we use slip rings (full rings) with which the ends of coil are in contact.
DC generator uses split ring type commutator (half rings) with which the ends of the armature coil are in contact.

(iv) **Brushes** There are two stationary metallic carbon brushes which are in contact with external device and rings.

- In an AC generator, **mechanical energy is converted into electrical energy**.

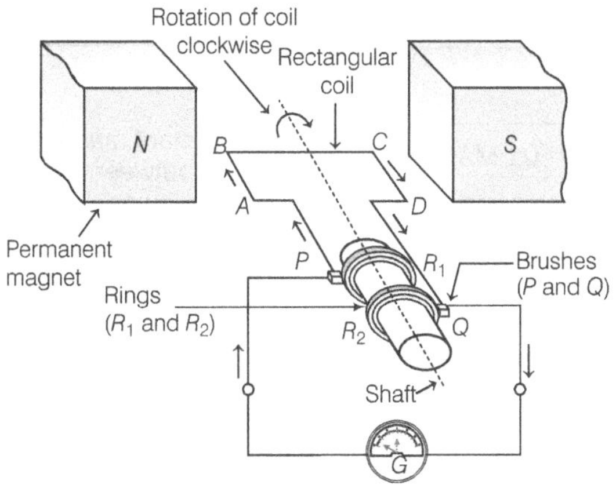

AC generator

Transformer

- It is a device which is used to increase or decrease the amplitude of an alternating emf without changing the frequency of AC.
- **Transformers work on the principle of electromagnetic induction**. It has two coils, primary coil and secondary coil. Input alternating current is supplied to primary coil while output current is received at secondary coil.
- The transformers are of following types
  (i) **Step-up transformer** The transformer which converts low voltage (high current) into high voltage (low current) is called step-up transformer. In this transformer, the number of turns in secondary coil (N_s) is more than the number of turns in primary coil (N_p), i.e. $N_s > N_p$.
  (ii) **Step-down transformer** The transformer which converts high voltage (low current) to low voltage (high current) is called step-down transformer. In this transformer, the number of turns in secondary coil is less than the number of turns in primary coil, i.e. $N_p > N_s$.

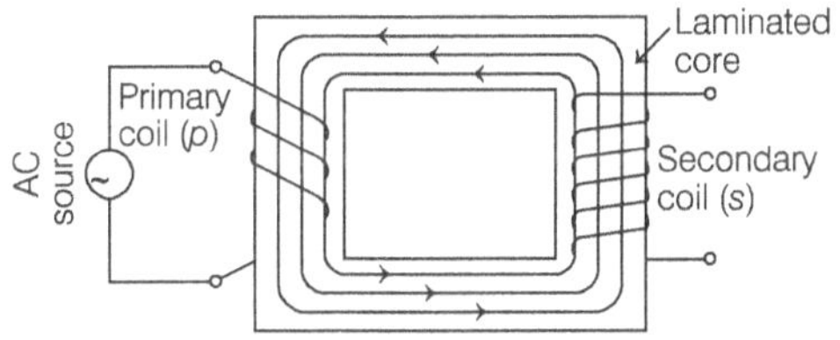

Step-up transformer

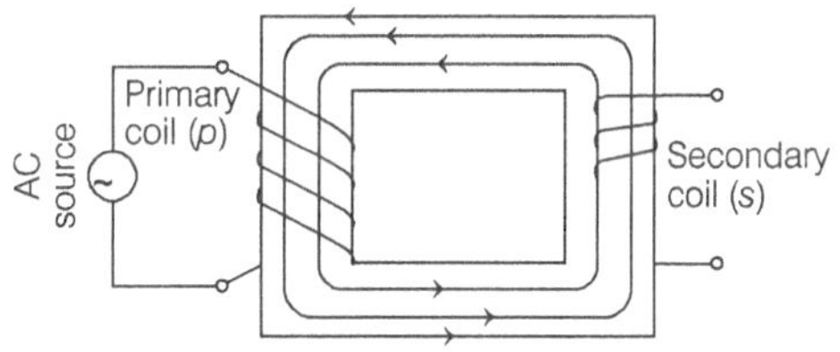

Step-down transformer

- For a transformer,

$$\frac{\text{Emf across the secondary coil } (E_S)}{\text{Emf across the primary coil } (E_P)} = \frac{\text{Number of turns in the secondary coil } (N_S)}{\text{Number of turns in the primary coil } (N_P)}$$

Or

$$\boxed{\frac{E_S}{E_P} = \frac{N_S}{N_P}}$$

- For an ideal transformer,

Power in secondary coil = Power in primary coil

or, $$E_S I_S = E_P I_P$$

$\therefore$ $$\boxed{\frac{I_P}{I_S} = \frac{E_S}{E_P} = \frac{N_S}{N_P}}$$

Uses of Transformers

Transformers are used in almost all AC operations. It is used in the induction furnaces and in the voltage regulators for TV, computer, refrigerator, etc.

EXAM ORIENTED QUESTIONS

TYPE - 1

01 Mark

Multiple Choice Questions

Q.1 The presence of a magnetic field at a point can be detected by

(a) a bar magnet
(b) a solenoid
(c) a current carrying loop
(d) a compass needle

Ans. (d) In the presence of a magnetic field, the needle of the compass rests only in the direction of magnetic field and only in the presence of earth's magnetic field, the needle rests in the North-South direction.

Q.2 If the strength of the current flowing through a wire is increased, the strength of the magnetic field produced by it **[ICSE 2023]**

(a) decreases
(b) increases
(c) remains the same
(d) first increases then decreases

Ans. (b) If the strength of the current flowing through a wire is increased, the strength of the magnetic field increases.

Q.3 By reversing the direction of current in a straight wire, the magnetic field

(a) will get reversed in direction
(b) will be increased
(c) will be decreased
(d) remains unchanged

Ans. (a) By reversing the direction of current in a straight wire, the magnetic field will get reversed in direction.

Q.4 Magnetic field due to a current through a straight conductor depends on

(a) current
(b) distance from the wire
(c) Both (a) and (b)
(d) cross-sectional area of wire

Ans. (c) Magnetic field (B) due to a current (I) through a straight conductor depends on the current and distance from the wire (r), i.e.

$$B \propto I \quad \text{and} \quad B \propto \frac{1}{r}$$

$$\Rightarrow \quad B \propto \frac{I}{r}$$

Q.5 The resultant magnetic field at point P situated midway between two parallel wires (placed horizontally) each carrying a steady current I is

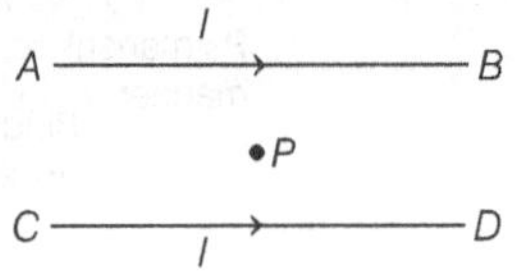

(a) in the same direction as the current in the wires
(b) in the vertically upward direction
(c) zero
(d) in the vertically downward direction

Ans. (c) The direction of magnetic field due to wires are opposite to each other at point P. So, the magnetic field will cancel out each other. As a result, the resultant magnetic field at point P will be zero.

Q.6 The strength of magnetic field lines due to a current flowing through a circular loop is

(i) inversely proportional to the radius of the coil.
(ii) directly proportional to the number of turns in the coil.
(iii) inversely proportional to the strength of the current flowing in the coil.
(iv) directly proportional to the radius of the coil.

(a) (i) and (iii) (b) (i) and (ii)
(c) Only (i) (d) Only (iv)

Ans. (b) The magnetic field produced by current- carrying circular wire is directly proportional to the amount of current, passing through it and the number of turns of the wire and inversely proportional to the radius of the coil.

Q.7 Current is flowing through a coil as shown in the figure. Which one of the given figures will correctly depict the magnetic polarity and the direction of the lines of force along the axis of the coil. **[ICSE Specimen 2025]**

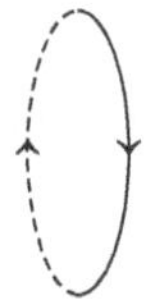

(a) 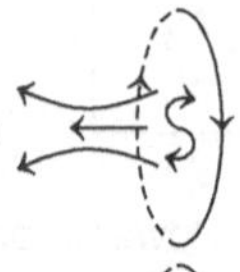

(b) 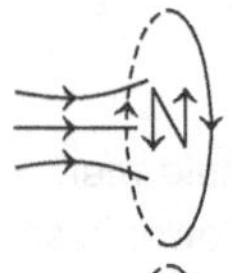

(c) 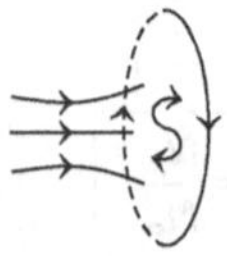

(d) 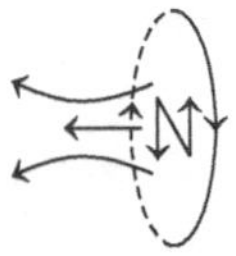

Ans. (c) According to Maxwell's cork screw rule, the figure given in option (c) will be correct.

Q.8 The strength of the magnetic field inside a solenoid decreases with
(a) increases the number of turns in the solenoid
(b) increasing the magnitude of current
(c) use of soft iron core
(d) increasing the gap between the turns of a coil

Ans. (d) By increasing the gap between the turns strength of magnetic field decreases in solenoid.

Q.9 The following figure shows a small bar magnet falling freely through a copper ring. For the observer at *A*, the direction of the induced current will be **[ICSE 2025]**

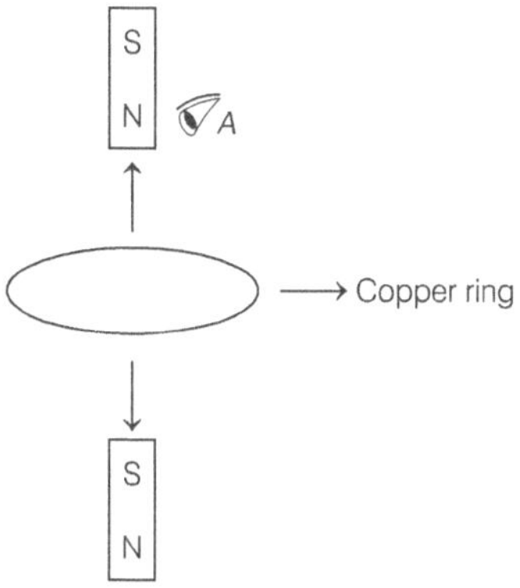

(a) clockwise when magnet is above and below the ring
(b) anti-clockwise when magnet is above and below the ring
(c) anti-clockwise when magnet is above the ring and clockwise when the magnet is below the ring
(d) clockwise when magnet is above the ring and anti-clockwise when the magnet is below the ring

Ans. (c)

Q.10 The pattern of the magnetic field produced inside a current-carrying solenoid is

(a) 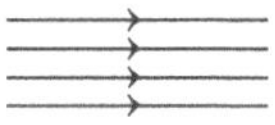
(b) 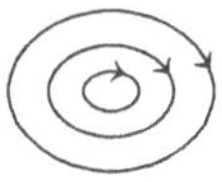
(c) 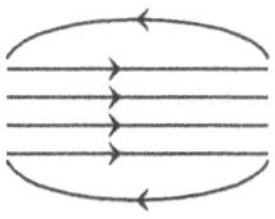
(d) 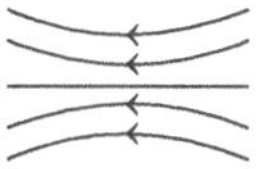

Ans. (c) The pattern of the magnetic field lines produced inside a current-carrying solenoid is parallel straight lines.

Q.11 Given below is a diagram of electromagnet showing magnetic field lines with points *X* and *Y*. Choose the correct statement.

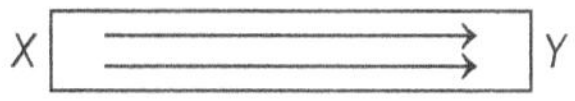

(i) *X* point is north pole
(ii) *Y* point is south pole
(iii) Magnetic field lines directed from *Y* to *X* outside the magnet.
(iv) Magnetic field lines directed from *X* to *Y* outside the magnet.
(v) *X* point is south pole.
(vi) *Y* point is north pole.
(a) (i), (ii) and (iv) (b) (iii), (v) and (vi)
(c) (v) and (vi) (d) Only (iii)

Ans. (b)

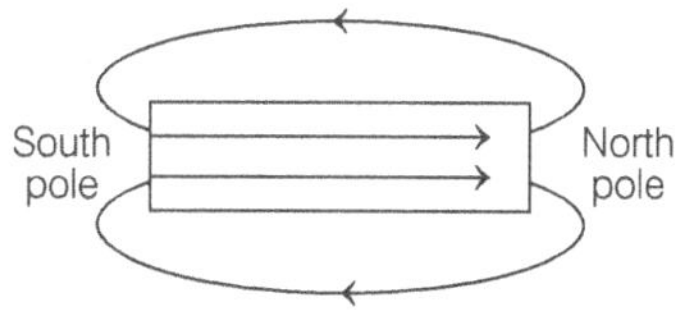

Q.12 When a proton beam enters in a magnetic field at right angle to it as shown in figure. The direction of force acting on the proton beam will be

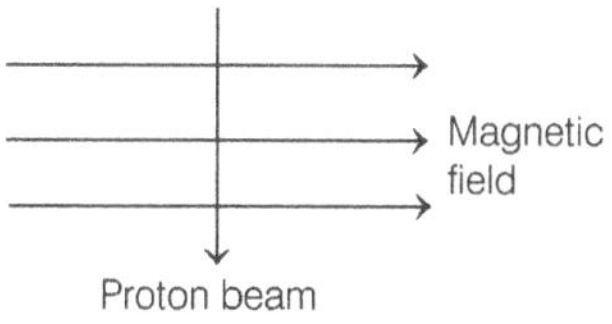

(a) to the right (b) to the left
(c) into the page (d) out of the page

Ans. (d) According to Fleming's left hand rule, the direction of force on a conductor is perpendicular to both the direction of the magnetic field and the current.
The direction of current is taken in the direction of motion of the proton beam and hence the force on the proton beam is directed out of the page.

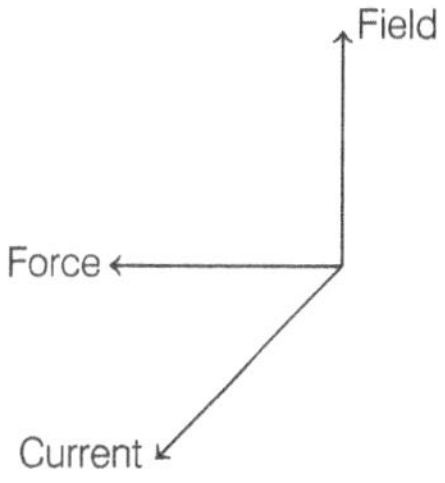

Q.13 A coil wound around a piece of soft iron can become an electromagnet only when **[ICSE 2022 (Sem-II)]**
(a) the circuit is open
(b) a magnetic compass is present in the vicinity
(c) a galvanometer is connected to the circuit
(d) a current flows in the circuit

Ans. (d) A coil wound around a piece of soft iron becomes electromagnet only when a current flows in the circuit.

Q.14 The magnitude of force on the current-carrying conductor increases when
(a) length of the conductor increases
(b) strength of current decreases
(c) external magnetic field strength decreases
(d) length of the conductor decreases

Ans. (a) The magnitude of force increases, when length of conductor increases, strength of current and magnetic field strength increase and the magnetic field lines do not intersect each other.

Q.15 A conductor *AB* is kept along North-South direction of the earth above a magnetic needle as shown below. When the key *K* is closed, then **[ICSE 2022 Sem-II]**

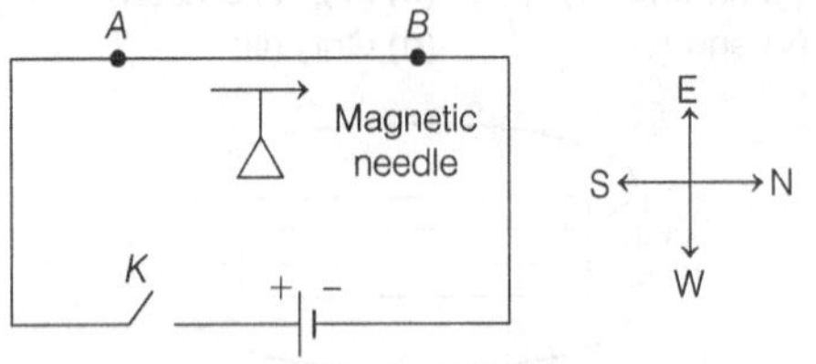

(a) the needle will not show any deflection
(b) the needle will deflect towards East
(c) the needle will turn in the opposite direction, i.e. towards South
(d) the needle will deflect towards West.

Ans. (b) From the figure we can see that the magnetic needle is kept below the conductor *AB* which is kept at North-South direction. We can see that the current is in clockwise direction and from the right hand thumb rule, the direction of magnetic field will be from East to West. Hence, according to Fleming's left hand rule, the deflection produced will be towards East.

Q.16 A magnetic compass is present on a small table, very close to the wall in a room. A man enters the room and switches ON the Air conditioner fitted near the ceiling. He observes that the needle in the compass shows immediate deflection. Identify the most probable reason for the deflection. **[Competency Based Que.]**
(a) Air blowing in the room.
(b) Current starts flowing through AC wire concealed in the adjacent wall.
(c) Vibrations are produced when the man starts talking to his wife in the kitchen.
(d) Vibrations were produced due to a file in his hand that fell on the ground.

Ans. (b) Since, current starts flowing in the wire concealed in the adjacent wall, a magnetic field is produced around the wire which makes the compass needle move.

Q.17 The diagram below shows a free conductor *AB* is kept in a magnetic field and is carrying current from *A* to *B* (To avoid confusion, complete path of the circuit is not shown). The direction of the force experienced by the conductor will be **[ICSE Specimen 2022 Sem-II]**

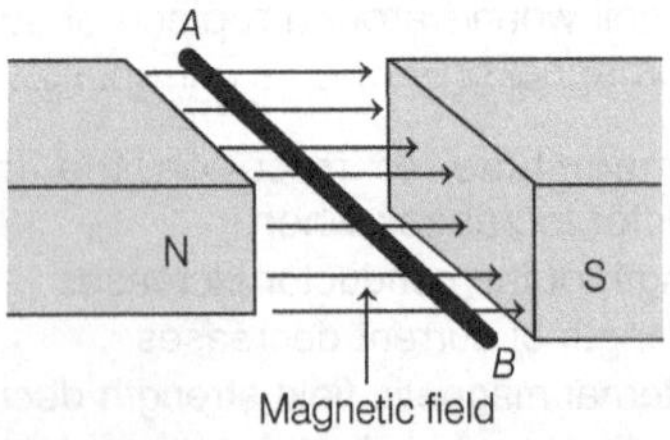

(a) up (b) down (c) towards N (d) towards S

Ans. (a) According to the Fleming's left hand rule, the direction of force experienced by the conductor will be up.

Q.18 When a conductor carrying current is placed in a magnetic field, perpendicular to it, then the direction of the force experienced can be found out using **[ICSE Specimen 2023]**
(a) Lenz's law
(b) Fleming's left hand rule
(c) Fleming's right hand rule
(d) right hand thumb rule

Ans. (b)

Q.19 Which of the following has its working based on electromagnetic induction?
(a) DC motor (b) AC generator
(c) Transformer (d) Both (b) and (c)

Ans. (d) Both AC generator and transformer works on the principle of electromagnetic induction.

Q.20 The direction of induced current is obtained by
(a) clock rule
(b) Fleming's left hand rule
(c) Fleming's right hand rule
(d) right hand thumb rule

Ans. (c) The direction of induced current is obtained by Fleming's right hand rule.

Q.21 The diagram below shows a magnet moved near a coil along its axis. Which of the diagram shows correct flow of current during this motion?

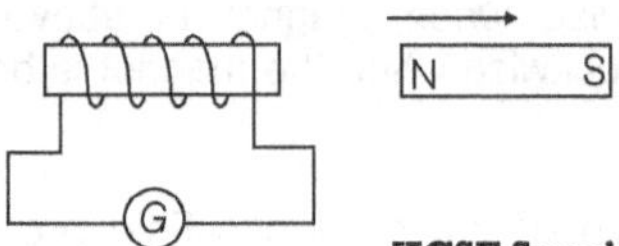

[ICSE Specimen 2022 Sem-I]

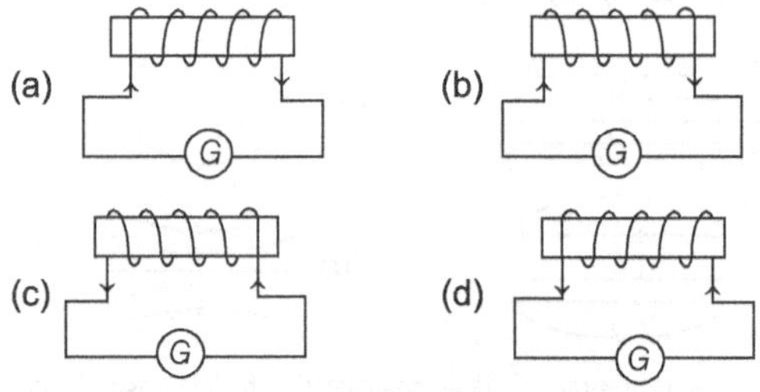

Ans. (c) According to the Fleming's right hand rule, the direction of induced current in the coil near to N-pole will be clockwise. It is shown correctly in option (c).

Q.22 The given rods will attract each other when:

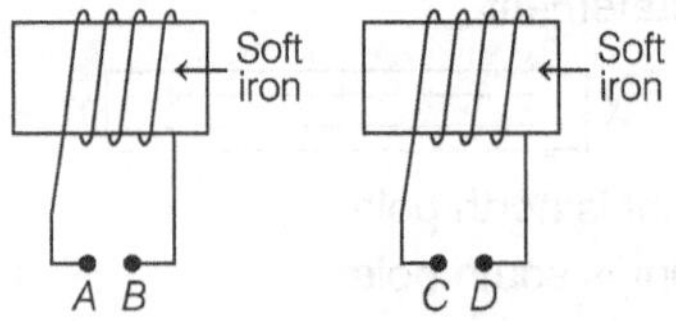

(a) *A* and *C* are connected to positive terminal of the battery.
(b) *B* and *C* are connected to the positive terminal of the battery.
(c) *A* and *D* are connected to the positive terminal of the battery.
(d) *A* and *D* are connected to the negative terminal of the battery. **[Competency Based Que.]**

Ans. (a) When *A* is connected to the positive terminal, the current flows in the clockwise direction with respect to the right face of the bar attached with the wire *AB*. Therefore, this pole behaves as a south pole.

When *C* is connected to the positive terminal, the current flows in the anti-clockwise direction with respect to the left face of the bar attached with the wire *CD*. Therefore this pole behaves as a North pole.

Hence, they attract each other.

TYPE - 2 — 01 Mark

Assertion-Reason Type Questions

Directions (Q. Nos. 1-7) In the following questions, a statement of assertion (A) is followed by a statement of reason (R). Mark the correct choice as

(a) Both A and R are true and R is the correct explanation of A.
(b) Both A and R are true but R is not the correct explanation of A.
(c) A is true but R is false.
(d) A is false but R is true.

Q.1 Assertion (A) A compass needle is placed near a current carrying wire. The deflection of the compass needle decreases when the magnitude of an electric current in the wire is increased.

Reason (R) Strength of a magnetic field at a point near the conductor increases on increasing the current.

Ans. (d) As a wire's current increases, the magnetic field around it strengthens, causing the deflection of a compass needle increase rather than decrease.

Q.2 Assertion (A) A compass needle is placed near a current carrying wire. The deflection of the compass needle decreases when the compass needle is displaced away from the wire.

Reason (R) Strength of a magnetic field decreases as one moves away from a current carrying conductor.

Ans. (a) A current carrying wire produces a magnetic field around it and a compass needle aligns itself with the magnetic field lines. The magnetic field strength decreases with increases in distance from the wire, which causes the compass needle's deflection to decrease.

Q.3 Assertion (A) When current is passed through a wire, a magnetic field is generated around the wire.

Reason (R) Whenever there is a change of magnetic flux linked up with the coil, the induced current is generated in the coil.

Ans. (b) Both A and R are true but R is not the correct explanation of A because even though the two phenomena are connected but they don't explain each other.

Q.4 Assertion (A) The magnetic field inside the solenoid is non-uniform.

Reason (R) The magnetic field produced by a current-carrying solenoid is independent of its length and cross-section area.

Ans. (d) Magnetic field is uniform inside the solenoid. The magnetic field produced by a current-carrying solenoid is independent of its length and cross-section area.

Q.5 Assertion (A) A current carrying conductor placed perpendicularly in a magnetic field experiences a force.

Reason (R) DC motor acts according to this principle.

Ans. (b) The force on a conductor in magnetic field is given by

$$F = IBl \sin\theta$$

here $\theta = 90^\circ$

$$F = IBl$$

But, DC motor works on the Fleming's left hand rule.

Q.6 Assertion (A) A direct current shows magnetic effect.

Reason (R) Alternating current varies with time.

Ans. (b) Both alternating as well as direct current shows magnetic effect and alternating current changes its direction periodically.

Q.7 Assertion (A) Soft iron is used to make electromagnets.

Reason (R) Soft iron loses all of its magnetism when current in the coil is switched off.

Ans. (a) Electromagnets are temporary magnets and the material which can loses all of its magnetism immediately after withdraw of current is required.

TYPE - 3 — 01/02 Marks

Fill in the Blanks

Q.1 The magnetic field produced by a straight current carrying wire is inversely proportional to .... [current (*I*) / distance (*r*) from the wire] **[1]**

Ans. distance (*r*) from the wire.

Q.2 In a step-up transformer the turns ratio is .... (more than 1/less than 1/equal to 1) **[1][ICSE 2025]**

Ans. more than 1

Q.3 The device that converts AC into DC is called as .... [diode / rectifier / transformer]. **[1]**

Ans. rectifier

Q.4 In an electric motor, energy is transferred from .... [electrical energy/mechanical energy] to .... [electrical energy/mechanical energy]. **[2]**

Ans. electrical energy, mechanical energy

Q.5 The transformer which converts .... [low voltage / high voltage] into .... [low voltage / high voltage] is called step-up transformer. **[2]**

Ans. low voltage, high voltage

TYPE - 4 02 Marks

Very Short Answer Type Questions

Q.1 The diagram below shows a loop of wire carrying current *I*.

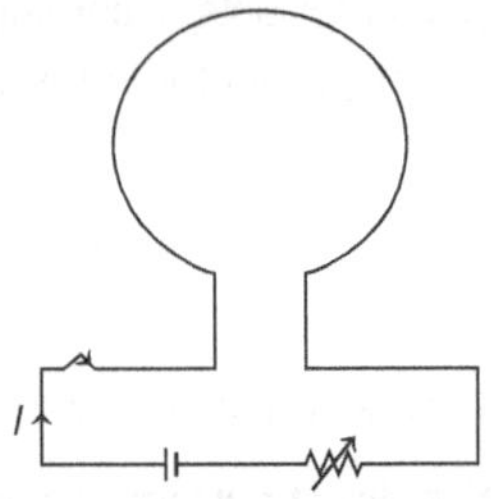

(i) What is the magnetic polarity of the loop that faces us? **[1]**

(ii) With respect to the diagram, how can we increase the strength of the magnetic field produced by this loop? **[1] [ICSE 2020]**

Ans. (i) The direction of current flowing through the loop is shown below.

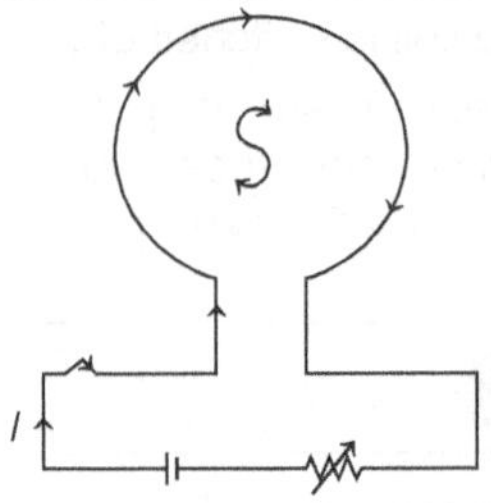

Since, direction of current in the loop is clockwise, hence it behaves as a South pole.

(ii) The strength of magnetic field produced by the loop is increased by decreasing the resistance (or increasing the current) with the help of rheostat.

Q.2 A compass needle is positioned close to a wire carrying an electric current. Observe and explain the outcomes in the following scenarios

(i) The electric current in the wire is increased. **[1]**

(ii) The compass needle is moved farther from the wire. **[1]**

Ans. (i) Magnetic field is directly proportional to the current. So, the deflection of the compass needle increases.

(ii) Magnetic field is inversely proportional to the current. So, the deflection of the compass needle decreases.

Q.3 The diagram below shows a copper conductor placed along the east-west direction. Magnetic compass *P* is present above the conductor, and *Q* is below the conductor. If current is passed through the wire from *A* to *B*. then which of the two compasses will show prominent deflection and why?

[Competency Based Que.]

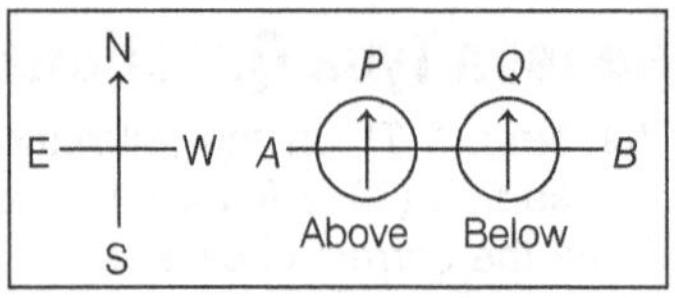

Ans. This is because the direction of magnetic field produced around the conductor for compass *Q* is in the same direction but it is opposite to the compass *P* so in order to align in the direction *P* will show deflection.

Q.4 How does the strength of a magnetic field produced by a straight current-carrying wire depend upon the perpendicular distance from the wire?

Ans. Magnetic field intensity (*B*) is inversely proportional to the perpendicular distance (*r*) from the current-carrying wire i.e., $B \propto \frac{1}{r}$.

Q.5 A magnet kept at the centre of two coils *A* and *B* is moved to and fro as shown in the figure given below. The two galvanometers show deflection. **[ICSE 2019]**

Show with reason whether : $x > y$ or $y > x$.

[*x* and *y* are magnitudes of deflection.]

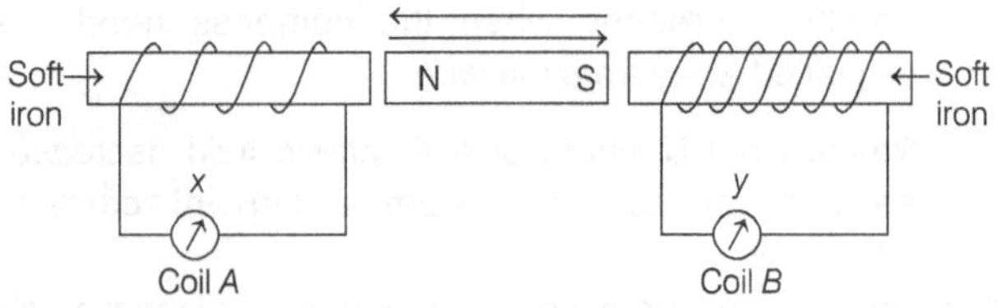

Ans. In the figure, the number of turns in coil *B* is greater than coil *A*. Hence, deflection in coil *B* will be greater than deflection in coil *A*, i.e. $y > x$.

Q.6 A straight wire is passed vertically through cardboard sprinkled with iron filings.

(i) When current is passed through the wire in the upward direction, it is seen that the iron fillings are arranging themselves in a definite pattern. Why? **[1]**

(ii) What would happen to this arrangement if more current were passed through the wire? **[1]**

[Competency Based Que.]

Ans. (i) When the current is passed through the wire, a magnetic field is generated around the wire.

(ii) The concentration of magnetic field lines will increase/the number of concentric circles will increase up to a greater distance.

Q.7 The figure given below shows an electromagnet.

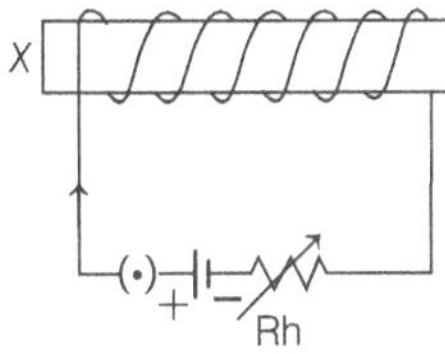

(i) What will be the polarity at the end *X*? **[1]**

(ii) Suggest a way by which the strength of the electromagnet referred in the question, may be increased. **[1] [ICSE 2009]**

Ans. (i) The polarity at end *X* is North polarity.

(ii) The strength of the electromagnet can be increased by increasing the strength of the current or by decreasing the resistance in the rheostat.

Q.8 Given differences between electromagnets and permanent magnets. **[2]**

Or State any two advantages of an electromagnet over a permanent magnet. **[ICSE 2018]**

Ans. Comparison between Electromagnet and Permanent Magnet

Electromagnet	Permanent Magnet
It is a temporary magnet.	It is a permanent magnet i.e., cannot be demagnetised easily.
It is made up of soft iron.	It is made up of steel.
It produces the magnetic field as long as current flows in its coils, i.e. it produces temporary magnetic field.	It produces permanent magnetic field.
The magnetic field strength can be changed.	The magnetic field strength cannot be changed.
It can produce very strong magnetic field.	It produces comparatively weak magnetic field.
Its polarity can be reversed.	Its polarity cannot be reversed.

Or

The two advantages of an electromagnet over a permanent magnet are

(i) The polarity of an electromagnet can be changed by reversing the direction of current in the solenoid while polarity of a permanent magnet can never be changed.

(ii) An electromagnet can produce a stronger magnetic field than a permanent magnet.

Q.9 (i) Which of the two, alternating current or direct current, produces a varying magnetic field when it flows through a conductor?

(ii) State the frequency of the alternating current supply in India **[ICSE 2025]**

Ans. (i) Alternating current would produce a varying magnetic field when it flows through a conductor.

(ii) Frequency of alternating current supply in India is 50 Hz.

Q.10 A copper conductor is placed over two stretched copper wires whose ends are connected to a DC supply as shown in the diagram. **[ICSE 2023]**

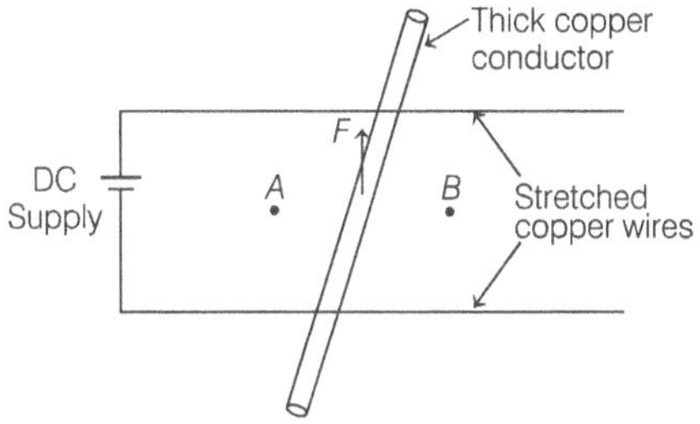

(i) What should be the magnetic poles at the points *A* and *B* lying on either side of the conductor to experience the force in the upward direction? **[1]**

(ii) Name the law used to find these polarities. **[1]**

Ans. (i) The magnetic poles at *A* and *B* should be of opposite polarity. Specifically, the pole at point *A* should be North (N) and the pole at point *B* should be South (S).

(ii) The law used to find these polarities is the Fleming's left hand rule for DC electric motors. This rule relates the direction of force on current-carrying conductor in magnetic field to the direction of current and the direction of magnetic field.

Q.11 When a current carrying conductor is placed in a magnetic field, it experiences a mechanical force. What should be the angle between the magnetic field and the length of the conductor, so that the force experienced is **[ICSE 2020]**

(i) zero and **[1]**

(ii) maximum? **[1]**

Ans. (i) A current carrying conductor placed in uniform magnetic field experiences no force (zero force), if the angle between the magnetic field and the length of the conductor is 0° and 180°.

(ii) A current carrying conductor placed in uniform magnetic field experiences maximum force, if the angle between the magnetic field and the length of conductor is 90°.

Q.12 (i) Name the principle of AC generator. **[1]**

(ii) State its one use. **[ICSE Specimen 2025][1]**

Ans. (i) An AC generator converts mechanical energy into electrical energy by using the principle of AC generator.

(ii) It is used to generate AC current in household supplies.

Q.13 **A transformer is used to change a high alternating emf to a low alternating emf of the same frequency.**

(i) Identify the type of transformer used for the above purpose. **[1]**

(ii) State whether the turns ratio of the above transformer is = 1or > 1 or < 1.

[ICSE Specimen 2025][1]

Ans. (i) The transformer used to change a high alternating emf to a low alternating emf of same frequency is called step-down transformer.

(ii) As, turns ratio, $r = \frac{N_s}{N_p} = \frac{E_s}{E_p}$

For step-down transformer,

$$E_s < E_p \Rightarrow \frac{E_s}{E_p} < 1$$

$\therefore$ ratio < 1(less than 1)

Q.14 **Two long straight vertical wires *X* and *Y* pass through a horizontal card, as shown in Figure a.**

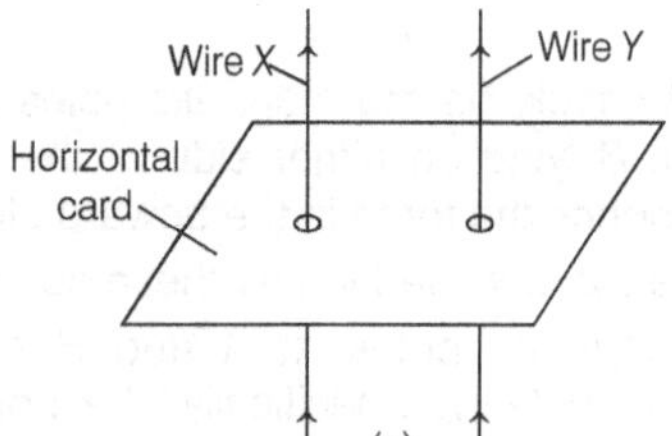

(a)

The current in each wire is in the upward direction, The top view of the card, seen by looking vertically downwards at the card, is shown in Fig. b.

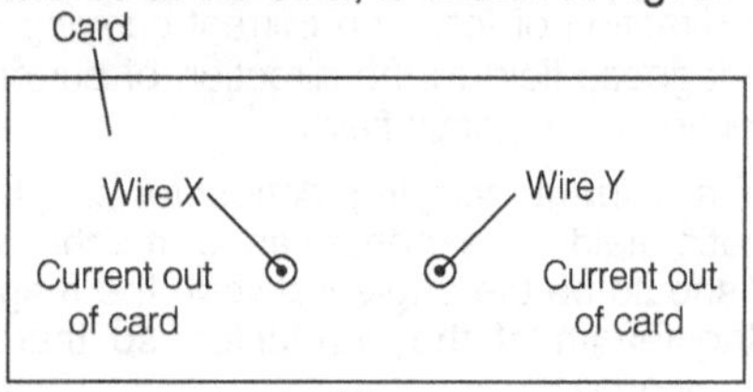

(b)

On Fig. b,

(i) Draw four field lines to represent the pattern of the magnetic field around wire *X* due solely to the current in wire *X*, **[1]**

(ii) Draw an arrow to show the direction of the force on wire *Y* due to the magnetic field of wire *X*. **[1]**

Ans. (i)

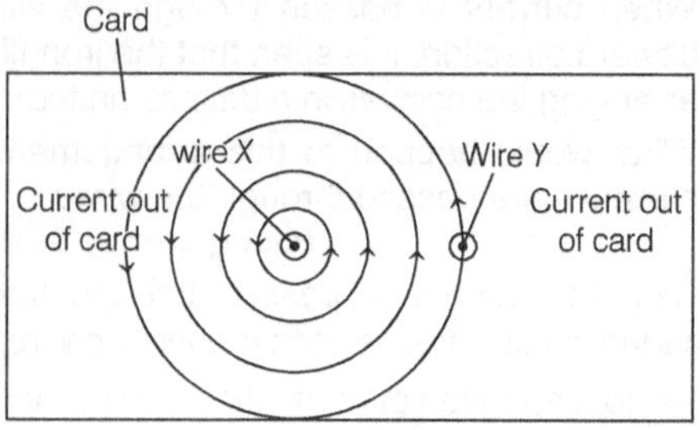

(ii)

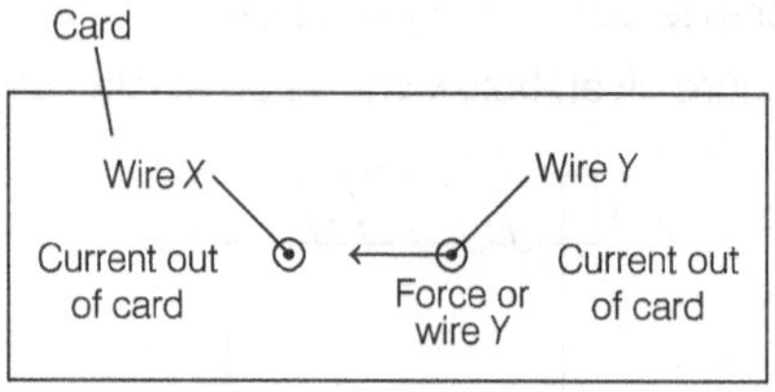

TYPE - 5

03 Marks

Short Answer Type Questions

Q.1 The diagram below shows a magnetic compass kept closer to a coil *AB* wound around a hollow cylindrical cardboard. **[ICSE 2022 Sem-II]**

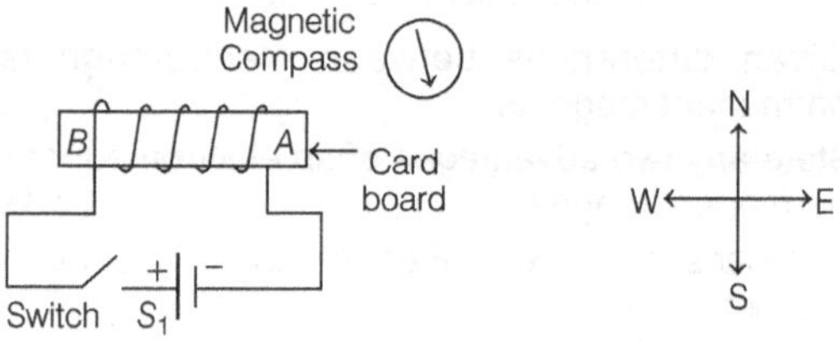

(i) After studying the circuit and the magnetic compass carefully, state whether the switch S_1 is open or closed. **[1]**

(ii) How did you arrive at the conclusion in part (i)? **[1]**

(iii) What is the purpose of placing the magnetic compass in the above setup? **[1]**

Ans. (i) The switch S_1 is open because no current is passing through the circuit. Since, the compass does not show any delfection.

(ii) As the switch does not have a wire connected to the circuit, thus we can say that the circuit is open or the switch is open.

(iii) The purpose of placing a magnetic compass is to study the deflection and to find out the direction of current.

Q.2 Given below is a current to study the magnetic effect of electric current. *ABCD* is a cardboard kept perpendicular to the conductor *XY*.

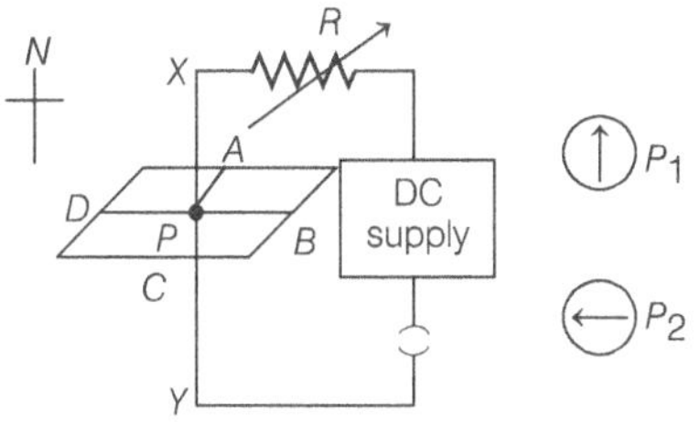

A magnetic compass is placed at the point *P* of the cardboard. P_1 and P_2 are the positions of the magnetic compass, before and after passing a current through *XY*, respectively.

(i) Name the rule that is used to predict the direction of deflection of the magnetic compass. **[1]**

(ii) State the direction of current in the conductor (*X* to *Y* or *Y* to *X*) when the circuit is complete. **[1]**

(iii) If resistance *R* is increased, then what will be the effect on the magnetic lines of force around the conductor ? **[1] [ICSE 2024]**

Ans. (i) Right hand thumb rule

(ii) *X* to *Y*

(iii) Magnetic field is inversely proportional to the resistance *R*. So, if resistance *R* is increased, the magnetic lines of force decreases

Q.3

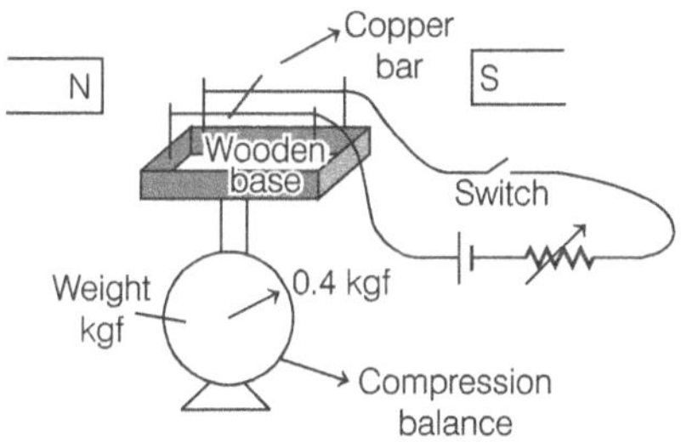

The above circuit diagram illustrates a copper bar placed on two copper wires stretched over a wooden base placed between two poles of magnets. This entire setup is placed on a compression balance, which shows a weight of 0.4 kgf.

(i) What will be the observation of the compression balance when we close the switch?

(ii) How will this observation change, when we increase the current in the circuit?

(iii) Name the rule used to come to the conclusion in (a).

Ans. (i) The reading in the compression balance will increase as the magnetic force on the copper wire acts in the downward direction.

(ii) The reading in the compression balance will further increase as the magnetic force is directly proportional to the current passing through the conductor.

(iii) Fleming's left hand rule.

Q.4 The diagram shows a coil wound around a U-shape soft iron bar *AB*.

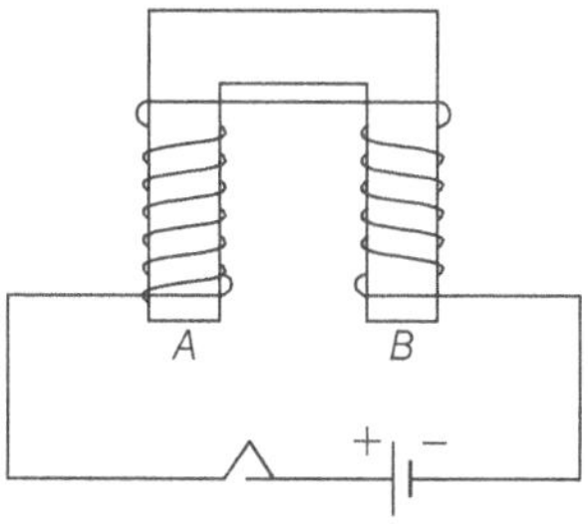

(i) What is the polarity induced at the ends *A* and *B* when the switch is pressed? **[1]**

(ii) Suggest one way to strengthen the magnetic field in the electromagnet. **[1]**

(iii) What will be the polarities at *A* and *B*, if the direction of current is reversed in the circuit? **[1] [ICSE 2018]**

Ans. (i) Current enters at point *A* (clockwise rotation) and leaving from point *B* (anti-clockwise rotation). Hence, *A* will be South pole and *B* will be North pole.

(ii) Increasing the number of turns of coils, increases current.

(iii) *A* = North, *B* = South.

Q.5 In the given diagram, *X* represents a conductor carrying current into the plane of the paper and kept in a magnetic field *N* and *S* represent the poles of a magnet and concentric circles of the magnetic field produced by the conductor.

(i) State the direction of the force experienced by the conductor. **[1]**

(ii) Explain the cause of the above-said force. **[1]**

(iii) Name the law used to determine the direction of the force in the conductor. **[1]**

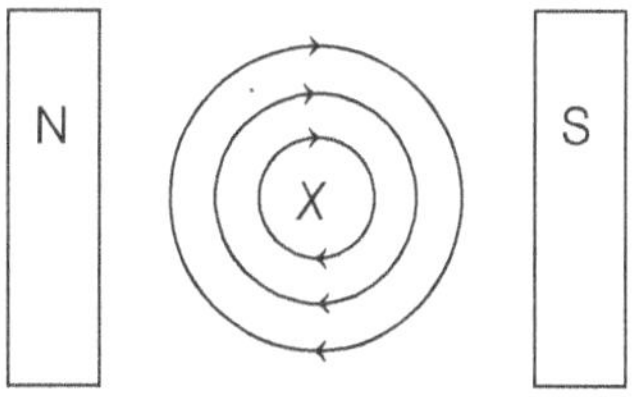

Ans. (i) The force experienced will be in the downward direction.

(ii) The force arises due to the current flowing in the circuit and the magnetic field around the conductor, which is also known as the magnetic force.

(iii) Fleming's left hand rule.

Q.6 (i) **Two circular coils *P* and *Q* are kept close to each other, of which coil *P* carries a current. If coil *P* is moved towards *Q*, will some current be induced in coil *Q*? Give reason for your answer and name the phenomenon involved.** **[1]**

(ii) **What happens, if coil *P* is moved away from *Q*?** **[1]**

(iii) **State few methods of inducing current in a coil.** **[1]**

Ans. (i) When coil *P* is moved towards *Q*, current will be induced in coil *Q*.

This is because on moving *P*, the magnetic field associated with *Q* increases and so a current is induced. The phenomenon is electromagnetic induction.

(ii) If *P* is moved away from *Q*, the field associated with *Q* will decrease and a current will be induced but in the opposite direction.

(iii) Some of the methods of inducing current in the coil are

(a) moving a magnet towards or away from the coil.

(b) moving a coil towards or away from a magnet.

(c) rotating a coil within a magnetic field.

Q.7 **Read the excerpt from a story and answer the questions that follow:**
On stage, a soft iron box sits a top a hidden copper coiled platform, conductive to electricity. I summoned a man who fancied himself a modern-day Hercules onto the stage and challenged him to lift the iron box. With ease, he lifted it up. Then, with a wave of my magic wand and a hidden switch activated, I said, "I'm going to take away your strength." When I asked him to lift the box again, he struggled, unable to budge it.

(i) **Explain the secret behind the magic.** **[1]**

(ii) **If you are asked to design the same magic in your science lab, give the necessary circuit diagram.** **[1]**

(iii) **Give any one device that works on the same principle.** **[1]**

Ans. (i) When the switch is put ON, the copper coil acts as a magnet and attracts the iron box.

(ii)

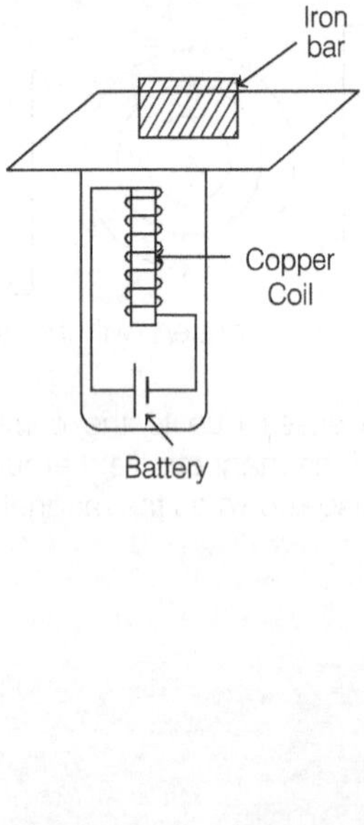

(iii) AC generator acts on the principle of electromagnetic induction.

Q.8 **Copper wire is wound around a steel bar *FT*. Current is allowed to pass through the coil for some time and then the bar is removed.** **[2]**

(i) **Draw only the magnetised bar *FT* and mark its poles.**

(ii) **Trace two magnetic lines of force around *FT* clearly indicating the direction.**

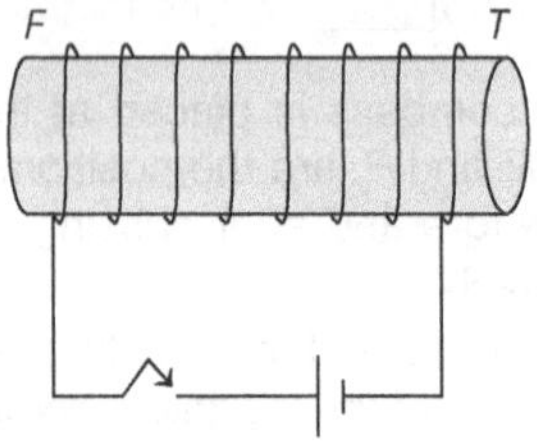

Ans. (i)

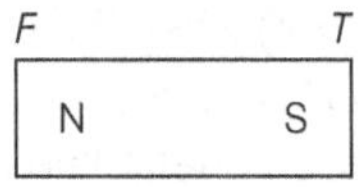

(ii)

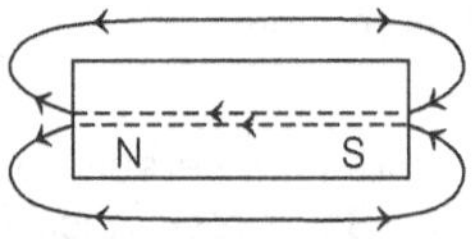

Q.9 (i) **Draw a neat and labelled diagram to show the structure of an AC generator.** **[2]**

(ii) **State the energy conversion taking place in the AC generator when it is working.** **[1]**

Ans. (i) The labelled diagram of an AC generator is shown below

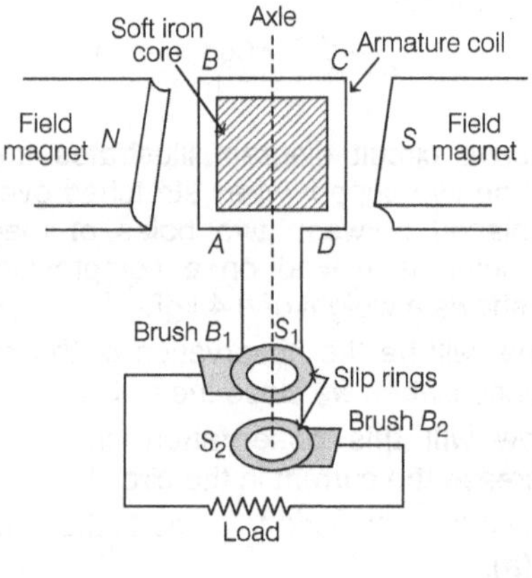

(ii) In the AC generator, mechanical energy of the rotation of the coil converts into electrical energy.

Q.10 Below is the diagram of a transformer

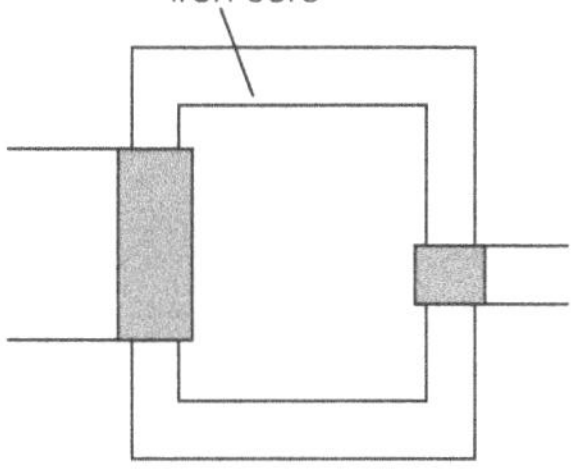

(i) Identify the type of transformer. **[1]**

(ii) In this type of transformer, which of the wire is thicker, the primary or the secondary? Give a reason. **[2] [ICSE 2024]**

Ans. (i) Step-down transformer

(ii) Secondary coil

The reason is that, secondary coil of a step-down transformer has greater current than primary coil. So, secondary coil is thicker as compared to its primary coil.

Q.11

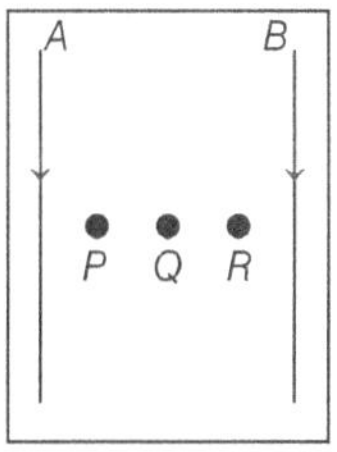

The diagram above shows two parallel wires carrying current in the downward direction. The magnitude of the current in wire *A* is greater than in wire *B*. It is also observed that the wires exert force on each other.

(i) State the direction of the force experienced by wire *A*. **[1]**

(ii) Name the law/laws used to come to the conclusion in (a).

(iii) When a compass is placed in between the two wires, it does not remain along the direction of the magnetic field wire *A* or wire *B* at one of the points *P*, *Q*, or *R*. State with a reason at which point you will observe this. **[1]**

[Competency Based Que.]

Ans. (i) Towards *B*

(ii) Right hand thumb rule and Fleming's left-hand rule.

(iii) At point *R*

Neutral point will always be formed near the weaker magnet.

TYPE - 6 — 04 Marks

Long Answer Type Questions

Q.1 The diagram below shows a cardboard on which iron filings are kept. A wire bent in the form of a loop is seen passing through the cardboard. When current flows through it, the iron filings arrange themselves as shown below. **[ICSE 2023]**

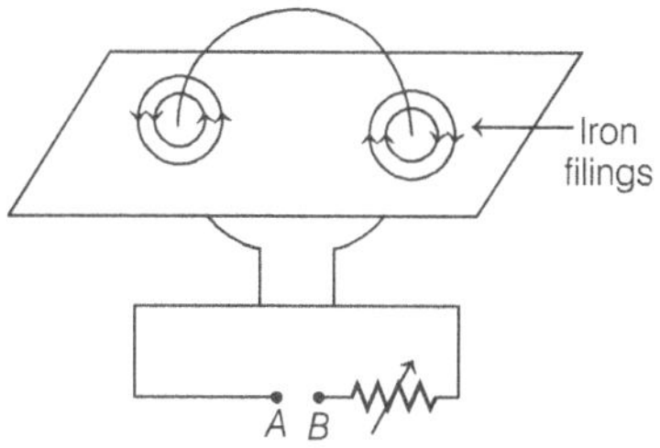

s

(i) State the polarities of the battery at *A* and *B*. **[1]**

(ii) State the effect on the magnetic field if an iron rod is held along the axis of the coil. **[1]**

(iii) State one way to

(a) Change the polarity of the coil. **[1]**

(b) Decrease the strength of the magnetic field around the coil. **[1]**

Ans. (i) A is +ve terminal and *B* is – ve terminal. At *A*, current is upward, so magnetic field line is anti-clockwise and it has North polarity. At *B*, current is downward, so magnetic field line is clockwise and it has South polarity.

(ii) If an iron is held along axis of the coil, the strength of the magnetic field is increased.

(iii) (a) The polarity of the coil can be changed by reversing the direction of the current.

(b) The strength of the magnetic field around the coil can be decreased by decreasing the current which can be achieved by increasing the resistance.

Q.2 The figure below shows a magnetic needle kept just below the conductor *AB* which is kept in North-South direction.

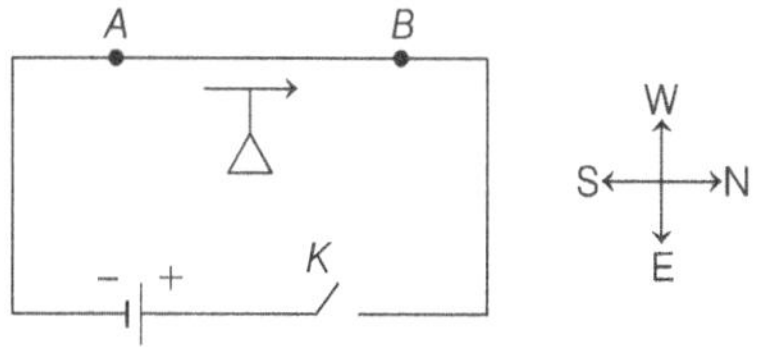

(i) In which direction, will the needle deflect when the key is closed? **[1]**

(ii) Why is the deflection produced? **[1]**

(iii) What will be the change in the deflection, if the magnetic needle is taken just above the conductor AB? **[1]**

(iv) Name one device which works on the principle of electromagnetic induction. **[1]**

Ans. (i) East direction

(ii) The needle aligns itself in the direction of the magnetic field lines. Since, the field lines are towards the east below the conductor. So, the compass deflects from North towards East.

(iii) The North pole of the compass needle deflects towards West.

(iv) Electric generator

Q.3 Figure shows a simple transformer used to light a lamp. The lamp is labelled 24 V, 36 W.

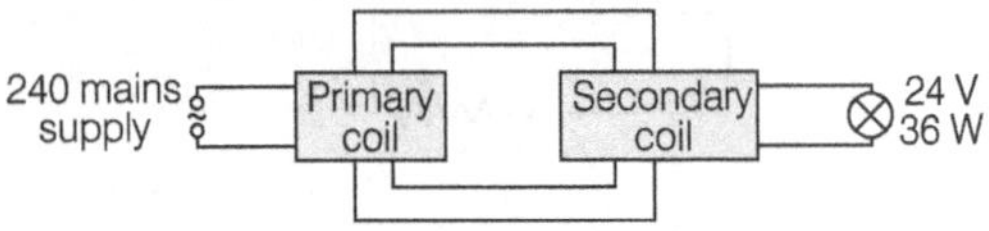

When the mains supply is switched ON, the lamp is very dim.

(i) State two ways in which the potential difference across the lamp can be increased without changing the mains supply. **[1]**

(ii) Explain why the core is made from iron rather than steel. **[1]**

(iii) For the lamp operating at the correct brightness, calculate **[1]**

(a) the current in the secondary coil, **[1]**

(b) the current in the primary coil. Assume that the transformer is ideal. **[1][Competency Based Ques]**

Ans. (i) 1. Increase the number of turns in the secondary coil.

2. Decrease the number of turns in the primary coil.

(ii) Iron magnetises and demagnetises easily.

(iii) (a) Secondary current $= \frac{P}{V} = \frac{36}{24} = 1.5$ A

(b) Primary current $= \frac{P}{V} = \frac{36}{240} = 0.15$ A

Q.4 (i) Draw a simple labelled diagram of a DC electric motor. **[1½]**

(ii) What is the function of the split rings in a DC motor? **[1½]**

(iii) State one advantage of AC over DC. **[1] [ICSE 2013]**

Ans. (i)

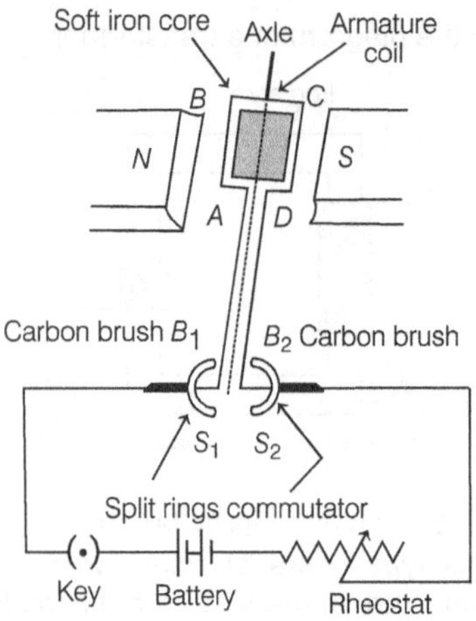

(ii) It acts as commutator in a DC motor, when the coil rotates, the split ring rotates with it to flow the current in the armature coil in such a way that it always keeps on rotating in the same manner.

(iii) AC can be transported to a large distance without much loss.

Q.5 (i) Draw a labelled diagram to show the various components of a step-down transformer. **[2]**

(ii) State the main difference between a step-up and step-down transformers. **[2]**

Ans. (i) The sketch of step-down transformer is shown below.

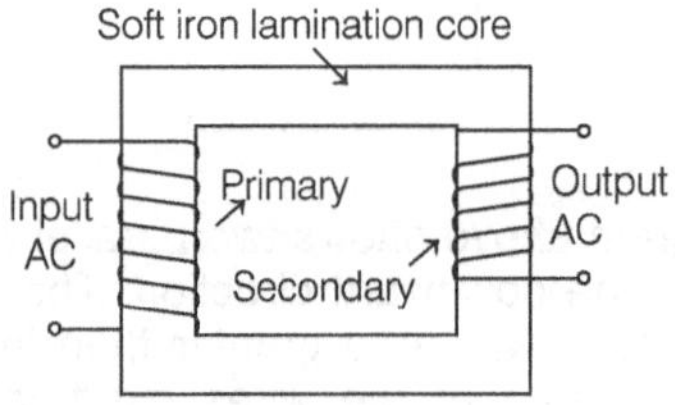

$N_p > N_s$

(ii) The difference between step-up and step-down transformers are given below.

Step-up Transformer	Step-down Transformer
It is used to change a low voltage alternating emf to high voltage alternating emf.	It is used to change a high voltage alternating emf to low voltage alternating emf.
The number of turns in primary coil is less than the number of turns in secondary coil.	The number of turns in primary coil is greater than the number of turns in secondary coil.

Q.6 Figure shows a coil *ABCD* that can turn between the two poles of a magnet. Bare metal paper clips support and pass current into and out of the coil.

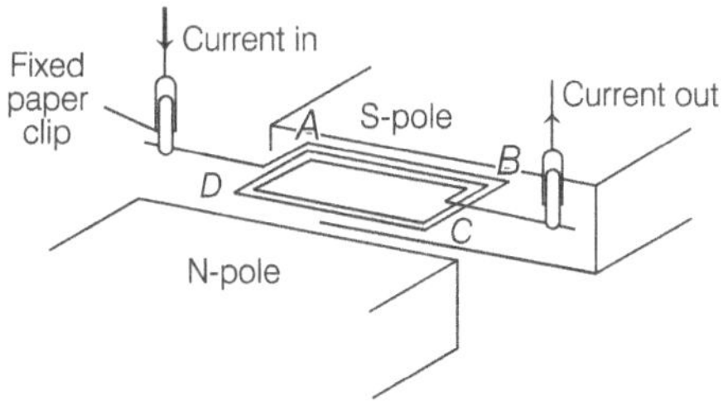

(i) (a) State the direction of the force on the side *AB*. **[1]**

(b) Explain the reason for your choice of direction. **[1]**

(ii) A student turns the coil through 180° so that *AB* is close to the N pole of the magnet.

(a) State the direction of the force on side *AB* of the coil. **[1]**

(b) The student releases the coil. Explain, why the coil does not rotate continuously. **[1]**

[Competency Based Que.]

Ans. (i) (a) Upwards.

(b) By using Fleming's Left hand Rule.

(ii) (a) Upwards.

(b) After the coil rotates past an angle of 90°, the magnetic forces acting on the coil produces a moment whose direction is opposite to the direction of motion of the coil.

Q.7 A copper rod *PQ* carrying-current is kept in a magnetic field as shown in the diagram. **[ICSE 2025]**

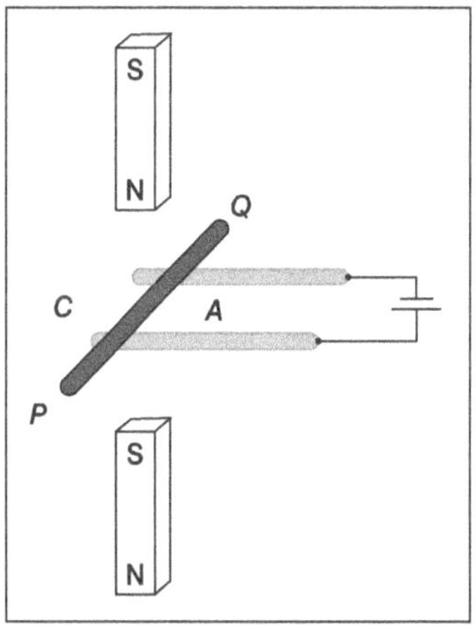

(i) The copper rod *PQ* will move towards *C*. State true or false.

(ii) Name the law used to determine the direction of motion of *PQ*.

(iii) What will be the effect on the force experienced, if the rod *PQ* is replaced by another copper rod of same length but of greater cross-sectional area?

(iv) Justify your answer in (c).

Ans. (i) True

(ii) Fleming's left hand rule

(iii) Remains same

(iv) Since $F \propto l$, where l is the length of the rod so it will not be affected due to the increase in cross - sectional area since the length remains same.

TYPE - 7 — 03/04 Marks

Case Based Questions

Q.1 In 1820, Hans Christian Oersted discovered that a magnetic needle is deflected by a current-carrying wire. For many years, he had expected to find a connection between electricity and magnetism. Before his discovery, Oersted had imagined the magnetic field to be a straight line along the direction of the wire with the north pole at one end and the south pole at the other. This was a major reason why he took so long to discover electromagnetism.

The figure below shows how Oersted would have arranged his wire and magnetic needle in his early experiments.

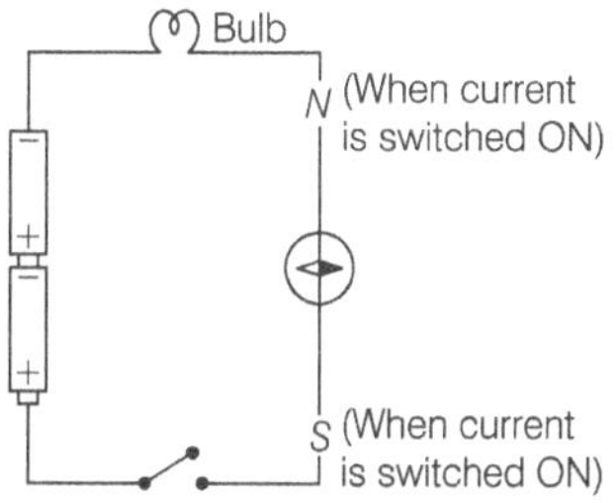

(i) Draw a diagram to show the observation that Oersted would have expected when switching ON the current, if his hypothesis had been correct. **[1]**

(ii) Based on our current knowledge of the magnetic field around a wire, explain why his experiment failed. **[1]**

(iii) If a neutron moves perpendicular to a uniform magnetic field, will it feel any force? Why? **[1]**

Ans. (i) He expected the magnetic field to be straight line along the direction of wire.

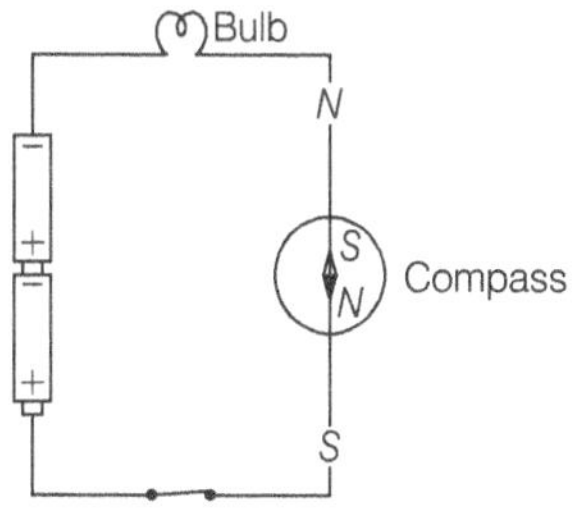

(ii) (a) The magnetic field due to the current is perpendicular to the wire.

(b) Since the needle is already pointing in a direction perpendicular to the wire, it will not get deflected.

(iii) No, neutron will not feel any force because neutron is a neutral particle having no charge.

Q.2 **A student was asked to perform an experiment to study the force on a current carrying conductor in a magnetic field. He took a small aluminium rod *AB*, a strong horse-shoe magnet, some connecting wires, a battery and a switch and connected them as shown. He observed that on passing current, the rod gets displaced. On reversing the direction of current, the direction of displacement also gets reversed. On the basis of your understanding of this phenomenon, answer the following questions:**

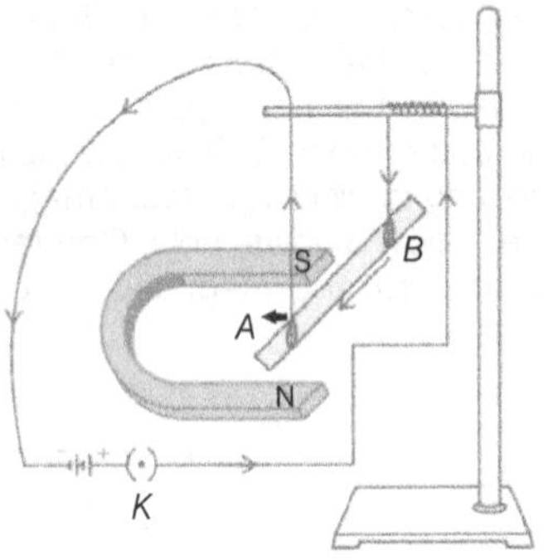

Read the above passage carefully and give the answer of the following questions:

(i) Why does the rod get displaced on passing current through it? **[1]**

(ii) State the rule that determines the direction of the force on the conductor *AB*. **[1]**

(iii) (a) If the U-shaped magnet is held vertically and the aluminium rod is suspended horizontally with its end *B* towards north, then on passing current through the rod from *B* to *A* as shown, in which direction will the rod be displaced? **[1]**

(b) Name any two devices that use current carrying conductors and magnetic field. **[1]**

Ans. (i) When a current carrying conductor is placed in a magnetic field, a magnetic force is exerted on the conductor which displaces the rod.

(ii) Fleming's left hand rule determines the direction of force on the conductor *AB*. According to this rule, stretch the thumb, forefinger and middle finger of your left hand such that they are mutually perpendicular. If the forefinger points along the direction of external magnetic field, middle finger indicates the direction of current, then thumb points in the direction of force acting on the conductor.

(iii) (a) Towards the left

(b) Electric motor and electric generator.

Q.3 **An electromagnet is a magnet consisting of a long coil of insulated copper wire wrapped around a soft iron core that is magnetised only when electric current is passed through the coil. Soft iron is used as core of an electromagnet because soft iron loses all of its magnetism when current in the coil is switched OFF. The strength of an electromagnet depends on a few factors such as number of turns in the coil, current flowing in the coil, etc.**

(i) Name two factors on which the strength of a magnetic field of an electromagnet depends. **[1]**

(ii) Which kind of energy change takes place in an electromagnet? **[1]**

(iii) Which material is used to make electromagnets and why? **[1]**

Ans. (i) The strength of an electromagnet depends on the number of turns in the coils and the strength of the current passing through the coil.

(ii) The energy change that takes place in an electromagnet is electrical energy to magnetic energy.

(iii) Soft iron is used to make electromagnets because soft iron loses all of its magnetism when current in the coil is switched OFF.

10

HEAT

Temperature

- It is the measure of degree of hotness or coldness of any body. Heat flows from a body at higher temperature to another body at lower temperature, until they reach on equal temperature. The SI unit of temperature is **kelvin** (K). Other units of temperature are **celsius** (°C) and **fahrenheit** (°F).

Temperature in kelvin scale = Temperature in celsius scale + 273.15

$$T\,(\text{K}) = T\,(^\circ\text{C}) + 273.15$$

Heat

- It is the form of energy which flows from one object at higher temperature to other object at lower temperature without any mechanical work. It measures the total internal energy possessed by the molecules.
  It is represented by Q.

Different Units of Heat Energy

- **One calorie** It is the amount of heat required to raise the temperature of 1 g of pure water by 1°C.
  $$1 \text{ cal} = 4.186 \text{ J} = 4.2 \text{ J}$$
- **One kilocalorie** It is the amount of heat required to raise the temperature of 1 kg of pure water by 1°C.
  $$1 \text{ kcal} = 10^3 \text{cal} = 4.2 \times 10^3 \text{J}$$

Thermal Capacity or Heat Capacity

- It is defined as the total amount of heat required to raise the temperature of a body by 1°C. It is represented by C.

$$\text{Heat capacity } (C') = \frac{\text{Heat supplied to the body } (Q)}{\text{Change in temperature } (\Delta t)}$$

- Its SI unit is joule/°C or joule/K. Its older unit is cal/°C or cal/K or kcal/°C.

Specific Heat Capacity

- It can be defined as the amount of heat energy required to raise the temperature of unit mass of a substance by 1°C. It is dependent on nature of the substance. It is represented by c.

$$\text{Specific heat capacity } (c) = \frac{\text{Heat energy supplied } (Q)}{\text{Mass of the body or substance } (m) \times \text{Change in temperature } (\Delta T)}$$

or Heat energy supplied $Q = mc\Delta t$

Relationship between Heat Capacity and Specific Heat Capacity

- The relationship between the thermal (heat) capacity C' and specific heat capacity (c) can be given as

$$C' = \text{mass } (m) \times c \text{ or } c = C'/m$$

- The SI unit of specific heat capacity is J/kg-K. The other units which is useful in calculation of specific heat is cal/g°C or kcal/kg°C.

Values of Specific Heat Capacity for Some Common Substances

Material	cal/g°C	J/kg-K
Water	1	4186
Ethanol	0.55	2302
Paraffin	0.51	2135
Ice	0.50	2093
Steam	0.46	1926
Copper	0.093	389
Lead	0.031	130

Consequences of High Specific Heat Capacity of Water

(i) In cold countries, temperatures can drop so low that liquids like wine or juice can freeze. To prevent this, people often place these bottles in a container filled with water, which acts as a heat reservoir. Due to high specific heat capacity of water it can absorb and release heat slowly. So, when the temperature drops, the water cools down gradually and helps in preventing the bottles from freezing too quickly.

(ii) Water in plants and animals helps to maintain a stable body temperature in all seasons by absorbing and releasing heat slowly. In summer, sweating, panting, and transpiration cool the body through evaporation. In winter, water acts as a thermal buffer, preventing heat loss and keeping vital organs warm. It also distributes heat through blood in animals and sap in plants, ensuring internal stability despite external temperature changes. This helps living beings survive and function efficiently.

(iii) Hot water bottles are used for fomentation because water, due to its high specific heat capacity, retains heat for a long time and releases it slowly, providing continuous warmth to the affected area. When applied to sore muscles or joints, the heat improves blood circulation, relaxes muscles, and reduces stiffness or pain.

(iv) Water is used as a coolant in car radiators because it can absorb and transfer heat efficiently without heating up too quickly. Its high specific heat capacity allows it to carry away excess heat from the engine and release it through the radiator, prevents overheating. Water also flows easily, ensuring smooth circulation and even cooling.

(v) Farmers fill their fields with water on cold winter nights because water releases heat slowly, preventing the soil temperature from dropping too much. Water has a high specific heat capacity, so it absorbs heat during the day and gradually releases it at night, keeping the air and soil warmer. This protects crops from frost damage by preventing sudden temperature drops that could harm plant cells and slow their growth.

Principle of Calorimetry

- According to the principle of calorimeter, when a hot body is mixed or kept in contact with a cold body, there is a heat transfer from hot body to cold body until they reach the same temperature. If no heat energy is exchanged with surroundings, then the heat gained by cold body is equal to heat lost by hot body.

  Heat lost by the hot body is always equal to the heat gained by the cold body.

$$\text{Heat lost } (Q_L) = \text{Heat gained } (Q_G)$$

or

$$m_1 c_1 \Delta T_1 = m_2 c_2 \Delta T_2$$

Change of State

- Normally, there are three states of matter solid, liquid and vapour (or gas). **The transformation of one of these states to another by absorbing or rejecting heat is called change of state.**

  There are two common changes of states of matter

  (i) Solid to liquid (and *vice-versa*)

  (ii) Liquid to gas (and *vice-versa*)

- The changes can occur when the exchange of heat takes place between substance and its surroundings.

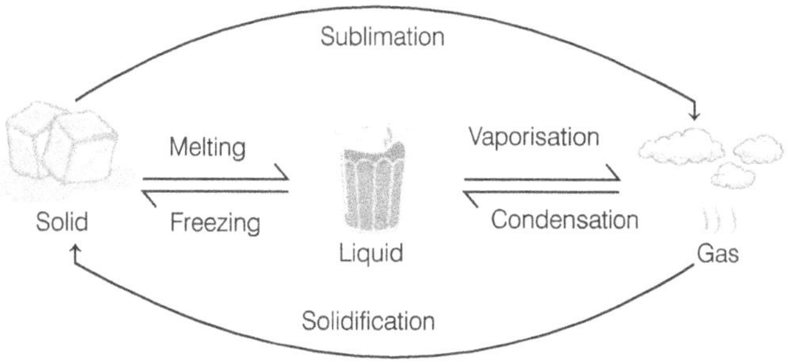

- The phenomenon of change of matter from one state to another and back to the original state by altering the conditions of temperature and pressure is called **interconversion of states of matter**.
  Following two factors (or any one of these) which makes it possible to convert one state of matter into another
  (i) Change in temperature (ii) Change in pressure

Terms Involved in Change of State

(i) **Fusion or Melting and Melting Point** The process of conversion of a matter from its solid state to its liquid state at specific conditions of temperature and pressure is called **fusion/melting**.

The definite temperature at which a solid starts melting is called the **melting point** of that solid, e.g., melting point of ice is 0°C or 273.16 K.

(ii) **Boiling and Boiling Point** The process of conversion of a matter from its liquid state to vapours (gaseous state) at specific conditions of temperature and pressure is called **boiling**. The temperature at which a liquid starts boiling at the atmospheric pressure is known as its **boiling point**.

(iii) **Sublimation** The process of change of solid state directly into gaseous state without passing through the liquid state upon heating and *vice-versa* on cooling is known as sublimation.

(iv) **Vaporisation** The process of conversion of a matter from its liquid state to gaseous state at specific temperature and pressure is called vaporisation.

(v) **Freezing and Freezing Point** The process of conversion of matter from its liquid state to solid state at specific conditions of temperature and pressure is called **freezing**. It is a reverse process of fusion/melting and the definite temperature at which a liquid changes into solid state by giving out heat energy at 1 atm is called the **freezing point**.

(vi) **Condensation** The process of conversion of matter from its gaseous state to liquid state at specific conditions of temperature and pressure is called condensation. It is a reverse process of vaporisation.

Latent Heat

- The amount of heat transferred per unit mass during the change of phase of a substance without any change in its temperature is called latent heat of the substance.
- Latent heat is denoted by L and its SI unit is J kg^{-1}. The value of latent heat is usually quoted at standard atmospheric pressure because it also depends upon the pressure.
- Thus, if a mass m of a substance undergoes a change from one state to the other, then the quantity of heat required is given by

$$Q = mL$$

i.e. $\boxed{\text{Latent heat, } L = Q/m}$

- Hence, during the phase change, the heat required by the substance depends on the mass m of the substance and heat of transformation Q.

Specific Latent Heat of Fusion

- It can be defined as the amount of heat required to convert a unit mass of solid into liquid without any change in the temperature.

Specific Latent Heat of Vaporisation

- It is defined as the amount of heat required to convert a unit mass of liquid into vapour without any change in temperature.

Some Natural Phenomena Involving Latent Heat of Fusion

Natural consequences of high specific latent heat of fusion of ice are as follows

(i) On the mountains in summer, snow melts very slowly. It is because every kilogram of snow requires 336000 J of heat energy in order to form water at 0°C. Therefore, there are no flash floods and the rivers contain the water for whole year.

(ii) During the snow storm, the weather becomes mild, it is because a large amount of heat energy is dissipated in the atmosphere due to the freezing of water vapour.

(iii) When the snow starts melting, the environment becomes bitterly cold, it is because every kilogram of ice on melting absorbs 336000 J of heat energy from the atmosphere.

(iv) The icebergs are carried on by ocean currents over very large distances because of high specific latent heat of fusion of ice.

Heating Curve for Water

- The curve given below shows the cycle in temperature when water transits from liquid state to gaseous state.

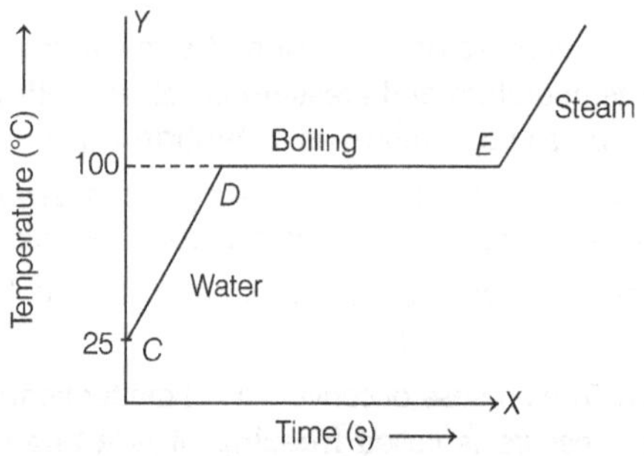

Heating curve of water

- From the curve, we can see that the temperature of water rises from 25°C to 100° C linearly with some absorption of heat as well as a rise in temperature.
- At point *D*, water starts boiling and it remains there for some times without any rise in temperature because during this time water changes its state from liquid to gaseous state which requires latent heat.
- Again at point *E*, temperature starts rising because all the water have been converted from the liquid state to gaseous state.

REVISION NOTES

EXAM ORIENTED QUESTIONS

TYPE - 1 01 Mark

Multiple Choice Questions

Q.1 Which of the following is not the unit of heat?

(a) Calorie (b) erg

(c) Torr (d) Joule

Ans. (c) Torr is not the unit of heat, it is the unit of pressure.

Q.2 Heat capacity of a body is the **[ICSE Specimen 2025]**

(a) energy needed to melt a body without change in its temperature.

(b) energy needed to raise the temperature of a body by 1°C.

(c) increase in volume of the body when its temperature increases by 1°C.

(d) total amount of internal energy that is constant.

Ans. (b) Heat capacity of a body is the heat or energy required to raise its temperature by 1°C.

Q.3 A metal piece of mass 5 g has thermal capacity 2.5 JK^{-1}. If the mass of the metal is tripled, then its specific heat capacity will be **[ICSE 2025]**

(a) 7.5 JK^{-1} (b) 2.5 JK^{-1}

(c) 1.5 $Jg^{-1}K^{-1}$ (d) 0.5 $Jg^{-1}K^{-1}$

Ans. (d) Specific heat capacity of the metal piece is

$$\frac{\text{thermal capacity}}{\text{mass}} = \frac{2.5}{5} JK^{-1}g^{-1} = 0.5\ JK^{-1}g^{-1}.$$

When the mass of the metal is tripled, the specific heat capacity remains unchanged as it is independent of the mass of the body.

Q.4 Identify the specific heat capacity of water.

(a) 4.2 $Jg^{-1}K^{-1}$ (b) 0.42 $Jg^{-1}K^{-1}$

(c) 4200 J $kg^{-1}K^{-1}$ (d) 420 J $g^{-1}K^{-1}$

Ans. (a) The specific heat capacity of water is 4.2 $Jg^{-1}K^{-1}$, which is the amount of heat required to raise the temperature of 1 g of water by 1°C.

Q.5 Which of the following liquids is most suitable for radiators in cars? **[ICSE Specimen 2023]**

(a) Liquid *P* with specific heat capacity 4000 $Jkg^{-1}K^{-1}$

(b) Liquid *Q* with specific heat capacity 2000 $Jkg^{-1}K^{-1}$

(c) Liquid *R* with specific heat capacity 1500 $Jkg^{-1}K^{-1}$

(d) Liquid *S* with specific heat capacity 2100 $Jkg^{-1}K^{-1}$

Ans. (a) Liquid *P* with specific heat capacity 4000 $Jkg^{-1}K^{-1}$.

Liquid *P* has a high specific heat capacity which means it can absorb a large amount of heat without much rise in its own temperature.

Q.6 The graph given below shows heat energy supplied against change in temperature when no energy is lost to the surrounding. **[ICSE 2024]**

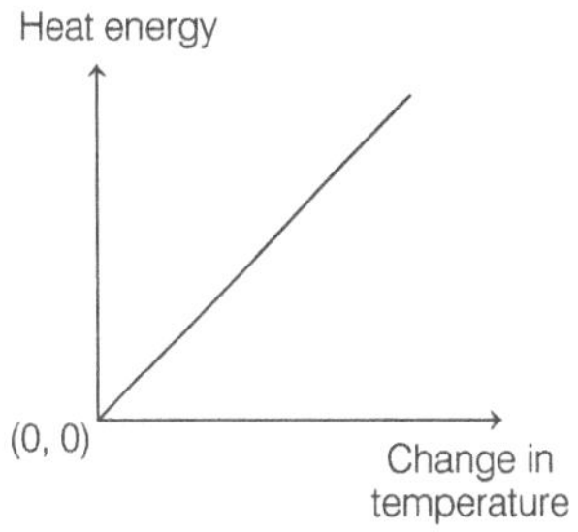

The slope of this graph will give

(a) specific heat capacity

(b) latent heat of fusion

(c) latent heat of vaporisation

(d) heat capacity

Ans. (d) $\Delta Q = C' \Delta T$

Heat capacity, $C' = \frac{\Delta Q}{\Delta T}$ = Slope

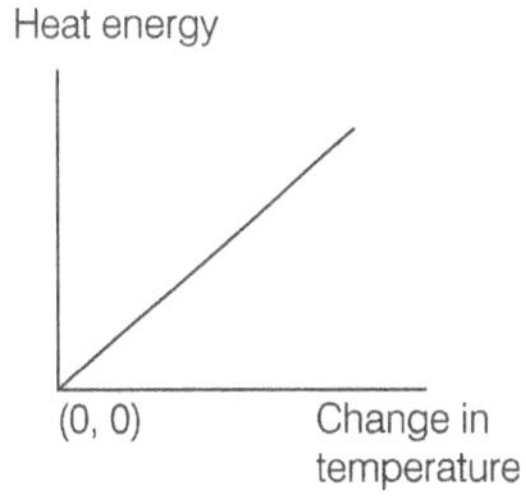

Hence, the slope of this graph will give heat capacity.

Q.7 The meaning of the statement specific heat capacity of water is 4200 $Jkg^{-1}K^{-1}$ is **[ICSE 2022 Sem-II]**

(a) Water needs 4200 J heat to raise its temperature by 1 K.

(b) To raise the temperature of water, 4200 J of heat is absorbed.

(c) 1 kg water absorbs 4200 J heat to increase its temperature by 1 K.

(d) 1 kg water needs 1 K temperature to absorb 4200 J heat.

Ans. (c) 1 kg water absorbs 4200 J heat to increase its temperature by 1 K.

Specific heat is the amount of heat required to raise the temperature of unit mass of a substance by 1 K or 1° C.

Q.8 Two substances, A and B, have the same mass. Substance A has a higher specific heat capacity than substance B. What consequences would you expect when these substances are subjected to the same amount of heat energy? **[Competency Based Que.]**

(a) Substance A will experience a smaller temperature change than substance B.
(b) Substance A will experience a larger temperature change than substance B.
(c) Both substances will experience the same temperature change.
(d) Either of them can show a greater change in temperature as the temperature change depends on factors other than specific heat capacity.

Ans. (a) Since $Q = mc\Delta T$, for the same mass and heat energy, the substance with a higher specific heat capacity (A) will have a smaller temperature change, while the one with a lower specific heat capacity (B) will have larger temperature change.

Q.9 Three metals, A, B and C, are supplied with the same quantity of heat. Their masses are in the ratio 2:3:4. If they show the same rise in the temperature, then the ratio of their thermal capacities will be **[Competency Based Que.]**

(a) 1:1:1 (b) 4:3:2
(c) 2:3:4 (d) 2:3:1

Ans. (a) Thermal capacity or heat capacity for a given mass of a substance is given as

$C = \frac{\Delta Q}{\Delta T}$, that is heat supplied per unit rise in temperature. Since, for all three metals, the quantity of heat supplied and the rise in temperature are the same, hence $C_A:C_B:C_C = 1:1:1$

Q.10 Water is used in car radiators because **[2022 Sem-II]**

(a) it is a good conductor of heat.
(b) it conducts heat faster as compared to the other substances and cools the engine quickly.
(c) its specific heat capacity is very low.
(d) its specific heat capacity is very high, so it can cool the engine without much increase in its own temperature.

Ans. (d)

Q.11 When substance transitions from solid to liquid, what happens to the kinetic and potential energy of its molecules ?

(a) Kinetic energy decreases, potential energy increases.
(b) Kinetic energy remains constant, potential energy increases.
(c) Kinetic energy and potential energy both increase.
(d) Potential energy decreases.

Ans. (b) When a substance changes from solid state to liquid state without change in temperature, average kinetic energy of the molecules does not change but the potential energy of the molecules increases as the average distance between molecules increases.

Q.12 The amount of heat energy required to melt a given mass of a substance at its melting point without any rise in its temperature is called as the **[ICSE Specimen 2025]**

(a) specific heat capacity
(b) specific latent heat of fusion
(c) latent heat of fusion
(d) specific latent heat of freezing

Ans. (b) The amount of heat energy required to melt unit mass substance at its melting point is called the specific latent heat of fusion.

Q.13 During melting of ice at 0°C, the **[ICSE 2024]**

(a) energy is released and temperature remains constant.
(b) energy is absorbed and temperature remains constant.
(c) energy is released and temperature decreases.
(d) energy is absorbed and temperature increases.

Ans. (b) During melting of ice at 0°C, the energy is absorbed and temperature remains constant.

Q.14 Which has more heat energy at 0°C,1g of ice or 1g of water?

(a) 1g of ice
(b) 1g of water
(c) Both have the same heat energy
(d) Ice has no heat energy

Ans. (b) 1g of water has 80 calorie heat energy more than 1g of ice at 0°C. 1g ice at 0°C requires 80 carlorie heat energy to be converted into 1 g water at 0°C.

Q.15 What prevents flash floods in river valleys during summer?

(a) Rapid evaporation of water.
(b) Slow melting of snow due to high latent heat of fusion.
(c) Absorption of heat by icebergs.
(d) Continuous rainfall in summer.

Ans. (b) The slow melting of snow ensures a steady flow of water, preventing sudden floods.

Q.16 A 250 g block of aluminium (specific heat capacity $C = 0.9\ Jg^{-1}K^{-1}$) is heated from 25°C to 75°C. Calculate the amount of heat absorbed by the block.

(a) 11.25 kJ
(b) 18 kJ
(c) 22.5 kJ
(d) 15 kJ

Ans. (a) Heat absorbed,

$$Q = mc\Delta T$$

Given, $m = 250$ g,

$$c = 0.9\ Jg^{-1}K^{-1}$$
$$\Delta T = 75 - 25 = 50°C$$
$$Q = 250 \times 0.9 \times 50$$
$$= 11250\ J$$
$$= 11.25\ kJ$$

Q.17 Which of the following substances A, B and C has the lowest heat capacity, if heat is supplied to all of them at equal rates? The temperature *versus* time graph is shown.

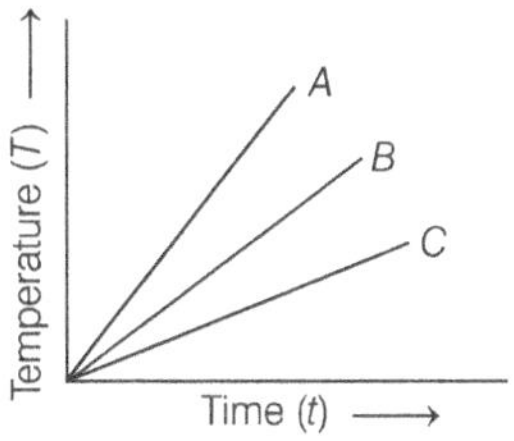

(a) C (b) B
(c) A (d) None of these

Ans. (c) Substances having more heat capacity take longer time to get heated to a higher temperature and longer time to get cooled. Here, substance A has the highest rise in temperature in a shorter interval of time.
So, A has the lowest heat capacity.

Q.18 If water absorbs 4000 J heat to increase the temperature of 1 kg of water through 1° C, then the specific heat capacity of water is **[ICSE 2022 Sem-II]**

(a) $4 \text{ Jkg}^{-1\circ}\text{C}^{-1}$ (b) $400 \text{ Jg}^{-1\circ}\text{C}^{-1}$
(c) $4 \text{ Jg}^{-1\circ}\text{C}^{-1}$ (d) $4.2 \text{ Jg}^{-1\circ}\text{C}^{-1}$

Ans. (c) Heat gained $= m \cdot c \cdot \Delta T$

$$4000 = 1000g \times c \times 1^\circ \text{C}$$
$$4 \text{ Jg}^{-1\circ}\text{C}^{-1} = c$$

$\Rightarrow$ Specific heat capacity of water $= 4 \text{ Jg}^{-1\circ}\text{C}^{-1}$

Q.19 Two identical calorimeters A and B contain equal quantity of water at 20°C. A 5g piece of metal X of specific heat $0.2 \text{ cal g}^{-1\circ}\text{C}^{-1}$ is dropped into A and a 5g piece of metal Y into B. The equilibrium temperature in A is 22°C and in B is 23°C. The initial temperature of both the metals is 40° C. Find the specific heat of metal Y in $\text{cal g}^{-1\circ}\text{C}^{-1}$.

(a) $\frac{27}{85}$ cal/g°C (b) 26 cal/g°C
(c) $\frac{85}{27}$ cal/g°C (d) 27 cal/g°C

Ans. (a) Given, calorimeters A and B are identical in size.
Quantity of water is same in both the calorimeters $= x$
Temperature of water = 20° C
For metal X, Mass = 5 g
Specific heat, $c_1 = 0.2 \text{ cal g}^{-1\circ}\text{C}^{-1}$
Initial temperature = 40 °C
Final temperature = 22 °C
For metal Y, Mass = 5 g
Specific heat, $c_2 = c \text{ cal g}^{-1\circ}\text{C}^{-1}$
Initial temperature = 40° C
Final temperature = 23° C
Now, for metal X,
Heat lost by X = Heat gained by water

$$\Rightarrow \quad 5 \times 02 \times (40 - 22) = x \times 1 \times (22 - 20)$$
$$\Rightarrow \quad 5 \times 02 \times 18 = x \times 2$$
$$\Rightarrow \quad x = \frac{5 \times 02 \times 18}{2} = 9 \text{ g}$$

As, calorimeter B also contains equal amount of water, i.e. 9 g.
$\therefore$ Heat lost by metal Y = Heat gained by water

$$5 \times c \times (40 - 23) = 9 \times 1 \times (23 - 20)$$
$$5 \times c \times 17 = 9 \times 3$$
$$\Rightarrow \quad c = \frac{9 \times 3}{5 \times 17} = \frac{27}{85} \text{ cal/g°C} = 0.32 \text{ cal/g°C}$$

Q.20 How many grams of ice at – 14° C are needed to cool 200 g of water from 25°C to 10°C? (Take, specific heat of ice = $0.5 \text{ cal g}^{-1\circ}\text{C}^{-1}$ and latent heat of ice = 80 cal g^{-1})

(a) 20 g (b) 27 g
(c) 30 g (d) 31 g

Ans. (b) Heat gained by ice = Heat lost by water
Let m = mass of ice
$L_{ice} = 80$ cal/g
$c_{ice} = 0.5$ cal/g/°C
Temperature of ice = – 14°C
Heat gained by ice

$$= mL + mc_{ice}\Delta t + mc_{water}\Delta t$$
$$= m(L + c_{ice}\Delta t + c_{water}\Delta t)$$
$$= m[80 + 0.5(0 + 14) + 1 \times (10 - 0)]$$
$$= m(80 + 7 + 10)$$
$$= m \times 97 \quad \ldots\text{(i)}$$

Heat lost by water

$$= 200 \times 1 \times (25 - 10)$$
$$= 200 \times 15 \quad \ldots\text{(ii)}$$

From Eqs. (i) and (ii), we get

$$m \times 97 = 200 \times 15$$
$$\Rightarrow \quad m = \frac{200 \times 15}{97} = 30.97 \text{ g}$$

Q.21 Each of the substances given below is supplied with same amount of heat. **[ICSE 2025]**

Which one will attain the highest temperature?

Substance	Lead	Aluminium	Copper	Iron
Specific heat capacity (cal/g°C)	0.031	0.21	0.095	0.115

(a) Aluminium (b) Copper
(c) Iron (d) Lead

Ans. (d) Since, lead has the lowest specific heat capacity, so the rise in temperature in case of lead will be the highest.

Q.22 The diagram represents two blocks of copper *A* and *B*. When same amount of heat is supplied, the temperature of *A* rises to half that of rise in *B*.

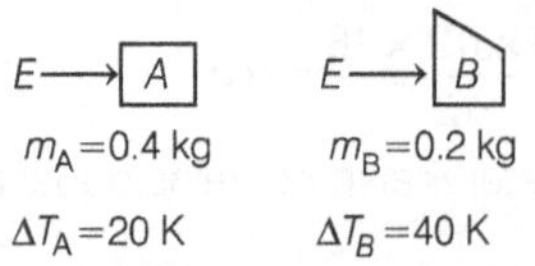

Which statement is correct about the above information?

(a) The specific heat capacity of *A* is twice that of *B*.
(b) The heat capacity of *A* is same that of *B*.
(c) The heat capacity of *A* is half that of *B*.
(d) The heat capacity of *A* is twice that of *B*.

Ans. (b) $Q_A = Q_B$

$$m_A c_A \Delta T_A = m_B c_B \Delta T_B$$
$$0.4 \times c_A \times 20 = 0.2 \times C_B \times 40$$
$$C_A = C_B$$

Q.23 Hot water at 70°C is mixed with cold water at 10°C in the ratio 3:1. What is the final temperature of the mixture?

(a) 30°C (b) 40°C (c) 50°C (d) 60°C

Ans. (c) The heat lost by hot water equals the heat gained by cold water. Using this formula

Heat lost = Heat gained

$$3m \times (70 - T) = m \times (T - 10)$$

Simplify the equation,

$$210 - 3T = T - 10$$
$$4T = 220 \Rightarrow T = 55°C$$

Q.24 During the change of state of a substance from solid to liquid, heat is absorbed by a body, but its temperature does not rise. Which of the following statements explains the phenomenon? **[Competency Based Que.]**

(a) Only KE of the molecules increases, but PE remains the same.
(b) Only PE of the molecules increases, but KE remains the same.
(c) Both KE and PE of the molecules increase.
(d) There is no increase in the PE and KE of the molecules.

Ans. (b) During melting, the heat energy absorbed is used to break intermolecular bonds, increasing the potential energy (PE) of the molecules. Since temperature remains constant, the kinetic energy (KE) does not change.

Q.25 Rivers which originate from the glaciers at high altitudes have a supply of water throughout the year. This is because ice in high mountains does not melt all at once. This is due to **[Competencey Based Que.]**

(a) high specific heat of ice.
(b) low specific heat of ice.
(c) low specific latent heat of fusion of ice.
(d) high specific latent heat of fusion of ice.

Ans. (d) Ice takes a lot of heat to melt completely because it has a high specific latent heat of fusion. This makes the melting process slow and steady, ensuring the rivers to get water supply throughout the year.

Q.26 The graph of temperature *versus* heat supplied for a material is given below

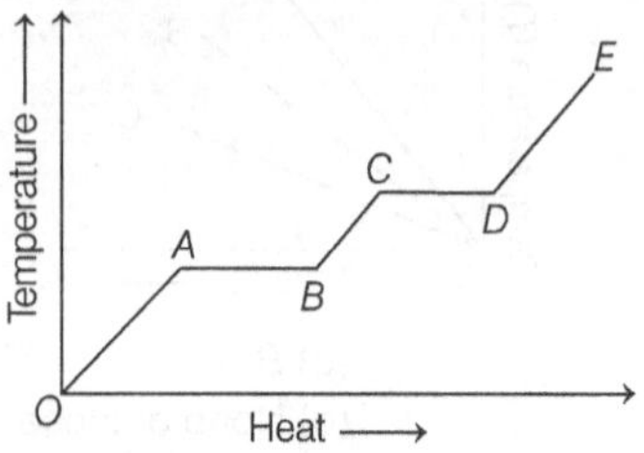

Which of the following statements is incorrect?

(a) Slope *DE* represents reciprocal of heat capacity.
(b) *AB* and *CD* lines represent phase change.
(c) Slope $OA > BC$, which means specific heat of liquid is greater than that of specific heat of solid.
(d) None of the above

Ans. (d) The material gains temperature as heat is supplied and its temperature keeps increasing until phase change occurs. At phase change, temperature does not increase, therefore the curve *AB* and *CD* are parallel to *X*-axis. The slope of the curve gives specific heat of material at different phases. From the analysis, all options are correct.

TYPE - 2

01 Mark

Assertion-Reason Type Questions

Directions (Q. Nos. 1-5) In the following questions two statements are given as Assertion and Reason.

(a) Both A and R are true and R is the correct explanation of A.
(b) Both A and R are true but R is not the correct explanation of A.
(c) A is true but R is false.
(d) A is false but R is true.

Q.1 **Assertion** (A) Heat energy is transferred from one body to another due to a temperature difference between them.
Reason (R) Heating a substance causes a rise in temperature.

Ans. (b) Both the statements give us the fact that there is a change in temperature when heat is supplied to a substance but there is no explanation to the fact.

Q.2 **Assertion** (A) The specific heat capacity of water is higher than most liquids.
Reason (R) Water requires more heat to raise its temperature by 1°C compared to other liquids.

Ans. (a) Water has a high specific heat capacity, which makes it an efficient thermal reservoir, requiring more energy to heat than most other liquids.

Q.3 Assertion (A) The temperature of boiling water remains constant even though heat is continuously supplied.

Reason (R) The heat supplied during boiling is used as latent heat of vaporization.

Ans. (a) During boiling, the heat energy converts water to steam without raising the temperature, as it is used as latent heat to change the potential energy.

Q.4 Assertion (A) Radiators in car and generators use water for cooling.

Reason (R) Water has a very low specific heat capacity.

Ans. (c) Radiators and generators use water for cooling because water has a high specific heat capacity.

Q.5 Assertion (A) For ice, the specific latent heat of fusion is 336000 J kg^{-1}.

Reason (R) 1 kg of ice at 0°C absorbs 336000 J of heat energy to convert into water at 0°C.

Ans. (a)

TYPE - 3 01/02 Marks

Fill in the Blanks

Q.1 Heat absorbed during change of phase depends on .... (mass/change in temperature/specific heat capacity) of the substance. **[ICSE 2025]**

Ans. specific heat capacity

Q.2 When a substance changes from liquid to vapour state, its temperature .... (increases, decreases, remains constant) **[1]**

Ans. remains constant

Q.3 The specific latent heat of fusion of water is approximately .... (334 J/g, 420 J/g) **[1]**

Ans. 334 J/g

Q.4 During the heating curve of water, at 100°C, water starts boiling and changes into .... (liquid/gas) phase. **[1]**

Ans. gas

Q.5 The temperature at which a substance starts to change from solid to liquid is called .... (melting point, boiling point) and the heat involved is called .... (latent heat of fusion, specific heat). **[2]**

Ans. melting point, latent heat of fusion

Q.6 The heat required to convert 1 kg of ice at 0°C to water at 0°C is known as .... (specific latent heat of fusion, specific latent heat of vaporisation) and its unit is .... (calorie, Jkg^{-1}) **[2]**

Ans. specific latent heat of fusion, Jkg^{-1}

TYPE - 4 02 Marks

Very Short Answer Type Questions

Q.1 (i) How can a temperature in degree celsius be converted into SI unit of temperature? **[1]**

(ii) A liquid X has the maximum specific heat capacity and is used as a coolant in car radiators. Name the liquid X. **[1][ICSE 2018]**

Ans. (i) The SI unit of temperature is kelvin. To convert temperature in degree celsius to kelvin, 273.15 is added to celsius. $T(\text{in K}) = T(°\text{C}) + 273.15$

(ii) Liquid X will be water as water has a high value of specific heat capacity.

Q.2 Given difference between

(i) Heat and temperature **[1]**

(ii) Heat capacity and specific heat capacity **[1]**

Ans. (i)

Heat	Temperature
It measures the total internal energy possessed by the molecules of the body.	It measures the degree of hotness or coldness of any body.
Its SI unit is Joule (J).	Its SI unit is kelvin (K).
By using the principle of calorimetry, this quantity can be measured.	By using the thermometer, this quantity can be measured.
It is an additive quantity.	It is not an additive quantity.

(ii)

Heat capacity	Specific heat capacity
It is the amount of heat required to raise the temperature of the whole body by 1 °C.	It is the amount of heat required to raise the temperature of unit mass of the body by 1 °C.
Its SI unit is JK^{-1}.	Its SI unit is $J\,Kg^{-1}\,K^{-1}$.
It depends on the material and mass of the body.	It is the characteristics of the material of the body, so it does not depend on the mass of the body.

Q.3 Thermal capacities of substances A and B are same. If mass of A is more than mass of B then

(i) which substance will have more specific heat capacity? **[1]**

(ii) which substance will show greater rise in temperature, if the same amount of heat is supplied to both? **[1] [ICSE 2023]**

Ans. (i) $M_A C_A = M_B C_B$

$$\frac{M_A}{M_B} = \frac{C_B}{C_A} \Rightarrow C_B > C_A$$

∴ B has more specific heat capacity.

(ii) Thermal capacities are being same, both A and B will show same rise in temperature.

$$C'_A \Delta t_A = C'_B \Delta t_B$$
$$C'_A = C'_B$$
$$\Delta t_A = \Delta t_B$$

Q.4 State whether the specific heat capacity of a substance remains same, when its state changes from solid to liquid. **[1]**

Ans. Specific heat capacity of a substance is its intrinsic property which changes when the phase of the substance undergoes a change.

Q.5 Why does stone lying in the sun get heated up much more than water lying for the same duration of time? **[2][ICSE 2020]**

Ans. The water does not get heated up as quickly as compared to stone. It is because water requires about five times more heat energy than stone for the same rise in temperature, i.e. water has higher specific heat capacity than stone.

Q.6 What do you understand by the following statements?

(i) The heat capacity of the body is 60 JK^{-1}. **[1]**

(ii) The specific heat capacity of lead is 130 $Jkg^{-1}K^{-1}$. **[1][ICSE 2016]**

Ans. (i) The heat capacity of the body is 60 K. It means that 60J of heat is required to raise the temperature of the entire body by 1°C.

(ii) The specific heat capacity of lead is 130 J/kg-K. It means that 130J of heat is required to raise the temperature of 1kg of mass by 1°C.

Q.7 On a hot summer day, we often put ice cubes to cool the water. Why? **[2][Competency Based Qus.]**

Ans. We put ice cubes into the water because every 1g of ice at 0°C extracts 336 J of heat from hot water as its latent heat of fusion.

Hence, the temperature of the water falls sharply.

Q.8 What is the reason of spraying water on the roads in the evening during the hot summer? **[2]**

Ans. Since, water has the highest specific heat capacity of 4.2 $Jg^{-1}{}^{\circ}C^{-1}$. Therefore, water absorbs a large amount of heat from the roads, but its own temperature does not rise much. Due to this, the road gets cooled.

Q.9 Why are burns caused by steam more severe than those caused by boiling water at the same temperature? **[2]**

Ans. As the latent heat of vaporisation is more than specific heat of boiling water, so burns caused by steam are more painful than boiling water.

Q.10 Calculate the amount of heat absorbed by 200 g of paraffin wax to melt completely at its melting point [Specific latent heat of fusion of paraffin wax = 146 Jg^{-1}] **[2][ICSE 2025]**

Ans. Specific latent heat of fusion of paraffin wax = 146 Jg^{-1}.

∴ Amount of heat absorbed by 200 g of paraffin wax to meet completely is = (146 × 200) J = 29200 J.

Q.11 Explain, why one feels icecream at 0°C colder than water at 0°C? **[2][ICSE 2001]**

Ans. Icecream at 0°C extracts heat (latent heat of fusion) from the surroundings and freezes into its solid state without any rise in temperature. When we touch both the substances, more amount of heat is transfered from our hands to the ice-cream as compared to water at 0°C. Hence, ice-cream feels colder than water.

TYPE - 5 — 03 Marks

Short Answer Type Questions

Q.1 State in brief, the meaning of each of the following.

(i) The heat capacity of a body is 50$J^{\circ}C^{-1}$. **[1]**

(ii) The specific latent heat of fusion of ice is 336000 J kg^{-1}. **[1]**

(iii) The specific heat capacity of copper is 0.4 J $g^{-1}{}^{\circ}C^{-1}$. **[1]**

Ans. (i) The heat capacity of body is 50 J/°C, it means 50 J of heat is required to raise the temperature of body by 1°C.

(ii) It means the amount of heat is required to change the state of 1 kg of ice to water without any change in its temperature is 336000 J.

(iii) This means that 0.4 J of heat is required to raise the temperature of 1 g of copper by 1°C.

Q.2 (i) Write an expression for the heat energy liberated by a hot body. **[1]**

(ii) Some heat is provided to a body to raise its temperature by 25°C. What will be the corresponding rise in temperature of the body as shown on the kelvin scale? **[1]**

(iii) What happens to the average kinetic energy of the molecules as ice melts at 0°C? **[1][ICSE 2012]**

Ans. (i) The expression for the amount of heat liberated by a body is

$$\Delta Q = mc\Delta t$$

where, m = Mass of substance,

c = Specific heat capacity of substance,

Δt = Change in temperature,

ΔQ = Heat gained or lost.

(ii) The rise in temperature will be same in both celsius and kelvin scale, as 1°C change = 1K change

(iii) The average KE of molecules remains same when ice melts as the temperature of body remains same.

Q.3 (i) A certain amount of heat will warm 1 g of material *X* by 10 °C and 1 g of material *Y* by 40°C. Which material has higher specific heat capacity? **[3]**

(ii) Which material, *X* or *Y*, would you select to make a calorimeter?

(iii) The specific heat capacity of a substance remains the same when it changes its state from solid to liquid. State true or false. **[ICSE 2025]**

Ans. (i) Material *X* has a higher specific heat capacity.

(ii) Material *Y*

(iii) False

Q.4 Specific heat capacity of substance *A* is 3.8 J/gK, whereas the specific heat capacity of substance *B* is 0.4 J/gK.

(i) Which of the two is good conductor of heat? **[1]**

(ii) How is one led to the above conclusion? **[1]**

(iii) If substances *A* and *B* are liquid, then which one would be more useful in car radiators? **[1]**

Ans. (i) Substance *B*

(ii) Since, the specific heat capacity of *B* is less than *A*. so, *B* is a good conductor of heat.

(iii) Since, the specific heat capacity of *A* is higher than that of *B*, so it can absorb more heat without much rise in temperature. Therefore, it is useful in car radiator.

Q.5 (i) Why does it become colder after a hailstorm than during or before the hailstorm? **[2]**

(ii) If two bodies have the same specific heat capacities, then they will always absorb the same amount of heat if their temperature increases by the same amount. State whether the given statement is true or false. **[1][ICSE 2022 Sem-II]**

Ans. (i) Before and during the hailstorm, there is plenty amount of heat present in the atmosphere. But after the hailstorm, ice absorbs a large amount of heat for melting, from the surrounding. So, the temperature of the surroundings fall and we feel cold.

(ii) The given statement is false as the heat absorbed also depends on the mass of the two bodies.

Q.6 (i) Define calorimetry. **[1]**

(ii) Name the material used for making a calorimeter. **[1]**

(iii) Why is a calorimeter made up of thin sheets of the above material answered in (ii)? **[1][ICSE 2019]**

Ans. (i) Calorimetry is the science associated with determining the change in energy of a system by measuring the heat exchanged with the surroundings.

(ii) Copper

(iii) It is because copper is a good conductor of heat, so it soon acquires the temperature of its contents and thin copper sheet has low heat capacity, so it takes only small amount of heat from its contents.

Q.7 (i) What is the principle of method of mixtures? **[1]**

(ii) What is the other name given to it? **[1]**

(iii) Name the law on which the principle is based. **[1]**
[ICSE 2016]

Ans. (i) According to the principle of mixtures, heat lost by the hot body must be equal to heat gained by the cold body, provided there is no heat loss to the surroundings.

(ii) The other name of principle of mixtures is principle of calorimetry.

(iii) Principle of mixture is based on the principle of conservation of energy.

Q.8 (i) Heat supplied to a solid changes it into liquid. What is this change in phase called? **[1]**

(ii) During the phase change, does the average kinetic energy of the molecules of the substance increase? **[1]**

(iii) What is the energy absorbed during the phase change called? **[1][ICSE 2018]**

Ans. (i) Heat supplied to solid changes it into liquid. This change in phase is called melting.

(ii) During the phase change, average kinetic energy of the molecules does not change, because the temperature remains constant.

(iii) The energy absorbed during the phase change is called latent heat of fusion.

Q.9 The diagram below shows a cooling curve for a substance

(i) State the temperature at which the substance condenses. **[1]**

(ii) The temperature range in which the substance is in liquid state. **[1][ICSE Specimen 2025]**

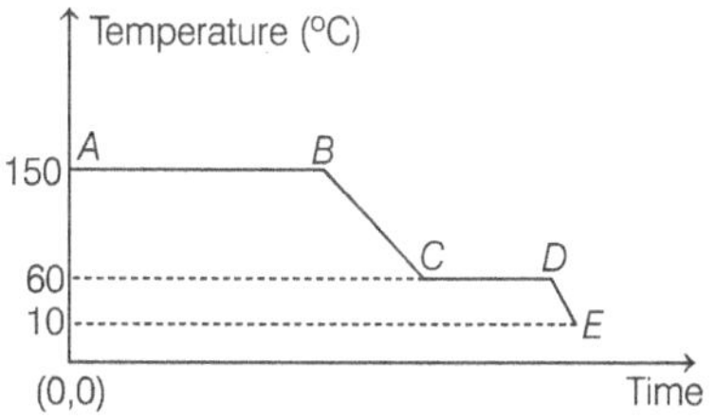

(iii) Why do we prefer ice to ice-cold water for cooling a drink? **[1]**

Ans. The cooling curve for the substance is shown below

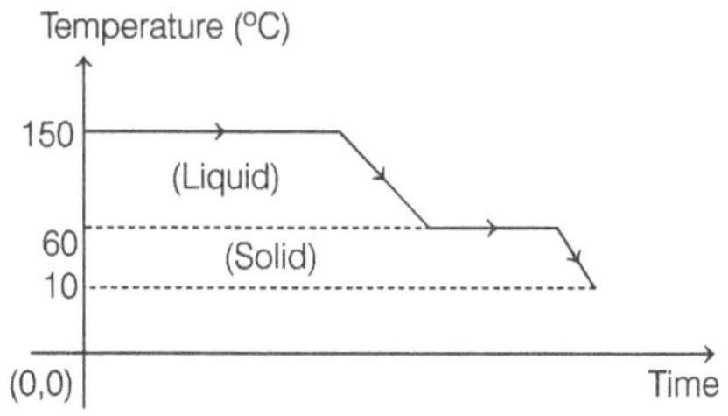

(i) The substance is condensed at the temperature of 150°C solidifies at 60°C.

(ii) The temperature range for which the substance is in liquid state is 60°C to 150°C.

(iii) Ice at 0°C would require a latent heat of fusion to change into water at 0°C. So, it absorbs a large amount of heat from the drink without raising its temperature. Hence, the drink is cooled faster.

TYPE - 6   04 Marks

Long Answer Type Questions

Q.1 If there is no heat loss to the surroundings, the heat released by the condensation of m_1 gram of steam at 100°C into water at 100°C can be used to convert m_2 gram of ice at 0°C into water at 0°C.

(i) Find

(a) the heat lost by steam in terms of m_1. **[1]**

(b) the heat gained by ice in terms of m_2. **[1]**

(ii) Form a heat equation to find the ratio of $m_2 : m_1$.

(Take, specific latent heat of vaporisation of steam = 2268 kJ/kg,

specific latent heat of fusion of ice = 336 kJ/kg,

specific heat capacity of water = 4200 J/kg°C) **[2]**

Ans. (i) (a) The heat lost by the steam is given by m_1L_s (where, L_s = Latent heat of steam) = 2268 m_1 kJ

(b) The heat gained by the ice is given by $m_2 L_i$ (where, L_i = Latent heat of ice)

= 336m_1 kJ

(ii) According to the principle of calorimetry,

Heat taken by ice = Heat given by steam

$$m_2L_i = m_1L_s$$

$$\Rightarrow \quad \frac{m_2}{m_1} = \frac{L_s}{L_i} = \frac{2268}{336} = \frac{27}{4}$$

$$\Rightarrow \quad m_2 : m_1 = 27 : 4$$

Q.2 (i) How is the transference of heat energy by radiation prevented in a calorimeter? **[2]**

(ii) You have a choices of three metals A, B and C, of specific heat capacities 900 J kg^{-1} $^{o}C^{-1}$, 380 J kg^{-1} $^{o}C^{-1}$ and 460 J kg^{-1} $^{o}C^{-1}$, respectively. To make a calorimeter, which material will you select? Justify your answer. **[2][ICSE 2017]**

Ans. (i) Calorimeter surface (outer) is highly polished, so as to minimise the heat loss due to radiation as polished metallic surfaces are poor absorber and poor emitter of heat.

(ii) Metal B should be selected to make a calorimeter because B has the lowest specific heat capacity as compared to A and C and hence it will easily reach the temperature of the calorimeter without absorbing much heat from its contents.

Q.3 (i) Water in lakes and ponds do not freeze at once in cold countries. Give a reason in support of your answer. **[2]**

(ii) What is the principle of calorimetry? **[1]**

(iii) Name the law on which this principle is based. **[1]**

[ICSE 2015]

Ans. (i) This is because the specific latent heat of fusion of ice is sufficiently high (336 J/g). So to freeze water, a large quantity of heat has to be withdrawn, hence it freezes slowly.

(ii) Total heat given by a hotter body equals to the total heat received by colder body, i.e. heat lost by hotter body = heat gained by colder body.

(iii) It is based on law of conservation of energy.

Q.4 (i) Heat supplied to a solid changes it into liquid. What is this change in phase called? **[1]**

(ii) During the phase change does the average kinetic energy of the molecules of the substance increase? **[2]**

(iii) What is the energy absorbed during the phase change called? **[1]**

Ans. (i) The change in phase is called melting.

(ii) During the phase change, average kinetic energy of the molecules does not change because the temperature remains constant.

(iii) The energy absorbed during the phase change is called latent heat of fusion.

Q.5

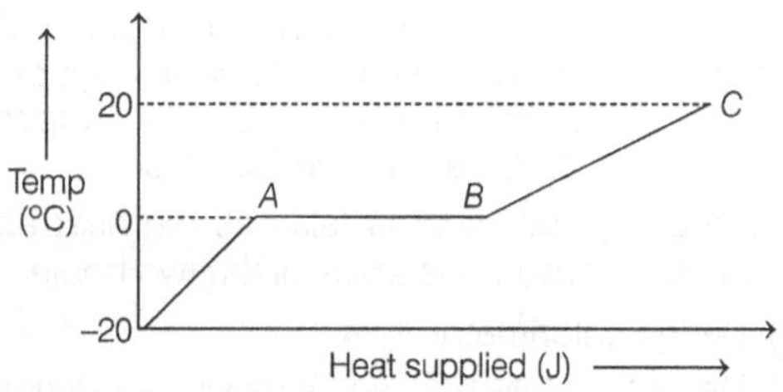

In the graph, a given quantity of ice is converted to water.

(i) What does the portion AB represent?

(ii) Why is the portion AB parallel to the time axis?

(iii) Why is the slope OA steeper than the slope BC?

Ans. (i) The portion AB represents the melting of ice.

(ii) The portion AB is parallel to the time axis because during melting though heat is supplied from outside, the temperature remains constant.

(iii) The slope of *OA* is steeper than *BC* because the specific heat capacity of ice is less than the specific heat capacity of water. Hence, ice needs less quantity of heat than water for the same rise in temperature.

TYPE - 7 — 03/04 Marks

Case Based Questions

Q.1 Water's high specific heat capacity plays a significant role in various natural and practical applications. It prevents liquids from freezing, helps organisms to maintain body temperature, regulates soil temperature, and serves as a coolant in many systems. Wet soil and water bodies heat up or cool down more slowly than their dry counterparts or other materials.

(i) A farmer observed that crops near water filled field survived a sudden frost, while crops in dry fields were damaged. Using your knowledge of heat capacity, explain why this happened? **[1]**

(ii) In car radiator, water is used as a coolant. Why does the engine temperature remains stable even after prolonged use? Explain without directly stating the property of water. **[1]**

(iii) A researcher fills two identical bottles, one with water and the other with juice. Both bottles are left outside in freezing conditions. The juice freezes faster than water.

Analyze this observation based on thermal properties? **[1]**

Ans. (i) Water in the fields releases heat slowly during the cold night due to its high specific heat capacity. This prevents the temperature in the surrounding area from dropping below freezing point (0°C), protecting the crops. In contrast, dry fields lack this heart reservoir, leading to frost damage.

(ii) Water absorbs a large amount of heat from the engine without a significant rise in its own temperature. This ability to store and release heat efficiently prevents the engine from overheating during prolonged use.

(iii) Water can absorb and store more heat than juice without significant temperature changes because it has a higher specific heat capacity.

As a result, water resists freezing, while the juice, with a lower heat capacity, loses heat faster and freezes earlier.

Q.2 In the physics laboratory, various blocks of materials labelled *A* and *B*, each with masses ranging from 10 g to 50 g, are utilised to determine their respective heat capacities. Subsequently, a graph is plotted to depict the relationship between the heat capacity and the mass of the materials as shown. **[Competency Based Que.]**

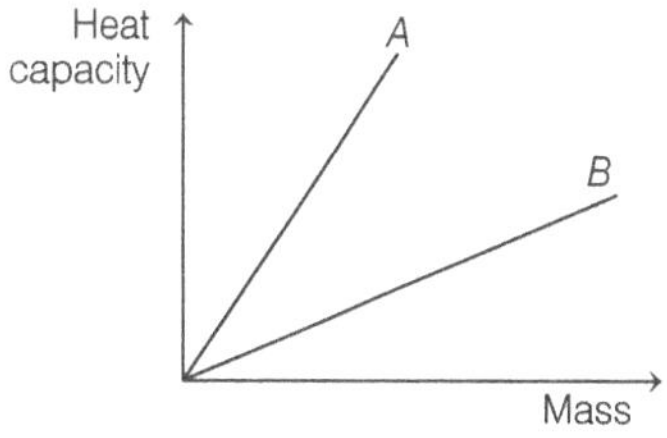

(i) Plot a graph illustrating the relationship between the mass and specific heat capacity of materials *A* and *B*.

(ii) Which material is a relatively better conductor? **[2]**

Ans. (i) Relationship between Heat capacity and specific heat capacity. The heat capacity H of an object is related to its mass (*m*) and specific heat capacity (*c*) by the formula.

$$H = mc$$

Looking at the graph,

For material *A*, the slope of the line represents H/m, which is the specific heat capacity (C) of material A.

Since, the line for *A* is a straight line passing through the origin with a constant slope the specific heat capacity of a material *A* is constant and relatively high.

Similarly the line for *B* is also a straight line passing through the origin with a constant slope, indicating that the specific heat capacity of material *B* is constant but lower than that of material *A* (because the slope is less steep).

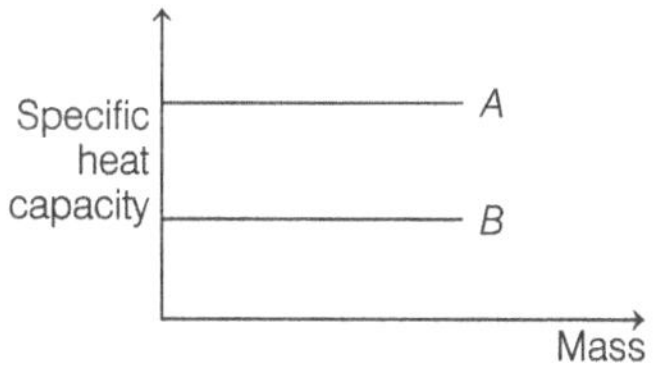

(ii) Material *B* has a lower specific heat capacity than material *A*. Therefore, material *B* is likely to be a relatively better conductor in the sense that its temperature will charge more significantly for a given amount of heat supplied as compared to material *A*.

Q.3 A child running a temperature of 101°F is given an antipyretic (i.e. a medicine that lowers fever), which causes an increase in the rate of evaporation of sweat from his body. The fever is brought down to 98°F in 20 minutes. Assume the evaporation mechanism to be the only way by which heat is lost. The mass of the child is 30 kg. The specific heat of human body is approximately the same as that of water and latent heat of evaporation of water at that temperature is about 580 cal g^{-1}.

(i) Calculate the heat lost by the child in the form of evaporation. **[2]**

(ii) What is the average rate of extra evaporation caused by the drug? **[2]**

Ans. (i) Given, mass of child,

$$m = 30 \text{ kg} = 30 \times 10^3 \text{ g}$$

Fall in temperature from fever,

$$\Delta\theta = 101° - 98° = 3° \text{ F} = 3 \times \frac{5}{9} = \frac{5}{3} °\text{C}$$

Specific heat of human

$$= \text{Specific heat of water} = 1 \text{ cal g}^{-1}{}^{\circ}\text{C}^{-1}$$

Heat lost by child in the form of evaporation (sweat),

$$Q = mc\Delta\theta = 30 \times 10^3 \times 1 \times \frac{5}{3} = 50000 \text{ cal}$$

(ii) If m'gram of sweat evaporates from the body of the child, heat gained by sweat $= m'L = m' \times 580$

(given, $L_{vap} = 580$ cal/g)

$\therefore$ Heat gained by sweat = Heat lost by child

$$m' \times 580 = 50000$$

$$m' = \frac{50000}{580} = 86.2 \text{ g}$$

Time taken by sweat to evaporate = 20 min

$$\therefore \text{ Rate of evaporation of sweat} = \frac{86.2}{20} = 4.31 \text{g min}^{-1}$$

Q.4 The three states of matter-solid, liquid, and gas-differ in terms of their particle arrangement and energy. In solids, particles are tightly packed with strong intermolecular forces, allowing only vibrations in fixed positions. Liquids have more energy, allowing particles to slide over one another while maintaining some mutual attraction. Gases possess the highest energy, where particles are far apart with negligible intermolecular forces.

During a phase change, such as melting or vaporisation, the energy supplied does not increase the kinetic energy of the particles. Instead, it is used to overcome intermolecular forces, leading to a change in potential energy. For example, energy is required to melt a solid to break its bonds, while vaporising a liquid demands even more energy due to greater intermolecular spacing in gases.

(i) Arrange the states of matter-solid, liquid, and gas in increasing order of their intermolecular forces. Explain your reasoning. **[1]**

(ii) Why does the temperature remain constant during a phase change, even when heat is being supplied continuously? **[1]**

(iii) Explain why the latent heat of vaporisation is greater than the latent heat of fusion for the same substance? **[1]**

(iv) What happens to the potential and kinetic energy of particles during melting and vaporisation? **[1]**

Ans. (i) Solid > Liquid > Gas

Solids have the strongest Intermolecular forces due to its tightly packed particles, while gases have negligible forces as their particles are far apart.

(ii) During a phase change, the energy supplied is used to overcome intermolecular forces, among the molecules of the substances so that it can change its phase. This is why, the temperature remains constant.

(iii) The energy required to convert a liquid to a gas is greater because particles in a gaseous state are much farther apart than in a liquid state. Overcoming these larger intermolecular distances require more energy compared to the transition from solid to liquid.

(iv) During melting and vaporisation, the potential energy of particles increases as intermolecular forces are overcome. However, the kinetic energy remains constant because there is no change in temperature during the phase change.

TYPE - 8

Numerical Questions

Q.1 Two metallic blocks P and Q having masses in ratio 2 : 1 are supplied with the same amount of heat. If their temperatures rise by same degree, compare their specific heat capacities. **[2][ICSE 2020]**

Ans. Ratio of masses of blocks P and Q,

$$m_P : m_Q = 2 : 1$$

$$\Rightarrow \quad \frac{m_Q}{m_P} = \frac{1}{2} \quad \text{... (i)}$$

We know that, heat supplied is given as

$$H = ms\Delta T$$

where, s is specific heat.

But $\quad H_P = H_Q$

$$\Rightarrow \quad m_P s_P \Delta T = m_Q s_Q \Delta T \Rightarrow \frac{s_P}{s_Q} = \frac{m_Q}{m_P} = \frac{1}{2} \text{ [from Eq. (i)]}$$

$$\Rightarrow \quad s_P : s_Q = 1 : 2$$

Q.2 The two metals A and B have their specific heat capacities in the ratio 2:3. If they are supplied to the same amount of heat, then

(i) which metal piece will show a greater rise in temperature if their masses are the same? **[2]**

(ii) calculate the ratio in which their temperatures rise, if the mass ratio of metal A and metal B is 3:5. **[2][Competency Based Qus.]**

Ans. (i) It is given that the rise in temperature is the same (Δt) and masses of the metals are different.

Let C_A and C_B be the specific heat capacities of metals A and B respectively.

Given the ratio of C_A and C_B is 2 : 3,
we write, $C_A = 2C$ and $C_B = 3C$

Now, both the metals are supplied with the same heat

$\therefore \quad Q = m_A C_A \Delta T_A$

Also, $\quad Q = m_B C_B \Delta T_B$

It is also given that, $m_A = m_B$

$\therefore \quad C_A \Delta T_A = C_B \Delta T_B$

$\Rightarrow \quad \frac{\Delta T_A}{\Delta T_B} = \frac{C_B}{C_A} = \frac{3}{2}$

$\Rightarrow \quad \Delta T_A : \Delta T_B = 3:2$

$\therefore$ Metal A will show a greater rise in temperature.

(ii) It is given that mass ratio, $\frac{m_A}{m_B} = \frac{3}{5}$

$\therefore$ Both metal are supplied with same amount of heat.

So we can write,

$m_A \times C_A \times \Delta t_A = m_B \times C_B \times \Delta t_B$

$\Rightarrow \quad \frac{\Delta t_A}{\Delta t_B} = \frac{C_B m_B}{C_A m_A} = \frac{3}{2} \times \frac{5}{3} = \frac{5}{2}$

$\Rightarrow \quad \Delta t_A : \Delta t_B = 5:2$

Hence, we can conclude that for metal *A* and *B*, the ratio in which their temperature rise is 5 : 2.

Q.3 **A solid of mass 50 g at 150°C is placed in 100 g of water at 11°C, when the final temperature recorded is 20°C. Find the specific heat capacity of the solid. (Take, specific heat capacity of water = 4.2 J/g°C)** **[2] [ICSE 2017]**

Ans. According to the question,

Mass of solid = 50 g,

Temperature of solid = 150° C,

Mass of water = 100 g

Temperature of water = 11° C,

Final temperature of mixture = 20°C

Specific heat capacity of water = 4.2 J g^{-1}°C^{-1}

Let specific heat capacity of solid = x

According to the principle of thermal equilibrium,

Q_L (heat lost) = Q_C (heat gained)

$\Rightarrow \quad 50x \times (150 - 20) = 100 \times 4.2 \times (20 - 11)$

$\Rightarrow \quad x = \frac{100 \times 4.2 \times 9}{50 \times 130}$

$\Rightarrow x = 0.582$ J g^{-1} °C^{-1}

$\therefore$ The specific heat capacity of the solid is 0.582 Jg^{-1} °C^{-1}.

Q.4 **Calculate the mass of ice required to lower the temperature of 300 g of water at 40°C to 0°C.** **[2] [ICSE 2016]**

Ans. According to question,

Mass of water $m_w = 300$ g

Temperature of water = 40°C

Latent heat of fussion of ice = 336 J g^{-1}

From principle of calorimetry,

Heat loss by the water at 40°C = Heat gain by the ice at 0°C

$\Rightarrow \quad m_w \times s \times \Delta t = m_{ice}(\text{mass of ice}) \times L$

$\Rightarrow m_{ice} = \frac{m_w \times s \times \Delta t}{L} = \frac{300 \times 42 \times 40}{336} = 150$ g

[$\because \Delta t = 40°$]

150 g of ice is required.

Q.5 **A hot solid of mass 60 g at 100°C is placed in 150 g of water at 20°C. The final steady temperature recorded is 25°C. Calculate the specific heat capacity of the solid. (Take, specific heat capacity of water = 4200 J kg^{-1}° C^{-1})** **[2][ICSE 2012]**

Ans. According to principle of calorimeter,

Heat gained = Heat lost

So, heat gained = $150 \times 42 \times (25 - 20)$ ...(i)

Heat lost = $60 \times c \times (100 - 25)$ ...(ii)

From Eqs. (i) and (ii), we get

$60 \times c \times 75 = 150 \times 4.2 \times 5$

$\Rightarrow \quad c = \frac{150 \times 4.2 \times 5}{60 \times 75} = 0.7$ J/g°C

Q.6 **A solid metal weighing 150 g melts at its melting point of 800 °C by providing heat at the rate of 100 W. The time taken for it to completely melt at the same temperature is 4 min. What is the specific latent heat of fusion of the metal?** **[2] [ICSE 2018]**

Ans. Given, $m = 150\text{g} = 150 \times 10^{-3}$ kg = 0.15 kg

Power $P = 100$ W

Time $t = 4\text{min} = 4 \times 60 = 240$ s

The amount of heat supplied in 4 min is given as heat energy

$Q = P \times t = 100 \times 240 = 24000$ J

This heat energy is used in melting.

Let L be the specific latent heat of fussion of the metal

$\therefore \quad mL = 24000 \Rightarrow L = \frac{24000}{0.15} = 16 \times 10^4$ J kg^{-1}

Q.7 **How much heat is required to convert 500 g of ice at 0°C to water at 0°C .The latent heat of fusion of ice 330 Jg^{-1}.** **[2] [ICSE 2024]**

Ans. Given, mass of ice = 500 g

Later heat of fusion = 330 J/g

Heal, $Q = mL = 500 \times 330 = 165000$ J

So, 165000 J of heat is required to convert 500 g of ice at 0°C to water at 0°C.

Q.8 **Calculate the heat absorbed by 200 g ice at 0° C to change to water at 60° C. [Specific heat capacity of ice = 2100 J kg^{-1} K^{-1}, Specific heat capacity of water = 4200 J kg^{-1} K^{-1}, Specific latent heat of ice = 336000 Jkg^{-1}]** **[2][ICSE 2023]**

Ans. Latent heat of ice (L_i) = 336000 Jkg^{-1}

Specific heat of the water (C_w) = 4200 Jkg^{-1}

Total heat absorbed by 200 g of ice to change to water at 60 °C is equal to H.

Also, H = Heat absorbed by ice at 0°C to change into water at 0°C + Heat absorbed by water at 0°C to change into water at 60°C.

$$\therefore\ H = \frac{200}{1000} \times 336000 + \frac{200}{1000} \times (60^\circ - 0^\circ) \times 4200$$
$$= (67200 + 50400)\ J$$
$$= 117600\ J.$$

Q.9 **From the graph of heating curve given below, state the melting point and boiling point of the substance.** **[2][Specimen 2022 Sem-II]**

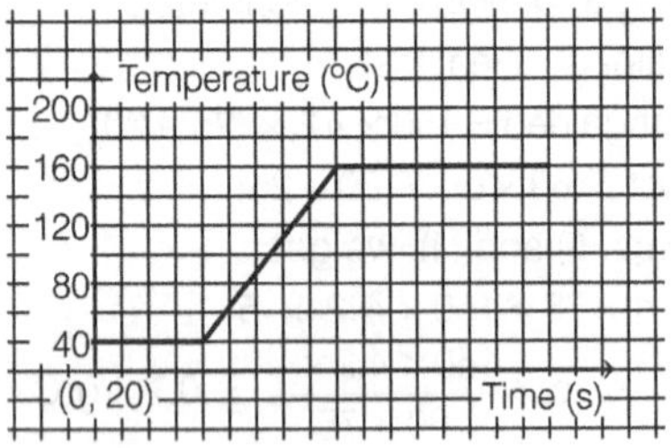

Ans. The melting point of the given heating curve is 40°C.
The boiling point of the given heating curve is 160°C.

Q.10 **What mass of ice at 0°C added to 2.1 kg water, will cool it down from 75°C to 25°C ? Given, specific heat capacity of water = 4.2 $Jg^{-1}\ °C^{-1}$, specific latent heat of ice = 336 Jg^{-1}.** **[ICSE Speciemen 2025]**

Ans. Heat lost by water = Heat gained by ice

$$m_\omega C_\omega \Delta T_\omega = m_i L_i + m_i c_\omega \Delta T'$$
$$2.1 \times 4200 \times (75 - 25) = m_i \times 336000 + m_i \times 4200(25 - 0)$$
$$21 \times 420 \times 50 = m_i(336000 + 105000)$$
$$m_i = 1\text{kg}$$

Q.11 **Water falls from a height of 50 m. Calculate the rise in temperature of water, when it strikes the bottom. (Take, $g = 10\ ms^{-2}$, specific heat capacity of water = 4200 J/kg°C)** **[2]**

Ans. Let the mass of water striking the ground per second be m kg.

Now, Heat energy gained at the bottom = Potential energy lost at the bottom

$$mc\Delta t = mgh$$
$$\Rightarrow\ c\Delta t = gh$$
$$\Rightarrow\ \Delta t = \frac{gh}{c} = \frac{10 \times 50}{4200}$$
$$= 0.12^\circ\ C$$

Therefore, the rise in temperature of water at the bottom is 0.12°C.

Q.12 **The difference between the temperature of water at the bottom and the top of a waterfall is 0.2 °C. Calculate the height of the waterfall. [$g = 10\ N\ kg^{-1}$, Specific heat capacity of water = 4200 J $kg^{-1}\ °C^{-1}$].** **[Competency Based Que.]**

Ans. $Q = mc\Delta T$

PE = mgh

Now, the heat gained equal to the potential energy lost

$mc\Delta T = mgh$

$$\Rightarrow\ c\Delta T = gh$$
$$\Rightarrow\ h = \frac{c\Delta T}{g}$$
$$\therefore\ h = \frac{4200 \times 02}{10} = 84\ m$$

Q.13 **Calculate the mass of ice needed to cool 150 g of water contained in a calorimeter of mass 50 g at 32°C such that the final temperature is 5°C. (Take, specific heat capacity of calorimeter = 0.4 J/g°C, specific heat capacity of water = 4.2 J/g°C and latent heat capacity of ice = 330 J/g)** **[3][ICSE 2017]**

Ans. Let the mass of the ice needed be m grams.

Heat gained by ice at 0°C to change into water at 0° C = (m × 330) J.

Heat gained by m grams of water at 0°C to change into water at 5°C = $m \times (5^\circ - 0^\circ) \times 42$

$= (m \times 21)$ J

Heat lost by 150 g of water to cool from 32°C to 5°C = $150 \times (32^\circ - 5^\circ) \times 4.2$

= 17010 J

Heat lost by calorimeter to drop its temperature from 32°C to 5°C = $50 \times (32^\circ - 5^\circ) \times 0.4 = 540$J

Now, according to the principle of calorimetry,

$m \times 330 + m \times 21 = 17010 + 540$

$$\Rightarrow\ m = \frac{17550}{351}\ g = 50\ g.$$

∴ Mass of ice required = 50 g

Q.14 **30 g of ice at 0°C is used to bring down the temperature of a certain mass of water at 70 °C to 20 °C. Find the mass of water (Specific heat capacity of water = 4.2 $Jg^{-1}\ °C^{-1}$ and specific latent heat of ice = 336 Jg^{-1})** **[ICSE 2025]**

Ans. Let the mass of the water required be m grams.

Heat released by water = Heat absorbed by ice

$$\therefore\ m \times 42 \times (70 - 20) = 30 \times 336$$
$$\Rightarrow\ m = \frac{30 \times 336}{4.2 \times 50}$$
$$= \frac{10080}{210} = 48\ g$$

∴ The mass of water required = 48 g

Q.15 (i) Give an important reason for copper to be used as a material for a calorimeter. **[1]**

(ii) Calculate the thermal capacity of 40 g of water. [Specific heat capacity of water = 4200 $Jkg^{-1}{}^{\circ}C^{-1}$] **[1] [ICSE 2022 Sem-II]**

Ans. (i) As copper has low specific heat capacity, so it can be used as a material for a calorimeter.

(ii) Thermal capacity = $m \times c$

$$= 40 g \times 42 \ Jg^{-1 \circ}C^{-1} = 168 J \ {}^{\circ}C^{-1}$$

Q.16 The diagram below shows a cooling curve for 200 g of water. The heat is extracted at the rate of 100 Js^{-1}. **[ICSE 2022 Sem-II]**

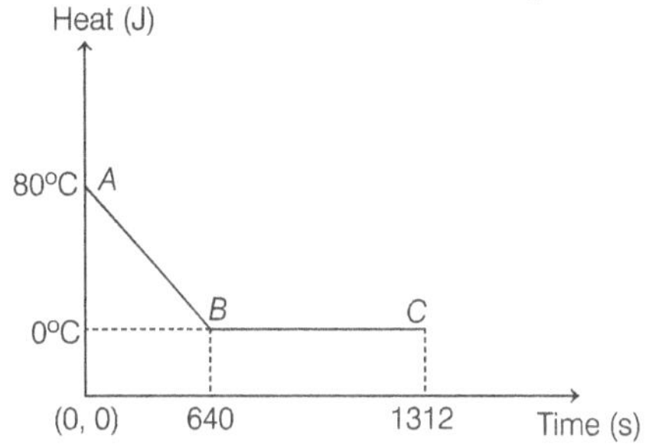

Calculate

(i) specific heat capacity of water. **[2]**

(ii) heat released in the region BC. **[1]**

Ans. (i) In the part of AB,

Temperature change = Δt = 80° C

Mass of water m = 200 g

The rate of heat extraction = 100 Js^{-1}

Heat extraction in 640 s

$$Q = P \times t = 640 \times 100 = 64000 \text{ J}$$

From the relation, $Q = mc\Delta t$

$$100 \times 640 = 200 \times c \times 80$$

$$c = \frac{100 \times 640}{200 \times 80} = 4 \text{ J/g}^{\circ}\text{C}$$

(ii) Heat lost in the part BC, $Q = p \times t$

$$= 100 \times (1312 - 640) = 67200 \text{ J}$$

Q.17 Two metals A and B have specific heat capacities in the ratio 2 : 3. If they are supplied same amount of heat, then

(i) which metal piece will show greater rise in temperature given their masses are the same? **[1]**

(ii) which metal piece will have greater mass, if the rise in temperature is the same for both metals? **[1]**

(iii) If the mass ratio of metal A and metal B is 3 : 5, then calculate the ratio in which their temperatures rise. **[1]**

(iv) if specific heat capacity of metal A is 0. 26 $Jg^{-1 \circ}C^{-1}$, then calculate the specific heat capacity of metal B. **[1][ICSE SQP 2022 Sem-I]**

Ans. (i) Refer to Sol. of Question 2 on page no. 178-179

(ii) Given that, $\Delta T_A = \Delta T_B$

$\therefore \quad m_A c_A = m_B c_B$

$\Rightarrow \quad \dfrac{m_A}{m_B} = \dfrac{c_B}{c_A} = \dfrac{3}{2}$

So, metal A will have greater mass.

(iii) Refer to Sol. of Question 2 on page no. 179.

(iv) $\dfrac{c_A}{c_B} = \dfrac{2}{3}$

$\therefore \quad c_B = \dfrac{3}{2} \times 0.26 = 0.39 \ Jg^{-1 \circ}C^{-1}$

Q.18 (i) A refrigerator converts 100 g of water at 20°C to ice at – 10° C in 35 min.

Calculate the average rate of heat extraction in terms of watts. **[2]**

Given, specific heat capacity of ice = 2.1 J $g^{-1}C^{-1}$, specific heat capacity of water = 4.2 J $g^{-1 0}C^{-1}$ and specific latent heat of fusion of ice = 336 Jg^{-1}.

(ii) The temperature of 170 g of water at 50°C is lowered to 5°C by adding certain amount of ice to it. Find the mass of ice added. **[2]**

Given, specific heat capacity of water = 4200 J $kg^{-1 0}$ C^{-1} and specific latent heat of ice = 336000 J kg^{-1}

Ans. (i) The mass of water to be converted m = 100 g.

The temperature drop of water

$$\Delta T = 20^{\circ} C - 0^{\circ} C = 20^{\circ} C$$

Latent heat of fusion of ice L = 336 J $g^{-1}{}^{\circ}C^{-1}$

Specific heat capacity of water,

$$C = 402 \ Jg^{-1}{}^{\circ}C^{-1}$$

Specific heat capacity of ice,

$$C' = 2.1 \ Jg^{-1}{}^{\circ}C^{-1}$$

The temperature drop of ice,

$$\Delta T = [0 - (-10^{\circ})] = 10^{\circ} C.$$

$\therefore$ From conservation of energy,

$$mc\Delta T + mL + mC'\Delta T' = P \times t$$

where P is the power or average rate of heat attraction per second,

$$100 \times 4.2 \times 20 + 100 \times 336 + 100 \times 2.1 \times 10$$
$$= P \times 35 \times 60$$
$$44100 = P \times 2100$$
$$P = 21 \text{W}$$

(ii) From the principle of equilibrium,

Heat lost by water to cool from 50°C to 5°C = Heat gained by ice at 0°C + Heat gained by water at 0°C to raise its temperature to 5°C.

Let the mass of ice required by m kg.

$$\therefore \quad \frac{170}{1000} \times 4200 \times (50° - 5°) = m \times 336000$$
$$+ m \times 4200\ (5° - 0°)$$

$$\Rightarrow \quad m = \frac{17 \times 42 \times 45}{357000} = \frac{90}{1000}\ \text{kg}$$

or $m = 90$ gram.

Q.19 Heat energy is supplied to 120 g of water, causing its temperature to rise by 10 K. The specific heat capacity of water is 4200 J/Kg K. The same amount of heat energy is then given to 60 g of oil, raising its temperature by 40 K.

Calculate

(i) the amount of heat energy (in joules) supplied to the water. **[1]**

(ii) the specific heat capacity of the oil. **[2]**

Ans. (i) Heat energy given to water = mass of water × specific heat capacity of water × rise in temperature

$$= \frac{120}{1000} \times 4200 \times 10 = 5040\ \text{J}$$

(ii) Heat energy given to the oil = 5040 J (given)

Let C be the specific heat capacity of oil,

$$\text{then } C = \frac{\text{amount of heat energy given to oil}}{\text{mass of oil} \times \text{rise in temperature}}$$

$$= \frac{5040}{\left(\frac{60}{1000}\right) \times 40} = 2100\ \text{J Kg}^{-1}\ \text{K}^{-1}$$

Q.20 (i) It takes a much longer time to boil off (change to steam) a certain quantity of water, rather than bring it to its boiling point from room temperature, say 25°C. Explain the reason for this. **[1]**

(ii) A hot solid of mass 60 g at 100°C is placed in 100 g of water at 18°C. The final steady temperature recorded is 20°C. Find the specific heat capacity of the solid. **[2]**

Ans. (i) The amount of heat required per gram of water to bring it to 100°C from 25°C is =

$= 42 \times (100°\text{C} - 25°\text{C})$

$= 315\ \text{Jg}^{-1}$.

The latent heat of vaporisation of steam on the other hand is around $2260\ \text{Jg}^{-1}$.

Therefore, it requires a huge amount of heat per gram of water to convert it into steam as compared to raising its temperature is 100°C.

(ii) Let the specific heat capacity of solid be s. So, according to the principle of calorimetry,

Heat taken by water = Heat given by solid

$\Rightarrow 100 \times 1 \times (20 - 18)$

$= 60 \times s \times (100 - 20)$

$$\Rightarrow \quad s = \frac{100 \times 2}{60 \times 80}$$

$$\Rightarrow \quad s = \frac{1}{24} = 0.041\ \text{cal / g° C}$$

Specific heat capacity of the solid, i.e. $s = 0.041$ cal/g°C

Q.21 A thermo flask of negligible heat capacity contains 100 g of ice and 30 g of water.

(i) Calculate

(a) the mass of steam at 100°C needed to condense in the flask to just melt the ice. **[1]**

(b) the amount of water in the flask after condensation. **[1]**

(Take, specific latent heat of vaporisation of steam = 2260 J/g, specific latent heat of fusion of ice = 336 J/g, specific heat capacity of water = 4.2 J/g°C)

(ii) Is it possible to condense the water formed, back to ice by adding ice at 0°C? Explain, giving a suitable reason to justify your answer. **[1] [ICSE 2004]**

Ans. (i) (a) Let the mass of the steam be m grams.

Latent heat of vapourisation of steam

$= 2260\ \text{Jg}^{-1}$

Mass of ice = 100 g

Latent heat of fusion of ice = $336\ \text{Jg}^{-1}$

∴ From the law of equilibrium,

$m \times 2260 = 100 \times 336.$

$$\Rightarrow \quad m = \frac{33600}{2260} = 14.86\ \text{g} \simeq 15\ \text{g}.$$

(b) The total mass of water in the flask after condensation

$= (30 + 100 + 15)\ \text{g} = 145\ \text{g}$

(ii) No, it is not possible to condense the water formed, back into ice because heat energy contained in ice at 0°C is more than the heat energy contained in water at 0°C. We know that heat energy always flows from a higher energy region towards a lower energy region to come into equilibrium.

Hence, ice will release heat energy to melt into water and not otherwise.

Q.22 50 g of ice at 0°C is added to 300 g of a liquid at 30°C. What will be the final temperature of the mixture when all the ice gets melted? The specific heat capacity of the liquid is $2.65\ \text{Jg}^{-1}°\text{C}^{-1}$, while that of water is $4.2\ \text{Jg}^{-1}°\text{C}^{-1}$. (Take, specific latent heat of fusion of ice = $336\ \text{Jg}^{-1}$) **[4]**

Ans. Given, mass of ice = 50 g

Mass of liquid = 300 g

Temperature, $t_1 = 0°$ C

Temperature, $t_2 = 30°$ C

Temperature of mixture, $T = ?$

Specific heat of liquid = $2.65\ \text{Jg}^{-1}°\text{C}^{-1}$

Heat energy given by liquid = Heat taken by water + Heat used to melt ice

$\therefore$ Heat used to melt ice $= m \times L$

$= 50 \times 336 \qquad (\because L = 336 \text{ J/g})$

$= 16800$ J

$\therefore$ Heat energy given by liquid

$= m \times c \times \Delta T$

$= 300 \times 2.65 \times (30 - T)$

By principle of calorimetry,

$300 \times 2.65 \times (30 - T) = 16800 + 50 \times (T - 0) \times 42$

$\Rightarrow \quad 795 \times (30 - T) = 16800 + 210T$

$\Rightarrow \quad T = 7.014^\circ\text{C} \simeq 7^\circ\text{C}$

Q.23 How many grams of ice at -14°C is needed to cool 200 g of water from 25°C to 10°C ? (Take, specific heat of ice $= 0.5 \text{ cal g}^{-1\circ}\text{C}^{-1}$ and latent heat of ice = 80 cal g^{-1}) **[4]**

Ans. Heat gained by ice = Heat lost by water

Let, m = mass of ice in grams

$L_{ice} = 80$ cal/g

$c_{ice} = 0.5$ cal/g/°C

Temperature of ice = – 14°C

Heat gained by ice to get converted into water at 10°C

$= m \times [0^\circ - (14^\circ)] \times 0.5 +$

$m \times 80 + m \times 1 \times (10^\circ - 0^\circ)$

$= 7\text{m} + 80\text{m} + 10\text{m}$

$= 97$ m

Heat lost by 200 g of water to reduce its temperature from 25° C to 10° C $= 200 \times (25^\circ - 10^\circ) \times 1 = 3000$ J

By the principle of calorimetry,

$3000 = 97$ m

$\Rightarrow \quad m = \dfrac{3000}{97} = 30.93 \text{ g} \simeq 31 \text{ g}$

$\therefore$ 31g of ice is required.

Q.24 A vessel from which the air is rapidly being pumped out contains 100 g of water at 0° C. The intensive evaporation causes a gradual freezing of the water. What part of the original water can be converted into ice by this method? **[4]**

Latent heat of vaporisation of water at 0°C,

$= 2.10 \times 10^3$ J/g

Latent heat of fusion of ice,

$L_2 = 3.36 \times 10^2$ J/g

Ans. Let mass of ice formed = m g

Then, mass of water evaporated = $(100 - m)$ g

As no water is left in the vessel,

Therefore, heat gained by water in evaporation = Heat lost by water in freezing

$(100 - m) L_1 = mL_2$

$(100 - m) \times 2.10 \times 10^3 = m \times 3.36 \times 10^2$

$\Rightarrow \quad m = 86.2$ g

In terms of percentage, it will be 86.2%.

RADIOACTIVITY AND NUCLEI

Nucleus

- In every atom the **positive charge** and **mass** are densely concentrated at the centre of **atom**, called nucleus of the atom.
- The overall dimension of a nucleus is much smaller than that of an atom.
- Nucleus is not a composite body, it consists of elementrary particles namely neutrons and protons.
- The **positive charge** of nucleus is due to the protons present in it.
- Neutrons are neutral particles which, along with the protons, contribute to the overall mass of the nucleus and hence the atom.
- **Atomic Number** (Z) Atomic number of an atom is the **number of proton present in its nucleus** (which is same as the number of electrons in that atom). It is denoted by Z.
- **Mass Number** (A) The **total number of protons and neutrons** present in the nucleus is called atomic mass number of that atom. It is denoted by A. Hence, number of neutrons $(N) = A - Z$
- **Isotopes** The atoms of the **same element**, having **same atomic number** (Z), but **different mass numbers** are called isotopes. e.g. Protium (^1_1H) and deuterium (^2_1H) are isotopes having same atomic number ($Z = 1$) and different mass number 1 and 2.
- **Isotones** Atoms (nuclei) with the **same neutron number *N*** but **different atomic number** Z are called isotones. e.g. $^{23}_{11}Na$ and $^{24}_{12}Mg$ are isotones having same neutron numbers (12).
- **Isobars** Atoms (nuclei) of **different elements having same mass number** A but **different atomic numbers** Z are called isobars. e.g. $^{23}_{11}Na$ and $^{23}_{12}Mg$ are the isobars having same mass number 23 and different atomic numbers 11 and 12.

Radioactivity

Radioactivity is a **spontaneous nuclear phenomenon** in which an unstable nucleus undergoes a decay with the emission of some particles (α, β) and electromagnetic radiation (γ-rays).

In nature, three types of radioactive decay occurs, which are given below

(i) **α-decay** In α-decay, a helium nucleus ^4_2He is emitted.

(ii) **β-decay** In β-decay, electrons or positrons (with the same mass as electron) are emitted.

(iii) **γ-decay** In γ-decay, high energy ≈ 100 keV photons are emitted.

Radioactivity as a Spontaneous Disintegration

- **Radioactive decay rate is independent of any physical changes** such as the change in pressure or temperature or any other chemical changes such as extreme heating, freezing, action of strong electric or magnetic fields, etc.
- Hence, **radioactivity is a nuclear phenomenon** in which radioactive elements disintegrates by spontaneously emitting radiations like α, β and γ.

Properties of α-Particles

- α-particle consists of a helium nucleus. It is denoted by $_2He^4$ (atomic number 2 and mass number 4). It is a positively charged particle.
- They have **least penetration power** and **highest ionisation power**.
- They **cannot penetrate skin** but are harmful for the human body if inhaled, ingested or absorbed through wounds.
- α-particles **affect** a photographic plate.
- α-particles **cause fluorescence** on striking a fluorescent material.
- These are **affected by electric and magnetic fields**.

Properties of β -Particles

- β-particles are **highly energetic electrons**, which are released from inside of a nucleus. It is denoted by $_{-1}\beta^0$(atomic number – 1and mass number 0)
- β-particles are negatively charged and they have a negligible mass.
- For the emission of a β-particle, a neutron changes into a proton and an electron, inside the nucleus.
- β-particle has **greater penetration power** as compared to α-particle.
- It has **less ionisation power** but is still harmful.
- β-particles **affect a photographic** plate.
- β-particles **cause fluorescence** on striking a fluorescent material.
- These are **affected by electric and magnetic fields**.

Properties of γ-Rays

- The electromagnetic waves from the high frequency end of electromagnetic spectrum **which do not have mass** are called γ-rays.
- It is **neutral in nature** and is denoted by $_0\gamma^0$. They are chargeless and massless.
- It is **highly penetrating in nature** as compared to α and β-particles. It is very harmful to the living cell and cause mutation.
- These radiations **affect a photographic plate**.
- These radiations **cause fluorescence**, when they strike a fluorescent material.
- These rays are **not affected by electric and magnetic fields**.

Radioactive Decay (Changes Within the Nucleus)

- A radioactive nucleus (parent nucleus), decays by particle emission into another nucleus (daughter nucleus), this phenomenon is called **radioactive decay**.

α-Decay

- In α-decay, the mass number of the daughter (product) nucleus decreases by four, while the atomic number decreases by two, with respect to the parent nucleus.

  The decay can be written as $^{A}_{Z}X \longrightarrow ^{A-4}_{Z-2}Y + {}_2He^4$

  where, X is the parent nucleus and Y is daughter nucleus.

  e.g. $_{92}U^{238} \longrightarrow {}_{90}Th^{234} + {}_2He^4$
- α-decay occurs with nuclei that are **very heavy**, hence unstable. So, by emitting alpha particles, mass number decreases and it **moves towards stability**.

β-decay

- **β^--Decay** In β^--decay, the mass number of the daughter (product) nucleus remains same but atomic number increases by one.

REVISION NOTES

The decay can be written as

$${}_Z^AX \longrightarrow {}_{Z+1}Y^A + \beta^-({}_{-1}e^0)$$

e.g. $${}_6^{14}C \longrightarrow {}_7^{14}N + \beta^-$$

γ-Decay

In γ-decay, there is **no change in mass number and atomic number** of parent nucleus but energy in form of **electromagnetic radiation** is released in this decay.

The decay can be written as ${}_Z^AX \longrightarrow {}_Z^AX + \gamma$ (gamma radiation or energy)

e.g $${}_{38}Sr^{87*} \longrightarrow {}_{38}Sr^{87} + \gamma \text{ (gamma)}$$

Uses of Radioactivity- Radioisotopes

- There are some elements with atomic number $Z < 82$, whose isotopes are also radioactive. These isotopes are called **radioisotopes**. e.g. Potassium ${}_{19}^{40}K$ and carbon ${}_6^{14}C$, etc., are the radioisotopes.
- Radioisotopes has its applications in different fields, they are discussed as follows

Medical Uses

(i) Diseases like leukemia, cancer, etc., can be cured by radioisotopes.

(ii) γ-rays emitted by ${}_{27}^{60}Co$ are used to kill the cells in malignant tumour of patient.

(iii) The weak radioactive tracers of isotopes such as radioisotopes of NaCl, I, etc., are used to diagnose the brain tumour, blood clots etc. before they become dangerous.

Industrial Uses

(i) To avoid the accumulation of charge on moving parts of machine due to friction, radioactive isotopes are used. Due to ionisation effect, charges accumulated on moving parts will be neutralised.

(ii) The radioactive isotopes have such an ionisation effect that they can be used in making luminescent signs.

(iii) Radioactive tracers are used to check the underground pipelines.

(iv) Radioisotopes in the form of nuclear fuel are used to produce power.

Scientific Uses

(i) The radioisotopes are used in determining the age of rocks containing carbon, by measuring the percentage of C^{12} and C^{14} in them.

(ii) The age of old objects not containing carbon can be determined by measuring the percentage of isotope atoms present in them.

(iii) These are used in α-particle gold foil experiment in order to study the structure of atom.

(iv) Radioactive sources of elements N, P, K are used in agriculture science to study the growth of plants with respect to manure.

Harmful Effects of Radioactive or Nucleus Radiation

- Radioactive or nucleus radiation are very harmful for human beings, i.e. they can cause diseases like sore throat, loss of hair, cancer, leukemia, etc.
- They also have effect on genetics which can appear in later generations.
- There are three main sources from where we get the harmful radiations.

(i) **Radioactive Fall out from Nuclear Power Plants and Other Resources** The nuclear power plants act as a major source of electricity in the world. In case any accident occur in the reactor of these plants, radioactive radiations will escape into the atmosphere in a large amount. It will not only affect the population around the plant but also affect the life at far off places where they can reach with air currents.

(ii) **Nuclear Waste** When the activity of the fuel rods used in nuclear power reactor decreases, they get rejected. But still, these rods are quite radioactive in nature. If these are thrown in an open garbage dump, they can contaminate water and soil and hence can affect the living organisms.

(iii) **Cosmic Radiations and X-rays** Cosmic radiations from the sun enter the earth's atmosphere from outer space. Out of these radiations, substantial amount of uncharged radiations such as γ-ray and X-ray, etc., enter the earth's atmosphere.

These radiations are also very harmful for human beings.

Background Radiations

- All the radiations which are present in the atmosphere, even **if there is no radioactive source present** are called background radiations.

  The sources of these radiations are

  (i) cosmic radiations.

  (ii) natural and artificial radioactive isotopes.

  (iii) products after nuclear explosion.

  (iv) traces of radioactive substances present in the earth i.e. rocks.

Nuclear Energy

- Nuclear energy is the energy released during the **transformation of one nucleus to another nucleus**.
- Two distinct ways of obtaining nuclear energy from nucleus are as follows

  (i) **Nuclear Fission** Nuclear fission is the phenomenon of **splitting of a heavy nucleus** (usually $A > 230$) into two or more lighter nuclei by the bombardment of proton, neutron, α-particle, etc. In fission, a heavy nucleus like ${}^{235}_{92}U$ breaks into two smaller fragments by the bombardment of thermal neutron (low energy or slow moving).

  e.g. $${}^{235}_{92}U + {}^{1}_{0}n \longrightarrow {}^{141}_{56}Ba + {}^{92}_{36}Kr + 3\,{}_0n^1 + Q$$

  [Energy released]

  (ii) **Nuclear Fusion** Nuclear fusion is the phenomenon of **fusing two or more lighter nuclei** forming a single heavy nucleus.

  e.g. $${}_1H^2 + {}_1H^2 \longrightarrow {}_2He^3 + {}_0n^1 + 3.27 \text{ meV}$$

  Fusion of hydrogen nuclei into helium nuclei is the source of energy of most of the stars including the sun.

Safety Precaution While Using Nuclear Energy

Some of the safety precautions which are required to be undertaken while using nuclear energy are as follows

Safety Measures for Handling the Radioactive Materials

(i) Each type of radiations should have some safety limits and that should be known to each and everyone, so that **no one get exposed beyond the safety limit** in any case.

(ii) People working with radioactive materials should **wear special lead lined aprons and lead gloves**.

(iii) In order to stop radiations from spreading all around, **the radioactive substances must be kept in thick lead containers** with a very narrow opening.

Safety Measures for Establishment of Nuclear Plants

When a nuclear power plant is going to be established to generate the electricity, proper care must be taken, so that the people working in it are not exposed to the nuclear radiations.

Given below are some safety measures which are to be followed during the establishment of nuclear power plants.

(i) The housing of nuclear reactor must be done in an air-tight building of strong concrete structure which can with stand earthquakes, fires and explosion.

(ii) For backup, a cooling system must be there for the reactor core for safety in case of failure.

Safe Disposal of Nuclear Waste

Nuclear wastes are the wastes found after use of radioactive material. It is obtained from different places like laboratories, power plants, hospitals, scientific establishment.

So, it must be first kept in thick cases and then must be buried in the specially constructed deep underground stores.

EXAM ORIENTED QUESTIONS

TYPE - 1 01 Mark

Multiple Choice Questions

Q.1 Mass number of an element is
(a) the number of neutrons in the nucleus.
(b) the number of protons in the nucleus.
(c) the total number of protons, electrons and neutrons.
(d) the total number of protons and neutrons in the nucleus.

Ans. (d)

Q.2 Heavy stable nuclei have more neutrons than protons. This is because of the fact that
(a) neutrons are heavier than protons
(b) electrostatic forces between protons are repulsive
(c) neutrons decay into protons through beta decay
(d) nuclear forces between neutrons are weaker than that between protons

Ans. (b) Heavy stable nuclei have more neutrons than protons because protons are positively charged and repel each other. This repulsive force has to be balanced by the strong nuclear force between the nucleons which is achieved by increasing the number of neutrons in the nucleus of the atom.

Q.3 To study the age of excavated material of archaeological significance we study the rate of decay of an isotope of **[ICSE 2022 Sem-II]**
(a) uranium (b) cobalt
(c) carbon (d) chlorine

Ans. (c) The age of excavated material is determined by archaeologists with the help of an isotope of carbon (Carbon-14).

Q.4 A radioactive element *P* emits one α-particle and transforms to a new element *Q*. What will be the position of the element *Q* in the periodic table? **[ICSE 2025]**
(a) One group to the left of *P*
(b) One group to the right of *P*
(c) Two groups to the right of *P*
(d) Two groups to the left of *P*

Ans. (d)

Q.5 The nuclear radiation which gets deflected towards negatively charged plate in an electric field is **[ICSE Specimen 2022 Sem-II]**
(a) gamma (b) ultraviolet (c) beta (d) alpha

Ans. (d) α-particles are positively charged particle. That's why, it is deflected towards the negatively charged particles.

Q.6 Which of the following radiations suffer maximum deflection in a magnetic field? **[ICSE 2023]**
(a) Alpha radiations (b) Beta radiations
(c) Gamma radiations (d) X-radiations

Ans. (b)

Q.7 The radiation with maximum penetrating power is **[ICSE Specimen 2022 Sem-II]**
(a) γ (b) β
(c) X-radiation (d) α

Ans. (a)

Q.8 The heaviest nuclear radiation is **[ICSE 2022 Sem-II]**
(a) X-radiation (b) α-radiation
(c) γ-radiation (d) β-radiation

Ans. (b) The heaviest nuclear radiation is the α-radiation. It is the helium nuclei.

Q.9 A radioactive element is placed in an evacuated chamber. Then, the rate of radioactive decay will **[ICSE Specimen 2024]**
(a) decrease
(b) increase
(c) remain unchanged
(d) depend on the surrounding temperature

Ans. (c) The rate of radioactive decay will remain unchanged as the rate of disintegration is a nuclear phenomenon and does not depend upon environmental factors.

Q.10 For the given equation

$$^{A}_{Z}X \longrightarrow A + ^{0}_{-1}e$$

where, *A* is
(a) $^{A}_{Z+1}Y$ (b) $^{A+1}_{Z}Y$ (c) $^{A+1}_{Z+1}Y$ (d) $^{A-1}_{Z+1}Y$

Ans. (a) Given equation is an emission of beta particle. The mass number remains unchanged and *Z* is increased by 1.

Q.11 In a nuclear reactor, 48 kJ of energy is produced per minute. If the energy released per fission is 3.2×10^{-11} J, then the number of fission which would be taking place in a reactor per second will be
(a) 2.5×10^{13} (b) 4.5×10^{12}
(c) 2.56×10^{11} (d) 3.25×10^{15}

Ans. (a) Given, power $= \dfrac{\text{Energy}}{\text{Time}} = \dfrac{48 \text{ kJ}}{60 \text{ s}}$

$\Rightarrow \quad \dfrac{4}{5}$ kJ/s

Energy released per fission = 32×10^{-11} J

∴ Number of fission per second

$$= \frac{\frac{4}{5} \times 10^3 \text{ J}}{3.2 \times 10^{-11}}$$

$$= \frac{0.8}{32} \times 10^{14} = 025 \times 10^{14}$$

$$= 2.5 \times 10^{13} \text{ fission per second}$$

Q.12 The process of splitting a heavy nucleus into two lighter nuclei is called

(a) fusion

(b) fission

(c) radioactive decay

(d) beta decay

Ans. (b)

Q.13 Which of the following combinations correctly shows the charges on the particles? **[Competency Based Que.]**

	$+1.6\times 10^{-19}$C	-1.6×10^{-19}C	$+3.2\times 10^{-19}$C
(a)	proton	neutron	alpha particle
(b)	alpha particle	electron	neutron
(c)	proton	electron	alpha particle
(d)	electron	proton	alpha particle

Ans. (c)

Q.14 A nucleus of an atom consists of 146 neutrons and 95 protons. It decays after emitting an alpha particle. How many protons and neutrons are left in the nucleus after an alpha emission? **[ICSE Specimen 2025]**

(a) Protons = 93, neutrons = 142

(b) Protons = 95, neutrons = 144

(c) Protons = 93, neutrons = 144

(d) Protons = 95, neutrons = 42

Ans. (c) Given, $p = 95$ and $n = 146$

$$A = p + n = 95 + 146 = 241$$

Now, ${}_{95}X^{241} \longrightarrow {}_{93}X^{237} + {}_2He^4$

Number of neutrons $= A - Z = 237 - 93 = 144$

Number of protons, $Z = 93$

Q.15 Which of the following equations are correctly balanced?

A. ${}^{q-1}_{p-5}X \longrightarrow {}^{q-5}_{p-3}Y + {}^4_2He$

B. ${}^{q-4}_{p-4}Z \longrightarrow {}^{q-4}_{p-5}X + {}^0_{-1}e$

C. ${}^{q-1}_{p-5}X \longrightarrow {}^{q-5}_{p-7}Y + {}^4_2He$

D. ${}^{q-4}_{p-7}Z \longrightarrow {}^{q-4}_{p-5}X + 2\,{}^0_{-1}e$ **[Competency Based Que.]**

(a) Only D (b) Only C

(c) Both A and B (d) Both C and D

Ans. (d) C. ${}^{q-1}_{p-5}X \xrightarrow{{}^4_2He} {}^{q-1-4}_{p-5-2}Y \longrightarrow {}^{q-5}_{p-7}Y + {}^4_2He$

D. ${}^{q-4}_{p-7}Z \xrightarrow{2\,{}^0_{-1}e} {}^{q-4}_{p-7+2}X \longrightarrow {}^{q-4}_{p-5}X + 2\,{}^0_{-1}e$

Q.16 The mass number of four different elements *A*, *B*, *C* and *D* are 2, 35, 135 and 239, respectively. Which of them would be the most suitable for nuclear fission?

(a) *A* (b) *C*

(c) *D* (d) *B*

Ans. (c) Element *D* would be most suitable for nuclear fission. As, it has greater mass which therefore will be converted into energy by producing lighter nuclei.

TYPE - 2

01 Mark

Assertion-Reason Type Questions

Directions (Q. Nos. 1-5) In the following questions, a statement of assertion (A) is followed by a statement of reason (R). Mark the correct choice as

(a) Both A and R are true and R is the correct explanation of A.

(b) Both A and R are true but R is not the correct explanation of A.

(c) A is true but R is false.

(d) A is false but R is true.

Q.1 Assertion (A) ${}_6C^{14}$ and ${}_7N^{14}$ are isobars.

Reason (R) The atoms of different elements which have the same mass number (*A*) but different atomic number (*Z*) are called isobars.

Ans. (a) Carbon has 8 neutrons and 6 protons whereas nitrogen has 7 neutrons and 7 protons in its nucleus but their mass number is same and hence they are isobars.

Q.2 Assertion (A) Out of α, β and γ radiations, α-particles have maximum penetrating power.

Reason (R) The α-particles are the heaviest among the three.

Ans. (d) Out of α, β and γ radiations, γ-radiation has the maximum penetrating power.

Q.3 Assertion (A) Electrons present in the nucleus are emitted as beta radiation.

Reason (R) The mass number of the nucleus remains unchanged during beta emission.

Ans. (d) Electrons are not located in the nucleus. During beta emission, a neutron transforms into a proton and an electron. As a result, the number of neutrons decreases while the number of protons increases, leaving the mass number unaffected.

Q.4 Assertion (A) Nuclear reactors mainly utilise nuclear fusion for energy production.

Reason (R) Nuclear fission reactions in nuclear reactors generate significant heat, which is converted into electrical energy.

Ans. (d) Nuclear reactors primarily rely on nuclear fission, not fusion, for energy production. In nuclear fission, heavy atomic nuclei are divided into lighter nuclei, releasing substantial energy in the process. This energy heats water to create steam, which powers turbines and generators to produce electricity. While nuclear fusion holds promise as a future energy source, current nuclear reactors mainly use nuclear fission to generate energy.

Q.5 **Assertion** (A) The ionisation power of β-particles is roughly $\frac{1}{100}$th times that of α-particles and nearly 100 times that of the γ-radiation.
Reason (R) The penetration power of β-particles is more than that of α-particles but less than that of γ-radiation.

Ans. (b) Both A and R are correct, but both are individual properties of the β-particles which are independent of each other.

TYPE - 3 01/02 Marks

Fill in the Blanks

Q.1 The nuclear radiation with lowest ionising power is .... (α / β / γ). **[ICSE 2025]**

Ans. γ

Q.2 An isotone of ${}_6C^{14}$ is .... [${}_8O^{17}$, ${}_6C^{13}$, ${}_8O^{16}$] **[1]**

Ans. ${}_8O^{16}$

Q.3 The isotope of hydrogen commonly involved in nuclear fusion is .... [deuterium / tritium]. **[1]**

Ans. deuterium

Q.4 The penetration power of the α-particles is the .... [most/least], whereas the penetration power of the γ-radiations is the .... [most/least]. **[2]**

Ans. least, most

Q.5 Nuclear .... [fission/fusion] is the process in which two lighter nuclei combine to form a heavy nucleus and the temperature required for the above process is .... [10^4 K/10^7 K]. **[2]**

Ans. fusion, 10^7 K.

TYPE - 4 02 Marks

Very Short Answer Type Questions

Q.1 In the following atoms, which one is radioisotope? Give one use of this isotope.
$O^{16}, C^{14}, N^{14}, He^4$ **[ICSE 2024]**

Ans. C^{14} is a radioisotope and it is used in agriculture to increase the yield of crop seeds.

Q.2 An atom of the isotope chlorine-35 contains 17 protons. For an atom of the isotope chlorine-37, state the number of
(i) protons **[1]**
(ii) neutrons **[1]**

Ans. (i) Number of protons = 17
(ii) Number of neutrons = 20

Q.3 State the number of
(i) electrons in a neutral atom of the isotope ${}_3^7Li$, **[1]**
(iii) nucleons in an atom of the isotope ${}_{82}^{208}Pb$. **[1]**

Ans. (i) Number of electrons = 3
(ii) Number of nucleons = 208

Q.4 Two isotopes of hydrogen are written as ${}_1^1H$ and ${}_1^2H$.
(a) Complete the table to show the number of protons and neutrons in one nucleus of each of these isotopes of hydrogen.

	Number of protons	Number of neutrons	
${}_1^1H$			**[1]**
${}_1^2H$			**[1]**

[Competency Based Ques.]

Ans. (a)

	Number of protons	Number of neutrons
${}_1^1H$	1	0
${}_1^2H$	1	1

Q.5 Why is radioactivity considered to be a nuclear phenomenon? **[2][ICSE Specimen 2018]**

Ans. Radioactivity is the spontaneous random emission of particles from within the nucleus of an atom. Since, the radiations are emitted from nucleus of an atom, thus the radioactivity is considered to be a nuclear phenomenon.

Q.6 How is the radioactivity of a radioisotope affected, if it undergoes a chemical change? Give a reason for your answer. **[ICSE 2023]**

Ans. Radioactivity of an element is not affected by the chemical changes as radioactivity is a nuclear phenomenon and does not involve extra nuclear electrons.

Q.7 It is possible for a hydrogen (${}_1^1H$) nucleus to emit an alpha particle? Give a reason for your answer. **[ICSE 2019]**

Ans. No, it is not possible because alpha particle consists of two protons and two neutrons. However, none of the isotopes of hydrogen has the same or more number of protons and neutrons in its nuclei. Thus, they cannot emit an alpha particle.

Q.8 A nucleus $_{84}X^{202}$ of an element emits an α-particle followed by a β-particle. The final nucleus is $_aY^b$. Find the values of a and b. **[ICSE 2020]**

Ans. When an α-particle is emitted by a nucleus, then mass number of nucleus is decreased by 4 units, while atomic number is decreased by 2 units. Similarly, for β-particle emission, atomic number is increased by one unit while mass number remains same.

$\therefore \quad _{84}X^{202} \xrightarrow{-\alpha} {}_{82}Z^{198} \xrightarrow{-\beta} {}_{83}Y^{198}$

$\therefore \quad _aY^b = {}_{83}Y^{198}$

$\Rightarrow \quad a = 83$ and $b = 198$

Q.9 A radioactive nucleus undergoes a series of decays according to the sequence,

$X \xrightarrow{\beta} X_1 \xrightarrow{\alpha} X_2 \xrightarrow{\alpha} X_3$

If the mass number and atomic number of X_3 are 132 and 69 respectively, what is the mass number and atomic number of X?

Ans. According to the question, $_{72}X^{140} \xrightarrow{_{-1}\beta^0} {}_{73}X_1^{140} \xrightarrow{\alpha(_2He^4)} {}_{71}X_2^{136} \xrightarrow{\alpha(_2He^4)} {}_{69}X_3^{132}$

Q.10 (i) Name the radiations that are emitted during the decay of a nucleus, which has highest penetrating power? **[1]**

(ii) Does the emission of the above-mentioned radiation result in a change in the mass number? **[ICSE Specimen 2025][1]**

Ans. (i) γ (Gamma) – radiation

(ii) No, γ-radiation is an electromagnetic wave which does not affect the mass number of the element which emits it.

Q.11 State one industrial use of α, β and γ radiations. **[ICSE Specimen 2017]**

Ans. **α-radiation** As smoke detectors for industrial purpose.

β-radiation Monitoring paper thickness in industries.

γ radiation As tracers for detecting leakage in pipes.

Q.12 What are background radiations? **[ICSE Specimen 2023]**

Ans. All the radiations which are present in the atmosphere, even if there is no radioactive source present are called background radiations.

The sources of these radiations are

(i) cosmic radiations.

(ii) natural and artificial radioactive isotopes.

(iii) products after nuclear explosion.

(iv) traces of radioactive substances present in earth, i.e. rocks.

Q.13 (i) What do you understand by the term nuclear fusion? **[1]**

(ii) Nuclear power plants use nuclear fission reaction to produce electricity. What is the advantage of producing electricity by fusion reaction ? **[1][ICSE 2018]**

Ans. (i) In nuclear fusion, two light nuclei are combined to form a heavy nucleus and release energy.

(ii) In fusion per unit mass, more energy is released than fission, therefore it is more useful in producing electricity.

Q.14 What is nuclear waste? State one method to dispose it off safely.

Ans. Radioactive wastes produced from the fission of U-235 in nuclear power plant, which are called nuclear wastes are very hazardous to living beings. To prevent harm, it is securely sealed in steel containers and safely buried deep underground, away from open areas.

Q.15 Copy and complete the nuclear reaction by filling in the blanks. $_{92}U^{235} + {}_0n^1 \longrightarrow {}_{56}Ba^{\cdots\cdots} + {}_{\cdots\cdots}Kr^{92} + 3\,{}_0n^1$ **[ICSE 2024]**

Ans. Let $_{92}U^{235} + {}_0n^1 \longrightarrow {}_{56}Ba^x + {}_yKr^{92} + 3{}_0n^1$

For balancing,

$$235 + 1 = x + 92 + 3 \times 1$$
$$236 = x + 95$$
$$x = 236 - 95 = 141$$

Again, $92 + 0 = 56 + y + 3 \times 0$

$$y = 92 - 56 = 36$$

So, $_{92}U^{235} + {}_0n^1 \longrightarrow {}_{56}Ba^{141} + {}_{36}Kr^{92} + 3\,{}_0n^1$

Q.16 Complete the following nuclear changes.

(i) $_{11}Na^{24} \longrightarrow {}_{\cdots}Mg^{\cdots} + {}_{-1}\beta^0$ **[1]**

(ii) $_{92}U^{238} \longrightarrow {}_{90}Th^{234} + \ldots +$ Energy **[1]**

Ans. (i) $_{11}Na^{24} \longrightarrow {}_{12}Mg^{24} + {}_{-1}\beta^0$

(ii) $_{92}U^{238} \longrightarrow {}_{90}Th^{234} + {}_2He^4$ (α-particle) + Energy

TYPE - 5 03 Marks

Short Answer Type Questions

Q.1 (i) Define radioactivity. **[1]**

(ii) A radioactive substance is oxidised. What change would you expect to take place in the nature of its radioactivity? Give a suitable reason. **[2]** **[ICSE Specimen 2017]**

Ans. (i) Radioactivity is the spontaneous process by which a nucleus of an unstable atom decay by emitting radiations such as α, β and γ.

(ii) If a radioactive substance is oxidised, then it will not affect its radioactivity because oxidation is a chemical process involving electrons present outside the nucleus and radioactivity is the process happening inside the nucleus and it only affects the protons and neutrons.

Q.2 The nuclei of four neutral atoms are represented as.

$$^{12}_{6}C,\ ^{14}_{6}C,\ ^{14}_{7}N,\ ^{15}_{8}O$$

(i) Neutral atoms also contain electrons. State which of the four nuclei is surrounded by the greatest number of electrons. **[1]**

(ii) From the four nuclei, state the two nuclei having same number of

(a) protons **[1]**

(b) neutrons **[1]**

Ans. (i) $^{15}_{8}O$

(ii) (a) $^{12}_{6}C$ $^{14}_{6}C$

(b) $^{14}_{7}N$ $^{15}_{8}O$

Q.3 Explain, using ideas about electrons, neutrons and protons, why atoms of $^{1}_{1}H$ and $^{2}_{1}H$ are uncharged. **[Competency Based Que.]**

Ans. Each of the atoms of $^{1}_{1}H$ and $^{2}_{1}H$ contains one electron and one proton. As the size of the charge on one electron is equal to the charge of one proton, hence the negative charge on the electron neutralises the positive charge on the proton and the atom as a whole becomes uncharged. The neutron in the atom of $^{2}_{1}H$ is neutral and has no effect on the overall charge.

Q.4 A beam of α, β and γ rays are travelling through a certain region in space.

(i) Arrange them in ascending order of ionising power. **[1]**

(ii) Which of the above will pass undeviated, if subjected to an electric field? **[1]**

(iii) With respect to your answer to part (ii) above, what will be the change in the nucleus of an atom after such a ray is emitted. **[1]**
[ICSE Specimen 2022 Sem-II]

Ans. (i) $\gamma < \beta < \alpha$

(ii) γ-rays pass undeviated, if subjected to an electric field as they are not charged particle.

(iii) The nucleus of the atom does not undergo any change in the mass number and atomic number during γ-emission. So, γ-rays take no mass and no electrical charge from the nucleus.

Q.5 (i) Complete the following nuclear changes **[1]**

$$^{238}_{92}P \rightarrow \text{=} Q + ^{4}_{2}He \rightarrow \text{=} R + ^{0}_{-1}e$$

(ii) Name the nuclear radiation which has the highest ionising power. **[2] [ICSE 2023]**

Ans. (i) $^{238}_{92}U \rightarrow ^{234}_{90}Th + ^{4}_{2}He + \text{Energy}$

$$^{234}_{90}Th \rightarrow ^{234}_{91}Pa + ^{0}_{-1}e$$

(ii) Alpha particles have higher ionisation power as compared to the other two types of radiations owing to the fact that an α-particle is a double ionised helium nucleus, i.e. He^{2+}.

Q.6 (i) Copy and complete the following nuclear reaction.

$$_{86}^{-}Rn \rightarrow ^{218}_{-}Po + ^{4}_{2}\alpha$$ **[2]**

(ii) What will be the effect on the radiation emitted in the above reaction when it is allowed to pass through an electric field? [Be specific in your answer **[1][ICSE Specimen 2023]**

Ans. (i) Let,

$$^{X}_{86}Rn \longrightarrow ^{218}_{y}Po + ^{4}_{2}\alpha$$

Balancing the atomic number gives us,

$$X = 218 + 4 = 222$$

Again, balancing the mass number we get,

$$86 = Y + 2$$

$$\Rightarrow Y = 86 - 2 = 84$$

So, $^{222}_{86}Rn \longrightarrow ^{218}_{84}Po + ^{4}_{2}\alpha$

(ii) α-particles are positively charged particles. Hence, it is deflected towards negative plate or terminal.

Q.7 A smoke detector containing an alpha particle source is fixed to the ceiling in a room.
A technician removes the source from the smoke detector and measures the count rate of the source.

(i) Suggest two precautions that the technician should take when working with the source. **[2]**

(ii) The technician measures the count rate, in counts/s, five times. On each occasion, the arrangement of the equipment is the same.
The values obtained are : 81 77 80 83 and 79.
Suggest why the values are different. **[1]**
[Competency Based Que.]

Ans. (i) 1. The source should be handled with long tweezers.

2. The lead-lined clothing should be used when working with a radioactive source.

(ii) The slight variation in the count-rates is due to the random nature of the process of radioactive emissions.

Q.8 A radioactive nucleus X emits an alpha particle followed by two beta particles to form nucleus Y.

(i) With respect to the element X, where would you position the element Y in the periodic table? **[1]**

(ii) What is the general name of the elements X and Y? **[1]**

(iii) If the atomic number of Y is 80, then what is the atomic number of X? **[1][ICSE Specimen 2025]**

Ans. Let the atomic number of element X be Z and the mass number be A.

$$^{A}_{Z}X \xrightarrow{\alpha} ^{A-4}_{Z-2}X$$

and $$^{A-4}_{Z-2}X' \xrightarrow{2\beta} ^{A-4}_{Z}Y$$

(i) As, the atomic number of both the elements X and Y are same, so they are placed at the same position in the periodic table.

(ii) X and Y are isotopes.

(iii) Atomic number of X = Atomic number of Y = 80

Q.9 The graph (Fig. *A*) illustrates the correlation between the number of protons (*X*-axis) and the number of neutrons (*Y*-axis) for elements *A*, *B*, *C*, *D* and *E* in the periodic table. These elements are denoted by the letters rather than their conventional symbols. When the element *C*, depicted in the graph, undergoes radioactive decay, it releases radioactive rays. When these rays are directed into the plane of the paper in the presence of a magnetic field, as indicated in the (Fig. *B*), they experience deflection, causing them to move upwards. **[Competency Based Que.]**

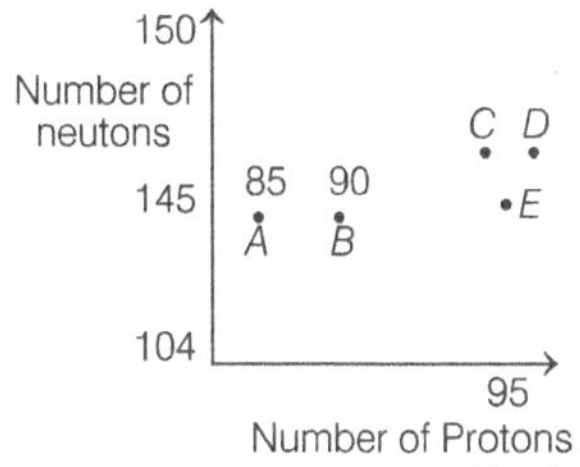

Fig. A

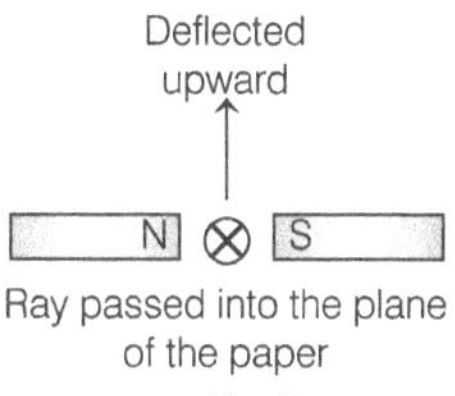

Fig. B

(i) Name the radioactive radiations emitted by the element *C*. **[1]**

(ii) Identify the daughter element from the graph. **[1]**

(iii) Name the law used to identify the radioactive radiations emitted by the element. **[1]**

Ans. (i) Beta

(ii) Daughter element *E*

(iii) Fleming's left hand rule

Q.10 Curium is a radioactive element with the symbol $^{247}_{96}Cm$ named in honour of Madam Curie. The graph of number of protons *versus* number of neutrons for some elements are shown below **[ICSE 2025]**

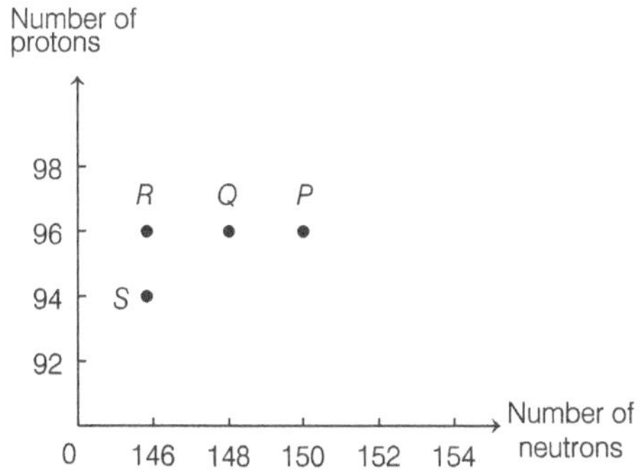

(i) Which point on the graph indicates the element Cm? **[1]**

(ii) Which point on the graph indicates daughter nucleus after Cm undergoes radioactive decay of 1α followed by 2β ? **[1]**

(iii) State the mass number of the daughter nucleus. **[1]**

Ans. (i) Point *P*

(ii) Point *R*

(iii) Mass number of the daughter nucleus is 243.

Q.11 The ore of uranium found in nature contains $_{92}U^{238}$ and $_{92}U^{235}$.

Although both the isotopes are fissionable, it is found out experimentally that one of the two isotopes is more easily fissionable.

(i) Name the isotope of uranium which is easily fissionable. **[1]**

(ii) Give a reason for your answer. **[1]**

(iii) Write a nuclear reaction when uranium 238 emits an alpha particle from a thorium (Th) nucleus. **[1]**

[ICSE 2018]

Ans. (i) $_{92}U^{235}$ is easily fissionable.

(ii) Fission of uranium with mass number of 238 is possible by only fast neutron but the fission of uranium with mass number of 235 is also possible by slow neutron.

(iii) $^{238}_{92}U \longrightarrow ^{234}_{90}Th + ^{4}_{2}He$ (α-particle)

Q.12 (i) When does the nucleus of an atom become radioactive? **[1]**

(ii) How is the radioactivity of an element affected, when it undergoes a chemical change to form a chemical compound? **[1]**

(iii) Mention one use and one harmful effect of radioactivity. **[1]**

Ans. (i) If the atomic number of an element is more than 82, then after it becomes radioactive. Atomic number between 82 to 92 are good radioactive elements.

(ii) There is no change in the radioactivity during the chemical reaction, because chemical reaction involves electrons in the outer shell of an atom, whereas radioactivity involves nucleons (i.e. neutrons and protons) in the nucleus of the atom.

(iii) Uses of radioactivity is in production of electricity in nuclear reactor and in carbon dating by (C^{14}) and in harmful effect is that, it can cause skin cancer and eye diseases.

Q.13 (i) Which nuclear radiation will travel undeviated in an electric field? **[1]**

(ii) How can one stop the radiations escaping from a nuclear reactor in a nuclear power plant? **[1]**

(iii) Name one internal source of background radiations. **[1][ICSE 2023]**

Ans. (i) Gamma radiations will travel undeviated in an electric field.

(ii) The steel containment vessel serves as a barrier to prevent leakage of any radioactive gases or fluids from the plant. An outer concrete building serves as final layer, protecting the steel containment vessel.

(iii) All people have internal radiation, mainly from radioactive potassium-40 and carbon-14 inside their bodies from birth.

Q.14 (i) **Complete the following radioactive reaction**

$$X \rightarrow Y + {}_{2}^{4}\text{He} \longrightarrow {}_{91}^{234}Z + {}_{-1}^{0}e$$ **[2]**

(ii) **Uranium is available in two forms U-235 and U-238. Which of the two isotopes of uranium is more fissionable?** **[1] [ICSE 2024]**

Ans. (i) ${}_{A}X^{B} \rightarrow {}_{C}Y^{D} + {}_{2}\text{He}^{4} \rightarrow {}_{91}Z^{234} + {}_{-1}e^{0}$

On balancing, $D + 4 = 234 + 0$

$D = 234 - 4 = 230$

$C + 2 = 91 - 1 = 90$

$C = 90 - 2 = 88$

Again, $B = D + 4 = 234$ and $A = C + 2 = 90$

So, complete equation

${}_{90}X^{234} \rightarrow {}_{88}Y^{230} + {}_{2}\text{He}^{4} \rightarrow {}_{91}Z^{234} + {}_{-1}e^{0}$

(ii) ${}_{92}U^{235}$ is easily fissionable. This is due to the fact that only fast neutrons can cause the fission of U-238, whereas slow neutrons can even trigger the fission of U-235.

Q.15 **Study the diagram given below and answer the questions that follow:** **[ICSE 2025]**

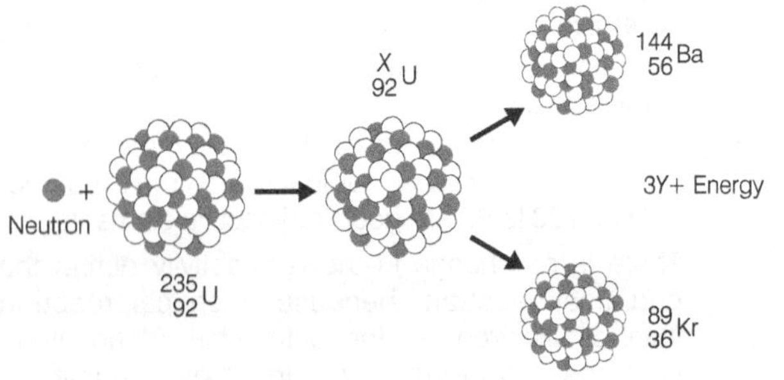

(i) **Name the process depicted in the diagram.**

(ii) **What is the value of X?**

(iii) **Identify Y. the missing product of the reaction.**

Ans. (i) Nuclear fission (ii) 236 (iii) ${}_{0}^{1}n$ (neutron)

Q.16 **In some power stations, nuclear fission is used as a source of energy.**

(i) **State what is meant by nuclear fission?** **[1]**

(ii) **The nuclear fission reaction produces neutrons. In the power station, the neutrons may be absorbed by rods made of boron-10. Complete the nuclear equation for the absorption of a single neutron by a boron-10 nucleus with the emission of an α-particle.** **[2]**

$${}_{5}^{10}\text{B} + \ldots\ldots\ldots \rightarrow {}_{3}^{\ldots}\text{Li} + \ldots\ldots\ldots$$

Ans. (i) Splitting up of a heavy nucleus into two intermediate nuclei along with the release of energy is known as nuclear fission.

(ii) ${}_{5}^{10}\text{B} + \overset{{}_{0}^{1}n}{\ldots\ldots\ldots} \rightarrow {}_{3}^{7}\text{Li} + \overset{{}_{2}^{4}\text{He}}{\ldots\ldots\ldots}$

TYPE - 6 — 04 Marks

Long Answer Type Questions

Q.1 A certain nucleus X has a mass number 14 and atomic number 6. The nucleus X changes to ${}_{7}Y^{14}$ after the loss of a particle.

(i) Name the particle emitted. **[1]**

(ii) Represent this change in the form of an equation. **[1]**

(iii) A radioactive substance is oxidised. What change would you expect to take place in the nature of its radioactivity? Give a reason for your answer. **[2]**

Ans. (i) β-particle; since during the ${}_{-1}\beta^{0}$ emission, there is gain in atomic number.

(ii) ${}_{6}X^{14} \xrightarrow{-1\beta^{0}} {}_{7}Y^{14} + {}_{-1}e^{0}$

(iii) There is no change in the nature of radioactivity during oxidation. Because oxidation is a phenomena in which involvement of electrons are there, whereas in radioactivity nucleons take part in the reaction.

Q.2 An atomic nucleus A is composed of 84 protons and 128 neutrons. The nucleus A emits an α-particle and is transformed into a nucleus B. **[1]**

(i) What is the composition of B? **[1]**

(ii) The nucleus B emits a β-particle and is transformed into a nucleus C. What is the composition of C? **[1]**

(iii) What is mass number of the nucleus A?

(iv) Does the composition of C change, if it emits γ-radiations? **[1] [ICSE 2020]**

Ans. (i) Number of protons in atomic nucleus, $A = 84$

$\therefore$ Atomic number of $A = 84$

Number of neutrons, $N = 128$

$\therefore$ Mass number of A,

$M = Z + N = 84 + 128 = 212$

$\therefore$ When an α-particle is emitted from a nucleus, then its mass number is decreased by 4 units and atomic number is decreased by 2 units.

$\therefore \quad {}_{84}A^{212} \xrightarrow{\alpha} {}_{82}B^{208}$

(ii) When a β-particle is emitted from a nucleus, then atomic number is increased by one unit and mass number is unaffected.

$\therefore {}_{82}B^{208} \xrightarrow{\beta} {}_{83}C^{208}$

(iii) Mass number of nucleus $A = Z + N = 84 + 128 = 212$

(iv) There is no change in the composition of C by the emission of γ-radiations.

Q.3 The graph illustrates the correlation between the number of protons (X-axis) and the number of neutrons (Y-axis) for element C in the periodic table. The element is denoted by letters rather than their conventional symbols. When element *C*, depicted in the graph, undergoes radioactive decay, it releases radioactive rays.

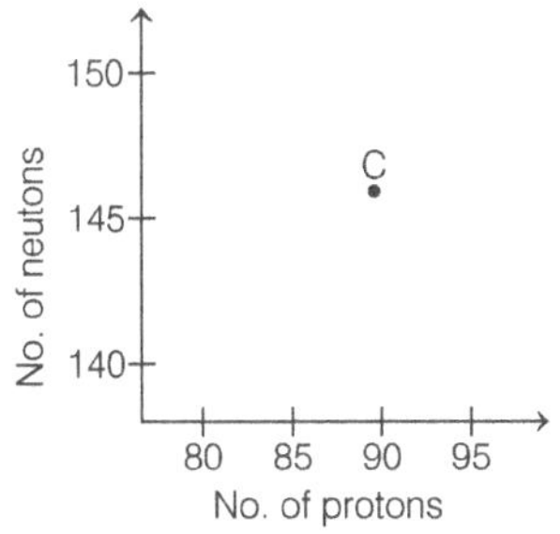

(i) Write the chemical symbol along with the mass number and atomic number for the element denoted as '*C*'. **[2]**

(ii) Plot on the graph,

(a) The daughter element after the emission of beta radiation by the element '*C*'. **[1]**

(b) The daughter element, as indicated in the previous answer, if it undergoes alpha decay. **[1][Competency Based Que.]**

Ans. (i) ${}_{92}C^{238} \longrightarrow {}_{92}U^{238}$

(ii) (a) ${}_{92}C^{238} \longrightarrow {}_{93}A^{238} + {}_{-1}\beta^{0}$

∴ For *A*, no. of protons = 93

no. of neutrons = 145

(b) ${}_{93}A^{238} \longrightarrow {}_{91}B^{234} + {}^{4}_{2}\alpha$

∴ For *B*, no. of protons = 91

no. of neutrons = 143

∴ Plotting them on graph, we get

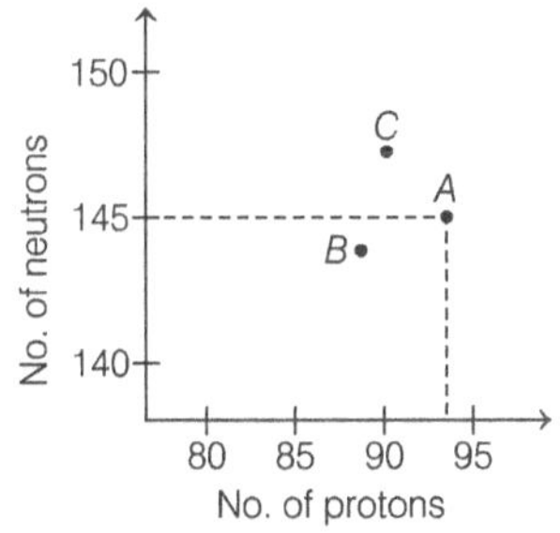

Q.4 (i) What is nuclear energy? **[1]**

(ii) After emission of a nuclear radiation, the atomic number of the daughter nucleus increases by 1. Identify the nuclear radiation. **[1]**

(iii) Write a nuclear reaction indicating the nuclear change mentioned in (ii). **[1]**

(iv) What is the special name given to the parent and daughter nucleus when this radiation is emitted? **[1]**

[ICSE 2022 Sem-II]

Ans. (i) Nuclear energy is the energy released during the transformation of nucleus into another nucleus.

(ii) The atomic number of the daughter nucleus increases by 1 in the β-decay.

(iii) Nuclear reaction for β-decay:

$${}^{A}_{Z}X \longrightarrow {}^{A}_{Z+1}Y + {}^{0}_{-1}e$$

(iv) Isobars

Q.5

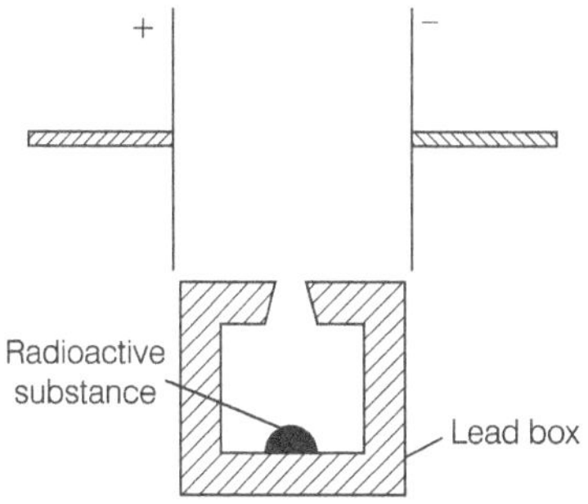

(i) Complete the diagram as given above by drawing the deflection of radioactive radiations in an electric field. **[2]**

(ii) State any two precautions to be taken while handling radioactive substances. **[2]**

Ans. (i)

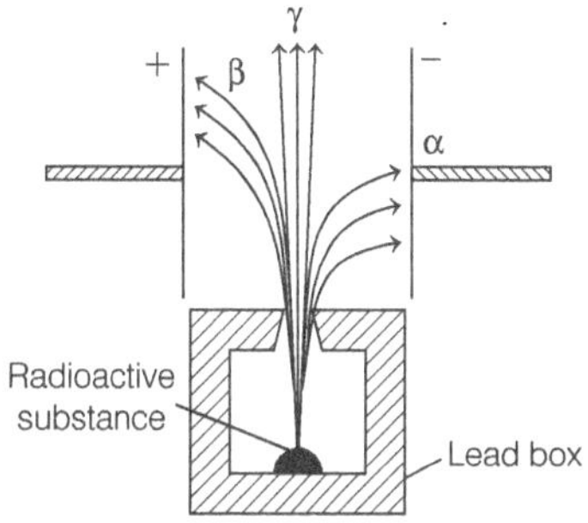

(ii) While handling the radioactive materials, following precautions must be taken

(a) Radioactive substances must be kept in a thick lead box.

(b) One should wear special protective lead coats and lead gloves while handling a radioactive substance.

Q.6 A process called nuclear fusion takes place in the Sun.

(i) Discuss the process of nuclear fusion taking place in the Sun. **[2]**

(ii) On Earth, solar panels and solar cells are powered by energy from the Sun. Describe how this energy from the Sun travels to Earth. **[2]**

Ans. (i) A nuclear reaction in which two light nuclei combined together to form a heavier nucleus with the release of enormous amount of energy is called the nuclear fusion. Most of the matter in the sun is in the form of hydrogen. In the core of the sun, the temperature and the pressure are so high that nuclear fusion occurs that converts its abundant hydrogen into helium releasing a tremendous amount of energy in the form of thermal energy.

(ii) The energy from the sun travels through the vacuum (space) in the form of electromagnetic radiation and reaches the earth.

TYPE - 7

04 Marks

Case Based Questions

Q.1 A researcher in a laboratory is conducting experiments with different radioactive isotopes. The lab contains samples emitting alpha, beta, and gamma radiation. To ensure the safety of the personnel and the lab environment, the researcher is using various detectors and shielding materials to study the properties of each type of radiation. The researcher observes the following during the experiments:

The alpha particles are emitted from a sample of radon gas. The beta particles are emitted from a sample of strontium-90. The gamma radiation is emitted from a sample of cobalt-60.

(i) What are the basic properties of alpha, beta, and gamma radiation. **[2]**

(ii) Why does a piece of paper block alpha radiation but not beta or gamma radiation? **[1]**

(iii) Why is plastic effective at blocking beta particles but not gamma radiation? **[1]**

Ans.(i) Properties of alpha, beta, and gamma radiation:

Alpha radiation Alpha particles consist of 2 protons and 2 neutrons. They have a low penetration power and can be blocked by a sheet of paper or the outer layer of skin. However, they can cause significant damage if inhaled or ingested.

Beta radiation Beta particles are high-energy electrons. They have a moderate penetration power and can pass through paper but are blocked by materials like plastic or a few millimetres of aluminium.

Gamma radiation Gamma rays are electromagnetic waves (high-energy photons) and have the highest penetration power. They require dense materials like lead or concrete to effectively shield them.

(ii) Alpha particles have low penetration power due to their larger mass and charge. The outer layer of skin or even a sheet of paper is enough to stop them. In the case of the experiment, paper is thick enough to absorb the alpha particles and prevent them from travelling further.

(iii) Beta particles are electrons, which are lighter and have more penetration power than alpha particles. Plastic, due to its density and thickness, is effective at stopping beta particles. However, gamma rays, being electromagnetic waves with high energy, pass through materials like plastic without significant attenuation.

Q.2 A scientist has discovered a new radioactive element $^{300}_{99}AB$, which emits three types of radiation: $^{6}_{3}\delta$, $^{0}_{2}\mu$ and $^{0}_{0}\gamma$. To study their characteristics, the scientist passed the radiation through strong electric and magnetic fields.

(i) Why is the element unstable? **[1]**

(ii) How do the radiations behave in a strong electric field? **[1]**

(iii) What will be the number of neutrons and protons present in the element? **[1]**

(iv) What happens when parent nucleus emit an $^{6}_{3}\delta$ particle? **[1]**

Ans. (i) The element is unstable because

number of neutrons >> number of protons

(ii) δ rays are deflected towards the negative plate because they are positively charged. μ rays are deflected towards the positive plate. And, γ rays remain undeflected as they are neutral.

(iii) Number of protons = 99

Mass number = 300

$\because$ Number of neutrons = $A - Z = 300 - 99 = 201$

(iv) After emitting a $^{6}_{3}\delta$ particle from parent nucleus

mass number = 300 − 6 = 294

and atomic number = 99 − 3 = 96

Q.3 One source of background radiation is cosmic rays. The cosmic rays that enter the Earth's atmosphere are known as primary cosmic rays. Most of these rays are fast-moving protons or fast-moving alpha-particles.

Both the Earth's magnetic field and the Earth's atmosphere reduce the number of primary cosmic rays that reach the Earth's surface.

(i) Name a source of background radiation apart from cosmic rays. **[1]**

(ii) State one effect of background radiation. **[1]**

(iii) State the number of protons and the number of neutrons in an alpha-particle. **[1]**

(iv) Explain how the Earth's atmosphere reduces the number of alpha- particles that reach the surface. **[1]**

Ans. (i) Active radioactive material in rocks in the earth crust.

(ii) This radiation causes cancer.

(iii) Number of protons = 2

Number of neutrons = 2

(iv) Alpha particles cannot penetrate the atmosphere as they cannot travel more than a few centimeters in air.

SAMPLE QUESTION PAPER
PHYSICS

General Instructions

Maximum Marks : 80

Time allowed : Two hours

Answers to this paper must be written on the paper provided separately.

You will **not** be allowed to write during the first **15** minutes.

This time is to be spent in reading the question paper.

The time given at the head of this paper is the time allowed for writing the answers.

Attempt **all five** questions.

The intended marks for questions or parts of questions are given brackets ().

You are advised to spend not more than 30 minutes in answering **Question 1** and 20 minutes in answering **Question 2**.

Section A

(Attempt all questions from this section) **[40 Marks]**

Question 1

Choose the correct answer to the questions from the given options **[15]**

(i) The radiation with maximum energy is

(a) γ-rays (b) β- rays (c) X-rays (d) α- ray

(ii) The $^{238}_{92}U$ isotope decays by α- emission and again further decays by β -emission. The final product is

(a) Pa (b) Ra (c) Sn (d) Th

(iii) If a swimmer inside water looks at an aeroplane in the sky, then which one of the following conditions is fulfilled?

(a) For the swimmer, the aeroplane will appear to be lower than it actually is.

(b) For the swimmer, the aeroplane will appear to be higher than it actually is.

(c) For the swimmer, the aeroplane will appear at its actual height

(d) For the pilot, the swimmer will appear to be at greater depth than it actually is.

(iv) Which of the following liquids is most suitable for radiators in cars?

(a) Liquid P with specific heat capacity 4000 J $kg^{-1}K^{-1}$.
(b) Liquid Q with specific heat capacity 2000 J $kg^{-1}K^{-1}$.
(c) Liquid R with specific heat capacity1500 J kg^{-1} K^{-1}
(d) Liquid S with specific heat capacity 2100 J $kg^{-1}K^{-1}$

(v) A boy P has a mass of 20 kg and is moving with a velocity of 5 ms^{-1}. Another boy Q has a mass of 5 kg and is moving with a velocity of 20 ms^{-1}. Calculate the ratio of the momentum of P and Q.

(a) 2 : 1 (b) 1 : 1 (c) 1 : 2 (d) 3 : 2

(vi) A radioactive nucleus is represented by $^{227}_{85}X$. It emits a β-particle and forms a different nucleus of element Y. Which of the following represents this new nucleus?

(a) $^{223}_{83}Y$ (b) $^{228}_{85}Y$ (c) $^{225}_{84}Y$ (d) $^{227}_{86}Y$

(vii) **Assertion (A)** The current is the rate of flow of charges.

Reason (R) Electric current will not flow between two charged bodies having same potential when connected.

(a) Both A and R are true and R is the correct explanation of A.
(b) Both A and R are true but R is not the correct explanation of A.
(c) Assertion is false but Reason is true.
(d) Assertion is true but Reason is false.

(viii) The diagram shows a coil wound around a U-shape soft iron bar AB. Which of the following statements is/are correct related to this.

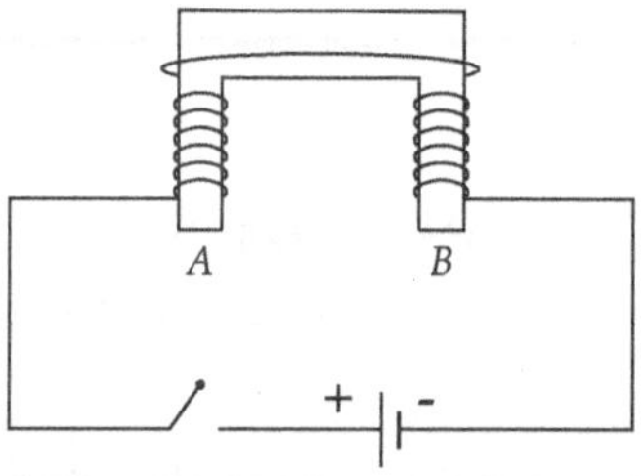

(a) Current enters at point A and leaves from point B.
(b) A will be south pole and B will be north pole.
(c) Increasing the number of turns of coils increases current
(d) All of the above

(ix) A body of mass m is accelerated with acceleration a. The kinetic energy in time t as it starts from rest is given by

(a) $\frac{mat}{2}$ (b) $\frac{m}{2}a^2t^2$ (c) mat^2 (d) $\frac{ma^2t}{2}$

(x) Which of the following wave has highest amplitude?

(a)
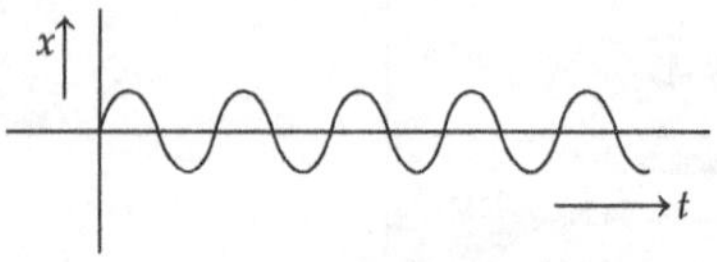

(b)

(c)
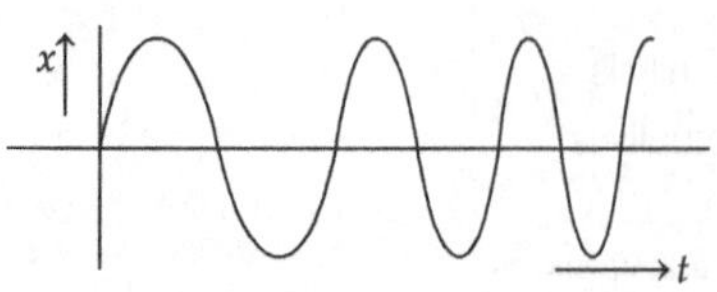

(d)
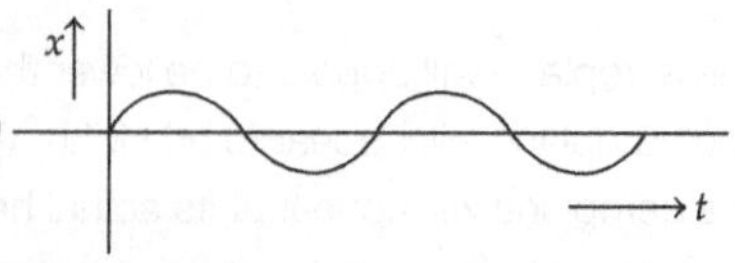

(xi) A battery of 10 V carries 20000 C of charge through a resistance of 20 Ω. The work done in 10s is

(a) 2×10^3 J
(b) 2×10^5 J
(c) 2×10^4 J
(d) 2×10^2 J

(xii) The diagram given below shows a ski jump, A skier weight 60 kg stands at *A*. He moves from *A* to *B* and takes off for his jump at *B*.

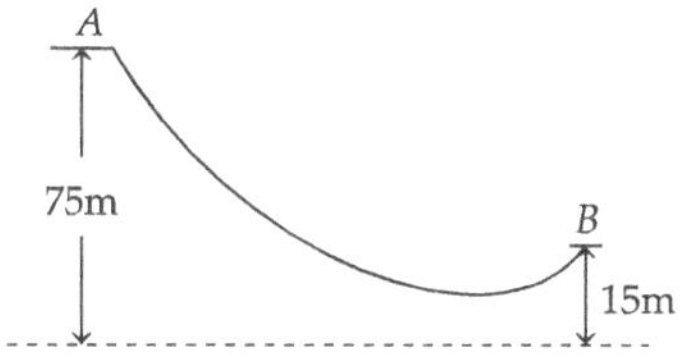

Change in potential energy of the skier between *A* and *B* is

(a) 2.6×10^4 J
(b) 3.6×10^4 J
(c) 4.6×10^4 J
(d) 5.6×10^4 J

(xiii) The temperature of 100 g of water is to be raised from 10°C to 40°C by adding steam at 100°C to it. The amount of steam required will be

[Take, latent heat of steam = 540 cal/g]

(a) 0.5 g
(b) 5g
(c) 10g
(d) 50g

(xiv) A double convex lens made of a material of refractive index μ_1, is placed inside two liquids of refractive indices μ_2 and μ_3 as shown, such that $\mu_2 > \mu_1 > \mu_3$. A wide and parallel beam of light is incident on the lens from the left. The lens will give rise to

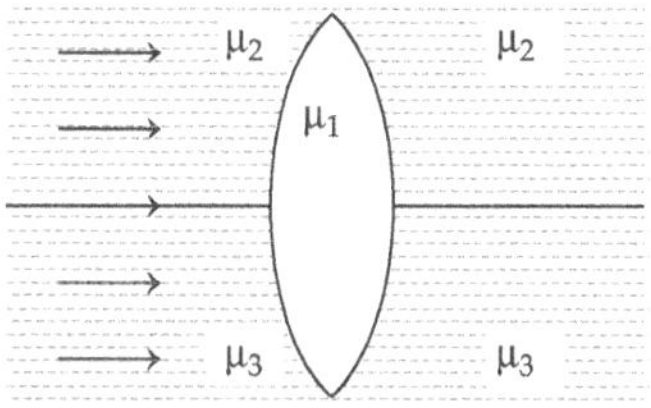

(a) a single convergent beam
(b) two different convergent beams
(c) two different divergent beams
(d) a convergent and a divergent beam

(xv) Figures given below show the shape of two different waves.

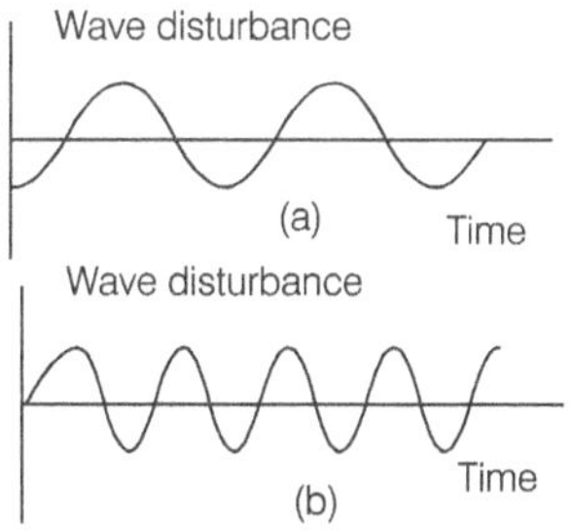

Figures (a) and (b) represent the

(a) low and high pitched sound respectively
(b) high and low pitched sound respectively
(c) only high pitched sound
(d) only low pitched sound

Question 2.

(i) Complete the following by choosing the correct answer from the bracket. **[6]**

(a) Speed of blue light in water is more than.........(green/orange/violet).

(b) Two sounds of same loudness and same pitch produced by two different instruments differ in ....(quality/intensity/frequency).

(c) In......... (bottle opener/ sugar tongs), load is situated between fulcrum and effort.

(d) A totally reflecting right angled isosceles prism can be used to deviate a ray of light through ...... (90°/30°/60°)

(e) In an electric bulb, the electrical energy is converted into......... (heat/chemical) energy and ....(kinetic/light) energy.

(ii) The nucleus *P* losses **[2]**

(a) one proton and

(b) one β -particle.

Write the symbol of the new nucleus in each case and express each change by a reaction.

(iii) The electrical resistivities of five substances *A*, *B*, *C*, *D* and *E* are given below. **[2]**

$A = 5.20 \times 10^{-8}\ \Omega$-m, $B = 110 \times 10^{-8}\ \Omega$-m, $C = 2.60 \times 10^{-8}\ \Omega$-m, $D = 10 \times 10^{-8}\ \Omega$-m and $E = 1.70 \times 10^{-8}\ \Omega$-m

(a) Which substance is the best conductor of electricity?

(b) Which two substances should be used for making electric wires?

Question 3.

(i) The figure below shows two parallel rays A (red) and B (violet) incidence from air, on air glass boundary. **[2]**

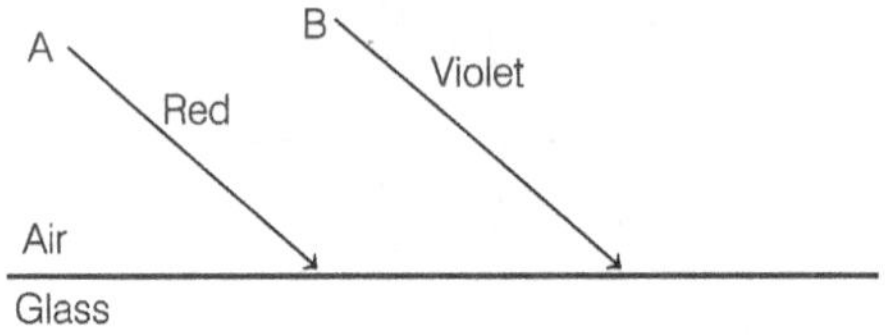

(a) How do the speeds of these rays differs in glass?

(b) Are the two refracted rays in glass parallel? (Give the reason)

(ii) Derive an expression for equivalent resistance in the following case **[2]**

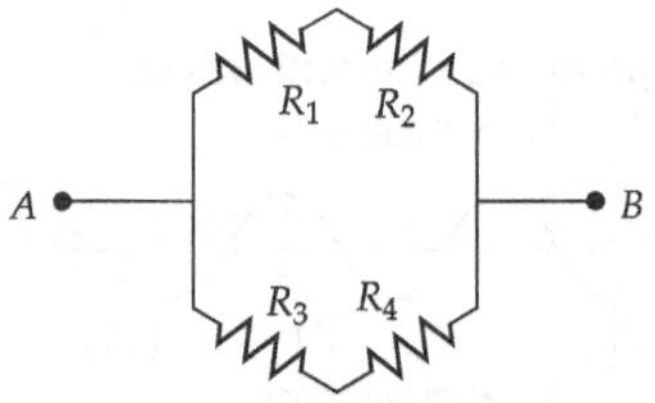

(iii) Copy the diagram given below and complete the path of the light ray till it emerges out of the prism. The critical angle of the glass is 42°. In your diagram, mark the angles wherever necessary. **[2]**

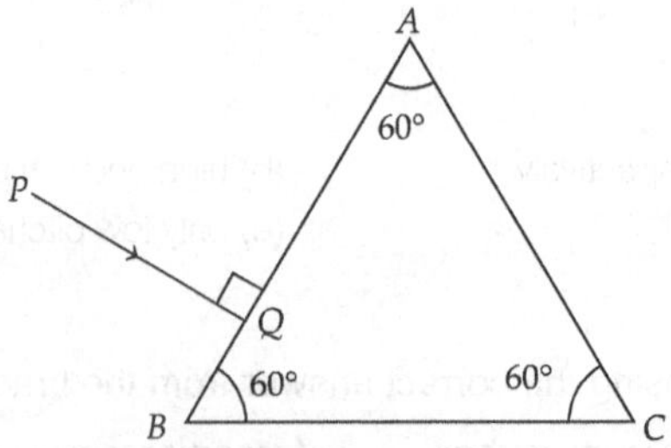

(iv) Three bulbs A, B and C are connected in parallel with a battery of 16 V and a switch, as shown in the figure below. Resistance of bulb A is twice of B but half of C. **[2]**

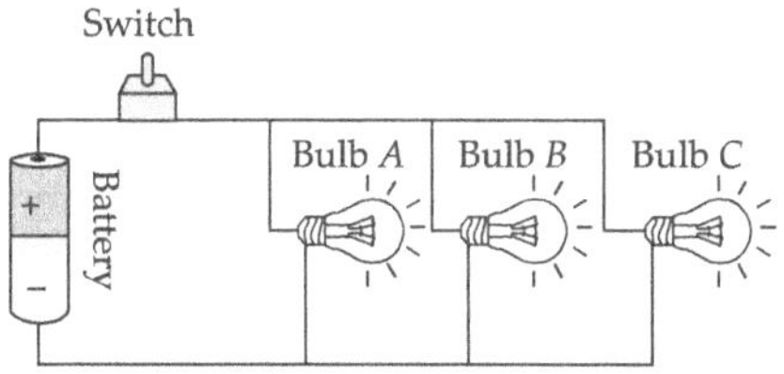

Which bulb will have more power in this arrangement? Justify your answer.

(v) A truck and a car are running with the same speed on a highway. If the ratio of their kinetic energies is 25 : 12, then what is the ratio of their masses? **[2]**

(vi) A lens forms an erect, magnified and virtual image of an object. Name the lens used and draw a labelled ray diagram to show the image formation. **[2]**

(vii) Uttam and Nitesh are standing at a distance of 12m and 20m respectively, from a cliff. They start shouting their names. They want to hear clear echo of their sounds.
[Take, velocity of sound in air = 340 m/s] **[3]**

(a) Will Nitesh and Uttam be able to hear a clear echo of their own sounds?

(b) Can you explain the condition for a sound to form an echo?

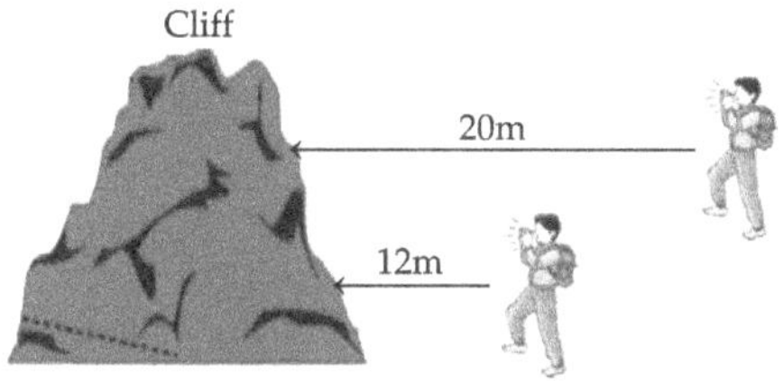

Section B

(Attempt any four questions from this section)

Question 4.

(i) Sachin and Anurag are performing an experiment to verify the principle of moments. Sachin took two pulleys and arranged as shown in diagram. Now, Anurag attached a weight w with pulley P_1.
(P_1 is movable pulley and P_2 is fixed pulley). **[3]**

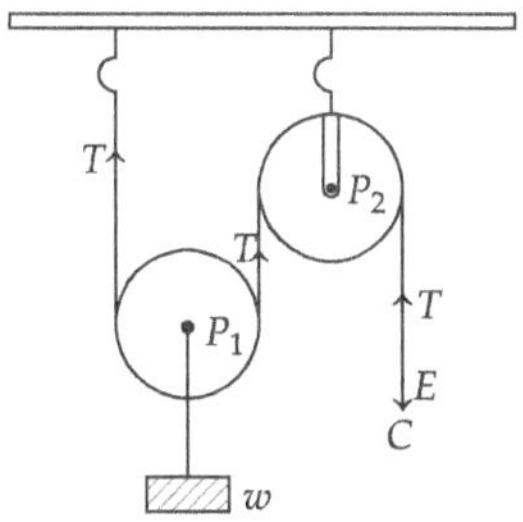

(a) If the free end C of the string moves through a distance x, by what distance is the load w raised?

(b) What effort E has to be applied at C to just raise the load $w = 20$ kgf? Neglect the weight of the pulley P_1 and the friction.

(ii) A 4 cm tall object is placed perpendicular to the principal axis of a convex lens of focal length 25 cm. The distance of the object from the lens is 40 cm.

By calculation, determine **[3]**

(a) the position and

(b) the size of the image formed.

(iii) (a) Two circular coils *P* and *Q* are kept close to each other, of which coil *P* carries a current. If coil *P* is move towards Q, will some current be induced in coil Q? Give reason for your answer and name the phenomenon involved. **[1]**

(b) What happens, if coil *P* is moved away from *Q*? **[1]**

(c) State few methods of inducing current in a coil. **[2]**

Question 5.

(i) A meter scale of weight 50 gf can be balanced at 40 cm mark without any weight suspended on it.

(a) If this ruler is cut at its centre, then state which part [0 to 50 cm or 50 to 100 cm] of the ruler will weigh more than 25 gf. **[1]**

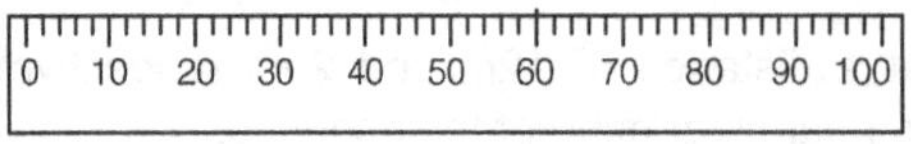

(b) What minimum weight placed on this meter ruler can balance this ruler when it is pivoted at its centre? **[2]**

(ii) (a) Water in lakes and ponds does not freeze at once in cold countries. Give a reason in support of your answer. **[2]**

(b) What is the principle of calorimetry? **[1]**

(iii) The refraction of a monochromatic ray through a prism as shown in the figure. **[4]**

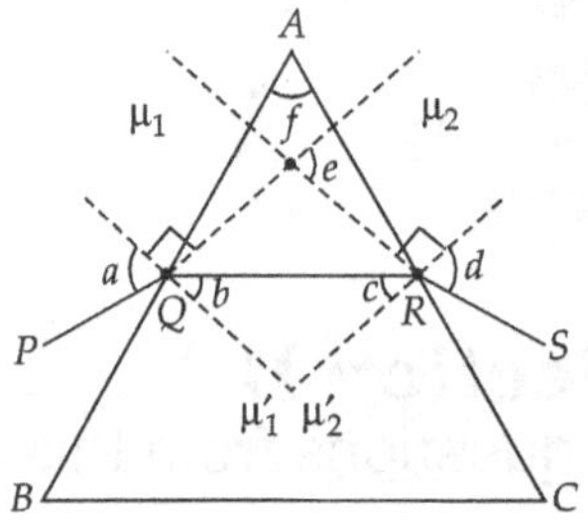

Complete the table using the labels from the figure. The first label is done for you

Description	Label
Angle of incidence	*a*
Angle of refraction	
Angle of emergence	
Angle of deviation	
Angle of prism	

Question 6.

(i)

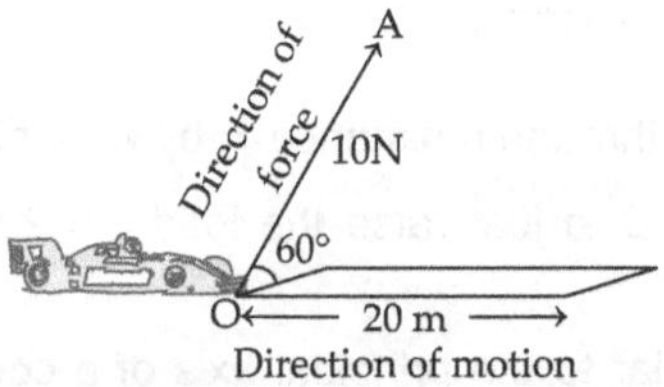

Monu pulls a toy car through a distance of 20 m on smooth and horizontal floor. The string held in Monu's hand makes an angle 60° with horizontal surface. If the force applied by Monu be 10 N,

(a) calculate the work done by the Monu in pulling the car. **[2]**

(b) If the string makes an angle 30° with the horizontal surface, then calculate the work done. **[1]**

(ii) (a) A thorium isotope $^{223}_{90}Th$ undergoes an α-decay and changes into radium. What is the atomic number and mass number of the radium produced? **[1]**

(b) If the radium undergoes a further disintegration and emits two β particles, represent this reaction in the form of an equation. **[1]**

(c) What is the source of energy released during the decay? **[1]**

(iii) Figure shows a steel ball placed at the periphery of a curved glass, in which a ball is released from point *A*.

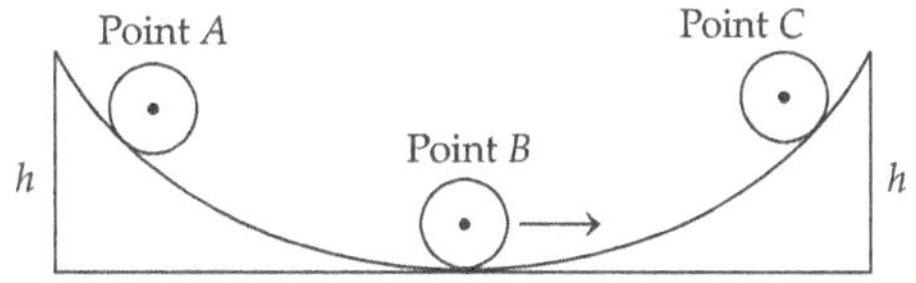

(a) Name the phenomenon involved in this. **[1]**

(b) At which point, kinetic energy will be maximum? **[1]**

(c) Explain with this example, how this phenomenon helps to understand energy conservation? **[2]**

Question 7.

(i) A girl puts her pencil into an empty trough and see the pencil from the position as given in the figure below.

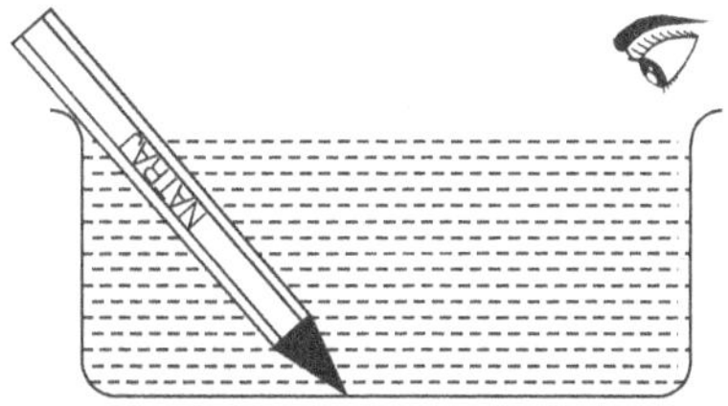

(a) What kind of variations will be noticed in the appearance of pencil when water is poured into the trough? **[2]**

(b) Mention the name of the phenomenon which accounts for the above stated observation. **[1]**

(ii) A virtual and diminished image is formed when an object is placed between the optical centre and the principal focus of a lens.

(a) Name the type of lens which forms the above image. **[1]**

(b) Draw a ray diagram to show the formation of the image with the above stated characteristics. **[2]**

(iii) Figure shows a uniform meter rule weighing 100 gf pivoted at its centre *O*. Two weights 200 gf and 350 gf are hanged from the meter rod as shown in the figure.

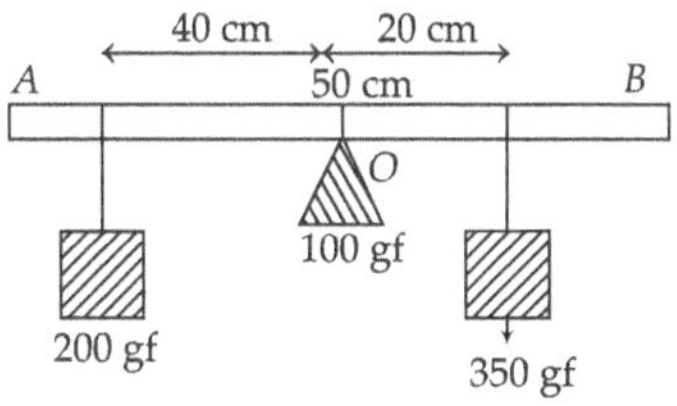

Calculate

(a) the total anti-clockwise moment about *O*. **[1]**

(b) the total clockwise moments about *O*. **[1]**

(c) the difference of anti-clockwise and clockwise moments about *O*. **[1]**

(d) the distance from *O*, where a 100 gf weight should be placed to balance the meter rule. **[1]**

Question 8.

(i) Shyam is trying to balance a meter rod on his finger as shown in the diagram. Two weights 50 gf and 200 gf are acting 40 cm and 95 cm respectively, and his finger is at 70 cm.

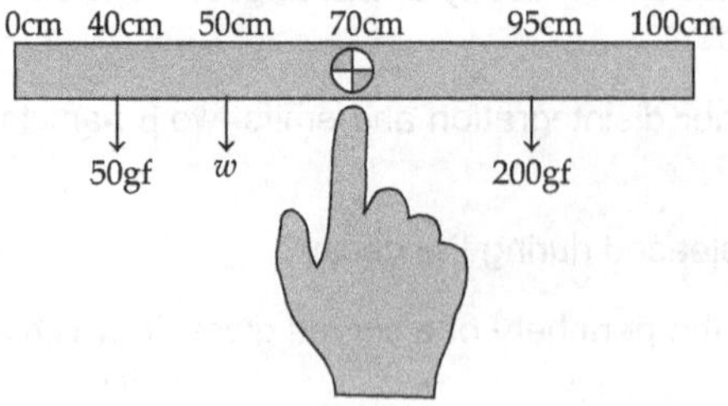

(a) Find the anti-clockwise moment and clockwise moment. [1]

(b) Find the weight of meter rod.

(ii) A student stands 330 m from a tall cliff which is 990 m from another tall cliff.

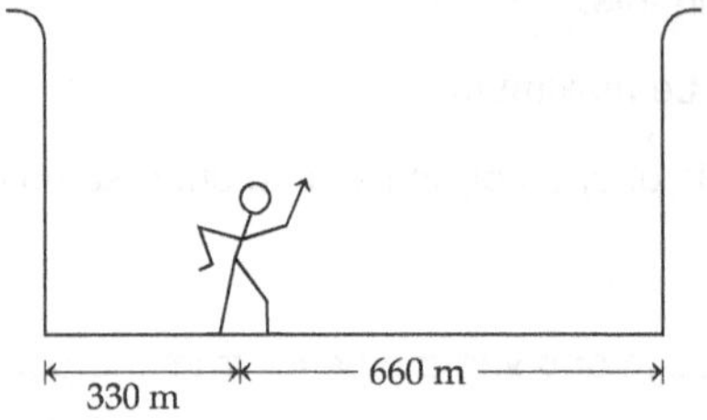

The student fires a pistol and hears some echoes. If the speed of sound between the cliffs is 330 m/s,

(a) what is the time taken by first echo to reach the student? [1]

(b) find the time interval between the first echo and the second echo. [2]

(iii) Sunita had to replace the electrical plug of her clothes iron. She bought a three-pin plug as shown below.

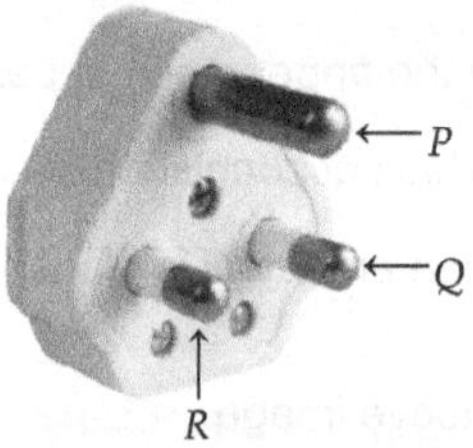

When she removed the old plug, she saw that there were three wires coloured red, black and green.

(a) To which pin on the plug should she connect the green wire? [1]

(b) To which part of the clothes iron is the green wire connected? [1]

(c) State the function of the green wire. [2]

Question 9.

(i) A nucleus $^{24}_{11}Na$ emits a β-particle to change into magnesium (Mg). [1]

(a) Write the symbolic equation for the process. [1]

(b) What are numbers 24 and 11 called? [1]

(c) What is the general name of $^{24}_{12}Mg$ with respect to $^{24}_{11}Na$?

(ii) The figures below show the displacement-time graph of two sound waves in air.

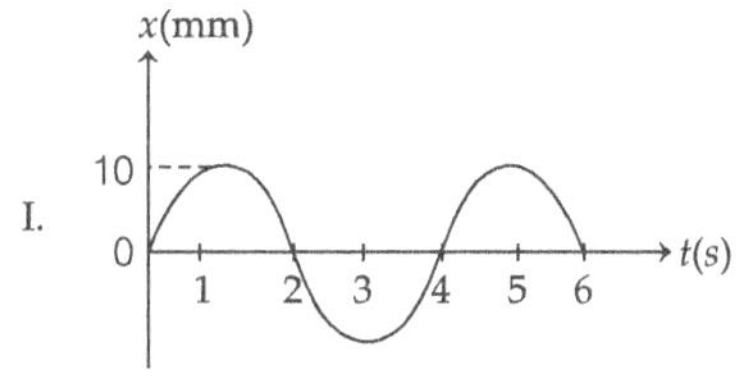

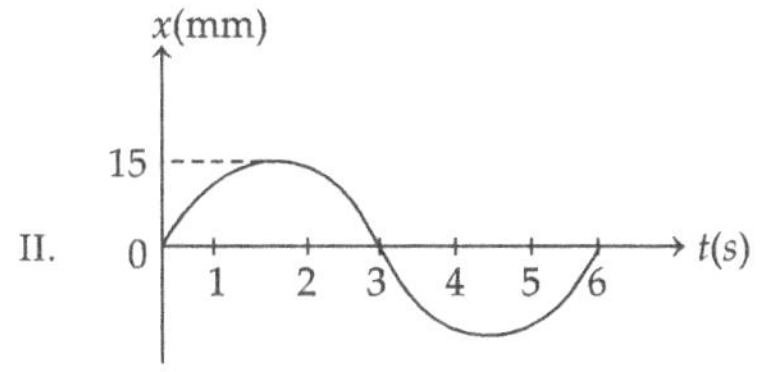

(a) Which wave will have greater loudness and why? **[2]**

(b) What is the ratio of frequency of (I) and (II)? **[1]**

(iii) *P* and *Q* represent two straight wires carrying equal current (*I*) in a direction perpendicular to the plane of the screen outwards. *K* is the mid-point of the line joining *P* and *Q*. The image shows the magnetic field lines around the wire. But the direction of the magnetic field is not marked.

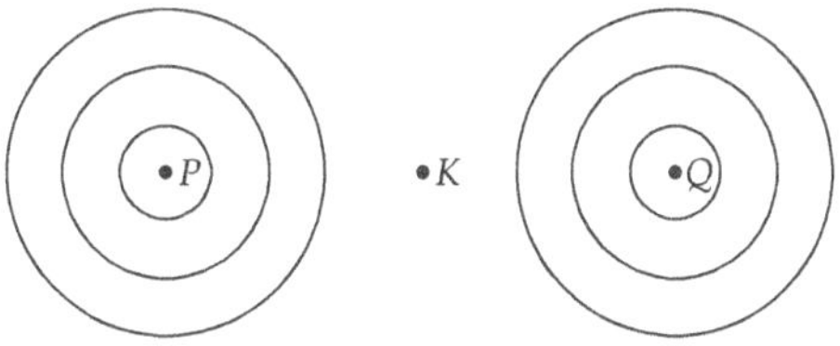

(a) Draw the above image and mark the direction of the magnetic field. **[1]**

(b) If the current in the wires is increased, how will the strength of the magnetic field around *P* and *Q* changes? Draw the magnetic field lines around *P* and *Q* to represent this change. **[1]**

(c) If B is the magnetic field at point *K* due to the current in wire *P*, what will be the magnetic field due to *P* and *Q* at the mid-point *K*? Give a reason for your answer. **[2]**

Answers

1.(i) (a) γ-rays have shortest wavelength or greatest frequency, hence it has maximum energy.

(ii) (a) The equation for α-emission is as follows

$$^{238}_{92}U \xrightarrow{-\alpha(^4_2He)} {}^{234}_{90}Th$$

The equation for β-emission is as follows

$$^{234}_{90}Th \xrightarrow{_{-1}\beta^0} {}^{234}_{91}Pa$$

(iii) (b) Water is a denser medium, so when light travels from water to air, i.e. denser to rarer, it will bend away from the normal, as a result of which aeroplane will appear to be higher than its actual position.

(iv) (a) More specific heat capacity means the liquid can absorb more heat before its temperature rises significantly, making it more effective for cooling the engine. So, liquid with high specific heat capacity is most suitable for radiations in cars.

(v) (b) For P, $m = 20$ kg, $v = 5$ m/s

For Q, $m = 5$ kg, $v = 20$ m/s

$$\frac{\text{Momentum of P}}{\text{Momentum of Q}} = \frac{20 \times 5}{5 \times 20} = \frac{1}{1}$$

(vi) (d) The process of decay can be written as

$$^{227}_{85}X \longrightarrow {}^{227}_{86}Y + {}^{0}_{-1}\beta$$

Therefore, the new nucleus formed will be $^{227}_{86}Y$.

(vii) (b) Electric current is the flow of electric charge and it flows from an area of higher potential to an area of lower potential.

When two charged bodies are at the same potential, it means they have an equal amount of charge and no potential difference between them.

In such a scenario, there is no driving force for charges to move from one body to the other, so no current will flow between them.

(viii) (d) current enters at point A and leaves from point B (anti-clockwise rotation). Hence, A will be south pole and B will be north pole.

Increasing the number of turns of coils increases current. Therefore, all options are correct.

(ix) (b) Given, the body starts from rest, i.e. $u = 0$

Now, velocity after time t, $v = u + at$

i.e. $v = at \quad (\because u = 0)$

Kinetic energy, $K = \frac{1}{2}mv^2 = \frac{1}{2}m(at)^2 = \frac{m}{2}a^2t^2$

(x) (c) Wave given in option (c) has highest amplitude as displacement (x) is higher in the wave.

(xi) (b) Workdone (W) = Charge × Potential difference = $20000 \times 10 = 2 \times 10^5$ J

(xii) (b) Given, mass of skier (m) = 60 kg

Loss in potential energy = $mg(h_1 - h_2)$

$$= 60 \times 10 (75 - 15) = 3.6 \times 10^4 J$$

(xiii) (b) Let m be the mass of steam,

Specific heat of water = 1 cal/g-°C

According to principle of calorimetry,

$$\text{Heat gain} = \text{Heat loss}$$

i.e. $100 \times 1 \times (40 - 10) = m \times 540 + m \times 1 \times (100 - 40)$

$$\Rightarrow \quad 3000 = 600\,m \Rightarrow m = 5 \text{ g}$$

Thus, 5 g steam is required to raise the temperature of 100 g water from 10°C to 40°C.

(xiv) (d) For $\mu_2 > \mu_1$

When the ray goes from denser medium to rarer medium, it bends away from the normal.

Therefore, the upper part of the lens will become diverging.

For $\mu_1 > \mu_3$

When the ray goes from rarer medium to denser medium, it bends towards the normal. Therefore, the lower half of the lens will become converging.

Hence, convergent and divergent beams are produced by lens.

(xv) (a) The faster the vibration of the source, the higher is the frequency and hence higher is the pitch.

The lower the vibration of the sound, the lower is the frequency and hence lower is the pitch.

Therefore, figures (a) and (b) represent the low and high pitched sound respectively.

2. (a) violet

(b) quality

(c) bottle opener

(d) 90°

(e) heat, light

(ii) (a) After the loss of proton, the mass number and atomic number of the nucleus $^{16}_{8}P$ will decrease by 1. The new nucleus will be $^{15}_{7}Q$ (say).

The nucleus $^{16}_{8}P$ changes to $^{15}_{7}Q$ (say) as follows

$$^{16}_{8}P \longrightarrow {}^{15}_{7}Q + {}^{1}_{1}p$$

(b) After the loss of one β-particle, the mass number will remain the same but the atomic number will increase by 1.

The nucleus ${}^{16}_{8}P$ change to ${}^{16}_{9}R$ (say) as follow

$${}^{16}_{8}P \longrightarrow {}^{16}_{9}R + {}_{-1}e^{0}$$

(iii) (a) E is the best conductor of electricity because of its least electrical resistivity.

(b) C and E should be used for making electric wires due to their low electrical resistivities.

3.(i) (a) The complete ray diagram is shown as below.

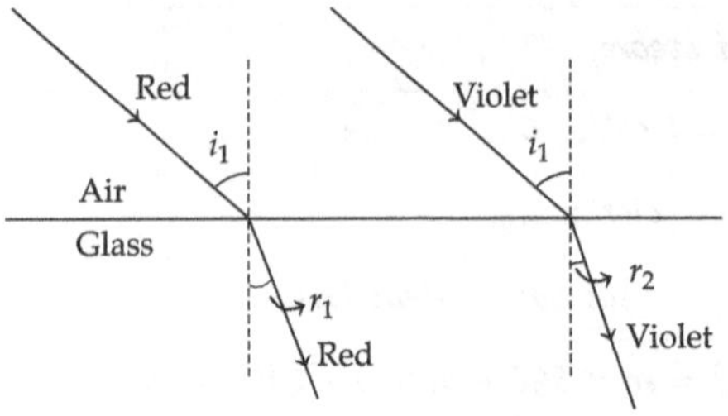

The two refracted rays inside the glass are not parallel because the refractive index of glass is less for red light while it is more for violet light. So, the red light (ray) is deviated less than violet ray, i.e. the angle of refraction for red ray is more than the angle of refraction r_2 for violet ray.

Since, $\mu_R < \mu_V$, so in the glass the red light travels faster than the violet light. Because refractive index is inversely proportional to the speed of light ray in a medium.

(b) No, the two refracted rays are not parallel to each other as their speeds vary in the glass. As red light with more speed bends less while violet light with slow speed bends more.

(ii) R_1 and R_2 are in series, thus for this combination, $R' = R_1 + R_2$

Similarly, R_3 and R_4 are in series.

So, $R'' = R_3 + R_4$

$\because$ R' and R'' are in parallel.

So, $$R''' = \frac{R'R''}{R' + R''} = \frac{(R_1 + R_2)(R_3 + R_4)}{R_1 + R_2 + R_3 + R_4}$$

(iii) The ray diagram is given below.

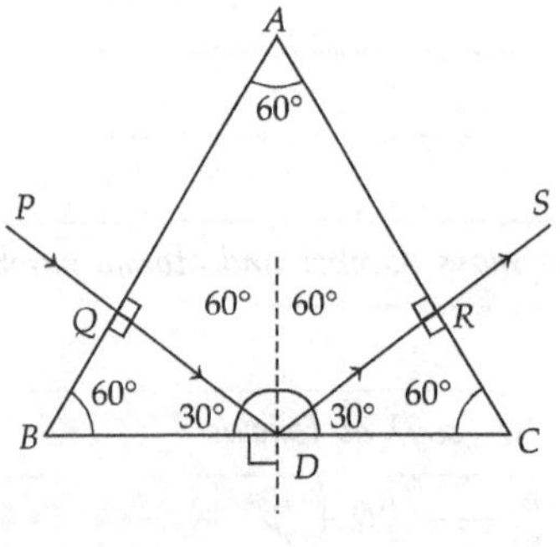

(iv) All bulbs are connected in parallel connections in this arrangement, so the potential of bulbs A, B and C will be same.

The power of bulb is given by

$$P = \frac{V^2}{R}$$

Since, the bulb B has lower resistance, so bulb B will have the highest power in this arrangement.

(v) The kinetic energy of a body,

$$KE = \frac{1}{2}mv^2 \Rightarrow m = \frac{2\,KE}{v^2}$$

Ratio of masses of truck and car is

$$\Rightarrow \quad \frac{m_1}{m_2} = \frac{2KE_1}{v^2} \times \frac{v^2}{2\,KE_2} = \frac{KE_1}{KE_2} = \frac{25}{12}$$

or $m_1 : m_2 = 25 : 12$

(vi) A convex lens forms this type of image of an object.

The ray diagram showing the formation of image is shown below.

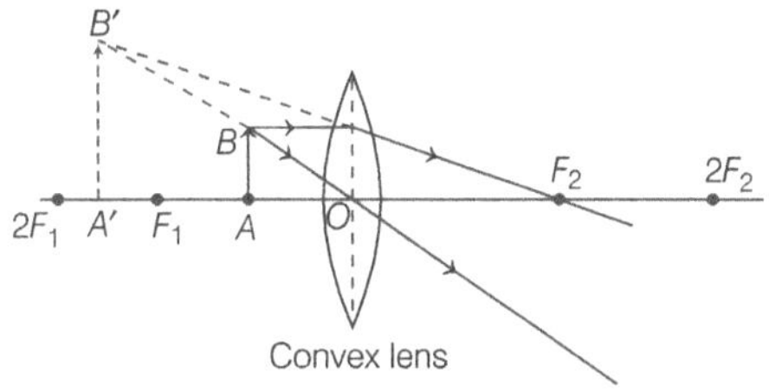

In this case, object is between optical centre O and focus F_1 of lens.

(vii) (a) We know that, we can hear two sounds separately, if the time gap between the two sounds is more than 0.1 s.

Now, check whether Uttam will hear his sound or not.

The time taken to hear the echo for Uttam,

$$t = \frac{2d}{v}$$

Here, $d = 12$ m, $v = 340$ m/s

$$\therefore \quad t = \frac{2 \times 12}{340} = 0.07 \text{ s}$$

Here, clearly observe that $0.07 \text{ s} < 0.1 \text{ s}$.

Therefore, Uttam will not be able to hear his clear echo.

Now, check whether Nitesh will hear his sound or not.

$$\therefore \quad t = \frac{2d}{v} = \frac{2 \times 20}{340} = 0.117 \text{ s}$$

Here, $0.117 \text{ s} > 0.1 \text{ s}$

Hence, Nitesh will be able to hear his clear echo.

(b) An echo is heard only if the distance between the person producing the sound and the rigid obstacle is long enough to allow the reflected sound to reach the person atleast 0.1 second after the original sound is heard.

4.(i) (a) If the free end C of the string moves through a distance x, the load w will rise by a distance $\frac{x}{2}$.

(b) Given, load, w = 20 kgf, E = ?

In equilibrium, w = 2 T and E = T

$\therefore$ Effort needed, $E = \frac{w}{2} = \frac{20}{2} = 10$ kgf

(ii) Given, height of object, $h_o = 4$ cm

Focal length of lens, f = 25 cm

Distance of object, u = − 40 cm

(a) Using lens formula, $\frac{1}{f} = \frac{1}{v} - \frac{1}{u} \Rightarrow \frac{1}{v} = \frac{1}{f} + \frac{1}{u} = \frac{1}{25} + \frac{1}{(-40)}$

$$\frac{1}{v} = \frac{8-5}{200} = \frac{3}{200}$$

$$v = \frac{200}{3} = 66.67 \text{ cm}$$

(b) $\therefore$ Magnification, $m = \frac{h_i}{h_o} = \frac{v}{u} \Rightarrow h_i = \frac{v}{u} \times h_o = \frac{66.67}{-40} \times 4 = -6.67$ cm

(iii) (a) When coil P is moved towards Q, current will be induced in coil Q. This is because on moving P, the magnetic field associated with Q increases and so a current is induced. The phenomenon is electromagnetic induction.

(b) If coil P is moved away from Q, the field associated with Q will decrease and a current will be induced but in the opposite direction.

(c) Some of the methods of inducing current in the coil are

I. moving a magnet towards or away from the coil.

II. moving a coil towards or away from a magnet.

III. rotating a coil within a magnetic field.

5.(i) (a) The part of the ruler that is cut from 0 to 50 cm has weight more than 25 gf.

(b)

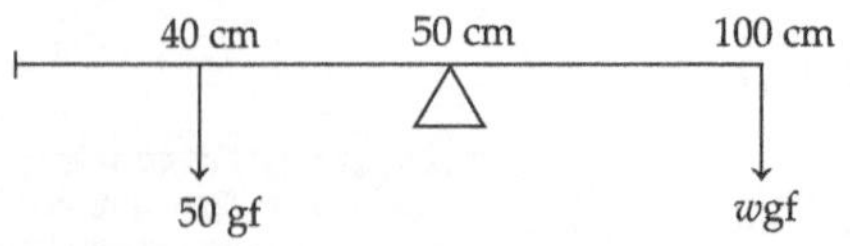

By principle of moments

$$50 \times 10 = w \times 50$$

$$\Rightarrow \quad w = 10 \text{ gf}$$

(ii) (a) The latent heat of fusion of ice is very high because of this a large amount of heat needs to be withdrawn for water in lakes and ponds to freeze. Hence, water in lakes and ponds does not freeze at once in cold countries.

(b) The principle of calorimetry states that when two or more bodies at different temperatures are brought into thermal contact and if no heat is allowed to escape to the surroundings, then the total heat lost by hot bodies must be equal to the total heat gained by cold bodies.

(iii)

Description	Label
Angle of incidence	a
Angle of refraction	b
Angle of emergence	d
Angle of deviation	e
Angle of prism	f

6.(i) (a) We know that, workdone when a body moves at an angle to the direction of force is, $W = Fs \cos\theta$

Here, $F = 10$ N, $\theta = 60°$, distance, $s = 20$ m

Now, $W = 10 \times 20 \times \cos 60° = 10 \times 20 \times 0.5 = 100$ J

(b) $W = Fs \cos\theta$

Here, $F = 10$ N, $\theta = 30°$, distance, $s = 20$ m

Now, $W = 10 \times 20 \times \cos 30°$

$$= 10 \times 20 \times \frac{\sqrt{3}}{2} = 200 \times \frac{\sqrt{3}}{2}$$

$$W = 100\sqrt{3} \text{ J}$$

(ii) (a) The atomic number is $90 - 2 = 88$ and the mass number is $223 - 4 = 219$.

(b) The required scheme of decay is as below.

$${}^{219}_{88}Ra \rightarrow {}^{219}_{90}Th + 2\,{}^{0}_{-1}e$$

(c) The difference in the mass of the reactants and the products is converted into energy according to Einstein's mass energy relation $E = mc^2$.

(iii) (a) Conservation of energy

(b) At point B, the kinetic energy of ball will be maximum.

(c) When a ball of mass m is released from point A, its energy is mgh. When the ball reaches at its bottom B, its energy is entirely kinetic.

As it moves towards C, its KE goes on decreasing and at C, its energy is entirely potential which is equal to mgh.

7.(i) (a) When water is poured into the trough, the appearance of the pencil will change. The pencil will appear bent or broken at the water surface.

(b) The phenomenon responsible for the above observation is known as refraction of light.

(ii) (a) Concave lens.

(b) Ray diagram

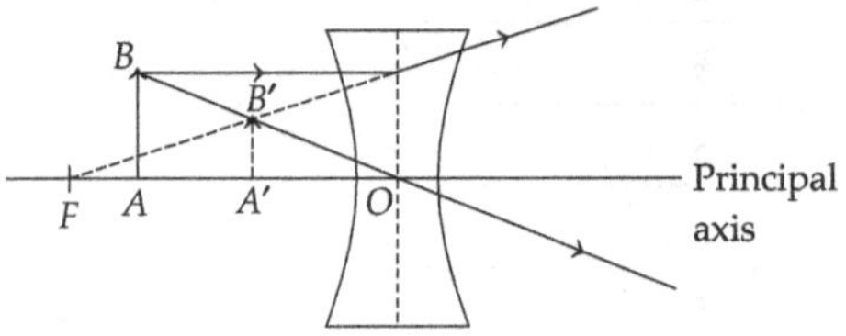

Concave lens

where, F = principal focus

and O = optical centre of lens.

(iii) According to the figure given in question, we get

(a) The moment of the weight of 200 gf $= 200 \times 40 = 8000$ gf-cm

(b) The moment of the weight of 350 gf $= 350 \times 20 = 7000$ gf-cm

(c) The difference of moments $= 8000 - 7000 = 1000$ gf-cm

(d) $200gf \times 40cm = 350gf \times 20cm + 100gf \times d$

$8000gf-cm = 7000gf-cm + 100gf \times d$

$1000 = 100d$

$d = 10$ cm on the right side of O.

$\therefore$ 100 gf should be placed 10 cm to right of O.

8. (i) (a) Let w be the weight of rod (for a uniform meter rod, its weight acts at 50 cm)

Clockwise moments $= [200 \times (95 - 70)]$

$= 200 \times 25 = 5000$ N-m

Anti-clockwise moments $= [50 \times (70 - 40)] + [w \times (70 - 50)]$

$= [50 \times 30] + [w \times 20]$

$= [1500 + 20w]$ N-m

(b) According to the principle of moment, when = rod is in equilibrium,

Anti-clockwise moment = Clockwise moment

$$1500 + 20w = 5000$$

$$\Rightarrow \quad 20w = 3500$$

$$\Rightarrow \quad w = 175 \text{ N}$$

(ii) (a) Time taken by first echo to reach student,

$$t_1 = \frac{\text{Distance}}{\text{Speed}} = \frac{2 \times 330}{330} = 2s$$

(b) Time for second echo to reach student,

$$t_2 = \frac{\text{Distance}}{\text{Speed}} = \frac{2 \times 660}{330} = 4s$$

$\therefore$ Time interval $= (t_2 - t_1)$

$= (4 - 2) = 2$ s

(iii) (a) Sunita should connect the green wire to the pin marked as P typically the pin with the longer leg.

(b) The green wire is connected to the metal carrying of the clothes iron.

(c) Green wire saves us from the electrical shocks.

9. (i) (a) The symbolic equation of this process is

$${}^{24}_{11}Na \longrightarrow {}^{24}_{12}Mg + {}_{-1}e^0$$

(b) 24 is the mass number and 11 is the atomic number.

(c) ${}^{24}_{11}Na$ and ${}^{24}_{12}Mg$ are isobars.

(ii) (a) The sound wave (II) has a larger amplitude = 15 mm

than the wave (I) (= 10 mm), therefore sound (II) will be louder than the (I) as loudness is

directly proportional to square of amplitude.

(b) Frequency of sound wave is given by, $f = \frac{v}{\lambda}$

where, v = velocity of sound wave.

As both the waves are travelling through the same medium, i.e. air, so both will have same velocity, i.e $v_a = v_b$

$$\therefore \quad \frac{f_1}{f_2} = \frac{\lambda_2}{\lambda_1} = \frac{6}{4} = \frac{3}{2}$$

(iii) (a) The direction can be found out using right hand thumb rule.

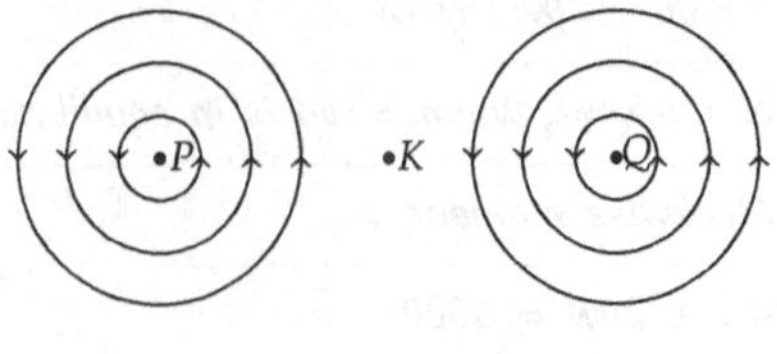

(b) If the current in the wires is increased, the strength of the magnetic field around P and Q will also increase.

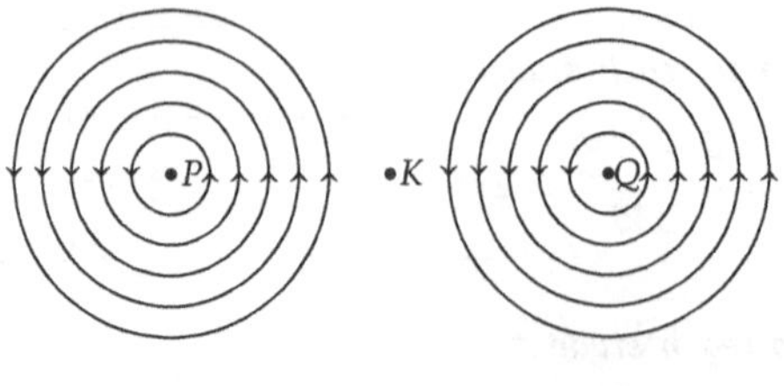

(c) The magnetic field at point K due to current in the wire P and Q are equal in magnitude but opposite in direction.

Therefore, these fields cancel each other and magnetic field due to P and Q at K is zero.

LATEST ICSE SPECIMEN PAPER
FULLY SOLVED
(PHYSICS)

General Instructions

Maximum Marks : 80

Time allowed : Two hours

Answer to this paper must be written on the paper provided separately.

You will not be allowed to write during first 15 minutes. This time is to be spent in reading the question paper.

The time given at the head of this paper is the time allowed for writing the answers.

Section A is compulsory. Attempt any four questions from Section B.

The intended marks for questions or parts of questions are given in brackets [].

Section-A

[40 Marks]

(Attempt all questions from this section)

Question 1

Choose the correct answers to the questions from the given options. **[15]**

(i) A moment of couple has a tendency to rotate the body in an anti-clockwise direction. Then, the moment of couple is taken as *Recall*

(a) positive
(b) negative
(c) maximum
(d) zero

(ii) The kinetic energy of a given body depends on the *Understanding*

(a) position
(b) centre of gravity of the body
(c) momentum
(d) displacement

(iii) For burning of coal in a thermoelectric station, the energy conversion taking place is *Recall*

(a) chemical to heat to mechanical
(b) chemical to heat to mechanical to electrical
(c) chemical to heat to light
(d) heat to chemical to mechanical

(*iv*) The adjacent diagram shows the movable block of a block and tackle system with effort in a convenient direction. From the diagram, we can conclude that the number of pulleys used in the fixed block are......... *Analysis & Application*

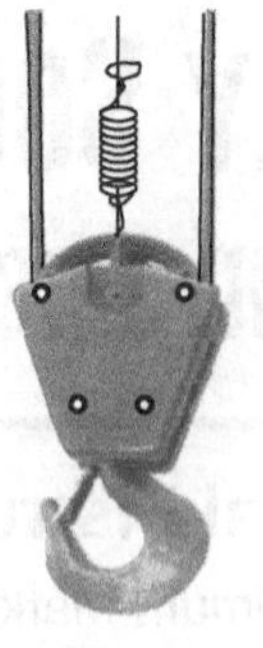

(a) 1 (b) 3 (c) 2 (d) 4

(v) White light is dispersed by a prism. Inside the prism, compared to the blue light, the red light *Analysis & Application*

(a) slows down less and refracts more
(b) slows down more and refracts less
(c) slows down more and refracts more
(d) slows down less and refracts less

(vi) An endoscope uses optic fiber to transmit high resolution images of internal organs without loss of information. The principle of light that is used by the optic fiber is based on *Recall*

(a) refraction
(b) reflection
(c) scattering
(d) total internal reflection

(vii) A convex lens has focal length 12 cm with an object at a distance of 20 cm in front of the lens. He obtains a blurred image on the screen placed at a distance of 23 cm in front of the lens. In order to obtain the clear image, he has to move the screen *Application*

(a) towards the lens
(b) away from the lens
(c) to a position very far away from the lens
(d) either towards or away from the lens

(viii) **Assertion** (A) Infrared radiations travel long distances through a dense fog and mist.

Reason (R) Infrared radiations undergo minimal scattering in the earth's atmosphere. *Understanding & Recall*

(a) Both A and R are true and R is the correct explanation of A.
(b) Both A and R are true and R is not the correct explanation of A.
(c) A is false but R is true.
(d) A is true but R is false.

(ix) Two sound waves *X* and *Y* have the same amplitude and the same wave pattern but their frequencies are 60 Hz and 120 Hz respectively, then *Understanding*

(a) *X* will be shriller and *Y* will be grave
(b) *X* will be grave and *Y* will be shriller
(c) *X* will differ in quality than *Y*
(d) *X* is louder than *Y*

(x) The graph of voltage *versus* current for four different materials is shown below.

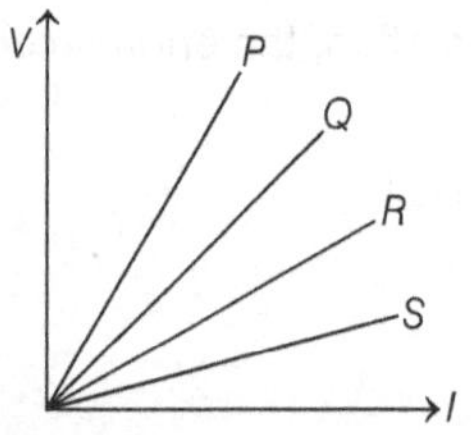

Which of these four materials would be used for making filament of a bulb? *Understanding & Recall*

(a) *Q* (b) *S* (c) *P* (d) *R*

(xi) According to the old convention, the colour of the earth wire is *Recall*

(a) black (b) green (c) yellow (d) red

(xii) Current is flowing through a coil as shown in the figure. Which one of the given figures will correctly depict the magnetic polarity and the direction of the lines of force along the axis of the coil. *Application*

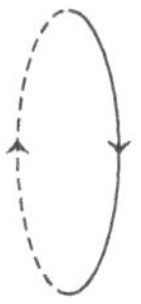

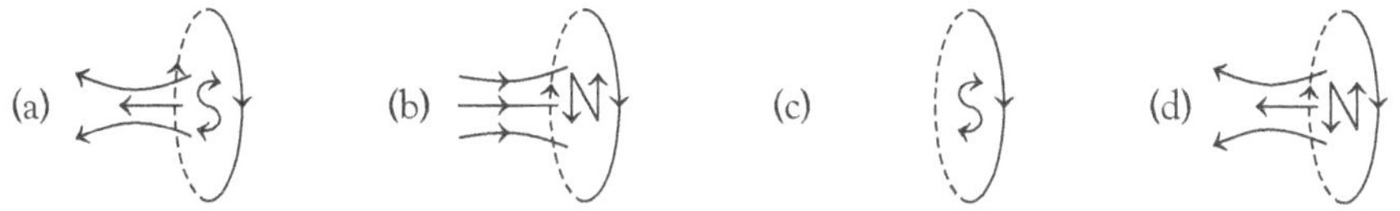

(xiii) Heat capacity of a body is the *Recall*

(a) energy needed to melt a body without change in its temperature.
(b) energy needed to raise the temperature of a body by 1°C.
(c) increase in volume of the body when its temperature increases by 1°C.
(d) total amount of internal energy that is constant.

(xiv) The amount of heat energy required to melt a given mass of a substance at its melting point without any rise in its temperature is called as the *Recall*

(a) specific heat capacity (b) specific latent heat of fusion
(c) latent heat of fusion (d) specific latent heat of freezing

(xv) A nucleus of an atom consists of 146 neutrons and 95 protons. It decays after emitting an alpha particle. How many protons and neutrons are left in the nucleus after an alpha emission? *Understanding*

(a) Protons = 93, neutrons = 142 (b) Protons = 95, neutrons = 144
(c) Protons = 93, neutrons = 144 (d) Protons = 95, neutrons = 42

Question 2

(i) Complete the following by choosing the correct answers from the bracket. **[6]**

(a) A .... [class I/class II/class III] lever will always have $MA > 1$.
(b) In a block and tackle system, increase in the weight of the movable block .... [decreases/does not affect/ increases] the efficiency of the pulley system.
(c) If the mass as well as the velocity of a body is doubled, then the kinetic energy of the body .... [is doubled/ becomes eight times/becomes four times] the initial kinetic energy.
(d) Unit of power used in mechanical engineering is .... [watt/horse power/erg per second].
(e) Two copper wires can have the different .... [resistivity/resistance] but will have same .... [resistance / resistivity]. *Recall & Understanding*

(ii) Draw a graph of potential energy *versus* height for a body thrown vertically upwards. [Assume no friction is present]. *Understanding* **[2]**

(iii) (a) Name the waves used for echo depth sounding.
(b) Give one reason for their use in the above purpose. *Recall* **[2]**

Question 3

(i) (a) Refer to the diagram given below. A lens with two different refractive indices is shown. If the rays are coming from a distant object, then how many images will be seen ? *Understanding*

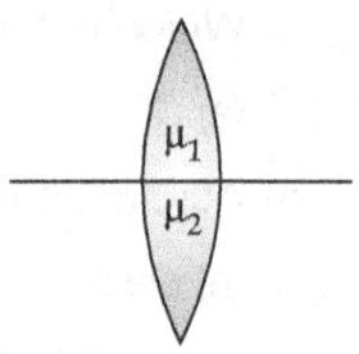

(b) A glass lens always forms a virtual, erect and diminished image of an object kept in front of it. Identify the lens. *Recall* **[2]**

(ii) If live wire makes an accidental contact with the metal case, which circuit (*A* or B) in the diagram, illustrating an electric iron, is considered to be safe for the user (assuming the fuse is present in the live wire in both circuits)? Justify your answer. **[2]**

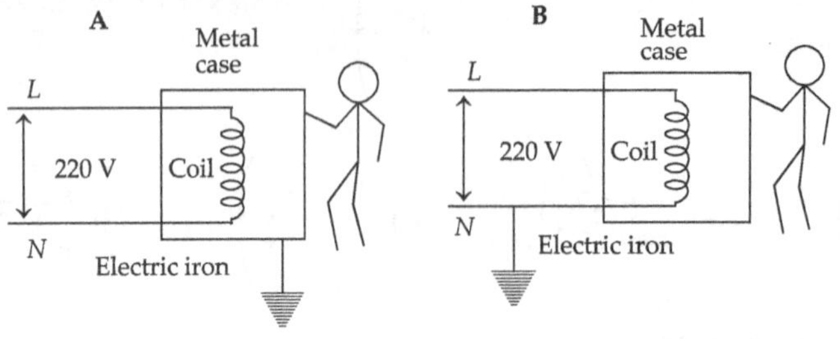

Application

(iii) A transformer is used to change a high alternating emf to a low alternating emf of the same frequency.

(a) Identify the type of transformer used for the above purpose. *Understanding*

(b) State whether the turns ratio of the above transformer is = 1or > 1or < 1. *Recall* **[2]**

(iv) A solid of mass 60 g at 100°C is placed in 150 g of water at 20°C. The final steady temperature is 25°C. Calculate the heat capacity of solid. [Specific heat capacity of water = 4.2 $Jg^{-1}K^{-1}$]

Understanding & Evaluate **[2]**

(v) (a) Name the principle of AC generator.

(b) State its one use. *Recall* **[2]**

(vi) (a) Name the radiations that are emitted during the decay of a nucleus, which have the highest penetrating power? *Recall*

(b) Does the emission of the above-mentioned radiation result in a change in the mass number?

Understanding [2]

(vii) The graph (Fig. A) illustrates the correlation between the number of protons (*X*-axis) and the number of neutrons (*Y*-axis) for elements *A*, *B*, *C*, *D* and *E* in the periodic table. These elements are denoted by the letters rather than their conventional symbols. When the element *C*, depicted in the graph, undergoes radioactive decay, it releases radioactive rays. When these rays are directed into the plane of the paper in the presence of a magnetic field, as indicated in the (Fig. B), they experience deflection, causing them to move upwards.

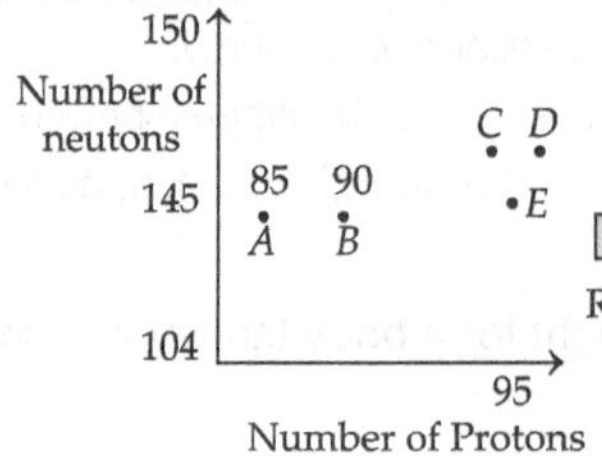

Fig. A

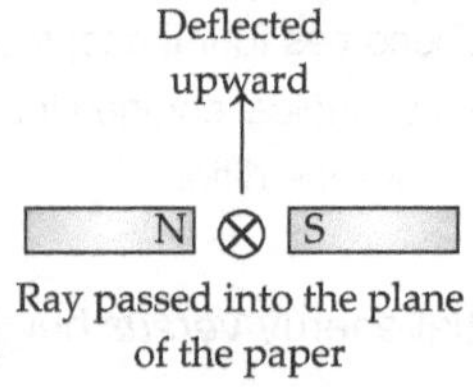

Fig. B

(a) Name the radioactive radiations emitted by the element *C*.
(b) Identify the daughter element from the graph.
(c) Name the law used to identify the radioactive radiations emitted by the element. *Application* **[3]**

Section-B

(Attempt any four questions from this section)

Queston 4

(i) The diagram given below shows a fish in the tank and its image is seen on the surface of water. **[3]**

(a) Name the phenomenon responsible for the formation of this image. *Understanding & Recall*

(b) A double convex lens with refractive index μ_1 inside two liquids of refractive indices μ_2 and μ_3 are shown in the diagrams below. The refractive indices are such that $\mu_2 > \mu_1$ and $\mu_1 > \mu_3$.

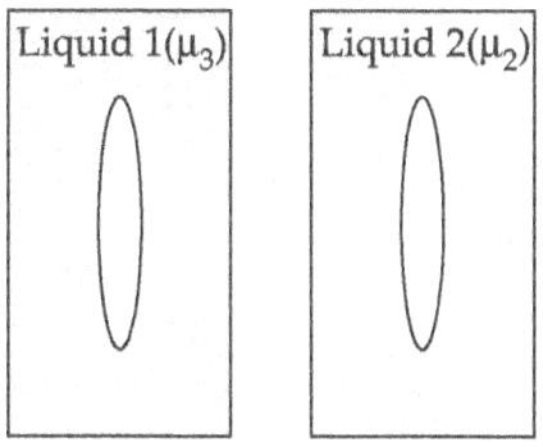

Fig. A Fig. B

How would a parallel incident beam of light refract when it comes out of the lens in each of the cases shown above? *Application*

1. In Fig. A. 2. In Fig. B.

(ii) The refractive index of water is 1.33 at a certain temperature. When the temperature of water is increased by 40 °C, the refractive index changes to x. **[3]**

(a) State whether $x < 1.33$ or $x > 1.33$. *Understanding*

(b) State two differences between normal reflection and total internal reflection. *Recall*

(iii) (a) Mixture of red+blue+green colours is passed through a convex lens as shown in the diagram below. State whether the ray passes through a single point or through different points on the principal axis after refraction. *Understanding*

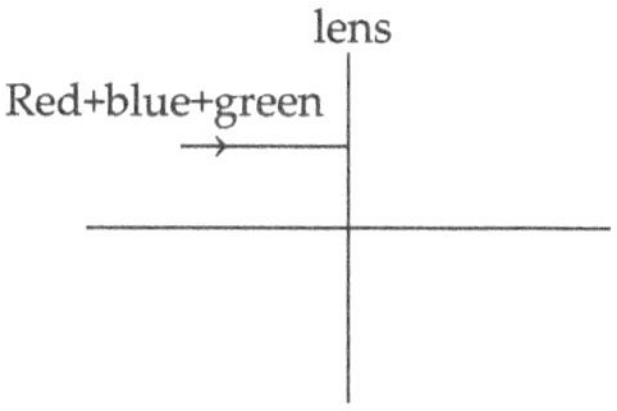

(b) Name the invisible radiations which are studied using the quartz prism. *Recall*

(c) State one use of these radiations. *Recall*

(d) Name one radiation having the wavelength longer than the wavelength of these radiations. *Recall* **[4]**

Question 5

(i) An object is placed at a distance 24 cm in front of a convex lens of focal length 8 cm.

(a) What is the nature of the image so formed?

(b) Calculate the distance of the image from the lens. *Understanding & Evaluate* **[3]**

(ii) When sunlight passes through water droplets in the atmosphere, it gets dispersed into its constituent colours forming a rainbow. A similar phenomenon is observed when white light passes through a prism **[3]**

(a) Which colour will show the maximum angle of deviation and which colour will show the minimum angle of deviation? *Recall*

(b) If instead of sunlight, a green-coloured ray is passed through a glass prism. What will be the colour of the emergent ray? *Understanding* **[3]**

(iii) *O* is a luminescent particle trapped inside a glass block. A student traces the path of rays coming out of it and reflecting over a plane mirror as shown in the figure below.

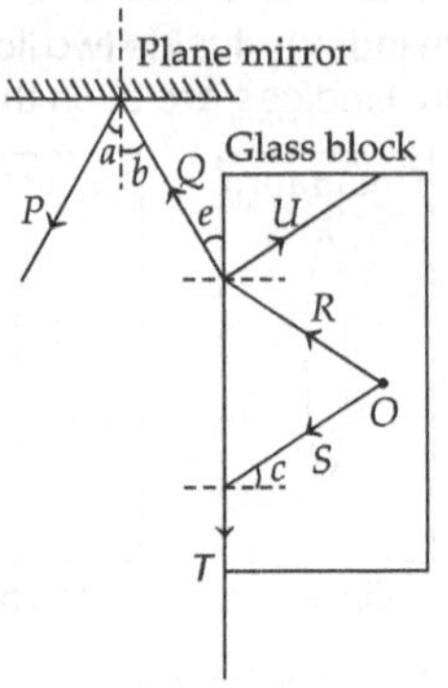

Complete the table using the labels from the figure. The first label is done for you.

Sr. No.	Description	Label
a.	an angle of reflection on the mirror	*a*
b.	a partially reflected ray in the glass slab	
c.	a critical angle	
d.	refracted rays	
e.	an angle of refraction of the ray *R*	

Understanding & Application [4]

Question 6

(i) A metal rod *AB* of length 80 cm is balanced at 45 cm from the end A with 100 gf weights suspended from the two ends.

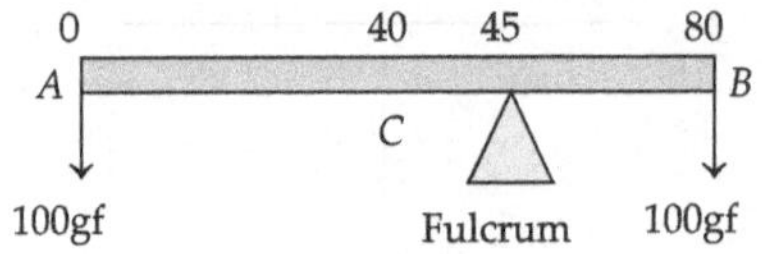

[3]

(a) If this rod is cut at the centre C, then compare the weight of *AC* to the weight of *BC*. *Understanding & Application*

(b) Give a reason for your answer in (a).

(ii) For each of the following scenarios, state whether the work done by gravity is positive, negative or zero. **[3]**

(a) A person walks on a levelled road.

(b) A person climbs a ladder.

(c) A car in neutral gear is coming down the slope. *Understanding & Recall*

(iii) The figure below shows a simple pendulum of mass 200 g. It is displaced from the mean position *A* to the extreme position *B*. The potential energy at the position *A* is zero. At the position *B*, the pendulum bob is raised by 5 m. **[4]**

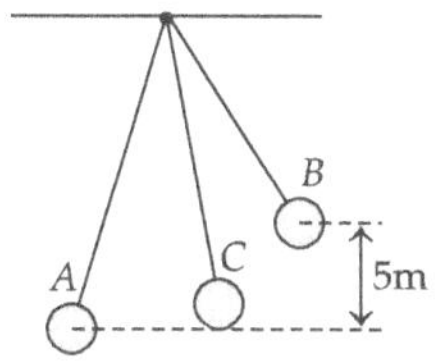

(a) What is the potential energy of the pendulum at the position *B* ? *Recall*
(b) What is the total mechanical energy at point *C* ? *Recall*
(c) What is the speed of the bob at the position *A* when released from *B* ? *Application & Evaluate*
(Take, $g = 10\ ms^{-2}$ and given that there is no loss of energy).

Question 7

(i) A block and tackle system of pulleys has velocity ratio 4. **[3]**
(a) Draw a labelled diagram of the system indicating clearly the direction of the load and effort. *Recall*
(b) Calculate the potential energy of the load 100 kgf lifted by this pulley to a height 5 m. (Take, $g = 10\ ms^{-2}$)
Understanding & Evaluate

(ii) A person standing in front of a cliff fires a gun and hears its echo after 3 s. If the speed of sound in air is $336\ ms^{-1}$, **[3]**
(a) calculate the distance of the person from the cliff.
(b) After moving a certain distance from the cliff, he fires the gun again and this time the echo is heard 1.5 s later than the first. Calculate the distance that the person moved. *Understanding & Evaluate*

(iii) The above picture shows a mother pushing her daughter sitting on a swing. The swing is going through the positions *A*, *B*, *C* where *A* and *C* are extreme positions and *B* is the mean position. **[4]**

(a) Which is the right position, i.e. at *A*, *B* or *C*, for the mother to give a constant periodic push to the swing every time in the forward direction to increase the amplitude of the swing?
(b) Name the phenomenon involved in this.
(c) Explain with this example, how this phenomenon helps to increase the amplitude of the swing.
Application

Question 8.

(i) The circuit depicted in the figure is employed for studying Ohm's Law. Instead of using a standard resistor, a student opts for a glass tube filled with mercury (tube 1), connected to the circuit through two electrodes E_1 and E_2. He records the readings of the ammeter and voltmeter, thereby calculates the resistance. The student repeats the experiment by substituting tube 1 with tube 2, where the same amount of mercury fills the tube 2.

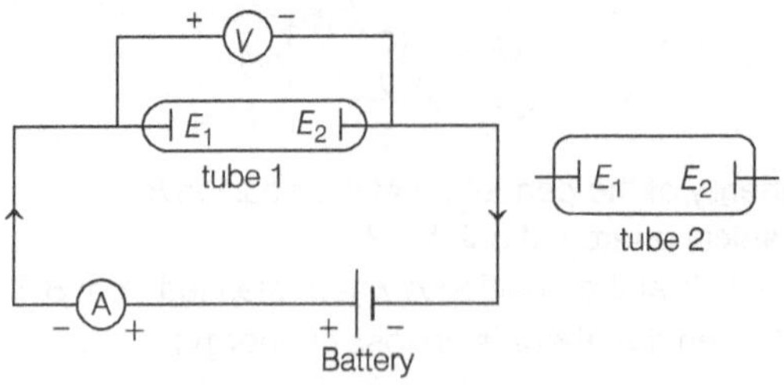

Neglecting internal resistance of the cell use (> or < or =) to compare

(a) the resistance in both the cases.

(b) the voltmeter readings in both the cases.

(c) the specific resistance in both the cases. *Understanding & Application* **[3]**

(ii) A radioactive nucleus *X* emits an alpha particle followed by two beta particles to form nucleus *Y*.

(a) With respect to the element *X*, where would you position the element *Y* in the periodic table?

(b) What is the general name of the elements *X* and Y?

(c) If the atomic number of *Y* is 80, then what is the atomic number of *X*? *Understanding & Recall* **[3]**

(iii) Observe the given circuit diagram and answer the questions that follow.

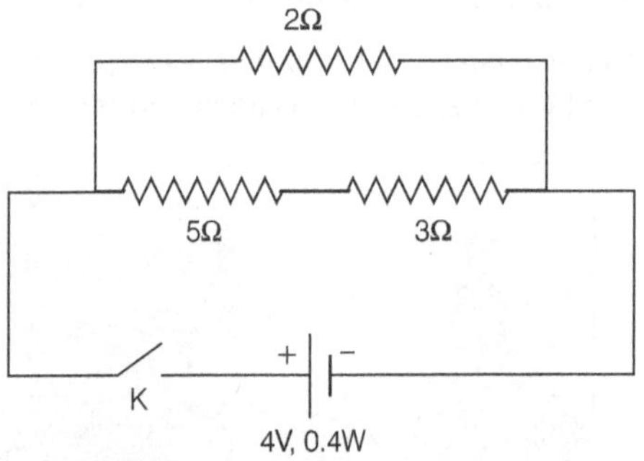

(a) Calculate the resistance of the circuit when the key *K* completes the circuit.

(b) Calculate the current through 3Ω resistance when the circuit is complete. *Understanding & Evaluate* **[4]**

Question 9.

(i) What mass of ice at 0°C added to 2.1 kg water, will cool it down from 75°C to 25°C? [Given, specific heat capacity of water = 4.2 $Jg^{-1}\,°C^{-1}$, specific latent heat of ice = 336 Jg^{-1}] . *Understanding & Evaluate* **[3]**

(ii) The diagram below shows a cooling curve for a substance. **[3]**

(a) State the temperature at which the substance condenses.

(b) The temperature range in which the substance is in liquid state.

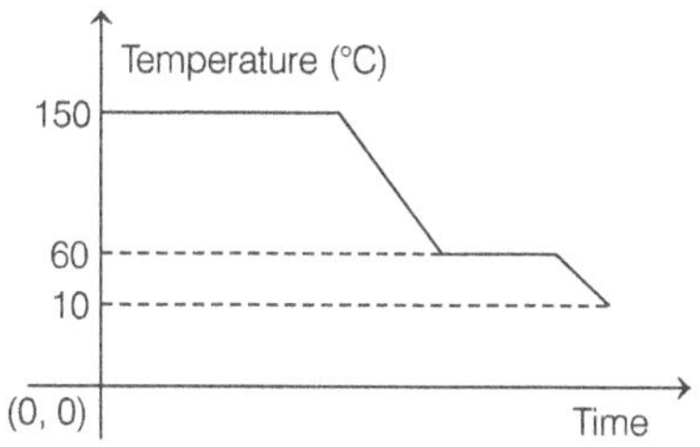

(c) Why do we prefer ice to ice-cold water for cooling a drink? *Understanding & Recall*

(iii) The diagram below shows a cardboard on which iron filings are kept. A wire bent in the form of a loop is seen passing through the cardboard. When current flows through it, the iron filings arrange themselves as shown below with the direction of magnetic field. **[4]**

(a) State the polarities of the battery at *A* and *B*.

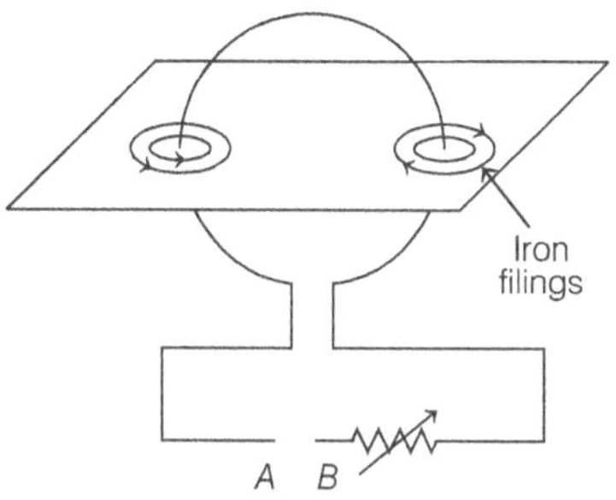

(b) State the effect on the magnetic field, if an iron rod is held along the axis of the coil.

Understanding & Application

(c) State one way to

1. change the polarity of the coil.
2. decrease the strength of the magnetic field around the coil.

Understanding & Recall

Answers

1.(i) (a) The anti-clockwise couple is taken as positive and clockwise couple is taken as negative.

(ii) (c) The kinetic energy of a body is

$$KE = \frac{p^2}{2m}$$

$$KE \propto (momentum)^2$$

(iii) (b) In thermoelectric station, the energy conversion taking place is chemical to heat to mechanical to electrical.

(iv) (c) From the diagram, we can conclude that the number of pulleys used in the fixed block are 2.

(v) (d) Inside the prism, compared to the blue light, the red light slows down less and refracts less because the wavelength of red colour is maximum.

(vi) (d) The phenomenon of light governing in optical fibre is based on total internal reflection.

(vii) (b) By lens formula,

For convex lens, $f = +12$ cm

$u = -20$ cm

$$\frac{1}{f} = \frac{1}{v} - \frac{1}{u}$$

$$\Rightarrow \quad \frac{1}{12} = \frac{1}{v} - \frac{1}{(-20)} \quad \Rightarrow \quad \frac{1}{12} = \frac{1}{v} + \frac{1}{20}$$

$$\Rightarrow \quad \frac{1}{v} = \frac{1}{12} - \frac{1}{20} \quad \Rightarrow \quad \frac{1}{v} = \frac{5-3}{60} = \frac{2}{60}$$

$$\Rightarrow \quad \frac{1}{v} = \frac{1}{30} \quad \Rightarrow \quad v = 30 \text{ cm}$$

Image will be formed at a distance 30 cm. So, in order to obtain a clear image, he has to move the screen away from the lens.

(viii) (a) Both A and R are true and R is the correct explanation of A.

The infrared radiations have long wavelengths, so they undergo minimal scattering in earth's atmosphere and travel long distances in dense fog and mist.

(ix) (b) The pitch or shrillness of a sound is directly proportional to its frequency.

∴ X will be grave and Y will be shriller.

(x) (c) Resistance, R = Slope of V-I graph = $\tan\theta$

As, $\theta_P > \theta_Q > \theta_R < \theta_S$

$\Rightarrow \quad R_P > R_Q > R_R > R_S$

The filament of a bulb is made up of high resistance material. So, material P is used to make its filament.

(xi) (b) According to old convention, the colour of live, neutral and earth wires are red, black and green respectively.

(xii) (c) According to Maxwell's right hand thumb rule, the figure given in option (c) will be correct.

(xiii) (b) Heat capacity of a body is the heat or energy required to raise its temperature by 1°C.

(xiv) (c) The amount of heat energy required to melt a given amount of substance at its melting point is called as the latent heat of fusion.

(xv) $p = 95,\ n = 146$

$A = p + n = 95 + 146 = 241$

Now, ${}_{95}X^{241} \longrightarrow {}_{93}X^{237} + {}_{2}He^{4}$

Number of neutrons $= A - Z = 237 - 93 = 144$

Number of protons, $Z = 93$

Hence, option (c) is correct.

2. (i) (a) class II (b) decreases

(c) becomes eight times (d) horse power

(e) resistance, resistivity

(ii) The potential energy of a body at height h,

$U = mgh$

$U \propto h$

$\therefore$ The graph of U versus h is given below

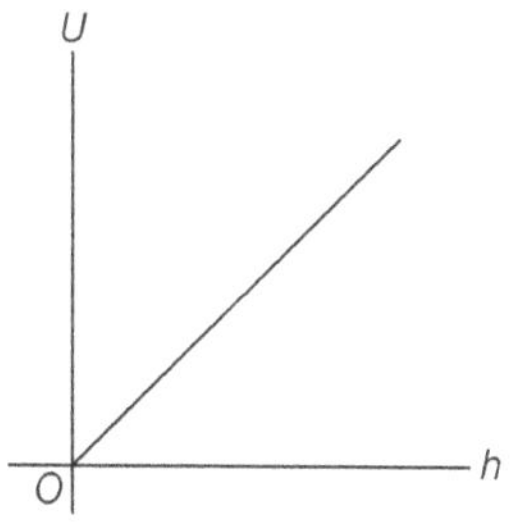

(iii) (a) The waves used for echo depth sounding are ultrasonic waves.

(b) Ultrasonic waves are used in echo depth sounding because these waves have very high frequency and short wavelength. So, these waves can penetrate undeviated through long distances in sea water.

3.(i) (a) As, the lens is made of two different refractive indices material so number of images formed will be two.

(b) In a concave lens, the image formed is always virtual, erect and diminished.

(ii) In circuit A, metal case is earthed. So, the person would not get electric shock but in circuit B, metal case is not earthed. So, the circuit will be completed through the body of the person giving him a shock. Therefore, circuit A is safe for the user.

(iii) (a) The transformer used to change a high alternating emf to a low alternating emf of same frequency is called step-down transformer.

(b) As, turns ratio, $r = \frac{N_s}{N_p} = \frac{E_s}{E_p}$

For step-down transformer,

$$E_s < E_p \Rightarrow \frac{E_s}{E_p} < 1$$

$\therefore$ $r < 1$ (less than 1)

(iv) Given, $s_w = 4.2 \text{ Jg}^{-1} \text{ K}^{-1}$

For solid, $m_s = 60$ g, $T_s = 100°C$

For water, $m_w = 150$ g, $T_w = 20°C$

Final temperature, $T_f = 25°C$

By principle of calorimetry,

Heat lost by solid = Heat gained by water

$$\Rightarrow \quad m_s \cdot s_s (T_s - T_f) = m_w s_w (T_f - T_w)$$

$\therefore$ Heat capacity of solid, $m_s s$

$$= \frac{m_w c_w (T_f - T_w)}{(T_s - T_f)}$$

$$= \frac{150 \times 4.2 \times (25 - 20)}{(100 - 25)} = 42 \text{ JK}^{-1}$$

(v) (a) Faraday's first law or principle of electromagnetic induction.

(b) AC generator is used as a power source in major power stations like wind turbines.

(vi) (a) Gamma radiations (b) No

(vii) (a) Beta (b) Daughter element E

(c) Fleming's left hand rule

4.(i) (a) The image formed of fish on the water surface is based on the phenomenon of total internal reflection.

(b) 1. Converge 2. Diverge

(ii) (a) As, refractive index $\propto \frac{1}{\text{temperature}}$

$\therefore$ $x < 1.33$

(b) Two differences between normal reflection and total internal reflection :

Normal reflection	Total internal reflection
In this reflection, light rays can be incident at any angle.	In this reflection, light rays must be incident at an angle greater than critical angle.
The energy of reflected rays is less than that of incident rays, i.e. there is loss of energy.	The energy of reflected rays is same as that of incident rays, i.e. there is no loss of energy.

(iii) (a) When mixture of red + blue + green colours is passed through a convex lens, each ray passes through a different points on the principal axis after refraction.

(b) Ultraviolet radiations are obtained by a quartz prism, as they are not absorbed by it.

(c) These radiations are used for killing bacteria.

(d) Visible radiation or infrared or microwaves or radiowaves.

5.(i) For convex lens, $f = 8$ cm, $u = -24$ cm

(a) As $u > 2f$, so the image formed is real, inverted and smaller size than object.

(b) By lens formula,

$$\frac{1}{f} = \frac{1}{v} - \frac{1}{u}$$

$$\Rightarrow \quad \frac{1}{8} = \frac{1}{v} - \frac{1}{(-24)}$$

$$\Rightarrow \quad \frac{1}{v} = \frac{1}{8} - \frac{1}{24} = \frac{1}{12}$$

$$\therefore \quad v = 12 \text{ cm}$$

(ii) (a) As, deviation $\propto \frac{1}{\text{wavelength}}$

∴ Violet colour will show maximum deviation and red colour will show minimum deviation because wavelength of violet colour is minimum and wavelength of red colour is maximum.

(b) When green-coloured ray is passed through a glass prism, then the colour of emergent ray will be also green because green light has not any component of light.

(iii)

Sr. No.	Description	Label
a.	an angle of reflection on the mirror	a
b.	a partially reflected ray in glass slab	U
c.	a critical angle	c
d.	refracted rays	Q,T
e.	an angle of refraction of the ray R	90 – e

6.(i) (a) Weight of AC < Weight of BC

(b) Since, the rod is balanced at F (fulcrum)

$$\therefore \quad W_{AF} = W_{BF}$$

Now, $W_{AF} - W_{CF} < W_{CF} \propto W_{BF} + W_{CF}$ [subtracting weight of CF from left and adding to right]

$$\Rightarrow \quad W_{AC} < W_{BC}$$

(ii) (a) No work is done.

(b) Negative work is done.

(c) Positive work is done

(iii) (a) The potential energy of the pendulum at point B

$$(PE)_B = mgh = 0.2 \times 10 \times 5 = 10 \text{ J}$$

(b) Applying conservation of mechanical energy,

$$E_A = E_B = E_C$$

∴ Total mechanical energy at point C,

$$E_C = E_B = (KE)_B + (PE)_B = 0 + 10 = 10 \text{ J}$$

(c) Applying conservation of mechanical energy at points A and B,

$$\frac{1}{2}mv^2 = mgh$$

$$\therefore \quad v = \sqrt{2gh}$$

$$= \sqrt{2 \times 10 \times 5} = 10 \text{ m/s}$$

7. (i) (a) A block and tackle system of pulley,

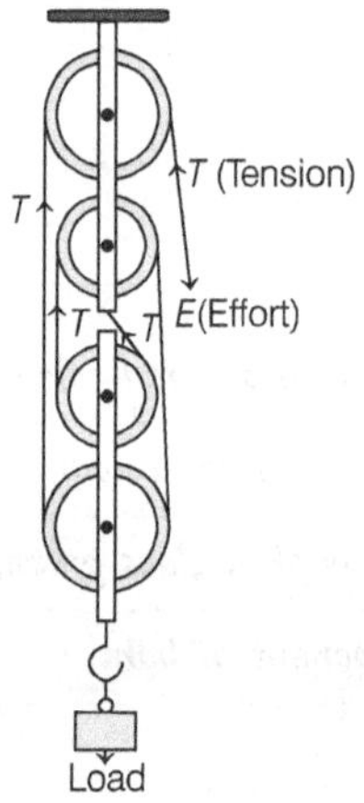

(b) Potential energy,

$$U = mgh = 100 \times 10 \times 5$$

$$U = 5000 \text{ J}$$

(ii) (a) Given, $t = 3$ s,

speed of sound, $v = 336$ m/s

Let d = distance of person from cliff.

$\therefore \; 2d = v \times t \quad \Rightarrow 2d = 336 \times 3 \quad \Rightarrow d = 504$ m

(b) Let the extra distance moved by person from the cliff = x

$$t = 3 + 1.5 = 4.5 \text{ s}$$

$$\therefore \quad 2(d + x) = v \times t$$

$$\Rightarrow \quad 2(504 + x) = 336 \times 4.5$$

$$\therefore \quad x = 252 \text{ m}$$

(iii) (a) At point A

(b) Resonance

(c) The natural frequency of the swing will equal the frequency of the force applied by mother. Due to which the amplitude of swing will increase.

8. (i) (a) $R_1 < R_2$ (b) $V_1 = V_2$ (c) $S_1 = S_2$

(ii) Atomic number Z and mass number A

$${}^{A}_{Z}X \xrightarrow{\alpha} {}^{A-4}_{Z-2}X \quad \text{and} \quad {}^{A}_{Z}Y \xrightarrow{2\beta} {}^{A-4}_{Z-2}Y$$

(a) As, the atomic number of both the elements X and Y are same, so they are placed at the same position in the periodic table.

(b) X and Y are isotopes.

(c) Atomic number of X = Atomic number of Y = 80

(iii) (a) When key K is closed, then the circuit diagram is as shown below.

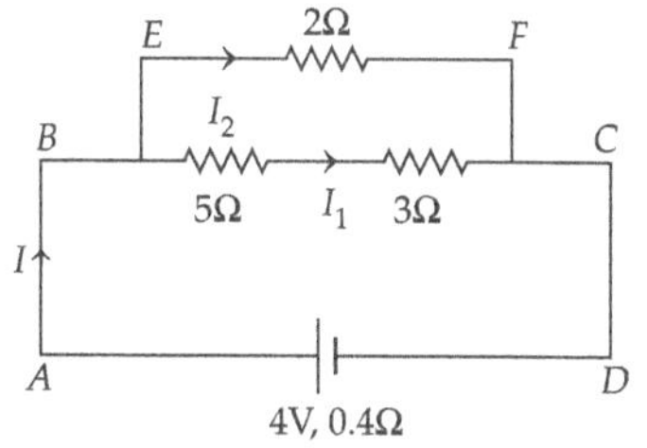

The resistance of the circuit is given by

$$R = \frac{2 \times (5 + 3)}{2 + (5 + 3)} + 0.4 = 2\ \Omega$$

(b) Current, $I = \frac{\varepsilon}{R + r} = \frac{4}{2 + 0.4} = 2\ A$

Current in 3 Ω, $I_{3\,\Omega} = \frac{IR_1}{R_1 + R_2} = \frac{5}{3} \times \frac{2}{[2 + (5 + 3)]}$

$$I_{3\,\Omega} = \frac{1}{3}\ A$$

9. (i) Given, $m_w = 2.1$ kg,

$(\Delta T)_{w,\ Heat\ lost} = (75 - 25) = 50°C$

$s_w = 4.2\ Jg^{-1}°C^{-1}$, $L_{ice} = 336\ Jg^{-1}$

Let m = mass of ice added at 0°C.

$\therefore$ By principle of calorimetry,

Heat lost by water from 75° to 25° C = Heat gained by ice at 0°C to water at 0° C + Heat gained by water at 0°C to water at 25°C

$\Rightarrow \quad m_w s_w (\Delta T)_{w,\text{ Heat lost}} = mL_i + ms_w (\Delta T)_{w,\text{ Heat gain}}$

$\Rightarrow \quad 2.1 \times 10^3 \times 4.2 \times 50 = m\,[336 + 4.2 \times 25]$

$\therefore$ Mass of ice, $m = 1000\ g = 1\ kg$

(ii) The cooling curve for the substance is shown below.

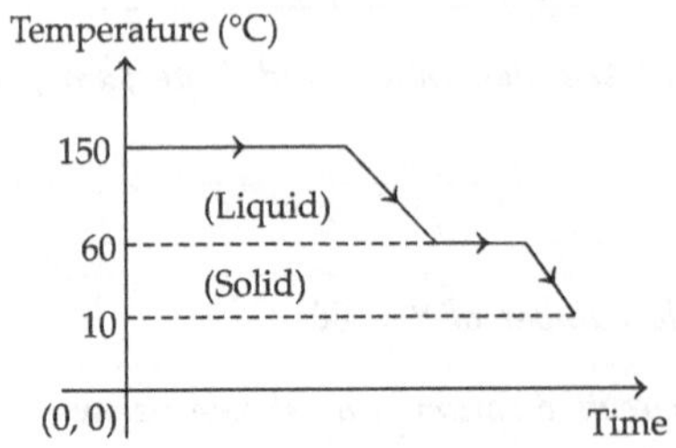

(a) The substance is condensed at the temperature of 150°C.

(b) The temperature range for which the substance is in liquid state is 60°C to 150°C.

(c) When ice melts to water at 0°C, it absorbs heat equal to latent heat of melting of ice and gets converted into water. This is the reason why drinks get even more colder when kept in ice as ice absorbs heat from the drink.

(iii) (a) A → Positive terminal

B → Negative terminal

(b) Magnetic field will expand in the direction of the held rod.

(c) 1. Reversing the direction of the current.

Or

Reversing the direction of the battery.

2. Reduce the potential difference across the coil.

Or Decreasing the strength of the current through the coil.

ICSE EXAMINATION PAPER 2025

PHYSICS

General Instructions

Maximum Marks : 80

Time allowed : Two hours

Answer to this paper must be written on the paper provided separately.

You will not be allowed to write during first 15 minutes. This time is to be spent in reading the question paper.

The time given at the head of this paper is the time allowed for writing the answers.

Section A is compulsory. Attempt any four questions from Section B.

The intended marks for questions or parts of questions are given in brackets [].

Section A **[40 Marks]**

(Attempt all questions from this section)

Question 1

Choose the correct answers to the questions from the given options. **[15]**

(i) A body is acted upon by two equal and opposite forces, that are not along the same straight line. The body will

(a) remain stationary
(b) have only rotational motion
(c) have only rectilinear motion
(d) have both rectilinear and rotational motion

(ii) Which among the following is a vector quantity?

(a) Work
(b) Power
(c) Energy
(d) Moment of couple

(iii) What is the correct energy transformation during burning of a candle?

(a) Heat → Kinetic + Potential
(b) Heat → Chemical + Light
(c) Chemical → Heat + Light
(d) Mechanical → Chemical + Heat

(iv) When a ray of light passes from one optical medium to another, which of the following physical quantities does not change?

(a) Amplitude of the wave
(b) Frequency of the wave
(c) Wavelength of the wave
(d) Speed of the wave

(v) Which one of the following combinations is the correct ascending order of electromagnetic waves in terms of wavelength?

(a) Gamma-rays, visible light, microwaves
(b) Microwaves, visible light, gamma-rays
(c) Gamma-rays, microwaves, visible light
(d) Microwaves, gamma-rays, visible light

(vi) For a lever, a graph is plotted with load on Y-axis and effort on X-axis. Which of the following represents the slope of the graph?

(a) Mechanical advantage
(b) Velocity ratio
(c) 1/ Velocity ratio
(d) 1 Mechanical advantage

(vii) For a real image formed by a convex lens, the ratio of

$I : O = 2 : 5$, then the object is I is the height of the image and O is the height of the object)

(a) between O and F
(b) beyond $2F$
(c) at F
(d) between F and $2F$

(viii) A ray of light is incident normally on a face of an equilateral prism. The ray gets totally reflected at the second refracting surface. The total deviation produced in the path of the ray is

(a) 30°
(b) 60°
(c) 90°
(d) 120°

(ix) In a closed circuit containing a bulb and a cell, the electromotive force (ε) and the terminal voltage (V) is related as

(Given, I is current and r is internal resistance)

(a) $V = \varepsilon + Ir$
(b) $V = \varepsilon - Ir$
(c) $V = \varepsilon \div Ir$
(d) $V = \varepsilon \times Ir$

(x) A metal piece of mass 5 g has thermal capacity 2.5 JK^{-1}. If the mass of the metal is tripled, then its specific heat capacity will be

(a) 7.5 JK^{-1}
(b) 2.5 JK^{-1}
(c) 1.5 $Jg^{-1}K^{-1}$
(d) 0.5 $Jg^{-1}K^{-1}$

(xi) **Assertion (A)** As the level of water in a tall measuring cylinder kept under running tap rises, the pitch of sound gradually increases.

Reason (R) Frequency of sound is inversely proportional to the length of the water column.

(a) Both A and R are true and R is correct explanation of A.
(b) Both A and R are true but R is not the correct explanation of A.
(c) A is true but R is false.
(d) A is false but R is true.

(xii) In the given circuits Y and Z, the resistors R_1 and R_2, are connected in

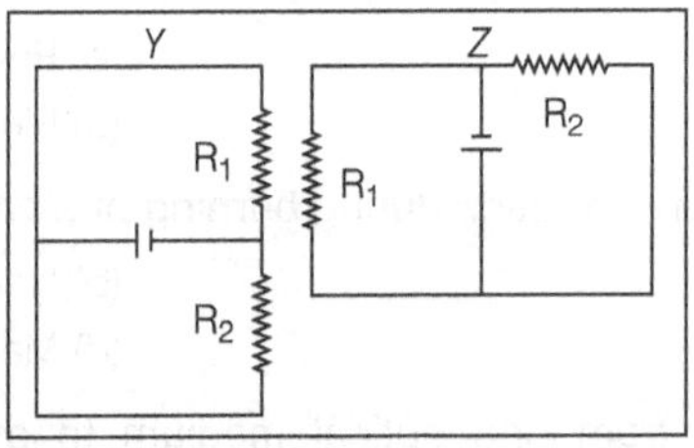

(a) series in both the circuits
(b) parallel in both the circuits
(c) parallel in Y and series in Z
(d) series in Y and parallel in Z

(xiii) A radioactive element P emits one α-particle and transforms to a new element Q. What will be the position of the element Q in the periodic table?

(a) One group to the left of P
(b) One group to the right of P
(c) Two groups to the right of P
(d) Two groups to the left of P

(xiv) Each of the substances given below is supplied with same amount of heat.

Which one will attain the highest temperature?

Substance	Lead	Aluminium	Copper	Iron
Specific heat capacity (cal/g°C)	0.031	0.21	0.095	0.115

(a) Aluminium
(b) Copper
(c) Iron
(d) Lead

(xv) The following figure shows a small bar magnet falling freely through a copper ring. For the observer at *A*, the direction of the induced current will be

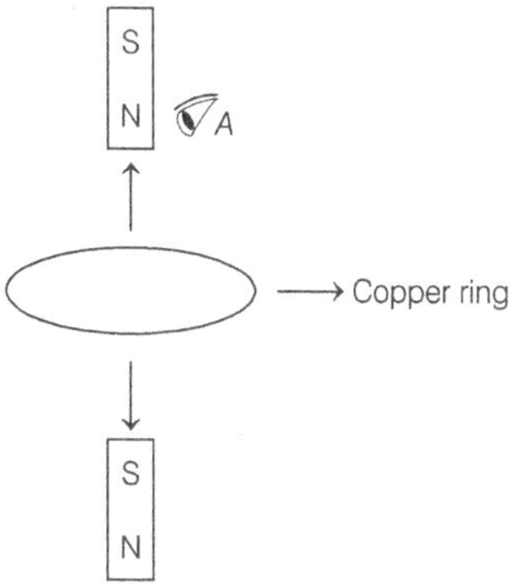

(a) clockwise when magnet is above and below the ring
(b) anti-clockwise when magnet is above and below the ring
(c) anti-clockwise when magnet is above the ring and clockwise when the magnet is below the ring
(d) clockwise when magnet is above the ring and anti-clockwise when the magnet is below the ring

Question 2

(i) Complete the following by choosing the correct answers from the bracket **[6]**

(a) In uniform circular motion the centrifugal force acts .... (towards the centre/away from the centre/along the tangential direction).

(b) Refractive index of a medium is independent of .... (temperature/angle of incidence/wavelength of light).

(c) Heat absorbed during change of phase depends on .... (mass/change in temperature/specific heat capacity) of the substance.

(d) Emf of a cell is .... (greater than / less than / equal to) the terminal voltage when the cell is in open circuit.

(e) In a step-up transformer the turns ratio is .... (more than 1/less than 1/equal to 1)

(f) The nuclear radiation with lowest ionising power is .... (α / β / γ).

(ii) A non-uniform kite is hanging freely from the branch of a tree as shown. Study the figure and answer the following **[2]**

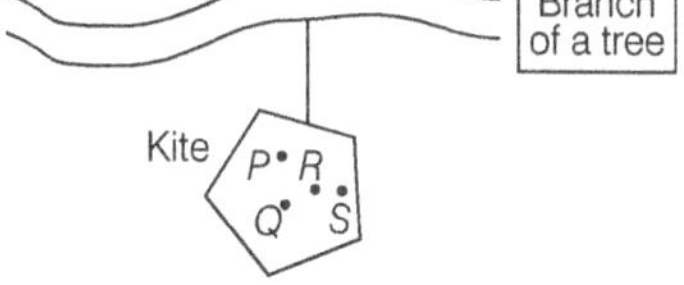

(a) Fill in the blank.

.... (*P*, *Q*, *R* or *S*) is the most probable position of its centre of gravity.

(b) Support your answer to (a) with a reason.

(iii) The displacement-time graph of a sound wave produced by a vibrating wire is shown below. **[2]**

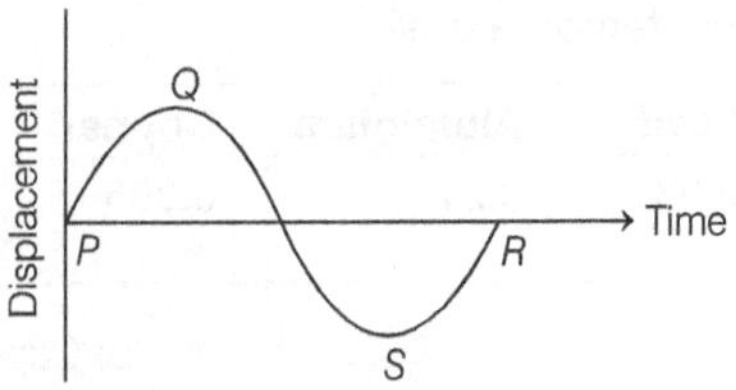

(a) How will you adjust the tension in the wire, to reduce the length of *PR*?

(b) Which characteristic of sound is affected by the reduction in the length of *PR*?

Question 3

(i) A ray of light enters a rectangular glass slab submerged in water at an angle of incidence 55°. Does this ray undergo total internal reflection when it moves from water to glass? Justify your answer. (The critical angle for glass-water interface is 54°.) **[2]**

(ii) According to the new colour convention which colour of wire is connected to **[2]**

(a) the metal body of the appliance

(b) the switch of the appliance?

(iii) (a) Which of the two, alternating current or direct current, produces a varying magnetic field when it flows through a conductor? **[2]**

(b) State the frequency of the alternating current supply in India

(iv) Calculate the amount of heat absorbed by 200 g of paraffin wax to melt completely at its melting point

[Specific latent heat of fusion of paraffin wax $= 146\ Jg^{-1}$] **[2]**

(v) Copper wire is wound around a steel bar *FT*. Current is allowed to pass through the coil for some time and then the bar is removed. **[2]**

(a) Draw only the magnetised bar *FT* and mark its poles.

(b) Trace two magnetic lines of force around *FT* clearly indicating the direction.

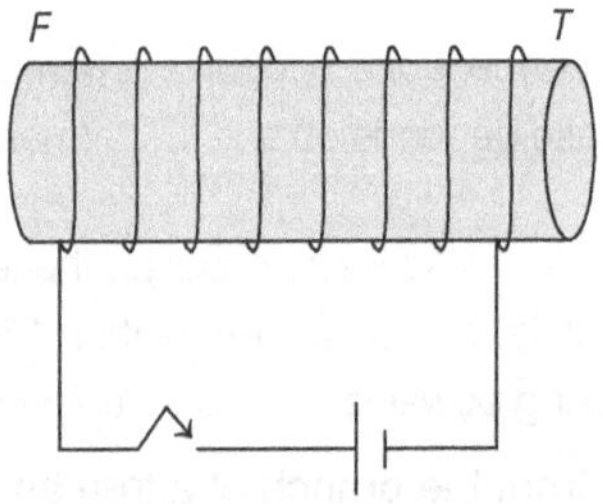

(vi) A current flows through a metallic conductor for a long period of time. State the change you would expect in its **[2]**

(a) Resistance

(b) Resistivity

(vii) Curium is a radioactive element with the symbol $^{247}_{96}Cm$ named in honour of Madam Curie. The graph of number of protons *versus* number of neutrons for some elements are shown below

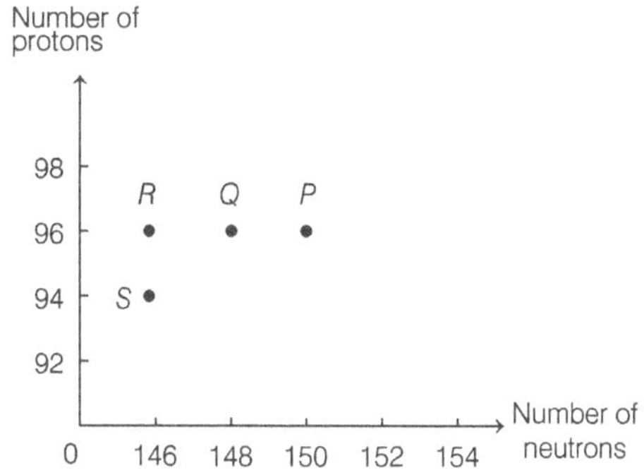

(a) Which point on the graph indicates the element Cm? **[1]**

(b) Which point on the graph indicates daughter nucleus after Cm undergoes radioactive decay of 1α followed by 2β? **[1]**

(c) State the mass number of the daughter nucleus. **[1]**

Section B

(Attempt any four questions from this section)

Queston 4

(i)

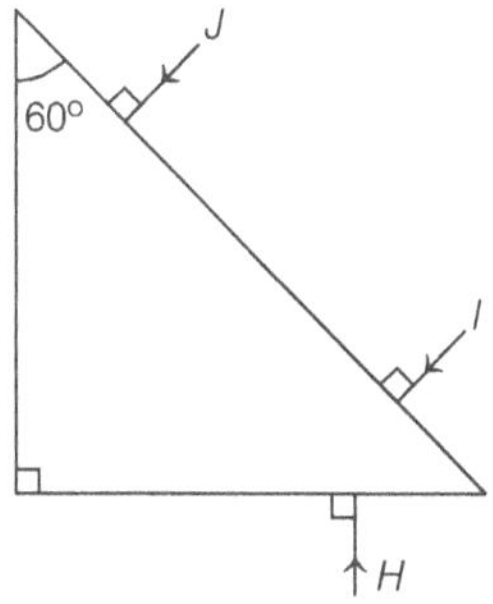

[3]

(a) Out of the three rays (*I*, *J*, *H*) shown in the diagram, which ray will suffer total internal reflection, while inside the prism? (Critical angle of the prism is 42°.)

(b) Copy the diagram to complete the path of the ray which you have named in (a) till it comes out of the prism

(ii) A rectangular glass block of refractive index 1.5 has an air bubble trapped inside it as shown in the diagram. When seen from the surface *AB*, it appears to be 4 cm deep. **[3]**

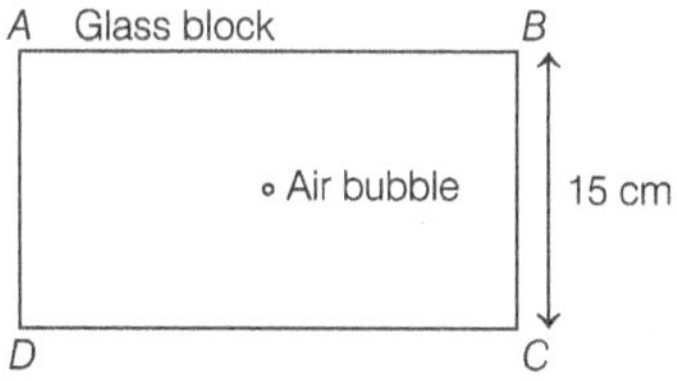

(a) Calculate the actual depth of the air bubble from the surface *AB*.

(b) For which colour of light, blue or yellow, the apparent depth will be greater?

(c) Turning the glass block upside down, does not change the apparent depth of the air bubble.
State true or false.

(iii) (a) An object is placed at 2*F* position of a convex lens. Draw a ray diagram showing the formation of the image.

(b) How will the size of the image change if we only replace the lens in the above arrangement with another lens of a greater focal length? **[4]**

Question 5

(i) An object is placed in front of a concave lens at a distance of 45 cm from it. If its image is formed at a distance of 30 cm from the lens, calculate the focal length of the lens? **[3]**

(ii) Two rays *PQ* and *RS* are incident on a rectangular glass block as shown in the diagram. Observe the diagram and answer the questions that follow. **[3]**

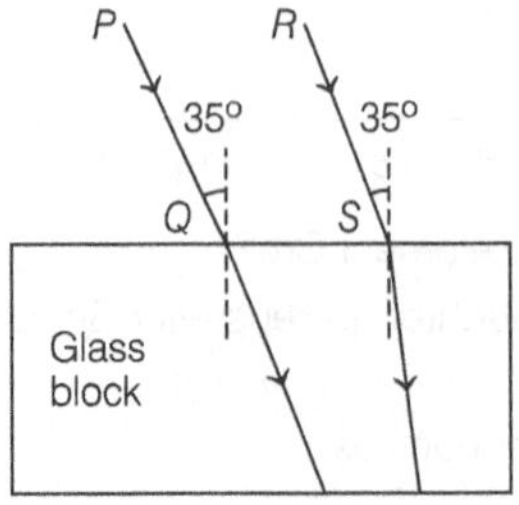

(a) Which of these two rays will have greater lateral displacement on emerging out of the block?
(b) travel with greater speed in the block?
(c) scatter more in the atmosphere?

(iii) (a) Name the radiations **[4]**
1. for which a quartz prism is used to study the spectrum.
2. which are used in remote sensing devices.
3. which are used in traffic signals in India.

(b) Name one property common to all electromagnetic radiations.

Question 6

(i) Akash takes a uniform meter scale and suspends a weight of 2 N at one end '*X*' and a weight of 5 N on the other end '*Y*'. He then balances the ruler horizontally on a knife edge placed at 70 cm from *X*. Draw a diagram of the arrangement and calculate the weight of the ruler. **[3]**

(ii) Three levers *X*, *Y*, *Z* of equal lengths are shown in the diagram. **[3]**

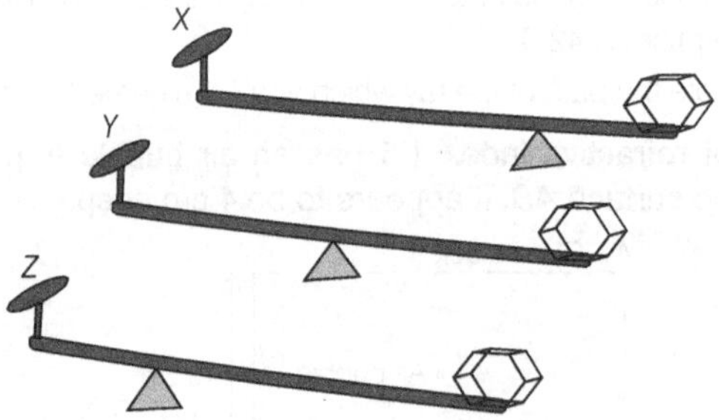

(a) Which class of lever do these belong to?
(b) Among these (*X*, *Y* or *Z*) which one will give the maximum mechanical advantage? Justify your answer.

(iii)

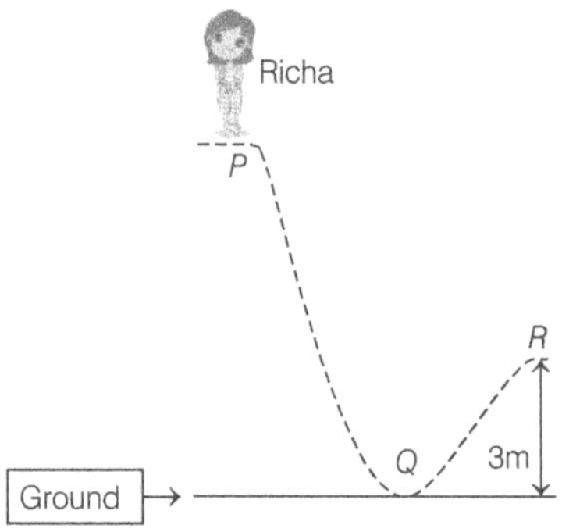

Richa weighing 40 kgf leaves point *P* on her skateboard and reaches point Q on the ground with velocity 10 ms^{-1}. Calculate **[4]**

(a) the kinetic energy of Richa at point *Q*.

(b) the vertical height of point *P* above the ground. (Use *g* as 10 m/s^2 and neglect friction)

(c) the kinetic energy of Richa at point *R*. (While moving from *Q* to *R*, she loses 500 J of energy against friction)

Question 7

(i) Draw a block and tackle system of pulleys with velocity ratio equal to 3. **[3]**

(ii) A submarine in the sea, sends ultrasonic ping and a stopwatch is started simultaneously. The stopwatch stops on receiving the reflected wave from an obstacle and reads 1 minute 40 seconds. Calculate the distance of the obstacle from the submarine. (Speed of sound in water 1500 ms^{-1}) **[3]**

(iii) The diagrams given below show two sound boxes *A* and *B* with wires of same length (*l*) and tension (10 kgf) but different cross-sectional areas. Simultaneously, vibrating tuning forks of frequency 300 Hz are placed on the boxes *A* and *B*. The paper rider falls off in case of *B* but not in case of *A*. **[4]**

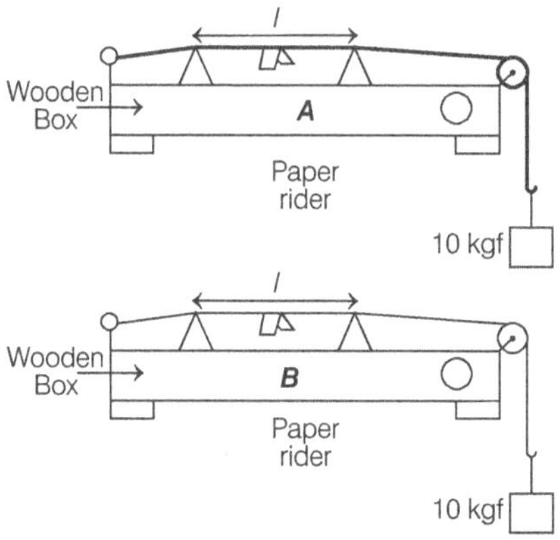

(a) Name and explain the phenomenon responsible for the falling off of the paper rider in *B*.

(b) The wire *A* resonates with a tuning fork of frequency *f*. Is *f* greater than, less than or equal to 300 Hz? Justify your answer.

Question 8

(i) The diagram shows wiring in a meter room of a building. **[3]**

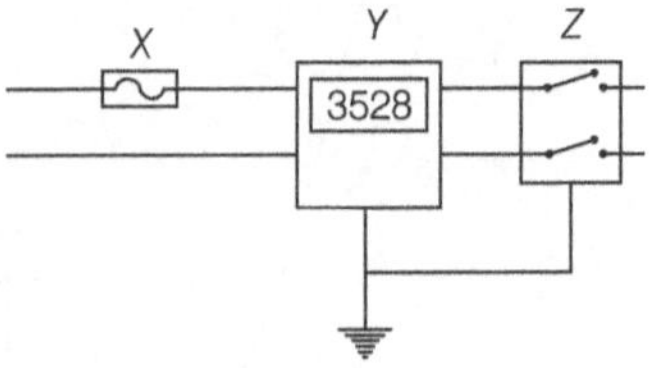

(a) What is the current rating of device *X*?

(b) What is the difference between the switch *Z* shown in the diagram and the switches you use to operate different appliances at home?

(c) What is the unit of the physical quantity displayed in *Y*?

(ii) Study the diagram given below and answer the questions that follow: **[3]**

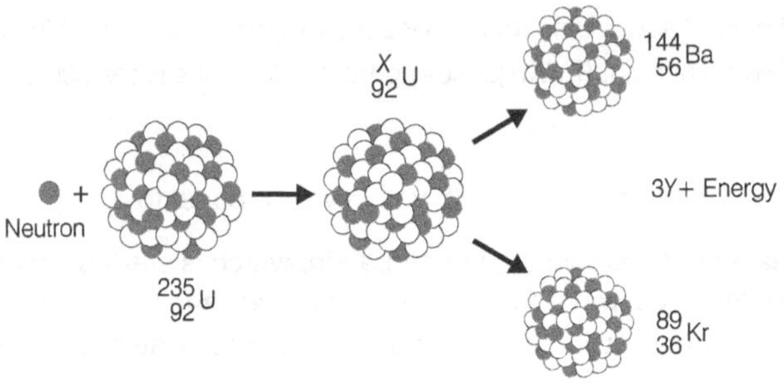

(a) Name the process depicted in the diagram.

(b) What is the value of *X*?

(c) Identify *Y*. the missing product of the reaction.

(iii)

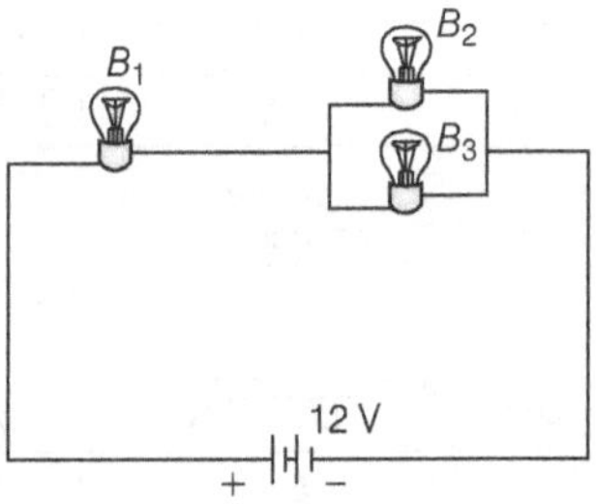

Three identical bulbs B_1, B_2, and B_3 each of power rating 18 W, 12 V are connected to a battery of 12 V. **[4]**

(a) Calculate:

1. the resistance of each bulb
2. the current drawn from the cell

(b) If the bulb B_3 is removed from the circuit, then will the brightness of the bulb B_1 increase, decrease or remain the same?

Question 9

(i) 30 g of ice at 0°C is used to bring down the temperature of a certain mass of water at 70 °C to 20 °C. Find the mass of water (Specific heat capacity of water = 4.2 $Jg^{-1}\,°C^{-1}$ and specific latent heat of ice = 336 Jg^{-1}) **[3]**

(ii) (a) A certain amount of heat will warm 1 g of material *X* by 10 °C and 1 g of material *Y* by 40°C. Which material has higher specific heat capacity? **[3]**

(b) Which material, *X* or *Y*, would you select to make a calorimeter?

(c) The specific heat capacity of a substance remains the same when it changes its state from solid to liquid. State true or false.

(iii) A copper rod *PQ* carrying-current is kept in a magnetic field as shown in the diagram. **[4]**

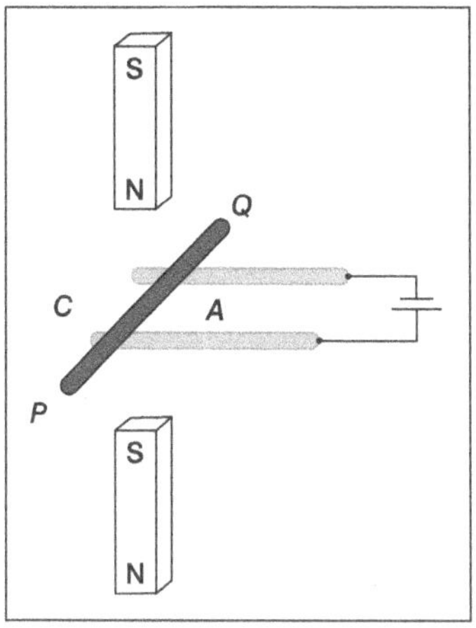

(a) The copper rod *PQ* will move towards *C*. State true or false.

(b) Name the law used to determine the direction of motion of *PQ*.

(c) What will be the effect on the force experienced, if the rod *PQ* is replaced by another copper rod of same length but of greater cross-sectional area?

(d) Justify your answer in (c).

Answers

1. (i) (b) When two equal and opposite forces not acting along the same line acts on a body, it forms a couple.

A couple is always needed to produce rotation in a body.

(ii) (d)

(iii) (c) When a candle burns, a chemical reaction occurs where wax reacts with oxygen which converts the chemical potential energy into heat and light.

(iv) (b)

(v) (a)

(vi) (a)

$$\text{Mechanical advantage} = \frac{\text{Load}}{\text{Effort}}$$

$$\text{and slope of a graph} = \frac{\Delta Y}{\Delta X}$$

(vii) (b) Here the image formed is real and diminished which depicts that the object is kept beyond 2F.

(viii) (d)

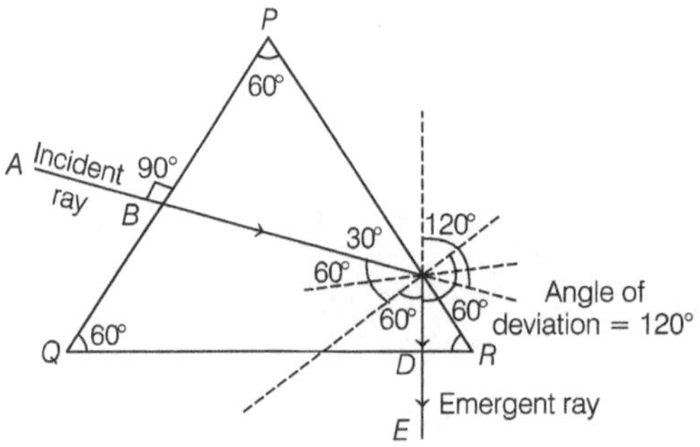

(ix) (b)

(x) (d) Specific heat capacity of the metal piece is

$$\frac{\text{thermal capacity}}{\text{mass}} = \frac{2.5}{5}\ JK^{-1}g^{-1}.$$

$$= 0.5\ JK^{-1}g^{-1}.$$

When the mass of the metal is tripled, the specific heat capacity remains unchanged as it is independent of the mass of the body.

(xi) (a) Both A and R are true and R is the correct explanation of A because as the water level rises, the air column decreases which increases the frequency of vibration of the air column thereby increasing the pitch of the sound.

(xii) (b)

(xiii) (d)

(xiv) (d) Since, lead has the lowest specific heat capacity, so the rise in temperature in case of lead will be the highest.

(xv) (c)

2. (i) (a) away from the centre

(b) angle of incidence

(c) specific heat capacity

(d) equal to

(e) more than I

(f) γ

(ii) (a) Q.

(b) For a stable equilibrium of a body, the centre of gravity should be as low as possible and also near the geometric centre of the body and in the above case Q is the most appropriate point for the centre of gravity of the kite.

(iii) (a) The frequency of note produced by a stretched string is related to the tension in the string as $f \propto \sqrt{T}$.

When the length PR is reduced, the wavelength of the wave is reduced thereby increasing the frequency of the wave.

So, the tension must be increased in case if PR has to be reduced.

(b) The pitch of the vibration of sound increases when the length PR is reduced.

3. (i) Yes, the ray will undergo total internal reflection as the critical angle of the glass-water interface is less than the angle of incidence of the ray of light.

(ii) (a) Green or Yellow (Earth).

(b) Brown (Live).

(iii) (a) Alternating current would produce a varying magnetic field when it flows through a conductor.

(b) Frequency of alternating current supply in India is 50 Hz.

(iv) Specific latent heat of fusion of paraffin wax = 146 Jg^{-1}.

$\therefore$ Amount of heat absorbed by 200 g of paraffin wax to meet completely is = $(146 \times 200)\ J = 29200\ J$.

(v) (a)

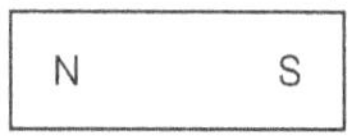

(b)

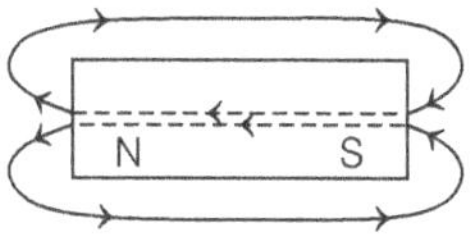

(vi) (a) Since the current flows for a long period of time so the resistance will increase due to the heating effect of current.

(b) Since, resistivity is also dependent on temperature and it increases with the increase in temperature so the resistivity is also affected in the above case.

(vii) (a) Point P

(b) Point R

(c) Mass number of the daughter nucleus is 243.

4.(i) (a) Ray J

(b)

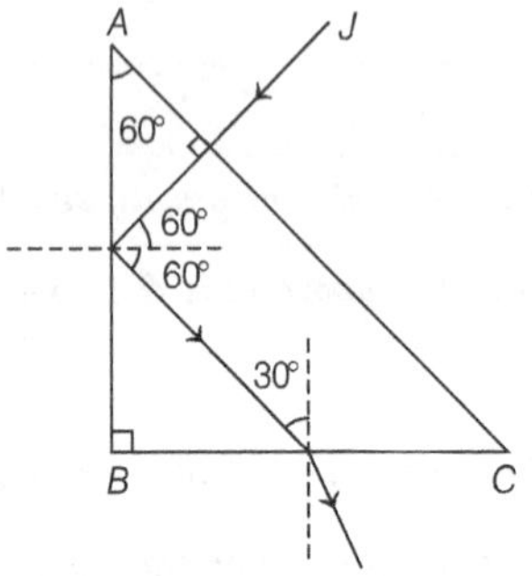

(ii) (a) Refractive index of a medium with respect to air,

$$\mu = \frac{\text{Re al depth or actual depth}}{\text{Apparent depth}}$$

$$\therefore \quad 1.5 = \frac{\text{Actual depth}}{4}$$

$$\Rightarrow \text{Actual depth} = (1.5 \times 4) = 6 \text{ cm}$$

(b) Apparent depth $\propto \frac{1}{RI}$

∴ The apparent depth will be greater for yellow light, since its refractive index for yellow light is lower.

(c) When the glass block is turned upside down, the real depth of the air bubble becomes 9 cm.

$$\therefore \text{Apparent depth} = \frac{9}{1.5} = 6 \text{ cm.}$$

∴ The statement is false.

(iii) (a)

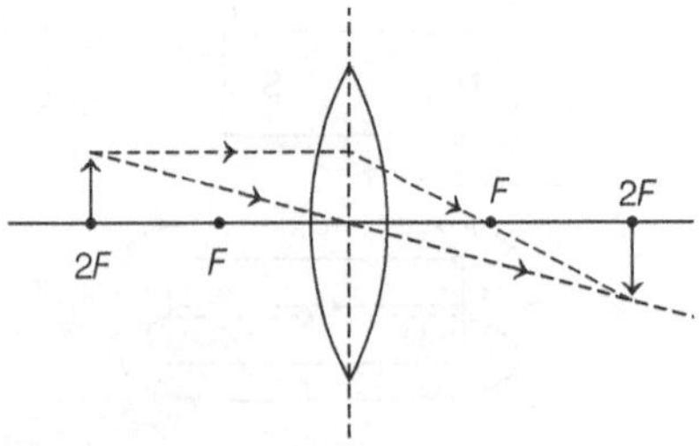

(b) Since the size of the image in the above case is same as that of the object so it will remain same even if the lens is replaced with a lens of a different focal length.

5. (i) From lens formula, we know that

$$\frac{1}{v} - \frac{1}{u} = \frac{1}{f}$$

where v is the image distance, u is the object distance and f is the focal length of the lens.

Here, v = – 30 cm, u = – 45 cm.

$$\therefore \quad \frac{1}{f} = \frac{1}{(-30)} - \frac{1}{(-45)} = \frac{-1}{30} + \frac{1}{45} = \frac{-1}{90}$$

$$\therefore \quad f = -90 \text{ cm}$$

∴ The focal length of the concave lens is 90 cm.

(ii) (a) Ray RS

Since, it bends more inside the glass block.

(b) Ray PQ.

Since, it bends less inside the glass block and hence has a lower refractive index as compared to ray RS.

(c) The light ray having greater refractive index will suffer less deviation as compared to the light having lower refractive index.

Therefore, PQ having lower refractive index will scatter more.

(iii) (a) 1. Ultraviolet radiation

2. Infrared radiation

3. Visible light

(b) All electromagnetic waves travel with the same speed in vacuum that is 3×10^8 m/s.

6. (i)

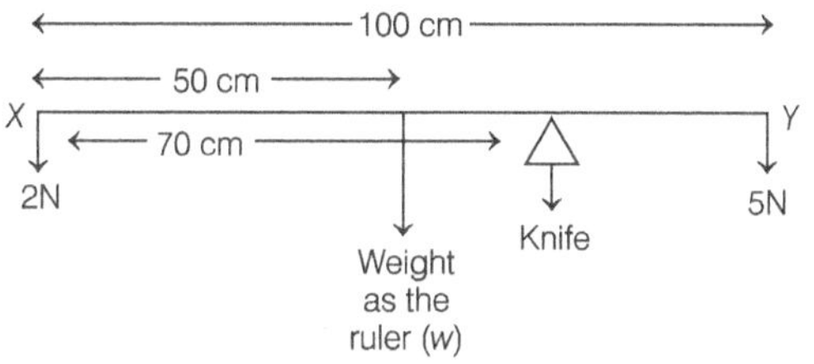

From the principle of moment, we know that

sum of anti-clockwise moment = sum of clockwise moment.

$$\therefore \quad (2 \times 70) + w \times 20 = 5 \times 30$$

$$\Rightarrow \quad 140 + 20w = 150$$

$$\Rightarrow \quad w = \frac{150 - 140}{20} = 0.5 \text{ N}$$

∴ The weight of the ruler is 0.5 N.

(ii) (a) Class I lever.

(b) Mechanical advantage $= \frac{\text{Effort arm}}{\text{Load arm}}$

Since the effort arm is greatest and the load arm is the least for 2, so 2 will have the maximum mechanical advantage.

(iii) (a) Weight of Richa = 40 kgf

$= 40 \times 10$ N

$= 400$ N

$\therefore$ Mass of Richa $= \frac{400}{10} = 40$ kg

$\therefore$ Kinetic energy of Richa when she reaches point Q $= \left(\frac{1}{2} \times 40 \times 10^2\right)$ J.

$= 2000$ J.

(b) From conservation of energy,

we know PE = KE

$\Rightarrow \quad mgh = \frac{1}{2} mv^2 = 2000$ J

where, h = length of PQ.

$\therefore \quad h = \frac{2000}{400} = 5$ m

(c) PE of Richa at point R = (400×3) J = 1200 J

Loss of energy = 500 J

$\therefore$ KE + 500 = 1200, by law of conservation of energy

$\therefore \quad$ KE = 700 J, at point R.

7. (i)

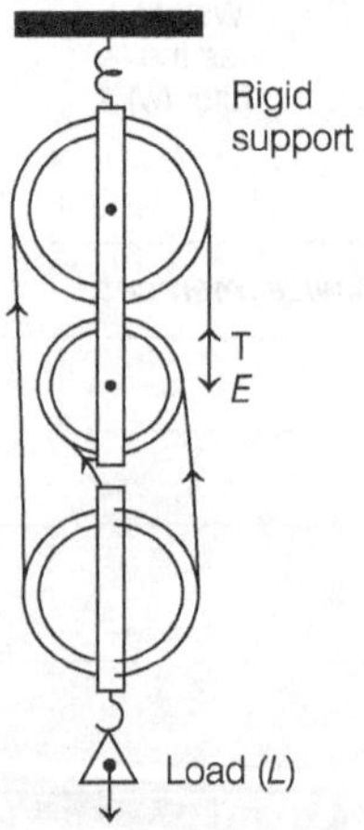